Public Policy and Higher Education

Public Policy and Higher Education, third edition, provides readers with the tools to examine how policies affect students' access and success in college. Rather than arguing for a single approach, the authors use research-based evidence and consider political and historical values and beliefs to examine how policymakers and higher education administrators can inform and influence change within systems of higher education. Raising new questions and examining recent developments, this fully updated edition is an invaluable resource for graduate students, administrators, policymakers, and researchers who seek to learn more about the crucial contexts underlying policy decisions and college access. This third edition includes updates across the board to reflect current policy contexts. Expanded historical frameworks allow readers to better understand the preparation, access, persistence, and development of state education systems. New considerations of state and national political ideologies help to inform contemporary contexts. Finally, refreshed cases, including an additional case about Florida and updated cases for California, Minnesota, Indiana, and North Carolina, equip readers with new ways to analyze complex state policies and their impact on higher education.

Special Features:

- Case Studies help readers build their skills in analyzing how political values, beliefs, and traditions influence policy decisions and adaptations within state systems.
- Reflective Questions encourage readers to discuss state and campus contexts for policy decisions and to consider the strategies used in a state or institution.
- Approachable Explanations unpack complex public policies and financial strategies for readers who seek an understanding of public policy in higher education.
- Research-Based Recommendations explore how policymakers, higher education administrators, and faculty can work together to improve quality, diversity, and financial stewardship.

Nathan J. Daun-Barnett is Associate Professor of Higher Education at the University at Buffalo, State University of New York, USA.

Edward P. St. John is Professor Emeritus at the Center for the Study of Higher and Postsecondary Education at the University of Michigan, USA.

Core Concepts in Higher Education
Series Editors: Marybeth Gasman, Stella Flores, and Edward P. St. John

Core Concepts in Higher Education is a textbook series for the education of new professionals, covering the core areas of study in the field of higher education and student affairs. This timely and dependable series provides the necessary tools to ensure practice is informed by theory and research. The books in this series invite students to think critically about the field to discover what has been left out and what needs to be learned, and also provides frameworks and constructs for addressing challenges facing higher education. The Core Concepts in Higher Education series moves thought, action, and scholarship forward by valuing, reconstructing, and building on the foundations of the field. Through a rich combination of research, theory, and practice, this series aims to move the field into a new generation of scholarship to better prepare students for authentic leadership of our colleges, universities, and academic communities.

Law and Social Justice in Higher Education
Crystal Renee Chambers

Qualitative Inquiry in Higher Education Organization and Policy Research
Penny Pasque and Vicente Lechuga

Understanding Community Colleges, Second Edition
Edited by John S. Levin and Susan T. Kater

Contemporary Issues in Higher Education
Edited by Marybeth Gasman and Andrés Castro Samayoa

A People's History of American Higher Education
Philo Hutcheson

Diversity and Inclusion on Campus
Supporting Students of Color in Higher Education, Second Edition
Rachelle Winkle-Wagner and Angela M. Locks

American Higher Education
Issues and Institutions, Second Edition
John R. Thelin

Organizational Theory in Higher Education, Third Edition
Kathleen Manning

Public Policy and Higher Education
Reframing Strategies for Preparation, Access, and College Success, Third Edition
Nathan J. Daun-Barnett and Edward P. St. John

For more information about this series, please visit: https://www.routledge.com/Core-Concepts-in-Higher-Education/book-series/CCHE

Public Policy and Higher Education

Reframing Strategies for Preparation, Access, and College Success

Nathan J. Daun-Barnett and Edward P. St. John

THIRD EDITION

Routledge
Taylor & Francis Group
NEW YORK AND LONDON

Designed cover image: BrendaStarrArt 2011 @ Getty

Third edition published 2025
by Routledge
605 Third Avenue, New York, NY 10158

and by Routledge
4 Park Square, Milton Park, Abingdon, Oxon, OX14 4RN

Routledge is an imprint of the Taylor & Francis Group, an informa business

© 2025 Nathan J. Duan-Barnett and Edward P. St. John

The right of Nathan J. Duan-Barnett and Edward P. St. John to be identified as authors of this work has been asserted in accordance with sections 77 and 78 of the Copyright, Designs and Patents Act 1988.

All rights reserved. No part of this book may be reprinted or reproduced or utilised in any form or by any electronic, mechanical, or other means, now known or hereafter invented, including photocopying and recording, or in any information storage or retrieval system, without permission in writing from the publishers.

Trademark notice: Product or corporate names may be trademarks or registered trademarks and are used only for identification and explanation without intent to infringe.

[First edition published by Routledge 2013]
[Second edition published by Routledge 2018]

ISBN: 978-1-032-72485-0 (hbk)
ISBN: 978-1-032-69303-3 (pbk)
ISBN: 978-1-032-72486-7 (ebk)

DOI: 10.4324/9781032724867

Typeset in Minion Pro
by KnowledgeWorks Global Ltd.

CONTENTS

Series Introduction *by Marybeth Gasman*   vii
Preface   ix
Acknowledgments   xvii

Chapter 1	Introduction	1
PART I	**REFRAMING HIGHER EDUCATION POLICY**	17
Chapter 2	Public Policy and Higher Education: Global Competitiveness, Political Divisions, and Reframing Strategies	19
Chapter 3	Reframing Policy Matters: Political Ideologies, Policy Studies, and Research Evidence	42
Chapter 4	Reframing Preparation: From Pathways to STEM Pipeline and Economic Stratification	70
Chapter 5	College Access: From Equal Opportunity to Economic Stratification	90
Chapter 6	Reframing College Success: Civic Leadership, Economic Uplift, and Financial Wellbeing	111
PART II	**STATE CASES**	135
Chapter 7	The Old Liberal Model: The California Case	137
Chapter 8	The Market Model Reconsidered: The Minnesota Case	164

Chapter 9	The Eroding Balanced Model: The Indiana Case	190
Chapter 10	From Merit Aid to MAGA Reforms: The Florida Case	219
Chapter 11	Conservative-Progressive Tensions: The North Carolina Case	247
Epilogue		272
Index		281

SERIES INTRODUCTION

In the third edition of *Public Policy and Higher Education*, Nathan Daun-Barnett and Edward St. John delve deeply into the issues that are central to the intersection of public policy and higher education. However, more than that—and unlike many scholars addressing public policy issues—they focus on how politics—even the brutal politics of the twenty-first century play out in higher education. They examine the ways that the clashes between the left and the right that we see on our televisions and on social media—and more recently in the streets and on campuses—"spill over" into the academy.

Having read editions one and two of this important book, I was struck by how much higher education has changed since the second edition. The nation and world have shifted in so many ways. As a historian, I'm always aware that there have been volatile times in the past, but in today's world, the changes and volitivity are coming at us faster and in real-time—almost immediately. As I read this third edition, I began wondering where we are going and if higher education will survive. In 2024, we are seeing a college close every week, and public dissatisfaction with higher education is at an unprecedented high.

Daun-Barnett and St. John explore all of the topics that are before us, with skill, compassion, and justice. While we often see public policy scholars taking a strange neutral stance on the issues of the day, the authors steer us in a direction that embraces justice and forces us to think about how we as a nation are losing when we don't embrace equity and prosperity for all.

As the Senior Series Editor for Core Concepts in Higher Education, I'm proud to have this important book in the series as it has the possibility of changing the way students and scholars approach higher education.

Marybeth Gasman
Samuel DeWitt Proctor Endowed Chair &
Distinguished University Professor
Senior Series Editor, Core Concepts in Higher Education

PREFACE

Higher education policy is framed and reframed at many levels of the polycentric, market-based, corporatized national network of colleges and universities connecting to diverse K-12 schools, communities of interest, and working environments. Public colleges and universities were central to the neoliberal education policy transition in 2010 when we began working on the first edition of *Public Policy and Higher Education: Reframing Access, Persistence, and College Success*. Marketization, the transition from competition between low-cost public colleges and financially challenged independent colleges to stratification of colleges for rich and poor, was well underway. We sought to explain the transition so that states and institutions could better craft strategies that promoted fairness in access. We developed viable frameworks for depicting how these fragmented, loosely networked enterprises could improve financial access. The trajectory toward inequality proceeded relatively unaltered. However, the book created frameworks for this purpose that are still relevant, especially if reframed for this new period.

The inequalities created by high tuition, high loans, and emphasis on STEM education for all are now apparent to most policymakers across higher education. Many, but not all, states are rebuilding technical pathways in K-12 and community, providing lower-cost options in community colleges, and increasing grants to ensure access for low-income students. Also, for the first time since 1980, college costs are declining, on average, but enrollment is lagging in many states. Colleges, states, and the federal government can no longer blame COVID for the current problems. Colleges and universities are preparing for an enrollment cliff, driven by a decline in the number of high school graduates projected for the coming age cohorts. They are also adjusting to the effects of a stubbornly strong labor market where vocational and technical pathways lead more directly to higher-paying jobs and a steep drop in public confidence, fueled by a conservative political backlash against the perceived liberal bias in higher education.

This new period of uncertainty, exacerbated by ideologies within schools, colleges, and the polity at large, differs dramatically from the neoliberal trajectory after 1980. We argue a dramatically different period of US education and economic engagement in a disrupted global economy began in 2015. Critics will argue that we are still firmly entrenched in a period of neoliberalism. While we do not disagree that many of the current policy priorities are rooted in neoliberalism, some of the changes we observe across states clearly show that a transition has begun. The contours of this new period are continuing to take shape as we write this volume, and these changes are the consequence of tensions between the growing progressive movement on the left and Donald Trump's version of populist nationalism on the right. The result, so far, is a set of volatile state political environments across the country.

CORE CONCEPTS FROM PRIOR EDITIONS

Consistent with prior editions, *Public Policy and Higher Education* introduces the rationales used in recent decades to change higher education policy (Part I) and places efforts to expand opportunity through improving preparation, access, and success into the policy contexts of states, developing frameworks for examining higher education (Part II). We encourage readers to reflect on and possibly reframe their assumptions about policies for improving equal opportunity and other higher education outcomes. However, we no longer have a Part III because we have substantially expanded the historical framework in Part I and the state contexts used across state cases in Part II; we conclude with an Epilogue focusing on emerging themes.

Part I continues to examine federal policy as a powerful force influencing the contexts of and incentives for state policy development and adaptation of K-12 and higher education but focuses on the new context. As before, we explain how federal policies create incentives that influence state and institutional policy decisions. To inform readers about this new period, we reexamine and update the arguments about national policy but continue to explain how policymakers crafted federally contracted researchers to align their findings with policy neoliberal policy arguments about preparation and access. The historical frame better illuminates how research informs policymaker arguments about linkages between policy decisions and educational outcomes. More than before, we focus on ideological beliefs held by policymakers who shape research and craft arguments for reform. Previously, we examined trends before 2008; now, we summarize findings on the late twentieth century and focus on this century up to the extent of current data, ranging from 2017 to 2023, depending on the source. National reporting of indicators has improved, so we use generally available data rather than generate our indicators, a strategy we tested in epilogues to Parts I and II in the second edition. We also believe this is a better strategy for those who want to use this text to assess other states' policies and politics. This third edition updates trends and integrates them into the text; we substantially revised or rewrote analytic chapters.

In the state cases (Part II), we encourage readers to consider how the frameworks implicit in state policy decisions have evolved by cutting Part III to make space for substantial changes to the framing in Part I and the historical framing of each case in Part II. We made the decision to add the Florida case (from the first edition) and updated cases for California, Minnesota, Indiana, and North Carolina. We made the decision to cut the Michigan case, given space constraints and the fact that we were over-represented in the Midwestern region of the country. This combination of states illustrates diverse adaptations to changing educational, social, and economic circumstances. Analyses and discussion of cases compare states to the national trends and other states, providing an engaging process to build skills in reframing when making policy choices and designing research studies to inform policymakers, scholars, and graduate students.

The state case studies encourage readers to build their skills in analyzing how political values, beliefs, and traditions influence policy decisions and adaptations within state systems. The case studies consider how local researchers and state officials have used research evidence about student outcomes related to preparation for, access to, and success in college as they craft and advocate for policy changes. We ask readers what they have observed about the relationships between state policy decisions and outcomes to encourage reflection and discussion of the frameworks recreated through adaptions to emerging conditions.

As readers compare cases, it will become evident that state policies on high school graduation, college admissions, and higher education finance influence who attends college and whether there is equal opportunity to enroll at four-year institutions within states. It is tough to hold together political coalitions that can sustain comprehensive and cohesive policy frameworks that promote equal opportunity, even when there is a history of success within a state. Indeed, we selected these state cases because they illustrate some of the ways state policy frameworks developed, adapted, and transformed over time. During the neoliberal turn in the 1980s, federal policy changes forced states and campuses to make changes as growing numbers of low-income, college-prepared students chose community colleges as the lowest-cost option. Stratification in college choice in the US resulted from policies that discriminated against low-income students, majority and minority, a radically different circumstance than the class-based stratification due to culture and aspirations evident in Western Europe in the same period (Meyer et al., 2013). The cases inform discussion about policy, research, and strategy because:

- Each state case addresses the evolution of policy rationales and trends in policy decisions and outcomes related to preparation, enrollment, and degree completion. We encourage readers to use the case evidence to test their assumptions about the linkages between policies and outcomes.
- The cases provide information on recent policy developments and encourage researchers to consider how those decisions may affect future outcomes. Policy issues change in states yearly, so case studies of the type presented merely provide background for contemporary policy analysis.
- Considering how researchers and policymakers in different states have approached puzzling policy problems in the past can help new generations of analysts and advocates to think critically and analytically about the policy problems they confront in their states.

The decline in equal opportunity evident during the transition to universal college preparation concerns us: It is also now apparent that state policies and the policies of other nations are the testing grounds for new access strategies. Throughout this book, we call readers' attention to how policies link directly and indirectly to students' choices about preparation for, enrollment in, departure from, and completion of different colleges and universities. While higher education research and policy studies of outcomes can be and have been used to inform policy decisions and educational practices, it is also essential to recognize research limitations. Too frequently, researchers and policymakers assume there are simple solutions to complex educational problems and social inequalities—mistakes we have made—partly because the logical models used in policy analysis and research oversimplify the complexity of education, governance, and student development.

WHAT IS NEW IN THE THIRD EDITION?

Although we retain and update the frameworks developed over a decade ago, this is a new book for a further period of this nation's history. We briefly outlined the latest and updated perspective on history, shifts in political ideologies, and analyses of trend analyses. The practice of policy analysis continued to change rapidly and dramatically, so we also encourage new, critical thinking about analytic methods used in policy research, an integral part of the questions posed in the chapters' conclusions.

Reframed Historical Perspectives

The reactionary positions advocated by the political right—the idea that the nation and states can return to the past—required us to think about historical legacies as we thought about the current chaos. Specifically, the idea that this nation's education system can move backward to some period of greatness is odd, at the very least. What may have been "great" for some was not for many Americans when many attended legally segregated schools and colleges. At the same time, the frontlines of advocacy for equity have also shifted as liberals defend diversity initiatives and goals. Starting education policy studies with a stronger sense of history is necessary.

While historians use different cut points to distinguish periods, we found five periods of K-12 and higher education policy (Table P.1) provide a historical framework for examining the evolution of policy issues, looking back to understanding history provided means of explaining differences. The chapters discuss how the legacy of decisions made during historic illuminate complexities now being contested in divisive debates about education nationally and in states. States' distinctive histories become legacies influencing the policy frameworks developed in response to neoliberalism and how they've evolved during this chaotic period.

The historical periodization of education policy provides a lens for illuminating the complexity of ideological and policy claims. During the neoliberal turn, policy advocates often arranged data in ways that built their false claims, a tendency that continues. More recently, the rapid progression of statistical methods used by mainstream scholars has often overlooked the impact of policy changes, especially the impact of economic policies on economic inequality (Piketty, 2014). We explain the historical periodization in analyses of the nation's discourse about preparation, access, and persistence (Chapters 2–6) and frame the origins and development of state education systems (Chapters 7–11). The historical perspectives on national issues and state policies across chapters add insight and nuance to analyses of tensions between Diversity, Equity, and Inclusion (DEI) and anti-woke across contexts.

Shifting Political Ideologies

We reconsider the history of political ideologies in states and nationally as they inform contemporary contexts for education. The first two editions focused on the shift from liberal policies of the 1960s and early 1970s to neoliberal policies to neoliberal policies that emerged in the late 1970s and early 1980s, leading to a new trajectory in K-12 accountability and higher education finance. With historical insight, we reconsider how both conservative and liberal policies promoted expansion in the 1950s, the ways the two approaches differed across state contexts, and how these histories influence contemporary debates about higher education, including efforts to reach a reconstructed middle ground in some states crafting strategies for promoting the promise of free community colleges. At the same time, the reactionary tensions by the Make American Great Again

Table P.1 Historical Periods Affecting Higher Education Development and Used to Inform Reframing of Contemporary Policy Issues

Period	Policy and Structural Developments in Higher Education
Early America Educational 1776–1870	• Early post-colonial education with the founding of community-based denominational colleges expansion westward. • Americanization of English governance followed the Supreme Court distinguishing public and independent colleges. • Conflict between Christian denominations in states led to state and regional differences in and higher education. • The Constitution left education development and governance to states. • Land Grants used to encourage education development as the US expanded into the Northwest Territories (now Midwest).
Formation of Public Systems 1870–1945	• "Public" education emerged from Protestant schools. • States excluded competing Catholic schools from public funding. • *Land Grant* colleges emphasized science and technology as a competitive force transforming both public and independent higher education. • The Great Depression created financial difficulties, including mergers, renaming, and repurposing colleges and universities. • In the 1930s, student protests paralleled public disputes about nationalist populism and international workers (communists).
Cold War: Progressive "Golden Age" 1940–1980	• The GI Bill rapidly expanded enrollment and ended *in loco parentis*. • New federal programs invested in research, science education, higher education facilities, and need-based student aid. • States developed state college systems, accelerated by federal support for state planning. • Merit-based admissions and need-based student aid evolved, adding to privilege-based tradition.
The Neoliberal Turn Global Transition 1980–2015	• The federal government formulated, and states implemented the STEM agenda for K-20 education. • The federal government shifted emphasis from need-based grants to loans. • College prices rose as purchasing power of need-based grants declined. • Research universities networked with international corporations in technology development. • State evolved distinctive approaches to promoting (or resisting) equity and fairness in access.
Post-Neoliberal Period 2015–present	• Federal K-12 and higher education continued the neoliberal framework. • States tested different approaches for contending with wealth stratification in higher education. • Internationalization of enrollment transformed with changes in international alliances, global migration, and wars. • Conflict between DEI advocates and anti-woke antagonists moved from political rhetoric into K-12 and higher education.

(MAGA) coalition undermine liberal efforts to promote the dream of citizenship by immigrants raised and attending schools in the US. Across contexts, paying attention to the historical roots of current tensions explains differences in the construction of policies and their timing in different states. States have unique political and cultural histories that explain how they became red or blue in the 2020s and how these tensions influence local educational opportunities and employment pathways.

Like educational opportunities in states and communities, their economies interface with local cultures and regional histories. Local cultures of immigrating, formerly enslaved, and marginalized indigenous cultures, interwoven in progressive policies promoting educational access, also influence regressive attitudes that deny opportunities to some groups. The current period of divisive political beliefs in the nation's polity magnifies local and national educational and economic challenges. These are deep cultural forces mirrored in debates about equity, inclusion, and denial of diversity.

We trace how the conflict between liberal and conservative values transformed as neoliberal compromises emerged and became confounded in different, often oppositional, claims in the current debates. The merging of technocratic and socially progressive values in the Science,Technology, Engineering, and Math (STEM) agenda and emphasizing loans for rising generations to pay their college costs resulted in an excessive debt burden for college dropouts and graduates, impairing their ability to buy homes, marry, and realize their capacity to support families. Liberals bought into the STEM agenda and overlooked the severe consequences of excessive debt, a public financing strategy that emerged from the minority position of liberals in the 1980s and 1990s. The STEM agenda added math and science courses in K-12, deemphasized civics, and pushed technical courses to the margin. Universities embraced the change because it increased the supply of college-prepared youth and increased tuition to adapt to declining government support. Progressives promoting low-cost college and MAGA conservatives seeking to eliminate pedagogies supporting diversity are now contesting these precariously crafted compromises.

Updated Trend Analyses

The first two edition's indicators documented policy changes and educational outcomes ending in 2010 (with modest updates in epilogues included in the second edition). They provided means for examining the neoliberal turn in K-12 and higher education in the decades at both ends of the turn of the twenty-first century. We summarized the findings from this earlier period and updated the indicators to focus on the twenty-first century. The comparison of the neoliberal turn and the current period illuminates new patterns that merit attention in states and nationally as this nation adjusts to a rapidly changing international economy.

The updated indicators reveal some of the flaws of neoliberal strategies, examined along with the review of evolving national and state economic forces affecting employment options. As part of the neoliberal turn, the education establishment supported the agenda set by *A Nation At Risk* (ANAR) (National Commission on Excellence in Education, 1983) and the elitist workforce development strategy that emerged from US trade policies and manifested in *Tough Choices, Tough Times* (Commission on the Skills of the American Workforce, 2007). The STEM agenda aligned college preparatory K-12 education with the idea that the US should educate the engineers and information systems creators providing the designs for products produced by lower-cost labor elsewhere. This nationalistic set of policies coalesced to marginalize and export working-class jobs and technical education was abandoned. However, the US was not the only nation focused on educating information scientists, business leaders, engineers, and lawyers. Outsourcing these skilled functions suddenly revealed the nation's economic dysfunction because declining earnings also hit white-collar Americans. The renewed union labor movement in the early twenty-first century suggests widespread support for these efforts to improve earnings for technical labor and more educated scriptwriters. In retrospect, these policy priorities were a knee-jerk response to growing competition during rapid economic globalization.

Higher education policy is badly in need of reform. This century, we have seen the development of new progressive ideas, versions of the dream, and promise ideals in states as the federal government stuck to outdated neoliberal policy trenches. The extreme clash of ideological beliefs on the political right and left—the great divide between now entrenched progressive views on diversity and equity and the reactionary beliefs that the nation would benefit from returning to the 1930s (i.e., the MAGA movement)—may be worse, metaphorically, than the oscillating Ukraine-Russian battle lines. Looking back to the formation of the public systems (1870–1945) provides a historical perspective, giving readers insights absent in the entrenched ideological battles in this post-neoliberal period (2015 and beyond).

Reframing Preparation, Access, and Persistence

These are troubling times, with conflicting education and social policies threatening the nation's stability and, possibly, its capacity to maintain democratic institutions. Although the content taught in schools and colleges is often at the center of the nation's political storms, education continues to be central to democracy. When we examine historical transformations and contemporary trends enlightened by thinking more critically about historical conflicts within education, we realize that education often responds to political changes rather than leading through content, teaching, and learning innovations. Since the history of schooling frequently places education as a leading force in social uplift, it is too easy to expect education to fix social problems. Unfortunately, inequality and social class conflict are part of American history and have been shaping forces in educational reform. We won't speculate about the future of American politics but look back for a clearer view of K-12 and higher education in contemporary society and the economy.[1]

NOTE

1 We have no known conflicts of interest to disclose for any of our chapters. Correspondence concerning the chapters in this book should be addressed to author Nathan J. Daun-Barnett.

REFERENCES

Commission on the Skills of the American Workforce. (2007). *Tough choices, tough times: The report of the new commission on skills of the American workforce*. National Center on Education and the Economy.

Meyer, H.-D., St. John, E. P., Chankseliani, M., & Uribe, L. (Eds.) (2013). *Fairness in access to higher education in a global perspective: Reconciling excellence, efficiency, and justice*. Sense Publications.

National Commission on Excellence in Education (1983). *A nation at risk: The imperative for educational reform*. U.S. Government Printing Office.

Piketty, T. (2014). *Capital in the 21st century*. Belknap Press.

ACKNOWLEDGMENTS

This third edition of *Public Policy and Higher Education* adapts previous frameworks but is primarily a new text. We benefited substantially from reviewers who had used prior editions. They point to the necessity of updating analyses and addressing contemporary political extremism. The policy issues in higher education have changed substantially in the past decade, requiring us to take a historical perspective to understand better the divisive issue now manifest nationally and across states. Prior editions benefited from funding from the Ford Foundation for Projects Promoting Equity in Urban and Higher Education at the University of Michigan's National Center for Institutional Diversity. An exceptional and creative data analyst, Karen Moronski-Chapman, compiled the analyses for the prior editions but was unavailable to continue with this edition because of her obligations on other projects. We thank Lariba Pakmoni, Qianqian Xu, and Jules Orcutt, graduate students at the University at Buffalo, for supporting data analysis, updating cases, and indexing for this edition. We sincerely appreciate thoughtful reviews by John Thelin, Professor Emeritus at the University of Kentucky, Gresham Collom, Assistant Professor at the University of Minnesota, Ontario Wooden, Senior Associate Dean in the University College at the University of North Carolina, and a colleague in Florida, who preferred to remain anonymous, given the current political environment in the state.

Finally, readers may notice a change in the order of authors. As the first author of the third edition, I would like to acknowledge the important contributions that Ed St. John has made that extend well beyond this publication. Ed and I have had variations of this conversation for over two decades, beginning when I was a graduate student presenting for the first time at the Association for the Study of Higher Education (ASHE) annual meeting. Each of us remembers that story slightly differently—he thought his comments as a discussant were overly critical, and as a second-year doctoral student, I was relieved that he had spared us justifiable criticism. One year later, he moved to the University of Michigan, and I was his first new advisee. This volume reflects our conversations and debates over the past two decades. Each of us has grown during that time and our relationship has evolved in the process. For those who have ever published with Ed, and there are many reading this volume, you know that it can be a humbling experience to work with a scholar so brilliant and prolific. I began as his graduate student, we have grown as colleagues, and he is now a dear friend. He will always be my mentor, and it may take several more volumes before I consider myself a peer.

Typically, we would assign authorship according to the relative contribution to the text. I suspect that Ed and I spent similar amounts of time on the production of this volume, and it was his wish that I serve as the first author. In truth, my contributions are an extension of his legacy. He was engaged in this public policy conversation well before I was even a college student. My contributions to the broader conversation are a small response to his enormous impact on the field.

As graduate students aspiring to careers as scholars, we are advised to separate ourselves from our advisors and establish ourselves as independent scholars. I am sure that is good advice when tenure and promotion are the goals. In fact, I am sure that I have shared similar advice with others on that path. When we wrote the first edition of *Public Policy and Higher Education*, I was on the tenure track, and Ed struggled to finish the volume. I was advised that spending my time this way would not benefit my career. I disagreed, but it was beside the point. My success as a scholar was attributable to him, and I realized I still had much more to learn from him. Given the generational nature of our work, what has made our relationship so powerful over the years is that we see higher education policy from two very different perspectives. Ed began his policy work during the transition from the liberal to the neoliberal periods, where I have only known neoliberalism as a policy context. At times, I think Ed may view me as a neoliberal, and he may be right; from my vantage point, I am a change agent in a neoliberal context. These different perspectives animate our work, enliven our conversations and debates, and inform how we have ultimately approached this text. I appreciate everything Ed has done to advance our thinking in this space, and I look forward to another 20 years of thinking with and learning from him.

1
INTRODUCTION

Uncertainty now prevails in US higher education policy due to clashes between the progressive left and conservative extremists embracing Donald Trump's populist movement to Make America Great Again (MAGA). The MAGA culture has captured the consciousness of many whites feeling disenfranchised and thrusting them into opposing social and political forces promoting equity across races and classes, known as the Diversity, Equity, and Inclusion (DEI) movement. The colleges and universities are battlegrounds for MAGA v. DEI, as the demand for opportunities at elite private and public colleges has turned into trench warfare in communities across the nation. After noting the current troubling context for higher education policy, we examine how this turmoil spills over into academic discourses, including the evolution of the higher education policy studies specialization, before introducing our approach to this edition.

SHIFTING CONTEXTS FOR CLASHING ACADEMIC DISCOURSE

Manipulation of policy studies by federal agencies fostered buy-in to the Science, Technology, Engineering, and Math (STEM) agenda by the education establishment in K-12 and higher education seeking new waves of federal support (Part I, Chapter 2). Promoting marketization of higher education aligned with the K-20 STEM agenda, federal policies transformed the education trajectory at the outset of the neoliberal period. Uncertainty now prevails in US higher education policy due to clashes between the progressive left and MAGA conservative extremists. After noting the current troubling context for higher education policy, we examine how this turmoil spills over into academic discourses, including the evolution of the higher education policy studies specialization.

As the neoliberal period unfolded, public deception became apparent, and the urban and rural poor experienced a regress in opportunities to attend four-year colleges. The new liberal education establishment continued to ignore the deceptions. The assumptions of marketization—the "global consensus" for higher education finance (Gore, 2000)—appealed to libertarians, a strong force among economists who advanced national government on economic globalization. The STEM pipeline appealed to the science establishment, long-favored disciplines in federal education and research funding. In short, the neoliberal trajectory reinforced oft-held views in economics, sciences, and education, the troika of academic power supporting the neoliberal education establishment. By 2015, the uneasy alliances began to break down, and a new period of economic globalization emerged.

Global higher education has entered a new period. The Israel-Hamas War seems as divisive for this generation as the Vietnam War had been for the Baby Boomers, the children of World War II (WWII) vets and Depression. Congressional meddling resulted in the ending of presidencies at Harvard and the University of Pennsylvania. Student unrest and conflict between students on campuses and between campuses and their various publics are reminiscent of the earlier period, but the financial context differs fundamentally. In the 1960s and 1970s, low- and middle-income students could study subjects of interest and graduate from college without substantial debt. Now, students graduate with excessive debt and the national price tag now exceeds more than $1.7 trillion (Hanson, 2023). As grandparents, the Boomer generation currently has grandchildren facing choices between excessive debt, increasingly too high to support a family after professional degrees, or a lifetime of navigating back and forth between employment work and technically acquiring new skills and certificates through web courses and exams.

In the 1980s, the federal government marketized higher education by emphasizing loans and tax credits for all students rather than adequately funding need-based grants during the neoliberal transition. Most states reduced the taxpayer share of college costs, resulting in higher tuition. The living standard for college graduates declined as college debt mounted. While these trends are still evident, our overemphasis on this weakness in the collective theories of the education establishment left too many issues unaddressed. Perhaps the two most significant developments during this period of chaos and disruption were the COVID-19 pandemic and the racial awakening following the murder of George Floyd at the knee of Derek Chauvin of the Minneapolis Police Department.

The nation was slow to respond after news of the first COVID-19 virus cases surfaced in Western media in early January 2020. The health systems were unprepared, given the prior experiences with other viruses, like the Avian flu, that never made it to the US. The scale of this pandemic exploded rapidly, and the national response followed. The *Coronavirus Aid, Relief, and Economic Security Act of 2020* (*CARES Act*) announced the shutdown of in-person courses at colleges and universities, and we expected to return to the semester within two weeks. It took longer to organize the response in the public health system. Despite his public opposition to COVID-19 vaccines, Trump signed the *CARES Act*. Weeks became months, and then months became more than two years of the public health crisis, which will have ripple effects on education and student mental health for the next generation.

George Floyd was murdered just two months into the public health crisis, on May 25, 2020. By this point, the Black Lives Matter (BLM) movement was already well underway, but his death was the spark that accelerated the movement toward racial justice. We know now that the fuel for this conflagration bubbled to the surface in response to the election of President Barack Obama and the subsequent shift in conservative politics to the populist nationalism embodied by the MAGA movement. Progressives drew renewed life from the Obama years and embraced a social justice agenda that called for more significant social and economic equity. At the same time, the new conservatism rallied against this new progressive social agenda, labeling it socialism, and cried out for a return to a time they felt embodied America's greatness. This post-neoliberal transition plays out at the federal and state levels in complex ways. It is unclear how this transition will unfold or what the new period will mean for higher education, but we must recognize our significant moment.

Before Floyd's murder, Trump had responded to fact-checking by labeling the mainstream media as fake news, demonstrating a remarkable ability to shift meanings. Via news reports in 2020, Eddie Glaude's (2020) *Begin Again: James Baldwin's America and Its Urgent Lessons for Our Own* briefly shed light on the big lie that held Blacks down for centuries, but the term "big lie" soon took opposing meanings. As the 2020 presidential election unfolded, Baldwin's original idea was that the "big lie" kept Blacks in their places in a racist society. Trump used the term "big lie," once the name of the mechanism for oppressing Blacks, in his description of Biden's November 2020 election. The aggressive responses to the BLM protest in Washington, District of Columbia (DC) illustrate a new meaning of the Bible as a political instrument, at least to Christian nationalists. January 6, 2021, when Trump supporters stormed the US Capitol Building, gave another meaning to the big lie.

In a pivotal moment, during June 1, 2020, BLM protest in Washington DC, the US Army cleared the streets of protestors so that Trump could hold a Bible in front of St. John's Church across the street from the White House. Biden's campaign claimed that Trump held the Bible upside down. It was backward, not upside down, a fact corrected by the *New York Times*, *The Houston Chronicle*, and various new media that used close-up shots confirming the Bible was top-up, but the cover faced Trump instead of the camera (Evon, 2020). The image, a symbolic gesture, and a nit-picking dispute about the picture reveal the unfortunate oppositional treatment of facts in campaigns. At the time, it had been years since fact-checking had made a difference in embarrassing Trump. Biden was engaged in the election battle, and the insurrection in the Capitol Building followed on January 20, 2021. False claims and perverse use of symbols continued to corrupt the public space. Symbols and false notions are disseminated through social media, pushing notions that accentuate social and political divisiveness in this nation's polity. As we finished this third edition, the battles over misinformation continued in the presidential debates four years later.

TROUBLED CONTEXTS FOR HIGHER EDUCATION POLICY

The polarity between the political left and right in the nation's polity, and with public disagreement, spills over into state government, school boards, and campuses. In higher education policy, these contemporary clashes can be viewed as the most recent episode in a long history of conflicting assumptions in periods of disruptions in academic discourses. Considering higher education policy within the context of these historical tensions helps understand DEI and MAGA on campus as part of the knowledge construction and reconstruction processes that evolve and transform paradigms across academic disciplines and professional fields (Table 1.1). The MAGA-DEI debates evolved from

Table 1.1 Historical Formation of Curriculum in Schools and Colleges and Communities of Resistance in Public and Academic Communities

Core Assumptions	Belief Traditions	Action Strategies
A. Formation		
1. Structures of academic fields	Additive knowledge, with breakthroughs: The structure and content of fields change as they develop new specializations (e.g., STEM)	Curriculum structure college-wide and in major programs for undergraduates, graduate, and professional fields build on core knowledge
2. Conflicting views within fields (possible catalysts for paradigm shift)	Critical studies and scientific studies testing assumptions question the core and may influence paradigm shifts (e.g., STEM pipeline)	Critical analyses provide voices of marginalized and excluded, a problem across primary fields and the professions
B. Resistance		
1. Western civilization	Eurocentric (originalist) Values education	Merit- and privilege-based admissions and aid
2. Diversity, Equity, and Inclusion (DEI)	Civil rights Critical theory	Resists discrimination Promotes social justice
3. Make America Great Again (MAGA)	White nationalism Christian nationalism	End affirmative action Remove diversity

prior evolutionary and revolutionary periods of scholarly practices, including additive scholarship on access and equity issues and related practices, the foundations (Part A). Just as historical periods of conflict sparked revolutionary changes in the structures of and beliefs about core assumptions in the disciplinary knowledge bases, these debates unraveled the pretense of consensus in disciplinary scholarly communities. The MAGA-DEI debates evolved from disputes about foundations, now criticized by both left and right extremes in academia and society (Part B). We outline the historical progress of scholarships at the core of the MAGA-DEI debate before delving into contemporary forms of resistance to curricula in K-12 schools and governance in academic communities at colleges and universities. Before discussing the foundations for MAGA v. DEI, the clashing strands resistance to them.

Conflicting Beliefs Obfuscating Rationality in Higher Education Policy

The dream of a distinctive national trajectory toward liberty for all through democracy and industry, the notion of American exceptionalism for social justice advocates, was shattered by these events and the tide of turmoil that overwhelms hope for a consensual polity with conflicting beliefs and increased acceptance of lies as truths. Perhaps Donald Trump's claims that Obama was not born in the US remains the marker event for the growing MAGA public's complacency with false narratives. The birther movement captivated the nation's discourse, though it was an obvious falsity (Pease, 2023). This clash overshadows current academic and cultural debates about educational content and governance. Before discussing reframing in the recent period of clashing perspectives of content and pedagogy in K-20 education below (Part A, Table 1.1), we examine the evolution of academic fields and the necessity of reframing policy issues to move toward fairer and more just policy decisions.

Evolution of Academic Fields
The evolving structure of curriculum evolved in parallel with historical periods of policy. A brief outline of periods is:

- *Early American Origins (1776–1870)*. Most colleges provided faith-centric liberal arts colleges for preachers, teachers, and civil servants. The body of knowledge (content) was considered finite in some fields (i.e., religion, humanities, and math). Still, the growth of expertise spurred the development of other fields, especially the new applied science fields of medicine and nursing.
- *Creation of Public Systems (1870–1945)*. The emergence of the "common" public schools hastened the secularization of school curricula. The new land grant universities accelerated science applications and the emergence of engineering, accelerating knowledge building as land grants and older campuses competed for students, faculty, and prestige.
- *Cold War (1945–1980)*. Massive infusion of (a) veterans accelerated student demand for applied fields; (b) advances in sciences fueled by federal research funding; and (c) Baby Boomers demanded new, critical social science knowledge. Higher education policy studies emerged in the 1960s as the federal government sought research informing education development.
- *Neoliberal Turn (1980–2015)*. The STEM pipeline solidified the domination of science, math, and engineering within university budgeting priorities. Economic stratification of access, as an artifact of differentiated pricing, fostered a new period of academic elitism. Higher education policy studies bifurcate into mainstream works informing the new system and critical studies voicing increasingly marginalized groups (e.g., minority, urban, and rural students).
- *The Post-Neoliberal Period*. Academe's unrest is characterized by renewed tensions between values in the civil rights movement, now manifest in DEI, and the inherent conservatism of the academic mainstream. Disciplinary preparation in graduate studies predisposes professors to support, ignore, or resist the trajectories of curriculum evolution on campuses, governing practices in academic departments, and regulations influencing academic mentoring.

The tension between clusters of mainstream and critical academics within fields continues as the public engages in the MAGA-DEI debates. New minority faculty members in departments with traditional norms face more extreme transitional challenges, a catalyst for hopeful advocacy for adopting more caring norms. The field of higher education policy has been swept along in these tensions as many writers align with the various streams of advocacy in K-12 and higher education.

Historical Foundations of Contemporary Conflict About Education
It is time to reframe the old assumptions to have a realistic hope of addressing contemporary education challenges. Both changes in the structure of higher education finance and the conflicting values in policy demand differ now from those used a decade and more ago. After four decades of the K-20 STEM agenda and marketization of higher education, it is time to examine evidence that contradicts the core assumptions and practices of education scholarship, policy, and practice. The current clashes in espoused beliefs on and off campuses barrage the public with the news; misinformation disseminated

through news and social media rehashed in conversations in families and classrooms. The texts questioned by the political right and the logic informing these critiques emanate from competing academic beliefs and traditions. So, it is time to reflect on the intellectual traditions that shape beliefs in scholarship. Rather than being a conflict between education and a contingent in the polity, the disputes grow out of conflicting academic discourses.

The implicit assumptions about culture and progress made by academic writers also foster siloed beliefs and constrained exchange using these assumptions. The exchanges within academic communities—on campuses, in departments, and during classroom discussions—are micro contexts that enable divisiveness, tacit acceptance of assumed truths, and silences by some students. Scientific constructs always faced underlying challenges, as conveyed in *The Structure of Scientific Revolutions*, Thomas Khun's (2012) oft-republished book on the evolution of knowledge as paradigms in primary scientific disciplines. Like the sciences, the social science and humanities disciplines and professional fields have paradigms with implicit beliefs partially supported by research, counterviews contesting assumptions, and inherently contradictory pedagogical content. The norms of sciences, humanities, social science, and other professional fields convey cultures of belief that affect knowledge creation. These norms are part of the cultures of disciplines that can also merit careful students, Michael Foucault's (2013) *The Archaeology of Knowledge*, also published in many editions, reveals the analytic tools for discerning bias require critical thought about the evolution of content, pedagogy, and practices within disciplines affecting professional practice within institutions, an analytical process often referred to as "postmodernism." The assumptions used in inquiry and the cultures that convey them are now disputed in K-12 education and conflicted in higher education.

Understanding the contemporary MAGA-DEI clash requires understanding the progression of conflicts about content and cultural traditions for research and action in professions, including behaviors in educational organizations as communities of scholarship. To deal forthrightly with the MAGA-DEI conflict, now seemingly earth-shattering in many contexts of college student life and professorial academic life, we need a historical perspective on the evolution of ideas and revolutionary leaps in beliefs underlying academic discourses. Like other basic and professional fields, higher education policy studies have paradigm conflicts and resistance to beliefs conveyed in the literature (research, policy reports, books on finance and policy, and textbooks). Specializations in higher education as a professional field of study draw from diverse academic disciplines. For example, higher education policy studies draw from law, government, economics, sociology, history, and other core academic fields. The evolving scholarship within the specialization is influenced by progress in paradigmatic thought in the disciplines and the specialized field as conveyed through the evolving norms in content pedagogies.

The evolving discourses in the study of higher education policy, intertwined with the debates in the core disciplines, shape and shake the foundational assumptions for this professional specialization. The emergence of the STEM pipeline prioritized the narrowing of pathways for all students and is at the center of MAGA-DEI disagreements. Rebuilding pathways between schools and colleges changes pedagogy in high schools and college entry courses within the disciplines. There are three patterns of resistance to the revised content structures for organizing high schools to provide college pathways through the curriculum. We briefly outline the history of higher education content before discussing the three prominent streams of resistance.

Western Civilization: Reclaiming a Legacy of Resisting Social Progress
Conservative academics reacted to the student movement and resisted institutional responsiveness to students' interests (Table 1.1, Part B.1). Student protests, critical scholarship, and social justice courses began marginalizing humanities in the traditional collegiate core curriculum. At Columbia, Daniel Bell led a planning group studying undergraduate curriculum in the Ivy League, an effort to retain the European core (Bell, 1966). This sentiment continued through the decades in elite academic circles and morphed as the K-20 STEM paradigm further marginalized the humanities.

Allan Bloom's *The Closing of the American Mind* (1987) made a persuasive argument that Western logics provide the basis for education in a democratic society. Built on his critique of the 1960s student protest, Bloom traced the Civil Rights movement in the early 1960s from the South to Northern campuses. He criticized the education of the early protesters because they had studied at Historically Black Colleges and Universities (HBCUs) and, he claimed, lacked proper foundations. The essence of the argument did not adequately deal with the roots of the Free Speech Movement in Berkeley, where the local social protests (in Oakland and San Francisco) were catalysts for campus unrest, or the Students for a Democratic Society (SDS) in Ann Arbor with a logic rooted students' and professors' recollections of John Dewey's legacy. Like *A Nation at Risk* (National Commission on Excellence in Education, 1983), Bloom's core argument set aside contemporary reasoning for social justice for diverse populations.

By the middle 1980s, the STEM-pipeline theory of the K-20 curriculum emerged at the intersection of the neoliberal education establishment and the corporate interests promoting economic globalization. In 1984, the neoliberal trajectory was in motion as William Bennett transitioned from the National Endowment for the Humanities to the US Department of Education. Reagan's first Secretary of Education, Ted Bell, sought to save the US Department of Education despite Reagan's campaign pledge to abolish the new Department, created in 1980 under President Carter. *A Nation at Risk*, a task force report, developed a strategy of compromise to design a new K-20 academic strategy centered on preparing all students for STEM fields. The objective of the group had been to set aside educational innovations designed because of student and social protest of the 1960s and instead encourage critical thought in K-12 and emphasize science and math (Ravitch, 2010), leading to a period of public deception in reporting of education statistics, acknowledged by a leader of the movement, Diane Ravitch.

Before becoming Secretary of Education, William Bennett (1984) wrote *To Reclaim a Legacy*. Much like *The Closing of the American Mind,* Bennett's report for the National Endowment for the Humanities advocated a return to Western humanities. Bennett ended up being both the steward for and critic of policies promoting the STEM pipeline. He also ardently advocated marketization to stimulate efficiency (St. John, 1994; St. John & Asker, 2003). Instead, the rising cost of educating STEM elite students got passed along to students, many of whom mortgaged their futures with debt to pay college costs.

The late 1980s was a period of growing public deception about K-20 education. ANAR was a report the education establishment could accept and support. Who could argue against math and science? The problems were many, however. The report had not told "the rest of the story." For example, it did not address the budget, and President Reagan was well into his savage funding cuts in Elementary and Secondary Education Act (ESEA) and the Higher Education Act (HEA) programs. A transforming neoliberal education quickly coalesced, supporting the K-20 pipeline while maintaining silence about student debt and cuts to vocational education. As the new Secretary of Education, Bennett led this new agenda. US Department of Education cut (reduced budgets or defunded) programs promoting social justice through reforms starting in the 1960s, but it did nothing to restore the humanities. The advocacy for Eurocentric values promoted by Bloom and Bennett languished as science and technology flourished as the priority in policy rhetoric and education budgets.

William Bennett did not stay silent after leaving the Department of Education. Instead, he became the voice for Eurocentric nationalism. In *The De-Valuing of America: The Fight for the Culture of Our Children*, one of several books after he served his term as Secretary, Bennett (1994) builds an ideological agenda for the new right in education. The values base for his vision harkened back to the period when reading instruction used Protestant biblical texts in the nation's early public schools. But he was Jesuit educated, having graduated from DC's vaunted Gonzaga High School. The push for high school graduation requirements under his leadership at the Department of Education in the early 1980s implemented the Catholic high school's curriculum, absent the religion courses, as a new national standard. The Eurocentric argument about curriculum united Protestants and Catholics in resistance to the STEM-inspired national education standards and fueled resistance to affirmative action. This ethos led to voter-mandated bans on Affirmative Action in Michigan and California, states that had once epitomized the movement toward progressive education for all. These beliefs favored merit and inherited privilege, or legacy of families, in admissions.

From Civil Rights to Diversity, Equity, and Inclusion (DEI)
The Civil Rights movement profoundly influenced social sciences and humanities courses on college campuses in the 1960s (Table 1.1, Part B.2). At UC Berkeley, San Francisco State, the University of Michigan, and campuses nationwide, students protested racial and gender discrimination and for coverage of social issues in the curriculum, sometimes advocating for new fields like gender and Black studies. It was a period of research, teaching, and curriculum innovation in higher education (Goodchild, 1997). A split between the academic mainstream and critical academic works opened across fields, divisions worsening in the current post-neoliberal period. The higher education literature promoted DEI as core issues (e.g., Winkle Wagner & Locks, 2013), expanding content in the field of study.

The Civil Rights Movement began during Reconstruction when an emergent National Association for the Advancement of Colored People (NAACP) began litigating to overcome reactionary policies and court decisions that segregated the nation. Also, following the Civil War, the women's right to vote movement gained momentum. Colleges provided spaces for social protest of inequality from the 1930s onward (Cohen, 1993). The 1954 *Brown V. Board of Education* decision resulted in federal efforts to desegregate public schools but not colleges. People of color and women marginalized across the history of higher education, especially before the 1960s, were strong voices in the student movements. The struggles from education opportunity and fair access—admissions practices that recognize centuries of educational cross-generation privilege denied—are central to the struggle in higher education.

Noted philosophers in their times, like Allan Bloom (1987) and Sidney Hook (1973), were critical of the Civil Rights movement on campuses, including urban riots and large-scale student protests, and its impact on liberalizing the curriculum. From the perspective of the left, in contrast, the Civil Rights movement was central to this trajectory toward liberty, freedom, and social justice. The core egalitarian ideals trace back to the American Revolution, the antislavery movement before the Civil War.

The anticommunist movement of right-leaning scholars in the US silenced the left during the Cold War (Bell, 1966). This conservative view of Western Civilization, like Bloom's lamenting critique of the student movement, became a logic for revising the core. In Europe after WWII, Marxist and liberal arguments provided competing foundations in the social sciences. After the fall of the Berlin Wall, however, the extremists of the anticommunist movement waned in the influence that dampened critique in the social sciences during the Cold War. The neoliberal turn in education also marginalized humanities, a conclusion often reached by conservative (e.g., Bennett, 1984) and critical (e.g., Nussbaum, 2000) humanists. The academic left adopted European neo-Marxist theories in social critique from the 1990s onward, recognizing extreme academic conservatism as social propaganda (Habermas, 1991), becoming a tool of the MAGA movement. Social critique, relying on social theory and humanist traditions, began to deconstruct and criticize assumptions lodged in the Eurocentric frameworks that treated knowledge as rooted in Western Civilization.

The twenty-first century's DEI movement builds on critical social science. Activists learn from research promoting equity and social justice but, more recently, sustained losses in affirmative action and women's rights cases in the Supreme Court. A core assumption in pedagogies promoting social justice is that ignorance, caused by prejudice, is mitigated by education and training (Adams et al., 2000). The University of Michigan successfully defended affirmative action, at least for an interim period, in the Supreme Court with research showing whites benefited from education with students of color (Gurin et al., 2002; Gurin et al., 2010). Pedagogies and practices continue to build on these findings as the DEI movement evolves. The evolving knowledge base influences curriculum in K-12 schools and organizational practices in higher education.

The DEI movement was also inspired by the dream of a post-racial society and accelerated by the election of Barack Obama as President. "Given our divisions today, however, Obama's premise appears implausible" (Leboeuf, 2019, p. 261). Obama's vision of hope for a civil, post-racial society proved unrealistic. The DEI movement's strategies for promoting hope through administrative regulation in higher education challenged assumptions of academics resistant to social progress because of foundational assumptions and beliefs formed in their graduate education. Like the Western Civilization movement, the MAGA critics of DEI focus on the limitations of the dream. In this book, we encourage readers to find neutral ground for moments of open conversation about policy, an aim increasingly challenging to actualize.

The assumption of ignorance, central to many social justice pedagogies, became a limitation of the DEI movement. As the Western Civilization advocacy demonstrates, outlined above, the advocates for Eurocentric education are not ignorant people. Educated in traditions of science, social science, and the humanities, many critics have knowledge-based frames. It is possible that when MAGA v. DEI tensions become part of policy deliberations, groups with mixed beliefs can create intellectual space for debate about predispositions. The reduction of the values about social justice to pedagogies and practices for all students across professions causes resistance, as does the prejudicial barriers created by Eurocentric and mainstream beliefs. Higher education is now in turmoil as intellectual conflict permeates into core knowledge and surfaces in microaggressions and disputes within and across academic fields.

The MAGA-DEI Clash Polarizing Academic Left and Right

The MAGA movement is based on beliefs—as untested propositions undaunted by facts—and is not predisposed to open discourse. (Table 1.1, Part B.3). Schools and colleges are caught in the tide of change propagated by the new right through themes advocated in social media. Three aspects of the MAGA movement—Christian nationalism, white nationalism, and gender discrimination—have fueled conflict over policies in education from K-12 to higher education and internationally.

Christian Nationalism

This movement integrates populist theology and political beliefs in religious education and popular media of the far right. Based on the faith-centric approach to the liberal arts tradition, it centers teaching in the humanities, social sciences, and sciences in faith-based views emphasizing nation-building. The interweaving of Christian doctrine and populist nation-building, as conveyed in many denominational schools and colleges, has a long history internationally as it does domestically. Doctrinaire beliefs form through evangelist Christian theology, networks of Christian activists, and social media, influencing new book bans and other local initiatives. This movement in the US is not new, nor is it a distinctively American phenomenon. Instead, in various differentiated forms, it is an international force in rightist populism.

Currently, Christian nationalism is a growing global force aligned with nationalist groups seeking to deconstruct international agreements on trade, peace, and environment; wars and cross-nation migration-immigration continue as global governance mechanisms are confronted by a new Cold War, with democratic values being challenges by autocratic expediency. Many Christian and Catholic college campuses have boards, administrations, and teaching faculty aligned with the Christian nationalist tradition, and they reinforce these values, beliefs, and ideologies. On secular campuses, faith-centered students learn to silence their views (Eckstein & Turman, 2002). Many students who enter secular colleges hold MAGA views and have college experiences that reinforce their beliefs. In contrast, Christian students' sense of belonging can conflict with humanities taught on secular campuses (Alvim, 2021). Creating cross-faith dialogue on secular campuses is troublesome due to extremes within faith traditions, from fundamentalist to liberationist views, complicating and often silencing diverse views on campuses (Small, 2011).

American (White) Nationalism

Before the Civil War, state Protestant denominations influenced state discourses and were intertwined with both the pro- and anti-slavery interests of states. During Reconstruction and in the following Jim Crow period, states' rights gained footing as a post-hoc rationale for the South's rebellion. But as Klan activism expanded in communities across the states and especially in the South, populist politicians like Huey Long and George Wallace tapped into nationalist white values. Ronald Reagan was the first to bring this festering resentment into the mainstream of a national party. Republicans continued to attract white nationalists, and Trump's political rise relied upon this group as the party's core.

In the US, because of the yearnings of some for the return to the academic roots of Western Civilization, it is evident that Eurocentrism is still a force in debates about methods and academic traditions. The moralizing of scholars like William Bennett fueled the links to Christian evangelizing, much the ways Eurocentric logic links to white nationalism. Patriotic themes de-emphasizing the trajectory toward race equity are aligned with policy lobbying about the K-12 curriculum, especially teaching history that aligns with patriotism and Christian-centric historical themes. Consider these findings from a recent analysis of school reform initiatives:

> Christian nationalism brings whites who identify with the ideological and political left into complete alignment with their conservative counterparts who are already more likely to support mandatory patriotic education. Our findings provide critical context for ongoing battles over public-school curricula and education's role in perpetuating social privilege.
>
> (Perry et al., 2023, p. 694)

White nationalism takes many forms on college campuses (Gavin, 2021). Nostalgia, legal originalism, closing the border, white idealism rooted in Western Civilization, and the foreign threat to higher education through international enrollment become real threats in the minds of citizens and students. Some professors, too, identify with these causes. The dissemination of these interests through social media becomes part of the educational content swirl, influencing swings of the public debates about education, as illustrated by Florida's anti-woke movement. Since teachers and students have different biases, those with populist beliefs may disregard inclusive content. Some Latinx, Black, and Asian students enroll in college with extremely conservative theological views as well, so the term "white nationalism" does not precisely fit the quasi-inclusive nature of the MAGA sentiments on campuses. Minorities can align with nationalist groups as they integrate into campus cultures that morph into nationalist frames and frameworks. Innovations in right-leaning critiques and practices are integral to streams of belief in American culture and education. Given these developments within education, discussions about improving educational opportunities are essential to education development and college life across the political spectrum, but they face a cacophony of entrenched beliefs.

"Me Too" and Gender Biases in the Mix of Ideological Turmoil

Trials of sexual predators capture attention in the confused mix of beliefs. The fall of icons like Bill Cosby and Harvey Weinstein ignited the "Me Too" movement, but Trump's E. Jean Carroll trials were ignored by the MAGA movement, by and large. The right-leaning response aligns with the long-standing protection of perpetrators within institutions and movements. Democrats also paid no heed to Clinton's sexual blunders and impeachment, further illustrating the role of collective bias and collective acceptance of institutionalized sexism.

Gender bias is a complex, confounding, and contested issue in education. Like Eurocentrism, it is rooted in the methods of inquiry in the sciences, humanities, and social sciences because white men were the primary writers in the Western intellectual tradition. Gender bias permeates academic cultures through behavioral norms and silences about harassment. Given the long history of professors dating and marrying students, much as doctors found paramours and wives in the nursing corps in hospitals, these cultural biases have been a long-standing problem. Senior male faculty suffered new self-image problems as Harvard and other universities adopted new policies on sexual harassment in the late twentieth century (e.g., Rosovsky, 1990). Like families with histories of child sexual abuse protecting themselves, academic cultural norms cover up and protect perpetrators.

Campus regulatory constraints on cross-gender faculty-student interaction increased over the past four decades. Fair treatment of people of diverse races and gender preferences, practices integral to contemporary DEI practices and guidelines, have not changed deeply entrenched norms that protect the privileged and powerful. The challenges are deeply embedded in documents, procedures, and practices, turning the new practices into enforcement. Even course evaluations, which typically allow professors to select most of the questions on evaluation questionnaires, carry forward gender biases (Khokhlova et al., 2023). In American culture, white nationalism aligns with the perpetuation of gender bias (Corcoran, 2019). Yet, it would be naive to place all the blame on rightists, nationalists, or conservatives. As the Clinton example so aptly illustrates, the defense of leaders cuts across value traditions. Churches and universities, especially, are bastions for protecting the elite.

The opening of dialogue and seeking remedies, promoted by the political left in this nation's institutions and polity, brings the MAGA into conflict with DEI. The arguments about gendered bathrooms by Republican presidential candidates in 2014 are reminiscent of George Wallace's claim he was not a racist, that he just wanted people to take a shower where they wanted to take showers, when he ran as an American Independent candidate. The fact that schools are at the center of these extremist arguments is not new, but instead is deeply rooted in diverse cultures and beliefs. Teaching history helps, as does reading Peggy Sue Wallace Kennedy's (2019) story as the daughter of George Wallace recalling her father's run for the presidency. Bathroom privacy is a metaphor for bias, now for outrage about gender affirming care and transition surgery, as it was for white segregationists.

PURPOSES, PEDAGOGICAL DESIGN, AND ORGANIZATION

The convergence of bias and silence in academic, civic, and political cultures underlies the complexities of MAGA v. DEI division in schools, colleges, and the communities they serve. The political power of MAGA extremists in the nation's polity influences K-12 and higher education curricula. School board meetings, opinion pieces, and social media become tools in alliance building. The rapid assault on the agenda of hope has caught many educators in the unexpected position of defending progressive histories in their core curriculum, guidelines for practice, and the cultures intersecting with educational institutions. The sources of the conflict are legacies from the past and are not limited to the US policy discourse. After the shock of polarizing disruptions subsides, the next step necessitates opening the discourse around pedagogical content and methods within schools, colleges, and the communities they serve. Listening rather than assuming ignorance is a difficult practice to learn for people across the political spectrum.

Purposes

Shifts in policy correspond with changing beliefs about society and education and have consequences for learning and attainment outcomes. Examining changes in policies and outcomes across periods, informed by history and shifting political rationales, we conclude chapters by discussing new issues, often related to problems overlooked during policy development. We also raise questions for policymakers considering alternative strategies, discussions about framing issues—in graduate classrooms and alliances of activist reformers—and researchers seeking to advance knowledge and inform practice.

While we care about and discuss equity and uplift for marginalized groups left behind by past policy choices, we do not argue for specific policies or actions. The lingering effects of the neoliberal policy framework are highly problematic, but some states have started testing new remedies to localized challenges. States with different dominant ideologies—the red and blue blotches on the national map—sometimes tackle similar problems with comparable methods. Comparing actions across states—and we used states with different political histories—provides new insights for researchers, students, and activists engaged in the national discourse. Comparing states to global issues provides an added, enriched perspective on governments' challenges in this period of lingering neoliberalism. The best course of action for this or other nations is not yet clear, at least for us, but we encourage thoughtful reflection of potential and possibilities.

Pedagogical Design

The analytic method across chapters encourages readers to think critically about their assumptions, situated in their lived histories, as they engage in conversations about issues. The content and issues addressed across chapters vary substantially, from legal history to beliefs and ideologies underlying historical and contemporary choices and decisions about policy to national matters about the future of educational opportunities and specific state programs and issues dealing with local challenges that emerge and history unfolds. While headings and titles vary across chapters, the pedagogical design includes consistent features.

Legal History Contextualizing Policy: A Starting Point for Reconceptualizing Strategies

Laws, regulations, and court cases shape the policy history of higher education and typically constrain policy choices and political decisions about action strategies. Given the nature of case law, history matters, and while Chapter 2 provides the overall legal framework underlying the historical periodization, each chapter starts by examining national and state histories developed within and pushing the boundaries of legal frameworks. Across chapters, readers are encouraged to ponder legal issues bounding the strategies they advocate as remedies to challenges facing diverse groups and cultures. The impact of the MAGA-DEI permeates into political interests and values judgments about strategies for public finance, outreach to marginalized groups, support of students seeking education uplift, and eventual opportunities for students and their capabilities to actualize the economic wellbeing of their families.

Beliefs, Ideologies, and Experience Shape Interpretation

When reviewing the history of policy choices in the abstract, the reader's first response is often belief-based until sharing evidence with people holding different frames. Listening to such bluster of initial reactions, as inner chatter of the mind or vocalized views in conversations, illuminates the diversity of opinions. Such views influence and are influenced by political arguments, especially in the context of MAGA-DEI battles in exchanges—the microaggressions that can linger in the minds of victims. As a second step in constructing chapters and focusing on Chapter 3, we use historical framing of conflicting beliefs and ideologies as the discourses evolved. We encourage readers to think about their inner framing of issues as they react to our construction of history. We recognize a range of historical interpretations, so we try to clarify how our views relate to other arguments; therefore, we are not claiming we've captured all points of view on critical issues.

Evidence of Correspondence Between Policies and Outcomes

Data analysis informing policy was sparse before 1960 because data and statistical methods were more rudimentary. After reviewing the history of policy studies in higher education, including conflicts about the "facts" used to craft neoliberal policies—manipulating data to disguise the ill effects of neoliberal policies—we define the straightforward method we use (Chapter 2). Past efforts to use systematic approaches repeatedly gave way to politics. Using national data, we present recent trends (2000–2020) for national issues and state cases (Chapters 7–11), providing readers with evidence for testing how well their assumptions hold up. As a third step, we encourage readers to consider shifts in outcomes that correspond with recent policy changes nationally and in states. Comparing periods (2000–2015 and beyond 2015) reveals a slowly unfolding new period of education history.

Reframing

The contested value sets of red and blue manifest as MAGA versus DEI as national discourses influence higher education policies. The polarities in the public polity hamper open discourse that might reframe national, state, and local strategies for promoting educational opportunity and economic wellbeing. We introduce ways of reframing educational opportunity and financial wellbeing as a conclusion to Chapter 2. Subsequent chapters carry forward this method of analyzing policy trends and outcomes to reach informed judgments about the consequences of policy choices.

Reflective Questions

At the end of each chapter, we ask questions, tailored to encourage readers to go through the pedagogical four-step thought exercise. We presuppose no answers. We encourage debate about the limitations of arguments and data analyses, including ours.

REFERENCES

Adams, M., Blumfeld, W., Castenda, R., Hackman, H., Peters, M., & Aunniga, X. (2000). *Reading for diversity and social justice: An anthology on racism, antisemitism, sexism, heterosexism, ableism and classism*. Routledge.

Alvim, H. G. (2021). When the church comes to campus: Christian convictions and the challenge toward authentic membership in the secular academy. *Growth: The Journal of the Association for Christians in Student Development, 20*(20), 51–64.

Bell, D. (1966). *The reforming of general education: The Columbia college experience in its national setting*. Columbia University Press.

Bennett, W. (1984). *To reclaim a legacy: A report on the humanities in higher education*. National Endowment for the Humanities.

Bennett, W. (1994). *The de-valuing of America: The fight for our culture and our children*. Simon & Schuster.

Bloom, A. (1987). *The closing of the American mind*. Simon & Schuster.

Cohen, R. (1993). *When the old left was young: Student radicals and America's first mass student movement, 1929–1941*. Oxford University Press.

Corcoran, E. (2019). The construction of the ultimate other: Nationalism and manifestations of misogyny and patriarchy in US Immigration Law and Policy. *Georgetown Journal of Gender and the Law, 20*(3), 541–576.

Eckstein, N. J., & Turman, P. D. (2002). Children are to be seen and not heard: Silencing students' religious voices in the university classroom. *Journal of Communication & Religion, 25*(2), 166.

Evon, D. (2020). Did Trump hold the bible upside down? All eyes were on the president as he appeared for a photo-op amid widespread anti-police-brutality protests in June 2020. *People Magazine*. https://people.com/politics/donald-trump-poses-bible-church-photo-op-after-police-clear-his-path-using-tear-gas/

Foucault, M. (2013). *Archaeology of knowledge*. Routledge.

Gavin, M. H. (2021). *The new White nationalism in politics and higher education: The nostalgia spectrum*. Rowman & Littlefield.

Glaude, E. (2020). *Begin again: James Baldwin's America and its urgent lessons for our own*. Crown.

Goodchild, L. F. (1997). Contemporary undergraduate education: An era of alternatives and reassessment. *Theory Into Practice, 36*(2), 123–131.

Gore, A. (2000). The rise and fall of the Washington consensus as paradigm for the developing countries. *World Development, 28*(5), 789–803.

Gurin, P., Dey, E. L., Hurtado, S., & Gurin, G. (2002). Diversity and higher education: Theory and impact on educational outcomes. *Harvard Educational Review, 72*(3), 330–366.

Gurin, P., Lehman, J., Lewis, E., Dey, E. L., Hurtado, S., & Gurin, G. (2010). *Defending diversity: Affirmative action at the University of Michigan.* University of Michigan Press.

Habermas, J. (1991). *The new conservatism: Cultural criticism and the historians' debate.* MIT Press.

Hanson, M. (2023). *Student loan debt statistics. Education Data Initiative.* Retrieved February 27, from https://educationdata.org/student-loan-debt-statistics

Hook, S. (1973). *Education & the taming of power.* Open Court Publishing.

Kennedy, P. W. (2019). *The broken road: George Wallace and a daughter's journey to reconciliation.* Bloomsbury Publishing.

Khokhlova, O., Lamba, N., & Kishore, S. (2023). Evaluating student evaluations: Evidence of gender bias against women in higher education based on perceived learning and instructor personality. *Frontiers in Education, 8.* https://doi.org/10.3389/feduc.2023.1158132

Kuhn, T., & Hacking, I. (2012). *The structure of scientific revolutions: 50th anniversary edition* (4th ed.). University of Chicago Press.

Leboeuf, C. (2019). "The audacity of hope": Reclaiming Obama's optimism in the Trump era. *The Journal of Speculative Philosophy, 33*(2), 256–267.

National Commission on Excellence in Education. (1983). *A nation at risk.* http://www.ed.gov/pubs/NatAtRisk/risk.html

Nussbaum, M. C. (2000). *Women and human development: The capabilities approach.* Cambridge University Press.

Pease, D. (2023). Preemptive impunity: The constituent power of Trump's Make America Great Again Movement. *Boundary 2: An International Journal of Literature and Culture, 50*(1), 13–67.

Perry, S. L., Davis, J. T., & Grubbs, J. B. (2023). Controlling the past to control the future: Christian nationalism and mandatory patriotic education in public schools. *Journal for the Scientific Study of Religion, 62*(3), 694–708.

Ravitch, D. (2010). *The death and life of the great American school system: How testing and choice are undermining education.* Basic Books.

Rosovsky, H. (1990). *The university: An Owner's manual.* W. W. Norton & Company.

Small, J. (2011). *Understanding college students' spiritual identities: Different faiths, varied world views.* Hampton Press.

St. John, E. P. (1994). *Prices, productivity and investment: Assessing financial strategies in higher education.* ASHE/ERIC Higher Education Report, Issue.

St. John, E. P., & Asker, E. H. (2003). *Refinancing the college dream: Access, equal opportunity, and justice for taxpayers.* Johns Hopkins University Press.

Winkle Wagner, R., & Locks, A. (2013). *Diversity and inclusion on campus: Supporting racially and ethnically underrepresented students.* Routledge.

Part I
Reframing Higher Education Policy

2
PUBLIC POLICY AND HIGHER EDUCATION

Global Competitiveness, Political Divisions, and Reframing Strategies

To make sense of higher education globalization and marketization, it helps to look back to before the Cold War to consider the federal role in developing colleges and universities in the US during the international era of empires. The early federal role started with the Continental Congress's passage of the Northwest Ordinance and the Supreme Court's distinction between public and independent colleges in their *Dartmouth* decision. These actions broke the links between central government control of college development—and the pattern within colonial systems across European nations' empires, including the American colonies before the Revolution.

Decentralized governance with public and private colleges emerged during the Early American period (Gadinger & Scholte, 2023). The federal government influenced this nation's distinctive path toward education development and periodically changed the trajectory of education development and access through legislation and regulations, direct funding through government programs, and the Supreme Court decisions with changing interpretations of the US Constitution. As globalization progressed, universities built international partnerships, and governments moved toward polycentric governance in higher education (Diamond, 2020). In recent decades, European higher education policy has adapted organizational and marketization strategies from the US, moving from institutional theory to decentralized models that rely on policy expertise instead of institutional knowledge (Vantaggiato & Lubell, 2022).

The history of federal policy in higher education is, therefore, increasingly informative to international discourse on the future of higher education. This chapter first examines the changing global contexts for higher education policy beginning with the Empire period. Next, we discuss issues emerging as states adapt to the continuation of the fiscally conservative federal educational pipeline policies. Finally, we consider strategies for reframing policy and research informing institutional, state, and federal policymakers seeking to improve education and career-development opportunities.

GLOBAL AND NATIONAL CONTEXTS FOR HIGHER EDUCATION POLICY

US higher education became the model for massification, informing the development of higher education pathways in Western Europe after World War II (WWII). As they built empires, European nations disseminated their models for organizing higher education within their empires (Clark, 1978, 1998). However, the legacies of organizational forms that evolved within alliances differed. The British, American, and German universities differed radically in their formal academic and administrative structures, but each had a substantial impact internationally during globalization (Meyer, 2016). After introducing the transforming global context for higher education, we examine how the historical development of federal education policy created lasting legacies distinguishing this nation's collegiate systems as they contend with the extreme inequalities created by this nation's K-20 education policies.

From Empires to Economic Globalization

International and national conflicts between globalism and nationalism, between neoliberals and neoconservatives, and between forms of academic governance in the Soviet and Western traditions have added to the current period of chaos. The realignment of nations after WWII influenced the development of higher education systems within nations during the eight following decades, as educational institutions navigated through historical transitions and readjusted to the new uncertainty (Table 2.1). Unlike most other countries, the US does not have national systems of education. Instead, the US is a constellation of "systems" comprising many institutions, a diversified supply of independent and public colleges creating collegiate opportunities in response to changing conditions. To compare education across nations, however, US education has been considered a system in international comparisons (Clark, 1978; Kerr, 1978). Prior transformations in political and economic alliances among nations situate the current uncertainty.

Transforming International Alliances Affecting Higher Education

The Russian alliance with Great Britain and the US defeated the Axis powers after German and Italian fascism swept most of Europe and Japan conquered most of the Far East. After the war, the conflict between the centralized Russian system of government and the Western decentralized democratic model evolved. Eastern Europe fell under Russian control as higher education, like Western systems, developed models of central control (Kerr, 1978), a legacy inhibiting the global competitiveness of universities in Soviet and post-soviet nations for decades thereafter (Chankseliani, 2013). Western Europe moved toward democratization, following the process set in motion by the Marshall Plan. Asian countries moved from education systems governed by colonial powers to their own domestic academic governance models (St. John, 1986). China followed the Russian script until that nation's democratic reforms of Mikhail Gorbachev. Unlike Eastern European countries in the former Union of Soviet Socialist Republics (USSR), China resisted democratic globalization but engaged in economic globalization with rapidly changing contexts for the flow of students and ideas.

In the early 1980s, the World Bank and International Monetary Fund promoted loans to expand college access as part of the "Washington Consensus" (Gore, 2000). The US shifted to a similar strategy in the late 1980s, using loans to expand opportunity,

Table 2.1 Transitions in Global for US Higher Education: Pre-WWII (Systemic Foundations), Cold War, Economic Globalization, and the New Uncertainty

Period	Empires Pre-WWII	Cold War (1945–1980)	Globalization (1980–2015)	New Uncertainty (2015–Present)
Economic & Social Forces (global)	Global Depression in (1930s); extreme poverty in the US & Europe; rise of the Axis nations	US & Western European sphere (with post-colonial nations) vs. Soviet sphere (w/ China)	EU develops as a global economic force; democracy movement; China engages in soviet corporatization	Globalism vs. Neonationalism: US–China conflict; COVID pandemic; breakdown
Civil Society and Discontent (US)	Mass unemployment: Labor conflicts influenced communists and nationalists: "Dust Bowl" and migration West	Nonviolent protests for Black voting rights; Vietnam protests; Urban riots; backlash (conservative); social divisions	De- and re-segregation; Systemic biases persist; Increased justice advocacy; Christian education increases	Open conflict: Extreme Right vs. BLM & Me Too; new classism; MAGA movement; anti-wok emerges Southern states
Education Policy Contexts (global)	Liberal arts and vocational postsecondary education in the US, Europe, and other nations	Mass access to higher education stimulates the US and European economies; education gap	China, the US, and the EU compete in a global economy; Russian cooperation in science (space)	Online learning during COVID shutdowns; change student flows; shifting partnerships
College Life, Curriculum, and Unrest (US)	Liberal arts (faith-based legacy) and vocational degrees; peace protests before Pearl Harbor	Federal programs support science, facilities, & student aid; student anti-war protests; ROTC expands	Shift to loans; curriculum wars (STEM & liberal arts advocacy); activists for diversity & affordability	Extreme economic segregation; Anti debt movement; Women's rights; end of affirmative action

deemphasizing need-based grants, and low tuition. The US also changed its K-12 policy, taking a different path than the European Union and other nations involved in the global supply chain (Yang & St. John, 2023). Placing the US—the federal and state policy shifts—in a comparative framing of policy changes across time illuminates the challenges governments and institutions face in this uncertain period.

Global Uncertainty Influencing in US Higher Education

The assault on democratic institutions reached a turning point in 2015 when the British voted to exit the European Union (BREXIT), and the US Senate refused to consider President Obama's nomination of Merrick Garland for the Supreme Court. BREXIT illustrated the fractured democratic trajectory of Europe that started after WWII—the failure of the Senate to ensure the continuity of our democratic traditions rather than promoting a new reactionary nationalist ideology. International information wars influenced both BREXIT and the Trump election (Stengel, 2019). The Trump Presidency further transformed the unstable neoliberal consensus, ending affirmative action. The US–China conflict disrupted the supply chain, COVID undermined the global economy, and climate change became a vivid global threat; fires, floods, hurricanes, and weather events illustrate that denial of science is an existential threat. Political scientists and historians now focus on the battle between authoritarianism and democracy in the US and nations across the globe. (Applebaum, 2020; Gerstel, 2022).

International wars now add to campus tension in the US. In the wake of the Russia-Ukraine War, Cold War tensions returned to Europe, and the US–China tensions accelerated, altering international education exchange. After two years of support from the West, Ukraine became a member of the EU in 2023, opening the door to new forms of exchange. Many other nations in the former USSR have also become part of the EU. Most critically, however, protests and violence on college campuses caught the ire of Congressional conservatives, leading to MAGA-inspired attacks on the leadership of elite universities. In response, university boards at the University of Pennsylvania and Harvard reconsidered the longevity of their presidents, as their campuses lingered on the edge of violence as the death toll in Gaza rose in the escalating Israeli-Palestinian military conflict.

Breaking Down Features of the Neoliberal Trajectory

The post-neoliberal controversies in the US have parallels in other nations, but the US pattern is distinctive. The federal government, states, and campuses now face the aftermath of high-tuition, high-loan strategies. Five decades of public finance now haunt working-class and low-income families with rising high-school students. Neoliberal political theory (Biebricher, 2019) argues liberalism started with the New Deal in the 1930s, followed by neoliberalism emerging in about 1980. Reconsidering federal policy and influential Supreme Court decisions across four historical periods reveals limitations of viewing the liberal transition to neoliberal policy without considering predecessor events to liberal policy and subsequent developments.

Before the Civil War: Public and Private Colleges

Passed originally by the Continental Congress, the *Northwest Ordinance of 1787* created a mechanism for the new territories to finance college development. Land grants—giving property taken from indigenous peoples to European immigrants and their dependents in new territories—became a mechanism for building schools and colleges. The Supreme Court's 1819 *Dartmouth* decision started an independent college sector early in the nation's history, creating diverse pathways to college development that had not yet evolved in Europe. Local donors and state land or territorial land grants subsidized the startup of new colleges. As Midwest states developed, the new government land grants and the option for starting independent colleges created pathways for public and private colleges.

Before the Revolution, England had chartered colleges based on appeals from the colonies. The federal government did not suddenly become a force influencing higher education development during the Cold War when education attainment became a factor in East-West competition, as might be assumed when considering that the Constitution did not mention education. Yet the federal government impacted the structure of the US system from the nation's founding. The Supreme Court ruled that the state of New Hampshire could not amend Dartmouth College's charter to make it a public institution because it would violate the contract clause of the US Constitution (Dartmouth University, 2024). States continued to charter colleges, but the Supreme Court's *Dartmouth* decision created an avenue for colleges as corporations independent of state control.

Communities, often spurred on by churches, could advocate for founding colleges with independent, nonprofit status, a new form of organization that evolved as an indirect form of public subsidy. The independent colleges were more dependent on tuition. However, some communities and states also taxed citizens to subsidize the educational delivery at some independent institutions, along with those that eventually became public. As legacies of this history, New York's Cornell University, the University of Pennsylvania, and other institutions evolved as hybrid organizations, with both independent governance and publicly-funded programs—private universities that had federally funded programs after the *Land Grant Act* (1862)—illustrating the complex and persistent legacy of the early period of founding. The British tradition of public–private cooperation in nation-building dates to at least 1600, with the formation of the East India Company (Roukis, 2004), and evolved over centuries (e.g., the building of roads, canals, and railroads connecting colonies and states). International public–private partnerships involving universities are now manifest in public–private cooperation emerging in the global economy.

The private colleges as an organizational form would take centuries to reach across the "pond" in higher education (Shattuck & Horvath, 2019); the case nearly immediately impacted the conception of private corporations in the US and England. By defining the rights of private corporations (Henshaw, 1837), the Supreme Court's *Dartmouth* decision also influenced the legal foundations of private corporations back in England. Before the end of the eighteenth century, the case was recognized in British common law (Doe, 1892), traveling back across the Atlantic, and eventually influenced international discourse on capitalism (Denham, 1909). Thus, the legal history of US higher education, emanating from the Board of a small New Hampshire college, had a global and national impact.

The *Dartmouth* case also had implications for the denominational conflicts that have been part of region-based culture across this nation's history. Virginia and other Southern colonies had religions aligned with the establishment claims in British common law (McConnell, 2002). Rebellions against the church's dominance of institutions influenced the religious wars in Europe, and the conflicting values crossed the Atlantic with the founding of New England colonies. Religious differences across states, a source of conflict in the colonies, meant that institutions' spiritual foundations differed across the Early American states (Silk & Walsh, 2008). The separation of church and state, implicit in the *Dartmouth* decision, set the stage for national identity development, as it did for the development of churches and colleges independent of state control.

Further, the assumption that leaving education out of the Constitution meant the federal government was not taking leadership in education may have disguised the very substantial role of the founders. The alignment of faith and colonies, enabled by British common law at the time, created insurmountable barriers to nationalizing an already diversified education establishment in the new states. In addition to the early federal legislators and courts creating pathways to independence for higher education from religious control in states, the founding fathers took an active interest in the founding of colleges: Thomas Jefferson founded the University of Virginia, and Benjamin Franklin co-founded the University of Pennsylvania. These are not the actions of founders who did not want to give a guiding hand to higher education. Instead, the potential for religious conflict across the states, an issue distancing the early Northern colonies for English education traditions—and potentially for Southern states—seems a better and wiser explanation. Martha Nussbaum's (2008) *Liberty of Conscience: In Defense of America's Tradition of Religious Equality* provides a compelling history of colonial sentiments reflected in subsequent tactics used by the founding fathers representing colonies with competing theocratic leanings.

Emergence of Public Systems: Land Grant Universities Compete with Independent Colleges

The first *Morrill Land Grant Act of 1862* gave federal land grants to states to develop colleges promoting agriculture and economic development (Table 2.2). Initially, the industrial North benefited more substantially from this legislation; the second Morrill Land Grant Act of 1890 extended the legislation to provide land grants for Black colleges, further empowering states to maintain segregated educational systems, particularly in the South. The foundation for segregated education emerged as an unholy, largely unspoken compromise, ending Reconstruction and the Civil War and jump-starting the role of higher education in nation-building.

Table 2.2 Federal Legislation and Court Decisions Creating Segregated Public Higher Education

Legislation Supporting University Development	Enabling Segregation
Morrill Land Grant Act of 1862, PL 37-130	The law provided land grants for colleges promoting agricultural and industrial development. It created market competition for students between new and old colleges.
Morrill Land Grant Act of 1890, PL 51-841	The second *Land Grant Act* created public colleges for Blacks, providing federal support for segregation.
US Supreme Court Decisions	
Plessy v. Ferguson, 163 U.S. 537 (1896)	Allowed segregated seating on trains. Legalized segregation in higher education.
Gaines v. Canada, 305 U.S. 337 (1938)	It forced Missouri to build a law school for one Black student, raising state costs of segregation.

In a pivotal Supreme decision influencing the evolution of public systems, *Plessy v. Ferguson* (1896) legalized segregation, removing legal barriers to developing dual systems of white and Black institutions. Southern and border states seized this opportunity by pursuing "separate but equal." The National Association for the Advancement of Colored People (NAACP) began challenging the doctrine in a series of Supreme Court cases, advocacy emphasizing "equal" opportunity. The *Gaines v. Canada* (1938) decision resulted in a one-room law school at Lincoln University for one Black student in Missouri. It was increasingly apparent the dual systems would be too costly, especially in border states. Still, the defense of dual systems lingered and haunts policy efforts to ensure equal educational opportunity.

Civil Unrest Before WWII

Prewar social and political turmoil, often overlooked in arguments about the origins of liberalism and nationalism, remains central to the contemporary understanding of divisiveness. Like European nations, the US populace, torn between nationalist and communist sentiments between world wars, resisted joining Britain in the war. A few of the most tumultuous forces merit attention relative to current divisiveness.

First, worker protests during the Depression were motivated by nationalist and communist agitation. The strong arms of industry and government fought for workforce stability as Italy and Germany fell to socialist nationalism, an ideology promoted by European fascists. These same ideological interests influenced college students in the US. The mass anti-war student protest movement in the 1930s was nationwide (Cohen, 1993). A national student walk-out for peace in the 1930s, before the US entered WWII, had a higher percentage of students protesting than the student Vietnam War protests in the 1960s (McGrath, 1971)—but the rate of protestors may have exceeded the threshold in the early 1970s.

Nevertheless, students' salient support for non-involvement in a war with Nazi national socialists and Russian communists fighting struggling democracies had lessons for rising generations. In the 1930s and 1960s, enlightened self-interests converged with idealism—as reactions to existential threats like war, mass violence, and environmental decline—to spur activism among some students in rising generations. Both progressive and conservative issues continued to draw students into activism after the 1960s (Cole & Heinecke, 2020; Rhoads, 1998).

Second, the US population, including college students, realigned their commitments to support the war effort. The American war effort in WWII was a remarkable shift from public despair and ideological conflicts before the war to a unified war effort. Italy and Germany fell into national socialism in response to austerity during the depression (Mattei, 2022). American icons, like Henry Ford and Charles Lindberg, were philosophically aligned with national socialism in the 1930s (Wallace, 2004). Yet, following Franklin Roosevelt's lead, the US engaged in manufacturing war supplies in the years before US engagement despite the internal national conflict. Indeed, the 1930s was a period of conflict about Roosevelt's social progressive agenda. Policy uncertainty about international politics—conflicting global and nationalist ideologies—was evident before engagement in WWII, as they are now. Universities that supported the war effort followed the shock wave of the bombing of Pearl Harbor via the exodus of students to join the war effort, ROTC, and research to support the war efforts.

Third, federal research funding excelled during WWII and accelerated after the war. University of Chicago, Columbia University, and the University of California, Berkeley

(UCB) were involved at the start of the National Institute of Education (NIE), building the atomic bomb, but more than 30 research sites were involved in the project during the war; there is an apparent rush to claim credit (e.g., Scherer, 2023) in the wake of the biopic, "Oppenheimer." Of course, UCB took the lead on the project, as it did in turning universities into multipurpose institutions (Kerr, 1963). In the 1960s and 1970s, the National Center for Education Statistics (NCES) reported on trends and special issues, while the National Institute of Education (NIE) funded basic and applied research. However, in the early 1980s, the Reagan administration cut education research funding and focused studies on topics supporting the administration's interest. The education community lobbied to restore these traditions (e.g., Justiz & Bjork, 1988), but the NCES research became increasingly political as neoliberal policies continued (Becker, 2004; Heller, 2004).

Fourth, influential Jewish social scientists also left Germany in the 1930s when they could; many found pathways in Western universities. Immigrating in 1934, Herbert Marcuse was world-renowned during the 1960s as a philosopher, social theorist, and political activist. Celebrated in the media as "father of the New Left," he was widely covered in the popular press. Yet the influence of the left was mitigated during the Cold War by the prevailing fear of communists among mainstream social theorists. In 1953, for example, Daniel Bell, David Reisman, Nathan Glazer, and other defenders of the narrow mainstream thought on the social order sought to promote a right-centered logic (Bell, 1963). They were critical of communist and right-wing extremism, especially the John Birch Society, but not academic work on the political right. Their logic held together political parties as they invested in expanding the public education system in the progressive period. At the other extreme, Leo Strauss became a political philosopher at the University of Chicago, influencing rising generations of US neoconservatives (Drury, 1997). These conflicts lingered through the Golden Age.

Cold War: Federal Support for Massification During the Golden Age
Pure gold does not tarnish with time, but the glimmer of the Golden Age of higher education was impure. Systemic inequality—both *de jure* segregation in the Southern and Border states and *de facto* segregation of other state systems limited the benefits of federal largess during this period of expansion. The federal investment in research and facilities and, significantly, the return of WWII veterans to college campuses accelerated the development of state higher education systems. The federal government also supported planning for state systems (Halstead, 1974). By the late 1970s, many policy experts predicted that many private colleges would close because it was challenging to compete with expanding low-cost public colleges; they advocated for more grant aid (Breneman et al., 1978).

After the Supreme Court's decision in *Brown v. Board of Education*, segregated higher education continued in Northern and Southern states (Table 2.3). The *Adams v. Califano* and *Adams v. Richardson (1977)* required states to desegregate public higher education and to provide equitable funding for Historically Black Colleges and Universities (HBCUs). Between 1977 and before the 1992 Supreme Court's decision in the *United States v. Fordice* case, Southern and Borders states were required to submit plans for desegregating public colleges and support institutional development at HBCUs. Mississippi, Alabama, and Louisiana—the Midsouth—resisted and were "saved" by the Supreme Court in *Fordice*. After the decision, public systems used merit admissions to

Table 2.3 Federal Legislation Supporting the Golden Age and Federal Court Decisions Constraining Desegregation Remedies

Legislation Expanding Access	Golden Age
Servicemen's Readjustment Act of 1944, PL 78–346	Provided portable grant aid for WWII veterans to attend college (portable grants)
National Defense Education Act of 1958, PL 85-864	NDEA created federal programs for need-based student aid and math/science education.
Higher Education Facilities Act of 1963, PL 90-575	Funding building academic facilities and dorms to expand campuses.
Elementary and Secondary Education Act, PL. 83–531	Established the Federal programs supporting special needs for students
Higher Education Act of 1965 became PL 89-329	The HEA established the federal role in student and institutional aid
Federal Court Decisions	**Desegregating Public Education**
Brown v. Board of Education, 347 US 483 (1954)	Ruled against legislated segregation. Forced desegregation of public education.
Adams v. Richardson, 356 F. Supp. 92 (D.D.C. 1973)	Extended desegregation requirements to public white colleges, mandated support for HBCUs, and required states with segregated systems to develop and gain approval for desegregation plans.
Adams v. Califano, 430 F. Supp. 118 (D.D.C. 1977)	
Bakke vs. California Board of Regents. 438 US 265 (1978).	The Court outlawed quotas as a means of achieving racial diversity.

claim they were desegrated without adjusting for inequalities in prior preparation or taking steps to encourage student diversity. In contrast, the public HBCUs had to develop programs that attracted whites to secure additional state funding necessary to offer programs of similar quality (St. John & Hossler, 1998; Williams, 1997).

Federal education programs expanded access and improved education equity. Starting with the *National Defense Education Act of 1958*, federal programs funded K-12 educational improvements, especially in math education, and created need-based financial aid programs for low-income students. In 1965, the *Elementary and Secondary Education Act* provided extra funding for supplemental instruction for low-income youth, and the *Higher Education Act* provided need-based grant aid. Supplemental K-12 education for disadvantaged students and need-based grants for low-income students became the pillars of education improvement and increased equity in college enrollment. The cases in the first edition of *Public Policy and Higher education* examined the increased educational equity in the late 1970s, providing a baseline for examining the impact of reforms—the changing trajectories in K-12 and higher education. In the third edition, these prior arguments are now documented history and we revised the cases to focus on education policy and outcome this century.

The Neoliberal Turn: Transforming the Trajectory Toward Inequality

The uneasy balance between segregation and expanding opportunity, the manifest destiny of expanding educational opportunity and the national development (1776 through 1980), gave way to new policies protecting the economic elite (i.e., lower taxes) and pitting the declining working class against other disenfranchised groups (1980 to present). The shift created by federal policymakers (Table 2.4) profoundly impacted racial equity.

Table 2.4 Federal Legislation and Supreme Court Decisions Altering the Trajectory of US Education from Expanding Opportunity to Ensuring Economic Stratification

Legislation Marketizing Higher Education	Legacy: Privatization of Public Higher Education
Middle Income Student Assistance Act of 1978, PL 95-566,	Eliminated family income thresholds for federal student grants and loans
Bayh-Dole Act of 1980, PL 96-517	Enabled universities to own, patent, and commercialize inventions funded by federal programs
Educational Consolidation and Improvement Act of 1981, 97th Congress, H. R. 9431	Consolidated programs and eased regulation, providing increased flexibility
No Child Left Behind Act of 1983, P. L. 107–110	Set the legal framework for the federal K-20 STEM pipeline
Higher Education Relief Opportunities for Students Act of 2003, Public Law (PL 108 - 76)	Gave Secretary of Education waiver authority on student debt in times of war and national emergency.
Court Cases on Affirmative Action	**Legacy: Constrained Opportunity**
United States v. Fordice, 505 US 717 (26 June 1992).	Allow states to use merit admissions criteria to achieve integration. The decision limited supplemental funding for HBCUs to programs attracting whites.
Gratz v. Bollinger, 539 U.S. 244 (2003). *Grutter v. Bollinger*, 539 U.S. 306 (2003).	The decisions upheld the use of race in admissions to universities. Suggested 25 year time limit affirmative action.

Most of the higher education literature arguing for and against affirmative action missed the underlying severe flaw noted by scholars (Law & Versteeg, 2012; Somers & Gera, 2023). Unlike most Constitutions in democratic nations, the US Constitution does not include a social welfare clause that provides a basis for affirmative action in many other countries. The originalist interpretive stance of the Courts constrained affirmative action mechanisms, one at a time, since the 1970s. Even after decades of federal legislation expanding opportunity during the tarnished Golden Age, the Courts protested the right of economic elites to gain access through the privilege of ancestry. They incrementally denied institutions opportunities to consider race as a factor in college admissions—the wave of federally supported collegiate desegregation waned to a final death. The fatal blow came after federal education legislation unleashed the period institutionalizing economic segregation.

Conflict about racial and ethnic diversity continues to haunt policy discourse—the persistent racial inequality and advocacy for fairness in admissions practices. *Regents of the University of California* v. *Bakke* ended quotas to promote diversity but supported using race as a factor in the admissions process. The diversity proponents initially opposed it, but eventually, it became core to rationales for continuing affirmative action. The Supreme Court's decision in the Michigan cases continued to support affirmative action as part of a holistic review of student applications. Still, it implied a 25-year sunset as part of Justice Sandra O'Connor's supporting opinion. The Supreme Court's recent decisions in the *Harvard* and *University of North Carolina* cases have effectively ended affirmative action as practiced under the limited constraints set by prior Supreme Court decisions.

Litigation over affirmative action provided a veil of ignorance over the complicated issue of higher education access and the growth of financial inequality throughout the neoliberal period. Litigation about affirmative action seldom focused on the financial aid strategies at campuses and in states pursuing diversity. However, the growing racial disparities that opened after 1980 corresponded with the reduced federal funding for need-based student grants; there were no significant changes in high school graduation requirements in the early 1980s when the gap opened (St. John & Noell, 1989). Increasing diversity depends partly on funding for need-based and merit grants for college students. Academically qualified majority and, minority low-income students benefit most substantially from grant aid. The strategy does not guarantee diversity among entering student cohorts, but there was equitable enrollment across racial groups when Pell Grants were adequately funded in the 1970s (St. John & Asker, 2003).

The primary neoliberal federal legislation creating the legal framework for transforming national policy on K-20 education occurred quickly between 1978 and 1983. Three laws passed during Jimmy Carter's presidency provided mechanisms for the neoconservative onslaught of cuts in trans that followed. Specifically, the *Middle Income Student Assistance Act of 1978* (MISAA) and the *Education Consolidation and Improvement Act of 1981* (ECIA) created new platforms for President Reagan to transform higher education finance through the budget process, consonant with his governing strategy in California.

As Governor and President, Ronald Reagan was a *regressive* conservative in education, advocating for budget cuts without creating new programs. California had a "blue line" budget process, allowing governors to cut funding. The blue line gave governors the authority to reduce the dollar amount of budget items, a more exacting budget authority than the widely advocated "line-item veto." Unlike his predecessors, Governor Reagan had no favorite programs he wanted to protect in the budget, especially in higher education, so he did not have to compromise like his predecessors (Evens, 1970). As President, Reagan promoted K-12 reforms without making a substantial new investment. His National Commission on Excellence in Education (1983) released a significant report, *At National At Risk*, that changed the course of education. Following the report, the *No Child Left Behind Act* created a new framework forcing states to adopt college-prep graduation requirements without making a substantial new investment to support the system changes necessary for compliance, including eliminating vocation diploma options.

In the White House, Reagan found ways to cut public funding, reshaping the federal role and education nationally. The *Bayh-Dole Act (1980)*, also passed under Carter, created new mechanisms for building university-corporate partnerships by allowing institutions to commercialize intellectual property generated through federally funded research, forming a fast lane to university engagement in economic globalization (Powers, 2004). *A Nation At Risk* (National Commission of Excellence in Education, 1983) was the final spoke in the wheel of change that led to the *No Child Left Behind Act of 2001*, George W. Bush's reauthorization of the ESEA, solidifying the legal enforcement framework for regressive education reform.

The impact of these laws and related changes in governing behaviors were twofold in education: (1) *marketizing higher education* through a regressive financial aid policy strategy (shifting from grants to loans), and (2) *nationalizing K-12 education* using a "college for all" model and limiting other educational pathways to college. All three editions of *Public Policy and Higher Education* examine the development of these federal policy mechanisms and state adaptions to changes in the federal government's funding strategies.

Before MISAA, public colleges were less expensive than independent colleges, but low-income students were eligible for federal student aid in both. The new law extended eligibility to middle-income students with financial need after college costs, a policy that relieved some of the stress on independent colleges. In the first year, colleges and universities moved federal Supplemental Educational Grants (SEOGs) to middle-income students even though Basic Educational Opportunity Grants (BEOG), now named Pell Grants, were not fully funded (St. John & Byce, 1982). At this point, it is crucial to recognize that the federal grant programs were designed as appropriated programs rather than entitlements, meaning Congress designated specific funding levels each year, and the program costs could not exceed the level of appropriations. MISAA expanded eligibility to more students. In the budget process that followed, even during the Carter years, the total funding level for the program did not increase for new students; thus, shifting need-based aid from low-income to middle-income students. By not meeting the allowable maximum award levels, the US Education Department could hold the program costs down and remove some middle-income students, reducing federal program costs consistent with the Reagan agenda. In subsequent budget requests, President Reagan extended this cost-cutting leverage by limiting Pell funding and cutting funding or eliminating some grant programs. Instead, both Reagan administrations pushed for the expansion of federal student loans.

The Carter presidency kept the South aligned with Democrats for four more years as neoliberalism emerged in education policy, but the 1980 election realigned the states. The turmoil foreshadowed the solidification of Red and Blue (Republican and Democrat) states. The state studies in Part II provide contrasting examples of adaptive policy reasoning, illustrating that states are discovering new pathways as they deal with political issues in their state. They show that higher education finance policies vary substantially and change over time as political parties and civic-minded activists react to the extent of educational opportunities and advocate for different paths. The engagement of researchers in state policy studies also influences state and institutional decisions.

The Intersection of Global Competition and Corporatized Neoliberalism

These historical federal policy periods have contemporary legacies integral to US higher education. The public and independent colleges are foundational, dating back to the Early American period. The two forms of institutions moved into the Northwest, but not into the new Southern states, as they expanded. In the North, giving lands that once belonged to indigenous people to Europeans for education became foundational to the expanding system. After the Civil War, systemic segregation evolved legally in the South and some Northern states. Cultural differences in the North, Midwest, West, and South had different regional effects on university development. The nation moved to mass higher education in the latter part of the tewntieth century, accelerated by federal funding. Yet integration was constrained by the Courts' limitations on affirmative action because, unlike other democratic countries that evolved in successive waves of reform, the Constitution did not have a clause emphasizing social justice and equity. Replacing the primary federal role of need-based grants to expand access equitably with loans for all was intended as a mechanism to stimulate competition leading to reduced prices (e.g., the Bennett hypothesis); instead, it altered the course toward equity by channeling high-need students into community colleges. Except for the support for massification, the other structural features of the federally constructed legal system governing higher education were uniquely American including the narrowing of high-school pathways to college prep as an American response to economic globalization. The challenge now is to expand opportunities for marginalized peoples in an economically stratified system. Given the extremely high cost of attending college, returning to a federal system that supports equal opportunity for qualified low-income students to enroll in all types of colleges without debt may not be feasible, if it is possible.

The current period of US education development is interwoven with the globalization of higher education and nations' economies, especially as they adapt to new international tensions. The marketization of higher education was a global trend, but the US K-12 reforms differed from rather than set the global trajectory. Most other nations retained technical high schools and postsecondary programs, but, like the US, they engaged in international testing of K-12 Students (Henry et al., 2001; Meyer & Benavot, 2013). Unlike the European Union and China, the nation's major economic competitors, the US moved toward nationalizing high-school graduation requirements and marginalizing vocational and technical education (Yang & St. John, 2023), which informed the formal recommendations of *A Nation At Risk*. When coupled with changes in trade policies that essentially expanded American industry, the K-12 policies undermined the working middle class.

The European Union took a fundamentally different approach to negotiating trade agreements. The EU protected trade for countries within the EU (Bollen et al, 2016), while the US strategy favored this nation's corporate elite and failed to protect the working class. When the parallel paths of trade policy, marketization of higher education, and nationalization of K-12 education accelerated wealth redistribution from the shrinking working- and middle-classes to the rising technical business elite who benefited from the new policies, the wealthy families holding land and stocks across generations, and, especially, the growing class of billionaires who mastered mechanisms for free trade and the supply chain.

THE CURRENT PERIOD: POLITICAL DIVISIONS AFFECT HIGHER EDUCATION POLICY

The current period has extreme political conflict. Instead of the neoliberal trajectory tying together Democratic and Republican voters, the current period of divisiveness creates barriers to finding consensual solutions to underlying conflict. There is no longer a commonly understood agenda for national higher education policy. In contrast, most EU nations preserved the working class rather than limiting taxes and constraining public funding for college students (Piketty, 2014; St. John, 2023). Northern and Western Europe moved toward mass higher education after WWII, but retained and improved their technical colleges as neoliberalism unfolded globally (Carpentier, 2019).

Presidents and the Courts in an Uncertain Period

Higher education finance at the federal level, especially the emphasis on loans, changed little, mainly due to budget constraints; the Obama Administration increased flexibility in K-12 accountability schemes, the Trump Administration emphasized privatization, and Biden found a way to forgive debt through regulatory change (Table 2.5).

Table 2.5 Federal Education Legislation and Court Decisions in the Period of Extreme Political Conflict (2015 and Thereafter)

A. Post-Neoliberal Legislation	Conflicting Policy Trajectories
Every Student Succeeds Act (ESSA) of 2015, Pub. L. 114–95	The ESSA takes effect beginning in the 2017–18 school year. It requires every state to measure performance in reading, math, and science, but gave states more flexibility.
Strengthening Career and Technical Education for the 21st Century Act of 2018, PL 115-224	Provided federal support for CTE programs and focused on improving CTE students' academic and technical achievement in high schools and colleges.
Coronavirus Aid, Relief, and Economic Security Act of 2020 (CARES Act), Pub. L. No. 116-136,	Signed on March 27, 2020, CARES provides additional support and flexibility on Title IV programs due to COVID-19.
Infrastructure Investment and Jobs Act of 2021, 117-58	Biden successfully implements most of his Build Back Better agenda in these laws, adding working-class jobs. His education reforms were primarily overlooked, including expansion and funding for technical education programs
CHIPS and Science Act of 2022, PL 115-368	
Inflation Reduction Act of 2022, PL 117-2	
B. Supreme Court Cases	**Reactionary Legacy**
Carson v. Makin, 596 U.S. 20-188 (2022)	Decided Main could not exclude families who send their children to religious schools from state-funded tuition reimbursement program
Students for Fair Admissions, Inc. v. President & Fellows of Harvard College (2023) & Students for Fair Admission, Inc. v. University of North Carolina, (2023), US 20-1199	Ended use of affirmative action in college admissions in independent (Harvard) and public (UNC) institutions
Biden, President of the United States, et al. v. Nebraska, 200 U. S. 321, 337 (2023)	Denied President Biden's first attempt to forgive excessive student debt
Loper Bright Enterprises v. Raimondo (2024), US 22-451	Shift authority for regulations from federal agencies to courts. Places President Biden's second loan forgiveness plan at risk.

Obama's Legacy

Through regulatory changes, the Obama administration altered the trajectory toward equity in high-school graduation, narrowing the race gap and raising the national graduation rate. These rates stabilized with only modest gaps after 2015 (Chapter 4). While the Obama Administration maintained accountability and consistency with ESEA at the time, it increased flexibility and encouraged state experimentation through regulations (Gross & Hill, 2016; McGuinn, 2016). Obama's *Every Student Succeeds Act of 2015*, passed as the neoliberal consensus broke down, extended the standards and testing approach, holding together the coalitions sufficient to pass the bill.

The current period of US education development is interwoven with the globalization of higher education and nations' economies, especially as they adapt to new international tensions.

Trump's First Term

President Trump's education agenda supported charters and proprietary education. He passed *Strengthening Career and Technical Education for the 21st Century Act of 2018*, extending Career and Technical Education (CTE) programs, including programs in for-profit institutions. Despite his resistance to national responses to the COVID crisis, the *Coronavirus Aid, Relief, and Economic Security Act of 2020* provided guidance and mechanisms for closing in-person college classes, illustrating a lingering Congressional capacity to reach consensus during crises. The emphasis on high tuition and student debt, outgrowths of the "Washington Consensus" of financing access, have influenced student unrest in the US and internationally, adding to political extremism (Johnston, 2015; Mir & Toor, 2023; Timmerman, 2019).

Trump's vocational education program funded for-profit schools along with projects in public schools and community colleges but did not change the STEM pathways agenda in the K-20 framework of curriculum alignment. In contrast, Biden's *Build Back Better* agenda included investment in vocational and career education programs. His first-term legislation included supporting infrastructure, computer chip production in the US, and new climate measures as part of inflation reduction, creating good middle-class jobs that do not require college degrees. Biden's plans to expand vocational education received only modest support from the education mainstream, an explanation for leaving it out of legislation.

Trump's version of privatization of vocational education and Biden's funding of career, vocational, and technical education suggest STEM stranglehold on K-12 education could chart different courses. Neither President has been able to gain substantial support in the education community. Forging a new vision or near consensus has not emerged, as was evident in the 1980 to 1983 period when Carter's new liberal agenda converged with Reagan's agenda for public education. However, state cases are beginning to demonstrate a shift toward academic pathways that value the CTE alternatives.

Biden's First Term

During the first two years of his Presidency, Biden delivered three laws enacting much of his Build Back Better agenda. The *Infrastructure Investment and Jobs Act of 2021* invested in national construction projects and jobs, many of which did not require college degrees. The *CHIPS and Science Act of 2022* protected core aspects of the computer industry, adding new protections on technology lost during decades of the nation's neoliberal trade policies. The *Inflation Reduction Act of 2022* delivered on other Biden promises. In the 2022 election, the House shifted to a Republic majority, bringing significant new legislation to a halt in a deadlocked Congress.

President Biden sought to deliver on a campaign promise to ease student debt. His first attempt was through the development of new regulations under the *Higher Education Relief Opportunities for Students Act of 2003*, a law that created loan forgiveness for veterans. The Supreme Court's 2023 decision in *Biden, President of the United States, et al. v. Nebraska* struck this down, a response to reactionary conservatives. The ideological battles of finding relief for student debt remain at the center of national political storms.

The Supreme Court Turns Education Further Right

The Supreme Court legalized public finance for private schools in 2022, ended affirmative action in 2023, and changed the prospects of improving opportunity through regulatory change. *Carson v. Makin (2022)* legalized state aid to religious school students, breaking the barrier between secular and faith-based education. The Supreme Court's decision on the combined affirmative action cases—*Students for Fair Admissions,*

Inc. v. President & Fellows of Harvard College (2023) & Students for Fair Admission, Inc. v. University of North Carolina (2023)—finally delivered to the segregationists, North and South, by ending the nation's constrained use of race-based affirmative action. The Supreme Court's decision on *Loper Bright Enterprises v. Raimondo (2024)* shifting final responsibility for approval of regulatory changes from federal agencies to the courts, placing Biden's efforts to reduce the student debt at risk.

The Troubled "Dream" and "Promise"

Promoting the agenda they sought in the Obama-Biden era at the waning of neoliberal dominance, President Biden introduced the *American Dream and Promise Act of 2023*, legislation also introduced in an earlier version by President Obama. Obama tried various ways to alter the high-loan trajectory. The *Promise,* a strategy that states, cities, philanthropists, and partnerships used to guarantee grants, took off without supporting federal legislation. Many Promise programs provide grants equaling tuition for lowest-income families, a strategy successfully used for many years in Indiana. However, Indiana was an anti-DREAM Act state (Chapter 9). The *DREAM Act* would guarantee that immigrant minors educated in the US would not pay out-of-state tuition, a federal idea that depends on state consensus and compliance. States across the nation have diverse, locally constructed attitudes, meanings, and policies related to the DREAM Act and Promise programs. Like Obama, Biden failed in his 2023 attempt to advance a new version of the legislation. The state's rights and segregation sentiments remain among legislators and their voters in districts and states across the nation.

Both strategies required state action through state-federal partnerships, if not through mandates. Earlier state-federal partnerships lingered as unfunded programs in the HEA, including earlier state-federal partnerships (Chapter 4). The Obama strategy would build state-federal partnerships, a process that existing laws or new ones could achieve; a conservative Congress cut this idea from the austere federal budget of the period. Had the Presidents from Reagan through Biden fully funded federal grant programs, the trajectory toward inequality would not have been as severe. The Supreme Court's rejection of Biden's attempt to forgive loans illustrates that creative attempts to reinterpret legislation or alter program effects through regulatory revisions frequently failed, especially if they emphasize socially progressive ideas.

The severity of the national challenge of financial inequality can be—and indeed has been—altered by some states during periods when bipartisan coalitions can be held together at least for constrained periods, as illustrated in the state cases (Part II). States have used various approaches to craft collegiate affordability, from California's master plan of the 1960s (Chapter 7) to the Carolina Covenant (Chapter 11) in recent times, a strategy adopted at diverse public and private colleges (Goward, 2018; Johnson & Collins, 2009).

State budget agreements are routinely reconstructed and subject to political ideologies; they are not set in state constitutions or maintained by legislation. Some states had constitutional language promising no or low tuition, but even these legal agreements fell apart as states adjusted to the federal financial aid policies (Lee et al., 1996). There is an apparent, possible silver lining to the role of state power. For example, Tennessee, a conservative state, and comparatively liberal California have versions of the Promise programs that provide free tuition all or most community colleges. Even when enacted, this approach continues economic stratification because it channels low-income students to community colleges, but it extends access incrementally.

A seemingly irreconcilable challenge—the capacity to craft collaborative strategies that mitigate the worst effects of federal political deadlock preventing meaningful reforms in higher education finance—now faces state and federal officials, college lobbyists and students, and concerned citizens aligning with interest groups sharing concerns about college affordability. Due to the excess debt burden, decline in middle-income earnings, and high housing costs, the current strategies for public finance are not working for low- and middle-income families. Breaking through barriers created by political conflict requires a collaborative reframing of the challenges informed by activist research that seeks to inform fragile coalitions.

Uncertainty on Campuses: Research, Student Aid, and Incentive Budgeting

Campuses and states adapted to changes in the federal role in financing higher education, from land grants in the Early American period through building mass systems after WWII to the current uncertainty. In addition to student aid, elite universities align academic strategies with anticipated federal research programs. For example, competition among research universities for faculty stars who can attract external research to fund graduate students now has a long and complicated history. This history may be as disheartening, from an egalitarian vantage point, as the shift from grants to loans. Fair and equitable funding for faculty across disciplines is now a long-lost practice in most leading universities. To illustrate this complexity, we review recent trends in federal research funding, discuss the decentralization of market influences into university budgeting and management, and reflect on political and academic divisiveness influencing the evolution of organizational strategies.

Federal Research

Along with the transformation in federal student aid policy, shifts in federal research priorities in science, health care, the environment, and warfare influence priorities within universities. Recent trends in federal funding for research further illustrate the complexity of these times. Most federal research funding is for defense, health, nuclear energy, and bombs (see Figure 2.1).

The trends illustrate a modest priority shift from defense to nondefense since 2015, a possible peace dividend coming about as US engagement in Middle East wars declined. President Trump's denial of the importance of vaccinations did not alter the changing trajectory. His and Obama's efforts to end the wars enabled the shift. Federal research funding is shifting away from universities to private corporations. Since the *Doyle-Bayh Act,* universities and private corporations have increasingly collaborated to bring innovations to the market, especially in science, health, and engineering. Universities focus on hiring faculty who can generate revenue. Experiences with patents are a stronger predictor of future success in licensing and profitability for faculty (Hsu & Kuhn, 2022), prioritizing recruiting successful professors rather than new junior faculty. These faculty stars, in turn, attract internal university resources as investments that seek further returns.

University Budget and Managerial Strategies Decentralize Politics and Markets

The complex relationships between external organizations and academics are often recognized in incentive budgeting with universities as they construct budgetary algorithms to distribute overhead and other resources and academic units within universities (Priest & St. John, 2006; Priest et al., 2002). Some universities also provide

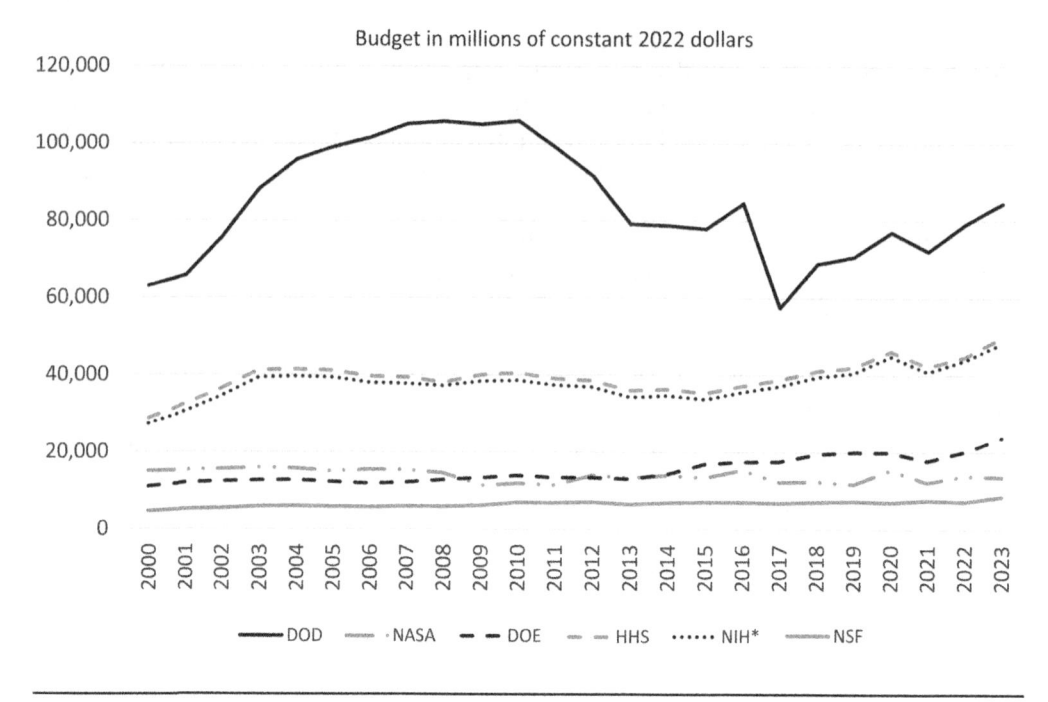

Figure 2.1 Trends in Federal Research and Development by Agency, 2000–2022
Source: American Association for the Advancement of Science (2023). Retrieved from https://www.aaas.org/programs/r-d-budget-and-policy/historical-trends-federal-rd

incentives for recruiting and retaining students in the internal market competitions for students as revenue (Hossler, 2006). The internal market forces interweave enrollment management tools for generating tuition revenue into academic and service units. Enrollment managers compete for resources for student grant aid, as do graduate deans and academic department chairs. The combined internal and external markets complicate efforts to promote diversity and recruit high-achieving students because of their mixed incentives.

In academic departments with teaching missions and student affairs service units, desterilized budgeting shifts responsibilities for enrollment management from admissions to practitioners. In theory, this practice provides opportunities for action inquiry supporting student persistence (Bean, 1990). The rapid move to privatization has made it difficult for academic and administrative units to actualize this potential (Paulsen & St. John, 2002). Instead, in too many instances, professors and administrators become managed professionals as accountability schemes trickle down university hierarchies (Rhoades & Slaughter, 1997). The infusion of new technologies has turned the transition of academic institutions into communities of managed professionals into a global phenomenon (Abad-Segura et al., 2020).

Divisive Politics Intrude into Academic Organizations

Universities are no longer the isolated communities immune from politics if they ever were. Indeed, the historical review of federal legislation and court cases above illustrates the shift in the political ethos of the nation and how its strategies for population growth, social uplift, and economic development have influenced colleges throughout its history. Now, with highly divisive politics on the MAGA right pushing for an end to DEI, a wave of reform in many red states is systematically banning policies that support and promote "woke" initiatives from curriculum and practice (Wong, 2023). Woke was used initially as a term for consciousness of racism, especially among Blacks in their vernacular. Florida's Governor Ron DeSantis turned the term into a dog whistle for MAGA Republicans nationally. While dealing with complex matters requiring academic and administrative units to respond to university budget incentives as they compete for students, the political battles about political correctness have invaded higher education at virtually every level of the complex enterprises. The following chapters focus on MAGA-DEI divisiveness in states and academic organizations.

REFRAMING STRATEGIES IN CHAOTIC TIMES

The combat between MAGA and DEI on campuses and in states is every bit as twisted and troubling as the national discourse. At times, the intensity of these matters pushes inequality aside as rhetoric reigns supreme in policy discourses in states and on campuses. Florida, North Carolina, Tennessee, and Texas were among the early states adjusting to new laws banning open discourse on the history of race and gender inequality (Wong, 2023). It is not hyperbole to conclude that MAGA is now at war with diversity, a growing problem this century (Crawford, 2000; Dobbin & Kalev, 2016). Winning the battle against affirmative action through court decisions was not enough to appease the populist anger.

The ideological battles on campuses add to challenges facing low-income families seeking uplift for their children, a process that requires breaking through educational, social, and economic barriers, in addition to paying the high net cost of college. The cross-generation social and economic uplift pattern changed as the neoliberal period progressed. Education attainment necessary for financial wellbeing transformed from basic literacy to a college degree; the screening device for good jobs shifted from high-school diplomas to college degrees, and the earnings of the middle class fell further behind the economic elite. Wealth disparities also increased in Western Europe, but wealth differences were not as extreme as in the US (Piketty, 2014).

Perhaps the most remarkable development of the neoliberal period was the explicit shift in the purpose of education, from emphasizing cross-generation uplift that promoted economic growth to education for all students to prepare for a STEM elite. Human capabilities theory, a progressive alternative to human capital theory (Sen, 2009), provides a frame for understanding contemporary challenges (Table 2.6). Higher education replaced high school as the screening mechanism for many jobs during the neoliberal period, as many college graduates took service jobs of various kinds instead of higher-prestige jobs.

The specter of debt now casts a shadow over student's life choices before, during, and after college. Graduate degrees are often now necessary for jobs sufficient to pay off the added debt of undergraduate degrees; students' choices about continuing versus dropping out or going to graduate school versus work are now affected by debt burden. The earnings differential between college and advanced degrees "are particularly high for African American and low socioeconomic status graduates, complicating simple conclusions

Table 2.6 Reframing Education Policy Development as Ensuring Financial Wellbeing from K-12 Education Through Graduate Education

Capability	Assess Capabilities Gaps	Build Support Networks
Financial Wellbeing	Minimum basic income for subsistence for individuals and families	Local agencies, businesses, schools, health care, and social services provide safety nets
College/Career Preparation	Local educational opportunities through K-12 schools, including localized preparation for college and work opportunities	Community engagement in schools, providing supplemental support for engaged learning, social services, and networking
Access to College and Career Pathways	Access to college, either academic or career education; guaranteed financial aid covering tuition when families cannot afford college costs	Social networks provide local and regional support; college networks linked to communities; technology access for distance learning
Successful Completion of College/Career Preparation	Opportunities in local, regional, and global collegiate & career pathways; appropriate employment opportunities	Partnerships among schools, colleges, nonprofits, and businesses supporting local economic and social development

about the stratification of debt at the postgraduate level" (Pyne & Grodsky, 2020, p. 20). Yet debt is also a severe problem for holders of advanced degrees at the start of their careers. Even physicians face early career stress, balancing family life with the massive debt necessary for many new MDs (Verduzco-Gutierrez et al., 2021). Student debt stress runs across the job hierarchy, from the top to the bottom, necessitating reframing strategies for college preparation, access, and success.

Questions

1. How did the Northwest Ordinance and the *Dartmouth* decision create an implicit framework for poly centric governance in US higher education?
2. As European empires crumbled after WWII, how did the US movement toward mass higher education influence the emergence of the US as the model for the international development of higher education systems during the Cold War?
3. How did the federal policy development influence the segregation of higher education and the neoliberal trajectory toward economic stratification in college access?
4. How do federal legislation and Supreme Court decisions influence state policy debates about DEI?
5. What are the most workable legal and policy mechanisms for decreasing reliance on loans in the financial of higher education? What social and economic forces constrain efforts to remedy over-reliance on loans and relieve the severe consequences of debt burden for college dropouts and graduates?

REFERENCES

Abad-Segura, E., González-Zamar, M. D., Infante-Moro, J. C., & Ruipérez García, G. (2020). Sustainable management of digital transformation in higher education: Global research trends. *Sustainability, 12*(5), 2107.

American Association for the Advancement of Science. (2023). *Historical Trends in Federal R & D*. Retrieved January 6 from https://www.aaas.org/programs/r-d-budget-and-policy/historical-trends-federal-rd

Applebaum, A. (2020). *The twilight of democracy: The seductive lure of authoritarianism*. Doubleday.

Bean, J. (1990). Why students leave: Insights from research. In D. Hossler, & J. Bean (Eds.), *The strategic management of college enrollments* (pp. 147–169). Jossey-Bass.

Becker, W. E. (2004). Omitted variables and sample selection in studies of college-going decisions. In E. P. St. John (Ed.), *Public policy and college access: Investigating the federal and state roles in equalizing postsecondary opportunity* (Vol. 19, pp. 65–86). AMS Press, Inc.

Bell, D. (1963). *The radical right: The new American right expanded and updated*. Doubleday.

Biebricher, T. (2019). *The political theory of neoliberalism*. Stanford University Press.

Bollen, Y., De Ville, F., & Orbie, J. (2016). EU trade policy: Persistent liberalisation, contentious protectionism. *Journal of European integration, 38*(3), 279–294.

Breneman, D. W., Finn, C. E., & Nelson, S. C. (1978). *Public policy and private higher education*. The Brookings Institution.

Carpentier, V. (2019). Higher education in modern Europe. In *The Oxford handbook of the history of education* (pp. 259–274).

Carson v. Makin Supreme Court (2022), 596 U. S. 20-1088

Chankseliani, M. (2013). Higher education access in post-Soviet Georgia: Overcoming a legacy of corruption. In H. D. Meyer, E. P. St John, M. Chankseliani, & L. Uribe (Eds.), *Fairness in access to higher education in a global perspective: Reconciling excellence, efficiency, and justice*. Sense Publications.

Clark, B. R. (1978). Concepts, models, and perspectives. In J. H. Van de Graff (Ed.), *Academic power: Patterns of authority in seven national systems of higher education* (pp. 164–190). Praeger.

Clark, B. R. (1998). *Creating entrepreneurial universities: Organizational pathways to transformation*. Pergamon Press.

Cohen, R. (1993). *When the old left was young: Student radicals and America's first mass student movement, 1929-1941*. Oxford University Press.

Cole, R. M., & Heinecke, W. F. (2020). Higher education after neoliberalism: Student activism as a guiding ligh. *Policy Futures in Education, 18*(1), 90–116.

Crawford, J. (2000). At war with diversity: US language policy in an age of anxiety. *Multilingual Matters, 25*.

Dartmouth University. (2024). *Dartmouth College Case Decided by the US Supreme Court*. Retrieved April 3 from https://home.dartmouth.edu/about/dartmouth-college-case-decided-us-supreme-court

Denham, R. N. (1909). An historical development of the contract theory in the Dartmouth College Case. *Michigan Law Review, 7*(3), 201.

Diamond, P. (2020). Polycentric governance and policy advice: Lessons from Whitehall policy advisory systems. *Policy and Politics, 48*(4), 563–581.

Dobbin, F., & Kalev, A. (2016). Why diversity programs fail. *Harvard Business Review, 94*(7), 14.

Doe, C. (1892). New view of the Dartmouth College Case. *Harvard Law Review, 6*, 161.

Drury, S. B. (1997). *Leo Strauss and the American right*. St. Martin's Press.

Evens, J. (1970). The view from the state of California. *Change, 3*(5).

Gadinger, F., & Scholte, J. A. (2023). *Polycentrism: How governing works today*. Oxford University Press.

Gaines v. Canada, 305 U.S. 337 (1938).

Gerstel, G. (2022). *The rise and fall of the neoliberal order*. Oxford University Press.

Gore, A. (2000). The rise and fall of the Washington consensus as paradigm for the developing countries. *World Development, 28*(5), 789–803.

Goward, S. L. (2018). First-generation student status is not enough: How acknowledging students with working-class identities can help us better serve students. *About Campus, 23*(4), 19–26.

Gross, B., & Hill, P. T. (2016). The state role in K-12 education: From issuing mandates to experimentation. *Harvard Law and Policy Review, 10*, 299.

Halstead, D. K. (1974). *Statewide Planning in Higher Education*.

Heller, D. (2004). NCES research on college participation: A critical analysis. In E. P. St. John (Ed.), *Public policy and college access: Investigating the federal and state roles in equalizing postsecondary opportunity* (Vol. 19, pp. 29–64). AMS Press, Inc.

Henry, M., Lingard, B., Rizvi, F., & Taylor, S. (2001). *The OECD, globalization and education policy*. Pergamon Press.

Henshaw, D. (1837). *Remarks upon the rights and powers of corporations, and of the rights, powers, and duties of the legislature toward them: Embracing a review of the opinion of the supreme court of the United States, in the case of Dartmouth College, in New Hampshire, given in 1819*. Nabu Press.

Hossler, D. (2006). Student and families as revenue: The impact on institutional behaviors. In D. M. Priest & E. P. St. John (Eds.), *Privatization and public universities: Implications for the public trust* (pp. 109–128). Indiana University Press.

Johnston, A. (2015, December 11). Student Protests Then and Now: From 'Hey, hey, LBJ!' to 'Black lives matter!'. *Chronicle of Higher Education*.

Johnson, T., & Collins, S. (2009). *Low-Income Student Persistence to Timely Graduation as a Function of the Academic Experience* Center for Enrollment Research, Policy, and Practice. Retrieved March 10 from https://eric.ed.gov/?id=ED537403

Justiz, M. J., & Bjork, L. S. E. (1988). *Higher education research and public policy*. Macmillan.

Kerr, C. (1963). *The uses of the university*. Harvard University Press.

Kerr, C. (1978). *12 systems of higher education: 6 decisive issues*. International Council for Educational development.

Law, D. S., & Versteeg, M. (2012). Debating the declining influence of the United States constitution: A response to professors Choudhry, Jackson, and Melkinsburg. *New York University Law Review*, 87, 2118.

Lee, J. B., Zumeta, W., & St. John, E. P. (1996). *Feasibility of establishing private higher education charter institutions and issuing tuition vouchers*.

Loper Bright Enterprises v. Raimondo (2024), US 22-451

Mattei, E. E. (2022). *The capital order: How economists invented austerity and paved the way to fascism*. University of Chicago Press.

McConnell, M. W. (2002). Establishment and disestablishment at the founding, part i: Establishment of religion. *William & Mary Law Review*, 44, 2105.

McGrath, E. J. (1971). Student governance and disorder. *Change: The Magazine of Higher Learning*, 3(3), 10–68.

McGuinn, P. (2016). From no child left behind to the every student succeeds act: Federalism and the education legacy of the Obama administration. *Publius: The Journal of Federalism*, 46(3), 392–415.

Meyer, H. D. (2016). *The design of the university: German, American, And world class*. Routledge.

Meyer, H. D., & Benavot, A. (2013). *PISA, power, and policy: The emergence of global educational governanc*. Symposium Books.

Mir, A., & Toor, S. (2023). Racial capitalism and student debt in the US. *Organization*, 30(4), 754–765.

Morrill Land Grant Act of 1862, Public Law 37-130.

Morrill Land Grant Act of 1890, Public Law 51-841.

National Commission on Excellence in Education. (1983). *A Nation At Risk*. http://www.ed.gov/pubs/NatAtRisk/title.html

Nussbaum, M. C. (2008). *Liberty of conscience: In defense of America's tradition of religious equality*. Basic Books.

Paulsen, M., & St. John, E. P. (2002). Budget incentive structures and the improvement of college teaching. In D. M. Priest, W. E. Becker, D. Hossler, & E. P. St. John (Eds.), *Incentive-based budgeting systems in public universities* (pp. 222–236). Eward Elgar.

Piketty, T. (2014). *Capital in the 21st century*. Belknap Press.

Plessy v. Ferguson, 163 U.S. 537 (1896).

Powers, J. B. (2004). Commercializing academic research: Resource effects on performance of university technology transfer. *Journal of Higher Education*, 74(1), 26–50.

Priest, D. M., & St. John, E. P. (2006). *Privatization and public universities*. Indiana University Press.

Priest, D. M., St. John, E. P., & Tobin, W. (2002). Incentive-based budgeting: An evolving approach. In D. M. Priest, W. E. Becker, D. Hossler, & E. P. St. John (Eds.), *Incentive-based budgeting systems in public universities* (pp. 227–236). Edward Elgar.

Profeta, A., Balling, R., Schoene, V., & Wirsig, A. (2010). Protected geographical indications And designations of origin: An overview of the status quo And the development of the use of regulation (EC) 510/06 in Europe, with special consideration of the German situation. *Journal of International Food & Agribusiness Marketing*, 22(1/2), 179–198.

Pyne, J., & Grodsky, E. (2020). Inequality and opportunity in a perfect storm of graduate student debt. *Sociology of Education*, 93(1), 20–39.

Rhoads, R. A. (1998). *Freedom's web: Student activism in an age of culture diversity*. Johns Hopkins University Press.

Rhoades, G., & Slaughter, S. (1997). Academic capitalism, managed professionals, and supply-side higher education. *Social Text*, 51, 9–38.

Roukis, G. S. (2004). The British East India Company 1600-1858: A model of transition management for the modern global corporation. *Journal of Management Development*, 23(10), 938–948.

Scherer, S. (2023). *Manhattan Project research at Purdue propelled Chemistry Department's postwar growth*. Purdue University. Retrieved April 2 from https://www.chem.purdue.edu/history/manhattan_project.html

Sen, A. (2009). *The idea of justice*. Belknap.

Shattuck, M., & Horvath, A. (2019). *The governance of British higher education: The impact of governmental, financial and market pressures*. Bloomsbury Publishing.

Silk, M., & Walsh, A. (2008). *One nation, divisible: How regional religious differences shape American politics*. Rowman & Littlefield.

Somers, P., & Gera, H. (2023). Affirmative action around the world: Why the protest over affirmative action in the US? In E. P. St. John (Ed.), *In col-learning in higher education*.

St. John, E. P. (1986). Postsecondary policy and management in the far East: A comparative study. *Higher Education, 15*, 523–545.

St. John, E. P. (2023). Higher education in post-neoliberal times: Building human capabilities in the emergent period of uncertainty, *Education Sciences. 13*(5), 500. https://doi.org/10.3390/educsci13050500

St. John, E. P., & Asker, E. H. (2003). *Refinancing the college dream: Access, equal opportunity, and justice for taxpayers*. Johns Hopkins University Press.

St. John, E. P., & Byce, C. (1982). The changing federal role in student financial aid. In M. Kramer (Ed.), *New directions in higher education* (Vol. 40, pp. 21–40). Jossey-Bass.

St. John, E. P., & Hossler, D. (1998). Higher education desegregation in the post-Fordice legal environment: A critical-empirical perspective. *Race, the Courts, and Equal*, 123–155.

St. John, E. P., & Noell, J. (1989). The impact of financial aid on access: An analysis of progress with special consideration of minority access. *Research in Higher Education, 30*(6), 563–582.

Stengel, R. (2019). *Information wars: How we lost the global powers Battle against misinformation and what we can do about it*. Atlantic Monthly.

Timmerman, D. (2019). The abolition of tuition fees in Germany: Student protests and their impact. In W. Archer, & H. G. Schuetze (Eds.), *Preparing students for life and work* (pp. 204–219). Brill.

Vantaggiato, F. P., & Lubell, M. (2022). The benefits of specialized knowledge in polycentric governance. *Policy Studies Journal, 50*(4), 849–876.

Verduzco-Gutierrez, M., Larson, A. R., Capizzi, A. N., Bean, A. C., Zafonte, R. D., Odonkor, C. A., & Silver, J. K. (2021). How physician compensation and education debt affects financial stress and burnout: A survey study of women in physical medicine and rehabilitation. *Physical Medicine & Rehabilitation, 13*(8), 836–884.

Wallace, M. (2004). *The American axis: Henry Ford, Charles Lindbergh, and the rise of the Third Reich*. MacMillan.

Williams, J. B. (1997). *Race discrimination in public higher education*. Praeger.

Wong, A. (2023, March 23). DEI came to colleges with a bang. Now, these red states are on a mission to snuff it out. *USA Today*. https://www.usatoday.com/story/news/education/2023/03/23/dei-diversity-in-colleges-targeted-by-conservative-red-states/11515522002/

Yang, L., & St. John, E. P. (2023). Public investment in short-cycle tertiary vocational education: Historical, longitudinal, and fixed-effects analyses of developed and less-developed countries. *Education Sciences, 13*(6), 573. https://doi.org/https://doi.org/10.3390/educsci13060573

Young, A. R., & Peterson, J. (2013). The EU and the new trade politics. In *The European union and the new trade politics* (pp. 1–20). Routledge.

3

REFRAMING POLICY MATTERS

Political Ideologies, Policy Studies, and Research Evidence

Conflicting ideologies emerged after the Revolution, Civil War, and World War II (WW II), leading to new generations of policies promoting college development. After WWII, conservative and liberal states used federal support, developed using systems logic informed by research, to build mass-access college systems. In the 1980s, the Reagan administration amassed data and used unsupportable logic to promote STEM education and marketization. The MAGA-DEI debate overlooks trends in college preparation, educational stratification, and the economic wellbeing of graduates. After a historical review of ideological conflicts in education policy development, we explain how careful analysis of policy changes and linked outcomes can inform a new generation of discourse about policy options. We develop frameworks for using trend data to analyze whether the Reagan era claims were correct and to inform contemporary policy discussions about education development and reform.

CONFLICTING POLITICAL IDEOLOGIES ACROSS EDUCATION HISTORY

Conflicting political ideologies emerged in successive historical periods and transformed through social reconstruction across time. Conflicting political rationales give way to new policy preferences; they eventually converge through compromise into strategies used to restabilize policy until a further period of severe conflict occurs. Old ideologies and rationales don't disappear; they reappear and transform in academic narratives as part of theories, research, and histories—this recurring cycle evolves in higher education policy as other discourses, especially in social and economic upheaval periods. In addition to living through conflict, people learn from novels, movies, and cross-generation conversations. Higher education policy followed this cycle of conflicting and stabilizing forces across historical periods (Table 3.1).

The legal history (Chapter 2) outlined the evolution of the political infrastructure across periods. Political turmoil and leadership influenced the emergence of new

Table 3.1 Conflicting Political Ideologies Emerging Across Transitional Periods, Conflicting Rationales, and Policy Preferences for Higher Education

Period	Political Ideologies	Conflicting Political Rationales Emerge	Higher Education Policy Preferences
Early America & Public Systems (1776–1940)	Evangelism	• Communities of Faith • Education Alignment	• Faith Centric Colleges • Educate Teachers & Preachers
	Egalitarianism	• Freedom & Emancipation • Social Progressive National Vision	• Education for Women & Blacks • Education for Professions
Cold War & Progressive (1945–1980)	Conservative	• Economic Development • Low Taxes	• Classical Education • Science & Technology
	Liberal	• Social Progress • Cross-Generation Uplift	• Education for Social Good • Equal Opportunity
Neoliberal (1980–2015)	Neoconservative	• Cut Social Programs • Reduce Taxes	• No Frills Education • Merit Aid • Student Loans
	Neoliberal	• Markets & Efficiency • Human Rights	• STEM Pipeline • College Preparation for all
Post-neoliberal (2015–)	MAGA Republicans	• Reactionary • Nationalist • Working Class	• Privatization • Christian • Career & Technical
	Uncertainty New Progressive Democrats	• Restore Public Role • Expand Opportunity	• Reinvestment • Debt forgiveness • Free (Community) College

coalitions that stabilized the trajectory after the Civil War and WWII—the stable periods held together with coalitions that crafted policies nationally and within states. The emergence of neoliberalism through policies promoted by Presidents Carter and Reagan shifted the trajectory. Next, we explain how ideologies emerged in periods of conflict, became rationales used for policy advocacy, and eventually became part of the policy compromises in renewed periods of quasi-stability in higher education development.

Competing Beliefs from the Founding Forward

The tensions between evangelization and egalitarianism, two forces evident before the American Revolution, divided the nation before the Civil War and remained unreconciled until WWII and the Golden Age of progressive investment. The divisions within and across regions constrained the apparent irrevocability of belief traditions as they evolved across history (Table 3.1). Political ideologies re-manifest, along with recontextualized political arguments, building on lingering distrust of the "other." In the US, the North-South tensions coalesced advocacy for enslaving people and oppositional egalitarian views. These lingering core tensions evolved and transformed. The DEI-MAGA disputes about education policy are rooted in this history, as interest groups have constructed and reconstructed curricula on humanities and civics aligned and realigned with shifting core and oppositional values.

Deep Tensions from the Nation's Founding

Evangelism is a political ideology advanced by religious groups, much like contemporary Christian nationalism. Evangelist groups founded American colonies that aligned their governing systems with Christian denominations, including Puritan (a Calvinist religion), Quaker, and so forth, forming theocracies in some colonies (Ellis, 1888; Maclear, 1959). Others came to the colonies for religious freedom and were among the early advocates of egalitarianism, a political ideology supporting expanding rights to more people. College preparation for all is a legacy of early egalitarianism altered by neoliberals. Tensions between the two ideological traditions—evangelism and egalitarianism—cut across American history.

A Nobel Prize economist, Robert Fogel (2000), focused on historical swings in the dominant public ethos in *The Fourth Great Awakening and the Future of Egalitarianism.* He argued that the American Colonies were founded with an egalitarian zeal but emphasized the evangelization of new settlers; the ethos shifted to egalitarianism during the Revolution, at least in the North's advocacy to end slavery before the Civil War, and once again, the movement toward gender equality and women's right to vote. He argued these periods of egalitarianism follow periods of religious fever with people of faith evangelizing through policies regulating behavior. He argued that the evangelization of the Moral Majority in the late twentieth century would lead to a renewed emphasis on equality in the early twenty-first century, including a reinvestment in need-based student aid to promote education equity.

A quarter century after Fogel predicted a new period would restore funding for student aid, the reinvestment in financial assistance did not happen—neoliberalism resulted in a more sustained change than expected. With the rise in college prices, spending more on grants once again would not restore equity to a higher education system with no affirmative mechanism to address prior inequalities facing rural and urban, low-income students who attended under-funded schools. Instead, the tensions between the two extremes represent a polarity in values. There is reason to argue that faith and introspection can inform attitudes about social equity. A mass swing back to a majority progressive ethos now seems impossible, given the MAGA-DEI tension in society, education, and higher education.

A more nuanced view of the underlying conflict emerged in Martha Nussbaum's (2008) *Liberty of Conscience: In Defense of America's Tradition of Religious Equality.* She provides a particularly compelling analysis of faith traditions in New England. She argued that early Americans valued liberty in addition to sincerely held religious beliefs. The strong strand of liberty-seeking New Englanders was quite varied, as it turns out. Nussbaum focused on Rhode Island, where Roger William created a colony for freedom seekers in Calvinist New England.

Value differences were spread across the region, as evidenced by the timing of the colleges' founding and development. For example, Bates College, Maine's foremost liberal arts college, was founded as an abolitionist college with funds generated from slavery (Soler, 2020). In the wake of a recent mass shooting in the Lewiston community, Bates students now work with the local community on preventing gun violence and healing from the psychological wounds in a community committed to gun ownership but not to human gun violence (Philpott, 2023). Attempts to generalize about divisive values across and within college and university communities are valuable exercises but are fraught with exceptions. Nussbaum's argument of liberty and freedom as an ethos unifies amid diverse values merits reflection.

Conflict During the Progressive Cold War

The federal programs supporting research, facilities, and students were a Golden Age for higher education during the Cold War, a period when progressive ideas about educational development cut across liberal and conservative political frames (St. John & Parsons, 2004). After WWII, with federal support, states aggressively built higher education systems. Some took liberal approaches, using California's Master Plan as a model. Others chose more conservative paths, like Indiana. The contrast between California's and Indiana's strategies for developing mass systems is illustrative of the underlying progressive period.

In California, system-wide administrations, created to coordinate across campuses, evolved into elaborate structures. The state's three-tiered approach—universities, state colleges, and community colleges—was widely emulated. California's Master Plan for Higher Education became a model for other states that developed statewide systems for universities, state colleges, and community colleges. In contrast, Indiana minimized duplication by having Purdue University (Chapter 9) develop technical collegiate branch campuses across the state while Indiana University (IU) built similar extension campuses for the liberal arts. The central campuses provided the coordination; they had leaner administrative systems than the California approach. IU developed a state-wide medical school, while Purdue governed engineering programs across the state (Chapter 9). Indiana built a progressive system on conservative principles fostered by midwestern fiscal conservatives in the Republican and Democratic parties. California became the classic liberal state where Republican governors, like California Governors Hiram Johnson and Earl Warren, were progressive in the traditions of Republican Presidents Abraham Lincoln and Teddy Roosevelt. In contrast, Southern Democrats were conservatives, and their influence reached Indiana but not California. Democratic and Republican governors and legislatures encountered conflict about funding levels, but both parties supported Indiana's dual system strategy.

Conservative values guided Indiana's approach, but both centered on progressive goals. The other Midwest states were liberal regarding their investment in higher education, a holdover from the ethos of Northwest Territories' education legacy. In contrast, Indiana lagged in higher education investment and had more constrained tax increases. In addition to IU, Purdue, and a few state universities, Ivy Tech (now Ivy Tech Community College system) provided technical postsecondary education for the industrial cities (i.e., Gary, Terra Haute, and Indianapolis). In the early part of the Progressive Era, IU and Purdue were at the bottom of the Big Ten in state funding per student. In the 1970s, under the leadership of George Weathersby at the Indiana Commission for Higher Education, the state began to invest in need-based grants to improve the financial stability of public institutions and private colleges. Indiana became a model for a balanced approach to building a state system at a low cost for taxpayers (Chapter 9).

The nation continued a progressive trajectory in the public finance of education through Republican and Democratic Presidents until Ronald Reagan was elected President. Jimmy Carter was a Southern Democrat and brought conservative financial strategies for promoting progress, much like Democrats in Indiana during the same period. By the time Reagan was elected President, Carter's legislative framework created the legal foundation for the rapid shift to "neoliberal" national policy (Chapter 2). The reactionary shift that had swept Reagan into the Governor's office and reshaped public education in the states from the 1970s to the 2010s (see Chapter 7) became part of the new national trajectory and influenced the global shift to neoliberalism (Gerstle, 2022).

Neoliberalism: Efficiency, STEM Agenda, and Marketization

Educational attainment outcomes remained central in the policy rhetoric of neoliberal reformers, but their policies did not have research-based strategies linked to these outcomes. The marketization agenda relied on efficiency arguments, and it gained support from a higher education lobbying community willing to accept loan expansion as grant funding declined (King, 1999a, 1999b). The Department of Education vetted researchers' reports so they would support reform agendas for marketization and STEM education, policy agendas crafted based on biased research and falsification in policy reports.

Post-Neoliberal Malaise

The education mainstream has awoken to a challenge. The MAGA ideology, the catalyst for the conservative elements of the post-neoliberal period, also played a role in Ronald Reagan's Presidential campaign in 1980 (Morgan, 2019). An appeal to white nationalists, the core of Southern Democrat values in the 1930s, MAGA is the nationalist rationale that is now the dominant theme of the Republican party. Trump ran for president in 2015–20 on a MAGA ideology. The alignment between conservative Christian education aligns with the MAGA movement as well. Christian academies mushroomed and expanded after school desegregation through the 1970s. Private school vouchers and the charter movements provided public funding for Christian schools in many states (Bailey & Cooper, 2009; Greene et al., 1998). Multiple generations in many families have been educated in curriculum framing content in this tradition, adding a Christian nationalism to the MAGA frame supporting educational markets over older patterns of education finance (Whitehead & Perry, 2020).

As is evident in many states, conflicting values hamper consensus building and direction setting on California's public campuses. California continues to offer the lowest tuition rates for community colleges, at less than $1,500 per year—the state's four-year tuition is closer to the national average and above the in-state rates of 23 other states (Ma & Pender, 2023). The push for new progressive values: The California State University system is trying to reduce tuition and reduce hate crimes on its campuses in the wake of the Hamas-Israeli war (Smith, 2023). The push for free colleges has become a reality for many California Community Colleges (CCC) students, as campuses are taking advantage of the California College Promise Act and the broader College Promise legislation passed in 2017 (Picazo, 2023). The CCC also adopted accreditation standards for DEI in the wake of the demise of affirmative action. Still, faculty are litigating the new requirements because of the constraints on their freedom to teach (Cumming et al., 2023). The clash between conservative anti-woke and progressive advocates of DEI remains a significant issue in many states, and the conflict spilled over into the 2024 Presidential campaign.

Perhaps the most evident example of contemporary uncertainty is the ambiguous future of Career and Technical Education (CTE) in high schools and colleges. Pushed to the remote margins by the STEM pipeline, CTE may be the most evident point of convergence between Trump's and Biden's education policies. Yet the education establishment's commitment to the K-20 STEM logic has slowed a conversation. The political emphasis on CTE, a programmatic priority for both Trump and Biden, could realign education development with the social goal of rebuilding a working class, a social theme uniting the two extremes. Thus, reinvestment in career, vocational, and technical education—upgrading technician education for a new generation of working Americans—may become part of a new, post-neoliberal education trajectory. Since politics influence educational policy nationally and in states, we focus on themes emerging from the new progressive and MAGA agendas.

The political battles surrounding the college for all logic and the developing consensus around CTE may be the most robust evidence pointing to the early evolution of a post-neoliberal period in the political zeitgeist. As we discuss in greater detail in Chapter 4 on academic preparation, we are witnessing the swinging of the preparation pendulum from four-year college preparation for all to multiple pathways for high school completion. This shift has taken considerable pressure off high schools, and their graduation rates have increased. We describe it as a pendulum swing because the new secondary school context is reminiscent of the pathways and tracks in the comprehensive high school before *A Nation at Risk*. In contrast, the *Shopping Mall High School* (Powell et al., 1985) period has boutique courses to appeal to the array of student interests and preferences. This critique of the comprehensive high school in the 1970s and 1980s argued that trying to be all things to all students created winners and losers in the "education marketplace."

Today, the marketplace is different because college dropouts and graduates face high debt. Further, the labor market's needs have evolved. It is not yet clear whether shifting away from college preparation, a topic we explore in the cases as a dimension of college success will have a material impact on the equitable distribution of economic opportunities.

Research Evidence Informing Policy Choices

After WWII, the return of GIs brought new waves of students and federal spending to America's public and independent colleges. However, human capital theory had not yet emerged as a logic for public and private investment. Instead, the new wave of investment necessitated new logic, theory, and rationalizations for increased investment. The evolution of data collection and the uses of research to inform public policy on higher education is an open question rather than a set pattern. We examine how data collection evolved and its uses in policy studies before considering the uses of research to inform policy development. While education data collection and policy research now have a long history of advocacy for expanding and contracting budgets, more should be given to the purposes and uses of data analyses as a resource for breaking through ideologically contested and belief-driven approaches to policy development. We examine the evolution and uses of data systems after WWII before examining the uses and misuses of policy research at the outset of the neoliberal turn.

DATA COLLECTION AND POLICY STUDIES

The federal government started collecting education statistics from states and schools in 1870. Higher education enrollment statistics and funding colleges in states informed enrollment-based funding in some states, but these early surveys did not include the complete universe of postsecondary institutions. In 1940, almost one-quarter of adults had graduated high school, and under 5% had graduated college. During the decade before WWII, colleges were numerous and struggling financially as the nation fought to climb out of the depression sweeping the world. Planning for expanding enrollment was not a high priority for state and federal education agencies; information on the number of institutions and enrollment in colleges is limited. Many campuses survived financial crises by constricting programs, merging with other campuses, and renaming to broaden appeal (Platt et al., 2017). As colleges struggled to maintain enrollment during the Great Depression, they experienced a nationwide student peace movement and a walkout of approximately a million students (Cohen, 1993). The GI Bill changed the academic world; a flood of adults entered college campuses as the Golden Age started, and new progressive policies emerged. After WWII, federal support of college students, especially returning GIs and expansion in enrollment, corresponded with an economic boom, reinforcing human capital logic about return on investment.

We examine the history of policy research, focusing on how policy changes correspond with outcome trends as baseline information to inform policy decisions in politically contested organizations (i.e., state agencies and universities). We are careful about this analytic process precisely because most policy research fails to do so. Most quantitative studies examine statistical relationships between variables at a point in time without considering the links to how policy changes—and especially trends in funding levels in student aid and tuition charges—over time, related to changes in outcomes. While attempts to establish causality are an econometric art form, it is not a substitute for building an understanding of how implemented policies link to actual outcomes. Critical research, in contrast, usually provides histories of policies and outcomes without considering the linking structures per se. Critique of neoliberalism is of limited value when it does not provide evidence to inform ongoing policy decisions. Debates about statistical methods and political theory have value, mainly as measures of academic productivity, but their practical value in day-to-day decisions remains limited.

Thus, we aim to encourage more thoughtful analytic research informing policy decisions, institutional action, and evidence-based, actionable research instead of ideological advocacy. In the following chapters, our trend analyses use state and national data sources and systematic research reviews that consider the underlying linking structures to provide information. We used frameworks linking policy and outcomes, a methodological necessity overlooked in many academic publications. Knowledge of research and policy linkages, especially illumination of emerging inequalities, are both essential to understanding the consequences of the policy.

History of Analysis Informing Higher Education Policy
Planning for the GI Bill emerged "within the immediate political, social, and institutional contexts that shaped the proposals for a package of veterans' benefits near and shortly after the end of World War II" (Altschuler & Blumin, 2009, p. 5). Following the allies' victory in Europe after WWI, the US federal government failed to follow up on its commitment to veterans so riots ensued (Cohen, 2001). The discontent spilled over into the psychological malaise as many families migrated West during the Great Depression. Roosevelt's New Deal was a package of programs partially implemented before the US engaged in WWII. The *Serviceman's Readjustment Act* (known as the GI Bill) was a way through the problem—keeping vets in the colleges and universities provided the willing and able ways to advance themselves and society while also reducing the impact of service members taking jobs from the women who manufactured the war supplies for the allies.

Research-informed planning increased only gradually after WWII. First, a systems approach for planning, used in the British and American invasions of Nazi Europe, was adapted to social and educational planning (Schultz, 1968). The formal method—program planning and budgeting—developed at UC Berkeley was advocated in higher education (Balderston, 1974; Weathersby & Balderston, 1972). Planning for the HEA Title IV Programs used the logical method, but there was limited supportive research. Economics was still developing as an analytic field. Critics correctly counter-argued that politics rather than rational analyses prevailed (Lindblom, 1959, 1979; Wildavsky, 1979). President Jimmy Carter's Zero-Based Budgeting, used across education and social agencies in the federal government, was the first government-wide effort to utilize data and research on program outcomes in program planning. Instead of realizing the efficiency aims, government analysts learned to circumvent the process to advocate for programs.

Development of Databases and Analysis Methods

Data collection on higher and other postsecondary education has never included all postsecondary programs, colleges, and universities. Enrollment and funding levels were usually the only data considered, along with budget rationales written by staff. Analysts typically used planning modestly and made incremental adjustments based on historical funding.

Federal and state data sources have improved with time and can be used to inform policy more routinely and systematically than is typically the case. Three forms of data collection evolved:

- *Institutional Surveys:* The Higher Education General Information Survey (HEGIS), started in 1966, collected institutional data on fall enrollment, finances, and facilities. Approximately 3,400 accredited institutions received surveys, but not all institutions responded(Thurgood et al., 2003). Replaced by Integrated Postsecondary Education Data Surveys (IPEDS) in 1987, HEGIS provided the primary source of information for states, the USDE, and researchers for two decades. The surveys were paper forms automated by a federal contractor. Today, IPEDS provides comprehensive data on more than 4,400 colleges and universities in the US eligible for Title IV financial aid programs.
- *Longitudinal Student Studies:* Initiated in 1957, Project Talent provided a longitudinal student database on aspiration, college enrollment, and subsequent events. Longitudinal surveys also collected data on life course choices and outcomes for cohorts graduating from high school in the 1970s and 1980s. Since the 1980s, the National Center for Education Statistics (NCES) has conducted numerous large-scale longitudinal studies that have shaped the public policy conversations around K12 and higher education. Research using surveys informed political discourses and was frequently employed to reinforce the emerging neoliberal policy priorities of the time.
- *State Data Collections.* After the 1972 HEA, states received funding for supplemental data collection. The National Center for Higher Education Management Systems (NCHEMS) developed additional campus survey forms for campuses, but Washington, Indiana, Florida, and a few other states collected student records. These state systems have not been as universally accessible as the federal data sources. Still, many studies have emerged from researchers who have gained access to them, notably in states like Florida, Indiana, and Ohio.
- *Other Federal Studies.* The US Department of Education routinely funds research, including evaluation studies collecting new and statistical studies utilizing federal and state data collection.

Each type of data has uses and limitations. HEGIS (now IPEDS), the original cornerstone of the public accountability system, provided enrollment and financial planning data for traditional higher education (i.e., campuses included in the surveys). States used enrollment data, or more detailed information on spring and fall enrollment, in financial aid and enrollment. States have also used HEGIS/IPEDS in budget development and coordinated collection for the federal government.

In contrast, the longitudinal surveys expanded the universe of student college choices to technical postsecondary education options available to students, including programs and colleges not included in HEGIS. Pell grants increased market forces by extending the range of choices open to low- and middle-income students. The longitudinal studies became an essential source for estimating the impact of portable grants: awards made by the government to students that they can take to institutions. Unlike merit aid awarded on grades and test scores, the Pell Grant used needs analysis to calculate eligibility and award level. In contrast, vouchers, now used in many K-12 systems, provide awards to nearly all students so they can make school choices. The longitudinal high school cohort surveys provided a data source for tracing the impact of portable awards on students' college choices.

State student-record databases include larger student universes but are constrained to reporting institutions. The expanding institutional universe for data collection helps improve coverage but does not entirely solve the problem. Even with advances in data collection, research design remains a crucial issue when interpreting the meaning of study findings, an issue too often overlooked in the rush to find more sophisticated methods.

Estimating the Impact of Tuition and Grants

As the federal investment in student aid grew from the GI Bill, the Truman Commission considered expanding enrollment by investing in student aid (Zook, 1947). Congress created the National Commission on the Financing of Postsecondary Education (NCFPE) to assess the impact of the newly legislated grant program under Title IV and the Title I program that would provide grants to colleges based on enrollment. The Commission utilized HEGIS enrollment and finance data to estimate the effects of tuition and state subsidies on student enrollment. The staff used simulations to predict impact, generating a price response coefficient for tuition—and reduction through grants—from Radner and Miller's (1970) student demand analysis with HEGIS dates. Treating grants as tuition subsidies for students' tuition charges (or "net price"), the National Commission on the Financing of Postsecondary Education (NCFPE) (1973) estimated the impact of the new Pell Grant program and subsidies to colleges on enrollment, concluding that student grants would have a more substantial effect than funding colleges. In subsequent reauthorizations, the Title I program was not funded and was replaced by other programs.

The Carnegie Commission on Higher Education (1973) had advocated for the Title I program while a Nixon-appointed task force recommended the portable aid program—an idea that influenced the creation of Basic Educational Opportunity Grants (now Pell)—to stimulate innovation (Newman, 1971). The NCFPE report sealed the casket for direct federal support for institutions, leaving that role to states. After that, student aid became the primary federal role (Gladieux & Wolanin, 1976), with only a few direct grants to developing institutions—HEA Title III funds for HBCUs and HEA Title V providing direct grant funding for Hispanic Serving Institutions (HSI). Title V funding has a modest positive effect on the enrollment of minority students (Ortega, 2021; Santiago et al., 2016). Given all the changes in federal programs, state funding, and college prices since 1978, well-designed studies of the various funding sources are now long overdue.

Many arguments against the NCPFE findings were politically motivated by advocates of federal funding for colleges (e.g., Carnegie Commission on Higher Education, 1973). The most compelling critiques were from Stephen Dresch (1975), a researcher at Princeton. Dresch argued that 1) extrapolations from simulations using price response measures should not extend beyond the period and policy conditions studied (i.e., the range of prices and subsidies affecting the population studied) and 2) the choice of price response measures, or PRs, did not consider all possible options. A series of studies followed, developing and improving methods of calculating standardized price response coefficients (SPRCs) (Jackson & Weathersby, 1975; Manski & Wise, 1983; McPherson, 1978), averaging across studies the impact of net prices. By the time the disputes ended, it was evident that the single price response measure for the net price was no longer adequate as the shift to marketization took off.

The National Longitudinal Study of the High School Class of 1972 (NLS-72) and High School and Beyond (HSB) follow the 1980 and 1982 high school cohorts. First, Jackson (1978) used NLS-72 in a three-stage model of college choice, documenting the impact of grants. His work was part of the federal study of institutional grants and federal grant aid (Weathersby et al., 1977), confirming the importance of grant aid as the most effective means for the federal government to expand access and equalize opportunity. Jackson's study informed the development of college choice theories used in enrollment management (Hossler & Gallagher, 1987). Next, Manski and Wise (1983) used NLS-72 to estimate the impact of Pell on enrollment, concluding the Program expanded enrollment in community colleges and technical programs. They also found that the newly enrolled students were not prepared to enroll in four-year colleges, an interpretive finding that influenced the STEM movement just getting underway. In the early 1980s, research using HSB documented the impact of grants on enrollment and persistence (St. John, 1991; St. John & Noell, 1989). HSB was also used in a new round of studies on the impact of prices and subsidies, stimulating a new round of projections.

After the drop in federal grant funding in the 1980s and out of concern for social justice and the potential implications of these cuts, it was essential to examine the impact of grants and loans on enrollment and persistence across income groups (St. John, 1990a, 1990b), which were studied using differentiated price response measures for grants and tuition for high-, middle-, and low-income students (St. John, 1993; St. John & Starkey, 1995). Subsequent simulation studies used these measures to assess the impact of mid-year tuition increases at a state university (Trammell, 1995) and to examine the cross-state analyses that provided adequate information to inform policy decisions (DesJardins, 1999). While this slow progression in econometric scholarship was a modest step forward in improving the utility of price-response measures in enrollment studies, this prior work was not adequate to contend with the arguments about academic access that academic preparation and college access that swirled in policy discourses started by changes in finance policies in the 2000s.

Analyses of State Student Records

By the 1980s, a few states collected student records instead of the NCHEMS supplemental data collection. The state of Washington collected student-tracking data on state grants and loans along with credits completed and was the first state to use student records to evaluate the impact of an increase in grant aid. Research using that data demonstrated that an increase in grant aid improved persistence at four-year campuses and reduced gaps in degree completion for students of color compared to white students (St. John, 1999).

Indiana developed a comprehensive program that combined incentives for preparation, student and family support services, and a modest student grant supplement—the Twenty-first Century Scholars Program. If students completed the steps to prepare, the grant award was increased to the current year's tuition level, while similar full-need students received grants based on the prior year's tuition charge. The award differentials were small, so the program added a minuscule amount to the awards students would otherwise receive. The initial study found the Scholars who pledged to take steps to prepare for college (their commitment) proved more likely to enroll in community colleges and private colleges (St. John et al., 2004). Subsequent studies also found positive effects on persistence (St. John et al., 2006).

Further analyses examined the impact of services, finding that taking advantage of counseling improved the odds of enrolling in community colleges and participating in college visits modestly increased the likelihood of enrollment in four-year colleges (Fisher, 2013; St. John et al., 2011). The impact of enrollment in private four-year colleges and two-year colleges was more substantial than for public four-year colleges, an artifact of the effort private colleges made to recruit scholars. Taking advantage of services was linked, of course, to self-selecting into the Scholars program. The promise of state grants equaling tuition attracted low-income students into the program. Participation, perceived as an honor, was significantly associated with the involvement in campus visits for students and parents. The state of Indiana had a generous need-based grant program that Scholars would receive without participating in the TFCS program.

A subsequent study found a significant effect in the original research overestimated the impact of the program because it did not consider selection effects (Toutkoushian et al., 2015). The more advanced method, in contrast, did not consider the modest grant increases (a negligible price change) or the services students used. In pursuit of better econometric techniques, the Toutkoushian team also overlooked changes in the grant program that had reduced the value of grant awards in the period they studied compared to the original study (see Chapter 9). Sometimes, the econometric rush for better methods overlooks policy contexts. The shift in award calculation had subtracted Pell, reducing the state award after the state promised to cover a higher award amount. By ignoring the cut in grant funding (award amount maximum compared to tuition), the study team supported the cuts in funding by the neoconservative governor and legislators. The alignment of the study in support of cuts in grants may have been unintentional. Still, researchers must consider changes in policy and funding before reaching conclusions that inadvertently support regressive policies. This politicization of research by conflicting researchers should inform studies of free tuition and other new promise programs. It is crucial to consider policy context and policy changes when comparing findings across time, an idea that harkens back to Dresch's (1975) criticisms of the NCFPE's planning model.

From Equity to Policy Outcomes

Political ideologies shift, influencing changes in federal and state education and public finance policies. Policy studies typically examine links between policy and outcomes in the aggregate, with minimal consideration of how policy changes affect inequality in the short and long terms. In the first edition of *Public Policy and Higher Education*, we focused on changes in policy between the Golden Age and the Neoliberal period, a perspective updated in the second edition. Sufficient time and political turmoil have passed to take a further step by comparing policies and outcomes in the neoliberal period to the impact of program and funding changes in the post-neoliberal period.

More than a century after being collected in 1870, education statistical reports measured progress in expanding educational attainment. Equal education opportunities for people of color and women became social and political issues as the decades progressed; policies promoting equal opportunity became central to federal during the 1960s and 1970s. The neoliberal turn shifted the emphasis from equal attainment to higher test scores as equity in attainment dropped, and test scores languished and even declined, at least in some states, for periods following the implementation of higher graduation standards for all.

The Consequences of the Neoliberal Turn

During the Ronald Reagan presidency, the US Department of Education (USDE) shifted strategies for funding K-12 education from equalizing opportunity to using public funding to enforce compliance with newly mandated standards (Finn, 1990). Federal studies did not consider how policy changes linked to student outcomes; instead, USED used the correlates of outcomes to advocate for higher standards while cutting funding for programs providing supplemental education for high-need students. The shift appealed to poor whites who assumed that equity-based programs favored minorities and wealthy people who wanted to pay less taxes. Attempts to erase equity from reporting analyses of education statistics led to mathematical and logical errors shaping public support for both the STEM pipeline agenda and marketization, major policy shifts dismantling equity policies rationalized by studies that focused on correlates of outcomes and did not consider the ways policy changes linked to outcomes (Berkner & Chavez, 1997; Pelavin & Kane, 1988).

The marketization of higher education and the STEM agenda are contemporary manifestations of the neoliberal transition. Biased research, developed as advocacy for the STEM agenda—arguments that curriculum changes and parental encouragement would improve access—was used to obfuscate the adverse effects of rising net prices for low-income students. Logically, a college preparatory curriculum and encouraging mentoring could have an additive, possibly independent, impact on expanding opportunity and raising enrollment in senior colleges. Policy studies needed to consider the possibility that all three mechanisms—academic preparation, financial aid, and increased access to information and support—impact change rather than focus on a single cause and exclude others through blindered reasoning.

The Shift from Race Equity to Academic Preparation for All

From the 1960s through the early 1980s, many federal education policy studies focused on reducing race equity in achievement and attainment. In the late 1970s, Blacks, whites, and Hispanics attended college at nearly equal rates, but this emphasis rapidly faded in the 1980s (St. John & Noell, 1989). From 1965 through 1978, need-based student grants narrowed the enrollment gap. When it reopened in the early 1980s after the first waves of cuts to federal grant funding, ED sought explanations supporting the rationale built by *A Nation at Risk*. Two politically crafted policy reports illustrate researchers' role in constructing the STEM rationale. These reports, as many others crafted during the period, focused on factors correlated with the different enrollment rates of whites and minorities. Neither examined the impact of federal grants that were being cut during this period of spurious policy research. Political vetting by education agencies shaped the presentation of findings and researchers were at risk of losing funding if they considered alternative explanations (St. John, 2013).

In a pivotal report, the USDE's Office and Planning and Budge investigated the enrollment gap that opened for Blacks in the early 1980s and settled on differences in high school math courses completed to explain differentials of the Black-White differential in enrollment rates (Pelavin & Kane, 1988). The math courses students completed correlated with college enrollment, an artifact of tracking prior student generations. Students in the vocational and technical education (CTE) programs tended to go on to work instead of college. At the time, the CTE curriculum often failed to prepare students for the high-tech workforce, a problem not considered in the rush to eliminate and alter programs focusing on low-income students. At the urging of USED, the Pelavin and Kane report (1988) overlooked other research conducted in the firm that found the decline in funding for federal grants corresponded perfectly with the opening of the gap. The findings on the impact of cuts in grant aid—left out the official report on the enrollment gap (i.e., Pelavin & Kane, 1988) —were published in *Research on Higher Education* after academic peer review (St. John & Noell, 1989).[1] The problem within the evolving policy discourse was that math preparation had not changed in the early 1980s when the gap opened, so the requirements per se could not have caused the enrollment gap to open.

The contractor also completed a follow-up reform for the College Board, a monograph (Pelavin & Kane, 1990) arguing that requiring Algebra I by 9th grade would improve postsecondary access and degree completion, fueling advocacy for raising math requirements for graduation. The math-education research and teacher education communities supported the Algebra agenda, adding to the neoliberal establishment's support of the STEM agenda. We recognize that access to STEM education pathways may have been a crucial public priority in our shift toward globalization and a knowledge economy—and our findings support aspects of this proposition–but avoiding the equally important issues of the rising cost of college and the elimination of costly upgrades to technical education in K-12 schools distracted policymakers and school advocates from considering the very real tradeoffs as part of the new agenda and the reconstructed equity gaps that followed.

The second report, a study prepared for the National Center on Education Statistics (NCES), found that more first-year students attended four-year colleges than applied the prior year, concluding the applications, not student aid, explained enrollment gaps (Berkner & Chavez, 1997), adding to a substantial number of NCES studies overlooked the link between the decline in need-based grants and the growing inequality. The report's logic built on Pelavin and Kane's academic preparation argument, disguising the reasons for the gap between white and Black student enrollment that opened in the late 1970s. Berkner and Chavez concluded that "college-qualified low-income students, once accepted to four-year colleges, are as likely to enroll as middle- and high-income students." This crafty statement of findings essentially says if students prepare and apply then Black and white students attended college at the same rate. If low-income students cannot afford four-year colleges, they would choose to start in two-year colleges or choose not to attend at all. Of course, college acceptance by four-year colleges correlates with enrollment—the report merely stated the obvious, using correlates on enrollment to explain away income differences in opportunity resulting in increasing stratification evident during the 1980s and 1990s.

The Berkner-Chavez report (1997) and Pelavin and Kane's conclusion that requiring Algebra in eighth grade would reduce the enrollment gap (Pelavin & Kane, 1988) illustrate the *blame-the-victim* orientation of the deficit model used by USED to reframe education policy during the Reagan and GHW Bush administrations. After another decade, the Congressionally created Advisory Committee on Student Financial Assistance (2002) exposed statistical flaws in the USED research and the failure to address the growing inequality. However, the STEM agenda (i.e., emphasizing more math for all) and underfunding of need-based grants continued as states struggled to remedy the ever-increasing unmet need gap caused by reductions in federal grants, a problem complicated by their competing policy priorities (e.g., funding for prisons). The shift toward merit-based in some state financial aid programs further complicated the increasing inequality during the late twentieth century. If preparation was the problem, 40 years of new requirements should have resolved disparities. Instead, the legacy of the blame-the-victim policies still haunts education policy.

FRAMEWORKS FOR RELIABLE TREND ANALYSES

The following chapters analyze policy trends (e.g., costs, subsidies, and requirements) logically linked to outcomes for attainment by diverse groups. We encourage readers to consider the data and develop their views about possible remedies. We do not propose new policies but instead leave that practice to readers. This trend analysis method can inform graduate students, professors and teachers, administrators in schools and colleges, concerned citizens, and other researchers and analysts about transforming patterns of inequality. We used three frameworks: 1) a social politic framework liking policies and outcomes; 2) integration of academic and financial theory of change for investigating the effect of encouragement programs with academic and financial support for low-income students; and 3) a university finance model explaining how that us change revenue sources for undergraduate education. Their logic relies on research testing links between policy and outcomes, controlling for different social and economic forces. We explain our approach for:

- Analyzing trends in policy and outcomes.
- Linking public policies to educational outcomes.
- Reviewing pathways to college model for examining promise programs.
- Analyzing college budgeting for tuition and student aid.
- Cautions about using research evidence.

Trends in Policies Linked to Educational Outcomes

The attainment framework is a theoretical model informed by decades of social and economic research (Table 3.2). To understand the impact of education policy on attainment outcomes across racial and ethnic groups, we examine specific policy indicators and outcomes related to preparation for college and career, college opportunities, and success rates for completing college. The new reality informs the presentation and discussion of these indicators that the current period differs dramatically from the prior 40 years.

Table 3.2 Policy Indicators and Outcomes for Preparation, Access, and Success for 2000 to 2020 Using National and State Data Sources

Policy Indicators for Preparation (Chapter 3 and State Cases)	Preparation Outcomes (Chapter 3)
• High School Graduation Requirement (Math & Science Courses), Nation & States (*direct*) • College Costs: Tuition, plus Room & Board (Nation and states, public 2- & 4- year, private 4-year) (*indirect*) • Average Debt for College Graduates (Nation)	• SAT English Scores (National) • SAT Math Scores (National). • High School Graduation Rates by Race (Nation and State Cases) • College participation rates by race (National) • State-Based Indicators (State Cases)
Policy Indicators for Access • Tuition, Plus Room and Board in public and private, two-year (National and States averages) • Need-Based & Non-Need State Grants (National and State cases) • State & Local Subsidies for 2- and 4-year public colleges (National) • Purchasing power of Pell (Maximum Award and Unmet Need) (Nation) • High school requirements	**Access Indicators** • Percent High School Completers Enrolling in College by Race (National and State Cases) • College enrollment by race as a percent of the population (States) • Percent of the population enrolling in college by race by college type: 2- and 4-year, public and private (Nation and State Cases)
Policy Indicators for College Success (Chapter 5, References Indicators in Chapters 3 and 5 and State Cases) • Prior preparation • Tuition, • Student aid	**Success-Related Indicators (Chapter 5 and State Cases)** • 6-Year Graduate rates, by sector and race (nation and states) • Rates of education attainment (State Cases)

The 2000–2020 trend analyses illuminate states' roles in reshaping education attainment, either accelerating or reversing the neoliberal trajectory. The new figures present data for 2000 to 2020 so readers can focus on

1. *Preparation.* Recent changes in education attainment, comparing the past to the present. Given the stagnation of federal policy (Chapter 2), the new national trends in high school graduation rates emerged due to state policy changes. The state cases show how several states adapted their policies to address challenges after the neoliberal turn. In those cases, states loosened the constraints on graduation requirements, giving schools greater flexibility to allow students the choice to follow multiple pathways to the high school diploma.
2. *Access.* Analyses focus on how federal student aid policies changed and how they are linked to rising tuition, leading to increased reliance on loans—the core mechanisms and outcomes of *marketization*. A few, but not all, of the case states, responded to students' interest in reduced costs and debt, creating a series of natural experiments examined in the cases.
3. *College success,* Analyses focus on degree completion by race and ethnicity, the key consequence of both the STEM agenda and marketization. The severe financial challenges facing educated citizens in a rapidly evolving labor market are evident in the

national data. The state cases also focus on completion rates and the capacity of graduates to support their families (economic wellbeing), leaving a plethora of challenges for other studies.

Research Base for Assessing Impact of Federal and State Policy on Postsecondary Attainment

Federal policies on K-12 and higher education impact attainment outcomes in complex contexts. The state K-12 and higher education policies and programs have an impact, as do prices and subsidies. Figure 3.1 provides a conceptual framework for readers thinking about these links. Readers interested in the studies developing and testing the model can scrutinize the original work in *Education and the Public Interest: School Reform, Public Finance, and Access to College* (St. John, 2006). The analyses of the framework's logic used national data sources, longitudinal data, and multi-level models. Therefore, readers can use their interpretations of trend analyses in this book to make informed judgments about policy choices at the institution and state levels. We review and note new studies that add to the interpretive base in this edition.

In addition, the National Bureau of Economic Research (NBER) also initiated college access and completion studies in the early 2000s that consider how policies link to attainment outcomes. Susan Dynarski's (2000, 2002) studies of merit aid programs focus on the differential effects, distinguishing the impact of whites and Blacks. Her work informed policymakers about the stratifying and discriminatory effects of the shift from need-based to merit grants, further illustrating the consequence of rewarding talent instead of promoting equity (McPherson & Schapiro, 1999). The primary benefit of states' merit grant programs is retaining high-achieving students instead of losing talent to other states (Cornwell & Mustard, 2004). The NBER effort to address the impact of the shift to need-based grants stimulated a new wave of research informing state policy development. The NBER studies also examined alternative mechanisms for expanding access.

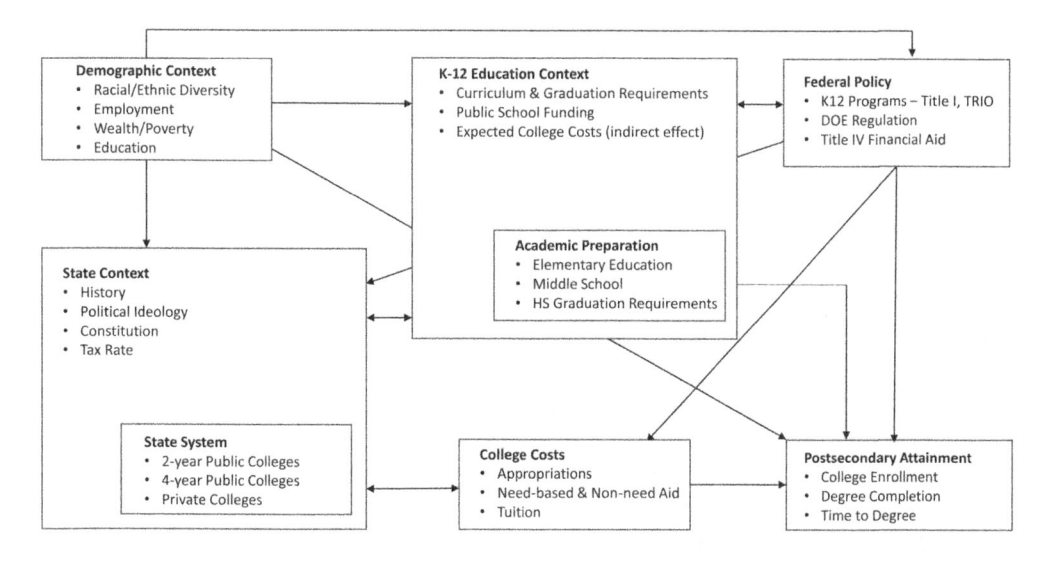

Figure 3.1 Framework for Assessing the Impact of Federal and State Policy on Postsecondary Attainment
Source: Adapted from St. John et al. (2004).

Eric Bettinger (2004) examined persistence, furthering the extant body of research documenting the impact of student aid on retention. Bettinger and Long (2009) investigated the effect of remediation on student collegiate outcomes. This work examines many of the linkages in our attainment model (Figure 3.1). Hoxby and Avery (2012) raised awareness that college-prepared low-income students were left behind and channeled into community college.

These studies add to the research base by informing linkages in the attainment mode. The NBER studies were careful to address the political contexts of their research; an issue often left out when new methods are introduced in higher education journals. This body of work confirms the need to consider policy contexts and logical linkages between policies and outcomes, our paramount concern across the editions of *Public Policy and Higher Education*. Graduate students and professors in this field must pay attention to contexts and linkages when they design studies and interpret results, lest their work lapses into the wasteland of ideological construction of the regressive social policy, the fate of too much education research during the neoliberal turn in higher education public finance policies.

Consistent with the many policy reports on the issues we examine, we use trend analyses, research review, and interpretations to inform readers. This approach does not substantially advance the methodological approach used by government planners. There is a difference, however. We critically examine assumptions made in the policy rationales instead of accumulating data to support an argument. Unlike the many studies that compile statistics to advocate a policy remedy, we critically analyzed policy arguments. We were careful to discuss how research informs policy judgments about linkages rather than advancing ideas without careful thought. We also address an underlying policy problem. Seife (2010) used the term "proofiness" to describe the use of faulty statistics to promote a new government agenda. This term aptly applies to the plethora of subtly crafted USED reports that essentially destroyed the progressive trajectory in American education as part of the neoliberal agenda. Studies developed by the Advisory Committee of Student Financial Assistance (i.e., Becker, 2004; Fitzgerald, 2004; Heller, 2004) exposed the statistical errors in the USED reports. However, given the period's politics—the lingering constraints of neoliberal haziness of neoliberalism—the Committee did not address the problem created by using the STEM access agenda to obfuscate the growing problem of unmet student financial need, the issue causing increased economic stratification in higher education access.

Complexities of Measuring the Impact of Promises, Guarantees, and Encouragement

Fortunately, many states and some cities now use encouragement programs and guarantees of student aid—as "Promise" programs—to urge students to prepare for and enroll in college. Research on Indiana's Twenty-first Century Scholars program considered local, state, and federal agencies' roles in encouraging underrepresented enrollment (e.g., St. John et al., 2011). Recent Tennessee studies of their program also illustrate the potential for bringing state-level studies into the national and international discourses on higher education policy. We briefly discuss these programs before discussing logical models for assessing their impact.

As engaged scholars, we value the efficacy of these programs but caution readers about assuming causality from research on these programs. Motivated students are more likely to choose to engage in these programs and take advantage of support services. Because of these characteristics, they are more likely to enroll than their otherwise average peers.

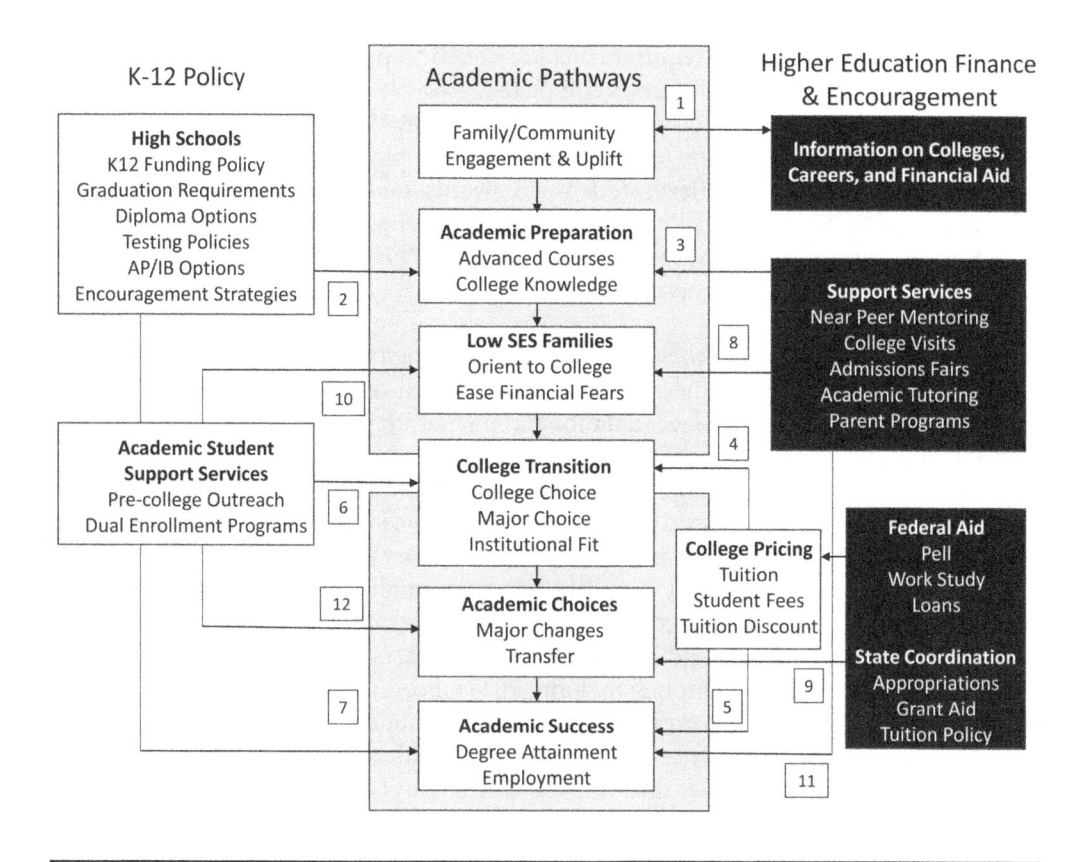

Figure 3.2 Academic Pathways and Theory of Change

In addition to money, and they may or may not receive more funding without engaging in the program, it is logically problematic to make causal claims about the monetary impact of these programs or to compare across studies. After presenting the logic for the pathways model, we discuss the early Indiana studies, recent Tennessee studies (e.g., Carruthers and Fox, 2016), and a few other noteworthy contributions. While we caution readers and researchers about making causal assumptions, the social value of these comprehensive programs exceeds the typically modest increments of funding they would receive without engaging in the promise programs.

The Pathways Model

Policy research on education attainment from K-12 and higher education increasingly uses student longitudinal databases to examine a single policy or program influencing high school graduation, college enrollment, or persistence. Since academic policies, support, and higher education influence these outcomes, we carefully review these studies in combination, comparing results and building a complete understanding of the impact of public policy and developments. The pathways to college model (Figure 3.2) focuses on these linkages:

- Guarantees of student aid to support the costs of attending encourage student preparation, enrollment, and college completion.

- High school graduation requirements are linked to preparation in high school, as measured by high school courses completed.
- Postsecondary encouragement programs that provide mentoring and other services influence preparation, especially courses completed.
- The cost of attending college, student aid awards, and other income sources (e.g., work and family support) link to college choice and persistence.
- Encouragement programs can improve the odds of high school completion, college transition, and college graduation.

Engaged Scholarship on Encouragement Program

The logic of the pathways framework was formed based on analyses using individual-student record data and state-level data for three separate programs—Indiana Twenty-First Century Scholars, Gates Millennial Scholars, and Washington State achievers—programs that delivered financially for students (St. John et al., 2011). Student engagement varies by the students, so collecting data on the use of services helps explain the impact (Fisher, 2013). Yet, services are not uniform across encouragement and promise programs; services and monetary support vary substantially from program to program and from site to site within programs. Encouragement programs that provide support without promises of financial aid have higher success rates in states that meet financial needs with student grants (Dalton & St. John, 2017). Programs that promise, guarantee, and provide aid remove the economic barriers but do not equalize prior inequalities in preparation and make up for systemic inequalities considered in program designs.

Two research-based examples illustrate the role of aim coupled with encouragement. The Tennessee Promise program provides coaching and last-dollar grants to all students, reducing reliance on loans. Carruthers and Fox (2016) examined the impact of the promise program on college enrollment, finding that program participated increased the likelihood of graduating high school and enrolling directly in college. They also modestly decreased chances of enrollment in four-year colleges. Unlike Tennessee, the Indiana studies found enrollment by low-income students increased in private colleges that collaborated with the Scholars program. A follow-up study in Tennessee found a 24-percentage point higher likelihood of receiving an associate degree, an insignificant effect on completing a four-year degree, and a negligible impact on earnings (Carruthers et al., 2023). Student record data collected by institutions, states, and national organizations has become increasingly important data sources for policy studies. Some statistical problems associated with sampling and response rates, always issues with longitudinal surveys, are eliminated because student records include information on the universe of enrolled students. Following students from K-12 to colleges, as in Tennessee, it is possible to provide comprehensive analyses of high school preparation and college.

Caution About Causal Assumptions in Program Advocacy

There are serious complicating factors in making judgments about promises, encouragement, and free college programs for two-year programs. Specifically, these programs include a promise of money, but students generally receive a similar award to what they would receive if they had not participated. The advantage comes through participation in counseling, college visits, and other services—students who do make the promise or make the pledge and take the same steps. The impact of these programs accrues from students' choices to participate and engage in support services, and it is exceedingly difficult to measure the impact of services (St. John et al., 2011). Despite research limitations, combining support services with financial aid adds to the impact of education programs and support services.

Local programs also have measurable effects on enrollment. Daun-Barnett's (2023) study of Buffalo adds substantially to understanding the process of reaching informed judgment based on data analyses. He finds that the improvement in preparation and access to postsecondary education among in Buffalo public school students was related to outreach services provided. As state-of-the-art research on programs, Daun-Barnett found a positive statistical association between the provision of support to complete the FAFSA in local schools with an increase in financial aid applications and the accuracy of those submissions. Perhaps more important, he found that authentic collaboration between the university and district partnerships was possible with sustained effort, continual communication, and a willingness to adapt to the local context.

Logical Model of College Finance

Since student aid is integral to the financing of public and private colleges. The cost of attending (tuition and hoisting cost) comprised most of the students' costs used to calculate financial needs. State and local funding, tuition, and endowments are the primary revenue sources for education expenditures. Our analyses of trends are based on a research-based model of college finance (St. John, 1991, 1994; St. John & Asker, 2003). Our logical model for funding college and universities, including community colleges, is as follows:

- *Cost of Attendance (COA)*. Tuition charges, room and board, books, and fees, set for each college as part of the Federal financial aid application and processing.
- *Education Expenditures*. Combines instruction (mostly faculty salaries and benefits), administrative, and library expenditures, along with an appropriate portion of facilities operating costs (shares also charged to revenue producing research and service).
- *Tuition and fees*. Student charges for the portion of educational costs (or education and related expenditures) paid for by students. Most public colleges also receive state subsidies for educational cost. Some private colleges use endowment and gift revenue to pay educational costs.
- *Room & Board*. Treated as an auxiliary cost by colleges in their budgeting, student charges cover these costs. These are auxiliary services that are supported by direct fees to students. State subsidies typically do not pay for dormitories.
- *Student Funding for Public Colleges*. Historically set at the average education cost per student in states with no tuition, now it is a shared cost with students through tuition charges.
- *Federal Need-Based Grants*. For undergraduates, most aid is provided by Pell grants.[2]
- *State Need-Based Grants*. Supported by federal partnership,[3] in theory at least, states can coordinate grant awards in changes to tuition charges, a process requiring cooperation in public and private colleges.
- *Merit (and other Non-Need Grants)*. Merit-based and other non-need grant programs are provided by states (considers below), foundations and other sources.

Historically, public and private colleges in some states constrained tuition but charged for room & board. Before 1980, most public and private colleges constrained their education and related expenditures and tuition charges; spending and tuition increased at about the inflation rate (St. John & Asker, 2023). After 1980, education and associated expenditures increased faster than inflation as colleges increased tuition and invested more in programs to attract students who could pay higher prices. The students' share of education costs also rose in the 1980s due in part to increasing costs of administrators and other educational expenses (Hansen & Guidugli, 1990; St. John, 1991), a pattern continuing in the following decades.

Except for the role of state funding, the trend analyses for public and private colleges use the same logical model. Both fund education expenditures from tuition, state subsidies (only at a few private colleges), and endowments (mostly at private colleges). Our analyses focus on state subsidies for public colleges, however, because state funding plays a key role in determining tuition charges. Pell grants are portable in the sense that students take their awards to colleges. The COA in higher, on average, at private colleges because of their reliance on tuition. However, public four-year colleges have "privatized" in recent decades as students' share of education costs increased.

Testing Beliefs with Research Evidence

If the history of policy research teaches us anything, it is that statistical models capture only a portion of the factors affecting student learning and educational attainment. State data systems do not include students' cultures, family histories, ambitions, motivations, and other factors influencing student choices. Cohort surveys capture some additional information but do not include older students when these data are used to examine traditional-age students transitions from high school to college. One-third of undergraduates are over 24 years of age (Hanson, 2024), which means that not all students continue without breaks for work, family, or other life issues. State and federal data collection typically captures all students, including adults, who return to college. Trend analyses for the percent of students enrolled by race and graduation rates by race include students of all ages, providing information representing actual outcomes for all students. Including adults in analyses of enrollment and attainment provides more realistic information on actual enrollment patterns than analyses using longitudinal surveys.

Techniques for analyzing students' behaviors leading to education attainment with state data have evolved over decades. Including selection variables is a poor substitute for sound reasoning and only modestly advances understanding of the complexity of the transition from high school to college. Racism, sexism, classism, and other biases screen students into and out of educational systems. Overcoming bias is a process of increasing opportunity. Government and foundation programs address specific social issues, and funding for students and institutions can be used to overcome barriers. Still, moving individuals, communities, states, and nations toward higher educational attainment and economic productivity is beyond the scope of academic and social policy.

REFRAMING ASSUMPTIONS ABOUT COLLEGE PREPARATION, ACCESS, AND COMPLETION

Habermas's (1979, 1984, 1985) theory of communicative action and his work on moral reasoning and public policy (1990, 1991) provide four lenses for framing linkages between policy and research practice (St. John, 2009a, 2009b, 2013): Instrumental, open strategic, closed strategic, and communicative. These four ways of framing provide ways to think about the links between political ideologies and policy studies. First, to make this link visible, we briefly return to topics in the two sections above. We restate our intention to encourage readers to reframe their understanding of the linkages between ideologies and research on preparation, access, and college success.

Framing Processes

Instrumental Ideology, Policy, and Research

Historically, empire-building from the ancient Greeks and Mongols to the early twentieth-century European colonialism treated people and emerging nations instrumentally. Monarchists frequently use authority instrumentally, expecting people to respond to rules externally imposed.

An intent of liberal education as it secularized and expanded after WWII was to provide students with skills to learn, think, and create. On the other hand, some factory-like schools in the early twentieth century treated students instrumentally (Rousmaniere, 1996). The school tracking schemes of the early twenty-first century used testing to sort children into career paths, an instrumental action when it did not involve consultation with parents. In contrast, the policy aims of equalizing opportunity for access, choice, and persistence in higher education during the mid-twentieth century emphasized freedom to choose based on academic ability rather than families' ability to pay, the antithesis of equity. The movement of education beliefs and values in education policy during the late twentieth century was away from instrumentalism. Even neoliberal school choice policies value family and student choice.

The MAGA movement to ban books treats schools and students instrumentally, based on extreme ideology, returning schools to the theocratic image of the early American Period. (see Florida case). The anti-woke movement claims that DEI is indoctrination, but the underlying theory of openness and democratic institutions of the literature on the exclusion lists defines the oversimplistic rationale. The re-emergence of dictatorial, monarch-like leaders in Western democracies raises fears of returning to authoritarianism (e.g., Applebaum, 2020).

Reagan's Department of Education treated researchers instrumentally in his second term, using political vetting to impose conclusions on researchers (St. John, 2013), as illustrated in this chapter's discussion of research on the race access gap that opened in the early 1980s. This approach to government control of education policy ran counter to social research traditions in the 1960s and 1970s, making it easier to conceptualize strategies aligned with the new conservative intellectuals who began the extreme critiques of socialism (Habermas, 1991).

Open-Strategic Ideology, Policy, and Research

Forged in debates among colonial Americans after the Revolution, the US Constitution exemplifies open-strategic action as an ideal. "A republic, if you can keep it," was Ben Franklin's response to the deliberations leading to the Constitutional Convention (Freedman, 2022). The response illustrates historical awareness; imagining, and especially maintaining, open processes for crafting a nation's strategies were rarities internationally at the time. Open exchange is not synonymous with democracy, but to some extent, the functioning of democratic institutions relies on the exchange of information and ideas between opposing positions. The social and economic theories of uplift of the 1960s emphasized research informing policy decisions about education development in a social democratic tradition.

The contested ideologies in academic discourse used research but mostly held to the principles of openness about education information (Chapter 2). NCES continued to develop statistics widely used in educational and social research, a practice that weathered the neoliberal turn in policy and manipulation of researchers through political vetting in the 1980s. The statistics remain trustworthy and open to diverse analytic frameworks. Data that can be used for analyses that use different points of view remain intact, as we illustrate in the following chapters. Openness of discourse has long been an academic ideal in education and policy research.

Closed-Strategic Ideologies, Policy, and Research

Problems quickly emerge when politics slip into autocratic logic; the idea that ends justify means has a long legacy, predating the idealistic social research of the 1960s. The academic debate between structural views of authority and social democratic frames of governance took a political turn in the middle nineteenth century when communist ideals became a manifesto for political action and revolution (e.g., Engles & Marx, 1848 [2002]). The US and Western democracies took an oppositional position against the spread of communism after WWII as Harvard political scientists took an overly anti-communist stance (e.g., Rostow, 1960). The ideological debates were overwhelmed by economic theories of globalization by the end of the Cold War (e.g., Dicken, 1998).

The "Global Consensus" promoted by international lending agencies (i.e., Gore, 2000) aligned international education policy with economic globalization (Henry et al., 2001). The emphasis on curriculum and testing in K-12 was global; however, Western Europe did not fall as perversely into the high tuition and loan strategy for higher education development as did the US and Latin America (Meyer et al., 2013). The debates about public funding of students and institutions versus the market approach should have informed openly examined evidence about policy options. However, federally constructed policy studies in the US fell into a closed-minded ideological trap.

Advocacy research plays an essential role in policy development. Still, we believe researchers should openly consider evidence even when conclusions recommend policies rather than crafting arguments intended to shape policy rather than inform policy choices. Although not our intent, we've both been in policy roles that slipped over the line into crafting rationales for reform. This book aims to inform open discourse instead of promoting any single viewpoint, a flaw of too many policy studies.

Communicative Ideology, Policy, and Research

Communicative analysis involves examining the foundational arguments of different points of view on morally problematic policy issues and encouraging discourse on what new moral standards, policies, and practices might enable resolution (Habermas, 1990, 1991; St. John, 2013). While we both aspire to this standard and realize it is needed now, especially in higher education policy research, it is exceedingly tricky to actualize; it depends on the exchange and discussion of ideas and evidence. Researchers can craft reports, articles, and books that provide information informing critical discourse.

However, concluding by advocating strategy is strategic compared to focusing on informing choices as the intent of communicative practices. The act of open exchange about evidence and morally problematic issues is the essence of communicative actions when viewed within this frame (Habermas, 1990).

Encouraging Open Exchanges About Troubling, Problematic Issues
In the earlier editions of *Public Policy and Higher Education,* we developed cases of distinctive models of strategic policy adaptations in states. The following chapters provide analyses of national trends and state cases illustrating that the policy contexts in US higher education are sometimes different than in 2010, the last data point in the previously examined trends. During the 2010s, states evolved new strategies as the federal government's policy frameworks remained relatively static. The policy contexts, state strategies, and educational outcomes have changed, so it is time to take a fresh look at adaptive policy change in states—some based on ideological beliefs, others as thoughtful changes when inequalities emerge. The trends in policy implementation and educational outcomes provide evidence that can inform reframing.

The time lags in data collection limit the time horizons for assessing the impact of ESSA flexibility and free tuition on student outcomes. The analyses of national trends and state cases illustrate new patterns of change after 2017 when ESSA went into effect; it was also the time that some of the ripple effects of Obama's support for Promise programs in states were taking hold in some states. States' responses to flexibility in federal policy were varied and influenced by ideologies that dominated legislatures and state houses. The national studies and state cases allow readers to set aside ideological beliefs to consider the likely effects of differential and nuanced changes in educational policies linked to access, retention, and economic success after college. Trend analyses do not rise to the level of well-designed evaluation studies, but the comparative insights gained from reviewing the evidence can inform such studies.

Questions

1. How does the history of education policy differences between states in the North and South before the Civil War inform your understanding of policy divisions in the MAGA-DEI debates?
2. What tactics can help us raise diverse points of view when the discussion of issues crosses the line into advocacy without consideration of evidence?
3. How can research best be crafted and used to inform discussion of moral dilemmas in educational policy and practice in this divisive MAGA-DEI period?
4. How do you distinguish between your *beliefs* about education policy—personal positions on issues that align with political ideologies—and *assumptions* about the possible effects of policy changes that can reexamined using statistical and other research evidence?
5. How can groups with different ideological beliefs about education policy create a safe discursive space for discussing critical issues in educational public policy?

NOTES

1. St. John and Noell examined national longitudinal studies to examine the impact of variations for preparation (i.e., comparison by high school tracks), aspirations, and student aid on access. The student aid decline was the best explanation for the enrollment gap that opened in the early 1980s. This paper reported for studies developed for the Pelavin and Kane report (1988) that essentially argued that ninth grade Algebra explained the gap.
2. There were multiple federal programs in the 1970s, including ED generally available program (e.g., SEOG,) along with specially directed programs in Social Security Administration, Health, Agriculture, and other agencies.
3. The federal government partnership with state, created in 1972, share a portion of state grants. The federal government pays a small share in most states.

REFERENCES

Advisory Committee on Student Financial Assistance. (2002). *Empty Promises: The Myth of College Access in America*.
Altschuler, G. C., & Blumin, S. M. (2009). *A new Deal for veterans*. Oxford University Press.
Applebaum, A. (2020). *The twilight of democracy: The seductive lure of authoritarianism*. Doubleday.
Bailey, M. J., & Cooper, B. S. (2009). The introduction of religious charter schools: A cultural movement in the private school sector. *Journal of Research on Christian Education*, 18(3), 272–289.
Balderston, F. E. (1974). Cost analysis in higher education. *California Management Review*, 17(1), 93–107.
Becker, W. E. (2004). Omitted variables and sample selection in studies of college-going decisions. In E. P. St. John (Ed.), *Public policy and college access: Investigating the federal and state roles in equalizing postsecondary opportunity* (Vol. 19, pp. 65–86). AMS Press, Inc.
Berkner, L., & Chavez, L. (1997). *Access to postsecondary education for the 1992 high school graduates*. In (pp. xii, 102). Washington, DC: U.S. Department of Education.
Bettinger, E. (2004). How financial aid affects persistence. *NBER Working Paper Series* (10242), 44. Retrieved November 30, 2010, from http://www.nber.org/papers/w10242
Bettinger, E., & Long, B. T. (2009). Addressing the needs of under-prepared students in higher education: Does college remediation work? *Journal of Human Resources*, 44, 736–771.
Bloom, A. (1987). *The closing of the American mind*. Simon & Schuster.
Carnegie Commission on Higher Education (1973). *Priorities for action: Final report*. McGraw-Hill.
Carruthers, C. K., & Fox, W. F. (2016). Aid for all: College coaching, financial aid, and post-secondary persistence in Tennessee. *Economics of Education Review*, 51(2), 97–112.
Carruthers, C. K., Fox, W. F., & Jepsen, C. (2023). What Knox achieved: Estimated effects of tuition-free community college on attainment and earnings. *Journal of Human Resources*. https://doi.org/10.3368/jhr.1220-11359R2
Chen, W., St. John, E. P., Hannon, C., & Li, X. (2018). *Actionable research for education equity and social justice: Higher education reform in China and beyond*. Routledge.
Cohen, D. (2001). *The war come home: Disabled veterans in Britain and Germany, 1914-1939*. University of California Press.
Cohen, R. (1993). *When the old left was young: Student radicals and America's first mass student movement, 1929-1941*. Oxford University Press.
Cornwell, C., & Mustard, D. B. (2004). Georgia's HOPE scholarship and minority and low-income students: Program effects and proposed reforms. In D. Heller & P. Marin (Eds.), *State merit scholarship programs and racial inequality*. The Civil Rights Project.
Cumming, T., Miller, M. D., & Leshchinskava, I. (2023). DEI institutionalization: Measuring diversity, equity, and inclusion in postsecondary education. *Change: The Magazine of Higher Learning*, 55(1), 31–38.
Dalton, R., & St. John, E. P. (2017). *College for every student: An educator's guide for building college and career skills*. Routledge.
Daun-Barnett, N. (2023). Say yes to education—Buffalo: A human capabilities approach to college access and local economic development. *Education Science*, 15(3), 472.
DesJardins, S. (1999). Simulating the enrollment effects of changes in the tuition reciprocity agreement between Minnesota and Wisconsin. *Research in Higher Education*, 40(6), 705–716.
Dicken, P. (1998). *Global shift: Transforming the world economy*. Paul Chapman Publishing, Ltd.
Dresch, S. P. (1975). A critique of planning models for postsecondary education: Current feasibility, potential relevance, and a prospectus for future research. *Journal of Higher Education*, 46(4), 246–286.
Drury, S. B. (1997). *Leo Strauss and the American right*. St. Martin's Press.
Dynarski, S. M. (2000). Hope for whom? Financial aid for the middle class and its impact on college attendance. *National Tax Journal*, 53(3), 629–661.

Dynarski, S. M. (2002). *The Consequences of Merit Aid*. National Bureau of Economic Research (9400).
Ellis, G. E. (1888). *The Puritan age and rule in the colony of the Massachusetts Bay, 1629-1685*. Houghton, Mifflin and Company.
Engles, F., & Marx, K. (1848 [2002]). *The communist manifesto*. Penguin Books.
Finn, C. E. (1978). *Scholars, dollars, and bureaucrats: Federal policy toward higher education*.
Finn, C. E. (1990). The biggest reform of all. *Phi Delta Kappan, 71*(8), 584–592.
Fisher, A. S. (2013). *When did public become the new private? Grappling with access to postsecondary education for low income students*. Ann Arbor, MI: University of Michigan.
Fitzgerald, B. F. (2004). Federal financial aid and college access. In E. P. St. John (Ed.), *Public policy and college access: Investigating the federal and state roles in equalizing postsecondary opportunity* (Vol. 19, pp. 1–28). AMS Press, Inc.
Fogel, R. W. (2000). *The fourth great awakening and the future of egalitarianism*. University of Chicago Press.
Freedman, E. M. (2022). *A republic, if you can keep it*. https://scholarlycommons.law.hofstra.edu/lectures_other/8/
Gerstle, G. (2022). *The rise and fall of the neoliberal order: America and the world in the free market era*. Oxford University Press.
Gladieux, L. E., & Wolanin, T. (1976). *Congress and the colleges: The national politics of higher education*. Lexington Books.
Gore, A. (2000). The rise and fall of the Washington consensus as paradigm for the developing countries. *World Development, 28*(5), 789–803.
Greene, J. P., Peterson, P. E., & Du, J. (1998). School choice in Milwaukee: A randomized experiment. In P. E. Peterson, & B. Hassel (Eds.), *Learning from school choice* (pp. 335–356). The Brookings Institution.
Habermas, J. (1979). *Communication and the evolution of society*. Beacon Press.
Habermas, J. (1984). *The theory of communicative action*. Polity Press.
Habermas, J. (1985). *Reason and the rationalization of society. Theory of communicative action* (Vol. 1). Beacon Press.
Habermas, J. (1990). *Moral consciousness and communicative action*. MIT Press.
Habermas, J. (1991). *The new conservatism: Cultural criticism and the historians' debate*. MIT Press.
Hansen, W. L., & Guidugli, T. F. (1990). Comparing salary and employment gains for higher education administrators and faculty members. *Journal of Higher Education, 61*(2), 142–159.
Hanson, M. (2024). *College Enrollment & Student Demographic Statistics*. EducationData.org. Retrieved March 15 from https://educationdata.org/college-enrollment-statistics
Heller, D. (2004). NCES research on college participation: A critical analysis. In E. P. St. John (Ed.), *Public policy and college access: Investigating the federal and state roles in equalizing postsecondary opportunity* (Vol. 19, pp. 29–64). AMS Press, Inc.
Henry, M., Lingard, B., Rizvi, F., & Taylor, S. (2001). *The OECD, globalization and education policy*. Pergamon Press.
Hossler, D., & Gallagher, K. S. (1987). Studying student college choice: A three-phase model and the implications for policymakers. *College and University, 62*(3), 207–221.
Hoxby, C., & Avery, C. (2012). The missing" one-offs": The hidden supply of high-achieving, low income students. *NBER Working Paper Series* (18586). Retrieved March 15, from
Jackson, G. A. (1978). Financial aid and student enrollment. *Journal of Higher Education, 49*(6), 548–574.
Jackson, G. A., & Weathersby, G. B. (1975). Individual demand for higher education: A review and analysis of recent empirical studies. *Journal of Higher Education, 46*(6), 302–327.
King, J. E. (1999a). *Financing a college education: How it works, how it is changing*. O. Press.
King, J. E. (1999b). *Money matters: The impact of race/ethnicity and gender and how students pay for college*.
Lindblom, C. E. (1959). The science of "muddling through". *Public Administration Review, 19*(2), 79–88.
Lindblom, C. E. (1979). Still muddling, not yet through. *Public Administration Review, 39*(6), 517–526.
Ma, J., & Pender, M. (2023). *Trends in College Pricing: 2023* (Trends in Higher Education Series, Issue, Issue. https://research.collegeboard.org/trends/college-pricing
Maclear, J. F. (1959). "The True American Union" of church and state: The reconstruction of the theocratic tradition. *Church History, 28*(1), 41–62.
Manski, C. F., & Wise, D. A. (1983). *College choice in America*. Harvard University Press.
McPherson, M. (1978). The demand for higher education. In D. W. Breneman & C. E. Finn (Eds.), *Public policy and private higher education*. The Brookings Institution.
McPherson, M. S., & Schapiro, M. O. (1999). *The student aid game: Meeting need and rewarding talent in American higher education*. Princeton University Press. http://www.loc.gov/catdir/toc/ecip0617/2006024115.html
Meyer, H. D., St. John, E. P., Chankseliani, M., & Uribe, L. (2013). *Fairness in access to higher education in a global perspective: Reconciling excellence, efficiency, and justice*. Sense Publications.
Morgan, I. (2019). Make America Great Again: Ronald Reagan and Donald Trump. In M. Oliva, & M. Shanahan (Eds.), *The Trump Presidency: From campaign trail to world stage* (pp. 59–82). Palgrave Macmillan.

National Commission on the Financing of Postsecondary Education (NCFPE). (1973). *Financing postsecondary education in the United States*.

Newman, F. (1971). *Report on higher education*.

Nussbaum, M. C. (2008). *Liberty of conscience: In defense of America's tradition of religious equality*. Basic Books.

Ortega, N. (2021). *An examination of the relationship between the developing Hispanic-Serving Institution (Title V) Program and six-year completion rates for Latino students at public four-year Hispanic-serving institutions (HSIs) in the United States*. Ann Arbor, MI: University of Michigan.

Pelavin, S. H., & Kane, M. (1988). *Minority participation in higher education*. U.S. Department of Education.

Pelavin, S. H., & Kane, M. B. (1990). *Changing the odds: Factors increasing access to college*. New York: College Board

Philpott, C. (2023, December 14). After mass shooting, Harward Center host gun violence prevention teach-inT. *The Bates College Student*. https://thebatesstudent.com/category/news/lewiston-mass-shooting/

Picazo, J. (2023). Tuition-free access expanding across California community college campuses. Ed Source. Retrieved March 15 from https://edsource.org/2023/tuition-free-access-expanding-across-california-community-college-campuses/699832

Platt, R. E., Chesnut, S. R., McGee, M., & Song, X. (2017). Changing names, merging colleges: Investigating the history of higher education adaptation. *American Educational History Journal*, 44(1/2), 49–67.

Powell, A. G., Farrar, E., & Cohen, D. K. (1985). *The shopping mall high school: Winners and losers in the educational marketplace*. Houghton Mifflin.

Radner, R., & Miller, L. S. (1970). Demand and supply in US higher education: A progress report. *American Economic Review*, 60(2), 326–334.

Rostow, W. W. (1960). *The stages of economic growth: An non-communist manifesto*. Cambridge University Press.

Rousmaniere, K. (1996). Teachers' work and the social relations of school space in early-twentieth-century North American urban schools. *Historical Studies in Education/Revue d'histoire de l'éducation*, 8(1), 42–64.

Santiago, D. A., Calderón, G. E., & Taylor, M. (2016). *From capacity to success: HSIs, Title V, and Latino students*.

Schultz, C. (1968). *The Politics of Public Spending*.

Seife, C. (2010). *Proofiness: The dark arts of mathematical deception*. Viking Press.

Smith, A. A. (2023). *Cal State leaders look to reduce tension, hate incidents on campus*. Retrieved March 15 from https://edsource.org/2023/cal-state-leaders-look-to-reduce-tension-hate-incidents-on-campus/700352

Soler, E. (2020). Founded by abolitionists, funded by slavery: Past and present manifestations of bates College's founding paradox. *Honors Thesis*, 321. https://scarab.bates.edu/honorstheses/321

St. John, E. P. (1990a). Price response in enrollment decisions: An analysis of the high school and beyond sophomore cohort. *Review of Higher Education*, 31(2), 161–176.

St. John, E. P. (1990b). Price response in persistence decisions: An analysis of the high school and beyond senior cohort. *Review of Higher Education*, 31(4), 387–403.

St. John, E. P. (1991). A framework for reexamining state resource management strategies in higher education. *The Journal of Higher Education*, 31(4), 387–403.

St. John, E. P. (1993). Untangling the web: Using price response measures in enrollment projections. *Journal of Higher Education*, 64(6), 676–695.

St. John, E. P. (1994). *Prices, productivity and investment: Assessing financial strategies in higher education* (ASHE/ERIC Higher Education Report, Issue.

St. John, E. P. (1999). Evaluating state grant programs: A case study of Washington's grant program. *Research in Higher Education*, 40(2), 149–170.

St. John, E. P. (2006). *Education and the public interest: School reform, public finance, and access to higher education*. Springer.

St. John, E. P. (2009a). *Action, reflection and social justice: Integrating moral reasoning into professional development*. Hampton Press.

St. John, E. P. (2009b). *College organization and professional development: Integrating moral reasoning and reflective practice*. Routledge.

St. John, E. P. (2013). Tools of state, using research to inform policy decisions in higher education. *International and Multidisciplinary Journal of Social Sciences*, 2(2), 118–144. https://doi.org/doi:10.4471/rimcis.2013.17

St. John, E. P., & Asker, E. H. (2003). *Refinancing the college dream: Access, equal opportunity, and justice for taxpayers*. Johns Hopkins University Press.

St. John, E. P., Gross, J. P. K., Musoba, G. D., & Chung, A. S. (2006). Postsecondary encouragement and academic success: Degree attainment by Indiana's twenty-first century scholars. In *Public policy and educational opportunity: School reforms, postsecondary encouragement, and state policies on postsecondary education*. AMS Press.

St. John, E. P., Hu, S., & Fisher, A. S. (2011). *Breaking through the access barrier: Academic capital formation informing policy in higher education*. Routledge.

St. John, E. P., Musoba, G. D., Simmons, A. B., Chung, C.-G., & Peng, C.-Y. J. (2004). Meeting the access challenge: Indiana's twenty first century scholars program. *Research in Higher Education, 45*(8), 829–871.

St. John, E. P., Chung, C. G., Musoba, G. D., Simmons, A. D., Wooden, O. S., & Mendez, J. (2004). *Expanding college access: The impact of state finance strategies*. Indianapolis: Lumina Foundation for Education.

St. John, E. P., & Noell, J. (1989). The impact of financial aid on access: An analysis of progress with special consideration of minority access. *Research in Higher Education, 30*(6), 563–582.

St. John, E. P., & Parsons, M. D. (2004). *Public funding of higher education: Changing contexts and new rationales*. Johns Hopkins University Press.

St. John, E. P., Simmons, A., Hoezee, L. D., Wooden, O., & Musoba, G. D. (2002). *Trends in higher education finance in Indiana compared to peer states and the U.S.: A changing context, critical issues, and strategic goals* (Policy Research Report, Issue.

St. John, E. P., & Starkey, J. B. (1995). An alternative to net price: Assessing the influence of prices and subsidies on within-year persistence. *Journal of Higher Education, 66*(2), 156–186.

Thurgood, L., Walter, E., Carter, G., Henn, S., Huang, G., Nooter, D., Smith, W., Cash, R. W., & Salvucci, S. (2003). *NCES Handbook of Survey Methods: Technical Report*.

Toutkoushian, R., Hossler, D., DesJardins, S., McCall, B. P., & Canche, M. G. (2015). The effect of participating in Indiana's twenty-first century scholars on college enrollments. *Review of Higher Education, 39*(1), 59–95.

Trammell, M. L. (1995). Estimating the enrollment effects of a mid-year surcharge. In E. P. St. John (Ed.), *Rethinking tuition and student aid strategies* (Vol. 89). Jossey-Bass.

Weathersby, G. B., & Balderston, F. E. (1972). PPBS in higher education planning and management: Part i, an overview. *Higher Education, 1*, 191–206.

Weathersby, G. B., Jacobs, F., Jackson, G. A., St. John, E. P., & Tyler, T. (1977). The development of institutions of higher education: Theory and assessment of four possible areas of federal intervention. In M. Guttentage (Ed.), *The evaluation studies review annual* (Vol. 2, pp. 488–546). Sage.

Whitehead, A. L., & Perry, S. L. (2020). *Taking America back for God: Christian nationalism in the United States*. Oxford University Press.

Wildavsky, A. (1979). *Speaking truth to power: The art and craft of policy analysis*. Little, Brown, and Company.

Zook, G. F. (1947). The president's commission on higher education. *Bulletin of American Association of University Professors (1915-1955), 33*(1), 10–28.

4

REFRAMING PREPARATION

From Pathways to STEM Pipeline and Economic Stratification

One of the signature policy priorities during much of the neoliberal period has been to increase state-level high-school graduation requirements in the core academic subjects of Math, Science, English Language Arts, Social Studies, and Foreign Languages (Allensworth et al., 2009; Daun-Barnett & St. John, 2012; Lee et al., 1997)—what we have described as the core of the STEM agenda (Daun-Barnett & St. John, 2012). While these state policies address the full array of core academic subjects, much of the emphasis has been on math and science and preparing for STEM disciplines in college. Today, states have shifted from a single minimum standard for all high-school graduates to multiple pathways that align with both college and career. The Education Commission of the States (2023) reported that 21 states now allow multiple pathways to high-school completion. The federal government eased restrictions constraining standard graduation during the Obama administration. A shift toward multiple pathways in policy is underway across the states but with more math courses required than in the 1970s. High-school graduation rates have risen consistently for the past 15 years or more, and the racial and ethnic gaps have narrowed to a difference comparable to the 1970s.

Postsecondary education should prepare students for careers in technical employment, academic fields, and professions that rely on advanced math and science. With the prospective revitalization of American industry—the expansion of good jobs for the working class—it is time to reemphasize technical education as an option in the college choice process, abandoning the money-maximizing goal of college choice theory, at least for enough time to read this chapter and to ponder its implications for people who are thinking about, working in, or reflecting on the constrained educational choices now evident. For almost four decades of neoliberal education policy, moving technical education into the new 4-year college model with community colleges as cooling out schools with some hope of transfer, the student choice paradigm subjugated to the STEM doctrine. The policy trajectory requires a fundamental rethinking of the links between high schools and preparation for financial wellbeing.

We use the concept of preparation for financial wellbeing—women and men having education sufficient for meaningful work to support their families—as an essential human capability requiring community support in contemporary society. Martha Nussbaum (1999) argued that education to a level sufficient for women to support their families is a capability standard globally, an opportunity denied in some theocracies. More recently, she developed a theory of human capabilities addressing financial, educational, and environmental issues facing people across nations (Nussbaum, 2011). Extending the capabilities framework to contemporary challenges facing education policy, we recognize that a capabilities standard for K-12 education should, at a minimum, be "localized preparation for college and work opportunities," a standard that requires "supplemental support for engaged learning, social services, and networking: (St. John, 2023, p. 89).

Reconstruction of arguments for preparing all students for STEM professions is long overdue. This chapter takes a first step; it starts with a historical view of preparation for financial wellbeing, turns to arguments for neoliberal reforms informed by a plethora of troubling federal reports, examines changes in policies and outcomes during the neoliberal turn and post-neoliberal period, and concludes by reconsidering preparation for financial wellbeing. We are encouraged by the shifts we see in high-school graduation requirements away from the strict college-for-all standard and toward a more balanced preference for multiple pathways, but more work is yet to be done.

COLLEGE AND CAREER PREPARATION

Since World War II (WWII), economists and employers have used education as a screening device for selection into well-paying jobs in the labor market. High-school diplomas were the screening device for most jobs during the Cold War, increasing economic incentives for students to complete high school (Taubman & Wales, 1974). When analyzing the decision to attend college, economists argued that forgone earnings were a "cost" that individuals weighed along with the "psychic" benefits of college (Becker, 1964). In the second edition of *Human Capital Theory*, Gary S. Becker (1975) expanded the theory to consider the costs of loans.

In contrast to loans, as a mechanism that delayed paying for the direct cost of attending college, need-based grants reduced the direct cost to students and did not require delayed payment. Like the GI Bill in the 1940s, new federal grants emerged through federal need-based grant programs in 1958 and 1964, but economists did not alter or challenge Becker's theory. Instead, economists and education finance experts extended the logic, starting with the National Commission on the Financing of Postsecondary Education (NCFPE) (1973). Enrollment management—marketing to students and reducing costs to attract more students who could pay tuition—had become core to academic business (Hossler, 1984; McPherson, 1978). The college finance game emerged, but students' choices were limited to community colleges and public technical colleges if they sought a quick transition into the workforce. Spiraling prices and strategic use of campus-funded grants not only raised revenue but also added to the inequalities in college access (Hossler, 2004; McPherson & Schapiro, 2006). Campuses employed tuition discounting practices designed to attract wealthier students who had access to better high schools and a stronger academic curriculum, and they shifted away from providing more need-based aid to those most in need of financial support—effectively leaving that responsibility to the state and federal governments. The racial and socioeconomic gaps grew as tuition rates rose and discounting favored wealthier students and families.

By the early 1980s, the STEM paradigm had emerged, pushing the idea of technical education out of the picture. The earlier editions of *Public Policy and Higher Education* focused on "college preparation," a notion consistent with the STEM transition that was underway. We were critical of the misuse of research in advocacy for the new standards. Still, we did not adequately consider the implications of the shift in the screening function of high schools and the aspirations of African Americans to break through barriers. These issues emerged in this edition when we used a historical frame. Education as preparation for meaningful work—education minimally sufficient to support a family—provides a socially just lens for considering evolving educational standards. In early America, literacy became part of the standard first, then high-school graduation during the Cold War. The three high-school tracks—honors/advanced, general, and vocational/technical—of the comprehensive high school provided some degree of choice, but many students had few choices regarding their high-school curriculum. The combination of racial segregation and tracking undermined equity in opportunity, especially for racially minoritized students. Assuming the best intentions of the STEM movement, consistent with the emergence of the neoliberal establishment, the movement sought to uplift racially minoritized students. Before considering how rising college net costs imposed new barriers for minorities, a topic in Chapters 5 and 6, the chapter reconsiders the shifting role high schools and postsecondary institutions play in preparing students for meaningful work that can support families.

In the early 1980s, the liberal education establishment of the Cold War that valued education for social uplift had been transformed into a neoliberal establishment promoting STEM education emphasizing 4-year degrees for all. Since the transition in core values was so rapid, restarting by looking back at how we got here makes sense. We use the idea of education for economic wellbeing, a human capability for all women and men, as the basis for reexamining our history (Table 4.1).

The legislative and judicial history in K-20 education (Chapter 2) and shifts in ideologies shaping public investment in schools, colleges, and low-income students (Chapter 3) inform this periodization of preparation. These periods also correspond with the shifting economic value of education in work opportunities as reflected by changes in attainment. Less than 2% of adults had graduated college in 1870, and 20% were literate. Reading, writing, and basic math—the education educational aims of common schools after 1870—were far from universal (Mintz, 2009). By 1870, all states had mandatory schools, and the federal government started collecting data on the K-12 education system. At the time, a small portion of the population graduated high school. We review how high schools developed in the early American period (before 1870), the development of competing collegiate systems and preparation pathways (1870–1945) before delving into the massification of education (1945–1980), and what happened in the 1980s as neoliberalism emerged, leading to contemporary chaos.

Origins and Legacies of Curriculum Reform Traditions

Despite the development of K-8 schools as "common" and accessible in most places, high schools per se were not widely available in the late nineteenth century (Peterson, 1985). Many teachers were young women, often with less than high-school themselves. Public-funded high schools expanded nationally from 1910 to 1940 (Goldin & Katz, 1998). In 1899, John Dewey addressed the challenge of creating a unified K-16 education system, illustrating the problem was far more complex than simply aligning the high-school

Table 4.1 College Preparation and Financial Wellbeing Across Historical Periods: Technical/Vocation, General Diploma, and Advanced Prep for Science and Engineering

Specializations/ Periods	Technical/ Vocational	General Education (Financial Wellbeing)	College Pathways
Early America (1776–1870)	From apprentice programs (formal and informal) to high-school programs	Some education (literacy) needed for good jobs and citizenship	Prep schools and universities provided opportunities for some aspirants
Public Systems (1870–1940)	High schools develop technical preparation; college teacher education for technical fields	Regional differences: more high schools in the North and urban areas, fewer in the South; race tracking	University leaders argue for raising standards, especially for liberal education and technical fields
Cold War (1945–1980)	Industrial, book-keeping, secretarial, arts, and technical support services	Mass high schools, graduation became screening devices for service & business	Clashes between technical prep and liberal arts in high schools and colleges
Neoliberal (1980–2015)	Shift to advanced math and sciences courses for all squeezed-out technical and arts	The college prep required; graduation rates drop after implementation; math education improves	College degrees became a screening mechanism, fewer industrial jobs, and the rise of high-tech
Post-Neoliberal (2015–present)	Renewed interest in career and technical education in high schools and community colleges	States modify graduation requirements and improve graduation rates	STEM continues; some STEM grads leave related jobs; conflicting social values

curriculum with college admissions standards (Orrill, 2001). He first articulated the different origins and subsequent trajectories of elementary and college education. Then, he demonstrated the complexity and variety of institutional structures that grew—including grammar schools, academies, high schools, technical/vocational schools, and normal schools—making the call for a unified educational standard elusive. Throughout the twentieth century, advocates of college preparation for all sought to increase the alignment of these two systems with marginal success. We reconsider the development of preparatory pathways in relation to evolving periods of federal impact on higher education.

Early America: Faith Traditions and Curriculum Diversity

The Colonial classrooms were centered on faith and led mainly by preachers (Meriwether, 1907). The early New England prep schools aligned with this tradition (Wheeler, 2019). Faith remained part of the Protestant "common school" until the federal courts constrained the practice, a gradual change litigated by states protecting their rights to maintain faith-based instruction. Unlike the common high schools, Catholic schools included science in the core curriculum much earlier than Protestant schools and universities. Influenced by Cardinal John H. Newman's ideas (1852), Catholics did not see as many contradictions between science and theology. This history is incredibly enlightening, given contemporary litigation over abortion and other ideas linked to the Christian view of science. The conflict between Protestant values in public schools and Catholic education persisted for another century.

As the schools evolved in the US, Catholic children interested in vocational fields were encouraged to attend public high schools. This history and the values-oriented culture of Catholic communities passed across generations in Catholic families probably explain why they performed better in statistical comparisons a century later (Bryk et al., 1995). Researchers did not consider the history of values education, which has intertwined with math and science for more than a century in Catholic high schools, or Christian advocacy for separate schools. Protestant Evangelists comprise 25% of the population, and Catholics are 21% (Pew Research Center, 2024): their influence is evident on Supreme Court appointments and policy on school vouchers.

The secularization of public schools was slow and had an extended legal history. In 1971, the Supreme Court's decision on *Lemon v. Kurtzman* established the three-part "Lemon Test" as the standard for public spending on education. This standard constrained public funding for schooling with (1) a secular purpose, (2) that would have a secular effect on learning, and (3) that would not entangle the government and religion (Pew Foundation, 2009). Under this standard, ESEA Title I could legally support supplemental math and reading education in religious schools if there were no religious artifacts in classrooms providing the instruction. This standard is now at risk and will undoubtedly be tested (Halper, 2024). For example, Louisiana recently required all classrooms to display the Ten Commandments.

The historical polarization between Catholics and Protestants influenced the history of high-school curricula—especially the now historic role of the courts in constraining religion in public schools—has many ironies and creates lingering challenges facing education and public discourse about schools. The contemporary Supreme Court has six conservative Catholic judges, making an extremist majority that is forcing educational policymakers to rethink the alignment of faith and education. In this century, the Christian education movement has absorbed advocacy for Catholic schools that can benefit from a new generation of public policy funding families choosing religious education for their children.

Christians, alienated by federal enforcement of desegregation and the Lemon standard, moved children into Christian schools or homeschooling for their children. By 2000, several states funded homeschooling, an option often used by Christian families; it was also a force for change in public education (Hill, 2000). As charters developed, religious schools found ways into funding schemes. The *Carson v Makin* (2022) Supreme Court decision created a legal pathway for states to provide scholarships for religious school students. The regressive decision is eerily reminiscent of the Supreme Court's decision on *Plessy*, which moved back to a segregated society in the late nineteenth century. In the early twenty-first century, the *Carson v. Makin* decision moves back to faith-based school choice, the pattern before the development of public schools after 1970. The Court now seems to value older, socially regressive legal constructs that can reshape education for decades.

Competing Systems: Vocational Curriculum in High Schools as They Developed
The Land Grant Act created the technical university that competed with and eventually transformed older, faith-centric colleges. The older colleges were not responsive to

industrialization and westward expansion of mining and agrarian society, especially evident in Northern and Western states. The planned Land Grant universities focused on technology for agricultural mechanization, extraction of mineral resources, and urban industrialization. Integrating new technologies into agriculture moved the masses from farms to the early industries decades after the promise of gold in the West. Land Grant colleges not only brought sciences, statistical methods of experimental analysis, and technology into higher education before the older colleges but also fostered vocational curricula in high schools. In the late nineteenth century, agricultural experimentation stations, a national set of enterprises operated by universities, expanded agricultural education into high schools (Moore, 1988).

Industrialization also brought new content to high schools. Europe, especially England, led the world in industrialization, including education reforms to support the emerging working class. Industrial education arose in the US and Europe during the late nineteenth and early twentieth century, with many advances intertwined through collaboration between US and European institutions (Fox & Guagnini, 1993). The American apprentice system also migrated into formal education (Douglas, 1968). The development of agricultural high schools sometimes included home economics education, creating high schools, career, and college opportunities for young women (Liddell, 1978). Educational development spawned by industrialization also expanded options for women. Secretarial and bookkeeping education, for example, created new pathways for women (Russon, 1983).

Education Expansion During the Cold War

In 1950, 30% of the college-age population enrolled, and only 3% of adults were illiterate. Both the general and vocational curricula were secular rather than faith-based early in the Cold War, before the *National Defense Education Act* (NDEA) *of 1958* passed. The NDEA provided funding for math innovations in K-12 schools and student aid for college students. The competing general high-school curriculum advanced as college prep options developed in many public high schools. Vocational education also expanded, but the dual pathways were used to channel whites and minorities into separate tracks in many cities (Oakes, 1985).

The debates about vocational versus general high school education emerged around the turn of the twentieth century (Grubb & Lazerson, 2005). As schools developed, channeling Blacks in vocational education was less threatening to whites, especially in the South. Options other than vocational ones were often more constrained for Black children. In addition to college prep and vocational education, graduates from the general track could go directly to work or attend community colleges and other programs that did not have rigorous admissions requirements. Still, as the multiple pathways developed, African Americans too often were channeled out of college preparatory options. Creating fair opportunities for Blacks became a foundation of neoliberal support of the STEM agenda (Oakes et al., 2006).

After years of decline in vocational high schools and pathways options in comprehensive high schools, career and technical education is gaining attention. Given recent developments in higher education finance and college going (discussed below), it seems time to rethink the STEM and CTE strategies. We compare the economic contexts of education and employment in the US and the European Union to reconstruct an understanding of preparation for career pathways (Chapter 6).

Neoliberal Turn: Nationalizing Education Standards
(and Increased Reliance on Loans)

A Nation At Risk (ANAR) (National Commission on Excellence in Education, 1983) was a conservative move away from progressive educational access and innovation (Ravitch, 2010). At the time of the report, the US still led the world in college access internationally and was deeply engaged in making up for the early history of unequal education. ANAR argued for shifting federal programs from equalizing opportunity for underrepresented groups to supporting all students, spreading constrained funds to more students, and deemphasizing supplemental instruction for students in families with less cross-generation educational attainment. As ANAR entered the policy discourse, a new, more equitable pattern was evident but was not firmly established. The pattern of incremental progress was at risk.

The national high-school graduation rate in 1969–1970, more than a decade before ANAR was published, was 78.7%, but it had incrementally dropped to 71.8% in 1979–1980 (National Center for Education Statistics, 2009). Had the study group that created ANAR focused on graduation rates as the problem, they might have advocated for different priorities. Raising requirements without recognizing the substantial financial investment required to provide the upgrade was irresponsible and inconsistent with the historical federal role in education. Expanding the college preparatory curriculum had been embraced by states mainly as a revenue-neutral or cost-cutting education reform strategy, which had likely undermined the effort. New personnel required to reform schools so they could provide advanced math and science for all was not possible without investing in supplemental math and reading.

Perhaps an extensive community-based strategy would have provided a support mechanism to assist students and parents through the transition from high school to college, coupling higher standards with engaging methods. ANAR did not mention expanding federal investment to improve math and science education in schools serving low-income communities. When states adopted the standards, they did not increase their investment commensurate with the increased cost. From 1965 through 1983, the federal government provided funding for improvement in educational opportunities, mainly through Title I. Following ANAR, Title I funds supported schoolwide reforms. Whole-class instruction methods, like the research-based *Success For All* (Slavin et al., 1990), were prioritized over the support of high-need students through ESEA Title I. *Success For All* schools used cooperative learning as the classroom instruction method instead of using professional reading and math teachers to accelerate learning for students challenged by the curriculum. High-achieving students—those quicker to understand lessons—instructed students who were slower to grasp the core concepts in required advanced math courses.

Cooperative learning may have been an appropriate instructional strategy, but schoolwide market schemes promoted by Title I were not effective, especially in urban schools (Gill et al., 2002). After decades of federally sponsored urban innovations through market schemes and Title I, high schools often had to double up by placing underprepared students in two math courses, reducing their opportunities to take courses aligned with career interests (St. John & Girmay, 2019). The combination of K-8 and high-school reforms did not work out as intended. Social and educational support for low-income high-school students was absent as schools and communities struggled to attain the new standards. Recent history suggests that social support partially compensates for the loss of education programs supporting equal opportunity (Chapter 5).

Despite federal studies utilizing "proofy" tactics and amassing data to support the transition, much of the academic research advocating new standards raised critical issues that must be addressed to improve schools. Oakes et al. (2006), for example, documented the inequities inherent in the tracking of students within high schools, especially after school desegregation, because students' experiences across those tracks and schools varied.

While a 9–14 integrated system does not provide an explicit remedy for this systemic bias, it does include language about multiple "pathways" through high school and college. In one sense, the language of pathways potentially transforms the meaning of tracks; however, the possibility of de facto tracking remains. For example, Anthony Carnevale (2007) noted the tracking problem in high schools when he argued that higher standards expanded opportunity: "The path of least resistance for reform is the current trajectory from high school up the education pipeline toward postsecondary education" (p. 21). The rise of dual college credit for advanced high-school courses improved the odds of access for some, but some courses did not meet the standard of prepared students for rigorous STEM programs at many universities (Field, 2021). Having credit for a college course does not mean that the course completed in high school will ensure preparation for the more advanced college courses that require and build on content knowledge. Thus, dual credit programs provide college credits and encourage college enrollment after high school, but they sometimes fall short of their intent, particularly if students and parents expect to reduce the cost of their education by lowering the number of credits they need while enrolled in college.

Another critique of the old system focused on the excessive testing within the K-12 accountability system, especially for high-school seniors. Kirst (2000), Kirst and Usdan (2003), and Kirst and Venezia (2004) argued that misalignment has resulted in a complicated array of tests, each serving a different purpose, with the result being an increased emphasis on preparation for end-of-course exams, mandatory exit exams, college admissions tests, and college level placement tests. This line of critique, based on Stanford's Bridge project, argued for a tighter alignment of the graduation requirements for high school with admissions standards for 4-year colleges, a topic examined in multiple states (Kirst & Venezia, 2004). The coalition supporting the 9–14 system emphasized high school and college alignment within a framework that included both K-12 *and* postsecondary education accountability.

US Department of Education's Argument for Higher Math Standards

After 1980, a period not considered in ANAR, a college enrollment gap opened for African Americans compared to whites. K-12 policies implemented in the late 1970s and early 1980s were not a possible cause, at least according to all analyses of policies and corresponding outcomes. ANAR did not consider the impact of cuts for the K-12 program—a rapidly developing problem—as a possible explanation for the decline in high-school graduation rates evident at the time. Instead, they invented a way to reduce the severity for middle-income families; ANAR claimed that K-12 was declining, putting the nation "at risk," and the report blamed K-12 schools.

Cuts to K-12 programs after implementing the *Education Consolidation and Improvement Act* were a plausible cause of the short-term decline. Still, ANAR or the USDE did not consider the mounting funding problems. Between 1980 and 1990, "Adjusted for inflation, funding for the office of elementary and secondary education decreased by

15 percent, and spending on programs in the office of postsecondary education declined by 24 percent" (Pitsch, 1991). Cutting taxes and funding for education and social programs was a priority in too many states and at the federal level. K-12 is labor intensive, so before the expansion of computer-aided instruction—a process that was often more, not less expensive—it was impossible to reduce funding without reducing teacher-student time for some students. It proved easy to cut specialized teachers as the feds moved to school-wide remedies. Higher education funding cuts reduced students' ability to pay for college, harming college access and persistence. Yet, contractors working for the US Department of Education (USDE) could not consider these issues if they wanted to keep their funding.

In the 1980s, the USDE used contractors to build this flawed argument that differences in middle school math explained the opening of the gap. There were well-established reasons to promote middle-school Algebra, but state policies on math requirements had not changed during the 1978–1983 period when the Black-White college enrollment gap opened. Without restoring federal grants for low-income students, providing improved math instruction had limited hope of improving enrollment in 4-year colleges.

Strategically crafted statistical reports were used in advocacy for raising standards, aligning K-12 and higher education, and marketizing through debt, the strategies that had low or reduced cost for the federal government. Indeed, many groups rationalize the new education agenda (e.g., the Commission on the Skills of the American Workforce, 2007, discussed above). These reports were also referenced extensively in policy advocacy reports. For example, writers in *Minding the Gap* (Hoffman et al., 2007) referenced these reports to build the case for more rigorous high-school courses. Many states adopted a minimum math requirement of Algebra I for high-school graduation. The final report of the Commission on the Future of Higher Education (U.S. Department of Education (2006), known as the Spellings Commission, referenced no fewer than ten statistical reports issued by the USDE.

Pathway Options in the 2020s

An espoused intent in policy advocacy for the STEM agenda that reconfigured high-school preparation was to prepare students for elite STEM professions that would lead the international labor market through design and engineering; participation in the twenty-first-century knowledge economy required an American workforce with science and math that could dominate "creative work" in research, development, design, marketing, and supply chain management, was an explicit aim of advocates of the STEM agenda (Commission on the Skills of the American Workforce, 2007). The strength of this economic rationale for pushing preparation and college for all has weakened, at least temporarily. The decades of encouragement for more students to prepare for and enroll in college have had an apparent impact on enrollment rates, which increased considerably after 1980. But the links between college degrees and employment after college weakened in the 2000s, partly due to an anemic labor market after the recession (Atherwood & Sparks, 2019). The current period of low unemployment is a further case for rethinking pathways through education systems to meaningful work.

Seizing on the flexibility in Obama's ESSA, many states created multiple pathways as they adapted math requirements and testing for accountability. The easing of federal regulatory standards opened avenues for adding diverse emphases in local schools while continuing the national agenda promoting educational improvement started by *A Nation at Risk*.

CHANGE IN POLICY AND GRADUATION RATES ACROSS PERIODS

The changes in educational outcomes following the standards movement are now a part of the historical record. We summarize findings from the earlier Public Policy and Higher Education editions to document policy changes and outcomes during the neoliberal transition. More recently, states have been coping with the educational consequences of neoliberalism in an uncertain period, which we describe as a post-neoliberal transition.

Adapting the STEM Agenda

The restrictions on math requirements did not ease during the Obama years, but states made adaptive changes that improved high-school graduation. The following analyses of policies and outcomes provide a substantial update. The trends in requirements from 2000 to 2020 (Table 4.2) are as follows.

- All 50 states continued to meet national math standards.
- The number of states requiring three or more math courses for graduation increased from 21 in 2000 to 42 in 2020.
- The number of states requiring at least Algebra I increased from 12 to 28.
- One fewer state had an honors diploma option in 2010 than in 2000.
- Local control of curriculum changed modestly during the two decades but was 5 in 2000 and 2010.
- The number of states requiring exit examinations for graduation peaked but was still higher in 2020 than in 2010.
- The percentage of high schools offering AP courses increased to 83% in 2020 from 58% in 2010, indicating college-level courses were more available.

Table 4.2 State Policy Indicators for Selected Years, 2000–2020

Policy-Related Variables	2000	2005	2010	2015	2020
State established content standards in math	50	50	50	50	50
Requires 3 or more math courses for graduation	21	28	31	43	42
Requires 1 or 2 math courses for graduation	24	17	13	3	3
Requires at least Algebra I or above	12	22	26	26	28
High-school curriculum is locally controlled	5	5	6	4	5
Offers an honors diploma	19	22	14	23	18
State offers multiple pathways to HS completion	–	–	–	–	21
Exam required for high-school diploma	14	19	28	24	17*
Percentage of schools participating in AP[§]	58%	62%	67%	81%	83%
Number of SAT Test-takers (1,000's)	1,414	1,575	1,547	1,637	2,198
Ninth grade cohort size (millions)	3.79	3.96	4.01	4.02	4.01
Outcomes of interest					
SAT verbal mean∞	505	508	500	495	528
SAT math mean∞	514	520	515	511	523
SAT combined∞	1019	1028	1015	1006	1051
Graduation rate[1]	71.7	74.7	79	84	87

* Based upon numbers reported by the Education Commission of the States. FairTest reports only nine states but counts those that suspended the test until 2024.

§ Reflects the median percentage of schools offering AP courses.

∞ These numbers reflect the national figures reported by Educational Testing Service.

1 Source is the National Center for Educational Statistics, Digest of Education Statistics, Table 219.46.

- SAT scores improved but changes in the test after 2017 discount the meaning of the change (see quote below).
- The percentage of students graduating from high school increased substantially, from 72% to 87%, a noteworthy change discussed further below and examined in the state cases.

High-school graduation rates for each race/ethnic group improved after 2000 for Hispanics (Figure 4.1). From 2005 to 2015, the gap for Blacks and other groups narrowed as well, a period that overlaps with the Obama administration. A closer look at how the USDE's regulations changed might reveal reasons for the rapid gains in minority student completion of high school:

- Through regulatory change, the Obama Administration eased accountability requirements and encouraged state experiments, reducing the gap in the early 2000s.
- After 2017 and the implementation of Obama's *Every Student Succeeds Act of 2015*, a sustained period of narrow gaps in opportunity to graduate ensued.

SAT scores did not increase, possibly an artifact of states' easing requirements for exit exams. With less stress on preparation for exams, students seem not to have been as well prepared for the combined SAT scores for math, reading, and writing: "The average score for the Class of 2015 was 1490 out of a maximum 2400 … down 7 points from the previous class's mark and was the lowest composite score of the past decade" (Anderson, 2017). The SAT exam changed after 2017, returning to the 1600 point scale, so it is impossible to track changes in scores after that.

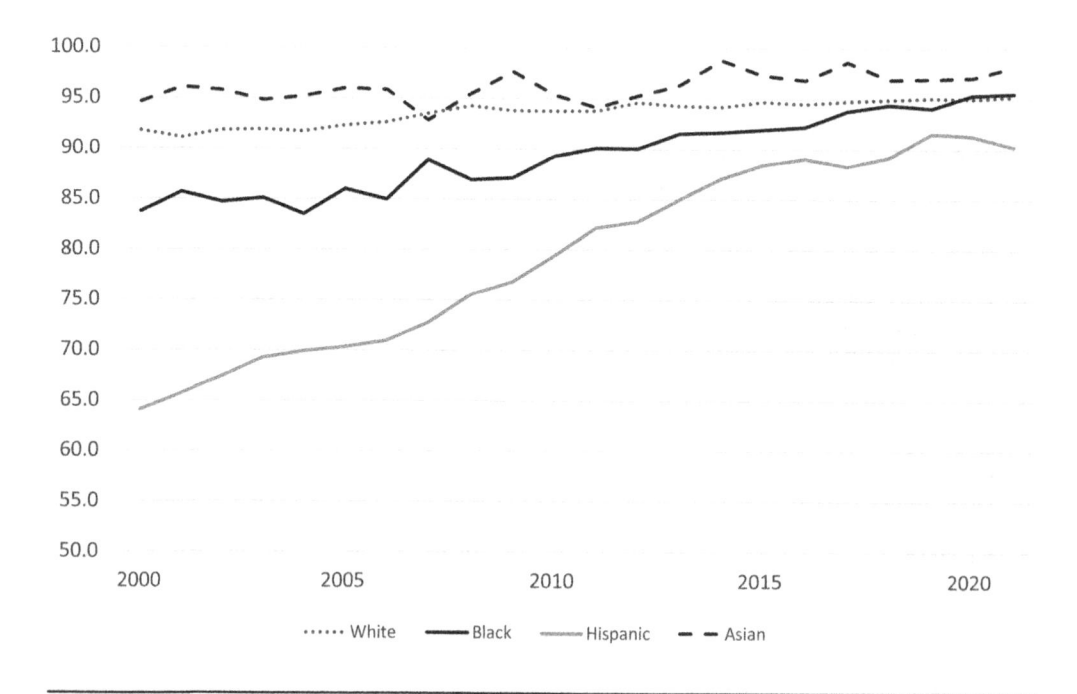

Figure 4.1 U.S. Public High School Graduation Rates for 9th Grade Cohorts by Race/Ethnicity

Source: NCES (2022) Digest of Education Statistics, Table 218.65. High-school completion rate of 18- to 24-year-olds not enrolled in high school (status completion rate), by sex and race/ethnicity: 1972 through 2021.

The ACT scores declined more substantially: "The class of 2023 had the worst ACT performance in more than three decades, according to newly released data from the nonprofit that administers the college admissions test" (Goldstein, 2023). The drop was, in part, an artifact of some states requiring all students to take the ACT as the state test. For example, average ACT scores in Michigan plummeted after the test was required (St. John & Girmay, 2019). Also, many colleges ceased using these tests for admissions. Thus, after 2015, college entrance exams were no longer useful measures of the impact of educational reforms.

The gains in graduation rates and completion of advanced math and science courses are evidence of actualizing the aims of ANAR, although increased state flexibility meant differential pathways and requirements were being used. The decline in scores and admissions tests runs counter to the STEM theory of change pushed by the ED. Still, the employability of graduates would be the crucial social and economic outcome of these agendas.

Comparing the Neoliberal Transition and the Post-Neoliberal Period

The contrast between the two periods raises questions about the sequence of policy arguments, policy changes, and educational outcomes. States responded rapidly to the STEM agenda and the threat of losing federal funds. The big stick approach—the severe financial consequences of not complying—explains the rapid change. Also, as some rational readers of the statistical reports projected, graduate rates declined, and math scores rose. The advocacy for higher standards by national associations simply was not based on the data. Instead, it was rationale building using "proofy" statistics and ideology, unfounded beliefs driven by the financial aims of state and corporate leaders seeking a "better prepared" workforce at low cost. In contrast, these agitating voices eased during the post-neoliberal adaptation period in states.

Preparation for Financial Wellbeing

With the gains in college-prepared high-school graduates during the past two decades—students completing more advanced science and math courses than graduates in the 1970s—we should increase college enrollment rates, a reality that did not materialize (Chapter 5). It is time to rethink the assumptions: the gains in preparation can be a positive development because this outcome links to preparation. The claim to rationalize the STEM agenda—that raising requirements would increase enrollment—became false because loans became the primary means of marketization.

Nonetheless, the gains in preparation merit consideration as a social good independent of the STEM claims. Adapting STEM requirements in math and science to meet the learning needs of career-oriented students seems a fruitful adaptation of educational social policy. Divorcing the two policy aims—improving high schools and college access—allows us to reframe preparation. To encourage readers to think creatively about preparation, this section:

1. Reexamines reasons for improving high schools, now and in the future.
2. Discuss alternatives pathways after high school that receive inadequate attention in the media and policy discourses.
3. Review the preparation debate from the perspective of African American education scholars.

RECONSTRUCTED REASONING ABOUT COLLEGE PREPARATION

Improvement in mathematical reasoning at all levels of education is no doubt crucial to public understanding of the impact of tuition, loans, and grants on avenues for and barriers to college and career preparation. Today, we are more likely to recognize the significance of college cost as a barrier to postsecondary participation, mainly because enrollments are declining overall as the labor market strengthens, costs continue to rise during a troubling inflationary period post-pandemic, and Americans are increasingly questioning the value of higher education, particularly those without a degree and those who identify politically on the conservative right (Kelderman, 2023).

Integrating Math into Career Preparation and Civics Education

After several studies of US vocational education and advocacy of integrating advanced content into career technical education (Hoachlander et al., 1992), Gary Hoachlander (1997) examined approaches to math education globally. Next, he refined his focus on integrated approaches in US vocational education (Hoachlander, 1999). Gradually, states and schools adopted the integrated approach, a topic of growing international interest (Çevik & Bakioglu, 2022). In addition to influencing the reform of vocational education in states, Hoachlander's integrated approach has gained attention internationally, including in Nordic nations with more advanced CTE education (Muhrman, 2022).

If vocational education regains public and government support in the US, it is reasonable to consider integrated instruction in math and other subjects, including science, English, and civics. A better-educated public requires corporate executives, government policymakers, educational leaders, and citizens not to be fooled by proofiness—using statistics to make false claims in research for government agencies (Seife, 2010). Captivated by simple, low-cost solutions to inequality in college access, education researchers and policymakers have advocated for moving Algebra I to eighth grade. Informed thinking about the meaning of numbers within their social and policy contexts could have paved the way to a better-reasoned path. Integrating sound mathematical reasoning about policy mechanisms into education and policy is part of reclaiming and maintaining democratic approaches in preparation for college and careers, including policy studies.

Adding Financial Wellbeing to College and Career Preparation

The labor market has changed education as a public good (what people think about the value of college and work), altering life possibilities. Many graduates delayed buying homes, getting married, and having children. Purchasing a new car had to be weighed against the monthly cost of repaying college debt. Growing student debt is the consequence. The Biden administration proposed two significant policies to address college affordability. The first, often debated strategy was the student loan forgiveness program. The Education Department began the program's rollout, but the Supreme Court ruled that the Biden administration did not have the authority to forgive that debt without more explicit permission from Congress. The Biden administration did successfully forgive more than $132 billion in student loans through regulatory mechanisms, including waiving loan eligibility requirements briefly for the Public Service Loan Forgiveness (PSLF) program and forgiving debt for students who attended now-defunct for-profit colleges (Rubin & Ettenheim, 2023). After extended political maneuvering, on February 21, 2024, President Biden forgave $1.2 billion for 153,000 borrowers: "The borrowers receiving relief are the first to benefit from a SAVE plan policy that provides debt forgiveness to borrowers who have been in repayment after as little as ten years and took out $12,000 or less in student loans" (The White House, 2024, p. 1).

Narrowing the purpose of high schools to STEM-prep, accompanied by trade agreements exporting working-class jobs, radically changed college and career pathways. To be clear, the evidence from historical and trend analyses suggests that moderation by states, reducing the extremism of aligned standards and tests, and easing methods of teaching advanced math narrowed the gap in high-school graduation for Blacks compared to whites. The narrative of the neo-liberal STEM movement argued that requiring more math was narrowing the college enrollment gap and overlooked the high-school completion gap. Given the rationalizing that fueled these reforms, the narrowed gap in high-school graduation rates is a considerable gain for the public good. This conclusion briefly considers how these trends confirm long-standing arguments by African American scholars before discussing how they inform strategies for improving preparation for college and careers.

The purpose of high school and college during the Early American Period is a fact that should not be overlooked when states make education reforms. In this conflicted period, knowledge of math, as the capacity to question false claims, is necessary for democratic citizenship. The fact that proofy statistics, creating myths rather than empirical facts, was utilized to guide policy for the STEM agenda illustrates that even the best educated were susceptible to false notions based on beliefs. This is the most salient reason for improving math education. Indeed, some argue informed democratic citizens should be an aim of education at all levels.

Pathways for High-School Graduates and Dropouts That Should Not Be Overlooked
The military actively recruited high-school graduates throughout this period, 1980–2024, offering pathways to careers and college without reliance on student debt. These options proved attractive to many Latinx immigrants, especially if they were not in a "DREAM" state offering them in-state tuition (Martinez & Huerta, 2020; McGlynn & Lavariega Monforti, 2010). As the middle east wars continued, many graduates faced choices between college with debt or going to war to gain delayed financial access through GI benefits (Kleykamp, 2006; McGlynn & Lavariega Monforti, 2010).

For too many high-school dropouts and graduates, prison became an unfortunate alternative pathway, in addition to college and war (Han, 2018). This was especially troubling because of the poor funding of many urban schools that withered in quality as they faced the challenge of providing advanced math and science to students who were not prepared to take these courses when they entered high school (Manheim & Nunnally, 2020; St. John & Girmay, 2019). Providing families with a safety net is crucial to uplifting education achievement in the highest poverty communities in both urban and rural areas.

The aim of improving financial wellbeing is more critical to children living in poverty. Reduction in poverty can improve education outcomes. According to the Census Bureau, "12.4% of Americans now live in poverty ... an increase from 7.4% in 2021. Child poverty also more than doubled last year to 12.4% from 5.2% the year before (U.S. Census Bureau, 2023)." The Census report went on to report: "This increase can be attributed to key changes in federal tax policy, including the expiration of temporary expansions to the Child Tax Credit (CTC) and the Earned Income Tax Credit (EITC) as well as the end of pandemic-era stimulus payments." These statistics and policy developments illustrate evidence that shows outcomes linked to policy. Improving the capacity of citizens to read and think about evidence is crucial to national wellbeing. These policy developments illustrate that the government knows how to lift students out of poverty but lacks the will.

Research on African American Uplift

When pondering these trends, readers should view the valuing of education with higher requirements from the viewpoint of African American scholars who've focused on these issues; we encourage the step below by reviewing key works by African American scholars too often set aside in the construction of the pipeline logic. We speculate about an alternative view based on extrapolation from the writings of senior African American scholars who supported strengthening academic preparation for Black youth. Still, they were concerned about the decline in grants as a cause of the growing disparity. Before examining the severity of stratification in college access in the next chapter, it is essential to reconsider the works of African American scholars who focused on preparation, social support, and reform in K-12 and higher education.

First, William T. Trent was a leader among a cadre of African American scholars who focused on academic preparation as a gateway to high-school completion and college preparation for fairness in college access. As he collaborated on the research team for the Gates Millennial Scholars Program, he argued for collecting and analyzing state and student data on high-school courses, including Advanced Placement, as a force for uplifting African American students into elite colleges (Trent, 2008; Trent et al., 2004). He examined success along the pathway for Scholars and a comparison group of students (students who met the academic qualifications but were not selected). His value set emphasized avenues for uplift and success over advocacy for GMS or any other intervention. He consistently testified on issues related to fairness in preparation for court cases on school desegregation. His work was within a long tradition of advocacy for rigorous academic support for African Americans' uplift.

Second, Walter Allen, a member of the GMS advisory team and Trent's long-time colleague, focused on social support for African Americans preparing for college (Allen, 1992; Allen et al., 2005). Allen pulled together a K-20 research team to build a cohesive, integrative argument about uplift, reconstructing education attainment theory (Allen et al., 1991). He also was a lead expert witness in college desegregation cases (Allen, 1994). Allen's research and arguments inform the development of leadership support in the GMS program (Wilds, 2004), the most extensive foundation grant program supporting undergraduate and graduate study for minorities.

Third, growing scholarship focuses on restoring the ethos of African American enthusiasm for education. The history of African American education in the South (Anderson, 1988) informed lines of inquiry that built an understanding of contemporary strategies for supporting African American students in the preparation process in schools and colleges. Venessa Siddle Walker (1996) studied the history of care of Black schools closed during segregation. She also collaborated on scholarship-informing strategies for integrating care into teacher education, public schools, and social programs (Walker &

Snarey, 2004). More recently, Leslie T. Fenwick (2022) traced the history of decline in Black schools, including the firing of well-educated and qualified teachers and leaders, as Black schools closed in the South.

These quantitative, qualitative, historical, and theory-informed studies inform outreach efforts and support programs in urban and rural schools, including GMS and high-school reforms funded by the Gates Foundation. These developments may explain the narrowing of the Black-White gap; progress empowered Black students' aspirations to complete more rigorous courses. Ignored by the neoliberal mainstream supporting the STEM agenda, these lines of inquiry illustrate that it is essential to reconsider these traditions, reconstruct theories and research methods, and improve strategies to recognize the challenges facing colleges seeking to enhance diversity, equity, and inclusion in K-20 education.

Reconstructing Theory and Practice

Based on reading and thinking seriously about the African American scholarship, we've speculated about reconstructing the logic used to view policy on preparation and access. The Algebra I conclusion reached by Pelavin and Kane used a deficit notion about Blacks—there had not been a decline in Black students completing Algebra, which would have been necessary for their reasoning for the opening of the enrollment gap to be true—but their advocacy for requiring the course may have had a positive impact of narrowing the gap. Informed imagination about the future, taking a step back to the past for a better view of the present may be necessary to see new possibilities for the future.

Interestingly, a study of career academies found positive, long-term income effects for low-income minority students from inner cities who attended these programs (Kemple, 2008), a forgotten part of the history of K-12 education as preparation. Learning to earn and develop skills was an important indicator of success historically. Access theory should begin with a reconstruction of preparation concepts, adding career preparation to the core notions and acceptable forms of practice. Biden's programs expand employment options, much as Franklin Roosevelt's programs created work opportunities and a safety net in the 1930s, before WWII. Career and technical education developed during the Cold War, the Golden Age of higher education, as did industrial jobs for an expanding working class. Biden's programs will not restore the working class, but they are a bold step in combination. In a sense, these actions should reconstruct concepts used in mainstream policy studies informing policy development. However, the struggle to overcome neoliberalism within the academic mainstream is not yet underway. For generations, rising Ph.D. students have learned research methods to confirm assumptions in the STEM agenda or reaffirm critical educational inequality theories.

The history of educational preparation for careers and colleges illuminates that the STEM doctrine was overly narrow and informed by flawed yet widely disseminated studies. The severe methodological errors opened the door for informed critique within the neoliberal education establishment (Advisory Committee on Student Financial Assistance, 2003) following analyses of the detrimental impact of funding cuts in federal grants (Advisory Committee on Student Financial Assistance, 2001a, 2001b). Understanding the centrality of student aid to access is only part of the challenge. Rather than narrowing down to a single pipeline, it is time to reconsider local pathways to financial wellbeing for families and communities. We encourage readers to engage with us in considering alternative ways of reframing preparation and access to fit the diverse education, social, cultural, and economic needs of current and prospective students.

> **Questions**
> 1. How did the tension between Egalitarianism and Evangelization, ideologies motivating creation of Early American schools and colleges, remanifest across the historical periods that followed?
> 2. How has competition between public and independent, private colleges and universities, been influenced by policy discourses on education development since the Civil War?
> 3. What role has and should research evidence pay in the development of education policy?
> 4. How did states adapt high-school requirements to create pathways while continuing to adhere to national standards?
> 5. What are the implications of recent changes diversifying high-school pathways for the college for all movement?

REFERENCES

Advisory Committee on Student Financial Assistance. (2001a). *Access Denied: Restoring the nation's commitment to equal educational opportunity.*

Advisory Committee on Student Financial Assistance. (2001b). *The impact of unmet need on low-income students.*

Advisory Committee on Student Financial Assistance. (2003). *Review of NCES research on financial aid and college participation and omitted variables and sample selection issues in the NCES research on financial aid and college participation.*

Allen, W. R. (1992). The color of success: African-American College student outcomes at predominantly white and historically black public colleges and universities. *Harvard Educational Review, 62*(1), 26–43.

Allen, W. R. (1994). The determinants of student choice and access in the Alabama state system of higher education. *Mimeo.*

Allen, W. R., Bonous-Hammarth, M., & Suh, S. A. (2005). Who goes to college? High school context, academic preparation, the college choice process, and college attendance. In E. P. St. John (Ed.), *Readings on equal education* (Vol. 20, pp. 71–113). AMS Press, Inc.

Allen, W. R., Epps, E. G., & Haniff, N. Z. (1991). *College in black and white: African American Students in predominantly White and historically Black public universities.* SUNY Press.

Allensworth, E., Nomi, T., Montgomery, N., & Lee, V. E. (2009). College preparatory curriculum for all: Academic consequences of requiring Algebra and English I for ninth graders in Chicago. *Educational Evaluation and Policy Analysis, 31*(4), 367–391. https://doi.org/10.3102/016237370934371

Anderson, J. D. (1988). *The education of Blacks in the South, 1860-1935.* University of North Carolina Press.

Anderson, N. (2017, September 3). SAT scores at lowest level in 10 years, fueling worries about high schools. *Washington Post.* https://www.washingtonpost.com/local/education/sat-scores-at-lowest-level-in-10-years-fueling-worries-about-high-schools/2015/09/02/6b73ec66-5190-11e5-9812-92d5948a40f8_story.html.

Atherwood, S., & Sparks, C. S. (2019). Early-career trajectories of young workers in the US in the context of the 2008–09 recession: The effect of labor market entry timing. *PLoS One, 14*(3), e0214234.

Becker, G. S. (1964). *Human capital: A theoretical and empirical analysis, with special reference to education* (Vol. 80). National Bureau of Economic Research.

Becker, G. S. (1975). *Human capital: A theoretical and empirical analysis, with special reference to education* (2nd ed., Vol. 80). National Bureau of Economic Research.

Bryk, A. S., Lee, V. E., & Holland, P. B. (1995). *Catholic schools and the common good.* Harvard University Press.

Carnevale, A. P. (2007). Confessions of an education fundamentalist: Why grade 12 is not the right end point for anyone. In N. Hoffman, J. Vargas, A. Venezia, & M. S. Miller (Eds.), *Minding the gap: Why integrating high school with college makes sense and how to do it*. Harvard University Press.

Carson v. Makin Supreme Court (2022), 596 U. S.

Çevik, M., & Bakioglu, B. (2022). The effect of STEM education integrated into teaching-learning approaches (SEITLA) on learning outcomes: A meta-analysis study. *International Journal of Progressive Education, 18*(2), 119–135.

Commission on the Skills of the American Workforce. (2007). *Tough choices or tough times: The report of the New Commission on the skills of the American workforce*.

Daun-Barnett, N., & St. John, E. P. (2012). Constrained curriculum in high schools: The changing math standards and student achievement, high school graduation and college continuation. *Education Policy Analysis Archives, 20*(5). http://epaa.asu.edu/ojs/article/view/907

Douglas, P. H. (1968). *American apprenticeship and industrial education*. Columbia University Press.

Education Commission of the States. (2023). *50 State comparison: High school graduation requirements*. Retrieved December 10 from https://www.ecs.org/50-state-comparison-high-school-graduation-requirements-2023/

Fenwick, L. (2022). *Jim Crow's pink slip: The untold story of black principal and teacher leadership*. Harvard Education Press.

Field, K. (2021). The rise of dual credit: More and more students take college classes while still in high school. That is boosting degree attainment but also raising doubts about rigor. *Education Next, 21*(1), 57–64.

Fox, R., & Guagnini, A. (1993). *Education, technology and industrial performance in Europe, 1850-193*. Cambridge University Press.

Gill, B. P., Timpane, P. M., Ross, K. E., & Brewer, D. J. (2002). *Rhetoric versus reality: What we know and what we need to know about vouchers and charter schools*.

Goldin, C., & Katz, L. F. (1998). *Human capital and social capital: The rise of secondary schooling in America, 1910 to 1940*. https://www.nber.org/papers/w6439

Goldstein, D. (2023, October 11). ACT reports record low scores as admissions landscape shifts. *The New York Times*. https://www.nytimes.com/2023/10/11/us/act-scores-college-admissions.html

Grubb, W. N., & Lazerson, M. (2005). Rally'round the workplace: Continuities and fallacies in career education. *Harvard Educational Review, 45*(4), 451–474.

Halper, J. (2024). When Life Takes Your Lemons: Resolving the Legislative Prayer Debate in School Board Settings in Light of Kennedy v. Bremerton School District. *Brooklyn Law Review, 89*(3), 933.

Han, J. (2018). Who goes to college, military, prison, or long-term unemployment? Racialized school-to-labor market transitions among American men. *Population Research and Policy Review, 37*(4), 615–640.

Hill, P. T. (2000). Home schooling and the future of public education. *Peabody Journal of Education, 75*(1/2), 20–31.

Hoachlander, G. (1997). Organizing mathematics around work. In L. Steen (Ed.), *Why numbers count: Quantitative literacy for tomorrow's America*. College Entrance Examination Board.

Hoachlander, G. (1999). *Integrating academic and vocational curriculum–Why is theory so hard to practice?* http://ncrve.berkeley.edu/CenterPoint/CP7/CP7.html

Hoachlander, G., Kaufman, P., Levesque, K., & Houser, J. (1992). *Vocational education in the United States: 1969–1990*. http://ncrve.berkeley.edu/CenterPoint/CP7/CP7.html

Hoffman, N., Vargas, J., Venezia, A., & Miller, M. S. (2007). *Minding the gap: Why integrating high school with college makes sense and how to do it*. Harvard University Press.

Hossler, D. (1984). *Enrollment management: An integrated approach*. College Entrance Examination Board.

Hossler, D. (2004). Refinancing public universities: Student enrollments, incentive-based budgeting, and incremental revenue. In E. P. St. John & M. D. Parsons (Eds.), *In public funding of higher education: Changing contexts and new rationales*. Johns Hopkins University Press.

Kelderman, E. (2023, September 5,). What the public really thinks about higher education. *The Chronicle of Higher Education*. https://www.chronicle.com/article/what-the-public-really-thinks-about-higher-education#:~:text=Nearly%2080%20percent%20of%20people,household%20income%20less%20than%20%2450%2C000.

Kemple, J. J. (2008). *Career academies: Long-term impacts on labor market outcomes, educational attainment, and transitions to adulthood*. https://eric.ed.gov/?id=ED631371

Kirst, M. (2000, Fall). The senior slump: Making the most of high school preparation. *National Crosstalk, 8*(4), 7.

Kirst, M., & Usdan, M. (2003). *Improving K-16 governance and student pathways*. National Governors Association.

Kirst, M., & Venezia, A. (2004). *From high school to college: Improving opportunities for success in postsecondary education* (1st ed.). Jossey-Bass. http://www.loc.gov/catdir/bios/wiley046/2003023724.html; http://www.loc.gov/catdir/description/wiley041/2003023724.html; http://www.loc.gov/catdir/toc/ecip0410/2003023724.html

Kleykamp, M. A. (2006). College, jobs, or the military? Enlistment during a time of war. *Social Science Quarterly, 87*(2), 272–290.

Lee, V. E., Croninger, R. G., & Smith, J. B. (1997). Course-taking, equity, and mathematics learning: Testing the constrained curriculum hypothesis in U.S. Secondary schools. *Educational Evaluation and Policy Analysis, 19*(2), 99–121.

Liddell, M. B. (1978). *Home economics: Past, present and future*. West Virginia University.

Manheim, F., & Nunnally, S. (2020). Black high schools of high quality prior to desegregation. *Journal of Negro History*

Martinez, E., Jr., & Huerta, A. H. (2020). Deferred enrollment: Chicano/Latino males, social mobility and military enlistment. *Education and Urban Society, 52*(1), 117–142.

McGlynn, A., & Lavariega Monforti, J. (2010). The poverty draft? Exploring the role of socioeconomic status in U.S. Military recruitment of Hispanic students. American Political Science Association, Washington, DC.

McPherson, M. (1978). The demand for higher education. In D. W. Breneman & C. E. Finn (Eds.), *Public policy and private higher education*. The Brookings Institution.

McPherson, M. S., & Schapiro, M. O. (2006). *College access: Opportunity or privilege?* Distributed by Holtzbrinck. http://www.loc.gov/catdir/toc/ecip0617/2006024115.html

Meriwether, C. (1907). *Our colonial curriculum, 1607-1776*. Capital Publishing Company.

Mintz, S. (2009). *Statistics: Education in America, 1860-1950*. The Gilder Lehrman Institute of American History. Retrieved April 2 from https://www.gilderlehrman.org/history-resources/teacher-resources/statistics-education-america-1860-1950

Moore, G. E. (1988). The involvement of experiment stations in secondary agricultural education, 1887-1917. *Agricultural History, 62*(2), 164–176.

Muhrman, K. (2022). How can students in vocational education be motivated to learn mathematics? *Nordic Journal of Vocational Education and Training, 12*(3), 47–70.

National Center for Education Statistics. (2009). *Table 103 – High school graduates, by sex and control of school: Selected years, 1869-70 through 2018-19*. Retrieved November 12 from http://nces.ed.gov/programs/digest/d09/

National Commission on Excellence in Education. (1983). *A nation at risk*. http://www.ed.gov/pubs/NatAtRisk/title.html

National Commission on the Financing of Postsecondary Education. (1973). *Financing postsecondary education in the United States*. Government Printing Office

Newman, J. H. (1852). *The idea of a university*. The Guttenberg Project. Retrieved March 12 from https://www.gutenberg.org/files/24526/24526-pdf.pdf

Nussbaum, M. C. (1999). *Sex and social justice*. Oxford, UK: Oxford University Press.

Nussbaum, M. C. (2011). *Creating capabilities: The human development approach*. Harvard University Press.

Oakes, J. (1985). *Keeping track: How schools structure inequality*. Yale University Press.

Oakes, J., Rogers, J. E., & Lipton, M. (2006). *Learning power: Organizing for education and justice*. Teachers College Press.

Orrill, R. (2001). Grades 11-14: The heartland or the wasteland of American education? In M. C. Johanek (Ed.), *A faithful mirror: Reflections on the college board and education in America* (p. 400). College Board.

Peterson, P. E. (1985). *The politics of school reform, 1870-1940*. University of Chicago Press.

Pew Foundation. (2009). *Shifting boundaries: The establishment clause and the government funding of religious schools and faith-based organization*. Retrieved March 12 from https://www.pewresearch.org/religion/2009/05/14/shifting-boundaries6/

Pew Research Center. (2024). *Religious landscape study*. https://www.pewresearch.org/religion/religious-landscape-study/#religions

Pitsch, M. (1991, June 5). Education spending declined during 80's, report says. *Ed Week*. https://www.edweek.org/education/education-spending-declined-during-80s-report-says/1991/06

Ravitch, D. (2010). *The death and life of the great American school system: How testing and choice are undermining education*. Basic Books.

Rubin, G. T., & Ettenheim, R. (2023, December 6). Biden has canceled about $132 billion of student loans despite Supreme Court Ruling. Here's How. *Wall Street Journal*. https://www.wsj.com/us-news/education/student-loan-forgiveness-amount-biden-ab289d75

Russon, M. (1983). How secretarial studies might evolve. *The Vocational Aspect of Education, 35*(90), 31–36.

Seife, C. (2010). *Proofiness: The dark arts of mathematical deception*. Viking Press.

Slavin, R. E., Madden, N. A., Karweit, N. L., Livermon, B. J., & Dolan, L. (1990). Success for all: First-year outcomes of a comprehensive plan for reforming urban education. *American Educational Research Journal, 27*(2), 255–278.

St. John, E. P. (2023). Higher education in post-neoliberal times: Building human capabilities in the emergent period of uncertainty. *Education Sciences, 13*(5), 500. https://doi.org/https://doi.org/10.3390/educsci13050500

St. John, E. P., & Girmay, F. (2019). *Detroit school reform in comparative contexts: Community action overcoming policy barriers*. Palgrave Macmillan.

Taubman, P., & Wales, T. (1974). Education on a screening device. In P. Taubman & T. Wales (Eds.), *Higher education and earnings: College as an investment and screening device*. National Bureau of Economic Research.

The White House. (2024). *FACT SHEET: President Biden cancels student debt for more than 150,000 student loan borrowers ahead of schedule*. Retrieved March 20 from https://www.whitehouse.gov/briefing-room/statements-releases/2024/02/21/fact-sheet-president-biden-cancels-student-debt-for-more-than-150000-student-loan-borrowers-ahead-of-schedule/

Trent, W. T. (2008). Looking for love in all the wrong places: High school racial composition, the implications of strategic recruitment, and becoming a GMS scholar. In W. T. Trent & E. P. St. John (Eds.), *Resources, assets, and strengths among successful diverse students: Understanding the contributions of the gates millennium scholars program* (Vol. 23, pp. 1–16). AMS Press, Inc.

Trent, W. T., Gong, Y., & Owens-Nicholson, D. (2004). The relative contribution of high school origins to college access. In E. P. St. John (Ed.), *Readings on equal education* (Vol. *20*, p. v). New York: AMS Press Inc.

U.S. Census Bureau. (2023). *United States Census Bureau*. Retrieved December 26 from https://www.cens

U.S. Department of Education (2006). *A test of leadership: Charting the future of U.S. Higher Education*.

Walker, V. S. (1996). *Their highest potential: An African American school community in the segregated South*. The University of North Carolina Press.

Walker, V. S., & Snarey, J. E. (2004). *Race-ing moral formation: African American Perspectives on care and justice*. Teachers College Press.

Wheeler, R. (2019). Archaeology in the classroom at a New England prep school. *Journal of Archaeology and Education*, *3*(2), 1.

Wilds, D. J. (2004). Improving access and college success for diverse students: Studies of the Gates Millennium Scholars Program. In E. P. St. John (Ed.), *Readings on equal education* (Vol. 20, pp. v–viii). AMS Press, Inc.

5
COLLEGE ACCESS
From Equal Opportunity to Economic Stratification

From this nation's founding until the neoliberal transition, privileged families, philanthropists, and student aid programs enabled qualified adolescents from impoverished backgrounds to pay college costs; similar opportunities extended to the mass of veterans returning from World War II (WWII) expanded college enrollment after WWII. The neoliberal Washington Consensus, promoted by the World Bank and the International Monetary Fund, encouraged governments to raise tuition and use loans to expand college capacity to enroll more students within nations to expand college enrollment globally.

During the development of mass higher education, states funded colleges based on enrollment, typically using equivalent-full-time-enrollment as the critical indicator. The *Education Amendments of 1972* explicitly identified *access*, college *choice*, and *persistence* as goals for equalizing education opportunities. The first two editions of *Higher Education and Public Policy* focused on reframing access, choice, and persistence as indicators states and institutions could use in partnerships promoting equal opportunity. However, as we rethought the context of public policy on higher education this century, we found that these terms did not fit the policy context created by neoliberalism. Of course, preparation for college and careers (Chapter 4) is a relevant indicator, along with enrollment (as a measure that includes first-time and continued or returning enrollment), and timely degree attainment is a more appropriate indicator than persistence in a period when student aid is inadequate to ensure opportunities for college completion. This chapter focuses on enrollment using data from the American Community Survey (ACS), conducted annually by the U.S. Census Bureau. It asks a representative sample of state residents about college participation for household members, providing a measure of enrollment rates and diversity among traditional college-age students. In addition to enrollment rates by traditional-college-age students (18-to-24 years of age), form ACS surveys and breaking down these indicators by race/ethnic group provides a more viable measure of college destinations of diverse groups than the underspecified indicators of access or choice, especially since many students qualified for 4-year college end up in 2-year college because of college costs.

This chapter starts by historically resituating the challenges created by the neoliberal transition, including discourse about declining postsecondary equity. Next, we compare outcomes that occurred during the transition to the current period of adaptations. The choice between 2-year and no college was not the payoff sold to generations of poor and middle-class students who bought into the STEM agenda's transformation of high schools. Placing the neoliberal turn in the historical framework provides a perspective for examining policy changes in the 2000–2020 period and resulting changes in educational outcomes. These analyses can inform reframing the current challenge: increasing opportunity and improving equity within the increasingly stratified colleges and universities.

UNDERSTANDING THE NEOLIBERAL TURN

Education professors and policymakers typically frame discussions of education enrollment opportunities using their historical and personal ideological understandings of higher education opportunities. Acting on beliefs, they use the evidence from contemporary and historical events to argue for strategies for policy and practices. Reconsidering the frames used to construct policy and investigating efficacy provides a starting point for analyzing the effects of policy shifts since 2000.

While techniques for developing colleges and promoting enrollment transformed across periods, the fundamental shift in the 1980s altered the trajectory (Table 5.1). The nation's two-century trajectory included the early American formation of colleges (1776 to 1870), the emergence of competition between new public and older private colleges (1870 to 1945), and the development of mass systems of higher education (1945 to 1980). Throughout these two centuries, colleges and states had incentives to keep tuition low and provide sufficient grants and scholarships to ensure low-income prepared students could afford to enroll. After 1980, enrollment grew because all high school graduates qualified, but the emphasis on loans and high tuition charges altered the trajectory toward inequitable enrollment opportunities for low-income students.

Pathway of Privilege: Early American Colleges (1776–1870)

College was for the privileged before the Civil War—private high schools and academies developed but charged tuition for attendance. In most colleges, the curriculum focused on traditional subjects aligned with local faith traditions, so the mobility of students and graduates was constrained; once founded, colleges' development, constrained by the limited supply of high school graduates who could afford college, was tied to evolving local school-college networks. The academy movement swept the North, expanding access to secondary schools for students who could pay tuition (Opal, 2004).

The college-founding movement emerged across the colonies before the Revolution, but the scope was more limited in the South because enslaved people and poor white men could not pay for high school or college (Knight, 1919). Local churches frequently operated grade schools but did not provide secondary education. In the Northeast, residential preparatory high schools began providing college pathways for wealthy families. The colleges in the new Northwest Territories struggled financially with few students as college opportunities expanded faster than student demand.

The localized school-to-college networks with philanthropic support for college preparation, outreach, and enrollment for low-income, academically prepared students constrained mobility across regions, especially in the new territory because faiths were

92 • Reframing Higher Education Policy

Table 5.1 Public Policy Shifts Affecting Higher Education ENROLLMENT: Student Demand, Colleges Opportunity, and Student Financial Aid Across Historical Periods

	Student Demand for Higher Education	College Opportunities	Financial Aid (Student Subsidies)
Early American Period (Before 1870)	College Curriculum Usually Aligned with Faith Traditions	Local Pathways; Population Growth; New Colleges in Northwest Territories	Philanthropy for low-income Students (State, Local, & Private Support)
Development of Competitive Public and Private Institutions (1870—1945)	General and technical high schools developed as the free-school movement reached all states.	Older colleges and the new land grants colleges competed; Science and career curricula options.	Land grants in the North after the Civil War; need-based aid expanded, and merit scholarships emerged
Cold War Expansion of Public Systems (1945–1980)	High schools became the screening device for good jobs. GIs flooded colleges, followed by equity-based fed student aid programs sustaining student demand.	Mass systems of 2-year and 4-year colleges developed; Private Colleges competed for students; equity-based grant programs emerged	GI Bill; Federal Need-based Aid Grants, Work, & Loans); National Need-Analysis & Merit Analysis Scholarships Develop
Neoliberal Turn (1980–2015)	Student demand accelerated by improved college preparation & decline of working-class jobs. Community college pipelines & decline of technical certificate options. Excessive loans.	Rising net prices of 4-year colleges increased reliance on loans. Increased public resistance to affirmative action. The 9–14 programs and community college transfer agreement expanded.	The federal government decreased grant funding, increased emphasis on loans, and pushed markets. States decreased college funding and competition for elite faculty with grants.
Post-Neoliberal (2015–present)	The high net cost of 4-year colleges limits opportunity. Students question the economic returns to higher education relative to the debt burden.	The STEM agenda's successes and failures, along with the shift in K-12 strategies focused on preparation, accelerating stratification.	States have created widely divergent pathways to college as quick fixes to the leaky STEM pipeline. Comparing states provides insight into possible directions.

in local communities in the new territories rather than states, the settlement pattern in the original states. Colleges that tried to break the tight links with faith sects were at risk of breaking up their networks. For example, Antioch College sought a cross-denomination approach to college development under Horace Mann's leadership. However, it was a tough sell to congregations and students. Eventually, Mann left—the noted educator's career ended in discord—and the college evolved its distinctive model (Clark, 1973; St. John et al., 2023).

Throughout the period, need-based scholarship aid awarded by campuses typically used state funds or philanthropic gifts: "Scholarships were prevalent, but cogent systems for measuring need or merit had not developed" (Fuller, 2014, p. 14). Some campuses also used loans. For example, in 1838, Harvard established a loan program with no interest accrued by students. Social class differences were pervasive in Early America and carried over into colleges, limiting the development of new pathways to high school and college. At Harvard, the dorms for low-income students were of lower quality than for wealthier students (Thelin, 2011). Poor students often faced discrimination from wealthier students, but education opportunities gradually expanded in local education networks.

Legacies of the privileged pathways created in the Early American period continue as historical legacies. The competition between colleges for high-achieving students emerged during this early period, evolved as competitive systems developed after the Civil War and the Cold War, and accelerated with marketing students during the neoliberal period. Disparities between housing quality for wealthy and poor students, ever-present, increased with the privatization of dormitories (Laidley, 2014).

Development of Competing College Systems (1870–1945)
Multiple high school pathways emerged as free schools expanded across the US (Chapter 4). Technical high schools developed nearby agricultural colleges, like traditional, faith-based education strategies in the early American period. Catholic academies emerged to prepare students for the universities, established as a pattern in the North before the Civil War. They evolved into private Catholic high schools aligned with Catholic universities (Power, 1954). The free school movement replaced the Protestant academies; the "public" system developed multiple diploma options, unlike the Catholic school pipeline, until, ironically, neoliberals sought to transform public schools into the Catholic model.

Land Grant universities emphasized sciences, forcing liberal arts colleges to provide these subjects so they could compete for students. There was a tension between the utility orientation of the Land Grant universities and the older academic colleges that persisted into the 1960s as Land Grant universities, like the University of California system, sought to have liberal arts as foundational for all (Cheit, 1975). During that time, the Ivy League struggled to retain a core curriculum in Western Civilization (e.g., Bell, 1966). The surfacing of these tensions in the two types of ivory towers, both were learning with their historic cores being challenged by student protests as universities responded to myriad social issues (Bennis, 1973).

After the Civil War, the national pension system provided subsidies for northern veterans to attend college (Fuller, 2014). The early precursor of the eventual national system of need-based grants and loan schemes slowly evolved through local state and local education networks of philanthropists, educators, and policymakers. The tradition of philanthropy for poor students continued, but older colleges developed merit aid for high-ability students to compete better with the new colleges. Elite colleges also found ways to compete for academic stars. In 1941, for example, Harvard started using the newly developed SAT for admissions and scholarships, a process adopted across the Ivy League by 1944, the start of merit as an alternative to using financial need as a basis for awarding scholarships. By the time the US entered WWII, college graduates were rare until the number of graduates rapidly expanded due to the new wave of veterans in public and technical colleges. The infusion of research funding for defense during WWII accelerated the development of research universities, an interlude when most colleges struggled as they competed for fewer students.

Cold War Expansion of Public Systems

The cross-generation impact of the GI Bill accelerated as the federal government invested in student financial aid for the next generation, starting with the *National Defense Education Act*. In most states, the compulsory education laws raised the required school attendance age to 16 or 18 (Justia US Law, 2024), creating a mechanism for keeping children in free schools. Completing high school also had economic value, as it became a screening device for good jobs (Taubman & Wales, 1974). High schools provided college pathways: vocational education prepared students for postsecondary technical certificates, the general diploma was sufficient to enter most state colleges and many liberal arts colleges, and an honors strand was offered mainly in the best urban and suburban high schools, giving high-achieving students head starts in engineering and science fields. With universal educational opportunities in place by the 1970s, with more than 70% graduating, student demand for colleges expanded.

State teachers' colleges and state universities ushered in the first wave of standardization in K-12 education. After WWII, states adopted new teacher licensure requirements, began requiring standardized tests, and expanded the use of testing and tracking in elementary and secondary schools (Baker, 2001). Daughters of women who had moved home from factories building war machines would go to college at higher rates than prior generations. The vision for racial justice after a desegregated military created hope, accelerated by the *Brown v. Board of Education* (1954).

Most states had developed mass public higher education systems by the late 1960s, with many states following the California model of research universities, state colleges and universities, and community colleges (Lee & Bowen, 1971, 1975). The comprehensive colleges comprised upgraded teachers and engineering colleges that expanded to offer comprehensive programs across the curriculum. In some states, like Florida, all 4- and 2-year colleges were in the same system. In others, one or more "flagship" research universities built new campuses, which is Indiana's approach. Locally developed junior and vocational colleges became part of state community college systems that assumed a larger share of funding for developing community colleges.

Expanding state systems accommodated the growing population of college-age students—the baby boom children of WWII veterans. Budget funding formulae became the cornerstone of rational state planning. There was extensive literature on developing state formulae, especially in the 1980s as states adapted to the end of the Baby Boom cohort (e.g., Breneman et al., 1978; Burke, 1994). As the shift to market systems occurred in the 1990s, many state budget officers resisted arguing for retaining rational models. However, market forces and arguments about taxpayer savings had already taken hold as researchers began to study the costs and benefits of higher education as a public investment (e.g., Hansen & Weisbrod, 1969). College tuition remained low in public colleges. In the early 1970s, for example, the Carnegie Commission on Higher Education (1973) argued that states should raise the tuition paid by students and families to 20% of educational costs. It was difficult for private colleges to compete with low-cost public colleges, so they lobbied for more federal student aid, resulting in the *Middle Income Student Assistance Act of 1978*. The clash between market forces, political advocacy, and rational funding analyses increased until the early 1980s.

The Neoliberal Turn (1980–2015)

The turn in policy during the neoliberal period altered the three-mechanism support, expansion, and equalization of student demand with enrollment opportunities. The STEM standards initially decreased high school graduation rates until states eased restrictions (Chapter 4); most 4-year colleges raised admissions requirements to align with the new standards, and community colleges and 9–14 programs provided courses that did not always meet 4-year college standards.

In the late 1980s, the Department of Education's advocacy for college preparation for all became the dominant narrative in advocacy for college access, replacing equal opportunity as the primary goal. By the end of the 2000s, foundations and government agencies were pushing for a new consensus for accountability, including content alignment from the 9th through the 14th grade. President Barack Obama, buying into the vision, set the goal of having 60% of the population complete college degrees as a response to the declining U.S. ranking in college access (De Neis, 2010). In his 2010 State of the Union speech, Obama evoked "sputnik" as an image to stimulate a deeper American resolve to improve competitiveness in education (Obama, 2010), much like 1958 when it stimulated passage of the *National Defense Education Act*.

Many locals developed 9–14 collaborative "pathways" through high school and college. For example, Anthony Carnevale (2007) argued that the tracking problem in high schools prepared one-third of the students for college, one-third for careers, and one-third for dropout. He also argued for standards that improved opportunity: "The path of least resistance for reform is the current trajectory from high school up the education pipeline toward postsecondary education" (p. 21). In theory, this pathways approach could include career-oriented options, but the STEM movement had already transformed the meaning of tracks into preparation for 4-year colleges. Too often, the 2-year systems and the high school pathways changed by focusing on 4-year preparation, 9–14 programs, and 4-year transfer programs. Theoretically, the new strategy made it easier to complete high school with courses that could transfer to 2-year colleges; in practice, it was too easy to transition to 2-year colleges for a period before dropping out or taking time off for work. Students who resisted loans moved back and forth between work and college, taking many years to complete an associate's degree, if they did so at all.

There was a significant disconnect between rhetoric about access and the funding mechanisms that ensure opportunity. Given the history of linking state funding to enrollment, it is essential to get past the faulty rhetoric of neoliberal education by recognizing that false facts distorted the meaning of access. The decline in federal grants and rising costs of attending college increased net prices for students and created a formidable barrier for first-generation college students seeking cross-generation uplift out of poverty. The decrease in available grant aid placed upward pressure on net prices, which resulted in greater reliance on loans, even among community college students. Public colleges increased prices when state per-student funding declined; they became destinations for upper-middle-income students in their states. Using prestige pricing, many private colleges catered to upper-income families seeking the frills of the good life for their children (Breneman, 1994).

Post-Neoliberal Uncertainty (2015–Present)

President Obama's voice was one of many calling for action on education reforms to expand preparation for college. The ESSA, passed in 2015 and implemented in 2017, established K-12 states' capacity to maintain flexible K-12 pathways, retaining an emphasis on math but including applied math options. The neoliberal postsecondary finance strategies continued, but he encouraged locales and states to develop promise programs providing additional student aid.

The rising net price for the typical student has interrupted choices about whether and where to attend college. As Promise programs developed and channeled low-income, academically prepared students into 2-year colleges, the "equal preparation for all students" movement, a neoliberal theme, had unequal effects on first-time and continued enrollment. The declining purchasing power of need-based grants became a dividing force. Too many college-prepared students could not get the support for 4-year degrees. Students must now consider the prospects of living with high student loan debt after college. The recent drop in prices by 4-year colleges suggests that significant changes in college finance will eventually be necessary despite deadlocked neoliberal education compromises in the near term. The trend analyses below examine how this challenging situation evolved.

Four-year colleges did not take advantage of the promise programs by raising tuition (Li & Katri, 2024), illustrating that adequate government aid constrains price increases. Given the power of government agencies to fund and vet research through politicized reviews, scholars, graduate students, and policymakers must delve into questions about politics, policies, and outcomes.

FINANCE POLICIES AFFECTING ENROLLMENT AND DIVERSITY

The inherent federal-state partnership in funding college students, built during the Golden Age, broke down during the Neoliberal Turn, and the future of public support appears uncertain as extreme conflict lingers between the neoliberal framework and arguments from both the left and right for reducing costs. These shifts in public finance substantially influence whether and where students attend college. We consider trends in:

- The cost of attending public and private colleges,
- The federal role in student aid (Pell Grants and debt burden),
- State Funding for colleges and students.

Cost of Attending Public and Private Colleges

The College Board provides annual reports on trends in college pricing, including tuition and fees which are the primary components of the Cost of Attendance (Figure 5.1). Additional costs include room and board, books, and other expenses allowed as part of federal need analysis. The cost of attending a 4-year college rose substantially in the 2010s and the 2020s but did not increase as fast as inflation after 2020. The constant dollar tuition rate appeared to drop while most colleges continued to make modest increases. It is

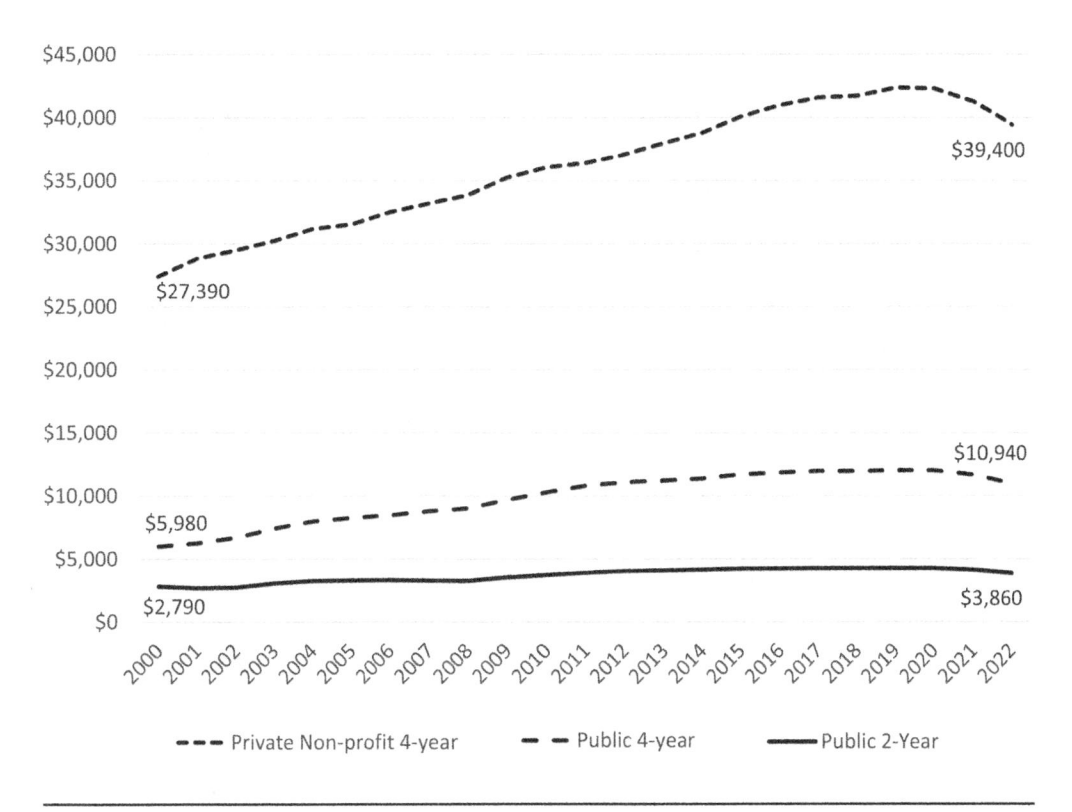

Figure 5.1 Trends in Average Undergraduate In-State Tuition & Fees per FTE in Higher Education in the U.S., by Sector, 2000–2022 (in 2022 Dollars)

Source: College Board (2023). Trends in College Pricing. Retrieved from https://research.collegeboard.org/trends/college-pricing

important to note that we report inflation-adjusted prices in this chapter and throughout the case studies and the data should be interpreted with caution. Adjusting our trend lines to 2020 dollars creates the impression that prices have declined in recent years, but we know that has not been the case. Instead, the declines are an artifact of slower price increases and a period of high inflation. Readers should be aware of that in the following case study chapters as well.

The combined cost of tuition and fees peaked in 2020 across the three types of colleges, reaching over $42,000 at private colleges in 2020, $11,990 in public 4-year colleges, and $4,250 in public 2-year colleges, when adjusting for inflation. Additionally, the costs vary substantially with each group, especially among private colleges. In 2020–2021, the University of Chicago was the highest-cost college (total cost of attendance), at over $84,000. Within states, the elite flagship campuses cost more than other state colleges. Public colleges also have higher out-of-state costs for non-residents, an issue driving advocacy for DREAM programs. Most students in community colleges live at home and have similar expected living costs they would have if they did not attend college. Room, board, and other costs vary substantially across locales and states.

The fact that inflation increased faster than college costs complicated college choices and enrollment decisions after 2020. Families' cost of living increased faster than college costs, so it was more challenging to pay for college. These conditions would likely increase pressure for students to borrow to pay their living costs. Thus, the early 2020s was an exceedingly uncertain time concerning paying college costs. The delay in processing of the Free Application for Federal Student Aid (FASFA) in 2023 further complicated enrollment prediction for the fall of 2024 (Conroy, 2023). Students had to wait to know how much aid they would receive.

Promise programs influence college pricing decisions by stimulating student demand through local pathways. California has over 120 promise programs that lower the cost of college for eligible students, which could be a force holding down tuition for community colleges in the state (see also Chapter 7). It is difficult to predict whether these political, inflationary, and social forces will have a sustained impact on the trajectory of college costs and students' enrollment decisions.

The Federal Role

Federal student financial aid policy lingers in the shadow of neoliberalism. The maximum Pell award is modest compared to the cost of attending college. Price increases did not raise more tuition revenue from Pell, except for the very few students at the margin of eligibility—those who qualify anew because of higher costs, a meager number of students. We examine trends in the purchasing power of Pell—the maximum award compared to the costs of attending a public 4-year college—and the debt burden of the average borrower.

The Purchasing Power of Pell Grants

Between 1973 and 1980, Pell Grants were the cornerstone of the market model, effectively increasing the purchasing power for qualified students who could not afford college. In 1978, MISAA opened the door to federal grants for middle-income students. Arguments about institutional waste and raising prices to maximize revenue from grants (Carnes, 1987; Finn, 1988a, 1988b) also created doubts about the federal role in a market model for higher education. Funding for other federal grant programs decreased substantially after 1980. The Bennett hypothesis was absurd when proposed (Bennett, 1987) because Pell's purchasing power was already declining, as was the case for other federal grant programs.

Federal funding for the Pell Grant Program is set annually by US Congressional approval of the maximum award, the means used to control costs. Pell-eligible students take their Pell awards to campuses as a quasi-entitlement, much like the GI Bill. Early in the Pell program, the Congressionally approved maximum followed the HEA-authorized level. Most other HEA Title IV programs provide grant amounts to campuses, so students receive awards from campuses. After the *Middle-Income Student Assistance Act*, the Carter administration constrained the Pell maximum to control federal spending on Title IV grant programs. Subsequent Presidential administrations used this mechanism to control costs. Presidents can appear liberal when signing HEA reauthorizations with high Pell funding before constraining costs in the annual budget development process in collaboration with Congress.

The maximum Pell Gant was nearly equal to the average cost of attending college (COA) at public 4-year colleges (i.e., tuition plus living expenses) in 1975 and 1980. There was a half-cost provision in the original Pell program, which meant Pell would only pay 50% of the cost of attending. The purchasing power of Pell Grants—the gap between the maximum award (the amount awarded to the highest-need student) and

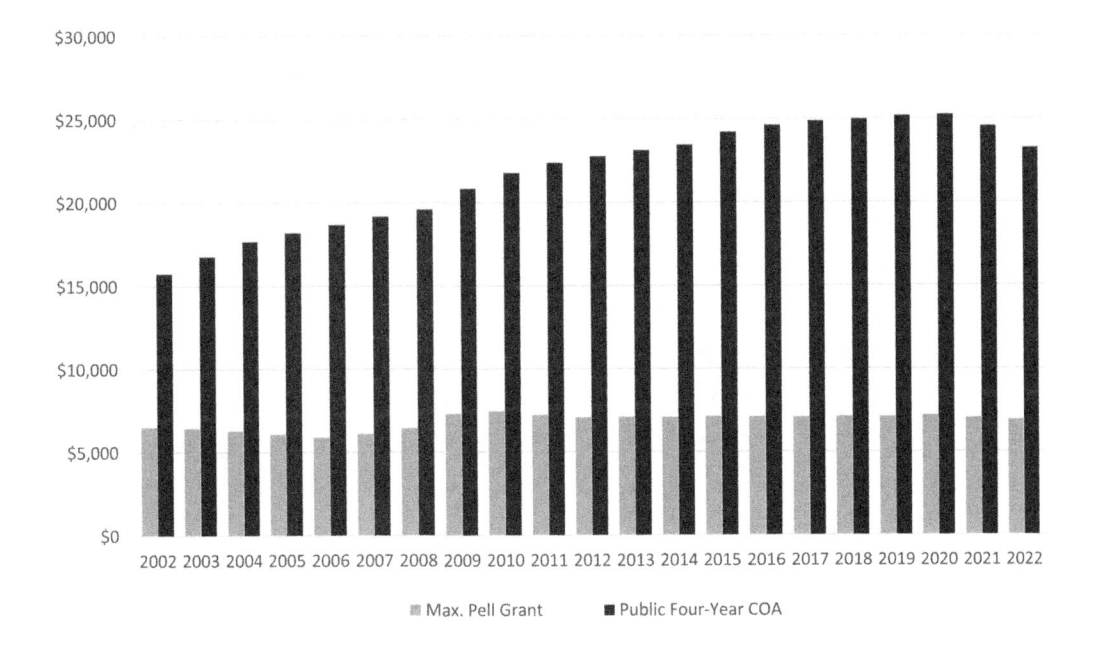

Figure 5.2 Gap Between the Maximum Pell Award and University Attendance Costs
Source: College Board (2023). Trends in Student Aid. Retrieved from https://research.collegeboard.org/trends/student-aid

the average COA—was seriously problematic after 2000 (Figure 5.2). The maximum Pell award, adjusted for inflation, kept pace with the cost of living after 2009, but the average public 4-year college COA rose substantially, increasing the gap. In contrast, the public college COA increased by about $5,000, considerably adding to the burden. The decline in Pell's purchasing power from 2002 to 2020 is primarily attributable to rising college costs. In 2021 and 2022, public 4-year college COA dropped modestly, but the burden after Pell remained substantial.

Trends in Student Debt

The massive debt for borrowers constrains their ability to pay off car and house loans and to feed families. The American dream of the 1950s and 1960s of having a single worker support a family—as a factory worker or college graduate in a job that may have more meaning—is a shattered dream.

The rapid rise in student borrowing (Figure 5.3) resulted in substantial, long-term debt, creating lifelong problems with repayment for many students. Since 2020, college costs have not grown as fast as inflation and wage growth has been faster than inflation. However, these trends have not overcome the affordability problem for many students, especially given the prospects of borrowing to enroll. A more complete rethinking of the human capital formulation—the individual's consideration of earnings, forgone wages, and prospects of jobs that provide financial wellbeing after debt—reflects the contemporary role of prospects of debt in student college choice. Rising generations learn about the consequences of high debt from parents and older siblings who have struggled to pay off loans, pay rent, and put food on the table.

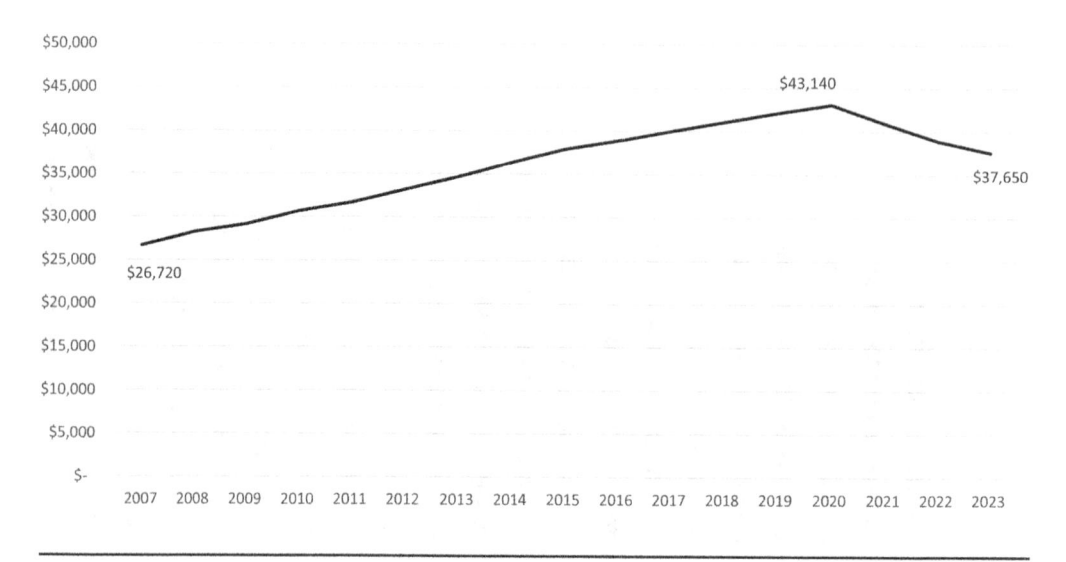

Figure 5.3 Average Federal Student Loan Debt per Borrower Over Time (2023 Dollars)
Source: College Board (2023). Trends in Student Aid. Retrieved from https://research.collegeboard.org/trends/student-aid

Trends in State Funding for Colleges and Students

Historically, public colleges in many states were free for students, but that period has long passed, as indicated in trends in COA (above). Both states and local governments fund colleges, with most local funds going to community colleges as jointly funded state and local institutions. We examine trends in subsidies to colleges and universities, state funding for need-based and non-need grants, and the ratio of grants compared to tuition charges as an indicator of the purchaser power of the average state grant.

State and Local Subsidies to Public Colleges and Universities

States and local governments share the costs of education with students (Figure 5.4). The amount of subsidy per FTE drooped annually between 2001 and 2012, as it had since 1980, but rose slightly after that. The average subsidy for 2022–2023 was still below 2001. State and local governments shifted college costs from taxpayers to students and their families. The average subsidy in 2022–2023 was $10,878 per FTE, approximately equal to students' COA that same year.

State Need-Based and Non-Need Grants

The average state funding per FTE for need-based and non-need grants was flat, adjusted for inflation in the 2000s, and increased slightly in 2010 (Figure 5.5). Information on state grant funding was not available after 2020, a period when the cost of attendance dropped modestly.

In the early 2010s, funding for need-based grants increased moderately and faster from 2015 to 2020, as the cost of attending public and private colleges increased. In 2020, the average need-based grant was less than $800, while the average COA at public 4-year colleges was almost $11,000, and the average borrower had nearly $40,000 in debt. From 2000 through 2020, the average gap in funding for state need-based grants increased compared to tuition charges.

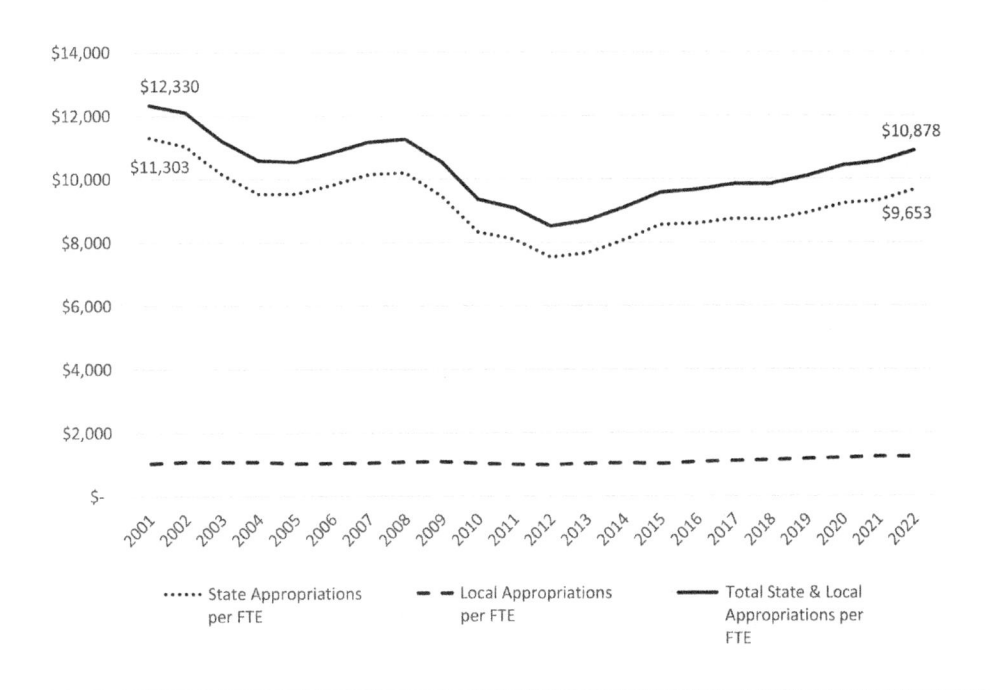

Figure 5.4 Trends in Average Annual State and Local Appropriations per FTE for Public Higher Education

Source: State Higher Education Executive Officers (SHEEO) (2022). State Higher Education Finance (SHEF) Annual Report. Retrieved from https://shef.sheeo.org/data-downloads/

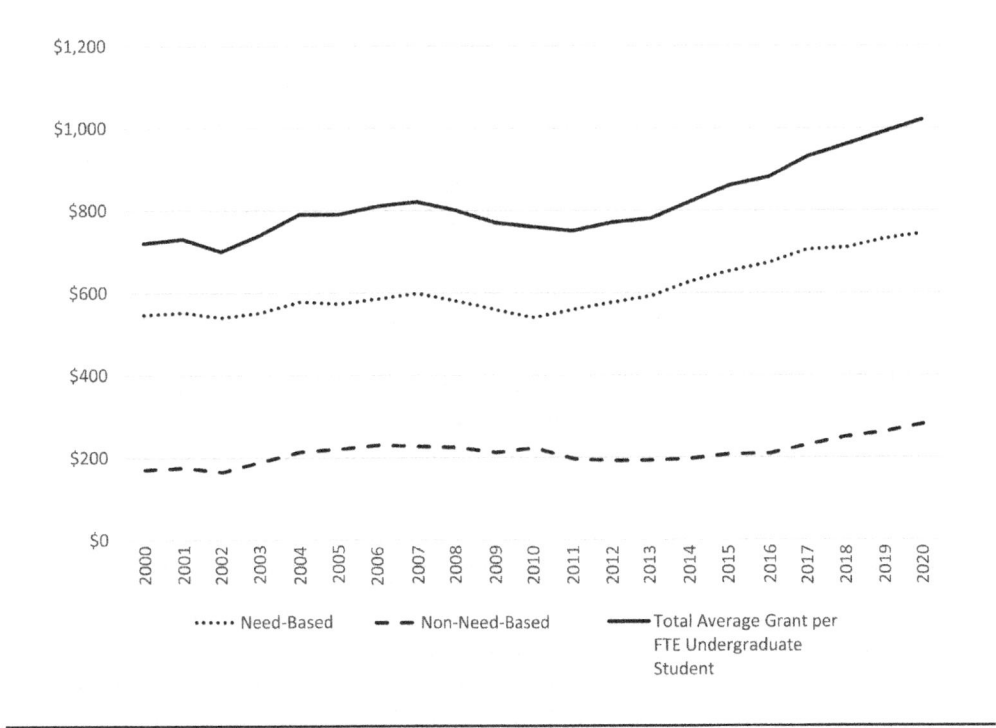

Figure 5.5 Trends in Average State Need-Based and Non-need-Based Undergraduate Grants per FTE, 2000–2020

Source: College Board (2023). Trends in Student Aid. Retrieved from https://research.collegeboard.org/trends/student-aid

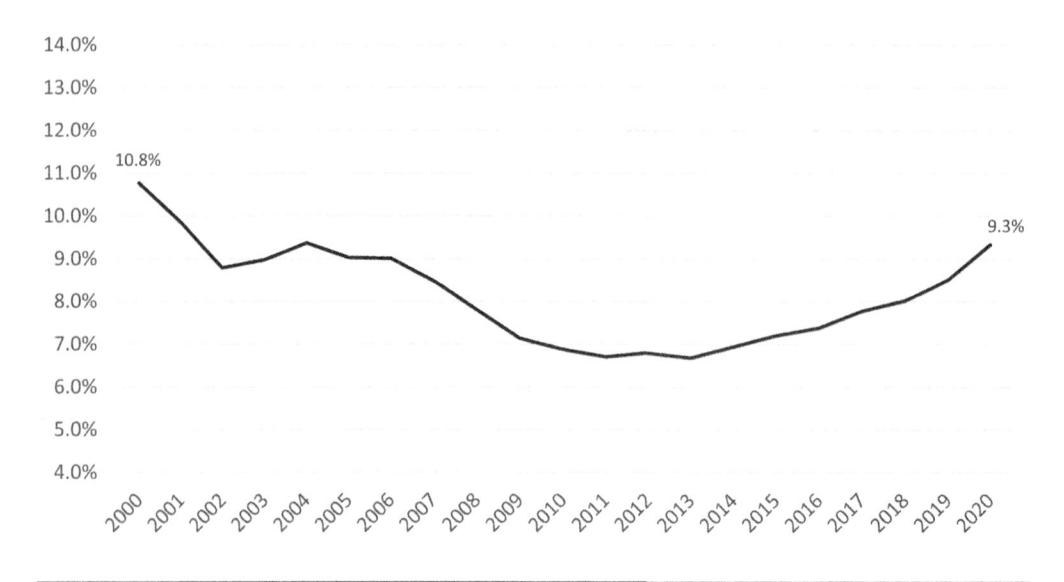

Figure 5.6 Trends in per FTE Funding of Need-based Grants as a Percentage of Average Public Full-Time Tuition
Source: College Board (2023). Trends in Student Aid. Retrieved from https://research.collegeboard.org/trends/student-aid

State funding for non-need grants, typically awarded based on merit (e.g., GPA or test scores), was also flat, adjusting for inflation. It increased slightly after 2015 but averaged less than $300 in 2020: a few states, especially Georgia and Florida, award the most merit grant aid.

The Purchasing Power of State Need-Based Grants
The state funding level of the average state need-based grant as a percent of the average tuition charge indicates trends in state grants' purchasing power and state efforts to keep public colleges affordable. The ratio dropped between 2000 and 2020 but dipped most substantially (7% or lower) between 2009 and 2015 (Figure 5.6). The ratio began to rise modestly, reaching 9.3% in 2020.

These trends indicate an overall shift in states' efforts to keep colleges affordable after 2015 when the average new public investment was modest and remained below the 2000 level and when need-based grant awards per FTE were 10.8% of the average tuition change. The overall trend indicates that states and the federal government did not make a substantial effort to keep public colleges affordable for low-income students between 2000 and 2020. Shifting patterns of enrollment demonstrate the consequences of states' policy choices.

ENROLLMENT, COLLEGE CHOICE, AND DIVERSITY

Federal and state funding and financial aid policies influence students, as do institutions' roles in marketing and providing student financial aid. Adult students typically take evening and weekend classes or enroll in online programs. During the worst of the COVID pandemic, most state colleges shifted to being primarily online. Earning a college degree became lengthy for many students who take courses periodically and part-time. In addition, a growing number of professionals in the workforce must continue to take content courses to keep current in their professions and trades. For the 2000–2021 period, we examine trends in enrollment of and diversity among college students.

Enrollment By Traditional-College-Age Students

The percentage of students enrolled in college during the fall after high school graduation is a typical measure of access. Enrollment provides an indicator of new and continuing students in the traditional college-age group, an indicator directly applicable to state financing of higher education (Figure 5.7). The college enrollment trends, broken down by racial/ethnic group, illustrate a narrowing enrollment gap and decline after 2015.

White and Asian high school graduates enrolled in college at higher rates than their Black and Hispanic peers during the 2000s. From Fall 2011 to Fall 2015, enrollment rates (about 70%) for whites, Blacks, and Hispanics were similar, but a gap reopened afterward. There was a decline in college enrollment rates for Blacks and Hispanics between 2016 and 2021 and for whites after 2018. Less than 60% of Blacks and Hispanics enrolled in 2020 and 2021, and white enrollment dropped to almost 60% in 2021.

College enrollment rates for Asian/Pacific Islander high school graduates hovered between 80% and 90% of high school graduation cohorts from 2004 to 2017, dipped below 70% in Fall 2018, but rose again. Except for 2002, when white high school graduates enrolled at a slightly higher rate, API high school graduates enrolled at higher rates than graduates in other racial/ethnic groups.

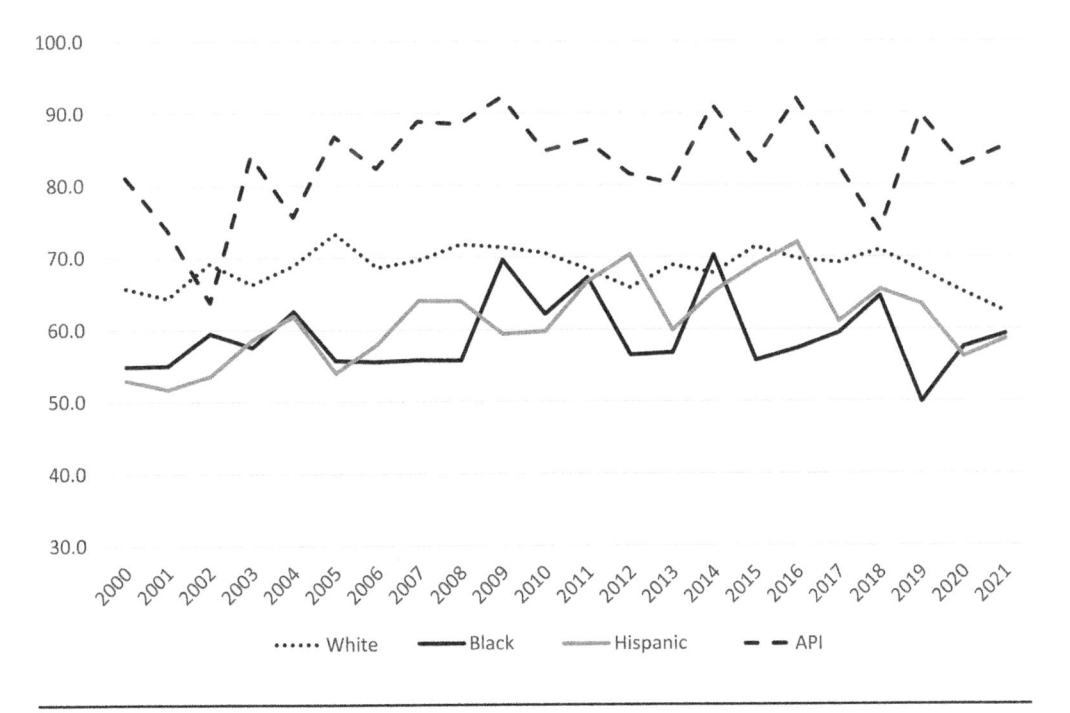

Figure 5.7 Trends in Percent of High School Completers Enrolled in College by Race/Ethnicity

Source: NCES (2023). Digest of Education Statistics. Table 302.20. Percentage of recent high school completers enrolled in college, by race/ethnicity and level of institution: 1960 through 2021. Retrieved from https://nces.ed.gov/programs/digest/index.asp

Colleges Choices: Enrollment by College Type

Community Colleges: The Front-Line of College Opportunity

At the turn of the twenty-first century, college choices varied substantially across racial/ethnic groups (Figure 5.8). In 2000, Asian/Pacific Islanders and Native Americans enrolled at about 1.6 times their representation of the US population, Blacks and Hispanics enrolled at rates approximately equal to the share of the population (1.0 ratio), and whites enrolled at a lower rate, about 90% of their share of the US population.

Since adults enroll in colleges along with traditional college-age students, we used the percentage of the population enrolled to examine racial differences in college choices. We discuss public 2-year and 4-year college enrollment trends from 2000 to 2020. The patterns of changing representation in community colleges tell different stories of educational opportunities across racial/ethnical groups in society. We briefly describe the pattern for each group:

- Across the 2000s, whites chose community colleges at a lower rate than other racial/ethnic groups. Their representation ratio dropped from 0.9 in 2000 to 0.8 in 2020. Given the relative affordability of community colleges, readers can assume white underrepresentation is an artifact of college choice.
- Native Americans had the highest representation rate in 2-year colleges until 2008 but fell to a rate lower than other groups except whites in 2020. Most tribal colleges offer only 2-year programs, so for Native Americans, 2-year colleges are the

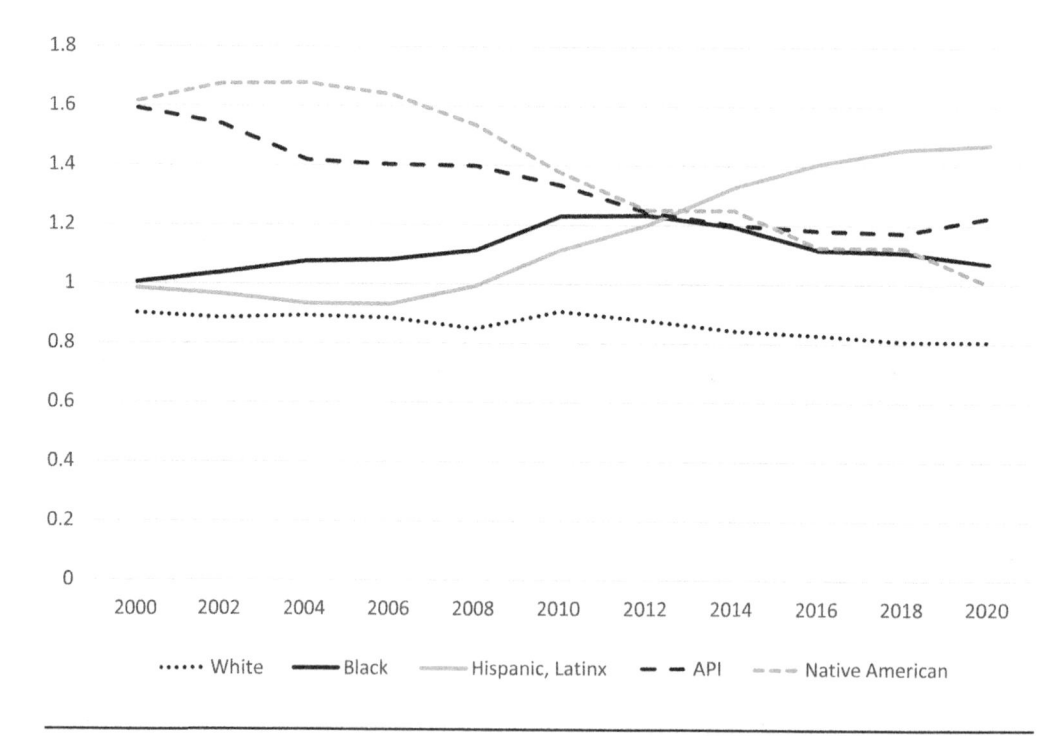

Figure 5.8 Racial/Ethnic Representation in All Public 2-Year Postsecondary Institutions as a Proportion of the U.S. Population

Source: NCES (2023). Digest of Education Statistics. Table 306.20 Total fall enrollment in degree-granting postsecondary institutions, by level and control of institution and race/ethnicity or nonresident status of student: Selected years, 1976 through 2021, Retrieved from https://nces.ed.gov/programs/digest/index.asp, and the Census Bureau Demographic and Housing Estimates, Retrieved from https://data.census.gov/

primary local enrollment opportunity. Native American representation in 2-year colleges dropped from 1.6 to 1.0 in 2020.
- The representation of Blacks in community colleges was higher than their percentage of the population across the two decades but rose from 2000 to 2010 and declined moderately by 2020. As a lower-income group, opportunities for Blacks relate to the threshold of equitable enrollment opportunity.
- Hispanic representation in community colleges increased substantially across the two decades, from representation equal to their share of the population by about 20 percentage points higher (to a 1.2 ratio).

Public 4-Year College: The Payoff for Prepared Students Who Can Pay

During the late twentieth century and early twenty-first century, preparation for enrollment in 4-year STEM programs had become the high school graduation standard. Of course, not all high school graduates plan to enroll in 4-year colleges, but equity in each group's representation indicates fairness (Figure 5.9). The patterns of racial representation varied most substantially for public 4-year colleges and changed considerably across the two decades:

- Substantially overrepresented across the 20 years, Asian/Pacific Islanders experienced a modest drop in the ratio, from 1.6 to 1.4, from 60 percentage points overrepresented to 40 percentage points. Pacific Islanders tend to be newer immigrants compared to Chinese, Indian, Japanese, and Korean families and tend to be more financially challenged, so there is substantial variation within this group.

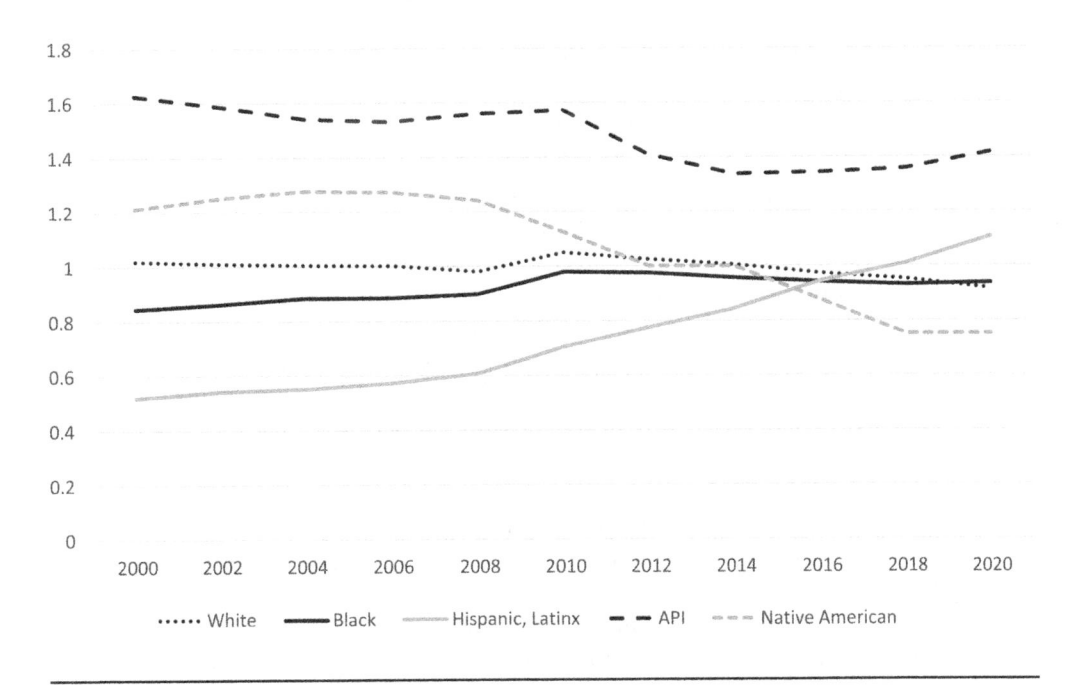

Figure 5.9 Racial/Ethnic Representation in All Public 4-Year Postsecondary Institutions as a Proportion of the U.S. Population

Source: NCES (2023). Digest of Education Statistics. Table 306.20 Total fall enrollment in degree-granting postsecondary institutions, by level and control of institution and race/ethnicity or nonresident status of student: Selected years, 1976 through 2021 Retrieved from https://nces.ed.gov/programs/digest/index.asp, and the Census Bureau Demographic and Housing Estimates, Retrieved from https://data.census.gov/

- Native American representation dropped across college types in the early twenty-first century, reversing the pattern in the late nineteenth century (Cahalan et al., 2022).
- Hispanics appear to be the success story in this, compared to other groups. From representation at about half their share of the US population in 2020, Hispanic enrollment in public 4-year colleges rose to a level where they are modestly overrepresented.
- White representation in public 4-year colleges dropped slightly across the two decades, from approximately equal to their share of the US population to the same rate as Blacks (0.94).
- Black representation in public 4-year colleges remained below their share of the US population over the two decades, but increased slightly in the 2010s compared to the 2000s, a five-percentage point rise (from 0.89 to 0.94).

REFRAMING

The change in the history of education, with a course-altering turn after 1980, a marker point, left the nation in turmoil in the 2020s. The meanings of diversity and fairness are also obfuscated by the neoliberal policy onslaught, floundered in many states, themselves besieged by MAGA-DEI battles over course content and behavioral regulations, are cracking the code that nationalized education. We quickly summarize the turning point in US education history and raise issues surfacing in the policy trends and outcomes before concluding with questions for readers.

A Turning Point in the History of US Education

For two centuries, the federal government created opportunities for colleges to expand enrollment through federal land grants and the Supreme Court's *Dartmouth* decisions distinguishing public and independent colleges. From 1945 through 1980, federal education programs also equalized educational opportunity. States, too, shifted patterns of public support from chartering public and private colleges to expanding opportunity from the Revolution until World War II by creating public schools that eventually provided K-12 education for all, developing mass systems of higher education in the 1960s and 1970s that provide college enrollment opportunities for all who wanted to attend college (in many states); and by providing need-based grants (especially in the 1970s)—the nation's possibility for global exceptionality in education changed abruptly.

The federal role changed starting in the transitional period (1976–1982), with a shift to marketizing strategies for

- *Research*: Encouraging university-corporate partnerships that accelerated economic globalization, e.g., the emergence of complex research-to-market strategies and the transformation of older approaches to science.
- *Student aid*: A fundamental shift from centuries of investment in population uplift through grants of various types to the utilization of loans, altering from taxing for uplift to mortgaging the future of poor and middle-class families with excessive student debt.
- *Nationalizing Education Through the STEM Agenda:* Rather than empowering communities and states to craft educational pathways that build local economies and

support social cohesion, albeit with segregated structural foundations, a national education agenda that supported large corporations in the development of global supply chains instead of local economies.

No research confirmed that such dramatic shifts would work as intended. When there are varied patterns of policy and practice, it is possible to estimate the impact of one policy type compared to the others, especially in student aid and the nationalizing high school curricula. Previously, the global exceptionalism case in education attainment and college quality was a lofty US status achieved through state and local practices. The federal government did not evaluate the impact of high school requirements on attainment or assess the effects of shifting from grants to loans for equal opportunity, the legislated intent of federal student aid. Advocates of economic globalization preached free markets, but education content and finance policies reduced freedoms. The new economic rationale scrapped the systemic legacy of the 1960s Civil Rights movement, hastening advocacy for DEI.

These nationalization and marketization stories (Chapters 2 and 3) are recounted here for their summative value. We encourage readers to look back to see the present more clearly. Introducing markets with public, quasi-public, and private schools offering the same required programs disguised the nationalized content, creating an illusion of choice. There was no longer a choice of pathways, so thematic schools developed to fill the void. Our narrative reconstructing of history can be—and indeed should be—questioned. We express extreme views now because we have tried to reconcile the evidence with our histories of advocating for some of the policies and programs reviewed. The time for turning to an evidence-based examination of policy history is overdue. It is time to set aside evangelistically disguised nationalization and marketization narratives that obfuscate inequality.

Policy Changes and Enrollment Stratification

The trends examined in Chapters 3–5 focus on this century—the aftermath of the radical change of policy on high schools' educational options and the financing of college enrollment—are recent and illuminate the aftermath. Finally, after some states started alternatives to the rigid national STEM recommendations, there was an upsurge in high school graduation and a reduction in the achievement gap across racial/ethnic groups, adding a modicum of flexibility as states varied programs based on local economic needs and social issues restored some sanity to an otherwise chaotic mess of K-12 education choices, as the case studies further reveal (Chapter 3, see also Part II).

This chapter focused on financial opportunity, the ongoing discrimination against poor people, as illustrated by enrollment stratification across racial/ethnical groups. Pell grants no longer cover a reasonable share of education costs facing low-income students whose parents do not have excess earnings to pay the unmet need to attend a public 4-year college without excessive borrowing. Students who prepare academically for 4-year colleges should have a fair opportunity to attend them. The excess cost of 4-year colleges after Pell translates to debt for low- and middle-income families. Trends with debt for the average borrower are troubling. Many community college students must borrow to attend full-time. Attending part-time leads to delayed degree attainment, at best, an outcome that affects lifetime earning potential (DesJardins et al., 2002).

The college transition rates for high school graduates provide a fair indicator of passing the minimum threshold for college enrollment, but the term access was redefined in the wake of *ANAR* and NCLB. The news is mixed. The gap in initial enrollment between whites and historically underrepresented minorities narrowed again in the 2005–2015 period—and readers could argue the patterns were equitable—but the gap reopened in a more recent period (after 2015). More troubling than the reopening of the gap is the decline in the rate of enrollment for whites and historically underrepresented minorities.

The recent decline in enrollment across groups is troubling. Good jobs that do not require college will make a difference in the future, although Biden's legislative success is too recent to impact the data we reviewed, as is the COVID shutdown of onsite enrollment. The decline in white enrollment and their apparent resistance to 2-year colleges may become the alarm that raises public interest. White middle-class alarm about Black enrollment was one of the triggers that set up MISAA and the subsequent fall of need-based grants. By extrapolation, the decline in white enrollment may also set off an alarm for the conservative interests now undermining public confidence in higher education.

The decline in Native American enrollment this century should be a matter of interest. Across the indicators reviewed, the decline in Native American enrollment is the most alarming. The cultural misfit (Oxendine et al., 2020), the prospects for and limitations of indigenizing curriculum (Waterman et al., 2023), coping with financial, social, and cultural challenges (Rodriguez & Mallinckrodt, 2021), and the appeal of the military (Hembrough, 2020), may be explanations, along with the end of affirmative action (Ly et al., 2022). It is also possible that the decline in Native American college enrollment is a leading indicator. Much like the "canary in the coal mine" this decline could be a harbinger of mistrust, doubt, and disinterest in these vital institutions. We hope this is not the case, but it is a question that merits asking.

Questions

1. How did the history of law and political ideologies influence the trajectory toward expansion and the neoliberal turn?
2. How did the federal marketization of higher education reshape state financing of higher education?
3. What policies—a combination of program changes and funding by states and the federal government—will likely improve diversity at public 4-year colleges, given the ban on affirmative action (affecting 4-year colleges) and quasi-segregated cities and suburbs (affecting 2-year colleges in many locales)?
4. To what extent is diversity in higher education a public good, a legacy of the Civil Rights movement, and/or an inappropriate policy goal?
5. Given the national debt and dependence on student loans, is economic stratification of college opportunities unavoidable? If so, is there a way to ease loan dependence for students in 2-year colleges? Are promise programs a viable, localized approach for promoting college choice?

REFERENCES

Baker, R. S. (2001). The paradoxes of desegregation: Race, class, and education, 1935-1975. *American Journal of Education, 109*(3), 320–343.

Becker, G. S. (1975). *Human capital: A theoretical and empirical analysis, with special reference to education* (2nd ed., Vol. 80). National Bureau of Economic Research.

Bell, D. (1966). *The reforming of general education: The Columbia College experience in its national setting*. Columbia University Press.

Bennett, W. (1987, February 18). Our greedy colleges. *New York Times*.

Bennis, W. (1973). *The leaning ivory tower*. San-Francisco: Jossey-Bass.

Breneman, D. W. (1994). *Liberal arts colleges: Thriving, surviving or endangered?* Washington, DC: The Brookings Institution.

Breneman, D. W., Finn, C. E., & Nelson, S. C. (1978). *Public policy and private higher education*. The Brookings Institution.

Brown v. Board of Education of Topeka, 347 U.S. 483 (Supreme Court of the United States 1954).

Burke, J. C. (1994). The proof is in the performance. *Trusteeship, 25*(May/June), 2–9.

Burke, J. C. (2002). *Funding public colleges and universities for performance: Popularity, problems, and prospects*. SUNY Press.

Cahalan, M. W., Addison, M., Brunt, N., Patel, P. R., Vaughan, T. III, Genao, A., & Perna, L. W. (2022). *Indicators of higher education equity in the United States: 2022 historical trend report*. https://files.eric.ed.gov/fulltext/ED620557.pdf

Carnegie Commission on Higher Education (1973). *Priorities for action: Final report*. McGraw-Hill.

Carnes, B. M. (1987). The campus cost explosion: College tuitions are unnecessarily high. *Policy Review, 40*, 68–71.

Carnevale, A. P. (2007). Confessions of an education fundamentalist: Why grade 12 is not the right end point for anyone. In N. Hoffman, J. Vargas, A. Venezia, & M. S. Miller (Eds.), *Minding the gap: Why integrating high school with college makes sense and how to do it*. Harvard University Press.

Cheit, E. F. (1975). *The useful arts and the liberal tradition*. McGraw-Hill.

Clark, B. R. (1973). The organizational saga in higher education. *Administrative Science Quarterly*, 178–184.

College Board. (2023). *SAT Suite of Assessments Report*. Retrieved February 4 from https://reports.collegeboard.org/sat-suite-program-results

Conroy, E. (November 16, 2023). FASFA Delay complicates student and colleges' financial aid processes. *Forbes*. https://www.forbes.com/sites/edwardconroy/2023/11/16/fafsa-delay-complicates-students-and-colleges-financial-aid-processes/

De Neis, J. (2010). *President Obama outlines goal to improve college graduation rate in U.S.: U.S. Ranks 12th globally, trailing Canada and Russia*. ABC News. Retrieved January 17 from http://abcnews.go.com/WN/president-barack-obama-outlines-college-education-goal-university/story?id=11359759

DesJardins, S., Ahlburg, D. A., & McCall, B. P. (2002). A temporal investigation of factors related to timely degree completion. *Journal of Higher Education, 73*(5), 555–581.

Finn, C. E. Jr. (1988a). Judgment time for higher education in the court of public opinion. *Change, 20*(4), 35–38.

Finn, C. E. Jr. (1988b). *Prepared statement and attachments*. Hearing before the Subcommittee on Postsecondary Education, Committee on Education and Labor, House of Representatives, 100th Congress, 1st Session.

Fuller, M. B. (2014). A history of financial aid to students. *Journal of Student Financial Aid, 44*(1), 4.

Hansen, W. L., & Weisbrod, B. (1969). *Benefits, costs, and finance of public higher education*. Markham Publishing Co.

Hembrough, T. (2020). A study of rural and Native-American college students' military identities, military family history, and reading interests. *Journal of Veteran's Studies, 6*(1), 46–63.

Justia US Law. (2024). *Compulsory Education Laws: 50-State Survey*. Retrieved February 24 from https://www.justia.com/education/compulsory-education-laws-50-state-survey

Knight, E. W. (1919). The academy movement in the south. *The High School Journal, 2*(7), 199–204.

Laidley, T. M. (2014). The privatization of college housing: Poverty, affordability, and the US public university. *Housing Policy Debate, 24*(4), 751–768.

Lee, E. C., & Bowen, F. M. (1971). *The multi-campus university: A study of academic governance*. McGraw-Hill.

Lee, E. C., & Bowen, F. M. (1975). *Managing multi-campus systems: Effective administration in an unsteady state*. Jossey-Bass.

Li, A. Y., & Katri, P. (2024). Does tuition-setting authority determine whether tuition increases at community colleges with new programs? *Journal of Higher Education*, 1–30. https://doi.org/https://doi.org/10.1080/00221546.2024.2301914

Ly, D. P., Essien, U. R., Olenski, A. R., & Jena, A. B. (2022). Affirmative action bans and enrollment of students from underrepresented racial and ethnic groups in US public medical schools. *Annals of Internal Medicine, 175*(6), 873–878.

Obama, B. (2010). *Remarks of President Barack Obama – As prepared for delivery address to joint session of congress*. The Whitehouse, President Barack Obama. Retrieved March 5 from http://www.whitehouse.gov/the_press_office/remarks-of-president-barack-obama-address-to-joint-session-of-congress/

Opal, J. M. (2004). Exciting emulation: Academies and the transformation of the rural North, 1780s–1820s. *The Journal of American History*, 91(2), 445–470.

Oxendine, S. D., Taub, D. J., & Cain, E. J. (2020). Factors related to Native American students' perceptions of campus culture. *Journal of College Student Development*, 61(3), 267–280.

Power, E. J. (1954). The formative years of catholic colleges founded Before 1850 and still in existence as colleges or universities. *Records of the American Catholic Historical Society of Philadelphia*, 65(1), 24–39.

Rodriguez, A. A., & Mallinckrodt, B. (2021). Native American-identified students' transition to college: A theoretical model of coping challenges and resources. *Journal of College Student Retention: Research, Theory and Practice*, 23(1), 96–117.

St. John, E. P., Bardzell, J., Chen, W., Hagan, R., & Samuel, E. (2023). Histories and futures. In E. P. St. John (Ed.), *Co-learning in higher education: Community wellbeing, engaged scholarship, and creating futures* (pp. 316–345). Routledge.

St. John, E. P., & Noell, J. (1989). The impact of financial aid on access: An analysis of progress with special consideration of minority access. *Research in Higher Education*, 30(6), 563–582.

Taubman, P., & Wales, T. (1974). Education on a screening device. In P. Taubman & T. Wales (Eds.), *Higher education and earnings: College as an investment and screening device*. National Bureau of Economic Research.

Thelin, J. R. (2011). *A history of American higher education* (2nd ed.). Johns Hopkins University Press.

Waterman, S. J., Lowe, S. C., & Shotton, H. J. (2023). *Beyond access: Indigenizing programs for native American student success*. Taylor & Francis.

6

REFRAMING COLLEGE SUCCESS

Civic Leadership, Economic Uplift, and Financial Wellbeing

With diverse origins and founding communities, US colleges and universities evolved with varying notions of success. Their founding communities and evolving constituents essentially defined success indicators through decisions to invest resources supporting their development and trusting them to educate rising generations of leaders in civil society and the industries employing graduates. In earlier editions of *Public Policy and Higher Education,* we used a narrow conception of academic success—college completion rates—as the purpose of public investment. Given the chaos of the current period, we restart with a new understanding of the historical patterns of college development, along with how their graduates and research contributed to social and political development.

A change process interwoven with social uplift and economic growth across historical periods, college development is challenged by political extremism on the left and right, leaving few opportunities for the compromises needed for cohesive national development. The overextended neoliberal education regime—governments, educational institutions, and corporations—creates and sustains social divisiveness that is unlikely to be resolved with or without significant changes in educational policy, at least in the near term, because of the growing political divide between the MAGA conservatives on the right and the DEI progressives on the left. Growing educational and economic inequality for the past four decades has seriously undermined this nation's social cohesion. The stratification created by neoliberal education policies creates barriers that will be difficult to overcome in the short term. Building on insights from prior chapters, we place the current chaos in a historical perspective before examining patterns of college completion this century and encouraging readers to reframe their assumptions about college success, starting with an understanding of the ways constituent communities defined success as they invested in colleges. As public colleges privatize, students pay a larger share of education costs. They must weigh their costs against rewards, especially if they and their families have limited financial resources to pay college costs.

HISTORICAL PERSPECTIVES ON COLLEGE SUCCESS

Over two and a half centuries since the nation's birth from the turmoil of the American Revolution, federal education policy has played a transformational, but often unseen and unrecognized, role in national development. From 1776 through 1976, the trajectory toward education development and equity in collegiate opportunity spurred social uplift and economic growth across the nation. Through an uneasy transition, Jimmy Carter's only term and Ronald Reagan's first term as President (1976–1984), the value of education as a public good was recast as notions that (1) market efficiency could squeeze colleges and universities and would reduce federal costs and (2) competition would stimulate college price reduction. Four decades of the neoliberal trajectory are enough, indeed too much, if we hope to reconstruct a vision that can hold the nation's diverse peoples together.

Looking back across historical periods provides insight into the ways patterns of college development were interwoven into community development, economic development, and social and political stress across historical periods (Table 6.1). Colleges developed as community-based institutions across US history. They also contributed to developing local, state, national, and international economies throughout our nation's

Table 6.1 College Development Interacts with Community Development, Economic Development, and Social and Political Stress Across Historical Periods

	Community Development	Economic Development	Social and Political Stress Indicators
Early America (Before Civil War)	Colleges provide moral foundations for leaders in schools, churches, and government	Legal apprenticeships with few university-based medical schools in some universities	North and South differences in economics, slavery, & education opportunity
Industrialization (After Civil War)	College education for trades and professions; math and science expand in liberal arts education	Mechanization of agriculture; industrial age; law, business, health, social service education	Labor disputes in mines and industry; prohibition & roaring 20s; stock crash; great depression
Golden Age (After WWII)	High school diplomas as screening for jobs; mass expansion of—and increased equity in—K-12 and college opportunities	Education attainment accelerates the economy; newer technical universities and older colleges competed	Development of the middle class; women go from work to home, to education; civil rights and anti-war protests
Neoliberal (End of Cold War)	High school as college prep; college for all movement; privatization of higher education	College for all movement; STEM degrees for the global economy; extreme income inequality	Growth of student debt; export of jobs erodes middle class; the "moral majority" enters politics
Post Neoliberal (After 2015, Extreme Divisiveness)	K-12 STEM with flexibility; states recreate pathways for working-class jobs	Attempts to rebuild infrastructure, health care, and computer chip industry	MAGA v. DEI; female medical care at risk; extreme debt; COVID shutdown

history. The constituencies of the colleges and the communities in the public and private sectors that they served also evolved. Political and social stressors also changed across periods. We reexamine the Early American, post-Civil War, the Cold War (i.e., the tarnished Golden Age), and the neoliberal turn (after 1980) before focusing on issues this century, since 2000, and highlight new developments informing the reader's reframing of public policy on higher education, as we transition into a post-neoliberal period.

Education Development in Early America
Looking back at the Early American period, especially the competitive forces between North and South before the Civil War, provides insight into the aims and images of college success that motivated college founding and development. In contrast to the comparatively well-funded English Universities at Oxford and Cambridge, the early US colleges were essentially local, as were the denominational sects of their founding communities—faith-based communities in the North and South before the Civil War. Protestant denominations in the North rebelled against the English Church before colonization, their colleges had weaker ties to the older English Universities and instead, were more aligned with Scottish traditions (Marsden, 1994). Still, the English Church and University model influenced college development, especially in Virginia and the Carolinas. Southern colleges had stronger ties to the English Church (Anglican/Episcopal) than Northern colleges because of the differences in faith between the founding churches and colonies. After the Revolution, the newly formed states evolved their governing arrangements, a process influenced by the *Dartmouth* decision (Dartmouth University, 2024; Denham, 1909).

Colleges and Community Development
The nation's fledgling colleges had poor relations with the English and Scottish universities that inspired the early waves of immigrants. The European institutions were much more prominent, with long histories of academic governance, while US colleges were finding their pathways with strong presidents (Meyer, 2016). The American model of department-based faculty governance did not develop until after the Civil War. From the nation's founding, churches and community leaders were the constituencies that invested in founding and maintaining colleges. Campuses built by slave labor, a practice that continued even after the Revolution, benefited from the severe human inequalities of the period. During the Revolution, the British recruited enslaved Black people into their ranks with the promised freedom after the war (Lanning, 2005). More Blacks fought for the British than the revolutionaries, choices that added to their precarious position across the states after the war. The churches and colleges evolved differently in the North and South, but the college-educated were among the privileged elite.

Churches exerted strong moral authority in communities and colleges, but this form of central control weakened as populations moved West. Before the influx of enslaved people, the Southern colonies relied on indentured servants in the early plantation pattern of agriculture, with tobacco as the export crop, before slavery became the stabilizing economic force. These indentured people were mostly Catholic Irish and Presbyterian Scotts who resisted Protestant control. When they finished servitude, they headed West to Appalachia. Like the flatland colonists, they fought Indigenous people and engaged in the early French Indian War that built the social and military capacity for the Revolution.

They had different attitudes about slavery and formal education than the European Americans running plantations; these regional differences are still evident with states in the old South.

Colleges and Economic Development

In *The Wealth of Nations*, published originally in 1776, Adam Smith (2002) argued that higher education played a vital role in the economic development of nations and offered a differing view of purpose and indicators of college success, emphasizing science and technology in addition to classical content. The push toward science and practical fields was slow before the Civil War. The first national institution at West Point aimed to educate military officers in engineering, military tactics, and infrastructure. The college supplied generals for the North and South, an unusual indicator of college success that lingers nonetheless (Morrison, 1974). The US had different economies in the North and South, so there was no single measure of success—support of industrial development was emerging in the North, the arguments leading to the *Morrill Land Grant Act* of 1862, while the South depended on the plantation economy and culture.

Early American colleges and professional schools contributed to the development of localized economies in the early American period. Besides West Point, engineering education did not develop as rapidly in England and the US as in Western Europe (Lundgreen, 1990). Before the war, there were diverse images of success in US medical education. Some early medical schools aligned with universities; others were private, even for profit. They also had diverse theories of medicine—homeopathic, osteopathic, and allopathic (Slawson, 2012; Snider & Micozzi, 2018). The severe treatment of wounds during the Civil War—amputation of limbs (an estimated 60,000)—created social pressure for change and contributed to the emergence of allopathy as "regular" medicine after the war (Figg & Farrell-Beck, 1993).

Legal education provides an interesting example of local adaptation before the Civil War. There were two forms of legal education: practice-based apprenticeships and collegiate-based and localized moral education in colleges. The English model influenced the evolution of localized early American apprentice legal education: "For centuries, English legal education relied exclusively on apprenticeship and affiliation with the venerable Inns of Court in London. The Inns of Court are a unique learning tradition, a combination of educational institution, boarding facility, and professional association" (Moline, 2004, p. 775).

Unlike Britain, the US evolved state legal systems in addition to American common law. Legal education occurred in decentralized apprentice-based legal education that did not have the stature or continuity of the British tradition. State laws on slavery and other critical matters differed. The arguments that state courts considered varied state interpretations of common law, rooted in the British legal system, followed different trajectories across states and regions. The religious, moral, and legal bases of law differed in courts and enforcement. Legal reasoning about important matters varied across regions, as did the relationships between colleges and local faith traditions, undermining the capacity for common grounding in moral foundations and legal issues before the Civil War.

Colleges Amid Social Stress Before the Civil War

Colleges in the North were increasingly supporting the end of slavery both as moral education and in admissions practices. Oberlin in Ohio and other colleges admitted Blacks. Newly formed colleges in the North were ardently opposed to enslaving people, a value rooted in the evolving faith traditions in the North. The founding of Wilberforce in 1856 for freed Blacks in Ohio, before the Civil War when the *Fugitive Slave Law* haunted communities promoting racial uplift, used this tactical process for Black college development, an altered blueprint followed by Northern religious groups fighting for Black uplift in the South during the decades that followed.

Early American colleges and private, professional schools differed substantially from the English and European institutions that were their predecessor images of education and college success. The *Dartmouth* decision freed many colleges from obligations to states, instead strengthening their reliance on the support of local constituents—the founding communities, churches, and philanthropists. Thus, the many and varied versions of college success were integral to the social and political stress before the Civil War, and their legacies linger in the minds of succeeding generations of their constituent communities across faiths, regions, and industries.

Successful College Development After the Civil War
As noted in prior chapters, the emergence of Land Grant universities during and after the Civil War added new, competitive images of college success. Competing to attract students, new programs, including doctoral studies and professional schools, reshaped the rapidly evolving industrial culture. The community-based and economic development roles of colleges and universities persisted and evolved, as did their intellectual and social contributions to the labor and anti-war movements.

Competition Between Land Grants and Traditional Colleges
The purposes of the new college differed from those of the older ones. Many older colleges were slower to change purposes but eventually competed with science education and alignment with professional education as they became multipurpose universities. The shifting ethos of founding communities and the constituents they served did not mean the older colleges changed their historical missions and purposes because of the competition. They integrated emphasis on math, science, and professional education, but the older liberal arts ethos frequently survived as a secular curriculum.

After the Civil War, some colleges remained fundamentally Christian; many older colleges evolved a community-based liberal ethos aligned with their supporting communities, businesses, and professions. The diversity of colleges was crucial, primarily as states and communities engaged in cultural conflict about the education of freed Blacks, integral aspects of the evolving economies in the South, North, Midwest (i.e., the maturing Northwest Territories), the Southwest, and the West. Of course, the nineteenth-century Indian wars were vital in opening the West, a story yet to be told as an integral part of college development (and the destruction of Native peoples and cultures). Still, one key element to the economic development of the North and South was the education of freedmen and women. Expansion of college for free Blacks transformed with the development of Black public colleges after the civil War. In 1833, Ohio's Oberlin College admitted free Blacks, opening the doors for W. E. B. Du Bois and other Black luminaries of reconstruction to colleges with traditional liberal arts programs (Lawson & Merrill, 1983). Du Bois advocated for access to high-quality higher education, which he described as dubed the talented tenth. After the Civil War, many advocates for Black higher education emphasized education for trades, more basic than the Northern land grants. The battles between the practical education vision for freedmen and the talented tenth ideal embraced by various faith communities motivated the development of Black colleges and universities (Esters & Gasman, 2024). The new institutions had varied allies and served diverse community interests.

Extreme unfettered capitalism unleashed after the Civil War enabled Northern industrialists to see the victory as a license to build a modernizing nation (Teitelman, 2020). Public-private partnerships built the railroads like the nation, created a flow of industrial goods, and expanded agricultural production. The fruits of the period were supported by developing Land Grant colleges in the North and West, along with help from states building their industrial base. The rebuilding of Southern colleges for whites, campuses destroyed in the war, took precedence over new college development in Alabama, Tennessee, Georgia, and other Southern states before the second Land Grant Act (1890) empowered the development of Black colleges for agriculture and engineering and made it possible to invest in Land Grant universities for whites as a new quasi-peaceful period of sustained college development pursued—all predicated on the evolution of the separate but equal doctrine codified in *Plessy v. Ferguson*.

Social and Political Stressors

The French and Indian War was central to building social networks among locally governed militias across the colonies, a form of social capital that made the Revolution possible (Stanley, 1998). Men who'd learned to fight, as did their Native American allies, were among the "minute men" who engaged the British beyond the battlefields. These stories are worth telling but are beyond the scope of our discussion of college development. The Republicans in the North, the legacy of the political plurality for the election of Lincoln, sought to bring Black men and women into public schools. Still, it led to often violent opposition from Southern whites (Boonshoft, 2022).

The troubled reconstruction eventually led to the development of segregated institutions supporting Black uplift in the South. At the time, political support for developing integrated schools and colleges in the North and West was weak, as segregated education swept the nation as an artifact of silence about racism. The marker events—the significant stressors in the social and political spheres—included the stock market crash in 1929 and the Great Depression of the 1930s, leading to extreme political turmoil. The Greatest Generation, the children of the Depression, became the forces for social change after WWII. Still, they, too, remained divided by racial tensions in the decades that followed as education transformed into compulsory K-12 and mass higher education in institutions segregated by the *de facto* practice of silence about racism.

The Cold War: Investing in Education Development

After World War II, the massive federal investment in higher education started with an emphasis on winning the next great war against communism at the outset of the Cold War. The success of the GI Bill spurred social and economic theorists to focus on social uplift and economic development as outcomes of public spending on education. When reconsidering measures of success for this significant shift in policy, it is crucial to recognize that government investment in higher education was a strategy for Western victory in the Cold War, especially after Russia launched Sputnik.

Expanding access through mass higher education was born during the Golden Age when nations invested in higher education to rebuild their economies after WWII. The idea that mass production of college-educated citizens would promote economic development took shape in the 1960s, along with social theories of cross-generational uplift and financial returns on investment (Becker, 1964; Blau & Duncan, 1967). The inequality in the structure of public higher education surfaced after scholars (Hansen & Weisbrod, 1969) examined who benefited from low-cost elite public colleges. The education revolution of nations supporting education equity was global, not just national (Meyer et al., 1977). The idea of local community development shifted to broader notions of social outcomes, including gains in attainment as products of spending strategies. With the historical perspective from prior periods, we reconsider notions of college success concerning community and economic development before outlining some of the emerging social and political stressors.

Community Development in Unequal Times

The 1950s and 1960s were a period of economic growth, and college students could look forward to employment opportunities constrained by implicit inequalities and bias that created barriers to uplift for minorities and women. Supplemental education in reading and math provided through ESEA Title I required parent advisory committees, but schools frequently controlled the selection of parents, limiting responsiveness to many communities. Access to basic math was denied to Black children in Mississippi, for example, as the Civil Rights movement generated community-based interventions, leading to the Algebra Project as a community-based math intervention (Moses & Cobb, 2001). Mechanization of agriculture in the West created new challenges for migrant workers as many were left to find new jobs and schools in the wake of the tomato picker machines (Hightower, 1973).

Universities engaged with communities and constituents on both sides of the cutting edge of technology and urbanization as divisiveness between the wealthy and poor persisted. For example, the UC Davis College of Engineering worked with local agriculture to develop automated tomato pickers. In contrast, the rural sociologists worked with displaced farmworkers to find pathways to new jobs and health care (St. John, 1994). Clark Kerr's (1963) multiversity campuses became dynamic institutions responding to the interests of many communities and constituents. The work of activists in UC extension services and marginalized university-based social science programs did not wield the influence of agriculturalists in the Central Valley or the emerging health care and computer industries in the San Francisco Bay Area. The corporations partnered with the UC campuses, Stanford, and USC, built a more robust state economy as inner-city neighborhoods located near university campuses experienced increasingly concentrated poverty.

Economic Growth and Investment in Education

Educated whites and Blacks benefited from the investment in education as a new Black economic elite emerged while the Black underclass was denied opportunity (Allen & Farley, 1986). Migrant farmworkers in the West and Midwest and inner-city Blacks in Chicago, Los Angeles, and other great American Cities had the most significant numbers left behind (Wilson, 1991). During the same period, rural whites also had income disparity compared to European Americans in the expanding suburbs and the wealthy urban elite.

Following the longitudinal cohorts through college and employment after college and considering the amounts of student aid awarded in the 1970s, a cost-benefit analysis found that the net present value in income from taxes was four times the program cost (St. John & Masten, 1990). The rate of return was four inflation-adjusted tax dollars for the feds for each dollar invested in grant aid, even with Reagan's lowered tax rates (St. John & Masten, 1990). Investing in early reading and math and need-based aid for college students—the pillars of the Federal education programs—helped build the economy. The Reagan administration did not emphasize tax revenue; instead, tax and program cuts were priorities. There was no interest in keeping cost-effective programs, a considerable difference from the Carter Presidency. The neoliberal wrath that shattered these effective strategies—redirecting supplemental support to market-based schools and shifting from grant to loan for college students—was ideological and did not align with the social and economic research that examined the impact of Cold War programs promoting education equity.

Social Stress Tarnished the Golden Glimmer of Education Investment

The social and economic development in the 1950s and 1960s was remarkable, but it also laid the foundations for the new age that followed. The women in The Greatest Generation worked in factories during the war, returned home so the veterans could work, and raised the children, so their daughters would attend college. The rising generation of women became the feminist generation's agitation for fairness in health and education opportunities. Black veterans returned to apartheid in the South: they and their children agitated for change. The image of the middle class portrayed on television—*Leave It to Beaver* and *Father Knows Best*—were not portrayals of the ordinary experience, even if commonly viewed.

The new opportunities for poor urban youth and other students who would not otherwise be able to pay for college reduced disparities but caused resentment. The Civil Rights movement sought to break barriers to education and voting in the South, the stranglehold placed on reconstruction by conservative court decisions in the late nineteenth century, including *Plessy*. On Northern and West Coast campuses, students organized and agitated to address civil rights, the failure of academic organizations to address contemporary issues like the Vietnam War.

Much like other periods of protests, students of the late 1960s and early 1970s were outraged by the hypocrisy. The hidden messages of liberal education texts from the Early American period, including the Bible, were about hypocrites who preached one value and acted on another. The fact the students from the South, North, and West voiced these agonies, making them visible on television, along with the *Beaver*, brought shock to the living rooms of aging WWII vets who'd fought to build a better world and were themselves outraged by Soviet communism sweeping large swaths of the planet after WWII.

Ironies of Neoliberalism

The messages from television and research were messy, complicated, and difficult to understand. By the middle 1970s, economists were warning that the nation had overinvested in education (Cartter, 1976; Freeman, 1975), but the economy and student's demand for education had not yet caught up with the supply of good jobs. Cartter's oversupply of PhD's turned into new scientists in the private sector and social scientists teaching for lower pay than their mentors had been paid at top universities. Labor markets are complex and difficult to predict, as is the demand for education.

Community Development Versus Nationalization

The swirling ideas from economists and social scientists influenced the initial stage of neoliberal reframing. Jimmy Carter, a Democratic President, thought there were more efficient ways to invest in education and health care. His programs created mechanisms that could transform education delivery by giving states more flexibility (Turnbull et al., 1981). Essentially, this argument would have reestablished links between education and their communities.

Instead, the Reagan administration nationalized education policies, only adding barriers between local constituents and their schools and colleges. Unlike Nixon and the prior Eisenhower administrations, Reagan cared less about research and more about cutting social programs. By his second term, his educational policy team had figured out how to manipulate research from education agencies, leading to severe disputes about statistical methods (Becker, 2004; Heller, 2004). The school marketization strategy established some local influence on school themes, but content remained virtually standardized rather than localized. In communities with high poverty, schools lacked funds to deliver, unlike the era of expanding education funding in the Johnson and Nixon administrations.

Education Attainment Amid Economic Uncertainty

The labor market for college graduates underwent a downturn in the early 1970s (Freeman, 1975) when students born after 1950 entered the labor market. The shooting of a student protester at Kent State in 1970 sent a shock wave through the protest movement, perhaps even quieting the student movements (Hall, 1985). Another coincidence is that people born before 1950 had upward mobility, while those born afterward faced cross-generation downward mobility, a statistical reality in the US and Western Europe (Breen & Müller, 2020). Many Boomers are grandparents, sometimes even great-grandparents, who've watched declining opportunity unfold across generations in their families. The cross-generation descent toward downward mobility corresponds with neoliberal policies redistributing wealth from the middle class to the economic elite, resulting from tax reforms favoring the rich. Whether lingering debt and excess of educated adults will affect lifetime opportunities for the generation now graduating from college is uncertain, but the outlook is bleak.

Enrollment predictions have always been a hazardous specialty in education; the expected enrollment decline at the end of the Baby Boom, for example, never materialized. Instead, institutions adapt to changes in society and policy, with factors challenging to imagine, let alone account for in predictive models. Despite a new generation of scholars testing new predictive methods (DesJardins & Flaster, 2013; Toutkoushian et al., 2015)—and perhaps even because of them—the neoliberal education policies have stuck, only with modest changes. Loans still predominate as a federal student aid strategy, and markets prevail over equitable school funding. The refinement in methods is noteworthy, yet a new generation of thought about remedies to the hypocrisies of education policy is essential.

Stressors in Uncertain Times

The MAGA-DEI divide, a theme discussed earlier (Chapter 3), overshadows serious challenges: the severe impact of debt on economic wellbeing and the uncertainty of the STEM agenda. These issues merit public attention unimpeded by ideological divisiveness.

By the early 1980s, it appeared the attitudes of rising generations ceased to value equity as did prior generations (Rokeach & Ball-Rokeach, 1989). In national opinion studies, there was a decline in antiracist and liberal attitudes. The instability of values set the stage for policy changes that cut funding for equity-minded programs, the "me" attitude that ushered in neoliberalism. The valuing of human capital as a reason for college also dropped as students reconciled social reasons for college with the growing dependence on loans (Johnson et al., 2016).

Perhaps more perplexing, the national policies promoting STEM majors have created complicated work-life patterns for college graduates in many locales. Social networks play increasingly important roles in college completion, especially for minority students (Mishra, 2020). An analysis of a longitudinal cohort found that underrepresented-minority STEM graduates were more likely to leave the STEM fields in part because of the local labor market (Lysenko & Wang, 2020). A survey of 2,000 graduating students found that they valued career- and study-related decision-making, when supported feedback and feedforward insights informing students' decisions about work (Bennett et al., 2020). Geo-analysis of employment by graduates reveals that in many locales, college graduates in STEM fields were often underemployed if they lacked the social networks to support moves to places with higher demand for STEM graduates, a plight more likely to impact women and minorities (Lysenko & Wang, 2023). This combination of findings suggests that rather than nationalizing education strategies and priorities, local alignment of workforce strategies should be a priority as a form of education support for community development.

TIMELY COLLEGE COMPLETION ACROSS RACE/ETHNICITY

The National Student Clearinghouse (NCS) provides data on timely completion of 2- and 4-year degrees, using a 6-year standard for both. We set aside the irony that this standard gives three times the time to degree to 2-year enrollment to examine college completion rates by race/ethnic group. First, however, we reconsider the meaning of educational attainment in the ongoing context of Federal STEM education policy.

Rethinking Persistence and Attainment

The 6-year degree completion rate measures timely degree attainment rather than persistence, a process previously conceived as continuous enrollment in the chosen college (Tinto, 1975). The NSC completion rate provides an outcome measure that includes transfer, a more inclusive measure considering both transfer and stop out. Given the accommodation to changes in choices for academic, financial, or personal reasons, the NSC 6-year rate provides a measure of timely completion related to degree attainment instead of focusing on persistence in one institution. Trends in preparation and access (Chapters 4 and 5) provide background for analyzing the NSC degree completion rate in policy studies. Three issues inform this analysis.

Family Finances, College Costs, and Reduced Grant Aid Have Transformed College Choice (Further Stratifying Opportunity)

When Federal student aid policy promoted equal education opportunity (Gladieux & Wolanin, 1976), they focused on three outcomes related to fairness: *access* (whether students enrolled), *choice of college* (unconstrained by cost), and *persistence* (as completion of a degree in the college of choice). As federal policy emphasized loans, some researchers redefined the persistence of continued enrollment from year to year, a measure that allowed for transfer or stopping out for a term (St. John et al., 1991). The NSC measure takes a step toward "timely attainment" by using a 6-year standard for completion rather than continuous enrollment or re-enrollment within a year.

Most currently enrolled students graduated high school after 1985, after curriculum nationalization with higher math and science standard. Thus, the NSC measure also indicates whether the new standard narrowed the race/ethnic gaps in attainment, an impetus for the rationale (Chapter 4). Further, since financial aid policies severely constrain choice, it is essential to recognize college opportunities because of college costs (Chapter 5). When they enroll, students plan to pay for college across the 2–4 years of anticipated enrollment. Low-income families are much more likely than middle- or high-income students to have federal loans as part of college packages, given that federal and state grants fell so far behind college costs.

Timeliness of Attainment Provides a Fairness Indicator

Considering preparation standard and stratified choices, it is reasonable to expect that timely attainment gaps would narrow if students could afford the college they enrolled in. Of course, other academic, social, and cultural factors can influence timely attainment; still, narrowing gaps in rates provides a measure of fairness in timely attainment, and widening gaps provides a measure of unfairness.

In addition to paying the direct costs of attending college with loans, the prospect of being able to pay off accrued debt is a financial factor that affects continued effort to complete college. If there is limited hope of being able to pay off loans, students are more likely to drop out, one of the possible reasons for the declining enrollment rate of Native Americans (Rodriguez & Mallinckrodt, 2021). A British study found that social class influences how students view employment opportunities (Burke et al., 2020), reinforcing the argument that differences in race and social class matter in students' estimations of the economic value of degrees. At the very least, the fear of debt is a possible explanation for not completing degrees and, therefore, contributes to unfairness when measured by changes in race/ethnic gaps in timely degree completion as an attainment process related to wellbeing in the national and local economies.

Timely Completion Is Appropriate for Comparing Systems (in States or Nations)

We used this measure of timely completion of degrees to compare states, a measure frequently considered across nations. Timely completion has long been a policy issue in the US (DesJardins et al., 2002), an emphasis spreading in Europe. A British study found timely college completion contributes to economic wellbeing after graduation and that social origins influence timely completion (Duta et al., 2021). An Italian study found that delayed graduation affects initial earnings, and wage differentials increase over time (Aina & Casalone, 2020). Given the increase in the European Union's crafting of economic and education policy, comparing EU nations is akin to comparing US states. Part II compares NCES completion rates for diverse groups in case-study states as a step toward understanding how policy influences timely degree attainment.

Degree Completion Rates Across Race/Ethnic Groups

Trends in preparation and college choice/stratification provide background for analyzing timely completion. The trend toward equity in college preparation corresponded with the widening gap in 4-year college enrollment by traditional-age students the year after high school:

- The gaps in high school completion rates across race/ethnic groups narrowed this century as states modified graduation course-content requirements in math and science (Chapter 5, Figure 5.1).
- A gap opened between Asian/Pacific Islanders and other groups in the early 2020s, with whites having the most substantial drop in college enrollment rates (Chapter 5, Figure 5.7).

The national rate of 6-year college-degree completion (Figure 6.1) differs for students across institutional types and age groups. The two population types—first-time enrollment by college-age first-year students and persistence to degree completion by all students—are not directly comparable. In contrast to what we observed in trends for high school completion and enrollment, the college completion rates remained stable across groups, but there were substantial and persistent gaps. Whites and A/PI students graduated college (about 70%) at consistently higher rates than the underrepresented minority groups (about 50% or less).

There was a slight improvement in rates for all groups except Native Americans, who showed a decline in enrollment in 2- and 4-year colleges this century. Unfortunately, there is not sufficient NSC data on Native American enrollment to include them in the comparison of groups across institutional types. Yet the combined findings are alarming, given that the decline in college opportunities for Native Americans appears to be related to debt and employment options.

The NSC completion rate is comparable to the racial representation in college enrollment since both statistics include all students regardless of age. Further, the adjustment for population representation provides a fairness indicator in the extent of opportunity, a factor in the intermediate conclusion that stratified opportunity was an artifact of higher education finance policies (Chapter 5). Racial/ethnic disparities in completion rates for public 2-year, public 4-year, and private 4-year colleges follow.

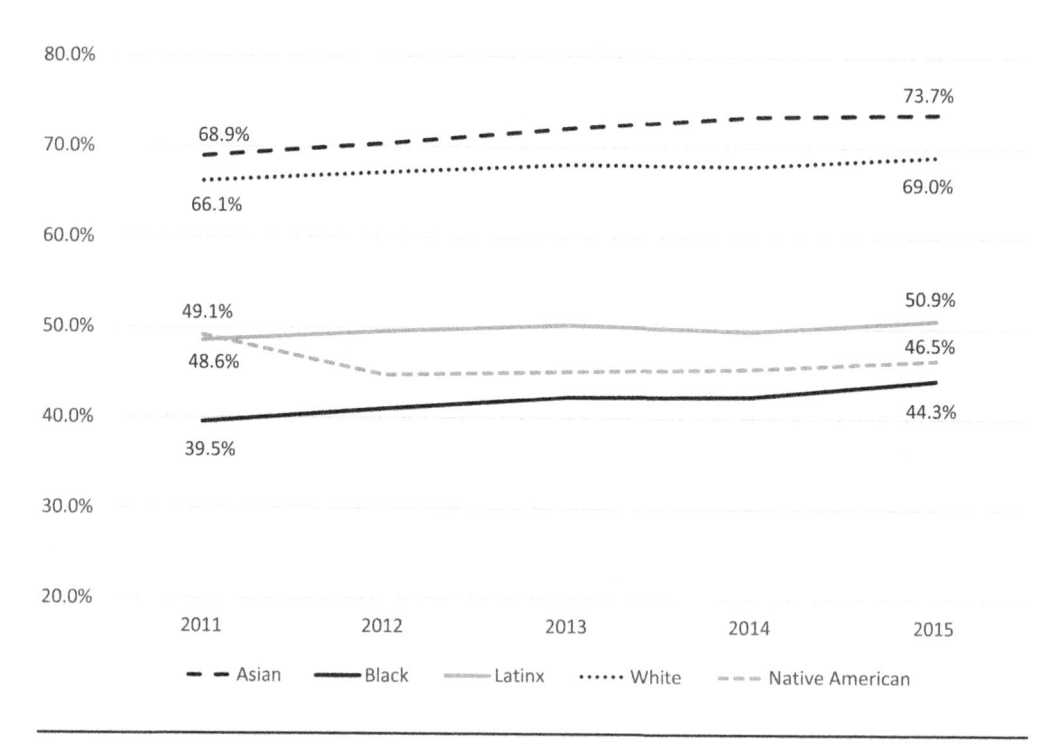

Figure 6.1 Trends in 6-Year Graduation Rates for All Postsecondary Institutions

Source: National Student Clearinghouse Research Center (2023). Completing College: National & State Reports. Retrieved from https://nscresearchcenter.org/completing-college/

Timely Completion at Public 2-Year Colleges

Blacks and Hispanics were consistently and increasingly represented at higher rates in the 2000s, while white and A/PI enrollment dropped (Chapter 5, Figure 5.8). Given the higher concentration of poverty among Blacks and Hispanics, the rising costs of attendance, and the shifting purchasing power of grants, it appears this widening gap was due to costs. College students during the period had complied with higher graduation standards, so lack of preparation, the narrative that shifted requirements, could no longer be the reason for limited enrollment in 4-year colleges.

Underrepresented minorities, Latinx and especially Blacks, completed 2-year colleges at much lower rates than white and A/PI students (Figure 6.2). Differences in the quality of prior education and socio-cultural differences could be factors, but concern about earnings and debt is also plausible and a more likely explanation for the disparity. If, for example, students only occasionally enrolled to improve skills for advancing employment, the behavior would be related to income disparities. US research supports the conclusion that community college students are especially loan-averse (Boatman & Evans, 2017). In England, debt aversion is much greater among lower SES students with lower earnings expectations (Callender & Mason, 2017; De Gayardon et al., 2019).

Timely Completion in Public 4-Year Colleges

Whites and Blacks were represented in public 4-year colleges this century at rates approximately equal to their percentage of the nation's population (Chapter 5, Figure 5.9). In contrast, Latinx increased representation and were overrepresented in the 2020s, illustrating substantial gains in opportunity possibly attributable to Federal funding for

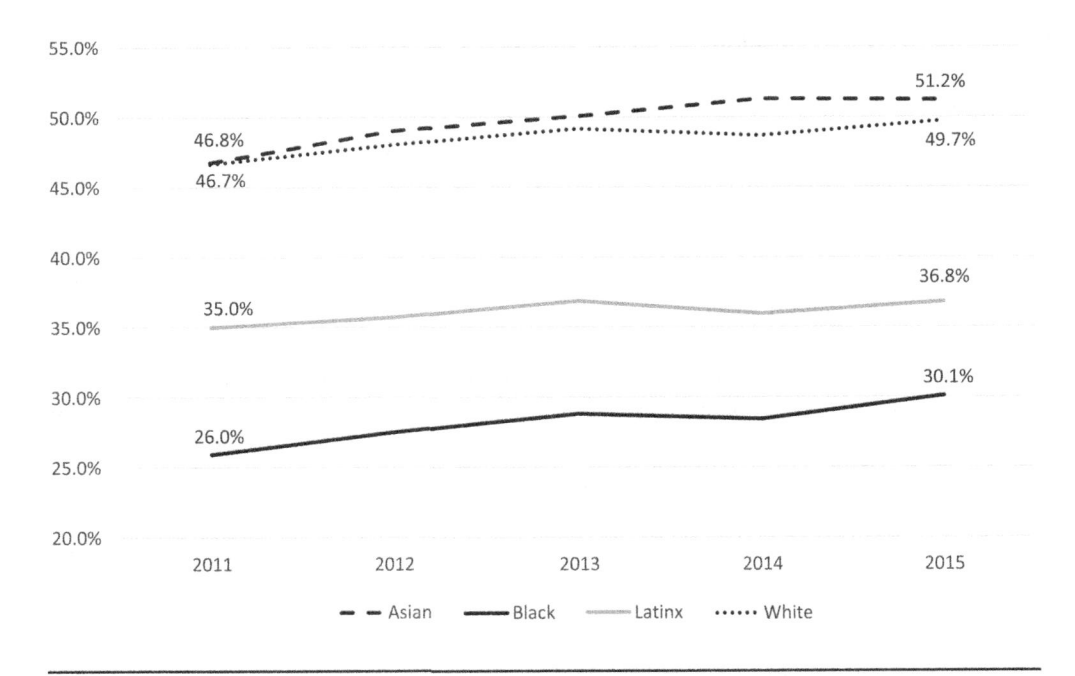

Figure 6.2 Trends in 6-Year Degree Attainment Rates for All 2-Year Postsecondary Institutions

Source: National Student Clearinghouse Research Center (2023). Completing College: National & State Reports. Retrieved from https://nscresearchcenter.org/completing-college/

124 • Reframing Higher Education Policy

[Figure: Line chart showing 6-year degree attainment rates from 2011 to 2015 for Asian, Black, Latinx, and White students]

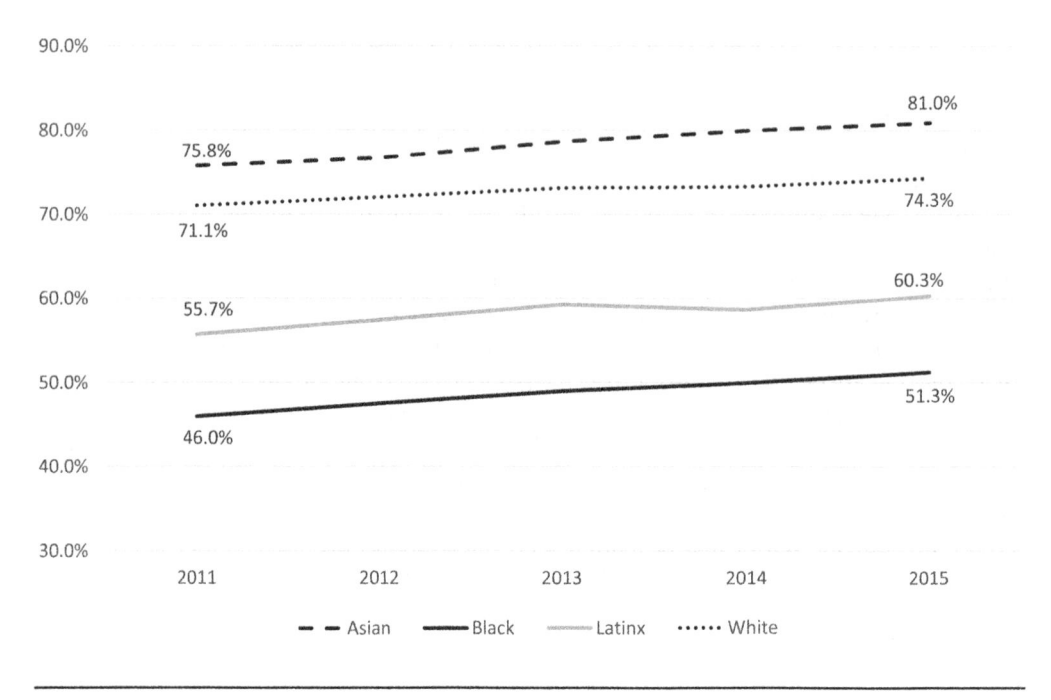

- Asian: 75.8% (2011) → 81.0% (2015)
- White: 71.1% (2011) → 74.3% (2015)
- Latinx: 55.7% (2011) → 60.3% (2015)
- Black: 46.0% (2011) → 51.3% (2015)

Figure 6.3 Trends in 6-Year Degree Attainment Rates for All Public 4-Year Postsecondary Institutions
Source: National Student Clearinghouse Research Center (2023). Completing College: National & State Reports. Retrieved from https://nscresearchcenter.org/completing-college/

Hispanic Serving Institutions (HSI) (D' Augustino, 2021). A/PI students consistently had the most substantial representation.

The 6-year completion rates for all groups improved in the 2010s (Figure 6.3), but substantial gaps persisted. A/PI and whites completed degrees at substantially higher rates than Blacks and Latinx students. For Latinx, the gains in enrollment and persistence, in combination, indicate improved opportunities, probably attributable to increased support for HSI's (Ortega, 2021). However, Latinx students continue to complete at more than 10 percentage points lower rate than whites and 20 percentage points lower than A/PI students. The gap for Blacks is even greater, well over 20 percentage points lower than for whites and about 30 percentage points lower than for their A/PI peers.

These lingering gaps in the opportunity to complete college degrees are troubling, especially for Blacks, the group with the lowest rate of enrollment in public 4-year colleges. It is worrisome because differences in Algebra completions were an excuse for differentials in college opportunity (Pelavin & Kane, 1990), a statistic used to build the case for raising requirements (see Chapter 3). College affordability—rising costs and declines in grants—continue to be the best explanation of the disparity, as it was for opening these gaps in 1980. The continued discriminatory impact of Federal and state finance policies is a public outrage, at the very least.

Disparities in Timely Completion in Private 4-Year Colleges

The enrollment analyses did not include information on enrollment in private 4-year colleges, a decision related to the focus on public finance, though they do rely on federal and state financial aid programs for their students. Private 4-year colleges have slightly

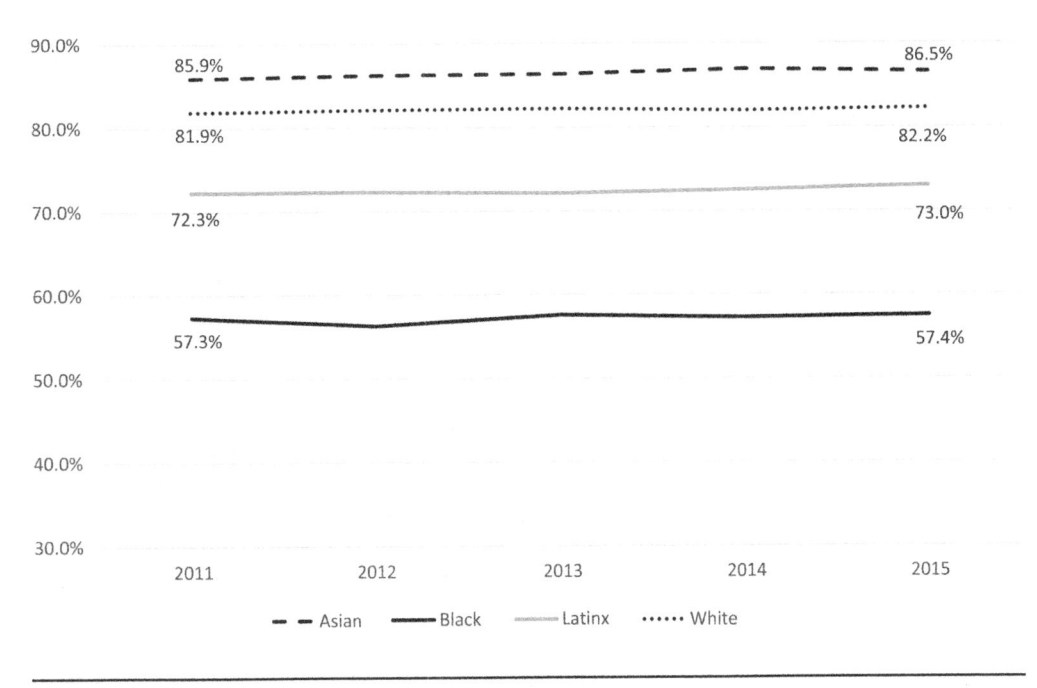

Figure 6.4 Trends in 6-Year Degree Attainment Rates for All Private Nonprofit Postsecondary Institutions
Source: National Student Clearinghouse Research Center (2023). Completing College: National & State Reports. Retrieved from https://nscresearchcenter.org/completing-college/

higher completion rates than public 4-year colleges (compare Figures 6.3 and 6.4), but gaps remain substantial and higher than in the public sector. More careful analysis of the diversity of opportunities in private colleges is critical and timely, especially given the history of price fixing in elite private colleges (Golden, 2007; Salop & White, 1991). In the aggregate, each group appears to graduate at higher rates from private nonprofit 4-year colleges than at their public counterparts, but as we will see in the state cases, there are differences for some racial/ethnic groups.

REFRAMING COLLEGE SUCCESS

In the *College Leadership for Community Renewal; Beyond Community-Based Education*, James Gollattscheck (1976), President of Valencia Community College in Orlando, communicated a vision of college success as renewal of the community. Interviews with his leadership team, including institutional leaders from the social welfare profession, revealed a shared institutional commitment to community development; they supported the inner-city community as they built a multi-campus system serving the growing urban area supporting a burgeoning entertainment and tourism industry (St. John, 1981). The idea of supporting community development was core to the Early American colleges, early colleges for teachers, lawyers, preachers, and other professionals, and the community service ideal of the Land Grant universities.

In these times of extreme haves and have-nots, community renewal efforts must include former students with debt, including graduates and peers who left college for work with a debt burden. The historical review illustrates that colleges have commitments to their founding communities, an idea obfuscated by the narrowing concept of STEM education in service of a global economic order. As colleges organize to serve the global economy, they still have an inherent obligation to support community development as part of the core missions, a necessity in all types of colleges and universities, not just community colleges. More specifically, they are responsible for linking their communities' needs to the broader global social and economic context. There are now three pillars of community building in colleges and universities: serving their communities through leadership development and service, supporting economic development through teaching and research, and collaborating with government agencies and businesses to ensure the financial wellbeing of graduates.

Civic Leadership

As has been the case across American history, many college-educated young adults remain in or return to their communities as teachers, doctors, lawyers, ministers, and in many other roles that support the social capital for community development. By the nature of their work, they have provided civic leadership supporting community building, but not all communities benefit equally, and the problem has worsened since the 1970s when Valencia Community College sought to promote an alternative vision of community renewal as integral to college development. Communities with high poverty have not proven to be able to create or attract job opportunities for STEM-educated adults who return (Hawley et al., 2014), a challenge adding to the extremes of wealth and poverty.

Concepts of civic leadership have evolved across the history of higher education and still motivate the enrollment of many students. The STEM paradigm and the ideal of college for all spread nationally in the 2000s, teachers and medical doctors frequently inspired prospective first-time college students as they were often the only college degree holders that low-income students see routinely (St. John et al., 2011). Mentoring programs expanded the exposure by bringing young professionals and college students into frequent contact with engaged students (Dalton & St. John, 2017). After decades of community-based efforts to expand opportunity, most high school students now know people—including parents, older brothers, sisters, and community members—saddled with debt after leaving college, a more severe reality in inner-city neighborhoods and rural communities.

Economic Uplift

The rhetoric of economic uplift has undergone the most substantial transformations across the two-and-a-half centuries of US higher education. In Early America, finding pathways to college, often through mentoring by tutors in academies, was a possibility for the privileged. Social and financial class uplift was less pervasive as a motivating factor than class reproduction. Families in power in the North, South, and territories moving West wanted to remain in power to ensure their children had opportunities. For the workers of the period, finding jobs that supported families was the shared goal. At the time, most family farms required all family members to work to make a profit and raise the standard of living, so college was usually beyond hope.

The idea of social and economic benefits of college was sold to rising generations for nearly five decades as part of the STEM agenda. At the time, however, the financial benefits of college graduation were in decline. Changes in the tax system favoring the wealthy over the middle class, the STEM agenda transformed high schools, the marketization of universities, and increasing dependence on debt over direct taxpayer support altered the trajectory of public universities. After 50 years of the neoliberal transformative trajectory, the notion of financial uplift has proven true for many college graduates and elusive to others, especially many of the low- and middle-income college students who bought into the dream and paid for it with loans. We use the 2020 Census data of attainment and earnings as the basis for both illustrating opportunities and challenges for graduates with high debt.

Degree Attainment for People 25 Years and Older

More than half of the adult population attended some college (Figure 6.5), less than one-third attained a bachelor's or degree or higher, and 29% had an associate's or some college. About half of the adults attending colleges did not complete 4-year degrees; 28% stopped after high school, and 13% had not completed high school. The extent to which degree attainment is an indicator of success depends on locales—communities, and states—as well as degree attainment as a national indicator of national economic development.

Earnings by Education Level

Adding earnings by degree level indicates the economic value of the individual's investment in paying college costs with family resources or debt. The national statistics combine the "some college" group with the "associates" into an earning category, grouping 2- and 4-year college departures with associate degree recipients. The median income for a high school graduate was $28,700, according to the 2020 Census; completing high school added about $8,000 to the median annual income (Figure 6.6) compared to a high school dropout. Since college costs have grown over the past five decades, older adults had lower debt, while younger adults faced higher college costs and higher debt when they borrowed. A critical question is whether, given the costs of college, completing an associate's degree improved the net income of the proximate half of college-educated

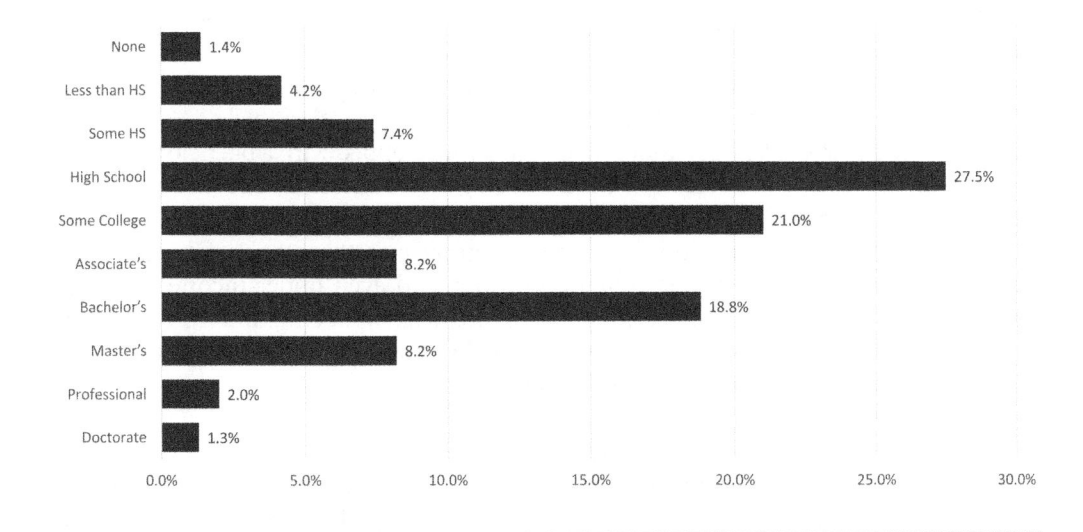

Figure 6.5 Highest Level of Educational Attainment for People 25 or Older in the US (2020)

Source: Statistical Atlas (2023). Educational Attainment. Retrieved from https://statisticalatlas.com/United-States/Educational-Attainment

Education Level	Median Annual Earnings
Graduate Degree	$67,800
Bachelor's Degree	$51,100
Some College	$34,400
HS Diploma	$28,700
No HS Diploma	$20,900
Total	$36,800

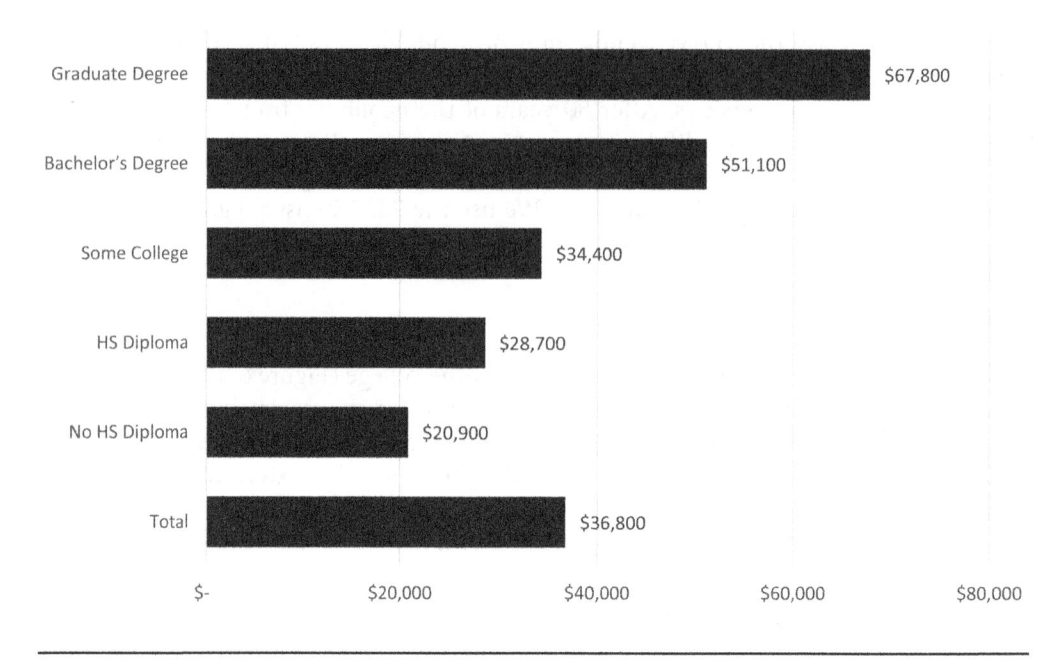

Figure 6.6 Median Annual Earnings by Level of Education (2023)
Source: Statistical Atlas (2023). Educational Attainment. Retrieved from https://statisticalatlas.com/United-States/Educational-Attainment

adults compared to those who completed some college. The answer, of course, depends on the college field of study and locale for employment.

Completing a bachelor's added substantially, about $16,000 annually, to median earnings compared to some college. Costs of 4-year colleges are substantially higher than those of 2-year colleges, but it appears that an additional 2 years has a payoff for individuals, especially after the debt is repaid. Further, completing college adds to the quality of life, at least that was assumed under the old human capital paradigm. Once again, it is necessary to consider debt, the field of study, and the context for employment, including whether graduates are willing to move to attain higher-paying jobs.

People with graduate degrees, about 12% of the adult population, have an additional median earning of about $17,000 more than adults who stopped with a bachelor's degree. Many of the middle-class professions, like nursing and education, encourage further degree attainment by providing higher pay, so many attended part-time. Sometimes, they must borrow to pay the additional costs, cutting into these financial incentives. Medical, business, and law degrees often cost more, and even upper-income students often borrow to pay the costs. The portraits of financial wellbeing among early- and mid-career adults with advanced degrees are complex and dependent on fields, specializations, locales of employment, and other factors.

Financial Wellbeing

The long-term financial wellbeing of people who leave college early or graduate with less than a bachelor's degree is lower if they borrowed in college. The problem is illustrated by recent information on loan repayment, attainment, and earnings. The average cumulative debt increased substantially in the past 15 years, especially for minorities (Welding,

2024). Only about 40% of students borrow, but minorities are more likely to borrow and enroll in 4-year colleges. In contrast, nearly half have some college or associate degrees. Borrowers likely faced loan repayment of $200 or more. Although loan repayment costs climb among borrowers with higher degrees, they also have higher earnings. It is crucial, therefore, to understand student debt burden along with expected earnings.

Loan Repayment

The monthly repayment for federal loans by associate's degree graduates who borrowed is $208 per month (Welding, 2024). The average cumulative federal debt is $19,140 for student borrowers with associate's degrees. Both debt and monthly repayment go up with degree level (Table 6.2). In addition to federal loans, it is not unusual for low-income students to borrow from other sources. The average monthly loan repayment cost declined from $500 in 2008 to $300 in 2020. The 2008 recession changed patterns of student borrowing, including more older Americans carrying student debt, some due to parent loans for undergraduates (Blagg & Cohn, 2022). More debt is now distributed across age and income groups.

The differential in median annual earnings for attaining some college but not a 4-year degree was $5,700 per year compared to a high school graduate. If individuals with some college borrowed and had average debt, the average loan repayment would be about $2,500 per year (12 × $208), nearly equal to half of the pre-tax income gain. In addition, forgone earnings for the enrollment period—accrued if students do not work or less when they work part-time to pursue a degree—add to the cost of education attainment. Given student departure rates, especially for 2-year colleges, the financial risks associated with borrowing to attend college are substantial.

The loan repayment differential for associate's degrees compared to bachelor's degrees is about $1,200 per year, which is favorable given the average earning differential (about $17,000 per year). There were also differences in the debt levels across different types of degrees. Again, contexts matter, such as the families' ability to pay, degree specializations, and locales.

Debt Burden Widening the Racial Wealth Gap

People of color borrow more and face higher monthly repayment costs than white, a doubly troublesome indicator of the growing wealth gap (Figure 6.7). The average debt narrative above best aligns with the experiences of whites who borrow (e.g., the proximate

Table 6.2 Average Student Loan Repayment by Degree (Circa 2020)

Degree Type	Average Cumulative Federal Debt at Graduation	Average Monthly Student Loan Payment (Standard Repayment)
Associate's	$19,140	$208
Bachelor's	$27,810	$302
Master's	$59,110	$688
MBA	$56,850	$662
Doctorate	$80,590	$938
Law Degree (JD)	$145,540	$1,694
Medical Degree (MD, DO)	$210,450	$2,449

Source: Welding, L. (2024). Best Colleges: Average Student Loan Payment. Retrieved from https://www.bestcolleges.com/research/average-student-loan-payment/.

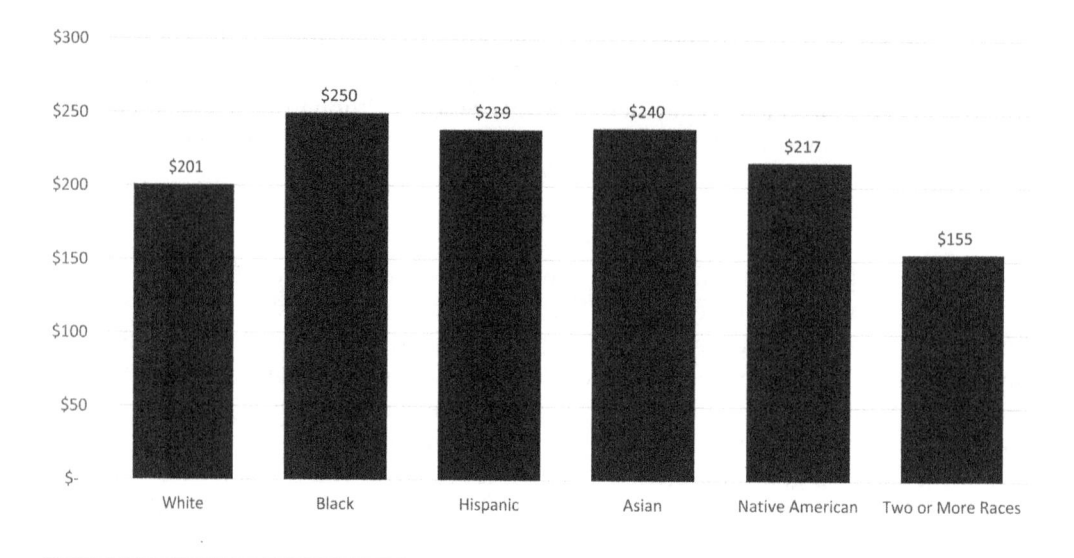

Figure 6.7 Average Monthly Student Loan Payments by Race, 2023

Source: Hanson, M. (2023). Education Data Initiative: Student Loan Debt by Race. Retrieved from https://educationdata.org/student-loan-debt-by-race

$200 monthly repayment). Blacks have substantially higher average monthly payments ($250) than Hispanics and Asians ($239 and $240). Native Americans have repayment closer to the average ($217), but the slippage in attainment in the past decades and the complex economic conditions of reservations complicate their situations.

Local contexts are an especially crucial issue when considering the impact of debt burden as a factor in racial and wealth disparities. The concentration of poverty and unemployment increased in urban minority neighborhoods in the 2000s (Kneebone et al., 2011). By 2021, these wealth differences were complicated by growing health disparities in the wake of COVID-19 (Chen & Krieger, 2021). These entrenched disparities are worsened by student debt, the burden that makes it more difficult for college-educated young adults to return to and support their communities.

College Success for Students in Their States

The long-term financial risks facing most low-income students when borrowing and enrolling are very high. The NSC retention data reveal that less than half of the underrepresented minority students with lower average family incomes will graduate in six years (Figures 6.1 and 6.2). The forgone earnings during years of enrollment, expected earnings, and expected debt made college enrollment a precarious proposition, a possible reason for the declining white enrollment. After more than four decades of federal advocacy for all students to prepare for and enroll in college and the STEM agenda, the pathways to success are far more complicated than envisioned by the advocates.

We are not suggesting abandoning STEM ideas in favor of a return to the 1970s. Instead, we argue for learning from history and evidence to reframe problems, practices, and policies based on that experience. The STEM agenda created fewer high school pathway options and recently broadened modestly in some states. It also pushed comprehensive community colleges toward being transfer programs for state universities, an issue in desperate need of reconsideration. In addition, the rush to raise the state of public 4-year institutions to national status too often glosses over local needs and issues. The workforce development notion is part of a framework for restarting and rethinking. We add to issues that merit attention when and if states begin to engage in this disparately needed process of focusing on workforce development. We examine education degree production as a process of promoting gains in attainment after considering severe problems related to the future of the working class.

Questions

1. Are the concepts of college success—civic leadership, financial uplift, and financial wellbeing—now in conflict because of student debt? How do they influence colleges' marketing strategies and students' college choices?

2. How can colleges align their academic and financial strategies to support student success and the development of aligned communities? How do colleges' diverse origins and purposes influence the competing images of college success?

3. Given the increasing reliance on debt as a cross-generation strategy for paying for college, how should students and their parents frame and discuss options? How significant is debt in adults' decisions to pursue advanced degrees or continuing professional education?

4. To what extent does—and should—the financial wellbeing of people in their local communities influence their academic and financial strategies? How do the missions of colleges (e.g., research universities, community colleges, liberal arts colleges) and their orientations toward local versus national markets relate to these strategic choices?

5. Given the growing economic stratification of communities within the states, variations in states' economies, and their investments in students and public colleges, what role should states play in campus pricing, marketing, and community outreach? How might these success factors—community leadership development, financial uplift of communities, and financial wellbeing of adults, given their student debt—be considered in state planning for higher education?

REFERENCES

Aina, C., & Casalone, G. (2020). Early labor market outcomes of university graduates: Does time to degree matter? *Socio-Economic Planning Sciences*, 71, 100822.

Allen, W. R., & Farley, R. (1986). The shifting social and economic tides of Black America, 1950–1980. *Annual Review of Sociology*, 12(1), 277–306.

Becker, G. S. (1964). *Human capital: A theoretical and empirical analysis, with special reference to education* (Vol. 80). National Bureau of Economic Research.

Becker, W. E. (2004). Omitted variables and sample selection in studies of college-going decisions. In E. P. St. John (Ed.), *Public policy and college access: Investigating the federal and state roles in equalizing postsecondary opportunity* (Vol. 19, pp. 65–86). AMS Press, Inc.

Bennett, D., Knight, E. W., & Bell, K. (2020). Graduate employability and the career thinking of university STEM students. *Teaching in Higher Education*, 25(6), 750–765.

Blagg, K., & Cohn, J. (2022). *How student loan borrowers have changed since 2008. Urban institute*. Urban Institute. https://www.urban.org/urban-wire/how-student-loan-borrowers-have-changed-2008

Blau, P. M., & Duncan, O. D. (1967). *The American occupational structure*. John Wiley & Sons, Inc.

Boatman, A., & Evans, B. J. (2017). How financial literacy, federal aid knowledge, and credit market experience predict loan aversion for education. *The ANNALS of the American Academy of Political and Social Science*, 671(1), 49–68.

Boonshoft, M. (2022). Histories of nineteenth-century education and the Civil War era. *Journal of the Civil War Era*, 12(2), 234–261.

Breen, R., & Müller, W. (2020). *Education and intergenerational social mobility in Europe and the United States*. Stanford University Press.

Burke, C., Scurry, T., & Blenkinsopp, J. (2020). Navigating the graduate labour market: The impact of social class on student understandings of graduate careers and the graduate labour market. *Studies in Higher Education*, 45(8), 1711–1722.

Callender, C., & Mason, G. (2017). Does student loan debt deter higher education participation? New evidence from England. *The ANNALS of the American Academy of Political and Social Science*, 671(1), 20–48.

Cartter, A. M. (1976). *Ph.D.s and the academic labor market*. McGraw Hill.

Chen, J. T., & Krieger, N. (2021). Revealing the unequal burden of COVID-19 by income, race/ethnicity, and household crowding: US county versus zip code analyses. *Journal of Public Health Management and Practice*, 27, S43–S56.

D' Augustino, K. (2021). *An exploration of enrollment and graduation rates as a result of Title V Funding at Hispanic-Serving Four-Year Universities*. University of Central Florida.

Dalton, R., & St. John, E. P. (2017). *College for every student: An Educator's guide for building college and career skills*. Routledge.

Dartmouth University. (2024). *Dartmouth College Case Decided by the US Supreme Court*. Retrieved from https://home.dartmouth.edu/about/dartmouth-college-case-decided-us-supreme-court

De Gayardon, A., Callender, C., & Green, F. (2019). The determinants of student loan take-up in England, *Higher Education*, 78, 965–983, https://doi.org/https://doi.org/10.1007/s10734-019-00381-9

Denham, R. N. (1909). An historical development of the contract theory in the Dartmouth college case. *Michigan Law Review*, 7(3), 201.

DesJardins, S., & Flaster, A. (2013). Non-experimental designs and causal analyses of college access, persistence, and completion. In L. W. Perna & A. Jones (Eds.), *The state of college access and completion: Improving college success for students from underrepresented groups*. Routledge Press.

DesJardins, S., Ahlburg, D. A., & McCall, B. P. (2002). A temporal investigation of factors related to timely degree completion. *Journal of Higher Education*, 73(5), 555–581.

Duta, A., Wielgoszewska, B., & Iannelli, C. (2021). Different degrees of career success: Social origin and graduates' education and labour market trajectories. *Advances in Life Course Research*, 47, 100376.

Esters, L. T., & Gasman, M. (2024). *HBCU: The power of historically black colleges and universities*. Johns Hopkins University Press.

Figg, L., & Farrell-Beck, J. (1993). Amputation in the Civil War: Physical and social dimensions. *Journal of the History of Medicine and Allied Sciences*, 48(4), 454–475.

Freeman, R. B. (1975). Overinvestment in college training? *Journal of Human Resources*, 10(3), 287–311.

Gladieux, L. E., & Wolanin, T. (1976). *Congress and the colleges: The national politics of higher education*. Lexington Books.

Golden, D. (2007). *The price of admission (Updated edition): How America's ruling class buys its way into elite Colleges–and who gets left outside the gates*. Crown.

Gollattscheck, J. F. (1976). *College leadership for community renewal; Beyond community-based education*. Jossey Bass.

Hall, M. K. (1985). "A crack in time": The response of students at the University of Kentucky to the tragedy at Kent State, May 1970. *The Register of the Kentucky Historical Society*, 83(1), 36–63.

Hansen, W. L., & Weisbrod, B. (1969). *Benefits, costs, and finance of public higher education*. Markham Publishing Co.

Hawley, C. E., McMahon, B. T., Cardoso, E. D., Fogg, N. P., Harrington, P. E., & Barbir, L. A. (2014). College graduation to employment in STEM careers: The experience of new graduates at The intersection of underrepresented racial/ethnic minority status and disability. *Rehabilitation Research, Policy, and Education*, 28(3), 183–199.

Heller, D. (2004). NCES research on college participation: A critical analysis. In E. P. St. John (Ed.), *Public policy and college access: Investigating the federal and state roles in equalizing postsecondary opportunity* (Vol. 19, pp. 29–64). AMS Press, Inc.

Hightower, J. (1973). *Hard tomatoes, hard times: A report of the Agribusiness Accountability Project on the failure of America's and college complex*. Schenkman Books.
Johnson, C. L., Gutter, M., Xu, Y., Cho, S. H., & DeVaney, S. (2016). Perceived value of college as an investment in human and social capital: Views of generations x and y. *family and consumer. Sciences Research Journal, 45*(2), 193–207.
Kerr, C. (1963). *The uses of the university*. Harvard University Press.
Kneebone, E., Nadeau, C., & Berube, A. (2011). *The re-emergence of concentrated poverty: Metropolitan trends in the 2000s*. Brookings Institution Metropolitan Program. Retrieved from http://staging.community-wealth.org/sites/clone.community-wealth.org/files/downloads/paper-kneebone-nadeau-berube.pdf
Lanning, M. L. (2005). *African Americans in the Revolutionary War*. Citadel Press.
Lawson, E. N., & Merrill, M. (1983). The antebellum "talented thousandth": Black college students at Oberlin before the Civil War. *Journal of Negro Education, 52*(2), 142–155.
Lundgreen, P. (1990). Engineering education in Europe and the USA, 1750–1930: The rise to dominance of school culture and the engineering professions. *Annals of Science, 47*(1), 33–75.
Lysenko, T., & Wang, Q. (2020). Race/ethnicity, gender, and earnings of early career STEM graduates in the US. *Geographical Review, 110*(4), 457–484.
Lysenko, T., & Wang, Q. (2023). College location and labor market outcomes for STEM graduates in the US. *GeoJournal, 88*(2), 1469–1491.
Marsden, G. M. (1994). *The soul of the American university: From protestant establishment to established nonbelief*. Oxford University Press.
Meyer, H. D. (2016). *The design of the university: German, American, And "world class."* Routledge.
Meyer, J. W., Ramirez, F. O., Rubinson, R., & Boli-Bennett, J. (1977). The world educational revolution, 1950–1970. *Sociology of Education, 50*(4), 242–258.
Mishra, S. (2020). Social networks, social capital, social support and academic success in higher education: A systematic review with a special focus on 'underrepresented' students. *Educational Research Review, 29*. https://doi.org/https://doi.org/10.1016/j.edurev.2019.100307
Moline, B. (2004). Early American legal education. *Washburn Law Journal, 42*(4), 775–802. https://heinonline.org/HOL/Page?handle=hein.journals/wasbur42&div=44&id=&page=&collection=journals
Morrison, J. L. (1974). Educating the Civil War generals: West Point, 1833–1861. *Military Affairs: The Journal of Military History, Including Theory and Technology, 38*(3), 108–111.
Moses, R. P., & Cobb, C. E. (2001). *Racial equations: Civil rights from Mississippi to the algebra project*. Beacon.
National Student Clearinghouse Research Center. (2023). *Completing College: A State-Level View of Student Attainment Rates*. Retrieved from https://nscresearchcenter.org/completing-college/
Ortega, N. (2021). *An examination of the relationship between the developing Hispanic-serving institution (Title v) program and six-year completion rates for latino students at public four-year Hispanic-serving institutions (HSIs) in the United States*. University of Michigan.
Pelavin, S. H., & Kane, M. (1990). *Changing the odds: Factors increasing access to college*. College Entrance Examination Board.
Rodriguez, A. A., & Mallinckrodt, B. (2021). Native American-identified students' transition to college: A theoretical model of coping challenges and resources. *Journal of College Student Retention: Research, Theory and Practice, 23*(1), 96–117.
Rokeach, M., & Ball-Rokeach, S. J. (1989). Stability and change in American value priorities. *American Psychologist, 44*(5), 775–784. https://doi.org/https://doi.org/10.1037/0003-066X.44.5.775
Salop, S. C., & White, L. J. (1991). Policy watch: Antitrust goes to college. *Journal of Economic Perspectives, 5*(3), 193–202.
Slawson, R. G. (2012). Medical training in the United States prior to the Civil War. *Journal of Evidence-Based Complementary & Alternative Medicine, 17*(1), 11–27.
Smith, A. (2002). *The wealth of nations*. Oxford, England: Bibliomania.com Ltd.
Snider, P., & Micozzi, M. S. (2018). Western Origins of natural medicines, nature cure, osteopathy, and naturopathy. In M. S. Micozzi (Ed.), *Fundamentals of complementary, alternative, and integrative medicine* (6th ed.). Elsevier.
St. John, E. P. (1981). *Public policy and college management: Title III of the Higher Education Act*. Praeger Press.
St. John, E. P. (1994). *Prices, productivity and investment: Assessing financial strategies in higher education*. ASHE/ERIC Higher Education Report, Issue.
St. John, E. P., & Masten, C. L. (1990). Return on the federal investment in student financial aid. *Journal of Student Financial Aid, 20*(3), 4–23.
St. John, E. P., Hu, S., & Fisher, A. S. (2011). *Breaking through the access barrier: Academic capital formation informing policy in higher education*. Routledge.

St. John, E. P., Kirshstein, R., & Noell, J. (1991). The effects of student aid on persistence: A sequential analysis of the high school and beyond senior cohort. *Review of Higher Education, 14*(3), 383–406.

Stanley, A. (1998). *European And native American warfare 1675-1815*. University of Oklahoma Press.

Teitelman, E. (2020). The properties of capitalism: Industrial enclosures in the South and the West after the American Civil War. *Journal of American History, 106*(4), 879–900.

Tinto, V. (1975). Dropout from higher education: A theoretical synthesis of recent research. *Review of Educational Research, 45*(1), 89–125.

Toutkoushian, R., Hossler, D., DesJardins, S., McCall, B. P., & Canche, M. G. (2015). The effect of participating in Indiana's twenty-first century scholars on college enrollments. *Review of Higher Education, 39*(1), 59–95.

Turnbull, B. J., Smith, M. S., & Ginsburg, A. L. (1981). Issues for a new administration: The federal role in education. *American Journal of Education, 89*(4), 396–427.

Welding, L. (2024). *Best colleges: Average student loan repayment*. Retrieved from https://www.bestcolleges.com/research/average-student-loan-payment/#:~:text=Data%20Summary,degree%2Dholders%20is%20about%20%24688

Wilson, W. J. (1991). Studying inner-city social dislocations: The challenge of public agenda research: 1990 presidential address. *American Sociological Review, 56*(1), 1–14.

Part II

State Cases

7

THE OLD LIBERAL MODEL

The California Case

In the progressive period after World War II, California became a national and international model for planning and financing higher education. The legacy of the California Master Plan for higher education is well-known among scholars of higher education globally. The 1960 plan for the three-segment system—a state system of community colleges providing local access for all, state universities as comprehensive colleges for mass higher education serving the top-third of all high school graduates, and research universities as the engine of economic development, accepting only the top 12.5%—became a model for planning in other states and nations. The agreement between President Clark Kerr of the University of California and Chancellor Glenn Dumke of California State Colleges resulted in a coordinated approach to the growth of the systems. It provided a framework for the state to become a national leader in public higher education quality and massification.

California's story of systemic educational transformation through political cooperation became an international narrative (Kerr, 1963; Smelser & Almond, 1974; Trow, 1973). The California Master Plan became a frequently told story of systemic educational transformation through political collaboration. The higher education landscape in California has changed dramatically over the past 50 years. The era of political cooperation has given way to contentious policy debates over affirmative action, the value of diversity on campus, the unionization of student workers, and issues impacting undocumented students who attend college.

But the landscape has changed radically, as portrayed in a 2009 press release: "The state's financial crisis is battering its world-renowned system of higher education, reducing college opportunities for residents and threatening California's economic recovery" (Chea, 2009, p. 1). In November 2011, the California crisis became national news when, at the UC Davis campus, campus police pepper-sprayed students protesting tuition increases, resulting in the resignation of the Chancellor. Once again, as if following a California student movement, college prices, and student debt surfaced as major national issues in the 2020 Presidential campaign.

DOI: 10.4324/9781032724867-9

This chapter untangles problems related to the causes of the late twentieth-century decline in the percentage of college-age students who enrolled, followed by recent changes that partially restored the state's lofty status this century. First, we revisit California's legacy of equity in higher education before examining recent trends in K-12 policy and public finance concerning trends in enrollment rates and racial/ethnic representation in the state's higher education system.

CALIFORNIA'S LEGACY OF EXCELLENCE AND EQUITY

The California Master Plan emerged during rapid growth after World War II as a rational remedy for schools and colleges' hodgepodge development. The tension between bottom-up equity, as a legacy of the Bear Flag Revolt, and elitist European Christian values had started with Spanish influence but rapidly transitioned into the American pattern of college development.

From Revolt to Public Systems

In Alta California, much like other Spanish territories in Mexico, education for natives was the primary research for starting Spanish-speaking schools in missions; dotting the state from San Diego to Sonoma, the missions sought to transform the natives into industrious Christian enslaved people (Allen, 2010). California Indians provided farm labor during the Spanish period of agricultural development as the state engaged in international free trade. Many immigrants arrived, mainly by clipper ships. By the 1840s, people with British and American surnames were among the recipients of land grants; Mexico's strategy for stimulating economic development.

The Bear Flag Revolt in 1846 was essentially an American conquest (Kelsey & Foy, 1946). The Gold found in Sacramento in 1848 transformed the economy and sparked Laborers to leave the rancheros for the gold fields, and new immigrants arrived overland. After the Bear Flag revolt, the new state rapidly followed the early American blueprint for education development, with primarily independent, faith-centric schools and colleges. The first English-speaking school started at the Santa Clara Mission before the Bear Flag Revolt and the Gold Rush. In 1851, the predecessor of the University of Pacific, a Methodist campus, started as a private high school in the Central Valley. Combining high school with collegiate education was also the pattern across the US. Founded in the 1950s, Santa Clara, Notre Dame de Namur, and the University of San Francisco were Catholic universities in the San Francisco Bay Area, the port for gold and grain before that. The Catholic influence on college founding illustrates the link between the Spanish heritage and the history of the missions, a different faith tradition than most American colleges founded during the period. Mills College for Women in Oakland and Stanford in Palo Alto, founded by a railroad builder, were also among the Bay Area colleges established in the 1850s.

The state's citizens actively engaged in advancing public education before the Civil War. A normal school in the 1850s established by the state legislature eventually became San Jose State University. Lowell High School, founded in 1856, is now the oldest public high school west of the Mississippi. After the Civil War, public education rapidly developed. In the first decade of the 1900s, agricultural colleges developed high schools in Davis, San Luis Obispo, Bakersfield, and other farming communities in California. Agricultural education also became part of high school textbooks (Howley et al., 2013).

The 1849 state constitution recognized the role of a state university with branch campuses. Still, it took the Land Grant Act for the state to create UC Berkeley through a public-private partnership. The College of California, founded in Oakland in 1855, merged with the new College of Agriculture and Mines in 1868 and became the University of California in 1870 (Britannica, 2024; Editors of the Encyclopaedia Britannica, 2024). It was a free public university open to all who met the admission standard, the founding faculty had classical admission standard emphasizing languages, and the campus was fraught with uncertainty and political battles during its first three decades (Douglas, 2018). UC San Francisco began as a medical campus in 1878, the Davis campus started as a farm in 1908, and UCLA began as a branch campus in 1919. The tensions between equity and quality became a core tension in the UC system as it began to compete with teachers' colleges emerging across the state.

Agricultural development in the fertile Central Valley and the expanding economy of Los Angeles became engines for population growth during the Great Depression as the push for education development took shape in the state. The Dust Bowl drove farmers west to become farmer laborers as the Agricultural industrial economy emerged in central California cities (Gregory, 1991); the severe discrimination against Mexicans created opportunities for Black laborers migrating to Los Angeles from the South (Sides, 1999), and New Deal projects created jobs in cities across the nation, especially in LA (Boustan et al., 2010). California education steadily developed before World War II, and even as the population moved westward in the Depression years, teacher's colleges were striving to become universities. Local communities advocated for normal schools, which became teacher's colleges and sought to become universities.

The legislature recognized the need for more postsecondary opportunities as the population grew in the early twentieth century. It authorized high school districts to create junior colleges in 1908, with the first starting in Fresno in 1910. Private colleges lobbied for support, especially given the low cost of public colleges (charging only registration fees, room and board, and other ancillary costs). When the GI Bill brought waves of Veterans to the state, public colleges swelled even more rapidly. The state student aid programs began in 1955 with programs that considered both merit and financial need (California Student Aid Commission, 2020).

The California Master Plan

California's Master Plan set the state on a trajectory to greatness in its higher education system. The differentiated system was not only a model for other states and nations, but California also had the best college enrollment rate in the nation and more top-rated research universities than any other state. Staying the course was often difficult since the system resisted change in the face of new challenges. This approach eventually resulted in eroding enrollment rate of college-age students during the late twentieth century, due to an acute financial crisis (Daun-Barnett & St. John, 2018). The University of California grew in academic distinction after a faculty revolt in 1919. Berkeley was the first university with the direct delegation of authority over academic matters given faculty, distinct from the strong-president model that dominated US higher education (Fitzgibbons, 1968; McConnell & Mortimer, 1970). As in many other states, higher education evolved largely based on community advocacy and competition among college campuses. By the 1940s, the University of California had developed a multi-campus system. Teacher normal schools (e.g., Chico State College) were combined with technical colleges (e.g., Pomona), and comprehensive colleges (Los Angeles) were formed into a state college system in the first half of the twentieth century; community colleges also emerged, usually in partnership with school districts.

With the return of World War II veterans to California campuses after the passage of the GI Bill, the campuses began to grow, especially the state colleges and universities. There was tension among the systems, but there was also plenty of opportunity to grow, given the rapid growth of the state population. Indeed, the Plan was a triumph of planning over chaos (Kerr, 1963; Smelser & Almond, 1974); it guided the development of three multi-campus systems: the University of California, California State Colleges and Universities, and California Community Colleges.

Within this scheme, state colleges and universities had an opportunity to grow, while the campuses of the University of California had the chance to concentrate on research excellence. UC Berkeley became the icon of the research university (Kerr, 1963), and UC Davis, UC San Diego, and UC Irvine also became leading research universities, often counted among the nation's top institutions. At the same time, California state colleges and universities and California community colleges also became models for developing state education systems. As part of the Master Plan, California committed to low tuition and high grant aid despite serious financial challenges (Lee & Bowen, 1971, 1975). California maintained a commitment to low tuition and high grant aid despite severe financial difficulties after neo-conservative tax policies constrained state funding and the UCs' opportunities for further growth.

California was more successful than most states in keeping tuition low and aid relatively high. As we will see below, the Great Recession challenged the California model and placed significant financial pressure on a system bursting at the seams with high student demand. For several years, California 4-year campuses raised their tuition rates dramatically, but they also made historic commitments to increasing need-based student aid. California remains a beacon for a more liberal approach to higher education finance. The state has also been a bellwether for critical issues facing higher education nationally, including the earliest debates over free speech, the role of affirmative action in college admissions, the use of the SAT in the college admissions process.

Weathering Political Storms

Soon after finalizing the Master Plan, the Free Speech Movement (FSM) started in 1964 at the University of California (Cohen & Zelnik, 2002), immediately impacting the political sphere. In his run for governor in 1968, Ronald Reagan campaigned against the protesters and the image of liberal intellectuals. Early in his first term, he focused on the UC budgets (Evans, 1) and implemented the first education fees. At the same time, students lobbied within campuses to use funding for student-oriented programs, including peer advising and other programs, to engage students. As at many universities, the institutions within the UC system weathered the storm of student protest by adapting and finding new ways to involve students in the governance mechanisms (McGrath, 1970; St. John & Regan, 1973). A new center was established at Berkeley that focused initially on governance, with an eye to UC becoming a national model (Glenny et al., 1975; McConnell & Mortimer, 1970).

After being pushed out of the presidency of the UC system by Governor Reagan, Clark Kerr went on to head the Carnegie Commission on Higher Education, providing a new phase of leadership to the nation (Carnegie Commission on Higher Education, 1973).

Kerr continued to provide national leadership in higher education (Kerr, 1978) and public commentary for the next two decades (Kerr, 1991, 1994, 2002). Kerr was not alone in leaving a leadership role in California higher education to go on to make national policy recommendations: Pat Callan, former commissioner of the California Postsecondary Education Commission (CPEC), has provided leadership in higher education finance (Callan, 2002, February; Callan & Finney, 1997), and former commissioners of California's student aid system have led national and international studies (Kipp et al., 2002; Marmaduke, 1988). Because of the California system's visibility and adherence to a distinctive model of governance and finance, leaders in the system frequently become national leaders in higher education.

Constrained Tax Revenue

Governor Reagan was the harbinger of a new era, implementing education fees for the time during his first term and constraining the authority of the UC Board of Regents. Reagan's conservative budget tactics jeopardized the constrained growth of the UCs and state colleges (Evans, 1971). After the passage of Proposition 13 in 1978, California capped property taxes, which has severely constrained tax revenues. As one *LA Times* reporter (O'Leary, 2009, p. 1) put it: "Before Prop 13, in the 1950s and '60s, California was a liberal showcase. Governors Earl Warren and Pat Brown responded to the population growth of the postwar boom with a massive program of public infrastructure—the nation's finest public college system, the freeway system, and the state aqueduct that carries water from the well-watered north to the parched South."

For decades, attempts by liberal leaders to get around the provisions of Proposition 13 failed (O'Leary, 2009, p. 1): "Beholden to a tax-averse electorate, the state's liberals and moderates have attempted to live with Proposition 13 while continuing to provide the state services Californians expect—freeways, higher education, prisons, assistance to needy families and, very important, essential funding to local government and school districts that vanished after the anti-tax measure passed."

Proposition 13 was not the only voter-passed ballot initiative constraining taxpayer support. The following year, Proposition 4, known as the Gann Amendment, limited most state and local government expenditures from tax sources: "The Gann limit, as it is often called, was not exceeded [i.e., limits on tax increases] until the 1986–87 fiscal year when $1.1 billion was refunded to taxpayers" (Institute of Governmental Studies, 2003). In addition, in 1988, California voters amended the State Constitution in Proposition 98 to establish "a minimum annual funding level for K-14 schools (K-12 schools and community colleges). Proposition 98-related funding constitutes over 70% of total K-12 funding and about two-thirds of total community college funding" (Legislative Analyst's Office, 2005). After Proposition 13 restricted increases in property taxes for schools, Proposition 98 ensured that other state revenues would be redirected to K-14 education, thus limiting tax revenues for colleges and other state functions. These later provisions provided modest protection for funding for public schools and community colleges but did not accommodate future enrollment growth; therefore, it was possible to cut funding per student to public schools as the school-age population grew. Further, the 4-year institutions did not have this minimal protection in a severely constrained tax environment.

Combined, these constraints handcuffed the state's efforts to fund higher education consistent with the Master Plan. There was substantial redirection of state tax revenues to local schools in subsequent years; the anti-tax contingent imposed several constraints on the state's ability to raise new taxes, causing a retracing in state financing of higher education along with other public enterprises in the state (St. John, 1994b). Indeed, it has long been evident in California that it would be necessary to restructure the higher education finance system to meet the expected student demand. Rather than engaging in a comprehensive restructuring of higher education, state leaders sought short-term fixes.

In California, there was a sustained pattern of resistance to market-based remedies to the financial constraints on growth. In the late 1980s, after an update to the master plan called for dozens of new universities that the state could not afford, St. John undertook a study for the California Postsecondary Education Commission (CPEC) that focused on state strategies to improve affordability. It became apparent that Minnesota's market model could be adapted to address the challenge in California (St. John, 1991). Analyses conducted initially for CPEC demonstrated that tuition increases, linked with increased investment in student aid, could be utilized to expand universities in response to growing student demand (St. John, 1994a). The problem in California, as in other states then, was that the historic commitment to low tuition represented a vital issue among liberals who constrained changes through the state's budgeting process. Other states adjusted incrementally to high tuition—and a few of these states (e.g., Minnesota, next chapter)—have made substantial investments in need-based student aid when desperately needed. However, California stuck to its goal of providing mass higher education with low tuition and state grants for high-achieving, low-income students who attended the state's private colleges. After decades of conflict and declining opportunity, California raised tuition dramatically and invested in grants; the impact on collegiate opportunity is now evident.

A Renewed Focus on Expanding Opportunity

During the 1990s and 2000s, higher education access was a significant topic among researchers and policymakers in California as the state engaged in debates about the renewal of the master plan. Much of the discussion has focused on expanding enrollment and equalizing opportunity, leading to growing problems with inequality, especially for the UC campuses. The demise of affirmative action and the problematic disparities in enrollment opportunities for low-income Latinx and Blacks have been lingering concerns for California, and both merit attention.

In 1996, California was the first state to ban affirmative action. The state entered the debates on affirmative action in the 1970s when UC Davis Medical School's admissions practices became a national issue. The Supreme Court's 1978 decision on *Regents of the University of California v. Bakke* established the framework for affirmative action—outlawing quotas but allowing consideration of race—that had held up legally for more than four decades until the recent *Students for Fair Admissions, Inc. v. Harvard College* Supreme Court decision. Now, selective colleges and universities nationwide are no longer allowed to consider race in college admission, codified in California law nearly two decades before the *Harvard* decision. The UC Board of Regents issued SP-1 and SP-2 in 1995, banning affirmative action in admissions and contracting. In 1997, California voters passed Proposition 209, effectively codifying the UC ban across the state (Chapa & Horn, 2007). In 2001, the Board of Regents rescinded both SP-1 and SP-2, but Proposition 209 made that decision largely symbolic by that point.

Within the UC system, utilization of subject-matter SAT scores was debated (Rothstein, 2002), but with excessive demand, the system simply did not adjust sufficiently.

UC stands in marked contrast to the University of Texas, which adapted to similar constraints by adopting a top 10% plan providing admission based on class rank—an approach that was more successful in maintaining existing levels of racial and ethnic diversity across the system (Chapa & Horn, 2007). The decline in representation of African Americans and Latinx in the UC system continued (Gándara, 2002, 2005; Gándara et al., 2006), which also occurred in Texas. The difference is that Texas was able to respond and adapt more effectively under its 10% plan than California was able to do under its subsequently adopted and more anemic 4% plan for admission to UC. The Texas plan was more effective as a remedy to the elimination of affirmative action in college admissions because it recognized that schools remained heavily segregated and that the guarantee to the top 10% of each high school class was likely to represent the local population of the school. Additionally, they could gain admission to the school of their choice, which placed considerable pressure on UT–Austin.

The decline in opportunity in the state and the fall from the top half to the lower half of states in college enrollment rates corresponded with increase enrollment disparities for California's underrepresented students (Gándara et al., 2006; Orfield, 1988). There has been extensive research on inequalities in opportunity in California, with most of these studies focusing on issues related to academic advising and advanced courses (McDonough, 1997; McDonough & Fann, 2007; Tierney & Hagedorn, 2002; Tierney et al., 2005). This wave of research has been compelling in revealing the links between school culture college aspirations. For example, Tierney and Venegas (2007) examined how high schools convey to students whether college is possible, including whether they provide information on college options and student aid. Cultural reproduction of an undereducated working class had evolved, especially in urban and rural parts of the state.

The underlying problem of public finance—how the state coordinates public funding to build campuses and fund students—received relatively little attention. Researchers have raised the topic of student aid (Fitzgerald & Kane, 2003) and the affordability of community colleges (Zumeta & Finkle, 2007). However, most commentaries remained critical of increasing tuition and grants as a coordinated strategy for expanding supply and improving affordability. Until recently, tuition at public colleges in California had been low compared with other states, but balancing appropriations with tuition and grants, a strategy that worked in other states (Hearn & Anderson, 1989, 1995; St. John, 1991, 2006), did not receive serious attention in California.

Demographic Changes

California is unique in the US; it has the largest population, is the most racially and ethnically diverse, and has the largest Gross State Product (GSP). However, the demographic context is complex and influenced by countervailing trends. Consistent with other states, California is becoming an increasingly educated labor force. In 2022, 44.8% of adults (aged 25–64) had attained at least an associate's degree, while 15.4% had not completed a high school credential (U.S. Census Bureau, 2023). In addition, the ethnic diversity of the state reflects both its position on the Mexican border, with a growing Latinx population, and its position on the Pacific Coast, with a relatively high Asian population.

California also has had two economies that depend on two different patterns of immigration: Latino/a immigrants, many of whom are undocumented, providing low-cost labor, and educated workers from other states and nations to fuel the state's high-technology economy in Silicon Valley and beyond. These conditions add to socioeconomic status, diversity, and social class extremes. These demographic factors help frame the state's K-12 and higher education policy issues.

Diversity in the State's Population. California became a "majority-minority state," meaning that white Californians have constituted less than half of the total state population since the 1990s. By 2006, more than 36% of California's population was Latinx and nearly 13% Asian Americans. In contrast, only about 6% identified as African American, down from about 8% in 1992, and less than 1% were Native Americans (St. John & Moronski, 2013). It is critical to keep this racial balance in mind when building an understanding of the policy discourse on race and education equity. These trends also suggest that the growing class differentiation in California may have racial undertones.

An Undereducated Working Class. The growing immigrant population across California has increased the percentage of the undereducated population during the 1990s. Like many states, Latinx have recently attended college in CA. The state has a sizeable undereducated population and, at the same time, plentiful jobs for citizens with college degrees. The percentage of the population that graduated from high school has fallen behind other states: the percentage of the population with a high school diploma in California grew to approximately 84% compared to 87% nationally (National Center for Education Statistics, 2023). More than 20% of the state population has completed only a high school diploma, including GED recipients, which is a difficult path to bachelor's completion. These undereducated adults work for low wages in agriculture, construction, and other trades and hold down wages for the traditional working class in the state until recently (Sumagaysay & Agrawal, 2023).

Legacy of Political, Social, and Economic Change

California has weathered waves of political and social transformations: from Spanish colonization to the Bear Flag Revolt; from waves of European and Asian immigrants mining gold and building railroads to a booming postwar economy; from master planning for rapid development of mass education to neoconservative public finance and tax constraints; from immigration with farm laborers and elite Asian STEM professionals to a renewed challenge to rebuild education with multiple pathways to education and economic success.

Now, California has a higher percentage of adults (between the ages of 25 and 64) with a bachelor's degree or above than the nation (U.S. Census Bureau, 2023). It is a globally recognized, knowledge-based, innovation-driven, high-technology economy that depends on an educated labor force. California has attracted college-educated workers from the rest of the US and from Asia, a pattern that contributed to new racial inequalities and economic disparities. In addition, California has had a relatively large Asian population since the late nineteenth century, when Chinese immigrants provided labor for railroads and other infrastructure development. Since the internment of the Japanese during WWII (Newton, 2006), California became an open-access education system for Asian Americans. Since voters decided to end affirmative action, higher education has transformed as Asian American/Pacific Islanders became the largest group on some UC campuses (Watanabe & Lu, 2020) and the state created new education pathways for the growing Latinx population (Contreras, 2019).

CALIFORNIA'S EDUCATIONAL POLICIES

The transitions in California's public policies and educational outcomes are complex and interrelated. Whereas a substantial portion of the problem with growing inequality and decline in opportunity in the state seems linked to tax constraints, the inability of the state to adjust state finance policies to new contexts accelerated the decline in the late twentieth century. After years of educational decline attributable to tax constraints, activism at the local and state levels created new tax laws and used funding for education and new environmental initiatives (Haggard & Kaufman, 2018). The latest wave of reform was not a product of central planning but of social action starting at the grassroots level.

It is not a pretty story, and it could have been better had the state recognized the structural problems created by tax revenue constraints and adapted public policies. In the prior version, we spoke more in-depth about eliminating affirmative action in college admissions in the state; since the *Harvard* case of 2023, race-based affirmative action is no longer allowed in any state. California's most significant higher education policy change has been its shift toward high tuition and aid—the model first embraced by Minnesota (next chapter).

High School Reform

In 1992, California was among a minority of states that required two math courses for high school graduation (Table 7.1). The state added Algebra I as a minimum graduation requirement in 2003 and a mandatory exit exam in 2006. California did not experience the enrollment gains these policies might have intended. However, the state has had difficulty maintaining adequate capacity to serve the needs of the growing high school graduate cohorts.

California was an early adopter of statewide high school graduation requirements. In 1986–1987, the California Education Code specified a minimum of courses students should complete during their high school career (left column, Table 7.1). Before that, students had two pathways to a high school diploma: a local set of requirements established by a district or the college preparatory curriculum, now referred to as the A-G requirements for admission to the University of California (UC) and the California State University (CSU) systems (right column, Table 7.1). What receives less attention is that California includes a provision that says, "The local governing board of the LEA, with the active involvement of parents, administrators, teachers, and pupils, shall adopt

Table 7.1 California High School Graduation Requirements

State Minimum Requirements	A-G Requirements (UC & CSU)
English—3 years	English—4 years
Math—2 years, inc. Algebra I	Math—3 years, Algebra I, Geometry, Algebra II
Social Studies—3 years	Social Studies—2 years, US History, + social science
Science—2 years Biological & Physical	Science—2 years, Biological & Physical with labs
Arts/World Language/CTE—1 year	Arts—1 year visual/performing arts
Physical Education—2 years	World Language—2 years same language
Ethnic Studies (2029)—1 year	Elective—1 year

Source: California Department of Education (2023c). State Minimum High School Graduation Requirements. Retrieved from https://www.cde.ca.gov/ci/gs/hs/hsgrmin.asp

alternative means for pupils to complete the prescribed course of study" and they provide several examples for those alternatives, including career technical education (CTE) courses, courses offered by regional occupational training centers, or some demonstration of practical skills or work experience (California Department of Education, 2023b), which is consistent with a growing shift toward providing multiple pathways for high school completion.

In addition to providing greater flexibility regarding course requirements for high school completion, California also eliminated its mandatory high school exit exam. The California High School Exit Exam (CAHSEE), approved by the California legislature in 1999 for the graduating class of 2006, aligned with the federal policy priorities of the time, first from the Clinton administration and then into George W. Bush and No Child Left Behind, his signature reauthorization of the Elementary and Secondary Education Act (ESEA). California suspended the test for three years, but in 2017, Governor Jerry Brown signed a bill abolishing the CAHSEE. Eventually, the state allowed students who had failed the test to earn their diplomas (Harrington & Fredberg, 2017). Exit exams remain a significant constraint that policymakers imposed on education through the neoliberal period, and California is not alone in eliminating or loosening this requirement.

Financing of Higher Education

The financing of higher education in California, historically a topic of national interest (Hansen & Weisbrod, 1969), has changed in recent decades. California maintained a historic commitment to low tuition and high aid until approximately 2008–2009 when significant increases in tuition and fees began for in-state students at 4-year public colleges and universities. As Figure 7.1 illustrates, the tuition increases were prominent between 2008 and 2012, corresponding with the timing of the Great Recession. Since then, the

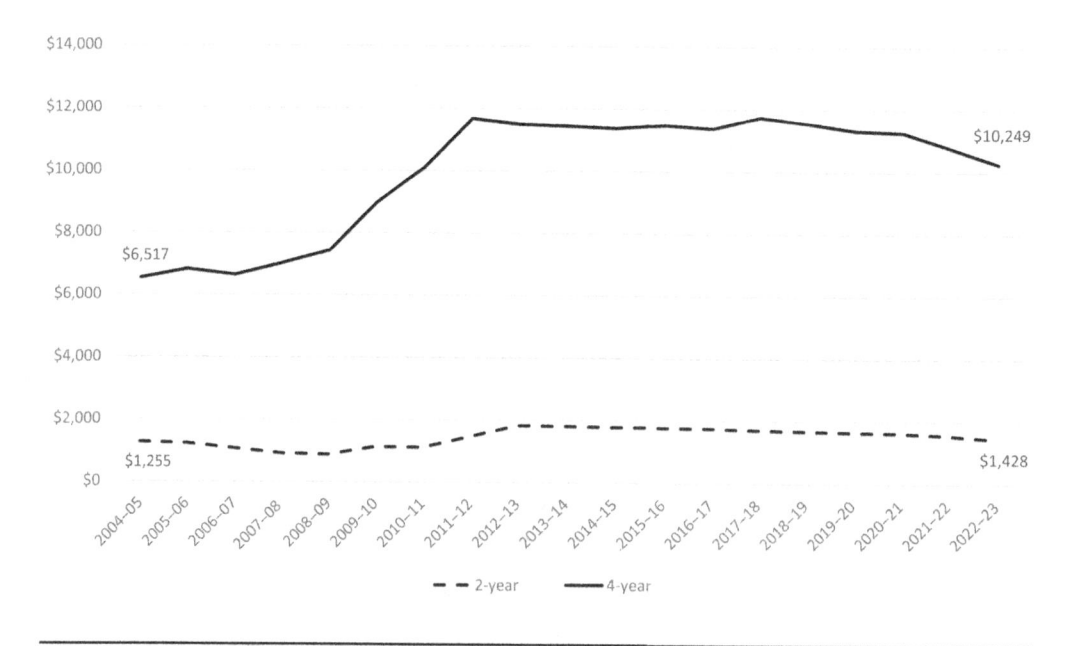

Figure 7.1 Trends in California Public Tuition & Fees (in 2022 dollars)
Source: Ma and Pender (2023). Trends in College Pricing and Student Aid 2023. New York: College Board.

rates have remained stable when adjusting for inflation. The apparent decline in tuition after 2020 is attributable to inflation increasing faster than tuition. Enrollments have declined nationally. Today, according to Ma and Pender (2023), California tuition rates at in-state public 4-year institutions are approximately $10,000, compared to the national average of $11,260. The trends suggest that California is moving toward a higher tuition model, like many other states, but there are two complementary trends to consider.

- California continues to provide the lowest price for a 2-year college education in any state, at $1,428, an approach that expands opportunity but channels low-income youth into community colleges.
- California has high out-of-state tuition premiums at approximately $25,000 above in-state rates. Given the limited space in the UCs, the middle class fought to ensure that out-of-state students paid their total cost (Clawson & Leiblum, 2008).

California's funding per FTE in public higher education was consistently higher than the national average from 1992 to 2000, and those trends continue today (Figure 7.2). In 2000, California spent over $8,000 per FTE on higher education (in 2020 dollars). That number dropped by nearly 20% to $6,300 per FTE in 2010 and has rebounded significantly in recent years to more than $8,100 in 2020. California's investment in higher education has also outpaced growing support for higher education across the country, spending nearly $1,500 per FTE more than the national average. Higher subsidies, in the form of state and local appropriations, per student are necessary for a state that maintains

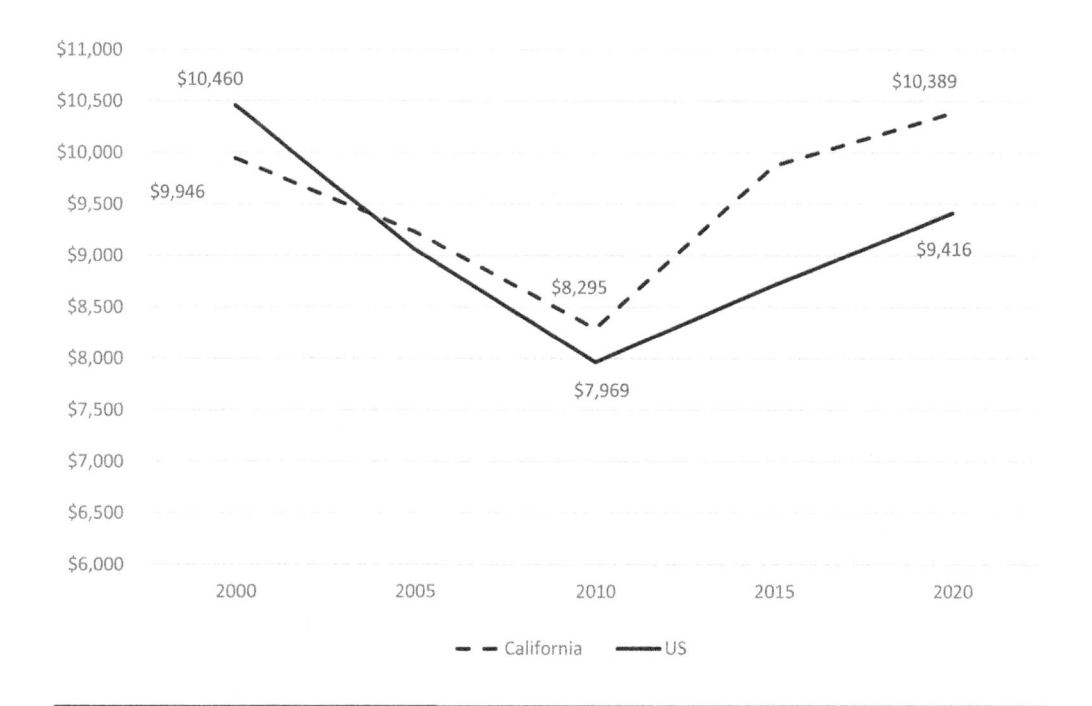

Figure 7.2 California Trends in State Appropriations per FTE (2020 Dollars)

Source: State Higher Education Executive Officers (SHEEO) Grapevine Annual Reports and NCES, Digest of Education Statistics (2023) Table 307.20.

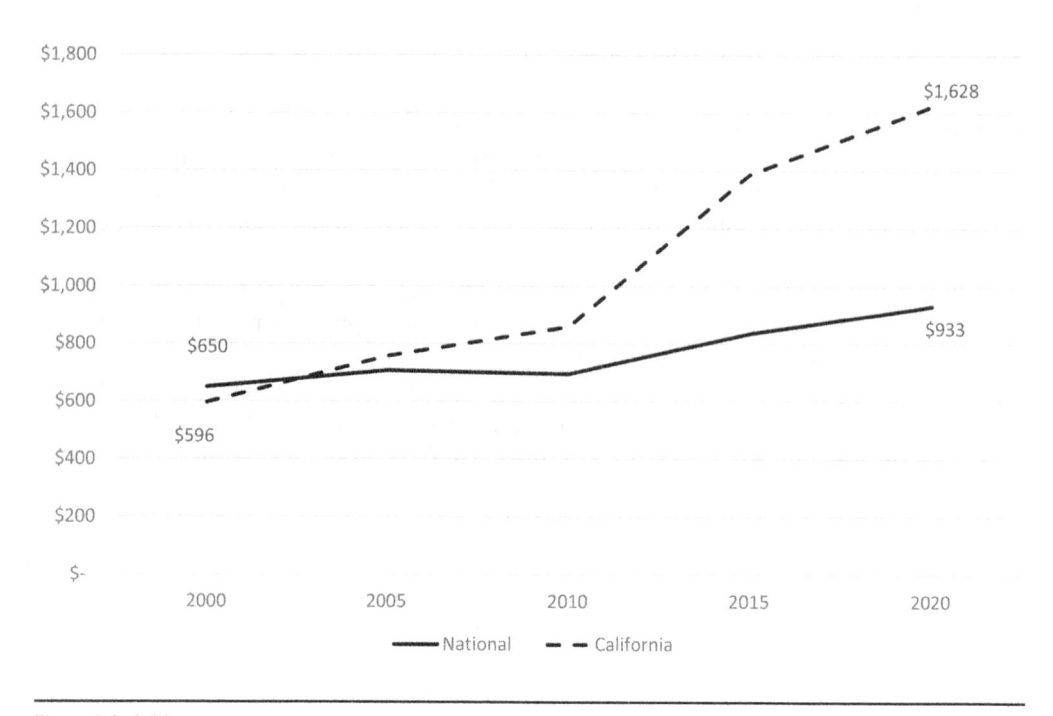

Figure 7.3 California Need-Based Aid per FTE (2020 Dollars)

Source: National Association of State Student Grant and Aid Programs (NASSGAP) (2023). Annual Survey Report. NCES, Digest of Education Statistics (2023) Table 307.20.

low tuition if the state seeks to maintain quality and competitive public campuses over the long term. Unsurprisingly, this increase in funding corresponds with a decline in inflation-adjusted public tuition and fees in the state.

The most significant changes in California pertain to its investment in need-based aid. The Cal Grant program is one of the largest and most comprehensive in the country, though in the early 2000s, growth in need-based assistance did not keep pace with rising tuition costs in the state. Since 2010, the story began to change dramatically (Figure 7.3). In 2005, California invested about $100 more per FTE than the national average of $505 (NASSGAP, 2023), and by 2010, California's investment continued to grow at a time when need-based aid was declining modestly across the country. By 2020, California's investment in need-based aid per FTE doubled from just over $595 per FTE to $1,628; California increased investment in students from slightly below the national average in 2000 to more than 50% higher than the national average in 2020.

California grant spending has been much higher than the national average in terms of total grant aid per FTE relative to tuition, and much of that investment is in need-based aid. California spends approximately $1 per FTE on non-need-based aid, compared to the national figures, ranging from $148 per FTE to $245 in 2020. While California has a merit aid program for students who have successfully completed the A-G requirements for UC and CSU, the amount spent on this program is negligible relative to the need-based Cal Grant programs. Although, in theory, low tuition and high grants (in relation to tuition) are the best possible combination for students, this combination of policies loses its practical value for students when their opportunity to enroll (i.e., the enrollment capacity of institutions) is constrained. Prior to 2010, capacity was very much an issue in

California public higher education. UC could not accommodate the top 12.5% of high school graduates, per the master plan, and it was turning students away from the community college system. Since that time, California has shifted to a high tuition, high aid model and it appears that trends in state and local appropriations and need-based aid, combined with declines in tuition and fees in public 4-year institutions and a renewed commitment to free community colleges suggests that California will be able to maintain its commitment to a lower financial burden for students from lower and middle-income families—something we were much less confident about a decade ago.

California rates higher than most other states in need-based aid funding per full-time-equivalent (FTE) student in higher education in relation to tuition charges. Owing to the history of low tuition charges in public institutions, the state directed most of its aid funding to students in private colleges. Now that California public tuition rates have risen considerably and they have significantly increased their investments in appropriations and need-based aid, we suspect the gap has narrowed in terms of the proportion of state financial aid flowing to private institutions compared to the state systems.

Through the years studied, California continued to fund its public colleges at a higher level per student than the average for other states. Even though the heavily subsidized UC system has not grown as fast as community colleges or state universities, this pattern has held up. The problems with this model, as it evolved in California, were (1) a comparatively higher taxpayer cost per student in the public system; (2) difficulty improving fairness in enrollment opportunities, given the high direct subsidies to existing colleges; and (3) the inability to overcome tax revenue constraints. We are optimistic about the trends in California over the past decade, though overall enrollments have not changed much, which may still be a consequence of inadequate system capacity to serve the needs of all students who could attend higher education in the state, or it could reflect more national trends in declining interest in postsecondary education.

TRENDS IN EDUCATION OUTCOMES

In California, as in most other states, there is a correspondence between changes in policy and education outcomes—particularly concerning curriculum requirements and mandatory exit exams. This section examines indicators of outcomes related to high school preparation, followed by trends in college participation rates and diverse representation within the state's system of higher education.

College Preparation
Implementing more rigorous requirements for high school graduation corresponded with improvements in outcomes related to academic preparation in California, but as we discussed above, so has the elimination of the mandatory exit exam and the embedded local discretion to modify curriculum requirements. The gains in high school outcomes are noteworthy, but it is less clear the role high school reform policies have played.

High School Graduation Rates
California's high school graduation rates improved from 1996 through 2005 but declined around 2006, corresponding with the implementation of CAHSEE, when the rate dropped to a low of 66%. In more recent reports, approximately 76% of high school

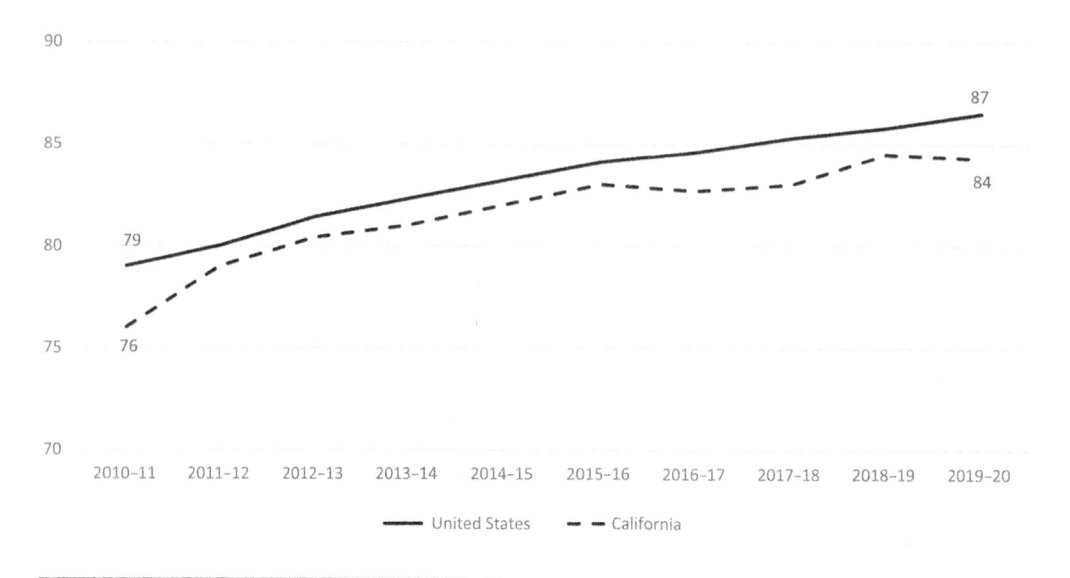

Figure 7.4 Public High School Graduation Rates (%) in California, 2010–11 Through 2019–20
Source: National Center for Education Statistics (2023). Digest of Education Statistics, Table 218.46.

students graduated high school in California in 2010, compared to 79% nationally. By 2020, high school graduation rates nationally grew approximately 8 percentage points to 87%, while California's rate lagged by about 3 percentage points at 84% (Figure 7.4) (NCES, 2023). California state data showed that racial gaps persist despite the overall improvement in high school graduation rates (California Department of Education, 2023a). Asian students graduate at 92% compared to 88% for white students, 82% for Hispanic students, and 77% for Black students.

The graduation rates continue to improve after the loosening of centralized academic requirements and the elimination of the mandatory exit exam. The percentages for all groups have improved significantly, but the gaps persist. We expected that once the education systems adjusted to the more rigorous curricular requirements, graduation rates would rebound, and the K-12 system would be able to adapt to the new expectations. That seems to have been confirmed, though eliminating the CAHSEE and allowing local discretion to create multiple pathways to a high school diploma has also been related to increasing graduation rates and emphasizing career and technical education (CTE).

College Admissions Test Scores

California has historically been an SAT state, and as such, it has also had considerable influence over the College Board as it made demands regarding changes to the test. Historically, California had a higher percentage of students taking the SAT than the national average; with 46% of high school students taking the SAT in 1992, California's rate was 4% higher than the national average (College Board, 2023). From 2004 through 2008, the rates of taking the test were nearly equal to the US average. From 2016 to 2020, SAT test-taking increased steadily in California, but in 2021, the number of test-takers dropped by more than 50% from 284,000 to 116,000. UC and CSU have dropped the SAT requirement from the admissions process (McDonnell Nieto del Rio, 2021) and predictably, the number of test-takers dropped again in 2022 to 102,000, though it rebounded slightly in 2023 to 122,000 test-takers. The scores rose from 1,048 to 1,100 in 2022 as the test-taking rates declined, and by 2023, the number of test-takers had increased, and the scores had dropped again.

California continues to exert considerable influence in debates around the value of college admissions test scores. They played an instrumental role in the brief addition of the writing assessment. Now that two of the largest higher education systems in the US have eliminated their use in the admissions process, others will likely follow. The elimination of the tests is consonant with the public discourse on using affirmative action in college admission. Many state systems and institutions are making similar decisions emerging from a global pandemic.

Higher Education Enrollment

College Participation Rates

In the 1960s, California had the highest college participation rate of any state nationwide. Those rates fluctuated through the late 1990s and early 2000s, but by 2013, the percentage of 18–24-year-olds enrolling in college was 46.4%, nearly 4 percentage points above the national average (Figure 7.5). In 2021, the rates were virtually identical, and California continued to enroll young adults more than most other states.

When we disaggregate those numbers by race, we find that while gaps have narrowed modestly since 2013, they remain large. Nearly 70% of Asian Americans between 18 and 24 attended college in 2021, fewer than 40% of Black young adults attend college, while 50% of white adults between 18 and 24 and 40% of Hispanic young adults enroll in college (Figure 7.6). Native American and Pacific Island students experienced much

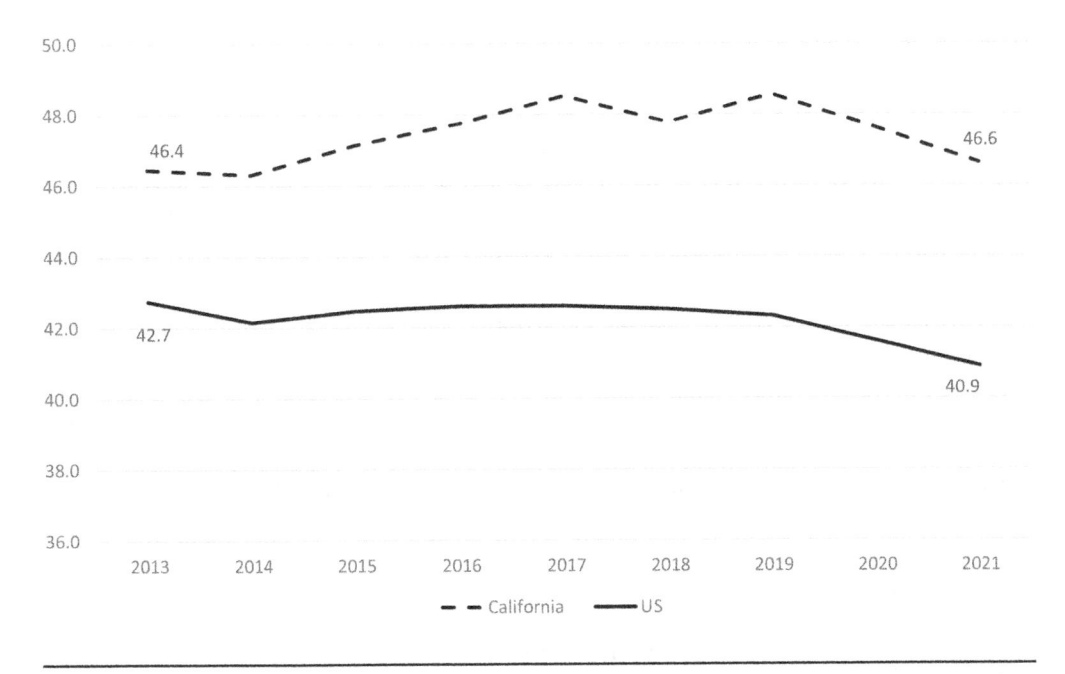

Figure 7.5 Percentage of 18- to 24-Year-Olds Enrolled in Degree-Granting Postsecondary Institutions: California & US
Source: National Center for Education Statistics (2023). Digest of Education Statistics, Table 302.65.

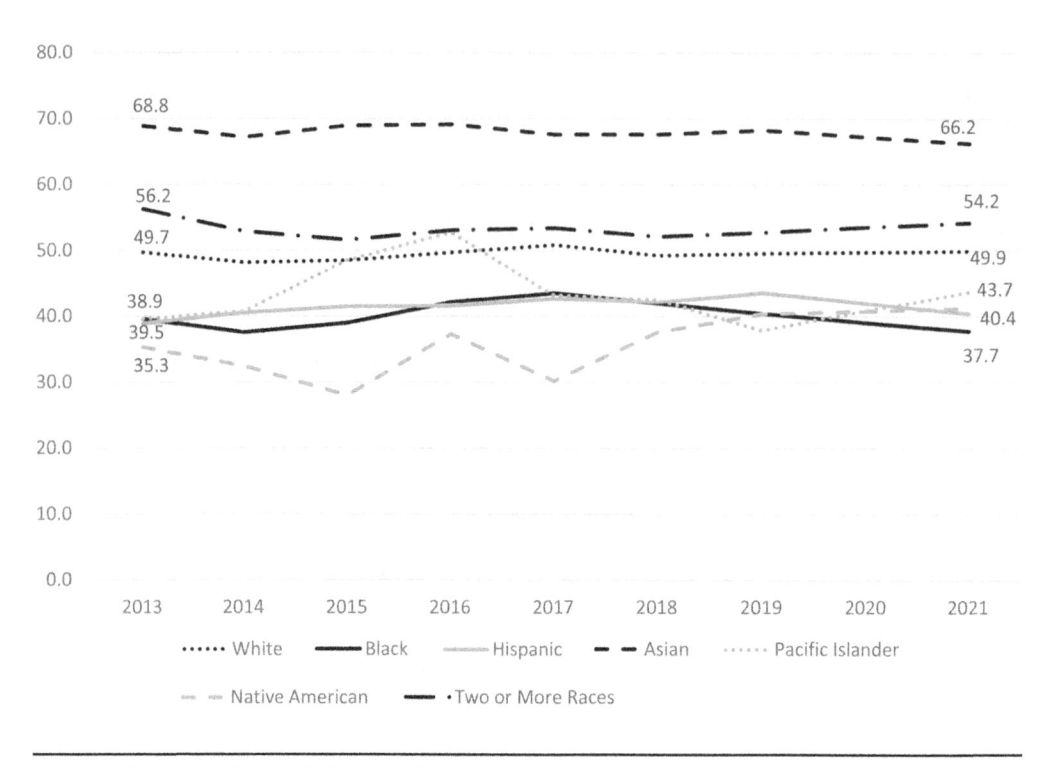

Figure 7.6 Percentage of 18- to 24-Year-Olds Enrolled in Degree-Granting Postsecondary Institutions, by Race/Ethnicity: California

Source: National Center for Education Statistics (2023). Digest of Education Statistics, Table 302.65.

more significant fluctuations in college enrollment during this period, but their rates were similar in 2021 compared to 2013.

The enrollment rate is not the only critical issue; equitable representation is also important. Our analyses in this subsection consider how well California maintained a diverse student population in the face of the political assault on affirmative action and the overall decline in opportunity. If we assume that a more substantial proportion of underrepresented students are on the margins in terms of qualifying for admission (the assumption made by critics of affirmative action), then we would expect that African Americans and Latinx would be the groups suffering the most substantially regarding college enrollment opportunity. As Figure 7.7 shows, Black and Hispanic students were over-represented relative to their percentage of the state population. Asian students were highly over-represented through the early 2000s, but their college enrollment rates equaled their proportion in the population by 2020. Meanwhile, white students have been under-represented in college enrollments in the state for more than a decade, and Native American students fell below representation a few years prior to 2020.

College Attainment

Success rates in California have remained relatively stable for the cohorts that began their college careers between 2013 and 2017. It is difficult to compare more recent trends

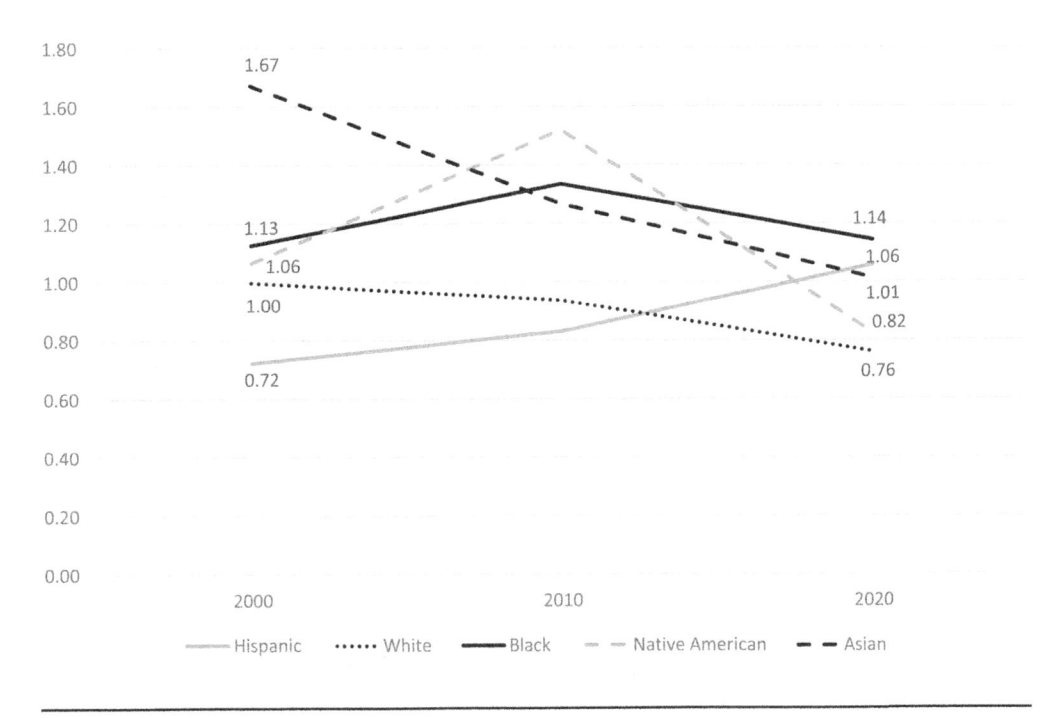

Figure 7.7 Racial/Ethnic Representation in California Postsecondary Education as a Proportion of the State Population

Source: National Center for Education Statistics (2023). Digest of Education Statistics, Table 306.70 & Table 266 & US Census Bureau (2020).

to what we observed during the late 1990s and early 2000s because the National Student Clearinghouse now provides more robust data on student completions. The trends have shifted slightly. Public 4-year institutions saw gradual increases across all subgroups, whereas the opposite was true for community colleges. Trends for both, and we also examine patterns for 4-year nonprofit colleges, are considered below.

College Attainment Rates by Race at 4-Year Public Institutions

For the cohorts that entered college in California in the early 2000s, we observed an overall increase of 6–10 percentage points in ten years, but we also saw persistent gaps that remained by 2008. Asian students graduated at 71%, while the 6-year completion rate for Black students was 45%—a gap of 36 percentage points. That gap shrunk by 4 percentage points compared to the 2002 entering cohort. Figure 7.8 provides more recent 4-year completion rates by race in California, which are slightly higher. Still, the gaps have once again only shrunk modestly, with one important exception. Latinx students improved their completion rates from 54% among the 2012 cohort to 67% for the entering class of 2017, effectively reducing the gap between Asian students by 10 percentage points and with white students to fewer than 5 percentage points. The graph shows a consistent drop in graduation rates for the 2016 cohort across racial and ethnic groups, which would have begun graduating in 2020 at the start of the Pandemic. The only exception was Latinx students, who continued to improve over that time.

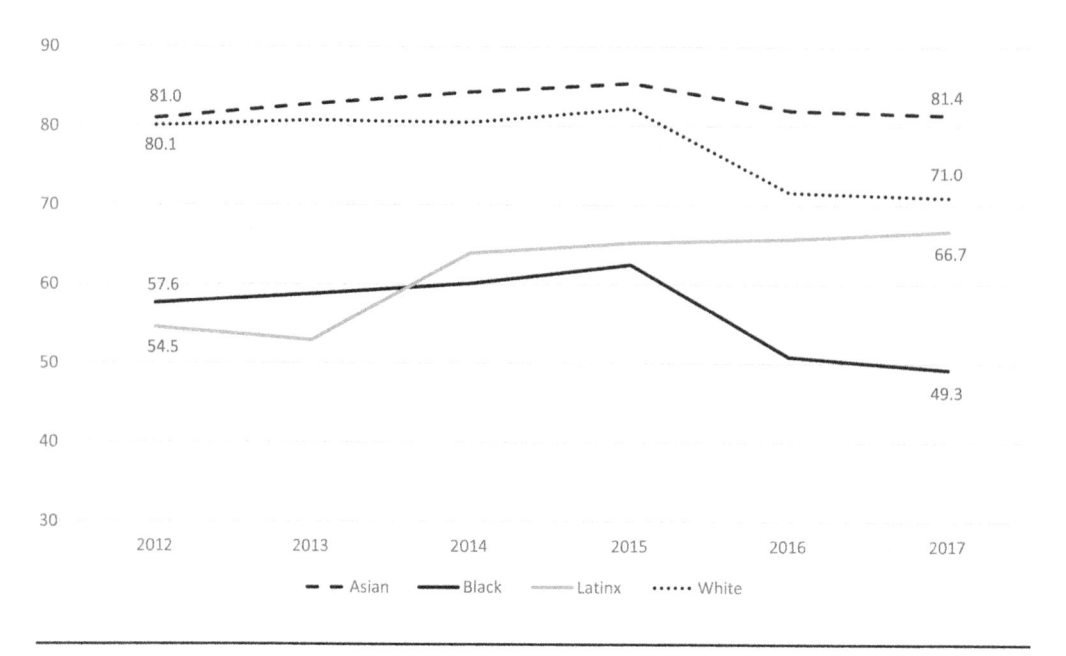

Figure 7.8 Trends in 6-Year College Attainment Rates for all California Public 4-Year Postsecondary Institutions
Source: National Student Clearinghouse Research Center (2022). Completing College: National & State Reports. Retrieved from https://nscresearchcenter.org/completing-college/

Graduation Rates by Race/Ethnicity at Private 4-Year Nonprofit Institutions
Completion rates for all students attending private 4-year colleges in California were higher than for the public institutions, and the gaps by race were narrower but equally persistent (Figure 7.9). Approximately 74% of Black students finished in six years among the 2013 cohort and that number was virtually identical five years later. Completion rates improved by approximately 2% among white students, were unchanged for Latinx students, but dropped by nearly 7 percentage points for Asian students. The gap between Black and white students in the 2017 cohort was only 12 percentage points, compared to 20 percentage points at public 4-year institutions.

Graduation Rates by Race at 2-Year Public Institutions
In contrast to the public 4-year colleges, the California community college system has much lower average completion rates and the pattern is slightly different than among students at 4-year institutions. We observed a decline among students who entered college in 2004, which likely was related to the great recession of 2008 and the funding volatility that ensued. During the early 2000s, the racial completion gaps at community colleges in California fluctuated between 15 and 20 percentage points, and that gap appears to have grown. As Figure 7.10 shows, among students who entered community college in 2013, 26% of Black students finished a degree in six years. In contrast, more than 48% of Asian students entering community colleges completed a degree in six years. Five years later, the gaps remained the same, but all groups improved by approximately 5 percentage points.

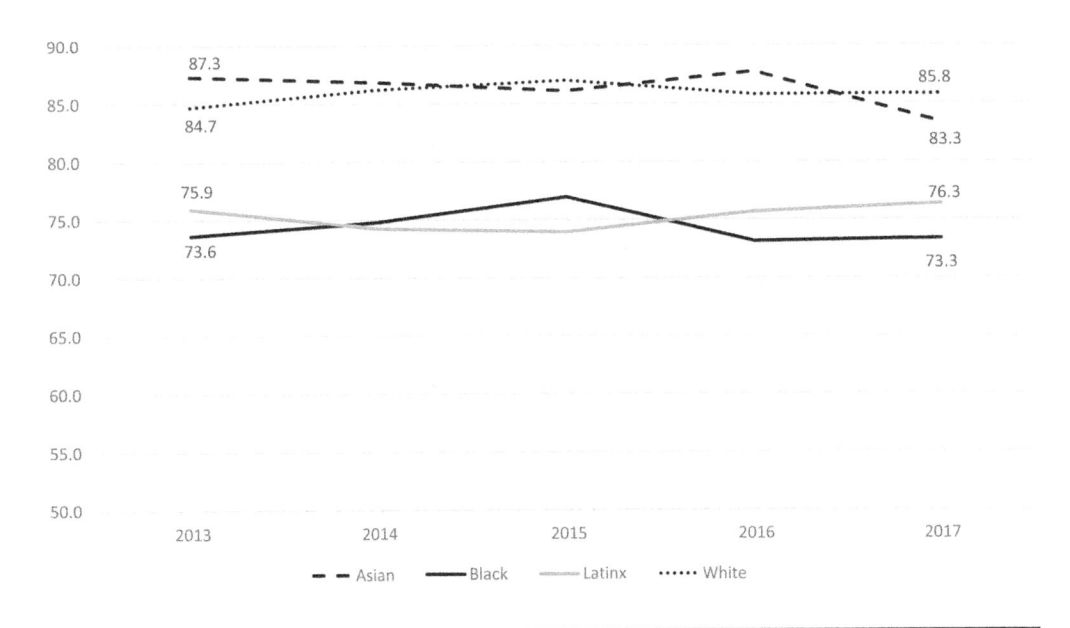

Figure 7.9 Trends in 6-Year College Attainment Rates for all California Private Nonprofit 4-Year Institutions
Source: National Student Clearinghouse Research Center (2022). Completing College: National & State Reports. Retrieved from https://nscresearchcenter.org/completing-college/

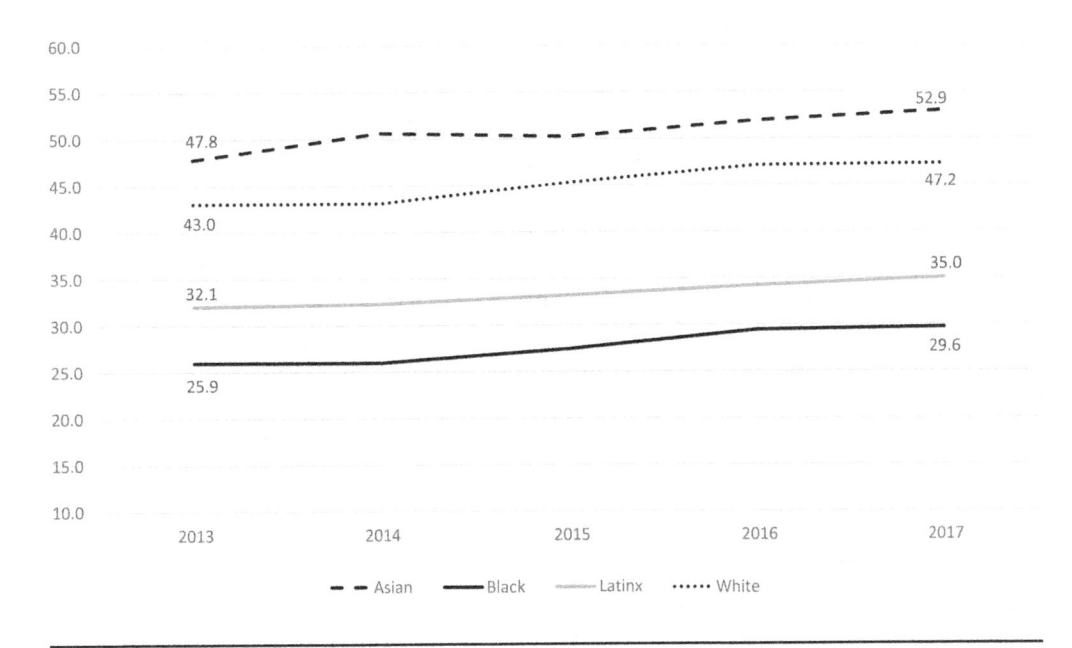

Figure 7.10 Trends in 6-Year Degree Attainment Rates for all California Public 2-Year Postsecondary Institutions
Source: National Student Clearinghouse Research Center (2022). Completing College: National & State Reports. Retrieved from https://nscresearchcenter.org/completing-college/

The degree completion data in California this century are mixed. In the aggregate, students from all racial and ethnic groups have completed college at higher rates. Latinx students even appear to have reduced the gaps at 4-year public institutions. Comparisons between the first decade of students and the more recent cohorts are difficult because the data are different. The data we use in this set of analyses are from the National Student Clearinghouse, and the advantage they have is that they can report on whether a student earns a degree, whether it was at the institution where they started. As a result, the more recent numbers are naturally higher. However, the trends among the more recent cohorts are still instructive. It is not surprising that graduation rates dropped among those who would have finished during the pandemic; it is surprising that Latinx students followed a different pattern and continued to improve in California during that difficult period.

CURRENT ISSUES IN CALIFORNIA

California has been a bellwether state for higher education policy and postsecondary opportunity and continues to be as we enter this new period for higher education. The state has been on the front lines of many of the critical political challenges facing higher education in the United States, including both affirmative action and in-state residency status for undocumented students. Through the DREAM Act, it was a national leader in terms of college opportunities for undocumented students. They created a legislative pathway for students who qualified for Deferred Action for Childhood Arrivals (DACA), granting them in-state tuition rates and making state and institutional financial aid programs available through alternative application processes. They have slowly developed system capacity to meet increasing student demand for postsecondary education in the state, and they have navigated the perilous terrain of dramatic tuition increases after the Great Recession. These were the significant policy issues we highlighted a decade ago. To a certain degree, these issues persist but have largely faded into the backdrop. In recent years, several new policy issues have become priorities.

Shift to High Tuition/High Aid

When we first examined the affordability issue in California, it was clear that tuition rates were rising quickly, and the state's historic commitment to low-cost higher education was in jeopardy; it was not yet clear whether they would find new ways to restore that commitment. In the decade since the recession and the dramatic increases in tuition rates at public 4-year institutions, the state has successfully shifted to what we would describe as a classical high tuition/high aid model. It is crucial, of course, to acknowledge that while tuition rates are much higher for California than in 2008, the in-state rates are still below the national average. California discovered, as did other states, that while high tuition and high aid are more efficient ways to utilize scarce tax dollars, historical precedent suggests that need-based financial aid seldom rises at rates that keep pace with rising tuition. As the Minnesota and Indiana cases illustrate (Chapters 8 and 9), it has been difficult for states to stick with high aid when extreme conservatives take over, a lesson learned in California in the wake of Reagan's election as Governor. For the moment, it appears that California has avoided this fate. Our analyses show that the state has doubled its per FTE investment in need-based aid over the past decade while tuition rates have leveled off and even declined modestly in recent years.

We view this as a positive development for California. Yet, context matters, and the state remains one of the most expensive in terms of cost of living, which has implications for college students. The cost of housing is at a premium across much of the state, which may affect students' choices of whether or where to attend college. Governor Newsome signed SB 4 in 2023 to allow private colleges more flexibility to build campus housing (Spitalniak, 2023). The potential downside of the high cost of living is that students may choose to under-match their choice of college to attend, relative to their academic profile, simply because of cost.

Elimination of SAT/ACT in Admissions at CSU

One of the crucial developments in college admissions recently has been the erosion of support for the continued use of college admissions tests in the application and admission processes. Several institutions had decided to move toward a test-optional policy well before the pandemic hit in 2020, but many more are making that choice today. The pandemic forced the issue for nearly all colleges and universities because students could not take the test safely in their schools or remote locations, and the College Board had not yet made fully remote test-taking a viable option. The decision for both CSU and UC to drop the SAT or ACT requirement from their admissions process is a significant change for the state (Zinshteyn, 2022). California is the first state in the nation to eliminate the use of admissions tests in its public 4-year institutions, a very different choice than going test-optional, as many more colleges have done throughout the pandemic and through 2024.

Critics of the testing industry would argue that the elimination of the test has reduced an important source of bias against low-income and racially minoritized students. The challenge now will be to see if eliminating tests changes the choice of institutions for many students. As Hamilton and Neilson point out, there is a prestige hierarchy, particularly in the UC system, and most students of color admitted to the system attend UC Merced, Irvine, and others at the less selective end of the system. One way to assess this change in the future will be to consider whether more low-income and racially minoritized students are admitted and choose to enroll at UC Berkeley or UCLA.

Free Community Colleges

California has never wavered in its commitment to low-cost community college education. As the data above indicate, the average cost of tuition at community colleges in the state is below $1,500 annually. There has been a growing movement nationally to make a community college education accessible for state residents. Tennessee has been the vanguard of that movement with its state Promise program. Community college in California has been free for many students since the passage of the California College Promise Grant, which waived tuition for students eligible for the DREAM Act; in 2017, the legislature also passed AB 19, creating the California Promise (Picazo, 2023). The bill provided additional resources for community colleges to invest in the success of their students. The colleges are not required to use those resources for tuition waivers, but many have chosen to do so. The only downside to this approach is that the message is not straightforward. The Tennessee Promise sends a clear and simple message to the residents of the state—if you attend a community college in the state, the cost will be covered. The California Promise does not work in that way. However, community college costs remain much more affordable than most states, even without the Promise.

UC Tuition Stability Plan

One of the contributing factors to the lower tuition and fees in California, relative to other states, may be the passage of the tuition stability plan by the UC Board of Regents in 2021 (University of California Admissions, 2023). A perennial concern for state higher education systems across the country is the relative unpredictability of the rising price of higher education. Some states limit the system's ability to raise rates but then periodically are forced to pass substantial tuition increases, often when state revenues are down. The tuition stability plan in California guarantees that tuition will remain flat for an incoming student for up to six years. Each new cohort of students may be subject to a higher rate, but they, too, will have that rate locked for up to six years.

REFRAMING SUCCESS

California is in a very different place today than a decade ago regarding postsecondary enrollment and college completion; it appears that it is committed to embracing a new version of the "Old Liberal Model." The state has loosened the curricular constraints on students by allowing greater discretion in the graduation requirements, and they have eliminated the CAHSEE, which, like many mandatory exit exams, served as an impediment to high school completion. These policy changes allow for multiple pathways to a high school diploma, enabling students to choose a college pathway through the A-G requirements or pursue CTE pathways that may align with opportunities in the labor market.

More than most states, California depends on educated and undereducated workers; it imports educated labor from inside and outside of the US but also attracts undereducated immigrants as laborers to maintain the agricultural economy. Yet, the state has a population decline due to high housing prices and the ability of educated workers to work from home (Leonard, 2023). Especially since the pandemic, once employed in high-tech firms, some employees can achieve a modicum of geographic freedom.

California maintains a two-tier education and employment economy. It has higher percentages of residents with less than high school educations than the national average. It has far fewer residents with only a high school diploma than the US as a whole; however, it exceeds the national average in some college, bachelor's, and graduate degrees but is somewhat below the national average with adults in an associate only, indicating a continuing pattern of attainment (Figure 7.11).

The state has strong economic incentives for education uplift. Californians with some college (including associates only), bachelor's, and graduate degrees earn more than the national average. At the same time, people with less than in high school diploma earn slightly less than the national average, but getting into college makes a difference (Figure 7.12). The education gains of Latinx residents illustrate the prospects of cross-generation uplift: children of laborers, even undocumented workers, can gain college admission. Latinx residents are also graduating from public 4-year colleges at increasing rates.

Although debt burden is a challenge for college graduates in California as it is in other states, the borrowing rate and median debt are lower than for the rest of the nation (Jackson & Starr, 2023). The rate of student borrowing is 10 percentage points lower than the rest of the country and is declining. The median debt on graduation varies from $13,200 at UC Davis to $18,000 at UC Riverside within the UC system and from $13,200 at Cal State LA to $25,000 at Cal Maritime in the CSU system. Even the highest median debt

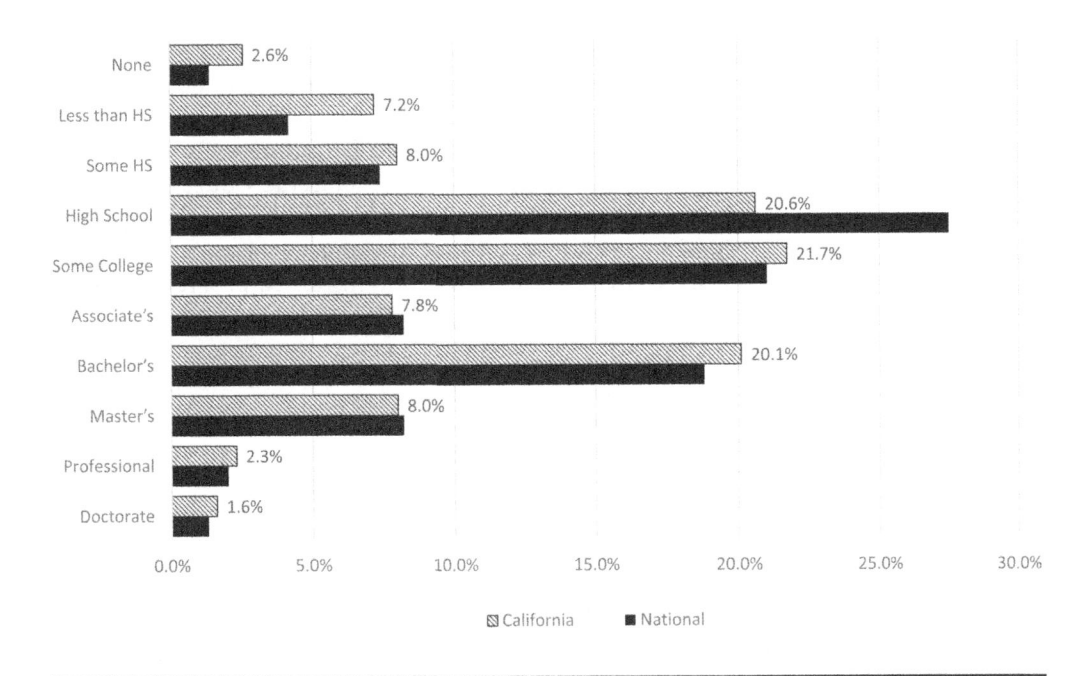

Figure 7.11 Highest Level of Educational Attainment for People 25 or Older in California (2020)
Source: Statistical Atlas (2023). Educational Attainment. Retrieved from https://statisticalatlas.com/United-States/Educational-Attainment

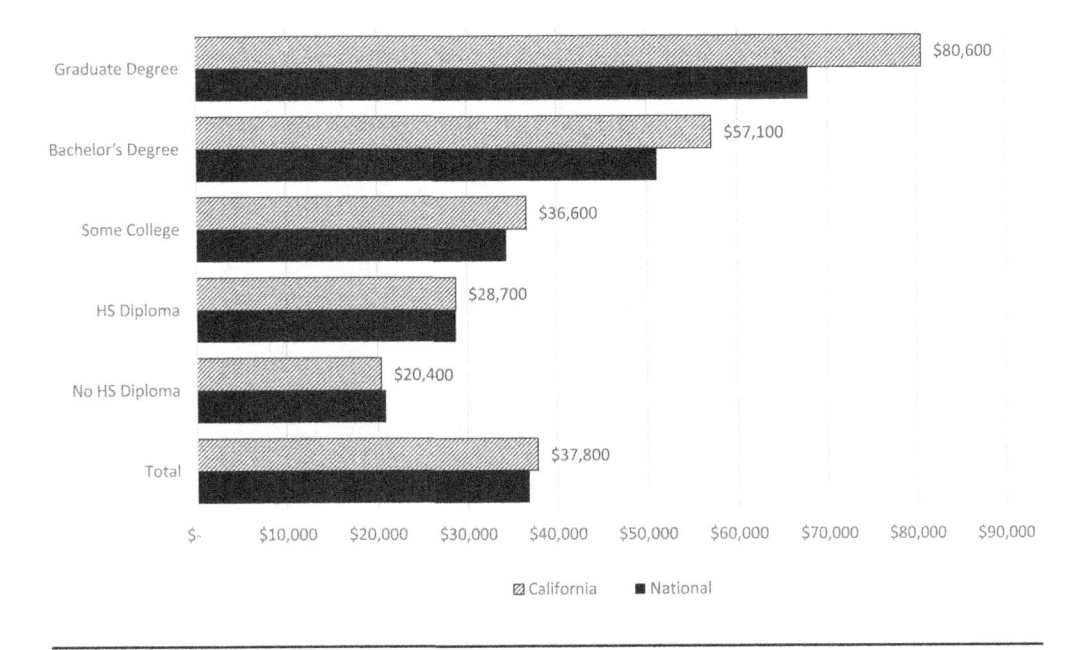

Figure 7.12 Median Annual Earnings in California by Level of Education (2020)
Source: Statistical Atlas (2023). Educational Attainment. Retrieved from https://statisticalatlas.com/United-States/Educational-Attainment

campus, Cal Maritime, a specialized campus, is at about the average for other states. Given the higher earnings for degree recipients in California, the student debt burden is not as severe a problem as in most states.

Thus, California has a racially discriminatory history in UC admissions and lost the tools of affirmative action more than a decade before the Supreme Court decision on *Students for Fair Admissions, Inc. v. Harvard College*. Opportunities gained through non-traditional avenues with extensive educational and social support suggest an alternative approach to social uplift. Thus, California may again be forging a new progressive model for promoting college development.

Questions

1. How did California's origins as a state, from the Bear Flag Revolt and Gold Rush to the Great Depression, influence the development of California's progressive educational system in the early twentieth century?
2. To what extent does the ethos of the 1960s Master Plan still provide a blueprint for education development, excellence, and equity in California?
3. How did California's history as the earliest state to experience neoconservative financial policies, a pillar of neoliberalism that emerged nationally in the 1980s, influence its capacity to adhere to the vision set in the Master Plan?
4. Does California's restructuring of higher education finance provide a model for other states? What does the model portend for historical tensions between whites and Blacks in the state and nation?
5. How has economic stratification in financial access to 4-year colleges for many, evident in California as it is nationally, influenced inequalities and opportunities across racial/ethnic groups? Do California's poor whites and Blacks have apparent overlapping interests in access to CTE in high school or community colleges?

REFERENCES

Allen, R. (2010). Alta California missions and the pre-1849 transformation of coastal lands. *Historical Archaeology, 44*(3), 69–80.

Boustan, L. P., Fishback, P. V., & Kantor, S. (2010). The effect of internal migration on local labor markets: American Cities during the great depression. *Journal of Labor Economics, 28*(4), 719–746.

Britannica. (2024). The editors of Encyclopaedia. "University of California." In Encyclopedia Britannica, 1 Feb. 2024.

California Department of Education. (2023a). *2020-21 data summary*. Retrieved from https://www.cde.ca.gov/ds/ad/datasummary.asp

California Department of Education. (2023b). *State minimum high school graduation requirements*. Retrieved from https://www.cde.ca.gov/ci/gs/hs/hsgrmin.asp

California Department of Education. (2023c). *State minimum high school graduation requirements*. Retrieved from https://www.cde.ca.gov/ci/gs/hs/hsgrmin.asp

California Student Aid Commission. (2020). *Cal Grant Handbook*. Retrieved from https://www.csac.ca.gov/sites/main/files/file-attachments/calgrant_handbook.pdf

Callan, P. M. (2002, February). Coping with recession: Public policy, economic downturns and higher education. National Center Report 02-2, Issue.

Callan, P. M., & Finney, J. E. (1997). *Public and private financing of higher education: Shaping public policy for the future*. American Council on Education/Oryx Press.

Carnegie Commission on Higher Education (1973). *Continuity and discontinuity: Higher education and the schools.* McGraw Hill Book Company.

Chapa, J., & Horn, C. L. (2007). Is anything race neutral? Comparing "race-neutral" admission policies at the university of Texas and the university of California. In G. Orfield, P. Marin, S. M. Flores, & L. Garces (Eds.), *Charting the future of college affirmative action: Legal victories, continuing attacks, and new research* (pp. 157–172). Civil Rights Project, UCLA School of Education. www.civilrightsproject.ucla.edu/research/college-access/affirmative-action/charting-the-future-of-college-affirmative-action-legal-victories-continuing-attacks-and-new-research

Chea, T. (2009, August). *Budget cuts devastate California higher education.* Associated Press. https://www.kpbs.org/news/economy/2009/08/05/budget-cuts-devastate-california-higher-education

Clawson, D., & Leiblum, M. (2008). Class struggle in higher education. *Equity & Excellence in Education, 41*(1), 12–30.

Cohen, R., & Zelnik, R. E. (2002). *The free speech movement: Reflections on Berkeley in the 1960s.* University of California Press.

College Board. (2023). *SAT Suite of Assessments Report.* Retrieved from https://reports.collegeboard.org/sat-suite-program-results

Contreras, F. E. (2019). *Becoming "Latinx responsive": Raising institutional and systemic consciousness in California's HSIs.* American Council on Education. https://www.equityinhighered.org/wp-content/uploads/2019/12/Conteras-Essay_FINAL.pdf

Daun-Barnett, N. J., & St. John, E. P. (2018). *Public policy and higher education: Reframing strategies for preparation, access, and college success.* Routledge.

Editors of the Encyclopaedia Britannica. (2024). *Encyclopedia Britannica.* University of California.

Evans, J. (1971). View from a State Capitol. *Change, 3*(5), 40–45.

Fitzgerald, B., & Kane, T. (2003, October). *Lowering barriers to college access in California and the nation: Opportunities for more effective state and federal student aid policies* the conference of the Harvard Civil Rights Project and the University of California, Sacramento, CA.

Fitzgibbons, R. H. (1968). *The academic senate of the University of California.*

Gándara, P. (2002). Meeting common goals: Linking k-12 and college interventions. In W. G. Tierney & L. S. Hagedorn (Eds.), *Increasing access to college: Extending possibilities for all students.* SUNY Press.

Gándara, P. (2005). *Fragile futures: Risk and vulnerability among latino high achievers.* Policy Brief, Issue.

Gándara, P., Orfield, G., & Horn, C. (2006). *Expanding opportunity in higher education: Leveraging promise.* SUNY Press.

Glenny, L. A., Bowen, F. M., Meisinger, R. J., Mogan, A. W., Purves, R. A., & Schmidtline, F. A. (1975). *State budgeting in higher education: Data digest.*

Gregory, J. N. (1991). *American Exodus: The dust bowl migration and okie culture in California.* Oxford University Press.

Haggard, S., & Kaufman, R. R. (Eds.). (2018). *The politics of economic adjustment: International constraints, distributive conflicts and the state.* Princeton University Press.

Hansen, W. L., & Weisbrod, B. (1969). *Benefits, costs, and finance of public higher education.* Markham Publishing Co.

Harrington, T., & Fredberg, L. (2017). California joins trend among states to abandon high school exit exam. Legislation. Retrieved from https://edsource.org/2017/california-joins-trend-among-states-to-abandon-high-school-exit-exam/588640

Hearn, J. C., & Anderson, M. S. (1989). Integrating postsecondary education financing policies: The Minnesota model. In R. H. Fenske (Ed.), *Studying the impact of student aid in Institutions* (Vol. 62, pp. 55–73). Jossey-Bass.

Hearn, J. C., & Anderson, M. S. (1995). The Minnesota financing experiment. In E. P. St. John (Ed.), *New directions for higher education: Rethinking tuition and financial aid strategies* (Vol. 89, pp. 5–25). Jossey-Bass.

Howley, M., Howley, A., & Eppley, K. (2013). How agricultural science trumps rural community in the discourse of selected US history textbooks. *Theory & Research in Social Education, 41*(2), 187–218.

Institute of Governmental Studies. (2003). *State financing of higher education.*

Kelsey, B., & Foy, M. E. (1946). The bear flag revolution. *The Quarterly: Historical Society of Southern California, 28*(2), 60–73.

Kerr, C. (1963). *The uses of the university.* Harvard University Press.

Kerr, C. (1978). *12 systems of higher education: 6 decisive issues.* International Council for Educational development.

Kerr, C. (1991). The new race to become Harvard or Berkeley or Stanford. *Change* (May), *23*(3), 8–15.

Kerr, C. (1994). *Higher education cannot escape history: Issues for the 21st century.* SUNY Press.

Kerr, C. (2002). *The future of the city of intellect: The changing American university in shock wave II: An introductory to the 21st century.* In S. J. Brint (Ed., pp. 1–19). Standford University Press.

Kipp, S. M., Price, D. V., & Wohlford, J. K. (2002). Unequal opportunity: Disparities in college access among the 50 states.

Lee, E. C., & Bowen, F. M. (1971). *The multi-campus university: A study of academic governance.* McGraw-Hill.

Lee, E. C., & Bowen, F. M. (1975). *Managing multi-campus systems: Effective administration in an unsteady state.* Jossey-Bass.

Legislative Analyst's Office. (2005). Proposition 98 Primer. Retrieved from http://www.lao.ca.gov/2005/prop_98_primer/prop_98_primer_020805.htm

Leonard, C. (2023, December 21). *The California exodus continues.* San Francisco Chronicle. https://www.sfchronicle.com/california/article/population-exodus-2023-18566180.php#

Ma, J., & Pender, M. (2023). *Trends in college pricing: 2023.* Trends in Higher Education Series, Issue, Issue. https://research.collegeboard.org/trends/college-pricing

Marmaduke, A. S. (1988). Beyond the borders: A discussion of student financial aid and educational opportunity in Texas, New York, and the Pacific Rim.

McConnell, T. R., & Mortimer, K. P. (1970). The faculty in university governance.

McDonnell Nieto del Rio, G. (2021, May 15). University of California will no longer consider SAT and ACT scores. *New York Times.* https://www.nytimes.com/2021/05/15/us/SAT-scores-uc-university-of-california.html

McDonough, P. M. (1997). *Choosing colleges: How social class and schools structure opportunity.* SUNY Press.

McDonough, P., & Fann, A. (2007). The study of inequality In P. Gumport (Ed.), *Sociology of higher education.* The Johns Hopkins University Press.

McGrath, E. J. (1970). *Should students share the power? A study of their role in college and university governance.* Temple University Press.

National Association of State Student Grant and Aid Programs. (2023). *53rd Annual Report on State-Sponsored Student Financial Aid.* https://www.nassgapsurvey.com/survey_reports/2021-2022-53rd.pdf

National Center for Education Statistics. (2023). Digest of Education Statistics. https://nces.ed.gov/programs/digest/2023menu_tables.asp

National Student Clearinghouse Research Center. (2023). *Completing College: A State-Level View of Student Attainment Rates.* Retrieved from https://nscresearchcenter.org/completing-college/

Newton, J. (2006). *Justice for all: Earl warren and the nation he made.* Riverhead Books.

O'Leary, K. (2009, June 27). The legacy of proposition 13. *Time.* www.time.com/time/nation/article/0,8599,1904938,00.html

Orfield, G. (1988). Exclusion of the majority: Shrinking college access and public policy in metropolitan los angeles. *The Urban Review, 20*(3), 147–163.

Picazo, J. (2023, November 1). Tuition-free access expanding across California community college campuses. *EdSource.* https://edsource.org/2023/tuition-free-access-expanding-across-california-community-college-campuses/699832#:~:text=As%20of%20the%20current%20semester,student%20at%20Folsom%20Lake%20College.

Rothstein, J. M. (2002). College performance predictions and the SAT.

Sides, J. A. (1999). Working away: African American migration and community in Los Angeles from the Great Depression to 1954.

Smelser, J. J., & Almond, G. (1974). *Gowth, structural change, and conflict in California higher education.* University of California Press.

Spitalniak, L. (2023, October 24). California passed a flurry of higher education laws. Here's what they'll do. *Higher Ed Dive.* https://www.highereddive.com/news/higher-education-laws-california-roundup/697561/

St. John, E. P. (1991). A framework for reexamining state resource management strategies in higher education. *The Journal of Higher Education, 31*(4), 387–403.

St. John, E. P. (1994a). Assessing tuition and student aid strategies: Using price response measures to simulate pricing alternatives. *Research in Higher Education, 35*(3), 301–335.

St. John, E. P. (1994b). *Prices, productivity and investment: Assessing financial strategies in higher education.* ASHE/ERIC Higher Education Report, Issue.

St. John, E. P. (2006). *Education and the public interest: School reform, public finance, and access to higher education.* Springer Press.

St. John, E. P., & Moronski, K. (2013). The late great state of California: The legacy of the master plan, the decline in access, and a new crisis. In E. P. St. John, J. Kim, & L. Yang (Eds.), *Privatization and inequality: Comparative studies of college access, education policy, and public finance* (pp. 175–213). AMS Press.

St. John, E. P., & Regan, M. C. (1973). *Students in campus governance: Reasoning and models for student involvement.* University of California-Davis.

State Higher Education Executive Officers. (2023). *State higher education finance annual report.* Retrieved from https://shef.sheeo.org/grapevine/?report_page=welcome

Sumagaysay, L., & Agrawal, S. (2023). New California laws raise the minimum wage for 2 industries. Others could see pay hikes, too, Cal Matters. Retrieved from https://calmatters.org/economy/2023/12/minimum-wage-2024/

Tierney, W. G., & Venegas, K. (Eds.). (2007). *The cultural ecology of financial aid decision making* (Vol. 22). AMS Press.

Tierney, W. G., Corwin, Z. B., & Colyar, J. E. (2005). *Preparing for college: Nine elements of effective outreach*. SUNY Press.

Tierney, W. G., & Hagedorn, L. S. (2002). *Increasing access to college: Extending possibilities for all students*. SUNY Press.

Trow, M. (1974). *Problems in the transition from elite to mass higher education*. McGraw-Hill.

U.S. Census Bureau. (2023). California Profile. Retrieved from https://data.census.gov/profile/California?g=040XX00US06#education

University of California Admissions. (2023). Tuition Stability Plan. Retrieved from https://admission.universityofcalifornia.edu/tuition-financial-aid/tuition-cost-of-attendance/tuition-stability-plan.html

Watanabe, T., & Lu, J. (2020, November 1). Affirmative action divides Asian Americans, UC's largest overrepresented student group. *Los Angeles Times*. https://www.latimes.com/california/story/2020-11-01/affirmative-action-divides-asian-americans-ucs-largest-overrepresented-student-group

Zinshteyn, M. (2022, March 31). Without SAT, ACT, what's next for Cal State admissions? *CalMatters*. https://calmatters.org/education/higher-education/2022/03/csu-entrance-requirement/

Zumeta, W., & Finkle, D. (2007). California community colleges: Making them stronger and more affordable.

8

THE MARKET MODEL RECONSIDERED

*The Minnesota Case**

Minnesota has two state systems—the University of Minnesota System and the Minnesota State Colleges and Universities System—which govern 4- and 2-year campuses. The state also has a thriving private sector comprised primarily of small liberal arts colleges, like the University of St. Thomas and Carlton College. Mainly due to planning for an enrollment drop that did not occur in the late twentieth century, the higher education system faced severe financial challenges and competition between sectors for state funding. In the 1980s, the state developed an equity-based market approach, which included mechanisms for coordinating state funding for campuses, tuition, and student grant aid for public and private higher education. Ironically, as documented below, Minnesota higher education faced enrollment declines due to COVID and transformations in higher education finance this century.

Minnesota adopted the high-tuition and high-grant aid market model for financing public and private higher education in the early 1980s after a crisis in state funding. Frequently characterized as a model for other states to follow, the equity-based market strategy is complicated for states to maintain (Hossler et al., 1997; Somers et al., 2004). In Minnesota, the plan worked relatively consistently for conservative and liberal gubernatorial administrations in the late twentieth century. However, the severe limitations are evident now: grant aid fell short of rising tuition costs in the early twenty-first century. After a summary of Minnesota's education history, this case reviews the development and current operation of the Minnesota model.

DEVELOPMENT OF MINNESOTA'S MARKET MODEL

The genesis of the market model for higher education in Minnesota is perhaps ironically informed by the internationally contested early settlement of the territory during European colonialism. France and England competed for the Minnesota territory for

---

* We thank Gresham Collom, Assistant Professor at the University of Minnesota, for his timely review of a draft of this case study.

more than a century. French traders entered through the St. Lawrence gateway into the upper Midwest; the English followed the Hudson Bay Company trade routes southward, extending conflicts from the old world to the new (Gluek, 1965). Placing French fur trading posts within English stockades became the ground for finding uneasy peace (Nute, 1930) before the region opened to Americans through the Northwest Territories before the Louisiana Purchase enabled settlers to expand West and North. The Native Americans and French traders worked in a market environment altered by the outcome of the French Indian War, moving the region from French to British colonial control. Gresham Collom (2024) describes the devastation of the Dakota-Indian War:

> Following the Dakota War of 1862 – in which over 300 Dakota people were sentenced to death and others were held within concentration camps – Minnesota signed legislation forcefully removing both the Dakota and Ho-Chunk people from the state and seized their lands. That same year the Morrill Act of 1862 revived the University of Minnesota – which closed in 1858 due to finances – and granted the institution the Dakota peoples' stolen lands.[1]

Like the other states in the Northwest Territory, Minnesota did have a few colleges before statehood in 1858. The founding and development of colleges followed the settlement of the territory. Hamline College, Minnesota Territory's first college, was founded by Methodist ministers in 1854 (Johnson, 2013). The Minnesota Territory had chartered the University of Minnesota in 1851, but it did not get started until 1858, the year Minnesota became a state. The state's first Lutheran college, Gustavus College, was founded in 1861. State colleges were established in St. Cloud in 1869 and Morehead in 1889. The foundations for cooperative public-private college development were evident by the early twentieth century.

Along with its neighboring state, Wisconsin, the people of Minnesota sought socio-economic transformations by challenging, confronting, and collaborating with corporate progressives seeking to limit the violence of the labor movement. The Scandinavian immigrants held progressive attitudes about social change, education, and research supporting economic development (Brye, 1977). Private liberal arts colleges played an essential role in the state's social and economic growth as the state began to expand the public system to meet growing demand in the 1960s (Jarchow, 1973). The University of Minnesota system developed five distinct campuses, including the Twin Cities campus with facilities on both sides of the Mississippi River; the state college system grew to seven universities with multiple campuses. The first junior college was established on the Fergus Falls campus in 1960 by a community group, leading to the development of regional community and technical college campuses.

Minnesota has a long history as a progressive state with a statewide planning system long before it developed the market-based funding model in 1984. Minnesota had higher-than-expected enrollment growth in the 1970s and severe revenue shortfalls in the 1980s. The progressive tradition of the state emphasized high-quality education to stimulate economic development. Unlike other Midwestern states with an industrial base, Minnesota had well-established research centers in the 1980s, emphasizing medical research and computer technologies. A high-tech state, planning for higher education emphasized excellence in the science, technology, engineering, and math (STEM) fields. The shift in federal policy from grants promoting equity to emphasizing loans was a development not considered by the planning groups, making it difficult for Minnesota to maintain its equitable approach to higher education.

Much like British control altered the French and Indian market for the fur trade after the French-Indian War, the shift in federal finance of higher education transformed Minnesota's higher education market in the 1980s and beyond. The traders moved their exchange into alignment with British control. The clash between Minnesota's grant-dependent market model and the Reagan Administration's loan-based market was more problematic than differences in theory. The change in federal strategy eroded the foundational assumptions of the state's financial plan—the declining federal investment in grants unexpectedly altered the state's trajectory. The research-informed state planning during the early 1980s, an exemplary model for collaboration at the time, had not considered the impact of the erosion of federal grants as the foundation of the state's market model, nor the long-term costs for students created by these changes.

Policy Developments Leading to the Market Model

Like many states, Minnesota responded to studies predicting a decline in enrollment after 1978 (Carnegie Commission on Higher Education, 1973). In 1977, the Minnesota Higher Education Coordinating Board (MHECB) implemented an enrollment bulge policy by freezing appropriations at 1977 levels (Minnesota Higher Education Coordinating Board, 1982). Although such plans seemed rational at the time, given the many reports claiming that higher education had unreasonable plans for growth (Balderston, 1974; Cheit, 1975), institutional adaptations to the policy were largely unanticipated.

The University of Minnesota (UM) System had a well-established research capability. Recognizing that the new context created new opportunities, the university capped enrollment and focused on raising quality. The system began to focus on generating revenue from other sources, including its hospital operation. During this period, there were also many special line-item allocations from the state for specific projects (St. John, 1991). Education researchers viewed this as an opportunity to test new approaches to managing internal costs and tuition charges. University of Minnesota Researchers supported the MHECB and sought the institution's best interests. For example, the system experimented with a differential pricing model, charging students more for high-cost STEM fields (Berg & Hoenack, 1987).

In contrast, state universities and community colleges seized growth opportunities, letting enrollment rise during the expected bulge to generate tuition revenue and resulting in lower total education revenue per student. The state universities absorbed excess demand generated by qualified students who were denied access to UM due to the enrollment cap. However, by 1982, it became clear that the average revenue per student had substantially declined in the state universities owing to the constraints on state funding. The community colleges also experienced enrollment gains, which was not as serious a problem because they relied less on state funding.

In 1979, the MHECB formed a task force to study enrollment and financing policy with funding from the Ford Foundation. In 1981, the task force invited national experts to discuss funding challenges in public postsecondary education and student financial aid. The task force considered financing alternatives, including an average-cost state finance plan that considered fixed and variable funding, student financial aid, and other approaches. After some deliberation, the task force (Minnesota Higher Education Coordinating Board, 1982) recommended a strategy that included (1) providing incentives for innovation and resource management, encouraging the governing board to anticipate changes in conditions; (2) equitably providing resources by assuring fairness in funding across sectors of higher education; (3) recognizing differing costs patterns, including the higher cost of STEM field education; (4) ensuring quality using identifiable measures of performance; and (5) encouraging increased productivity.

The Minnesota Market Model

Minnesota adopted a new approach to funding in fiscal year 1984 (St. John, 1991), establishing average cost funding for each institution based on an analysis of a 12-cell matrix (high-, medium-, and low-cost programs at the lower division, upper division, and graduate levels), with average costs based on full-year enrollment (fall enrollment adjusted for within-year attrition) in each of the cells. Studies of costs at peer institutions were used to set the funding target in each cell. In addition, the state set a goal of one-third funding from tuition and two-thirds from state appropriation. Most states had not yet allowed tuition to rise to even 20% of costs at the time, so this was a relatively high-tuition model (Carnegie Commission on Higher Education, 1973). The new Minnesota plan also had an explicit link between tuition and student aid policy. Need-based student grant aid covered students' costs minus Pell grants and expected student and family contributions. Following implementation, MHECB funded studies of the impact of the new policies on enrollment by low-income students, which documented the program's positive impact (Hearn et al., 1985; Minnesota Higher Education Coordinating Board, 1987).

Other problems occurred as the MHECB sought to build and hold together a political coalition supporting reform. The state legislature did not replace line-item funding with a general budget allocation with the new average-cost formula using the two-thirds state support because of the requested funding increases (St. John, 1991). After the average-cost funding model was adopted, a state auditor uncovered financial mismanagement, resulting in the resignation of the UM President in 1988 (St. John, 1991). During a period of tax revenue shortfalls, the university had failed to "inform the governor or legislature about excess revenues from the hospital. When the information finally became public in 1988, the University of Minnesota's system quality improvement campaign, 'A Commitment to Focus,' ran into political problems and was withdrawn from legislative consideration" (p. 275). However, amid this controversy, the MHECB launched a center in Rochester, Minnesota, involving cooperation between the university, state colleges, and the community college system.

Perhaps the most remarkable feature of the Minnesota model is that it has held together for nearly three decades, albeit with changes along the way. Hearn and Anderson (1989, 1995) conducted two studies of implementation, documenting that continued collaboration between researchers and policymakers played a role in maintaining the basic model in a policy environment. The ability to sustain political commitment to the model resulted from political support for all sectors, a coalition that has been difficult to hold together in most other states (Hossler et al., 1997). Coordinating mechanisms built into the Minnesota model included an emphasis on funding targets that assured adequate funding for campuses, a balance of tuition and student aid ensuring stability in the ability to meet demand as the state's share of funding declined gradually, and student aid sufficient to fund low-income students who enrolled in both public and private colleges.

The Evolution of Strategy

While Minnesota embraced a liberal market approach to funding higher education, it was never easy for the MHECB to hold together political coalitions to fully support the model (Hearn & Anderson, 1989). As the model evolved, decreasing the percentage of education costs subsidized by the state proved necessary. Over time, Minnesota's governors and legislatures frequently lacked the will to fund the coordinated scheme. The MHECB was dissolved and replaced by the Minnesota Office of Higher Education (MOHE), an agency with less overall budget authority and a more limited focus on the administration of state financial aid programs. The higher education system office assumed direct responsibility for proposing budgets and lobbying for its state funding. Student grant aid became less central to the shared agenda of all three systems. There was an effort to develop a policy center at the University of Minnesota to provide analyses for the state, but this vision was never fully realized. Due to these systemwide challenges, tuition rapidly rose to more than one-third of average costs. There were also changes in the basic precepts of the student grant program, which undermined its effectiveness, especially concerning student debt and student outcomes.

Student Aid Strategy Restructuring in 2010

By 2010, MOHE had developed a new scheme for coordinating state grants and tuition charges, using the logic of both explicit and implicit assigned responsibility. The model explicitly assigned family responsibility as the ability to pay, based on federal need analysis methods; taxpayer responsibility through aid to colleges and students; and student responsibility for a work/loan burden. In addition, students had an implicit responsibility for the costs of attendance beyond expected work/loan contributions, grants, loans, and other sources.

Since creating the average costs strategy, Minnesota has awarded state grants after the Pell Grants, reducing its obligation by the amount of money students received from that program (Hearn & Anderson, 1989). The 2010 strategy made explicit a student obligation to assume loans and work at a level approaching $8,000 per student, an extremely high amount to expect from low-income students whose families qualified for full Pell funding. Further, the maximum award, combining Pell plus state grant aid, was capped at $16,000. Because the state cap subtracted the grant award from its maximum award, the neediest students received a lower state grant than students in the lower-middle-income group. Thus, the new award scheme was not optimal for students in the lowest income group regarding their choice of institution or the purchasing power of their grant packages. Since the state maintained a maximum award and subtracted the Pell Grant award from the state grant amount, the state grant program tilted toward favoring middle-income students who did not qualify for the maximum Pell. With the rising tuition charges, the net cost after the combined aid increased, especially for low-income families. The emphasis on loans after 2010 was a significant departure from the original design of the Minnesota model. With cuts to Pell especially, the MOHE did not hold to old commitments when faced with the impact of federal finance policies.

The most severe problem with the restructured model was that Minnesota's explicit work/loan burden was substantially higher than the federal standard established in the Pell formula. In the federal need-analysis methodology, the student contribution was 50% of assets above $2,500. A second problem was that there was evidence that student borrowing, especially by lower- and lower-middle-income families, was excessive in Minnesota because of the combination of explicit and implicit costs. In 2007–2008, Minnesota participated in a national study of student borrowing. That year, Minnesota students enrolled in each type of institution had substantially higher debt than the national average for students enrolled in similar institutions, even community college students (Lydell, 2008).

TRENDS IN K-16 POLICIES

Minnesota has a distinctive history in K-12 education and in the market system used to finance higher education. The patterns of change in academic preparation, college access and diversity, and 6-year college degrees are reviewed below.

High School Preparation Policies

In 2019, the Federal Reserve of Minneapolis (Grunewald, 2019) issued a report on the state of educational achievement in Minnesota, finding that while overall, students outperformed their peers in most states, internally, gaps by race, ethnicity, and class were among the largest in the nation. The report considers outcomes across K-12 education, including standardized testing, graduation rates, and college readiness indicators, and in all cases, low-income and racially minoritized students scored well behind their white and Asian peers. The findings over time are more mixed. They show some modest improvements in closing achievement gaps and high school graduation rates by race and ethnicity but increasing gaps by income, as measured by free or reduced lunch eligibility. While Minnesota appears to perform well compared to other states, the system may be less equitable than others.

In the national discourse, advocates for higher graduation standards claimed the policy would reduce inequality in college access. Despite problems with the public financing of higher education in the past decade, Minnesota has maintained its K-12 preparation standard and outcomes. It has also been a leading state in implementing policies supporting college preparation (Table 8.1). The state implemented math standard in 1995 and required an exit examination beginning in 1997. It required three math courses for graduation by students in the high school class of 2007. Geometry became a requirement for the 2008 graduating class, a more rigorous standard than most states. The policy

Table 8.1 Minnesota High School Graduation Requirements

Course Requirements (21.5 credits)
English Language Arts—4 years
Math—3 credits, encompassing Algebra II, Integrated Math III or equivalent*
Social Studies—3.5 credits, including government & citizenship**
Science—3 credits, Earth & Space, Biological & Physical
Arts—1 credit
Personal Finance—1 credit**
Physical Education—local determination
Health Education—local determination
7 elective credits

* Grade 8 students are required to complete Algebra I
** Requirement applies to the class of 2028

Source: Minnesota Department of Education (2023). Graduation Requirements. Retrieved from https://education.mn.gov/mde/dse/gradreq/

landscape began to change in 2013. The state eliminated the mandatory exit exam as a graduation requirement (Hawkins, 2012), corresponding with a modest uptick in state high school graduation rates.

Today, Minnesota requires all students to complete 21.5 credits in high school, including three credits of math that extend through Algebra II or the Integrated Math III state equivalent, three credits of science that span the physical and life sciences, and 3.5 credits of social studies, including a course of government and citizenship (Minnesota Department of Education, 2023). In many ways, they have maintained a college preparatory curriculum for all, and unlike other states, they also require 8th-grade students to complete Algebra I as defined by state standard. In 2022, the state modified its standard, including a list of course equivalencies students could use to meet specific requirements. For example, economics taught in an agricultural and technical program could satisfy a half-credit social studies course, and either computer science or a Career and Technical Education (CTE) course could fulfill a math requirement. Minnesota has not established multiple pathways as other states have, but they have added flexibility to the state statutes. Even with the partial pathways approach, Minnesota has more combined science and math requirements than the national average (Chapter 4).

STATE FINANCING OF HIGHER EDUCATION

Minnesota incrementally abandoned its historic commitment to fully funding need-based grant aid to finance its postsecondary education market model. Further, Minnesota is a state with an exemplary history of academic preparation. Therefore, this case provides a unique window for the impact of reductions in student need-based grants and the emergence of high tuition, combined with high loans. We trace Minnesota's trends in public finance, enrollment rates, college success, and racial equity gaps below.

Funding Higher Education in Minnesota

Public In-State Tuition and Fees

Like most states, Minnesota has seen some increases in the price of public higher education after adjusting for inflation. Public tuition and fees in Minnesota are higher than the national averages for 4- and 2-year institutions; they are relatively more affordable at the 4-year level than for community colleges. Figure 8.1 shows the cost of tuition and fees at a public 4-year institution, which is nearly $13,000, compared to the national average of $11,260. Community colleges are 50% more expensive than the national average at $6,134 compared to $3,990. Both rates have declined modestly in the past two years but remain among the highest states in the nation.

State Funding of Public Higher Education

Minnesota has experienced considerable volatility in state appropriations for higher education over the past 20 years. The cyclical nature of state funding epitomizes the balance wheel function higher education plays in the state budget (Delaney & Doyle, 2007). Minnesota's state and local appropriations per FTE student to public colleges were higher than the national average in 2000 but lower than average by 2010 ($4,985 per FTE in 2022 dollars). As Figure 8.2 demonstrates, per FTE, spending in Minnesota has improved slightly over the past decade, mirroring gains that we have seen across the country.

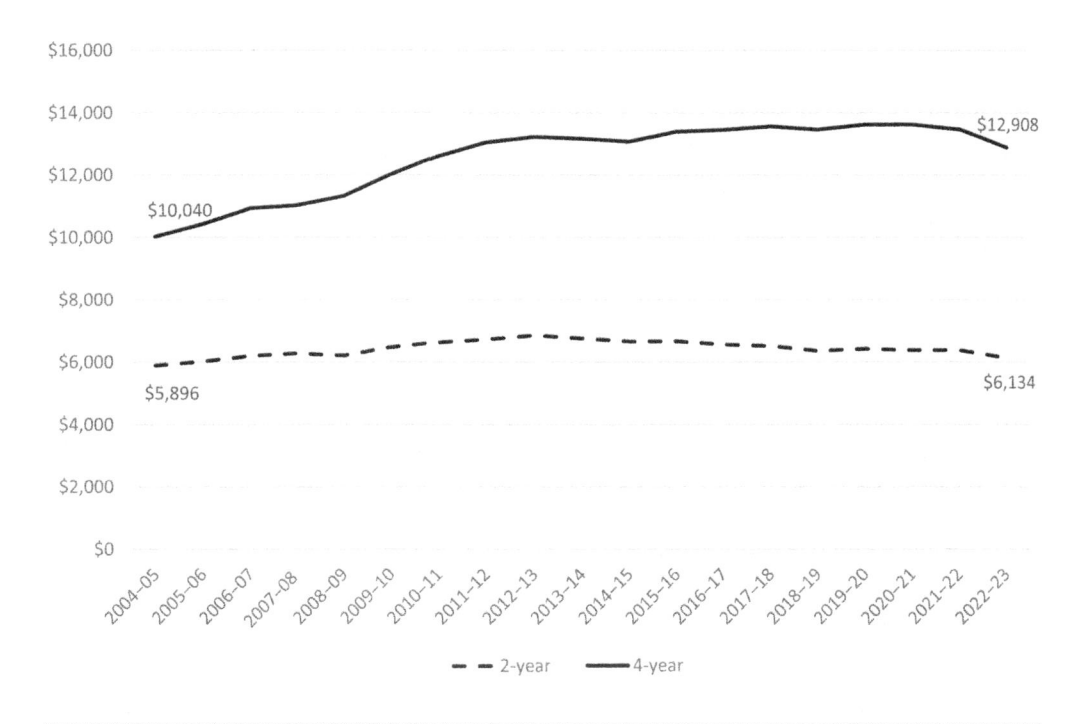

Figure 8.1 Trends in Minnesota Public Tuition & Fees (in 2022 dollars)
Source: Ma and Pender (2023). Trends in College Pricing and Student Aid 2023. New York: College Board.

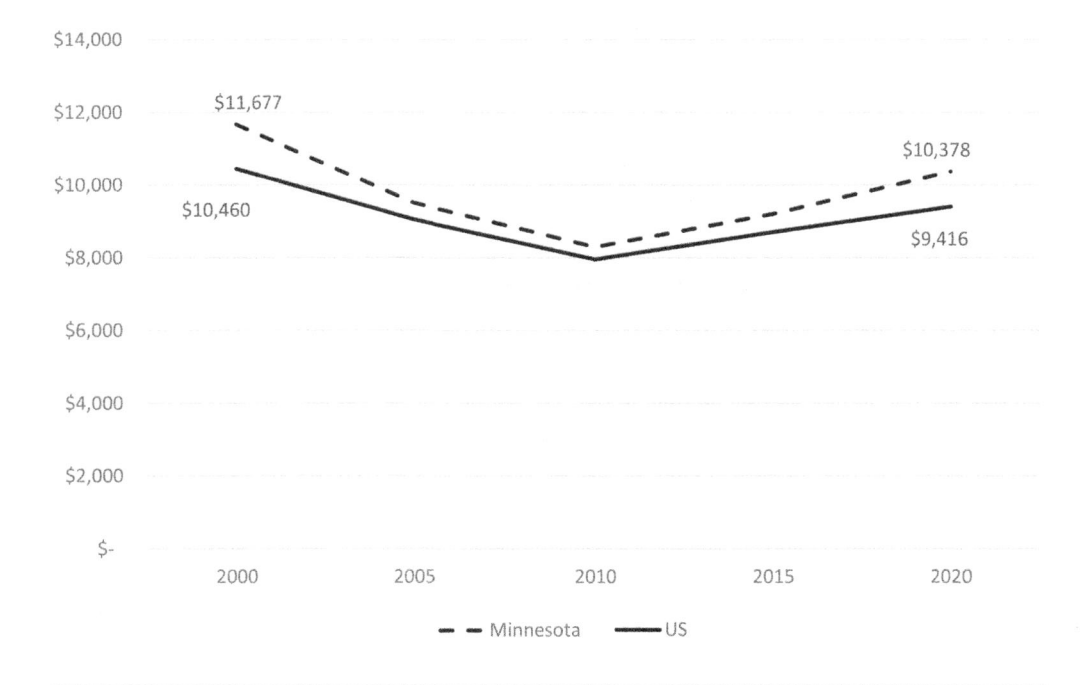

Figure 8.2 Minnesota State Appropriations per FTE (2020 Dollars)
Source: State Higher Education Executive Officers (SHEEO) Grapevine Annual Reports and NCES, Digest of Education Statistics (2023) Table 307.20.

172 • State Cases

Even with recent improvements, the 2020 funding levels remained behind the 2000 levels, but the direction is positive. The one caveat is that these numbers may be improving partly because of a decline in enrollments, which has been consistent across most states in recent years. Given the decrease in state funding from 2000 through to 2010, combined with only modest increases through 2020, Minnesota transferred college costs from taxpayers' direct subsidies to college to students in the form of tuition increases. Tuition increased while state appropriations declined between 2000 and 2020.

A Step Toward Restoring State Need-Based Grants

Coordinating increases in public tuition charges with increases in student grants reduces inequalities (St. John, 2006; St. John & Asker, 2003). That is the promise of the high-tuition, high-aid model. Minnesota embraced the high-tuition model, but the aid had consistently fallen short. State grant funding per FTE student in Minnesota's public and private higher education system began to drop even before college subsidies. In 1992, state grant funding per FTE student exceeded the national average ($904 compared with $441 in the United States). Figure 8.3 shows that Minnesota support for need-based aid per FTE hit a low in 2005 at approximately $650 per student and has grown about $100 per FTE over the past 15 years to $755 per FTE. Minnesota continues to invest more in need-based aid than the national average, but it has not recovered to the amounts invested 20 years ago. In fact, given the drop in the average state need-based grant award, the rise in student self-help (work and loans), and the rise in tuition is virtually the same as the national pattern.

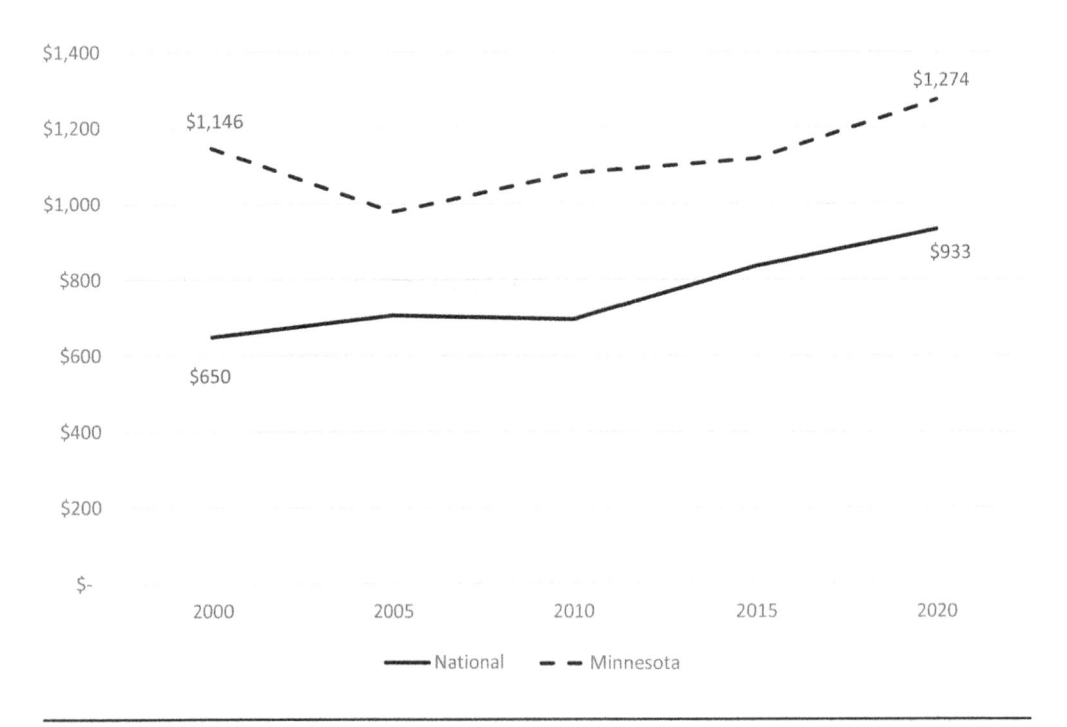

Figure 8.3 Minnesota Need-Based Aid per FTE (2020 Dollars)

Source: National Association of State Student Grant & Aid Programs (NASSGAP) (2022). Annual Survey Report. NCES, Digest of Education Statistics (2023) Table 307.20.

Minnesota has not invested much in non-need-based aid, so it does not fit Minnesota's affordability strategy. In 2000, Minnesota spent less than a dollar per FTE on non-need-based assistance, which only increased to about $6 in 2022. The amount is inconsequential for the state, considerably less than the national average of $245 per FTE. When we view increases in need-based aid coupled with increases in state appropriations per FTE, we may see why tuition and fees have declined modestly in recent years. Non-need grants were not central to Minnesota's market model's original design and intent.

When students' costs increase, elite public colleges rely more on providing merit aid to wealthy students from wealthier families, a vanity reward for students who can otherwise pay more. Therefore, it is essential to track aid practices at the University of Minnesota to explore whether campus aid policies contribute to income and racial stratification. The average tuition increased by nearly $3,000 in 2020 ($12,908) over 2000, but the increased appropriation for grants per FTE increased only about $130. With the decline in Pell's purchasing power, it is apparent that family wealth was an increasingly important part of financial access to public 4-year colleges in Minnesota.[2]

TRENDS IN STUDENT OUTCOMES

The three types of outcomes influenced by changes in state policies on preparation and higher education finance are high school graduation (directly related to preparation requirements), college enrollment (affected directly by finance policies and dual enrollment and indirectly by other preparation policies), and colleges degree attainment (affected directly by campuses policies and practices and state finance policies and indirectly by state academic preparation requirements). Trends related to these three types of outcomes are summarized below.

High School Graduation

One of the critical antecedents to college enrollment is the successful completion of the high school diploma or its equivalency. As we show earlier, national trends suggest that high school graduation rates are improving, and the gaps between racially minoritized students and those who identify as either white or Asian are closing. Unlike many other states, Minnesota had improved high school graduation rates for African Americans between 1996 and 2008. However, as the Federal Reserve report noted, those gaps have grown in recent years and are among the largest of all states in the country. In 2010, 77% of Minnesota high school students completed high school, compared to 79% nationwide (Figure 8.4). Both rates have improved over the last decade, and the gap remains roughly 2 percentage points. The Federal Reserve Bank of Minneapolis (Grunewald, 2019) estimates that the gap between Black and white students has declined from more than 30 percentage points 20 years ago to only 18 points in 2019, a considerable gap but consistent with the trends reported nationally. While graduation rates lagged the national average, the trajectory of improvement was similar. The high math and science requirement may be an explanation. The benefit would depend on whether there were gains in graduation rates, a factor observed in the national data (Chapter 4).

Student Academic Achievement

Like many Midwestern states, Minnesota utilizes the ACT for college admission more consistently than the SAT. In 2022, only 2,142 students took the SAT (College Board,

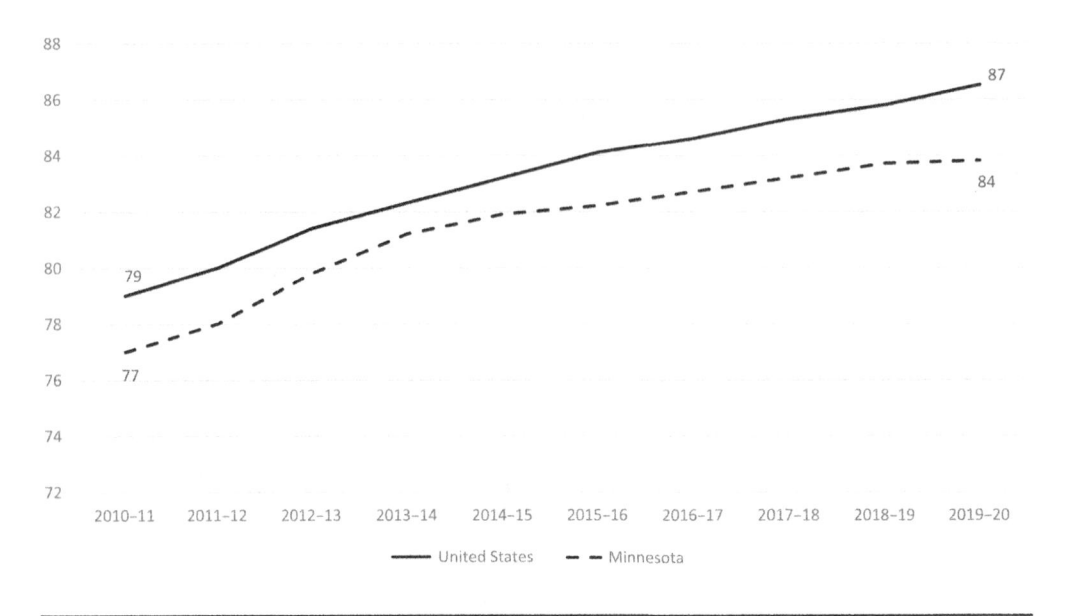

Figure 8.4 Public High School Graduation Rates in Minnesota, 2010-11 Through 2019-20
Source: National Center for Education Statistics (2023). Digest of Education Statistics, Table 218.46.

2023b), compared to 39,881 ACT takers (ACT, 2023). Reporting SAT scores is not meaningful because only 4% of students took the test. Consistently across states, the lower the percentage of students completing the test, the higher the average test scores, which is true in Minnesota. The average SAT composite score for Minnesota high school students was 1,225, compared to a national average of 1,050 (College Board, 2023a). Minnesota has consistently had higher test scores than other states, which is true for the ACT. According to ACT, 69% of Minnesota high school graduates took the ACT, and the average composite score was 20.8, compared to a national average of 19.5 (ACT, 2023). Assessing gaps by race and ethnicity is more challenging because ACT does not publish individualized state reports like the College Board. According to the 2018 state profile, the Black/white gap in ACT scores in 2018 was nearly 6 points (16.5 v. 22.2). A 22 ACT composite is roughly equivalent to an 1120 SAT score. In contrast, a 16 ACT is equivalent to an 890 SAT combined score—a larger difference than the Black/white SAT score gap nationally of 172 points (926 v. 1,098), which is consistent with the concerns raised by the Federal Reserve Bank of Minneapolis regarding racial equity gaps.

Access and Diversity

Access and diversity are closely intertwined policy issues that interact with the distribution of diverse groups within states. In Minnesota, most African Americans reside in the Twin Cities, and there is a growing Black immigrant population in St. Cloud and Rochester. There is geographic access for minoritized students in Minnesota. Still, preparation and the ability to pay for college—dependent, in part, on federal, state, and institutional aid—influence access among prepared students. Along with university campuses in these cities, Minnesota's community colleges, private colleges, and proprietary colleges also face the challenge of reaching out to provide better pathways to higher education for diverse students.

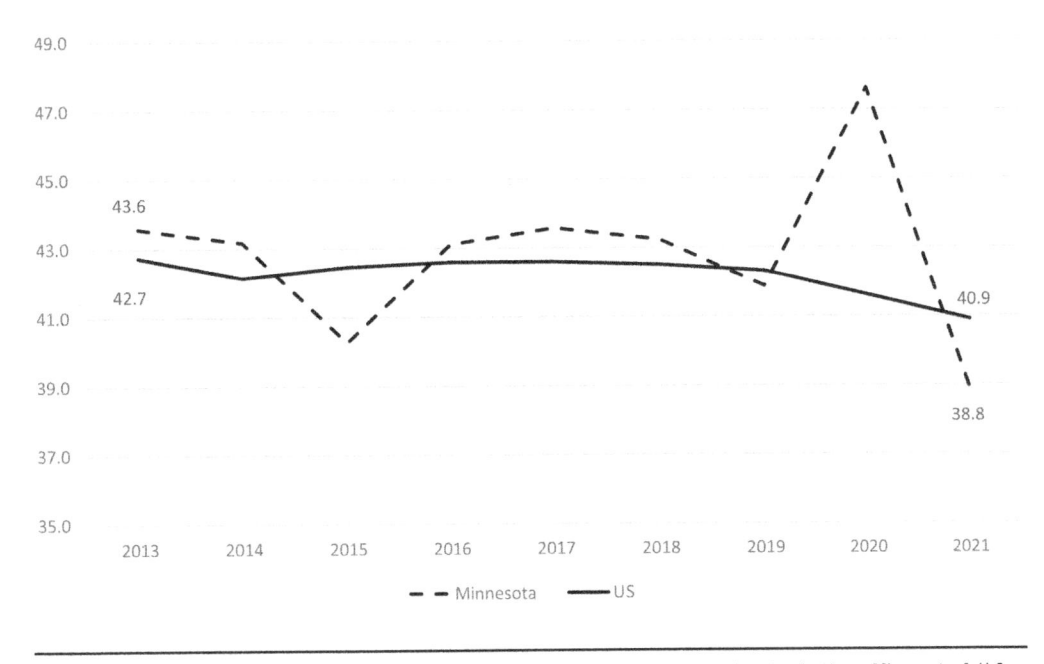

Figure 8.5 Percentage of 18- to 24-Year-Olds Enrolled in Degree-Granting Postsecondary Institutions: Minnesota & U.S.
Source: National Center for Education Statistics (2023a). Digest of Education Statistics, Table 302.65.

College Enrollment

In Minnesota, college participation rates of 18–24-year-olds have been consistent with national trends for nearly a decade. As Figure 8.5 illustrates, 43.6% of young adults in Minnesota enrolled in college compared to 42.7% nationally. In 2020, Minnesota experienced a spike of an additional 4 percentage points but dipped significantly in 2021 to a low of 38.8%. Some of this volatility is a consequence of the pandemic, but it is unclear why the Minnesota rates were much more variable than the national figures. From enrollment data and financial trends, there are reasons to suspect that Minnesota is falling short of this older policy goal set as part of the planning for the market model.

When we disaggregate college participation rates for 18–24-year-olds in Minnesota, we observe consistent gaps of 25–30 percentage points between Asian and Hispanic students until 2021, when participation rates drop for all groups and appear to reduce the gap considerably (Figure 8.6).[3] In that year, white students and those who identified with two or more races attended college at a rate of nearly 42%, compared to 25% for Hispanic students and 35% for Black students. It is unclear why participation rates among Asian students dropped so precipitously from 2020 to 2021. Xenophobic treatment Asian students received as backlash to the COVID pandemic is a plausible reason.

The drop in Black enrollment after 2017 is alarming, given the erosion of the market model. In addition, the decline of enrollment in degree-granting institutions raises another red flag. It is possible that students, families, and society's collective understanding of debt may have caught up with the eroding Minnesota market model. High tuition and inadequate need-based grants—including Pell and state grants—contribute to further stratification, channeling more students into 2-year colleges. Biden's good jobs

176 · State Cases

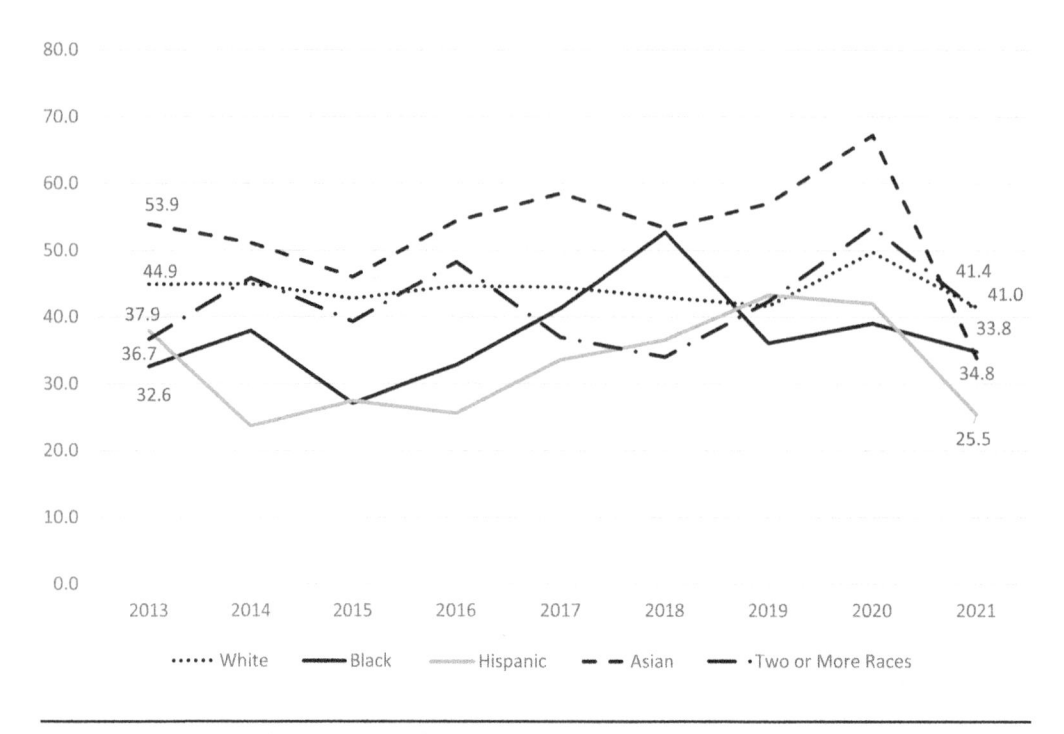

Figure 8.6 Percentage of 18- to 24-Year-Olds Enrolled in Degree-Granting Postsecondary Institutions, by Race/Ethnicity: Minnesota

Source: National Center for Education Statistics (2023). Digest of Education Statistics, Table 302.65.

policies may provide a viable alternative for young adults, though it may be too early to say by 2021.

Another perspective on equity in college enrollments is to compare college participation rates by race to their proportion in the state population. Figure 8.7 depicts these trends from 2000 to 2020. The data reveals that Black students have been over-represented in higher education relative to their proportion of the state population. This trend has shifted significantly from 2000, when they were only slightly over-represented, to the past decade, when they were twice as likely to be enrolled in college compared to their proportion of the state population. White students, however, have been underrepresented in higher education relative to their total population, a trend that has intensified over 20 years. Hispanic students, who were much less likely to attend college in 2000 relative to their population percentage, saw their representation increase by approximately 25% by 2020, exceeding expectations based on Minnesota's population demographics. It is crucial to contextualize these figures. Minnesota is predominantly white, and while it has become more diverse since 2000, over 75% of the population identifies as white (U.S. Census Bureau, 2023) (down from 88%, 20 years earlier). Our earlier data also indicated that Black students were over-represented in 2-year colleges and the for-profit sector, a trend likely persisting today, given national enrollment trends. Regrettably, we could not disaggregate racial disparities by the institution's sector.

No matter how the problem is sliced and diced, the dramatic climb in Black student enrollment at public 2-year colleges shows that economic stratification is a growing reality in Minnesota. Blacks, the lowest-income ethnic group in the state, attend 2-year

The Market Model Reconsidered • 177

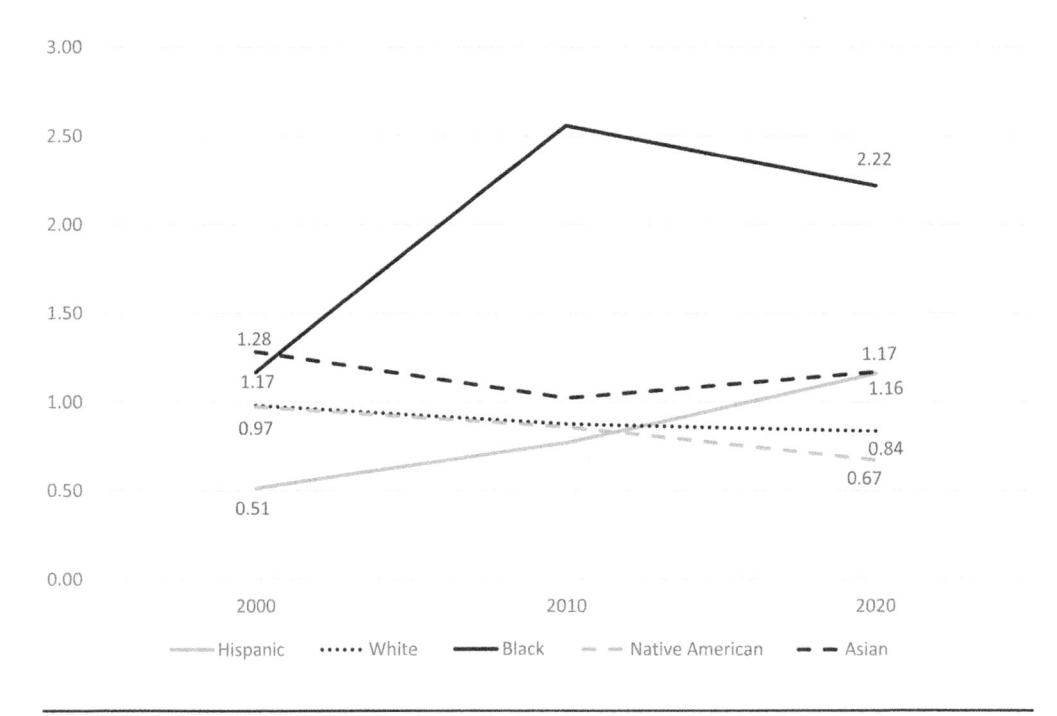

Figure 8.7 Racial/Ethnic Representation in Minnesota Postsecondary Education as a Proportion of the State Population
Source: National Center for Education Statistics (2023). Digest of Education Statistics, Table 306.70 & Table 266 & US Census Bureau.

colleges at two times the state average. This analysis uses percentages adjusted for the population, including students returning to college.

College-Degree Attainment Rates in Minnesota's Higher Education System

Timely attainment of degrees is vital for students' wellbeing through adulthood and states' social and economic development. College degree attainment rates are related to family background, academic preparation, initial college choices, and student financial aid. When states keep colleges affordable for low- and middle-income residents, students are likelier to have timely degree attainment (completion within six years). Trends in timely degree attainment rates are below, using 6-year graduation rates, whether students begin at 2- or 4-year institutions, based on National Student Clearinghouse (NSC) data.

Bachelors' Degree Attainment Rates by Race for Student Starting at 4-Year Public Institutions

The 6-year degree-completion rates for students who started their postsecondary education at a Minnesota public 4-year institution have remained relatively consistent for the 2012–2017 cohorts (Figure 8.8), except for the gain in attainment by Blacks over time. White students have consistently graduated around 80% of the time. Both Asian and Hispanic students experienced declines of 3–5% during the same period. On the other hand, Black students significantly increased their timely degree attainment by 10 percentage points from the 2012 to 2017 cohort. As a result, the racial gaps between Black and white students in Minnesota's college graduation rates have shrunk from approximately 25 percentage points down to 17 points.

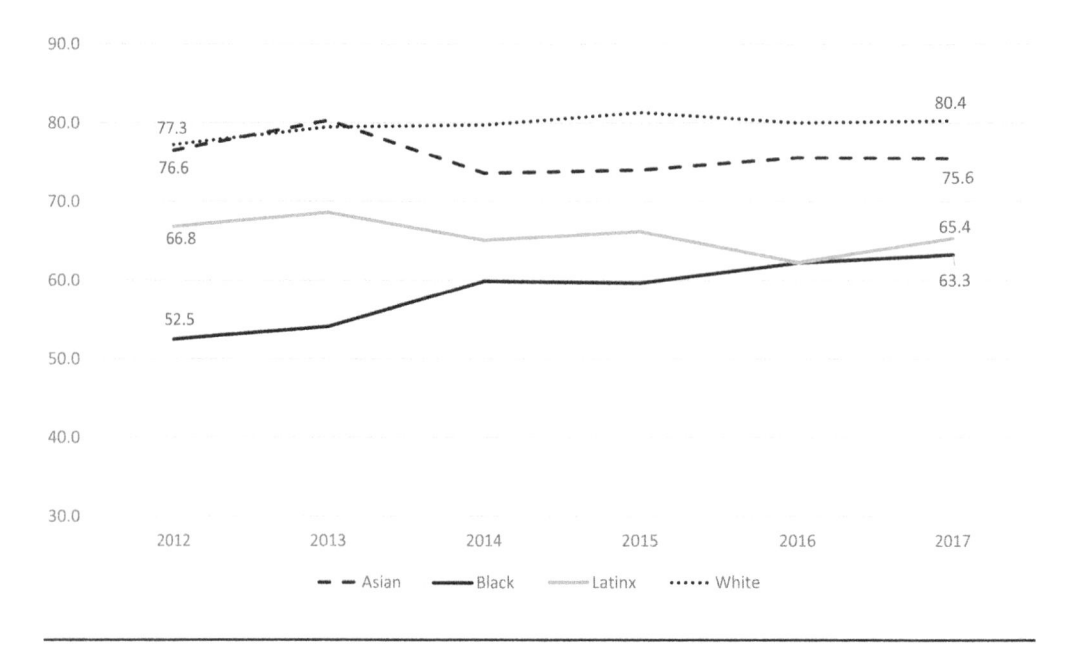

Figure 8.8 Trends in 6-Year Degree Attainment Rates for all Minnesota Public 4-Year Postsecondary Institutions
Source: National Student Clearinghouse Research Center (2022). Completing College: National & State Reports. Retrieved from https://nscresearchcenter.org/completing-college/

The gain in Black student degree attainment over this period is especially noteworthy and merits more attention. There are three possible explanations for these gains. First, perhaps campuses improved aid packaging for Blacks compared to other groups. Since such practices by universities are now essentially banned because of the Supreme Court decisions in the *North Carolina* and *Harvard* cases (see Chapter 2), if true, this finding might not reveal legal practices for the period ahead. The aid packaging hypothesis may be of historical interest and could perhaps inform the development of race-conscious aid programs (a topic discussed in the private college section below). Second, it is also possible that STEM requirements implemented in Minnesota benefited Black high school students who, in prior decades, would have been vocationally tracked, a hypothesis discussed in Chapter 6. The second explanation supports arguments that historical differences in preparation disparities in college-degree attainment had been caused by inadequate financial support for college (e.g., Allen, 1992; Chapter 2), an argument that differs in substance and intent from the access rationale developed by the US Department of Education in the 1990s (Chapter 3). Prior research also indicates that improvement in state aid reduces the white-Black persistence gap because more Blacks have financial need (St. John, 1999), but this is not relevant to the Minnesota case during this period. The second hypothesis merits the attention of higher education researchers. Trend analyses do not provide sufficient evidence to discern which of these hypotheses is better supported by empirical evidence, a question that requires a more sophisticated statistical analysis. Additionally, the prior research finding that improvement in state grant funding reduces white-Black persistence gaps merits attention as states debate policies promoting education attainment and workforce development.

More significantly, at least concerning state policy aims, the size of the gap in 4-year degree attainment rates for Latinx and Black compared to white and Asian students is troubling. The reduction in the white-Black degree attainment gap does not mean the size of the gap is not still a problem. The hypothesis that improved college preparation for Blacks explains the reduced white-Black attainment gap raises further doubts that financial aid packaging had an impact on gains in Black 4-year degree attainment in Minnesota. Further, the white-Hispanic attainment gap is especially troubling because of the decline in Hispanic racial representation in public 4-year colleges. The growing underfunding for high-need students in Minnesota could explain the persistent gap. While it is encouraging that the white-Black attainment gap declined, possibly because of improved preparation, the findings alter the conclusion that the state's grant aid was inadequate for low- and middle-income students with documented financial need, a seriously problematic conclusion for students and the Minnesota economy.

There is a troubling gap in 4-year college graduation rates for Latinx and Black compared to white and Asian students. The growing underfunding for high-need students in Minnesota could explain the persistent gap. The only encouraging sign is that the gap did not increase and even narrowed slightly. Improved STEM requirements may benefit Black students who, in prior decades, would have been vocationally tracked (a hypothesis discussed in Chapter 4).

Degree Attainment Rates by Race/Ethnicity for Students Starting at Minnesota's Private 4-Year Nonprofit Institutions

A large percentage of colleges in Minnesota are private nonprofit institutions. Out of 74 public, private, nonprofit 2-year, and 4-year institutions, 33 are private, compared to 13 public 4-year institutions and 28 community colleges. Overall, students who begin college at a private 4-year nonprofit college are slightly more likely to complete in six years than their public institution peers (Figure 8.9). More than 85% of white

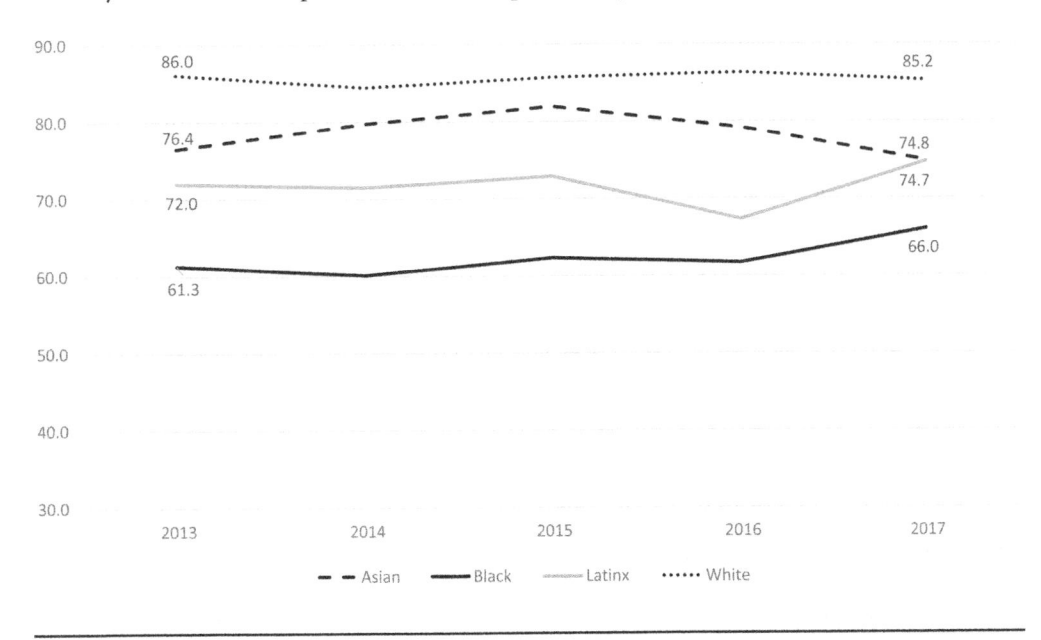

Figure 8.9 Trends in 6-year Degree Attainment Rates for all Minnesota Private Nonprofit 4-Year Institutions

Source: National Student Clearinghouse Research Center (2022). Completing College: National & State Reports. Retrieved from https://nscresearchcenter.org/completing-college/

students in the cohorts beginning college in 2012–2017 starting at Minnesota private 4-year colleges completed within 6 years, followed by Asian and Hispanic students (both at 75%) and then Black (65%) students (Figure 8.9). Graduation rates among Black students are similar whether they attend public or private 4-year colleges. Still, the rates are considerably lower for Hispanic/Latinx students (75% compared to 65% at 4-year public institutions).

The racial gaps are troubling, but the recent decrease is promising, given financial indicators. Private 4-year colleges may be targeting aid using their financial-need and other indicators that get support to students who can benefit from it. In addition, in some institutional and state cases, race-conscious student aid provided through state and campus programs can overcome disparities (St John el., 2007). For example, in Minnesota, Augsburg University maintains financial access for American Indians: "Augsburg's American Indian Recognition Full Tuition Program aims to support and promote the importance of American Indian students on campus. Unlike many public institutions, Augsburg's program does not limit eligibility to American Indian students who live in the state." The NSC data did not include American Indians. Given the national decline in enrollment by American Indians, better data collection and reporting are necessities for better-informed public policy. The 2023 Supreme Court decision in the *Harvard* case may have implications for the legality of race-conscious, campus-based scholarship programs, an issue for legal scholars to consider.

Degree Attainment Rates by Race for Students Starting at 2-Year Public Institutions
Consistent with national figures, students who begin at a community college are less likely to graduate than those at public or private 4-year institutions. Approximately 60% of white students in the five cohorts completed in six years; the percentage did not substantially change over the period considered (Figure 8.10). Graduation rates for racially minoritized students fluctuated slightly over that time, possibly attributed to their smaller proportions of the state population. Perhaps the more important finding is that the gaps between Black and white students have remained unchanged at approximately 23 percentage points, indicating persistent disparities. The low-degree attainment rates for Hispanics and Blacks, are seriously problematic for Minnesota higher education, the state's economy, and especially for students who chose 2-year campuses because it is the most affordable option.

It is difficult to compare these rates to those from earlier periods because the data available today are different than they were during our previous editions. The National Student Clearinghouse (NSC) data follows students through completion, whether they stay at the same institution or transfer to another, a critical issue for community colleges because transfer articulation is essential to their mission. To put this into perspective, we reported that a third of white students graduated from community colleges in 150% of the time in 2002 (a tighter window of time than what NSC reports), compared to only 12.7% of Black students. These numbers are much lower than what we are reporting for recent cohorts of graduates, but the gap between the groups has remained essentially the same. In 2002, the gap was 21 percentage points, and for the most recent cohort, the gap was about 22 points. The Federal Reserve Bank of Minneapolis (Grunewald, 2019), in its assessment of inequality in education in the state, did not consider college completion, but their concerns about persistent gaps remain accurate at this level.

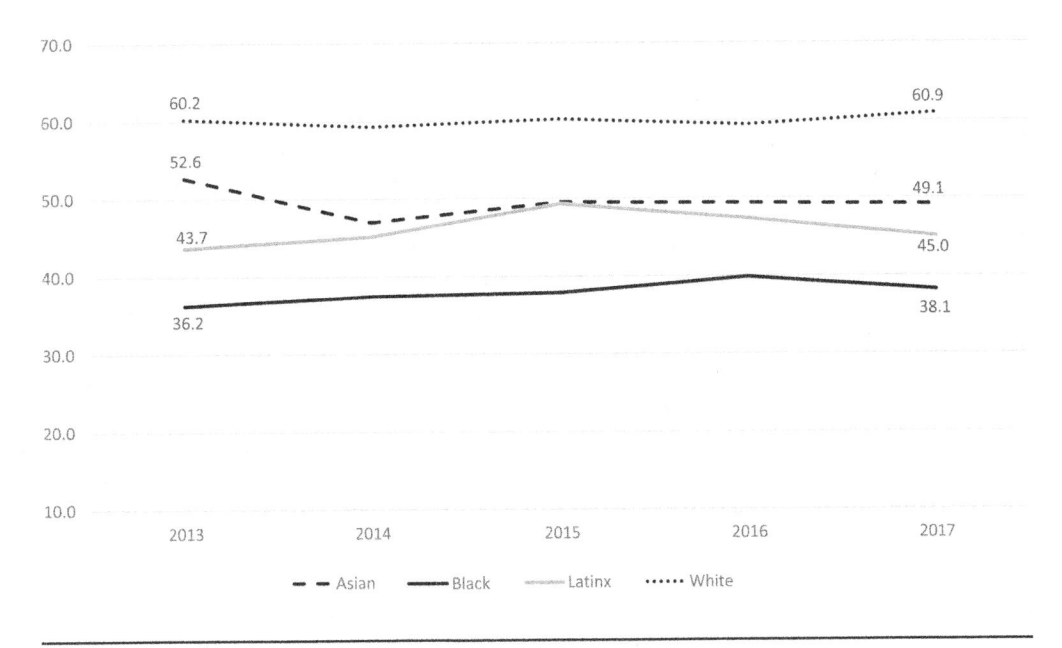

Figure 8.10 Trends in 6-Year Degree Attainment Rates for all Minnesota Public 2-Year Postsecondary Institutions
Source: National Student Clearinghouse Research Center (2022). Completing College: National & State Reports. Retrieved from https://nscresearchcenter.org/completing-college/

Improving Access and Success, but Gaps Persist

Earlier, we characterized Minnesota as providing constrained access to postsecondary education. Today, the trends are encouraging overall but problematic from an equity perspective. High school graduation rates are rising, college participation rates have improved, and degree completion is higher, even when we compare the more modest NSC numbers for completion at the same institution to earlier periods. The success rates include students who transfer institutions, providing a more complete picture of student success. Unfortunately, despite these gains, our assessment is consistent with that of the Minneapolis Federal Reserve Bank. Minnesota's overall success masks persistent racial gaps in our data and is likely consistent if we were to examine differences by family income as well. The facts that tuition is declining modestly and both appropriations and need-based aid per FTE are up suggests that the state may be returning to its market strategy of high tuition and high aid.

CURRENT ISSUES IN MINNESOTA

Minnesota has embraced a high-tuition/high-aid model for the funding of higher education, and, to date, they have fared reasonably well. In 2020, 39.1% of Minnesota adults above age 25 had attained a bachelor's degree or above—which is second only to Massachusetts and is 8 percentage points higher than a decade prior (U.S. Census Bureau, 2023). Tuition rates across the two public systems—particularly in the University of Minnesota System—have been higher than other states in the region, and their track record on funding for postsecondary education is mixed. In 2000, Minnesota state appropriations per FTE were approximately $8,400, which was about 10% higher than the national average. By 2005, the state had fallen behind the national averages, and even with increases since 2010, Minnesota lagged the nation by $450 per FTE. In 2011, in-state students paid $15,859 for tuition and fees at the Twin Cities campus of UM (National Center for Education Statistics, 2023b). The in-state tuition rates for the University of Minnesota, as the public flagship, have increased much more slowly since 2019 than was the case back in 2011, when the increases over four years were close to 30%. The Minnesota State College and University (MNSCU) System remains a relative bargain for in-state students at approximately $9,400 per year.

Minnesota's critical policy issues relate to its market orientation and commitment to a high-tuition/high-aid approach to funding higher education. Johnstone (2001) warned more than two decades ago that the danger inherent in the high-tuition/high-aid model is that the state will fail to keep its promise in terms of aid; this is where the Minnesota case is beginning to show some strain. Finally, like other states trying to reign in what they consider out-of-control expenses in public higher education, Minnesota has cut funding substantially and committed a small portion of those cuts to performance funding. It is essential to consider each of these policies, both in the context of the Minnesota case and relative to the challenges facing other states across the country. The two most significant policy changes in Minnesota pertain to eliminating the mandatory exit exam for high school and implementing the new North Star Promise Scholarship, which is following in a long line of promise programs designed to reduce costs for lower-income students and families.

Changing Graduation Requirements

Like many states nationwide, Minnesota increased its requirements for a high school diploma through the 2010s. The state requirements in 2024 are like the expectations more than a decade ago—21.5 Carnegie units in the core academic subjects, including English (4), Math (3), Science (3), and Social Studies (3.5). They even require Algebra II or Integrated Math III, among the more rigorous math sequences, to be aligned with state math standard. The difference we discussed earlier is the flexibility built into the exceptions the state policy allows, creating de facto pathways for students who may not find the traditional core college prep curriculum appropriate.

The more significant change in Minnesota was eliminating the short-lived mandatory exit exam. Students slated to graduate from high school between 2010 and 2014 were required to pass minimum competency exams in reading, writing, and math or an alternative set of requirements. All students were required to test as proficient on the three sections of the Minnesota GRAD test in 2015. As Fair Test (2017) reported, Minnesota eliminated the requirement as soon as it went into effect. The combination of the modifications to the graduation requirements and the elimination of the Minnesota GRAD Test has reduced the constraints placed upon the students and schools, allowing them greater curricular flexibility.

Changes in State Grant Programs

In the late twentieth century, Minnesota kept its promise of high tuition and aid. After 2000, however, the higher-than-average need-based aid did not offset the high tuition resulting from lower-than-average state appropriations per FTE commitments. In 2024, the Minnesota Office of Higher Education (2023) launched the North Star Promise, which "will create a tuition and fee-free pathway to higher education for eligible Minnesota residents, at eligible institutions as a 'last dollar' program by covering the tuition and fees remaining after other scholarships, grants, stipends and tuition waivers have been applied." In theory this would raise total federal and state grants to qualifying low-income students. If the state does carry through with its side of the promise, the lowest-income students would still have to borrow for living costs (i.e., room and board). It is a big step back toward the intent of the market model but may fall short of restoring fairness.

To be eligible for the North Star program, they must be a Minnesota resident, have an adjusted family income of less than $80,000, attend a Minnesota public institution or tribal college, and meet several academic stipulations regarding the number of credits and progress toward one's first degree. It is too soon to know how this program will affect the overall affordability picture in Minnesota. It does not reduce the sticker price, which is higher than average, but it will likely make college more affordable for lower-income students and their families.

Performance Funding

Minnesota is not a state with a long history of investment in performance funding, and it has proven to be a difficult policy to manage effectively. From 1994 to 2007, the legislature allowed for a 1% increase in funding for the state system, but that funding did not materialize (Gehring, 2016). In the 2008–09 fiscal year and from 2012 to 2017, the state distributed 1% of total appropriations based on performance metrics. These resources have been contingent upon improvements in graduation rates, institutional diversity, and other state priorities. In 2017, the state shifted from 1% to 5% conditional funding, which is a considerable increase but is on the lower end for states that have adopted performance funding strategies. Research on performance funding has generally found that the modest amounts states set aside do not significantly affect institutional behavior (Dougherty et al., 2016; Gehring, 2016), which could be the result for Minnesota. Performance funding aligns with the market orientation of Minnesota's higher education policies. It identifies the goal but allows institutions to develop the most cost-effective strategies to achieve the goal. Unfortunately, performance funding typically favors campuses most capable of reaching the benchmarks, which are institutions that frequently serve more privileged students (Hillman et al., 2015; Umbricht et al., 2015). The consequence may be that fewer resources are allocated to campuses most likely to serve underrepresented students.

REFRAMING SUCCESS

Instead of concluding as though the cases were a status report, we encourage readers to reflect on the implications of the updated Minnesota for the financial wellbeing of residents. As is the case in most other states, most college graduates who borrowed face economic challenges that are more severe than would have been true if the state had adhered to the original market strategy, developed in a planning process conducted in collaboration with researchers from the University of Minnesota and support by the Ford Foundation.

Focus on Financial Wellbeing

We consider earnings and college debt to affect the wellbeing of residents–college graduates, non-graduates, high school graduates, and those with no college. We discuss debt, attainment, and earnings considering three periods of higher education finance in Minnesota—the market model in the late twentieth century, the decline of the early twentieth century, and the hope that the North Star Promise will provide a better future.

College Debt by Minnesota Graduates

In the *Minnesota Reformer*, Madison McVan (2023) summarized the status of students in Minnesota, tying hope for improvement to the North Star Promise:

- Nearly two-thirds of Minnesota students who graduated with bachelor's degrees last year have student debt, and those who took out loans owe an average of $24,000.
- Students earning master's and doctoral degrees take out loans less frequently, but when they do, they borrow more money than undergraduates, according to a Minnesota Department of Higher Education report.
- Many students at for-profit universities, meanwhile, are beset with a financial albatross when they finish: Bachelor's students at for-profit universities take on the most debt by far—85% of students graduate with loans, with a median cumulative debt of more than $39,000.
- Overall, the median debt for Minnesota students earning associates and bachelor's degrees has decreased by more than 10% since 2012.
- Minnesota college debt could soon decrease even more starting in 2024 as the state's new North Star Promise scholarship program kicks in after the DFL-controlled Legislature passed it into law earlier this year. The program will cover tuition and fees for students whose parents make less than $80,000 per year—just above the median household income for Minnesota.

However, Minnesota has high poverty in many of the Black neighborhoods, a reality exposed by the news coverage of George Floyd's death and the trials that followed. With this alarming reality, we must also recognize that the inequality extends to college debt facing Black graduates: "Black students borrowed an average of $58,400 in 2020 from all higher-ed institutions, which was higher than the average amount borrowed from students who are Asian ($49,100), of two or more races ($43,400), white ($43,300), Hispanic ($41,700), or American Indian/Alaska Native ($36,900), according to the Nation Center for Education Statistics" (Minnesota Education Equity Project, 2023). Thus, the debt for Blacks more than doubles the state average, including white student debt, illustrating the consequence of the last dollar grant method, subtracting Pell award from the state grant maximum award when it falls so far below the cost of attendance. This practice denies low-income students the advantage of federal aid and increases their dependence on debt, a strategy that increases lifetime indebtedness and long-term wealth inequality.

Adult Education Attainment

Associates and bachelor's degree recipients in Minnesota were substantially overrepresented compared to the national averages (Figure 8.11), suggesting the state's undergraduate aid programs were relatively successful in mitigating the effects of college costs on adult postsecondary attainment. Minnesota's high level of undergraduate degree attainment appears to be the outcome of maintaining high academic standards in K-12 education and delivering education to its citizens. Academic attainment indicates a higher degree of success. High schools delivered on the educational promise of neoliberalism better than most states.

However, the erosion of the state's college finance strategy paints a more troubling picture, especially given the high debt burden facing African American college graduates. The late twentieth-century college students who benefited most substantially from Minnesota's

The Market Model Reconsidered • 185

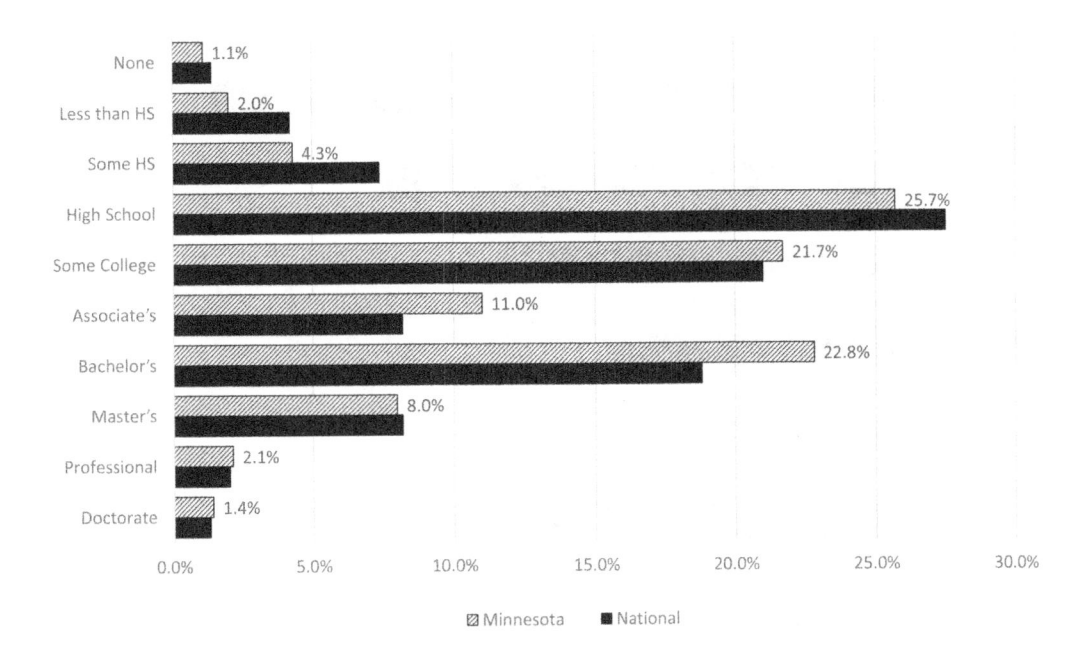

Level	Minnesota	National
None	1.1%	
Less than HS	2.0%	
Some HS	4.3%	
High School	25.7%	
Some College	21.7%	
Associate's	11.0%	
Bachelor's	22.8%	
Master's	8.0%	
Professional	2.1%	
Doctorate	1.4%	

Figure 8.11 Highest Level of Educational Attainment for People 25 or Older in Minnesota (2020)
Source: Statistical Atlas (2023). Educational Attainment. Retrieved from https://statisticalatlas.com/United-States/Educational-Attainment

adherence to the market model would be mostly mid-career or further along in 2020. It is possible, too, that as midcareer adults, they would have been able to invest in their children's education, the generation rising into college during the 2000–2020 period when the purchasing power of federal and Minnesota grants was declining; their loans may have filled the financial gaps that were building. The increased reliance on debt accentuated savage inequalities for Black Minnesotans who navigated into and through college.

Investment in rising student generations and the intent of the North Star Promise for the lowest-income groups may be sufficient to keep attainment levels rising. In terms of continuing attainment patterns, Minnesota may have found a path, for now at least.

Adult Earnings by Education Attainment Level

The comparisons of Minnesotans' earnings by education level (Figure 8.12) provide a slightly different twist to this (speculative) stargazing. People with no diploma, high school diploma, and some college had more substantial earning differentials over the national average than those with bachelor's degrees or higher. Given the debt burden of Minnesota students, this pattern of earnings raises intriguing issues in the Minnesota case.

First, the national data illustrate that borrowers with the highest attainment also had the highest debt and monthly repayment. To the extent that adherence to the market model in the late twentieth century reduced debt, mid-career and more senior people with advanced degrees would not have had as severe debt burdens during their early careers as their age-related peers in most other states or as high as younger working Minnesotans.

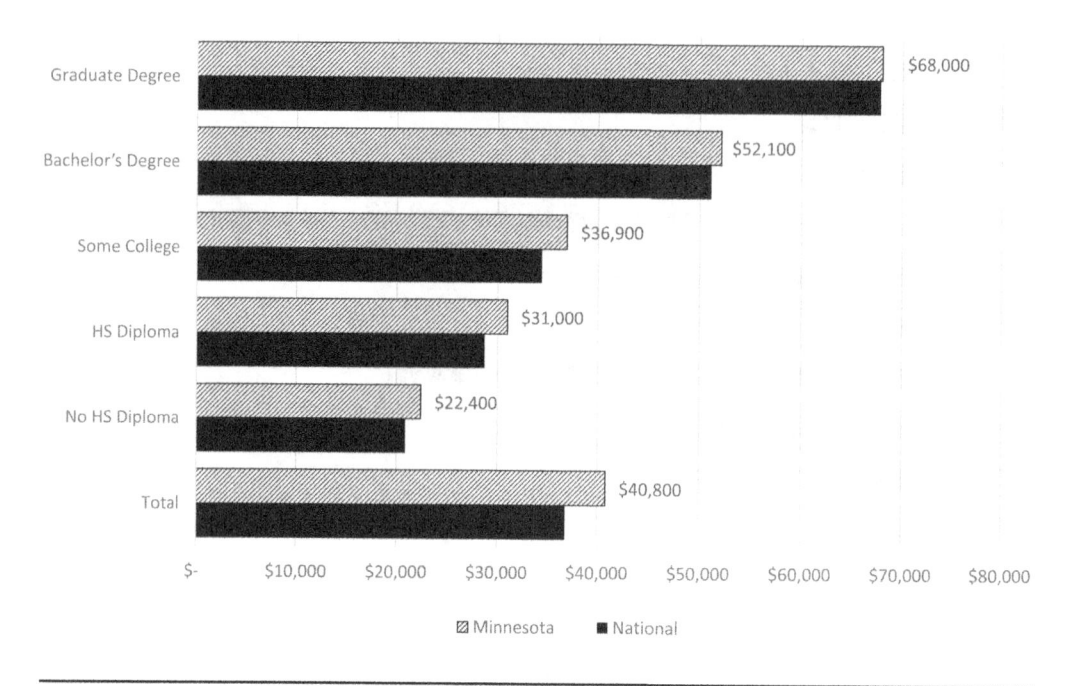

Figure 8.12 Median Annual Earnings in Minnesota by Level of Education (2020)
Source: Statistical Atlas (2023).

Second, the economic challenges would be more perplexing for the early-career Minnesotans who graduated during the 2000s. Minnesota college graduates are among the most severely indebted in the nation (Minnesota Education Equity Project, 2023). While some will benefit from Biden's debt forgiveness, most Minnesota graduates will continue with a high debt burden, and their earnings will not be higher than average. Thus, they face more severe circumstances than the early-career workforce nationally. Regardless of their postsecondary attainment level, debt burden remains an issue for most Minnesotans who borrowed to attain at least some college, undergraduate, and advanced degrees.

Finally, the patterns of earnings for students with less than bachelor's provide other twists to the puzzle:

- Adults with no high school diploma or a high school diploma but no college earned more than the average for similarly educated people nationwide. Thus, not enrolling in college and not borrowing provided some economic advantages for Minnesotans across adult working generations.
- Minnesotans with some college (associate or college non-completers) also earned more than their similarly educated peers nationally. The early career workers (people in the cohorts entering college in the 2000s) face the most perplexing situations because they face college debt that would impact their ability to get by economically. Returning to college could come at a very high long-term cost for them.
- Even if, on average, Black Minnesotans with some college or degrees earn the same average wage as their white peers, they have double the debt burden, and they were more likely to have borrowed. Thus, wage inequality, measured by net earnings after debt repayment, remains a bleak outcome of Minnesota's higher education finance policy.

Navigating Toward the North Star Promise

In Minnesota, as in other states, college debt adds to the challenges facing citizens who attend college whether or not they graduate. The strong Minnesota economy has provided more economic opportunity than most states, but not all Minnesotans have ventured into college since the state-aligned grants in the 1980s. Like other states, Minnesota had a history of racial inequality in K-12 and higher education. However, our reading of trends suggests that by delivering on the improved graduation requirements, Black students were better prepared and, therefore, had the academic background to improve their odds despite high college costs.

Statistics on education and earnings illustrate that Minnesota's adult population is better educated than the nation, a probable benefit of the aggressive pursuit of the market model in the late twentieth century. Earnings in 2020 were also higher for all education levels than for the nation. However, people with bachelor's and advanced degrees received a minor advantage over their national education peers than did people with some college or less.

Implemented in fall 2024 (Minnesota Office of Higher Education, 2023), the North Star Promise might mitigate the worst effects of the debt burden for rising generations of Minnesotans and restore trust in the Minnesota system. However, confidence in education is eroding nationally, and it remains unclear how states can restore hope for educational and economic uplift across generations. Minnesota provides a compelling case because of the progressive values underlying its higher education finance strategy in the late twentieth century. The case also illustrates that market theories have limitations, especially when the public lacks the will to stay the course, which is the pattern thus far this century in Minnesota. The imagery of the North Star relates to navigating the seas a night before more advanced technologies evolved. With the idea of equity in the public's mind, the state may find means for ensuring financial wellbeing for more citizens and immigrants to work and contribute taxes.

Questions

1. How does Minnesota's pioneering story add substance the state's evolving methods of financing education uplift?
2. How did Minnesota's late twentieth-century market model compare to the neoliberal model that evolved in the state?
3. Does the K-12 education system in Minnesota address social, racial, and economic inequalities compared to the nation's current trajectory for college preparation?
4. What lessons emerge from the erosion of Minnesota's market model in the early twentieth century?
5. How does the high education level of Minnesotans add or detract from the state's capacity to deliver on the North Star Promise? Does the plan address the problems inherent in the state's evolving higher education finance schemes?

NOTES

1 Gresham Collum provided this additional paragraph as part of his review. He discussed the treatment of Native American as part of his job talk at the University of Minnesota.
2 The North Star Promise pays tuition and fees for students from families with $80,000 adjusted or less (Minnesota Office of Higher Education, 2024), a progressive step forward that could overcome some of the disparities evident in the trends reviewed below.
3 Native Americans are not included in this table because they were not included in the data we used for this figure.

REFERENCES

ACT. (2023). *Average ACT Scores by State Graduating Class of 2022.* https://www.act.org/content/dam/act/unsecured/documents/2023-National-ACT-Profile-Report.pdf

Balderston, F. E. (1974). Cost analysis in higher education. *California Management Review, 17*(1), 93–107.

Berg, D. J., & Hoenack, S. A. (1987). The concept of cost-related tuition and its implications at the university of Minnesota. *Journal of Higher Education, 58,* 276–305.

Brye, D. L. (1977). Wisconsin Scandinavians and progressivism, 1900-1950. *Norwegian-American Studies, 27,* 163–193.

Carnegie Commission on Higher Education (1973). *Continuity and discontinuity: Higher education and the schools.* McGraw Hill Book Company.

Cheit, E. F. (1975). *The useful arts and the liberal tradition.* McGraw-Hill.

College Board. (2023a). SAT Suite of Assessments Report. Retrieved from https://reports.collegeboard.org/sat-suite-program-results

College Board. (2023b). SAT Suite of Assessments Report: Indiana. Retrieved from https://reports.collegeboard.org/media/pdf/2023-indiana-sat-suite-of-assessments-annual-report-ADA.pdf

Collom, G. (2024). *History of Minnesota Higher Education.* In E. P. St. John (Ed.).

Delaney, J. A., & Doyle, W. R. (2007). The role of higher education in state budgets. In K. Shaw, & D.E. Heller (Ed.), *State postsecondary education research: New methods to inform policy and practice.* Stylus.

Dougherty, K. J., Jones, S. M., Lahr, H., Natow, R. S., Pheatt, L., & Reddy, V. (2016). *Performance funding for higher education.* Johns Hopkins University Press.

Fair Test. (2017, November 2023). Graduation Test Update: States that Recently Eliminated or Scaled Back High School Exit Exams. https://fairtest.org/graduation-test-update-states-recently-eliminated/

Gehring, M. (2016). Performance-based Funding in Minnesota Higher Education. https://www.house.mn.gov/hrd/pubs/perffundhe.pdf

Gluek, A. C. (1965). *Minnesota And the manifest destiny of the Canadian northwest: A study in Canadian-American relations.* University of Toronto Press.

Grunewald, R. (2019). A Statewide Crisis: Minnesota's Education Achievement Gaps.

Hawkins, B. (2012, December 6). Few would likely mourn an end to Minnesota's high school exit tests. Minneapolis Post. https://www.minnpost.com/learning-curve/2012/12/few-would-likely-mourn-end-minnesotas-high-school-exit-tests/

Hearn, J. C., & Anderson, M. S. (1989). Integrating postsecondary education financing policies: The Minnesota model. In R. H. Fenske (Ed.), *Studying the impact of student aid in Institutions* (Vol. 62, pp. 55–73). Jossey-Bass.

Hearn, J. C., & Anderson, M. S. (1995). The Minnesota financing experiment. In E. P. St. John (Ed.), *New directions for higher education: Rethinking tuition and financial aid strategies* (Vol. 89, pp. 5–25). Jossey-Bass.

Hearn, J. C., Sand, H., & Urahn, S. (1985). *Targeted subsidization of post-secondary enrollment in Minnesota: A policy evaluation.* U. O. Minnesota.

Hillman, N., Tandberg, D., & Fryar, A. H. (2015). Evaluating the impacts of "New" performance funding in higher education. *Educational Evaluation and Policy Analysis, 37*(4), 501–519.

Hossler, D., Lund, J., Ramin, J., Westfall, S., & Irish, S. (1997). State funding for higher education: The sisyphean task. *Journal of Higher Education, 68*(2), 160–190.

Jarchow, M. E. (1973). *Private liberal arts colleges in Minnesota: Their history and contributions.* Minnesota Historical Society Press.

Johnson, F. L. (2013). Creating Hamline, Minnesota's first college. Retrieved from https://www.minnpost.com/mnopedia/2013/05/creating-hamline-minnesotas-first-college/

Johnstone, D. B. (2001). Financing higher education: Who should pay? In P. G. Altbach, R. O. Berdahl, & P. Gumport (Eds.), *American Higher education in the twenty-first century* (pp. 347–369). The Johns Hopkins University Press.

Lydell, L. (2008). *How families pay for college: An analysis of national and state-level survey research*. Minnesota Office of Higher Education. http://www.ohe.state.mn.us/pdf/SGR9-HowFamiliesPayforCollege.pdf

Ma, J., & Pender, M. (2023). Trends in College Pricing: 2023. Trends in Higher Education Series, Issue, Issue. https://research.collegeboard.org/trends/college-pricing

McVan, M. (2023). *Nearly two-thirds of Minnesota undergrads take out student loans*. Minnesota Reformer. Retrieved from https://minnesotareformer.com/briefs/minnesota-undergrads-take-out-student-loans/.

Minnesota Department of Education. (2023). Graduation Requirements. Retrieved from https://education.mn.gov/mde/dse/gradreq/

Minnesota Education Equity Project. (2023). What does Minnesota's student debt look like? https://www.mneep.org/2023/08/02/what-does-minnesotas-student-debt-look-like/.

Minnesota Higher Education Coordinating Board. (1982). Final Report of the Task Force on Future Funding of Postsecondary Education.

Minnesota Higher Education Coordinating Board. (1987). Headcount Enrollment by Racial/Ethnic Group.

Minnesota Office of Higher Education. (2023). North Star Promise Scholarship. Retrieved from https://www.ohe.state.mn.us/sPages/northstarpromise.cfm

National Association of State Student Grant and Aid Programs. (2022). 53rd Annual Report on State-Sponsored Student Financial Aid. https://www.nassgapsurvey.com/survey_reports/2021-2022-53rd.pdf

National Center for Education Statistics. (2023b). *College navigator*. National Center for Education Statistics. Retrieved from https://nces.ed.gov/collegenavigator/

National Center for Education Statistics. (2023a). Digest of Education Statistics. https://nces.ed.gov/programs/digest/2023menu_tables.asp

National Student Clearinghouse Research Center. (2022). Completing College: A State-Level View of Student Attainment Rates. Retrieved from https://nscresearchcenter.org/completing-college/

Nute, G. L. (1930). Posts in the Minnesota fur-trading area, 1660-1855. *Minnesota History*, 11(4), 353–385.

Somers, P., Woodhouse, S. R., & Cofer, J. E. Sr (2004). Pushing the boulder uphill: The persistence of first-generation college students. *Journal of Student Affairs Research and Practice*, 41(3), 811–828.

St. John, E. P. (1991). A framework for reexamining state resource management strategies in higher education. *The Journal of Higher Education*, 31(4), 387–403.

St. John, E. P. (1999). Evaluating state grant programs: A case study of Washington's grant program. *Research in Higher Education*, 40(2), 149–170.

St. John, E. P. (2006). *education and the public interest: School reform, public finance, and access to higher education*. Springer Press.

St. John, E. P., & Asker, E. H. (2003). *Refinancing the college dream: Access, equal opportunity, and justice for taxpayers*. Johns Hopkins University Press.

State Higher Education Executive Officers. (2023). State Higher Education Finance Annual Report. Retrieved from https://shef.sheeo.org/grapevine/?report_page=welcome

Statistical Atlas. (2023). Educational Attainment in the United States. https://statisticalatlas.com/United-States/Educational-Attainment

U.S. Census Bureau. (2023). Minnesota Profile. Retrieved from https://data.census.gov/table/ACSST1Y2022.S1501?q=Minnesota%20education

Umbricht, M. R., Fernandez, F., & Ortagus, J. (2015). An examination of the (Un)Intended consequences of performance funding in higher education. *Educational Policy*, 31(5), 643–673.

9

THE ERODING BALANCED MODEL

The Indiana Case

Indiana's comprehensive approach to promoting educational attainment combines the promise of student aid sufficient for low-income students to pay the costs of public colleges. The first state to develop a comprehensive approach to improving educational opportunities for low-income students, Indiana has undergone a shift toward extreme conservatism this century. The case starts with Indiana's story from the origins of the state higher education system, through the development of the comprehensive strategy, and to its evolution since 2005 when the state's balanced conservative-progressive political governance undermined the maintenance of this distinctive approach. Next, we examine policy and funding changes, educational outcomes (i.e., college preparation, enrollment, and attainment), and current policy issues and encourage readers to reframe meanings of college success as portrayed in the Indiana case.

THE INDIANA STORY

The comprehensive approach to promoting education attainment evolved during an innovative period of change in the 1990s and 2000s. After introducing the key features of the Indiana approach, we provide a historical perspective of the origins and evolution of Indiana's higher education system as a background for discussing the politics and processes involved in developing the state's approach, which is evolving now without integrated political support.

Key Features of the Comprehensive Approach

Indiana developed a comprehensive approach to increasing college attainment before any other state. At the time, most states responded to mandates for college preparatory curriculum independent of adaptations in college funding and student aid. The Indiana Education Policy Center (hereafter the "Center"), a politically non-partisan center founded by faculty at Indiana University with support from the Lilly Endowment, provided studies for the Indiana Department of Education, the Governor's Office, the Indiana Commission on Higher Education, the Governors, and legislative staff in the

1980s, 1990s, and 2000s, providing integrative information to diverse political interest groups (McCarthy et al., 2000). The Center and other research groups' studies provided evidence for integrative thinking and facilitated discussion in politically fragmented contexts. However, political action in the state develops the comprehensive model through an evolutionary, often disjointed political process. The three program features of Indiana's comprehensive approach provide background.

Integrative Approaches to School Reform

Center studies addressed a broad range of K-12 policy issues. Studies of teacher development, reading programs, and higher education finance fostered integrative thinking about reform, involving cross-agency, cross-party officials in thinking about and enacting reform strategies in K-12 education that provided evidence-based approaches that tested liberal and conservative ideas in planning and evaluation studies on professional development for teachers, integrated approaches to curriculum development, and evidence-based budget reform (Bull et al., 1994; St. John et al., 2003; Theobald, 2003). Center staff took jobs in state government as agency officials coordinated tactics on program proposals and funding. For example, the idea for improving K-12 graduation standards was developed by a legislator, encouraged by a staff member in the student aid agency, and integrated into the system before the state was required to mandate it. The evolution of graduation requirements is described below, after these reforms and contemporary issues are placed in historical perspective.

The Promise of Student Aid for Low-Income Students

A precursor to the Promise programs that now proliferate, the Twenty-First Century Scholars Program was the first state-level program to provide encouragement and guaranteed grant aid equaling tuition for low-income students who pledged to prepare for college. The common feature of Promise programs is the commitment to meet financial need, as a level of commitment ranging for tuition at public 2-year colleges to meeting costs at 4-year colleges. The Twenty-First Century Scholars Program provided extensive services along with an aid guarantee to pay college costs. The Scholars provided low-income students who took the pledge with encouragement for college preparation and college application support during a period when the state was creates a new college prep options for high school graduates and maintain student funding for need-based grants.

Support Servicing Supporting Underrepresented Students

Support services offered low-income students and their parents opportunities to learn how to help them prepare for and succeed in college. Governor Evan Bayh signed the program into legislation in 1990, but it was controversial and began as an unfunded mandate. In 1990, the Lilly Endowment partnered with the state by funding the parent component, and eventually, the state of Indiana funded its grant obligation. Twenty-First Century Scholars became a national model (Advisory Committee on Student Financial Assistance, 2002), with program features replicated in other states. Indiana's comprehensive strategy evolved from its fiscally conservative approach to building the public higher education system after World War II. The current wave of state Promise programs builds on Indiana's innovative history by adding guaranteed student aid into their strategies for promoting access and attainment.

The region that became Indiana entered the union after the French and Indian War via the *Northwest Territories Ordinance*. Making less investment in education than either Ohio or Illinois, the states of its Eastern and Western borders, Indiana found ways to innovate for less.

Early Foundations of Public and Private Colleges

Indiana followed the path of statehood pioneered by Ohio in the Northwest Territory but with less government investment. This ethos continued from humble beginnings through the twentieth century. Yet, Indiana found its path over time, minimizing state investment and maintaining diverse programs when possible. In recent decades, the nation has empowered states to return to theocratic principles of the founding colonies.

After Ohio became a state in 1803, the Northwest Territory was renamed the Indiana Territory and provided the starting point for expanding westward to Illinois, Wisconsin, and part of Minnesota. After a period as the frontier territory and gateway to the West, Indiana became a state in 1816. South Indiana became a conservative agrarian region before the Civil War. It continued with that legacy, as Northern Indiana became the home for the Boilermakers at Purdue and industrialization as part of the greater Chicago area, the chemical industry helped build Indianapolis, and the rural regions retained their religious foundations.

College Founding in the Early American Period

Public higher education began before independent colleges in the Northwest Territories. The second university in the Northwest Territories, Vincennes University, was founded in 1806 as a seminary for learning at an outpost for settlers moving west, opening pathways for settlers moving toward the Mississippi (Burnett, 1933). Similar to California's missions during the period, the founding documents focused on educating indigenous peoples as well as immigrant Europeans settling in the West. Vincennes remained a 2-year college and eventually became a partner in the state's community college system. Indiana University started as a seminary in 1820, after the state donated township land to service as a seminary of learning, focusing on Greek and Latin. The seminary ended in 1828 as the college expanded its curriculum (Woodburn, 1940).

Like Ohio, Indiana had private colleges founded by various faith groups, some founded before the Civil War and many afterward. Established in 1827 by Quakers, Hanover College is the oldest private college in Indiana. Eleutherian College, founded in 1848 to provide admission to whites and formerly enslaved Blacks, continued operating as a private, coeducational school until the mid-1880s (Indiana Division of Historic Preservation and Archaeology, 2024). Notre Dame started in 1842. Indiana now has about 60 private colleges. Many private college campuses, including Notre Dame and Indiana Wesleyan, maintain strong faith-based identities as the state evolved a strong Christian polity—Indiana is now a conservative, Christian state (Pew Research Center, 2024).

Public Higher Education After the Civil War

The end of the Civil War sparked a new era of education development. Two percent of the state's population had graduated high school in 1870, 6.4% in 1900, 26% in 1940, and 36% in 1950; despite the relatively slow growth of high schools, a diverse collection of colleges developed after the Civil War. Founded in 1869 with a gift of 100 acres from the university's namesake, John Purdue, Purdue University became the state's response to the Morrill Act. The university's first degree, awarded in 1875, was in Chemistry. The science orientation at Purdue versus the theological origins of IU reflects the history of their college founding and their conflicting missions after the Civil War. It also illustrates the substantial diversity of political and social interests in Indiana. The tension between science and Christian values, symbolized by the Lilly Endowment's support for Christian communities and education, created the context for channeling profits from medical chemistry into programs that strengthen Christian values in communities, colleges, and the state (Lilly Endowment, 2024).

Like Indiana University in the 1960s, Purdue developed 2- and 4-year college campuses across the states, some as IU-PU partnerships. Purdue University developed a statewide engineering school, and Indiana University created a statewide medical school, illustrating the state's effort to avoid duplicative costs of education development, the path taken in the liberal states in the region. This strategy enabled the state to develop multiple engineering programs under the direction of Purdue and medical education across the state under the direction of Indiana University. This strategy was a low-cost way for the state to expand high-cost education programs across locales without creating competing institutional interests.

The Indiana Technical College, founded as a for-profit college in 1930, nearly shut down during WWII when most men went to war but surged after the war as veterans took advantage of the GI Bill, using technical education to gain opportunities during industrialization after WWII. In the late 1940s, it reorganized as a nonprofit and eventually became IVY Tech, a state institution, in 1963. The IVY Tech system partnered with Vincennes to start the Indiana Community Colleges in 1995, illustrating the conservative, balanced approach to college development.

Restructuring Public Higher Education

Indiana's public higher education system developed a distinct set of generally accessible public colleges. The state's research universities—Indiana and Purdue—have branch campuses. Indiana University provided geographic access to 2-year degrees with guaranteed transfer to four-degree programs through their regional branch campuses. Joint Indiana-Purdue campuses developed in Indianapolis and Fort Wayne, with programs lodged organizationally at the two main campuses. Some thought that Indiana had an exemplary model of 4-year degree access. Indiana's state universities—Ball State, Indiana State, and the University of Southern Indiana—were independent of these two large state systems. The state also had well-established independent colleges, including the University of Notre Dame and several liberal arts colleges.

In the early 1990s, there was no public 2-year college system in the state, but the state had 2-year access across the state: Purdue, Indiana University, and Vincennes had 2-year degree offerings at their branch campuses. IVY Tech, the state's technical college system, had historically awarded technical certificates but not college degrees. Transfer students generally came from the regional campuses of IU and Purdue. Based on a review of access in the state, Gary Orfield (1997) argued that Indiana provided better access to 4-year degrees than states with separate 2- and 4-year systems.

A Period of Change

The Indiana Commission for Higher Education, formed in 1971, comprised a 14-member board of gubernatorial appointees representing the state's Congressional districts, a faculty representative, and a student representative. Historically, Indiana's agency had a strong research capability, a tradition established by George Weathersby, who left his faculty position at Harvard to become commissioner in 1976. The state had developed a student record system for public higher education and coordinated with the Independent Colleges of Indiana, Inc. when analyses included students in private colleges. Weathersby had been staff director for the National Commission on the Financing of Postsecondary Education in the early 1970s and had helped design a robust need-based grant system. The independent colleges had a strong lobbying presence in Indianapolis for the state's need-based grant programs. Purdue, Indiana, the state universities, and IVY Tech also actively lobbied for funding, but despite these pressures, the ICHE maintained a rational budgeting formula into the 1990s.

Stan Jones, a former state legislator and student body president at Purdue University, was appointed commissioner in 1995 and served through 2000. He was the first appointee who did not come from a background in higher education. During his term as commissioner, Jones oversaw several significant initiatives, including the Twenty-First Century Scholars Program and the state's community college system. Using the state grant program levers, he also established the Core 40 as Indiana's required high school curriculum to improve student preparation for college and workforce success.

During these years, the various branches of government collaborated to develop a comprehensive, coherent set of strategies, despite divided government—at that time, one of the legislative houses was Democrat, the other Republican. The superintendent was an elected Republican. A Democratic governor appointed Stan Jones, and the statehouse remained democratic until the end of his term. The Indiana Education Policy Center, an independent research organization housed at Indiana University, collaborated with the ICHE, the governor's office, legislative staff, and foundations in the state (i.e., Lilly Endowment and Lumina Foundation) on research supporting and informing policy development throughout most of this period (St. John et al., 2003; Theobald, 2003). The IEPC was a trusted source of research but generally did not make specific recommendations in their reports; instead, policy studies informed both political viewpoints to maintain political neutrality. The credibility of the research depended on providing balanced analyses, especially given the split control of the legislature. The Democrat-Republican legislative balance shifted after 2005 as the balanced approach to policy research waned.

Indiana's Balanced Approach

Indiana's balanced approach to providing access to higher education began to develop even before Stan Jones was appointed Commissioner. The cornerstone of the strategy was the Twenty-First Century Scholars program. At the time, Stan Jones was a state legislator who supported the unfunded initiative; he served as a special assistant on education to Governor Bayh. The key feature of the Twenty-First Century Scholars program was the pledge taken by low-income students in the federally subsidized lunch programs. Students agreed to take the steps to prepare for college, remain drug-free, and apply for college and financial aid. At the same time, the program committed scholarships equaling tuition at a public college. After implementation, a balanced approach to preparation and access emerged in Indiana, providing the basis for the Academic Pathways and Theory of Change Model (Figure 3.2, Chapter 3).

Another essential feature of Indiana's balanced approach was coordination with high school preparation. Under the leadership of Dr. Suellen Reed, superintendent for public instruction in Indiana from 1992 to 2008, the state had developed an honors diploma. When Stan Jones became Commissioner of ICHE in 1995, he advocated for the Core 40 in all high schools as a step toward preparing students for enrollment in 4-year colleges. By the late 1990s, all high schools provided the full Core 40 curriculum. A school finance committee comprised the governor's office staff, legislative staff for education and budget committees, and Indiana Department of Education representatives. With analytic support from the Indiana Education Policy Center (Theobald, 2003), the committee developed a funding formula that provided supplemental funding to schools with low-income students and incentive funding for schools to improve the percentage of students graduating with Core 40 and honors diplomas.

In the years before Jones was appointed Commissioner, there had been a concerted effort to build an infrastructure that supported encouragement services. Don Hossler, a Professor at Indiana University, was actively engaged as a researcher supporting the development of the early college information programs in the state, which led to the creation of the Indiana Career and Postsecondary Advancement Center (ICPAC), charged with providing information and encouragement services throughout the state (Hossler & Schmit, 1995). ICPAC assumed coordination of the support services for Twenty-First Century Scholars but also provided information to all potential college students in the state. ICPAC collected surveys from all middle-school students, providing data used in several studies on college preparation and success in Indiana (Hossler et al., 1999). Eventually, linking these surveys with the individual student data collected by the state provided a basis for evaluating the impact of the Twenty-First Century Scholars program on college enrollment and choice of institution (St. John et al., 2002a).

In the late 1990s and early 2000s, the support services provided for Scholars expanded (Evenbeck et al., 2004). There were regional centers across the state that provided mentoring for parents and students; an extensive telephone network supported inquiries (an early in-person call center); both students and parents had opportunities to visit college campuses; and Hossler's research demonstrated the impact of the Twenty-First Century Scholars Program, which quickly became a model for other federal initiatives including GEAR UP (Gaining Early Awareness and Readiness for Undergraduate Programs) and the federal Twenty-First Century Scholars college readiness intervention program.

The primary challenge for Indiana was to ensure funding for the aid guarantee as part of the annual budget process. Over time, a series of tactics emerged. Nick Vesper, formerly a researcher with the Indiana Education Policy Center (IEPC), took a research position with the State Student Aid Commission of Indiana (SSACI) in 1995. He provided researchers at the IEPC access to the extensive student aid data supplied as part of the state system, making it possible to develop a series of studies assessing the impact of state grants on retention (St. John et al., 2000). Vesper had also helped to create a funding scheme for state grants that differentiated amounts for students based on their diploma type: 100% of the base award for students with the honors diploma, 90% of funding for high-need students with Core 40, and 80% funding for the regular diploma. Central to the new funding policy was that the maximum award for the neediest students equaled the prior year's tuition charge (when fully funded); Twenty-First Century Scholars already committed to student aid funding as part of the grant program. The previous year's tuition charge was the maximum state grant award for low-income students; Scholars also received a modest top-off award amount equaling the current year's tuition increase over the prior year (i.e., the difference between the current and previous year's tuition charges).

Before 2005, the state's differentiated student aid award scheme had hybrid merit- and need-based aid features. The commitment to fully fund the maximum award (with a modest cap off for Twenty-First Century Scholars) was held together by conservatives favoring the merit features and liberals supporting the need-based features of the state grant program that provided the bulk of the grant award. Whereas the studies of student persistence may not have been otherwise persuasive to legislators in debates about maintaining full funding for student aid, they led to the formation of an informal working group to examine higher-education finance composed of staff from the governor's office. Researchers in the policy center worked with the higher education finance committee to discuss alternative policies to maintain balanced political support. Using federal data as a resource, the Policy Center developed comparative state indicators for a report comparing Indiana's financing strategy to peer states (St. John et al., 2002b). Released with a press statement by the governor's office in 2002, the report encouraged continuing the coordination of financial strategies, similar to the Minnesota model at the time.

For a few years, the state fully funded student grants, a process reinforced by the informal indexing of the maximum state grant to the prior year's tuition. The attention given to research on comparison states helped hold together the political will to fund grants. Without this collaboration among staff and researchers, Indiana's legislature would not have sustained its commitment to fully funding the state's need-based student grant program, the foundation for improving access in the late 1990s and early 2000s. The shifting political forces in 2005, along with career-change moves by staff in the Policy Center and key state staff positions in the legislature and governor's office, virtually wiped out institutional knowledge of these practices.

The 1999 high school cohort study in Indiana found that Twenty-First Century Scholars were substantially more likely to enroll in the newly developing public 2-year colleges or private colleges (St. John et al., 2002). Some private colleges recognized that the Twenty-First Century Scholars brought substantial financial resources with them and began recruiting and retaining them actively. The private colleges did not make up the difference when the bottom fell out of the state grant program (by subtracting Pell from the maximum). The public 4-year campuses did not substantially alter their recruitment procedures to attract Scholars, nor was there much evidence of campus-based efforts to provide academic support for low-income students (Lumina Foundation for Education, 2008; St. John et al., 2011).

Political Extremism Challenges the Comprehensive Approach

Before Indiana took an extreme conservative turn in 2005, it held to a progressive path toward college development, a legacy of the Northwest Territories. Unlike the other states in the region, Indiana did not seek the highest-quality or best-funded universities; instead, its conservative and liberal politicians combined to craft a conservative-progressive approach that, with support for the Lilly Endowment, pioneered a distinctive approach to expanding postsecondary opportunity in the early 1990s. The ability to compromise around the economic and academic method of improvement, created exemplary support services that became a model for a new federal program, Gaining Early Awareness and readiness for Undergraduate Programs (GEAR UP). GEAR UP, implemented nationally in 1998, which provides federal funding for local, campus, and statewide encouragement programs and became the primary funding source for Indiana's support services for school students preparing for college.

In 2005, the state of Indiana took a radical right turn in K-12 finance policies and struggled to maintain a balanced, comprehensive approach to higher education finance. A bright, shining star of a case in the earlier editions of *Public Policy and Higher Education*, the state fell from its lofty status. Neoliberal academic and finance policies continue in the state; the implementation of vouchers and reduced school funding undermined the hope generated during the earlier period of innovation.

This case continues the story of innovation but also reveals that 2005 was a critical point, marking change in direction. The nation's trajectory was theocratic from the Colonial period, gradually giving way to secularization (Smith & Smith, 2022). Recent federal policies and Supreme Court decisions made it easier for conservative states like Indiana to return to a modern version of the founding Christian values. Yet, Indiana has made some recent changes that suggest it might bring progressive education investment back into balance with the state's core conservative values.

New Hope for Indiana's Promise

We no longer have insider's knowledge of Indiana strategic planning for higher education. However, it appears that Indiana does not subtract Pell Grants from the Twenty-First Century Scholar Award. The state program information currently describes the award as follows:

> The 21st Century Scholarship is an opportunity for students to afford college in Indiana. The 21st Century Scholarship pays up to 100% of tuition at public colleges in Indiana and part of the tuition at private or independent colleges. Learn more about the schools, colleges, and universities that accept 21st Century Scholars. The scholarship does not cover the cost of books, room and board, parking fees, lab fees, or any other fees that are not assessed to all students.
> (Indiana Commission for Higher Education, 2022a, p. 1)

This description indicates that the state has increased its investment in the program. More public campuses now recruit Scholars and package their aid programs to align with the intent of the Scholars program. The trends in policy, funding, and related student outcomes update the Indiana Story.

TRENDS IN STATE POLICY AND FUNDING

Indiana made substantial gains in college access during the late 1990s and early 2000s. Their development and continuation depended on political negotiations and tradeoffs among liberal and conservative policymakers and individual change agents advocating for strategies to improve the state's overall standing. Indiana's policies for and outcomes on preparation, access, and retention follow.

Academic Preparation Policies

The high school graduation requirements (Table 9.1) implemented math standard, required at least two math courses for graduation by 1991, and required an exit exam in 2000. A study of the implementation of the exit exams revealed adverse effects on

Table 9.1 Indiana High School Graduation Requirements

General Requirements (Class of 2019)	Core 40 Requirements (Class of 2016)
English—3 years	English—4 years
Math—2 years, Inc. Algebra I	Math—3 years, inc. Algebra I, Geometry, Algebra II
Social Studies—3 years	Social Studies—2 years, US History, + social science
Science—2 years Biological & Physical	Science—2 years, Biological & Physical with labs
Arts/World Language/CTE—1 year	World Language—2 years same language
Physical Education—2 years	Arts—1 year visual/performing arts
Ethnic Studies (2029)—1 year	Elective—1 year

Note: two additional pathways are identified for Indiana Students: Core 40 with Academic Honors (AHD) and the Core 40 with Technical Honors (THD). Beginning in 2023, students are required to complete additional graduation pathway requirements that align with either college or career.

Source: Indiana Department of Education (2024a). Diploma Requirements. Retrieved from https://www.in.gov/doe/students/graduation-pathways/diploma-requirements/

high school completion among special education students (Manset & Washburn, 2010). In subsequent years, the policy modifications accommodated special needs students (Manset & Washburn, 2003). The Core 40 diploma, which required Algebra I, was the default curriculum. With parental approval, students could opt for a regular diploma type; however, student aid was substantially lower for students who did not complete the Core 40 program. By 2019, Algebra I became the standard for all students to complete the general requirements, and the Core 40 curriculum added Geometry and Algebra II as requirements for the high school diploma.

One distinctive feature of Indiana's approach was that all high schools were required to offer advanced diplomas and funded for this extra effort before the college preparatory curriculum (Core 40) became Indiana's default curriculum. As illustrated in Indiana's balanced model (Figure 4.1), K-12 policies can indirectly affect college enrollment through improved preparation, as evidenced by modest gains in test scores in Indiana. Another unique feature of Indiana's approach was developing a statewide organization to encourage academic preparation, especially for low-income students. The combination of guaranteed aid through Twenty-First Century Scholars and encouragement programming through ICPAC was significantly associated with improved enrollment rates by low-income students, as demonstrated by research on Twenty-First Century Scholars (St. John et al., 2004).

With the election of Mitch Daniels as governor, Indiana's commitment to adequate funding for K-12 education evaporated. In 2005, Indiana began cutting public funding for schools and scholarships for college students (Toutkoushian, 2019). By 2009, a court decided that education was not a "right" in Indiana, nor was the state obligated to provide adequate funding. School funding dropped substantially, and the state fell in rankings on achievement, college enrollment, and other outcomes. This century's trends in state higher education finance, enrollment, and diversity by type of institution follow.

State Financing of Higher Education

There was a surge in public funding for student grant aid in Indiana during the early 2000s. However, the state's balanced political ethos suddenly shifted from its historic conservative-progressive tradition to a neoconservative position on public finance.

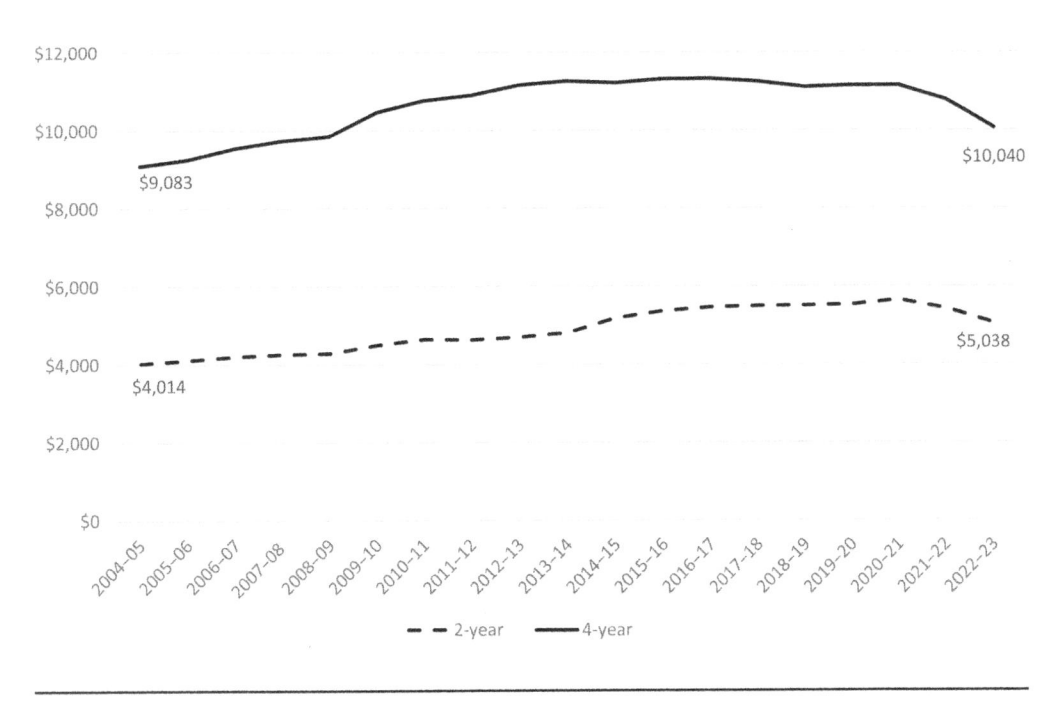

Figure 9.1 Trends in Indiana Public Tuition & Fees (in 2022 Dollars)
Source: Ma & Pender (2023). Trends in College Pricing and Student Aid 2023. New York: College Board.

Mitch Daniels's election as Governor in 2005 ushered in a new era of tax cuts and rollbacks in funding for higher education and other public services. As founding director of ICPAC, Scott Gillie observed that "the proportion of tax revenue for higher education in Indiana was the same in 2010 as in 1952."[1] These conditions have affected the financing of college access. The radically conservative change in state financing of higher education led to a difficult period, but as we note below, there are some recent signs of progress toward a more just future.

Public College Tuition Charges

In-state undergraduate tuition charges in Indiana were higher than the national average through the early 2000s, but by 2022, in-state tuition would be similar to the national average. Tuition and fees are relatively flat in Indiana for both 2- and 4-year public institutions from 2004 through 2023 (Figure 9.1). Consistent with trends across the country in recent years, tuition rates were down as demand for higher education has declined. Public 2-year colleges cost $5,308 in FY23, compared to $3,806 nationally. The first tier for college access was high, especially for low-income students who did not sign up for Twenty-First Century Scholars as youth. The link between the maximum state student grant award and the prior year's tuition charge also broke during this period.

Funding for Public Colleges and Universities

State funding for public colleges declined substantially in the early twenty-first century (Figure 9.2). In 2000, state appropriations were slightly higher than the national average ($7,812 per FTE). Both state and national averages declined through 2010, but

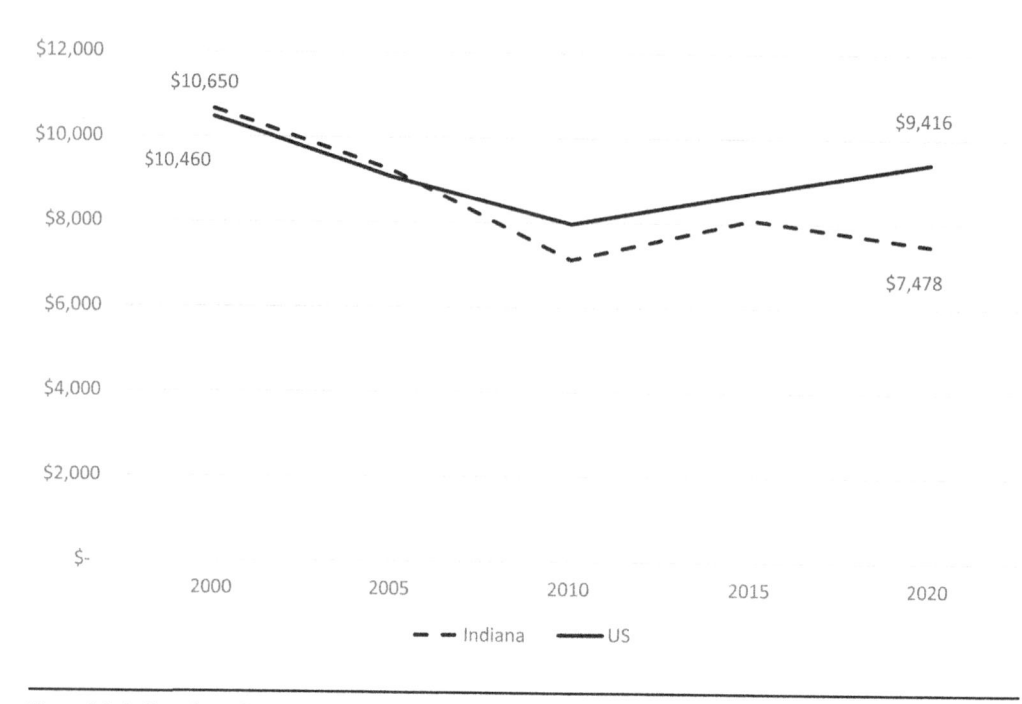

Figure 9.2 Indiana State Appropriations per FTE (2020 Dollars)
Source: State Higher Education Executive Officers (SHEEO) Grapevine Annual Reports and NCES, Digest of Education Statistics (2023) Table 307.20.

Indiana fell further by 2010 and has not improved substantially. While national figures had grown to $9,416 per FTE in 2020, Indiana peaked at almost $7,500 in 2020, at a rate nearly $2,000 per FTE lower than the national average.

The declines in national and state numbers reflect two significant trends. First, as one might expect, public investment in higher education has not kept pace with inflation in most years. Around the Great Recession, state investments in higher education declined in real dollars. Second and counter-intuitively, part of the decline resulted from growing enrollments. Many states do not typically allocate funds per FTE basis, so when enrollments grow, and state appropriations are not adjusted to reflect that change, the per-student funding declines because the denominator has grown more quickly than the numerator. Recent increases in per FTE appropriations illustrate the converse relationship; as enrollments decline, as they have between 2019 and 2023, even with no additional state support, per FTE appropriations go up.

State Funding for Need-Based Grants

Early increases in tuition charges raised the state's cost of funding Twenty-First Century Scholars, which was problematic for state policymakers. Since the program's early years, tuition rates grew slower and were beginning to decline by 2020, which may reflect political pressure to keep the cost of the programs relatively stable. Indiana significantly increased funding for need-based aid in the early 2000s (Figure 9.3).

The Twenty-First Century Scholars program seems to work more integrated than in the past—and may be more generous. For example, Indiana University (IU) Bloomington (2023) program indicates the "IUB 21st Century Tuition Scholarship covers:100% tuition

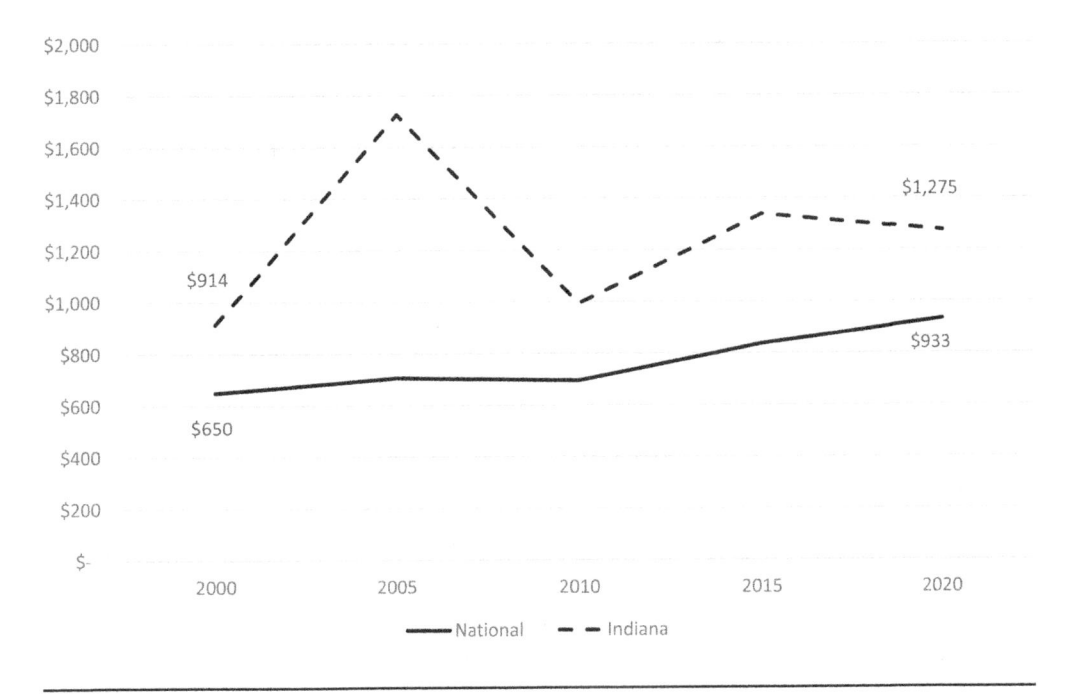

Figure 9.3 Indiana Need-Based Aid per FTE (2020 Dollars)

Source: National Association of State Student Grant & Aid Programs (NASSGAP) (2023). Annual Survey Report. NCES, Digest of Education Statistics (2023) Table 307.20.

and mandatory student fees (e.g., *activity, repair and rehabilitation fee, transportation, technology, and health*), the Common Application Fee, the IU Intent to Enroll Admissions Fee; IU et al., Fall/Spring Study Abroad with IU affiliated programs, and IU Intensive Freshman Seminar (IFS) tuition fee (if applicable) for incoming scholars." In the early 2000s, IU virtually avoided recruiting Twenty-First Century Scholars even after Ed St. John and Don Hossler, colleagues in the IU higher education program at the time, made presentations to the Board of Trustees encouraging more direct action in recruiting and marketing. The transition illustrates what seems to be a rapidly growing awareness of the importance of state-campus partnerships in student aid delivery.

Recovering the Comprehensive Approach

In earlier editions of *Public Policy and Higher Education*, Indiana's case provided evidence of a relationship between coordinated public investment and improvement in opportunity. The case also illustrated that it took decades to build a new trajectory, but policy changed rapidly after 2005, raising the possibility that the comprehensive approach might not hold together. The evidence on academic strategy held together, and financial strategy recovered, at least partially.

The story is uplifting. Indiana's tuition charges were consistently and substantially lower across the two decades of the twenty-first century. Need-based grants tumbled in Indiana after 2005 but recovered substantially, though not entirely. Controlling for inflation, the average grant rose between 2000 and 2020. The threat imposed by the extreme conservative shift in 2005, the period examined in prior editions, was a downward blip, not a lasting change in trajectory.

TRENDS IN STUDENT OUTCOMES

The case now demonstrates that swings in student outcomes don't constantly shift but follow policy shifts after radical policy changes. The widening opportunity gaps in Indiana now illustrate that failing to hold to the original design for local support for encouragement and fully funded state grants came at a high cost for minorities, especially Blacks.

Academic Preparation

The linkages between high school graduation requirements and achievement outcomes are well established (Chapter 5). We examine recent trends in graduation rates and test scores in Indiana below.

High School Graduation Rates

In early iterations of our work, K-12 reforms implemented in Indiana in the late 1990s and 2000s did not improve graduation rates or reduce inequalities across racial/ethnic groups. During that period, we observed gaps of as many as 50 percentage points between Asian and Black students. Graduations remained stable over time, and the gaps were persistent. Since then, we have seen both growth in high school graduation rates in the aggregate and reduced gaps by race and ethnicity. Figure 9.4 shows that while

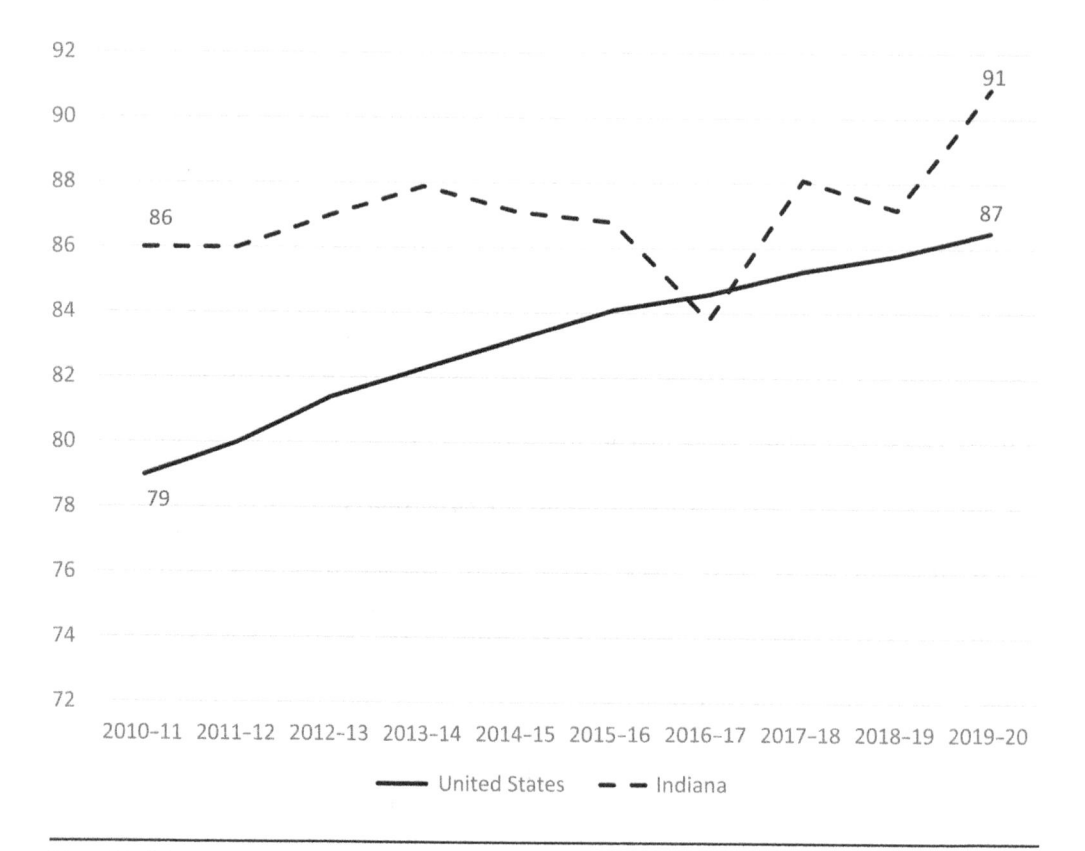

Figure 9.4 Public High School Graduation Rates in Indiana, 2010–11 Through 2019–20

Source: National Center for Education Statistics (2023). Digest of Education Statistics, Table 218.46.

Indiana has outperformed national averages since 2010 by a wide margin, it experienced a notable decline in 2016 before recovering and surpassing prior graduation rates at 91%, compared to the national average of 87%. Despite some volatility in the middle portion of the decade, Indiana's high school graduation rate improved since 2010.

In 2020, 91% of Indiana students graduated high school, a 5 percentage point increase from a decade earlier. NCES (2023) also shows that in 2020, the gaps in high school graduation rates had declined considerably. Asian and white students were still graduating at a very high rate (96% and 91%, respectively), but the gaps were less than 10 percentage points, with 88% Hispanic and 85% Black students finishing high school within four years. Indiana trends reflect national trends as well. The racial gaps have shrunk considerably as the overall graduation rates have improved.

SAT Test Scores

Indiana appears to be an anomaly compared to other states regarding participation in the SAT admissions test. Indiana has a more significant proportion of its high school students who take the SAT, which remains the case through 2023. Like other states, Indiana saw participation rates decline in 2021 and 2022. To put this into perspective, 49,000 students completed the test in 2019. By 2021, that number dropped to 32,000 (College Board, 2023). The drop was not as significant as in other states but followed a similar path. What appears to be very different is that in 2023, SAT participation rates not only returned to prior levels but exceeded them by nearly double. In 2023, 78,000 students in Indiana took the test—a much higher number of test takers than any prior year.

We focus less on the SAT because many institutions have shifted to test-optional admissions policies or eliminated the requirement. The participation rates dropped when fewer students needed SAT scores to gain admission to their institutions of choice. It is unclear why so many students would choose to take a college admission test in Indiana when these policies have changed. As of 2023, Indiana University shifted to test-optional; submission is not required but considered when submitted. Purdue continued to demand the SAT for admission to the main campus (National Center for Education Statistics, 2023). That may explain why test-taking returned to prior levels but not why it grew beyond prior rates.

The gaps in overall SAT scores have remained essentially unchanged. In 2023, Asian students earned combined scores of 1,092 on average, while white, Hispanic, and Black scores were 1,026, 914, and 864, respectively. The gaps in test scores may seem relatively less critical in an era when tests are optional. However, the tests may still significantly impact students' choices to pursue engineering and STEM disciplines, which are the focus at Purdue.

Gains in Preparation

The combination of higher-than-average graduation rates and the continued student engagement in admissions tests illustrates that the K-12 education system, a key feature of Indiana's comprehensive strategy, continued to have an impact across the first two decades of the twenty-first century. As noted above, Indiana continued as a low-tuition, high-grant state, a second part of the comprehensive strategy. We did not track changes in ICPAC and student support services; however, we lack insight into the status of the third feature of the comprehensive approach. However, in 2011, we heard alarming comments from Scott Gillie, the founding director of ICPAC and key innovator in these student-support initiatives in the 1990s. He was concerned about the shift to webpage support as a replacement for in-person counseling, homework support, and other in-person and telephone support.

Enrollment and Diversity

Enrollment is a key indicator of successful state policies promoting college access, diversity, and degree attainment. Indiana was a success story from the late 1990s to the early 2000s, with policy changes implemented around education reform and postsecondary finance. In 1994, Indiana was below the national average in college continuation rate—55% in Indiana compared with 57% in the United States. For the next decade, the rate climbed in Indiana while it declined in the United States overall, reaching 62% in Indiana in 2004 compared with a U.S. average of 56%. It is difficult to compare the available numbers today because NCES reports the percentage of 18- to 24-year-olds enrolled in a postsecondary institution rather than a measure of students who continue into college directly after high school. Enrollment includes both first time students and returning students, a combination of access and persistence.

The trends in the early twentieth century show that since 2013, enrollment of Indiana's college-age population has lagged behind the averages for other states (Figure 9.5). Indeed, Indiana's decline in access after 2013 compared to the national average illustrates that the decrease in educational opportunity followed the state's failure to follow up on the original, balanced approach to high school preparation and college finance.

In 2013, the proportion of 18- to -24-year-olds from Indiana enrolled in college was like the national average. However, in subsequent years, Indiana's rates dropped earlier and

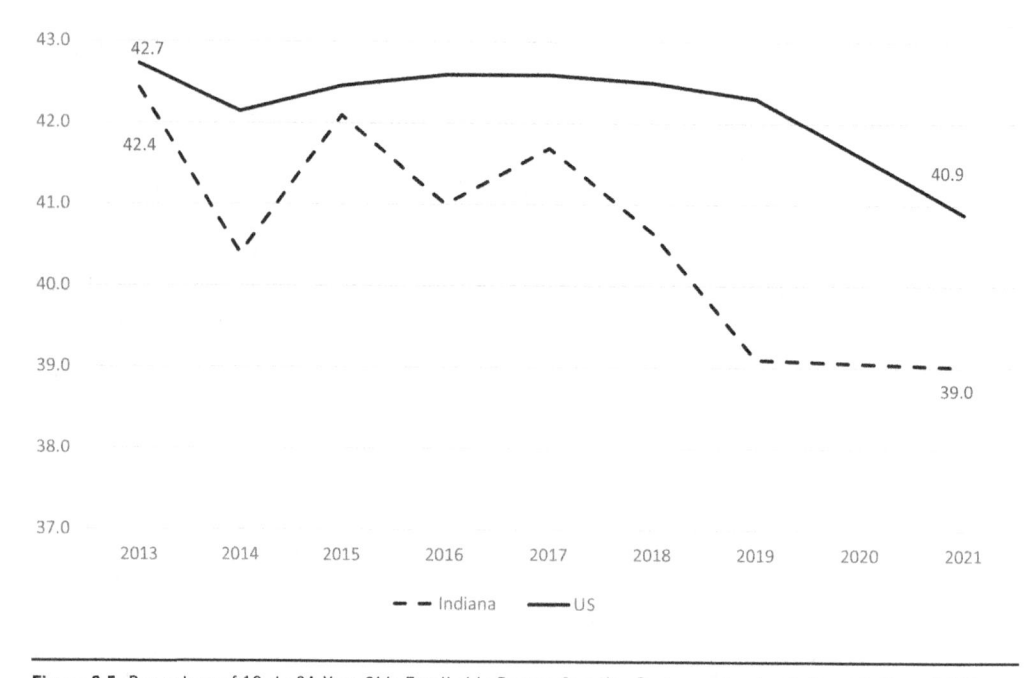

Figure 9.5 Percentage of 18- to 24-Year-Olds Enrolled in Degree-Granting Postsecondary Institutions: Indiana & U.S.
Source: National Center for Education Statistics (2023). Digest of Education Statistics, Table 302.65.

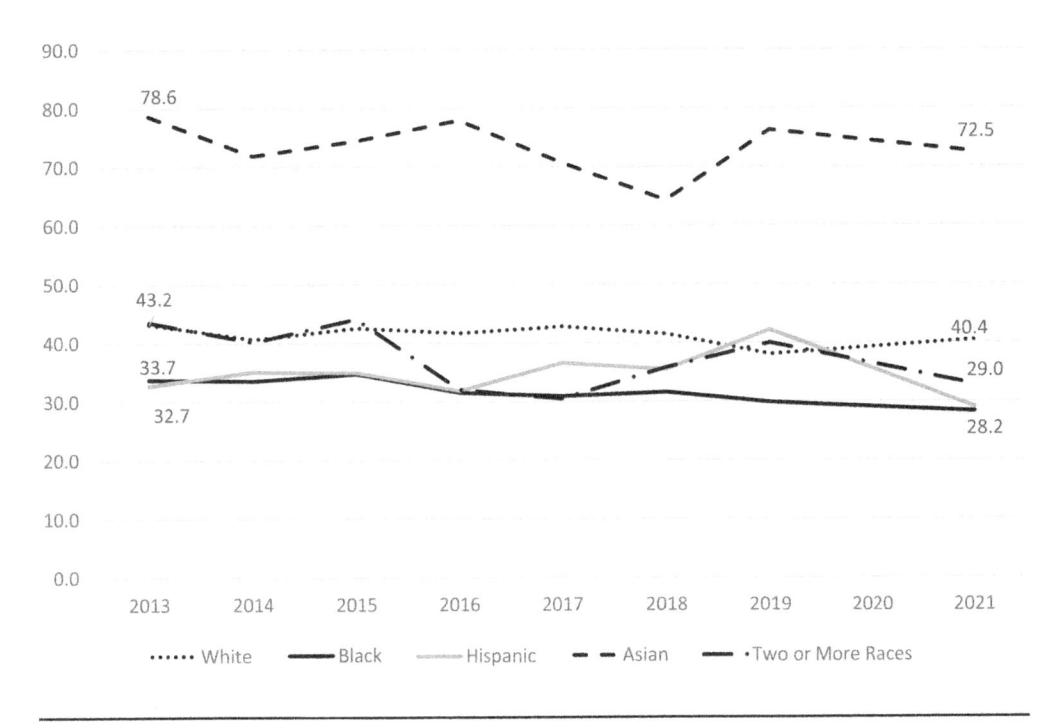

Figure 9.6 Percentage of 18- to 24-Year-Olds Enrolled in Degree-Granting Postsecondary Institutions, by Race/Ethnicity: Indiana

Source: National Center for Education Statistics (2023). Digest of Education Statistics, Table 302.65.

sharper than the national rates. By 2021, only 39% of young adults in Indiana enrolled in college compared to almost 41% nationally. In some ways, it appears Indiana has improved compared to the national averages, but when considering racial gaps in college participation, Indiana has not progressed (Figure 9.6).

Asian young adults attend college at much higher rates than their peers in Indiana. While their rates fluctuate between 70% and 80%, white students and those who identify with two or more races hover between 40% and 45% enrollment rates. Black and Hispanic students have seen mixed results. College enrollment rates for Black students have remained close to 30% for the entire period, with slow declines to 29% in 2021. By contrast, Hispanic students experienced much more volatility from 2013 to 2021. Hispanic enrollment rates have changed dramatically from their high of 41% to a low of 29%.

Trends have changed considerably regarding racial and ethnic representation in Indiana postsecondary education. Before 2000, white student enrollment was proportional to the state population, and the percentage of Asian students in college was roughly twice their proportion of the population. Since that time, Indiana has experienced some changes (Figure 9.7). In 2000, both Black and Hispanic students were under-represented in higher education, while Asian and Native American students were over-represented, but that had changed by 2020.

Whites are more than 80% of the state population. White students enrolled in college at a rate equal to their population representation, but by 2020, whites had dropped by 10 percentage points. In contrast, Black students were under-represented in 2000 but exceeded their proportion of the population in college by 20 percentage points in 2010

206 • State Cases

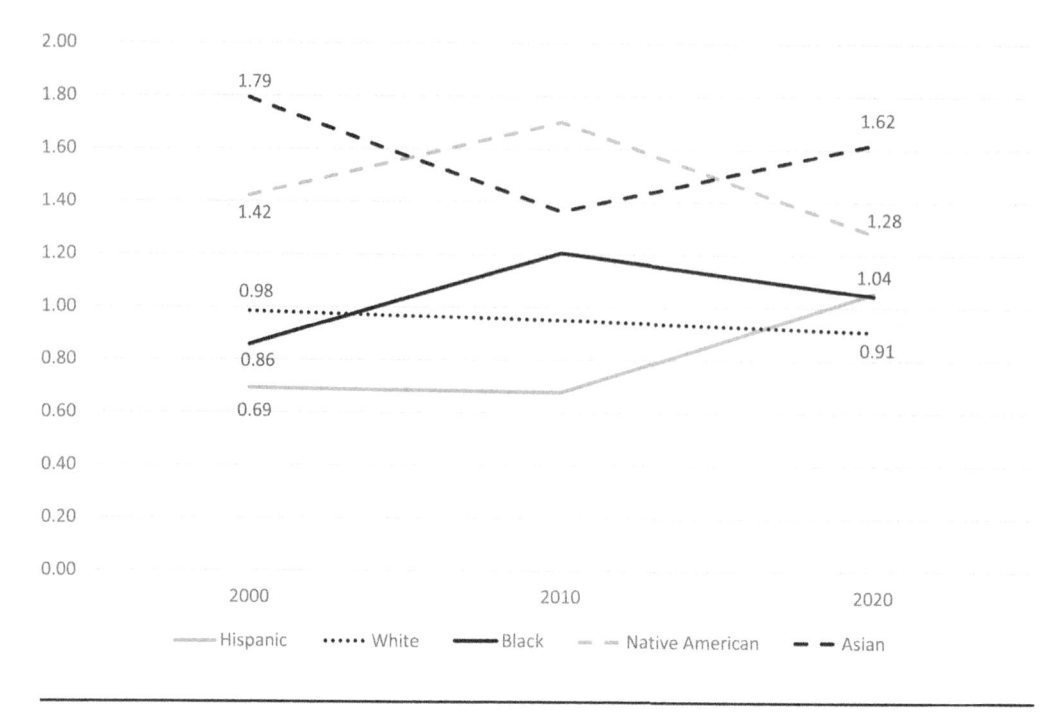

Figure 9.7 Racial/Ethnic Representation in Indiana Postsecondary Education as a Proportion of the Indiana State Population
Source: National Center for Education Statistics (2023). Digest of Education Statistics, Table 306.70 & Table 266 & US Census Bureau.

before returning to nearly proportional in 2020. Hispanic representation rate was equal to Black students in 2020, but they remained consistently under-represented before 2000 and in 2010. Blacks and Hispanics, relatively small percentages of the Indiana population, were not underrepresented in higher education compared to whites.

Decline in White Student Enrollment

Looking across the enrollment and diversity indicators, it is apparent that white college-age adults enrolled at lower rates than other groups. They were also underrepresented based on population in 2020, indicating fewer white adults above college age are also enrolling. The representational indicators suggest a drop in aspirations, commitment, will, or follow-through. Indeed, the drop in white enrollment may explain why the combined enrollment rates of college-age students were lower for Indiana than the average for the nation.

College Attainment Rates in Indiana Higher Education

Many factors can influence degree completion rates, including individual background, academic programs, college life, campus support services, and public finance policies. Other than sustaining a commitment to support institutions and students financially, a practice that creates stability in students' perceived ability to pay college costs, the impact of state policies is often modest and indirect.

The Indiana Project on Academic Success (IPAS) demonstrated that institutions could adapt institutional strategies to improve student success rates, but those efforts depend on institution and context (Hossler et al., 2009; Patton et al., 2006; St. John

& Musoba, 2010). In theory, the academic preparation standard of states have an indirect effect on college success, depending on other factors influencing the quality of preparation in high schools. The IPAS project also suggested that technical assistance and research support for campuses can also have an impact through support of innovation on campus (Hossler et al., 2009; St. John & Musoba, 2010). While IPAS was a 3-year project, the culture of using data to improve retention may have evolved positively in Indiana. The Lumina Foundation supported IPAS and continues to support innovations and best practices that support retention and degree completions in Indiana.

The IPAS legacy evolved into the Project on Academic Success (PAS), a collaborative initiative with the National Student Clearinghouse (NSC). PAS performed analyses using NSC data. The NSC collection process follows students for six years, even if they stop out or transfer. This approach is consonant with state policies that link to educational attainment as an outcome promoting social uplift and economic development. NSC data is used to generate trends in 6-year completion rates for student cohorts, starting in public 4-year, private 4-year, and public 2-year institutions in Indiana.

A recent study of the Twenty-First Century Scholars by the Regional Laboratory (Indiana University Northwest, 2023) carefully examined the program's impact on academic success during the first two years of college. Scholars had higher academic achievement during the first year and were more likely to return for the second year than students who received Pell only (equivalent students who did not take the preparatory steps required for Scholars). Students who return for the second year are more likely to earn degrees within six years than students who do not return for transfer.

Trends in 6-Year Attainment by Race for Student Cohorts
Staring in Indiana's 4-Year Public Colleges

Reporting on 6-year attainment by student cohorts improves upon the persistence percentages in earlier education using statistics provided by the National Center for Education Statistics (NCES). The NCES data provided an institutional vantage on degree completion, while the NCS college and reporting links directly to state goals of promoting degree attainment. We briefly state the findings from the early reports, when neoliberal policies were first implemented in states in response to federal education mandates and changes in federal grant and loan programs. After the summary, we examine trends using NSC data on attainment.

The NSC data indicate whether students have been successful in attaining a degree, even if they have left one institution and transferred to another (Figure 9.8). These numbers provide a more reliable estimate of attainment because they report on whether students completed degrees, and the percentages rose. Among the students in the 2012–2017 cohorts who began college in those years, 85% of Asian students graduated in six years, compared to 75% of white, 65% of Hispanic, and 48% of Black students. In addition, every group improved the cohort completion rate over the period. Black students have narrowed the gap slightly with white students in Indiana (nearly 30 percentage points for the 2012–2018 cohort compared to 25% for the 2017-2-23 cohort), but the gap remains substantial. The gap between Hispanic and white students fluctuated during that period, but the gap remained at less than 10 percentage points.

208 • State Cases

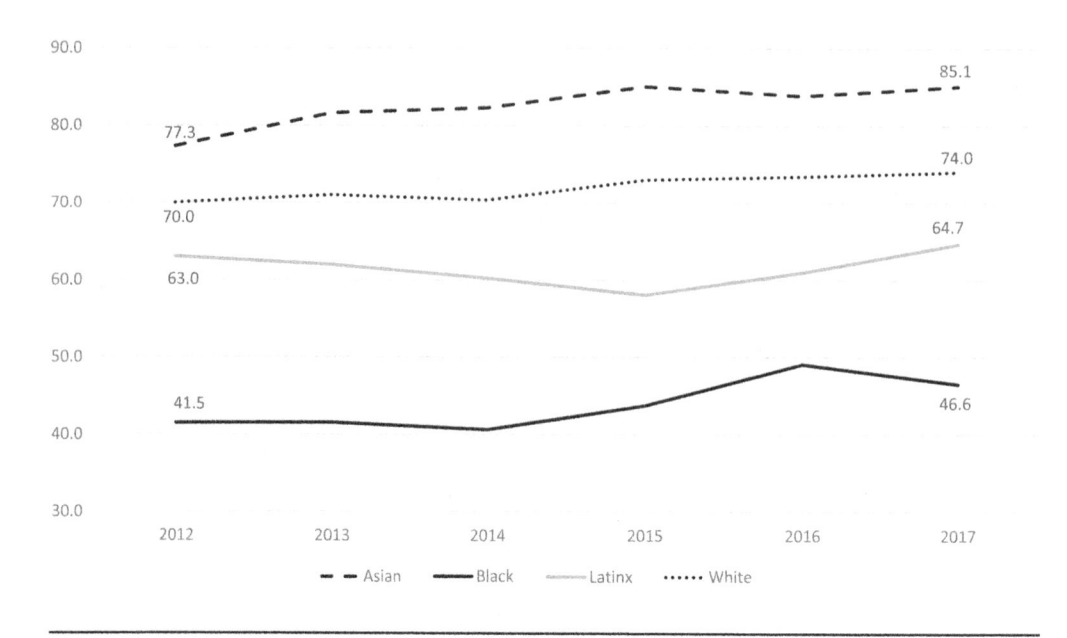

Figure 9.8 Trends in 6-Year Degree Attainment Rates for all Indiana Public 4-Year Postsecondary Institutions
Source: National Student Clearinghouse Research Center (2022). Completing College: National & State Reports. Retrieved from https://nscresearchcenter.org/completing-college/

Private Nonprofit Colleges and Universities

The most notable finding in the 6-year completion rates for private colleges may be that private colleges are better for some students than others in Indiana (Figure 9.9). White and Asian students graduated at higher rates from private colleges, consistent with what we have seen in national trends. Hispanic students graduated at similar rates, regardless of whether the institution is public or private (65% and 69%), but Black students may be at a disadvantage. Approximately 41% of Black students in the 2012 cohort graduated from private nonprofit colleges in six years, compared to 48% from their public counterparts. The lower rates of Black attainment align with the declining commitment to state student grants. In the aggregate, public institutions in Indiana are doing a better job graduating Black students. Indeed, the exceedingly low college completion rates for Blacks in Indiana's private colleges after 2013 are alarming by any standard of fair and equitable educational opportunity.

Public 2-Year Colleges

In our prior analyses of 3-year graduation rates of community college students, we found meager rates across the 2-year college system (St. John et al., 2018), when fewer than 20% of any sub-group of students graduated within 150% of the time to degree (i.e., completing a 2-year program in three years).

The NSC did not report any data for college completions at Indiana's 2-year institutions, which may reflect that IVY Tech has not elected to participate in the NSC data exchange. While more than 95% of all colleges and universities participate today, the NSC data will always under-report when students attend colleges that do not report to the NSC system. However, a report from the Indiana Commission for Higher Education (2022b) indicates that approximately 18% of community college students earn a

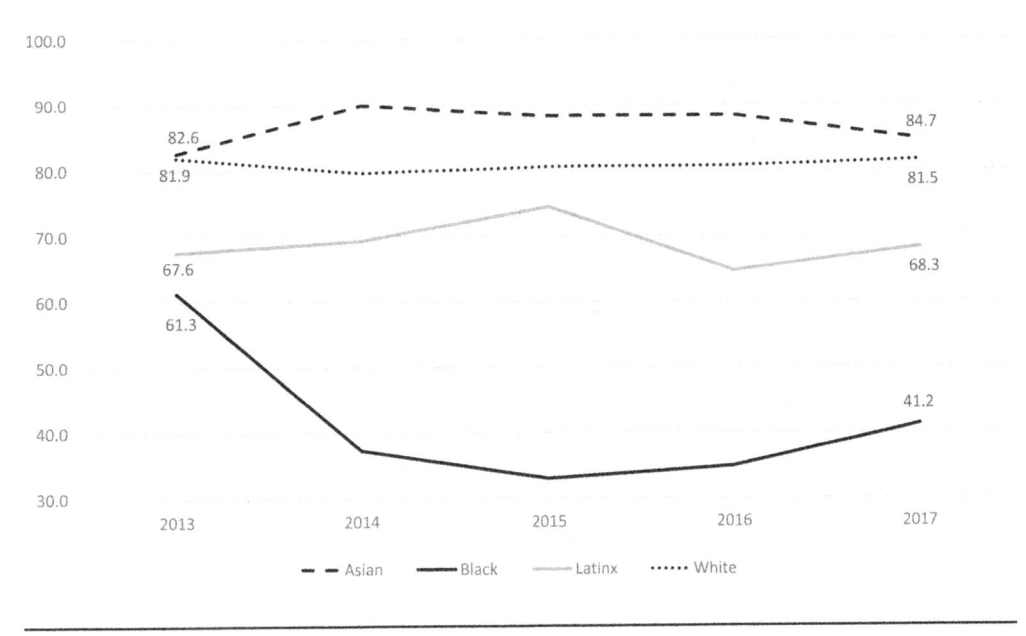

Figure 9.9 Trends in 6-Year Degree Attainment Rates for all Indiana Private Nonprofit 4-Year Institutions
Source: National Student Clearinghouse Research Center (2023). Completing College: National & State Reports. Retrieved from https://nscresearchcenter.org/completing-college/

credential on time, and nearly 42% will earn a degree in six years. In terms of racial/ethnic gaps, Hispanic students graduate slightly below the state mean, while Black students graduate at about 24 percentage points behind the state average for community colleges.

Delivery on Promises with Ambiguous Outcomes

Indiana's high school graduation rates remained above the national average. Students who graduated had met higher standard than most other states, many of which had created more flexible pathways. The Indiana promise was that the new curriculum was mandated for all rather than considered an option, as it had been when Twenty-First Century Scholars for elementary students in Federal free and reduced cost lunch programs, the lowest income students in the state. Eventually, low-income middle school students who had not signed up for elementary school could sign up, making the promise to complete school, remain drug-free, and not break the law. Students from low-income families were eligible for support services through high school, and those who participated in the program were more likely to attend college (St. John et al., 2011). However, the decline in white enrollment is a perplexing development in Indiana.

The graduation rates for Blacks attending private 4-year colleges were much lower than in public 4-year colleges, and public 2-year colleges were worse. Public 2-year colleges, the destination for too many urban Blacks lacking preparation and opportunity, were much worse in the 2010s than at the turn of the twenty-first century. In the late 1990s, private colleges had taken advantage of generous grants from the state, including recruiting Twenty-First Century Scholars from urban districts. In contrast, public colleges did not use this approach (St. John & Musoba, 2010). With the declining purchasing power of federal and state grants, Blacks have not fared well in any sector of Indiana higher education. However, the current inequity of private colleges is especially troubling given the historical success in the 1990s and early 2000s. After the glory of providing the model for GEAR UP, Indiana slid into the dismal portrait of educational inequality this century.

The state developed a high-tuition community college on a system from a technical college with only a modest infusion of new academic capital, with few full-time academic faculty and minimal student support services (St. John et al., 2011). For a sustained period, the state provided counseling, college trips, homework support, and other services in school-based programs, along with the backing of a state-wide service center (a call center). Eventually, the human services gave way to a web-based system, and Indiana's financial promise to these low-income families eroded as the years progressed. Not all low-income students have computers or the skills to use the transformed web-based support program. Over time, the high school graduation requirements for scholars rose, the support declined, and student aid faded in value. Most gains in enrollment over ordinary Pell recipients were in community colleges (St. John et al., 2011).

Indiana invested more per student in need-based aid than the national average for 2000 by approximately $200. By 2005, the state investment grew to more than $1,200 per FTE, primarily driven by the investment in grants. Between 2005 and 2020, Indiana's funding for need-based grants dropped by over $700 per FTE. During the same period, grant appropriations per student fell, and tuition increased, especially in public 4-year colleges. The state found clever ways to reduce the financial value of the monetary payoff, like Pell from the total award. Politically, this was a crucial period in Indiana when it was adjusting to a neo-conservative governor, breaking from the balanced approach built through years of policy collaboration and research. The appropriation for grants per FTE was about $500 per student lower than in 2020, but less grant money went to the lowest-income children, whether they would take the pledge or not. In-state tuition had risen by over $1,200 in public 4-year colleges. The hope promised by Twenty-First Century Scholars—that students with Federal Free and Reduced Cost lunch would get state grants equaling tuition plus a Pell award when they enrolled in college—was far from reality and has not been restored despite modest progress in the recent past.

By 2010, those numbers returned to near 2000 levels before they grew again over the decade from 2010 to 2020, when Indiana invested $300 per FTE more than the national average. The higher-than-average need-based aid per FTE is a positive development but does not offset losses in state appropriations per FTE over the same period. The net impact is a higher proportion of cost absorbed by students and parents, particularly middle-income families who are not eligible for need-based programs.

The decline in the purchasing power of state grants (i.e., the growing gap between tuition changes in state per FTE funding for grants) may be a severe problem in Indiana, as it is nationally, especially given the persistent inadequacy of Pell. The fact that Indiana and other states subtract Pell from state grants means that state student aid favors students with modest needs, not those with the most substantial financial need—the haunting legacy of the Twenty-First Century Scholars program.

CURRENT ISSUES

The Indiana strategy for postsecondary access and success was, by most accounts, comprehensive, but proved impossible to sustain given shifts in state politics. The state utilized a balanced framework for identifying and addressing the challenges students faced when engaging in the college choice process; the state initiated substantial changes that addressed access and persistence barriers. The Twenty-First Century Scholars program was the signature initiative designed to eliminate costs as a barrier for low-income families and engage students earlier in the choice process. The Core 40 diploma, established to raise the academic threshold for preparation, sought to increase the successful completion of a college education. These policies remain in place and are central to the Indiana story. However, decreased school funding and a decline in the value of grants, especially for Twenty-First Century Scholars and other low-income students, gutted these noble intentions, starting with budget changes in 2005. As the outcome trends illustrate, there was no substantial improvement in college graduation. College completion rates for Blacks and Latinx did improve modestly, a probable impact of higher graduation standard, but gaps persisted.

In 2011, the state launched a school voucher program for low-income students, and with recent legislation, the state opened that program to nearly every student in the state. At the same time, higher education is a growing target of ridicule from the conservative legislature. A Senate Bill, introduced in 2023 and still under consideration, would address what they perceive as viewpoint discrimination in higher education. Both pieces of legislation indicate that the conservative state is moving further to the extreme, which already has implications for education at all levels.

Indiana School Choice Voucher Program

In 2011, Indiana launched a statewide voucher program created the Choice Scholarship, which gave funds to approximately 4,000 students across the state and further drained financial support for public schools. At that time, only students whose families were at or below 100% of the free or reduced lunch (FRL) eligibility threshold ($44,863/year for a family of four at that time) (McInerny, 2016). Students, in turn, would be eligible for a scholarship covering most of their private school tuition. The eligibility criteria have changed several times over the past decade, including the proportion of school funding that could follow the student. Expanded in 2016 under Governor Mike Pence, a second-tier scholarship was created for families whose income was as high as 200% of the FRL level (as high as $90,000 for a family of four) (McInerny, 2016). Public school leaders have opposed the legislation since its inception, noting the likely impact on the state's funding for public K12 schools.

In 2017–18, Indiana created a program that gave vouchers to low-income students attending religious schools. Independent research found that high-quality private schools refused to accept voucher students. Students who opted into the programs improved less than peers who stayed in the public systems (Sude et al., 2018), findings consistent with prior national research (Dynarski & Nichols, 2017). The Indiana Education Evaluation and Policy Center reported the voucher program has influenced more than 500 student transfers in 2022–23: "The data reveal that 53% of the transfers were from public to non-public schools. The remaining 47% were from public to other public schools, including public charter school transfers." (Hamid et al., 2024, p. 1).

During the 2023 legislative session, the state passed a more sweeping expansion of the law, now allowing Choice Scholarships to follow any student whose family income is at or below 400% of the FRL threshold, which is approximately $220,000 for a family of four (Indiana Department of Education, 2024). In the prior legislative cycle, the state removed a $4,800 cap for the maximum voucher and changed it to 90% public school allocation for that student in their neighborhood school (Smith, 2023). In more than a dozen years, the Choice Scholarship will grow from several thousand low-income students in 2011 to as many as 95,000 students whose families are upper-middle income or below, projected for 2024, once these changes go into effect. These changes mean fewer resources will flow to the local schools, and the state will invest significantly more resources into this voucher program, which will subsidize increasingly wealthier families.

SB 202 Bill to Eliminate Viewpoint Discrimination

Indiana is not the first state in the nation to consider legislation to eliminate "viewpoint discrimination" in the college classroom; it is among the most recent to consider the move. The conservative majority in the state Senate is calling for significant changes to the ways they believe colleges and universities are creating a hostile environment for students with more conservative values and viewpoints. Conservative lawmakers view this legislation as an opportunity to address a growing divide in how the public perceives the value of higher education; as Brenan (2023) reports that public confidence in higher education has declined considerably in recent years—particularly among Republicans and those without a college degree. In 2015, 56% of Republicans reported great confidence in higher education, but by 2023, that percentage had dropped 37 points to only 19%. Democratic confidence declined from 68% to 59%, but the 40-point gap along the political continuum has fueled a backlash against higher education in recent years.

The American Association of University Professors (AAUP) and the chapter membership from the two flagship public universities—University of Indiana, Bloomington, and Purdue University, West Lafayette—have spoken out forcefully against the law, recognizing they share a common concern regarding public trust, but they argue the provisions would undermine academic freedom and damage the quality and vitality of the institution without improving free speech on campus (American Association of University Professors - Purdue, 2024). The policy calls for post-tenure review of faculty, it would call for the expansion of diversity to reflect all under-represented students rather than specifically underrepresented minority students with conservative viewpoints, and it would change the makeup and function of Boards of Trustees by giving the legislature more power of appointment and to remove faculty who they perceive are not valuing a diversity of viewpoints in their classrooms (Smith, 2024).

REFRAMING SUCCESS

In the spirit of innovation promoting equity and economic development, Indiana's balanced approach resulted in gains in college access, with growth in rankings among students, through the late 1990s and early 2000s. The data suggest that the state kept pace with a higher percentage of young adults attending college than the national average. While the early trajectory was toward success, erosion of the state's conservative progressivism reversed the trajectory to success toward the reverse image of success.

From a racial equity perspective, the results are especially troubling. Indiana's legacy of innovation with a balanced conservative-progressive approach changed after 2005 as the political winds shifted. Christian nationalist policies transformed Indiana's education progress this century from a balanced approach to access to an ineffectual approach to

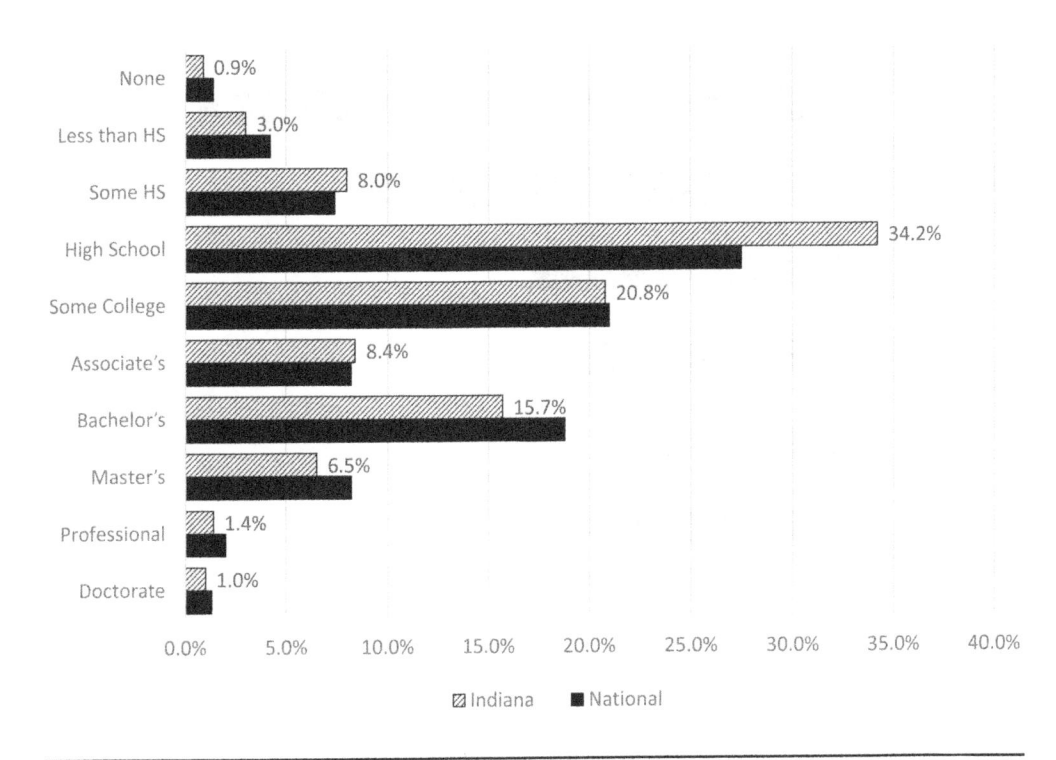

Attainment	Indiana	National
None	0.9%	
Less than HS	3.0%	
Some HS	8.0%	
High School	34.2%	
Some College	20.8%	
Associate's	8.4%	
Bachelor's	15.7%	
Master's	6.5%	
Professional	1.4%	
Doctorate	1.0%	

Figure 9.10 Highest Level of Educational Attainment for People 25 or Older in Indiana (2020)
Source: Statistical Atlas (2023). Educational Attainment. Retrieved from https://statisticalatlas.com/United-States/Educational-Attainment

ensure access and equal opportunity. The past two decades have undermined the progress in educational attainment supporting economic development. The goal of building an educated workforce with uplifted lifetime opportunities gave way to living with debt: the low- and middle-income students who borrowed entered a job market that often did not offer financial reward for their education attainment. National Census data in 2020 show that Indiana is not an economic environment that pays off after paying college prices with loans.

Attainment and Economic Development

Over one-third of Indiana's adults did not choose college after high school, a rate far exceeding the national average in 2020 (Figure 9.10). The percentage of the state's population with some college and associates degrees mirrored the national average. However, baccalaureate and advanced degree attainment lagged far behind the national average. This pattern confirms that Indiana's senior public institutions, a strategy emphasized at Indiana University (Hossler, 2004), continued treating students as a source of revenue rather than supporting the aim of increasing attainment.

Adults with high school diplomas or some high school earned more than their educational peers nationally in 2020 (Figure 9.11). The effort to build an educated force, an idealism manifest in Stan Jones's leadership at the Commission, did not materialize in Indiana. Comparatively undereducated, Hoosiers with college and graduate degrees also earn less. Adults with some college (including associate's), bachelor's, and advanced degrees earned substantially less than similar-educated adults nationally.

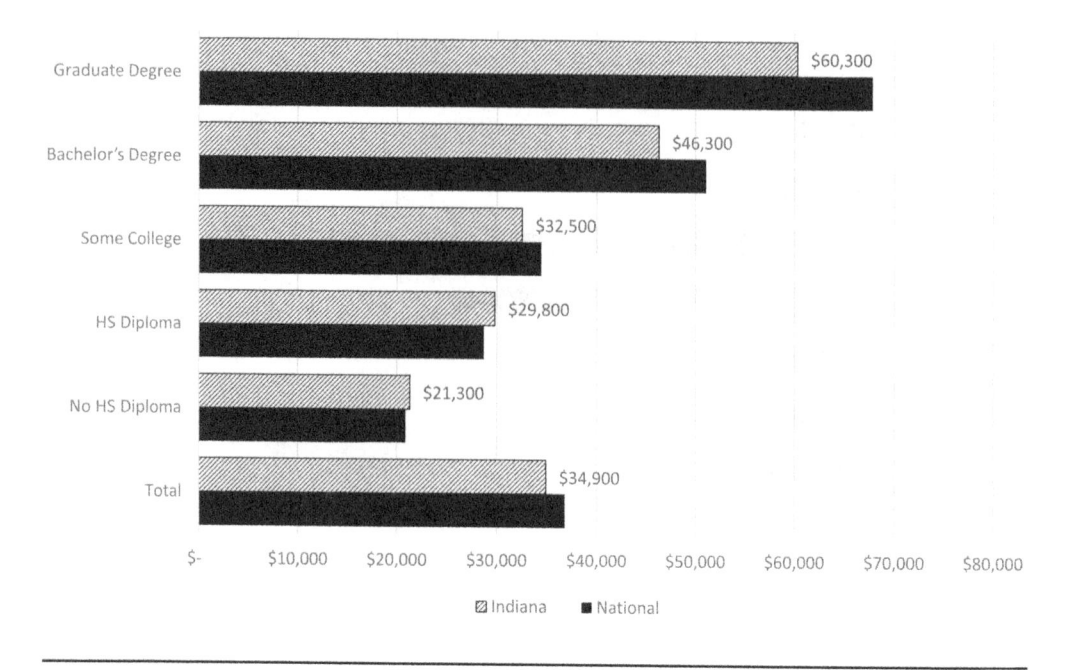

Figure 9.11 Median Annual Earnings in Indiana by Level of Education (2020)

Source: Statistical Atlas (2023). Educational Attainment. Retrieved from https://statisticalatlas.com/United-States/Educational-Attainment

Indiana's college graduates earn less than average but borrow at about the same rate and level as college students in other states. The Indiana Commission for Higher Education (circa 2023) estimates the average debt for 2- and 4-year college borrowers is $25,000 for borrowers, and 61% of Indiana's degree earners borrowed. Adults with high school or less earn more than their national peers and have no college debt. In contrast, adults with some college (associates degree or drop out), bachelor's, and advanced degrees earn less than their national peers. If they borrowed, as did most recently finishing college students, they face difficult life choices with income prospects that barely increase net income after debt repayment.

From Political Balance to Reactionary Conservatism

Indiana has pursued an ideologically conservative approach over the past two decades, faith-based rather than a knowledge-based social and educational approach. The innovation period in the late 1990s and early 2000s had limited impact in terms of degree attainment. The vision for a statewide effort to uplift through education and promote economic development, an ideal underlying ICPAC and the Twenty-First Century Scholars (Hossler et al., 1999), was not actualized due to the state's radical ideological turn. The comparison of Indiana's outcomes with other states with substantial Evangelist Christian polities (see the North Carolina and Florida cases) can inform discussion of economic conservatism instead of being guided by pollical ideology without comparative insight.

The expansion of conservative values and ideologies should not be surprising, but they will impact education moving forward. Changes to the state voucher program in recent years will likely significantly impact public schooling, diminishing the state's capacity to deliver its educational standard. The expansion of eligibility and the elimination of the award cap will place significant pressure on the state education budget and is likely to be a zero-sum for schools, given the conservative preference to support lower taxes. The call for post-tenure review and the political consolidation of the power to appoint Boards of Trustees reflects growing trends in conservative states nationwide. As the AAUP noted, it may have a chilling effect on academic freedom on college campuses in the state. How that is likely to impact access to college or successful completion of a college degree remains to be seen. Still, the K-12 market strategy will probably affect the quality of the educational experiences for students across public and private K-20 education.

The social and financial wellbeing of citizens resides in the space between the legacy of balanced politics and reactionary policies, the return to the American period, a period when emerging public colleges competed with older schools and colleges. In Indiana, the religious foundations of schooling were Quaker, Catholic, and Protestant. The early schools in Vincennes and South Indiana served Native people and formerly enslaved people along with immigrant Europeans, although few in any of these groups had the opportunity. Today, educational challenges are different but rooted in the history and patterns of settlement in the Northern and Southern parts of the state. For generations, forethought informed compromise, building education policies utilizing a cos-efficient logic of compromise. As this extreme conservative period continues, with limited tax dollars following students to private religious schools, Indiana's capacity to maintain college affordability is increasingly constrained. Many young adults now enter Indiana's job market with college debt constraining their life choices. This pattern accelerates as the state's polity seeks new common values supporting uplift and expanded opportunity that guided the state's educational and economic plans at the turn of the twenty-first century.

Will Indiana Find Balance Once Again?

Indiana's case, informed by insights about recent changes in the Twenty-First Century Scholars Program (Evenbeck et al., 2004; Indiana University Bloomington, 2023), suggests that campus-state partnerships in recruitment and retention are evolving. Perhaps such development harkens back to a movement into a balance of progressivism with the state's conservative trajectory. If the state does find a new balance, it will likely involve reconciling progressive and Christian national values.

Indiana has two major foundations promoting new directions. Lilly Endowment, the nation's fourth-largest foundation, supports causes in community development, education, and religion. Lumina Foundation is the nation's largest foundation that is solely dedicated to expanding the portion of American learning beyond high school. With substantial portions of the funds devoted to Indiana, they are shaping forces, and their legacies help explain the Indiana story narrated above. Perhaps more than any other state, Indiana is positioned to generate a renewed vision of progressive development that embraces the core values of faith. Yet the challenges of diversity, inclusiveness, and taxpayer willingness to sustain progressive initiatives are now subject to ideological extremism. Finding a shared, inclusive vision beyond the extremes remains a hope, dream, and possibility.

Questions

1. How did federal education policy during the Early American period (i.e., *Northwest Territories Act* and *Dartmouth* case) influence the pattern of college development in Indiana? (How does the pattern of development compare to California and Minnesota?)
2. How did conservative, liberal, and Christian values influence college development in Indiana? (How does Indiana Compare to California and Minnesota?)
3. How does Indiana's strategy for developing accessible higher education systems compare to the nation, California, and Minnesota?
4. How does Indiana's comprehensive encouragement, academic, and financial strategies compare to the changing patterns in California's liberal model and Minnesota's market model? How successful were the approaches to promoting equity (the old liberal, market, and comprehensive) compared to the national high-loan approach?
5. How are the politics of the post-neoliberal period, including increasing religiosity and efforts to support private school choice, impacting family choices and possible student outcomes in the current period to the balanced conservative-progress period? To what extent is the modest delivery of college success, as measured by timely degree attainment, an outcome related to the sociopolitical ethos of the polity?

NOTE

1 Quoted from an email for Scott Gillie to Ed St. John sent on November 28, 2011, sent as part of the review process for the first edition of this book.

REFERENCES

Advisory Committee on Student Financial Assistance. (2002). *Empty Promises: The Myth of College Access in America.*

American Association of University Professors - Purdue. (2024). *Joint statement of IU-Bloomington and purdue-West Lafayette AAUP chapters on senate bill 202.* AAUP. Retrieved from https://aauppurdue.org/2024/02/joint-statement-of-iu-bloomington-and-purdue-west-lafayette-aaup-chapters-on-senate-bill-202/

Brenan, M. (2023). *American's confidence in higher education is down sharply.* Gallup. Retrieved from https://news.gallup.com/poll/508352/americans-confidence-higher-education-down-sharply.aspx.

Bull, B., Buechler, M., Didley, S., & Krehbiel, L. (1994). *Professional development and teacher time: Principles, guidelines, and policy options for Indiana.* Indiana Education Policy Center.

Burnett, H. R. (1933). Early History of Vincennes University. The Indiana Magazine of History, 114–121. https://www.jstor.org/stable/27786602.

College Board. (2023). *SAT Suite of Assessments Report: Indiana.* Retrieved from https://reports.collegeboard.org/media/pdf/2023-indiana-sat-suite-of-assessments-annual-report-ADA.pdf

Dynarski, M., & Nichols, A. (2017). More findings about school vouchers and test scores, and they are still negative. https://www.brookings.edu/wp-content/uploads/2017/07/ccf_20170713_mdynarski_evidence_speaks1.pdf

Evenbeck, S., Seabrook, P. A., St John, E. P., & Murphy, S. (2004). Twenty-first century scholars: Indiana's program of incentives for college going. In R. Kazis, J. Vargas, & N. Hoffman (Eds.), *Double the numbers: Increasing post-secondary credential for under-represented youth* (pp. 169–174). Harvard University Press.

Hamid, M., Moore, M., & Lubienski, C. F. (2024). Examining the impact of school choice programs on enrollment shifts: Winners and losers in Indiana. *Policy Brief, 24*(1). https://ceep.indiana.edu/education-policy/policy-briefs/2024/school-choice-in-indiana.html

Hossler, D. (2004). Refinancing public universities: Student enrollments, incentive-based budgeting, and incremental revenue. In E. P. St. John & M. D. Parsons (Eds.), *In public funding of higher education: Changing contexts and new rationales*. Johns Hopkins University Press.

Hossler, D., & Schmit, J. L. (1995). The Indiana postsecondary-encouragement experiment. *New Directions for Higher Education, 89*, 27–39.

Hossler, D., Schmit, J. L., & Vesper, N. (1999). *Going to college: How social, economic, and educational factors influence the decisions students make*. Johns Hopkins University Press.

Hossler, D., Ziskin, M., Gross, J. P. K., Kim, S., & Cekic, O. (2009). Student aid and its role in encouraging persistence. In J. Smart (Ed.), *Higher education: Handbook of theory and research* (pp. 389–425). Springer.

Indiana Commission for Higher Education. (2022a). 21st Century Scholars. https://learnmoreindiana.org/scholars/

Indiana Commission for Higher Education. (2022b). Indiana College Completion Report: 2022. https://www.in.gov/che/files/2022_College_Completion_Report_10_03_2022.pdf

Indiana Department of Education. (2024). Indiana Choice Scholarship Program. https://www.in.gov/doe/students/indiana-choice-scholarship-program/

Indiana Division of Historic Preservation and Archaeology. (2024). Eleutherian College. https://publichistory.iupui.edu/items/show/314?tour=36&index=5

Indiana University Bloomington. (2023). 21st Century Scholars Program. Retrieved from https://21centuryscholars.indiana.edu/index.html

Indiana University Northwest. (2023). Academic Success and Achievement Programs. Retrieved from https://northwest.iu.edu/academic-success/21st-century-scholars/index.html.

Lilly Endowment. (2024). Strengthening religious institutions and networks. Retrieved from https://lillyendowment.org/our-work/religion/religious-networks-and-institutions/

Lumina Foundation for Education. (2008). Indiana's Twenty-first Century Scholars program: A statewide story with national implications. Results and Reflections, Issue.

Manset, G., & Washburn, S. J. (2003). Inclusive education in high stakes, high poverty environments: The case of students with learning disabilities in Indiana's urban high schools and the graduation qualifying examination. In L. F. Miron, & E. P. St. John (Eds.), *Reinterpreting urban school reform: Have urban schools failed, or has the reform movement failed urban schools* (pp. 33–52). SUNY Press.

Manset, G., & Washburn, S. J. (2010). Equity through accountability? Mandating minimum competency exit examinations for secondary students with learning disabilities. *Learning Disabilities Research & Practices, 15*(3), 160–167.

McCarthy, M., Jones, B. A., & St. John, E. P. (2000). *University-based policy research centers*. Policy Bulletin No. PB-26. Indiana Education Policy Center.

McInerny, C. (2016, August 19). Five Years Later, Indiana's Voucher Program Functions Very Differently. State Impact Indiana. https://indianapublicmedia.org/stateimpact/2016/08/19/years-indianas-voucher-program-functions-differently/

National Center for Education Statistics. (2023). College Navigator. *National Center for Education Statistics*. Retrieved from https://nces.ed.gov/collegenavigator/

National Center for Education Statistics. (2023). *Digest of Education Statistics*. https://nces.ed.gov/programs/digest/2023menu_tables.asp

National Student Clearinghouse Research Center. (2023). *Completing College: A State-Level View of Student Attainment Rates*. Retrieved December 20 from https://nscresearchcenter.org/completing-college/

Orfield, G. (1997). Going to college. In K. K. Wong (Ed.), *Indiana Youth opportunity study: A symposium* (Vol. 3, pp. 3–32). JAI Press.

Patton, L. D., Morelon, C., Whitehead, D. M., & Hossler, D. (2006). Campus-based retention initiatives: Does the emperor have clothes? In M. Wilkerson, & E. P. St. John (Eds.), *Reframing persistence research to improve academic success* (pp. 9–24). Wiley Periodicals.

Pew Research Center. (2024). Religious Landscape Study. https://www.pewresearch.org/religion/religious-landscape-study/#religions

Smith, C. (2023, April 27). Indiana Nears Universal 'School Choice' in New Budget. Indiana Capital Chronicle. https://indianacapitalchronicle.com/2023/04/27/indiana-nears-universal-school-choice-in-new-budget/.

Smith, C. (2024). College Faculty Overwhelmingly Oppose Bill Seeking to End "Viewpoint Discrimination." Indiana Capital Chronicle. https://indianacapitalchronicle.com/2024/02/15/indiana-college-faculty-overwhelming-opposed-to-bill-seeking-to-end-viewpoint-discrimination/.

Smith, H. Z., & Smith, H. Z. (2022). The Plymouth company and Massachusetts bay company (1622–1639): Establishing theocratic corporate governance. In H. Z. Smith (Ed.), *Religion and governance in England's emerging colonial empire, 1601–1698* (pp. 71–111). Springer.

St. John, E. P., & Musoba, G. D. (2010). *Pathways to academic success in HIgher education: Expanding opportunity for underrepresented students*. Routledge.

St. John, E. P., Daun-Barnett, N., & Moronski, K. (2018). *Public policy in higher education* (2nd ed.). Routledge.
St. John, E. P., Hu, S., & Fisher, A. S. (2011). *Breaking through the access barrier: Academic capital formation informing policy in higher education*. Routledge.
St. John, E. P., Hu, S., & Weber, J. (2000). Keeping public colleges affordable: A study of persistence in Indiana's public colleges and universities. *Journal of Student Financial Aid, 30*(1), 21–32.
St. John, E. P., Loescher, S. A., & Bardzell, J. S. (2003). *Improving Reading and literacy in grades 1-5: A resource guide to research-based programs*. Corwin.
St. John, E. P., Musoba, G. D., Simmons, A. B., & Chung, C.-G. (2002a). Meeting the access challenge: Indiana's twenty first century scholars program.
St. John, E. P., Musoba, G. D., Simmons, A. B., Chung, C.-G., & Peng, C.-Y. J. (2004). Meeting the access challenge: Indiana's twenty first century scholars program. *Research in Higher Education, 45*(8), 829–871.
St. John, E. P., Simmons, A., Hoezee, L. D., Wooden, O., & Musoba, G. D. (2002b). Trends in higher education finance in Indiana compared to peer states and the U.S.: A changing context, critical issues, and strategic goals. *Policy Research Report, Issue.*
Statistical Atlas. (2023). *Educational Attainment in the United States*. Retrieved April 10 from https://statisticalatlas.com/United-States/Educational-Attainment
Sude, Y., DeAngelis, C. A., & Wolf, P. J. (2018). Supplying choice: An analysis of school participation decisions in voucher programs in Washington, DC, Indiana, and Louisiana. *Journal of School Choice, 12*(1), 8–33. https://doi.org/10.1080/15582159.2017.1345232
Theobald, N. (2003). Reinterpreting urban school reform: Have urban schools failed, or has the reform movement failed urban schools. In L. F. Miron, & E. P. St. John (Eds.), *Reinterpreting urban school reform: Have urban schools failed, or has the reform movement failed urban schools* (pp. 77–93). SUNY Press.
Toutkoushian, R. (2019). Education funding and teacher compensation in Indiana: Evaluation and recommendation. Retrieved from https://ihe.uga.edu/sites/default/files/inline-files/Indiana-Report-on-Funding-for-K-12-Education.pdf
Woodburn, J. A. (1940). *History of Indiana University*. In (pp. 3–25). Indiana University Press.

10

FROM MERIT AID TO MAGA REFORMS

The Florida Case

The grassroots Make America Great Again (MAGA) movement evolved across conservative states, like Indiana, as Florida's Governor Ron DeSantis led a legislative assault on "woke" curriculum in schools and colleges. The MAGA legislative attacks on the mainstream curriculum in schools and colleges shake the foundations of higher education, as professors risk termination if they speak out against dropping diversity, once the core to the missions of the schools of education in Florida universities, or if they speak out too strongly about the changes within their institutions. Recent legislation's threat to academic freedom now shakes the foundations of public higher education in Florida (Altschuler & Wippman, 2023). These recent developments are transforming Florida's public higher education in the short term and will likely influence educational choices for rising student generations over decades ahead.

Florida's earlier wave of conservative postsecondary reforms focused on merit aid to retain high-achieving white students in the state colleges. Following the Georgia HOPE program, many conservative states adapted the scheme to fit the higher education systems in their states (Heller, 2002). Proponents of merit grants argue that these programs retain high-achieving residents in the state and improve access, arguments for which there is some empirical support (e.g., Dynarski, 2002). But merit programs are also associated with inequality, making it more difficult for low-income, first-generation, and racially minoritized residents who frequently have access to lower-quality schools to attend 4-year colleges if they do not meet the academic requirement for scholarship eligibility (Chapter 5). Given the wide use of merit grants as a model for expanding college access and encouraging academic preparation (Bishop, 2005), policymakers need to ponder the strengths and limitations of merit grants as a political strategy for financing access to higher education.

Before the MAGA assault, Florida's Bright Futures was a distinctive merit aid strategy. The merit program aligned the award with the state's K-12 reforms, providing students with financial incentives for academic preparation. We examine the development of these grants as part of a comprehensive state-level reform strategy promoting preparation and college access improvement. Florida Bright Futures program has been controversial, with vociferous support coupled with serious critiques from Florida citizens and external experts; DeSantis's anti-woke reforms are now further fracturing the foundations for education in Florida. This case reviews the historical development of Florida higher education, the emergence of Bright Futures, current policies and preparation and finance, and related outcomes before the overview of current issues and reframing issues related to the economic wellbeing of Florida's residents.

EDUCATION DEVELOPMENT SOUTH OF THE SOUTH

Louisiana and Florida were Southern states with strong Spanish cultural influence before becoming territories of the United States. Caribbean links are still strong in Florida, with Cubans making up 7% of the state's population. The primarily white Cubans combine Latin culture with conservative political values. We briefly summarize education developed before the Civil War, the state's struggle with desegregation, and the mixed legacy of progressive values leading to Bright Futures.

From Spanish Origins to the Civil War

The history of Europeans in Florida began, and as historical myth informs school children, when Spaniards arrived looking for the fountain of youth (Olschki, 1941). Large Florida land grants awarded by the King of Spain were the first wave of European intrusion into Native cultures (Martin, 1944). As in California, some Natives were enslaved, along with imported Africans. Black Caribe, Black Seminole, and Afro-Indians populated early communities in Florida before the territory aligned with the US (Bateman, 1990). At the time, Native Americans, enslaved Africans, and whites lived in a Spanish-Caribbean culture. The early origins of the state's population add to the mysterious alchemy of the contemporary anti-woke movement.

Negotiations between Spain and the US started in 1802 and concluded in 1818 with an agreement for Florida to become a territory of the US. The negotiations did not cover the future of enslaved people, which was not considered despite the differences in the evolving slave laws in the two nations; there was no way to know the number of enslaved people in Florida at the time (Bates, 1928). The transfer became official in 1821; the movement of whites to Florida was slow, so agriculture continued to depend on its distinctive slave economy.

Higher education evolved in the Florida territory, like the path to statehood in the Northwest Territories, the federal law structuring requirements for statehood. In 1851, the state legislature authorized the establishment of two seminary schools—East Florida Seminary and West Florida Seminary—the former became Florida State University in Tallahassee, and the latter became the University of Florida in Gainesville (Kleinberg, 2019). The West Florida Seminary opened its doors in Ocala in 1853 and eventually moved to Gainesville, whereas East Florida Seminary began educating students in 1857, long after the gentlemanly education strategy had evolved in the South. Nominally a state institution, "for many years nearly all of its students were from Tallahassee and vicinity, and it was a Tallahassee school" (Dodd, 1948, p. 1). Florida A&M, the state's first public historically Black college, was founded in 1887, a few years before the *Morrill Land Grant Act of 1890*.

As a Southern territory, it followed the laws and traditions of the Old South. The Plantation culture was not pervasive in Florida before the Civil War, but the slave codes were strict because whites feared a slave revolt. Disillusioned whites moved further South after the Civil War, as did free Blacks. Racial tensions were integral to education development during Reconstruction. For a brief period after the War, Blacks in the South influenced education development, but it didn't last (Tyack & Lowe, 1986). Following the legal framework of the No*rthwest Territories Act*, Florida became a state in 1848. The state had about 140,000 people in 1860 (Census Bulletin, 1890).

Developing Public Education in the Segregated South

Florida grew from 269,493 people in 1870, the first year when all states had free schools for some, to 752,619 in 1910, the period Jim Crow shaped segregated education in the South. Florida's state-local struggle over uniform textbooks and teaching methods started in 1868. These conflicts extended into the 1960s (Black, 1964), so the MAGA-DEI battle over textbooks is not new from a historical perspective. A segregated system evolved and continued, becoming a legal issue in the 1940s when the NAACP focused on the "equal" side of separate but equal. Nationally, Black schools had older textbooks when they had them, and in Florida, the battles narrowed the funding gap before *Brown v. Board of Education*: "In 1940, Florida had expended, yearly, $62.78 per white student and $27.63 per Black student for educational purposes. In 1952, the figures were $195.01 for each white student and $153.24 for each Black student." (Tomberlin, 1974, p. 457). It was still a substantial gap; Black schools received less than half the funding of white schools, and they received about 80% by the time the *Brown* case changed the national discourse.

The desegregation struggle did not ease white-Black tension in Florida. Battles over school desegregation flared up across the state. Hard-line segregationists dominated the state government in the 1960s, a legacy that continues in the state's political structure (Winsboro & Bartley, 2014). The state's compliance with the federal desegregation requirement was tokenism instead of real change. Many whites left the public schools to attend Christian schools, and churches became segregated as well. The state Baptist convention, for example, developed a biblical justification for segregation and closed their church doors to Blacks (Newman, 1999). Religion became the rationale for fighting desegregation, dividing the populace, and setting the stage for increasingly sophisticated education policies favoring white isolation, a theme supported by the growing population of white Cubans in Miami and Southern Florida.

BRIGHT FUTURES IN THE SUNSHINE STATE

The Bright Futures program, implemented in 1997, promoted academic preparation for college, rewarded high-achieving students, and encouraged more students to enroll in Florida colleges. Critics argued that it undermines college access for minority students. Funded by state lottery receipts and well utilized, by 2011, the program costs rose higher than the funds the lottery generated.

The Bright Futures program remains a central feature of state education policy, impacting students' opportunities to attend college and earn a degree. More recently, Florida became a bellwether state for conservative education priorities. The school-choice backlash morphed into resistance to diversity, equity, and inclusion (DEI) initiatives. With a history of textbook wars, Florida's anti-woke movement became a catalyst for using book banning as a national tactic for MAGA activists. The state has passed several laws that change the context for college choice and constrain academic freedom for faculty and students in classroom discourse. Liberal-minded, high-achieving students will have increased incentives to consider out-of-state college options.

Florida has been a purple state politically, but MAGA conservatism has been growing. In 2019, the legislature passed the Family Empowerment Scholarship-Educational Options program to increase school choice across the state. The program is primarily open to all parents of K-12 students in foster care or households earning less than 185% of the federal poverty level, followed by those below 400% (Florida Department of Education, 2023b). In 2023, the Governor signed an additional piece of legislation expanding school choice by eliminating the enrollment cap and the financial eligibility restrictions.

In 2022, the conservative legislature and Governor took steps to weaken tenure for teachers and college faculty in public institutions. Undergirded by his belief that the state's higher education system is indoctrinating students into a more liberal ideology, Governor DeSantis signed a bill to require post-tenure review after five years (Ceballos, 2021). When combined with the Governor's activism around removing and replacing Trustees with conservative ideologues, the move may have a chilling effect on the scholars whose work focuses on DEI, gender studies, or even sociology more broadly. In 2024, the Florida State Board of Education voted to prohibit spending on DEI programs across the 28 state colleges because, as Governor Ron DeSantis has claimed, the programs are wasteful and "hostile to academic freedom." (Moody, 2024). The year prior, Governor DeSantis removed the Board of Trustees from the New College and replaced them with conservative supporters who cut the DEI office and the gender studies program (Moody, 2024).

During the 1970s, Florida had two major public universities (University of Florida and Florida State University), a major historically Black college (Florida A&M University)—all three of whom are public land grant universities—several regional public universities (e.g., Florida International, Central Florida, and Florida Atlantic), all organized under the umbrella of the State University System of Florida's Board of Governors, and a community college system. There were 28 districts in the Florida Community College System, many of which represented multiple counties. There is a long history of articulation between 2-year colleges and state universities in Florida, making it easy for students to maintain dual enrollment in a community college and 4-year institutions as a cost-saving strategy. By 2010, some community colleges in Florida had developed 4-year degree programs as a lower-cost alternative to the state college system, as described later in this chapter. The state had a history of funding both merit- and need-based grants but was not among the leading states in either program type.

THE BRIGHT FUTURE GRANT IN CONTEXT

Florida was one of the early states to adopt more rigorous high school graduation requirements. By 1997, when the state started Bright Futures, Florida had a mandatory state exit exam, required three math courses for graduation, and had adopted national math standards from the National Council of Teachers of Mathematics (NCTM). In 1998, it implemented Algebra I as a minimum requirement for graduation, and from that point, there was an alignment between what was generally considered a rigorous high school standard and Bright Futures.

The Florida Bright Futures program has been in place for over two decades and has served more than 950,000 students (Office of Student Financial Assistance, 2023).

It is Florida's signature financial aid program tailored to specific criteria. For a student to be eligible for any of the awards, they must be a US citizen or eligible non-citizen, complete the Florida Financial Aid Application (FFAA) before the fall semester begins, earn a high school diploma or its equivalent, have a clean criminal record with no felony convictions, been accepted to an eligible institution in Florida, and apply within five years of graduating high school (Office of Student Financial Assistance, 2023). The Bright Futures program offers five different awards, tailored to the specific needs of each student but with a focus on merit-based criteria for eligibility. The Florida Academic Scholarship (FAS) and the Florida Medallion Scholars (FMS) awards require students to complete 16-course credits in the core academic subjects, which reflects the state graduation requirements and includes two years of a foreign language. The two programs differ based on GPA, college admissions test scores, and required service or work hours. The Florida Gold Seal Vocational (FSV) award and the Gold Seal CAPE Scholars are intended for students attending vocational or applied technology programs in Florida that is eligible for an associate degree. In all cases, students must achieve a minimum GPA and credit requirements in college that differ depending on the award level and will be covered for a limited number of time or credits, reflecting the program's expectations.

Program Features of Bright Futures Merit Grants

The Florida Bright Futures program makes awards to Florida residents who enroll in eligible public and private programs within three years of high school graduation. The Bright Futures program has the following components:

- *Florida Academic Scholars (FAS).* The award requires a 3.5 GPA; 1340 SAT/29 ACT/96 CLT; or IB diploma; National Merit, Achievement, National Latino Scholar, or Home Education; and 75 hours of public service and a college prep HS diploma. The award covered 100% of tuition and fees.
- *Academic Top Scholar.* Awarded to one top-ranked initial FAS per county.
- *Florida Medallion Scholars (FMS).* It requires an HS standard diploma or GED, a 3.0 GPA in 15 college prep courses, 1210 SAT/24 ACT/84 CLT, and at least 75 hours of community service. In exchange, students receive coverage of 75% of the cost of tuition and fees. The test score requirements and service expectations have increased since the program started, mainly because the program's cost quickly exceeded the state's lottery revenues. For example, in addition to raising the eligibility requirements, Florida eliminated the $1,500 to cover expenses in the first year.
- *Gold Seal Vocation Scholars (GSV).* It requires an HS standard diploma or GED, a 3.0 GPA in non-elective courses in high school, a minimum 3.5 GPA in three vocational courses, and at least 30 hours of community service or 100 hours of paid work. Award equals 75% of tuition and fees.
- *Gold Seal CAPE Scholars (GSC).* This program requires an HS standard diploma or GED, a 3.0 GPA in non-elective high school courses, a minimum of 5 postsecondary credit hours through CAPE industry certifications that articulate for college credit, and at least 30 hours of community service or 100 hours of paid work. The award equals 75% of tuition and fees. After successfully launching the first three programs, this program was designed specifically for industry-certified postsecondary programs.

Students must maintain a 3.0 GPA for FAS and 2.75 for FMS and GSV, with at least 6 hours per term, to keep their awards. The award equals 75% of tuition and fees. Students who attend private institutions receive an amount equivalent to what they would have received for a public institution, depending on the number of credits they take and whether the institution is on a semester or quarter system.

The award criteria set preparation thresholds for students in different high school tracks, encouraging an alignment between their academic preparation and the financial opportunity to enroll in college. Low-income students are the most likely to respond to embedded financial incentives. For example, students with grades above 2.75 but below 3.0 might consider taking a vocational course if they have financial need, an option in the Bright Futures program but not in some other state and federal grants.

The financial incentives created by Florida's Bright Futures are complex, attempting to align different patterns of student preparation with enrollment in various colleges and programs. Although the GPA requirements to maintain grants can influence major choices, students choose majors less likely to put their scholarship at risk due to low grades (Zhang et al., 2013); these intermediate program effects are not a primary focus of this review. Given the extensive commentary on the program in the popular press, we focus on the program's potential effects on preparation (the initial program intent) and equity in college access (an unintended consequence of the program). Bright Futures may improve upon the Georgia HOPE model from an access perspective, given the range of awards and eligibility criteria; the trade-off is that the program is complex, making it difficult for students to understand whether they are eligible or which program best fits their situation. Ultimately, the lack of a clear signal to students regarding their likely net cost of college may negatively affect college participation compared to straightforward criteria for Georgia's HOPE awards.

Critiques and Reform Efforts

While the Bright Futures program intended to encourage academic preparation, most criticisms focused on enrollment effects. Research suggests (Harkreader et al., 2008) that the program's impact on academic preparation will indirectly affect enrollments via the choice of institution attended. The literature includes the following commentary:

- Scholars and the press have documented the gap in awards for African Americans and Latinos/as compared with whites, arguing that the program adds to disparities in the opportunity to enroll in college are well documented (Dynarski, 2002; Heller, 2002, 2004; Heller & Rogers, 2003).
- The program has also been criticized because of the qualification standards. Some reports have argued that the test scores required for awards are too low (McGrory, 2014).
- Research indicates that low-SES families benefit less from Bright Futures than high-SES families in Florida (Heller, 2004b; Stranahan & Borg, 2004) for two reasons: fewer students from low-income families choose to attend college, even when they finish high school, and fewer low-SES students qualify for the programs. When they qualify, it is for the less generous variations of the program.
- The indexing of awards to tuition may influence tuition increases, thus constraining funding for public universities (Colavecchio-Van Sickler, 2007), an argument made a decade earlier about the Pell Grants by former Secretary of Education William Bennett (1987).

- The program is criticized in the press as a reverse Robin Hood program (Borg & Borg, 2007), generating money from low-income families through the lottery to pay for the college costs of students from wealthy families.

The Florida Bright Futures program provides financial rewards to students who take specific pre-college courses and receive high grades in them; it doesn't specify which courses students should take. Since only the number of advanced math courses is specified, students can avoid challenging courses if they are near the grade point threshold for qualifying for the program.

College students are among the most politically active advocates for the program because they depend on the grants. Yet college students' advocacy for the program is appropriately viewed as being in their self-interest. In contrast, most of the criticisms of the program raise issues related to social justice and inequality. To untangle the implications of these arguments, we examine trends in preparation and college access and review changes, if any, in other policies that could influence preparation or college enrollment by diverse groups of students.

A capacity issue in the state has fueled some of the movement to create the state college system and enable community colleges to award baccalaureate degrees. With this limited capacity for growth, keeping more talented students in Florida (reducing the brain drain) would reduce access to 4-year colleges, especially for low-income students who qualify for a 4-year college but do not earn the Bright Futures award.

Why Examine Bright Futures?

When we chose the Florida case for the first edition, the literature on programs like Bright Futures overlooked the intent and outcomes of implementing merit aid. Doyle's (2006) analysis of the diffusion of merit aid programs was the exception. He also considered the implications of merit aid for the continued support of need-based programs (Doyle, 2010). Doyle tested several competing theories for why states adopt merit aid programs and found that some states with low college continuation rates adopted merit programs, contrary to the policy trajectory in northern states. Indiana, another state with a history of low college enrollment, chose the need-based approach. The contrast between these states' progressive notions about financial aid nearly disappears when we examine policy on social issues.

We left Florida out of the second edition of *Higher Education and Public Policy* because of the length limitation on the updated manuscript. Repeating research documenting inequalities associated with merit aid was too much at the time. However, Florida's movement from the conservative merit approach to the new, extremist MAGA philosophy raised the importance of the case from the perspective of political analysis, not just enrollment effects. We analyze trends of policy indicators below as a relatively straightforward method of examining policy implementation and linked outcomes, consistent with our approach. We included Florida again to trace the evolution of the state's conservative movement. The revised case now fills gaps in understanding conservative policy on social regulation and educational progress.

Florida higher education has entered an uncertain period. Enrollment in the Florida college system in 2022–2023 was 285,288 students, lower than it had been since 2002–2003. While enrollment dropped after the pandemic, the decline started over a decade ago. "The number has been on decline generally since a peak in the fiscal year of 2010–2011, where there were 375,292 FTE students" (Sachs, 2023, p. 1). Lower-cost community college offering 4-year degrees may account for some of the change in enrollment patterns. However, the political climate is the primary reason liberal high school students across the nation are not considering Florida:

> A survey done by Arts and Sciences found that one in four students ruled out attending a college in a state because of the political climate in the state; this was true of both liberal and conservative students. Conservative students tended to rule out attending college in California and New York, while liberal students tended to mark Florida, Texas, Alabama, and Louisiana off their lists. For liberal students, the main issues are abortion and reproductive rights, lack of concern about racial equity, LBGTQ+ laws, and ease of getting guns, while for conservative students, the reasons were more general.
>
> (Lapovsky, 2023, p 1)

Not only are more high-achieving students choosing to go out of state, but a decline in Bright Futures Scholars is attributable to stricter standards and the lower portion of college costs covered by the Scholarships. In 2023, recognizing that the Bright Futures Scholars program faced severe problems, Governor DeSantis made this plea to the state legislature when arguing for relaxing requirements, "By improving the existing opportunities available, this bill secures Florida's greatest legacy, its children, and ensures they are set up on the path to their brightest future regardless of economic background," (quoted by Sterling, 2023, p. 1). The program changes in HB 25 reduced the size of the grant and weakened the requirements to expand awardees and induce more enrollments.

TRENDS IN POLICY IMPLEMENTATION

There is a substantial body of research in higher education that links public policies to education outcomes, but few studies examine trends within the political histories of states. This section examines trends in education policy and higher education finance in Florida, including but not limited to the Bright Futures program.

State Policy Related to Academic Access

The policy environment for public high schools in Florida has not changed significantly in the past decade, except for some approved alternatives to the course requirements, particularly in math and science. There was a similar pattern of easing restrictions across the US. The more significant change in this area is the addition and expansion of school choice across Florida.

Florida "bars instruction on gender identity and sexual orientation. The state law, known by its opponents as 'Don't Say Gay,' bars instruction on gender identity and sexual orientation" (Woo et al., 2024). In addition to banning books from the school libraries, the state-mandated textbook changes and classroom discussions. Other laws have radically changed teacher education: "Since 2021, Florida has passed legislation that radically redefines how educators address race-related topics in the university classroom. Two laws in particular, HB 7 (Stop WOKE Act) and HB 999, which outlaws DEI programs at Florida universities, have led the charge" (Russell-Brown, 2024). Although these laws change the culture and context of education, we cannot track content and culture changes with the statistics reported below. However, a new state testing option aligns merit awards with the new curriculum ideology.

Another law expanded school choice across Florida. In the book's first edition, Florida had not yet passed legislation to fund school vouchers, but in 2024, the state voucher program is already 5-years-old. It has expanded significantly to allow nearly every family in the state to be eligible. By September 2012: "Nearly 123,000 new students have received private-school vouchers after state lawmakers this year pass a major expansion of voucher programs, while a group that administers the programs says they will not bring an "exodus" from public schools as critics have predicted" (News Service Florida, 2023). Although the graduation and college enrollment statistics track students who transfer schools, this program is too recent to include students in the data reported below.

High School Graduation Requirements

Florida has regular, accelerated, and special diploma options (Florida Department of Education, 2023a), consistent with the tradition of comprehensive high schools in the United States. However, there is variability in the extent to which the courses required for each high school diploma are available to all students. Research that controls for state context using time-series data indicates that raising state graduation requirements is positively associated with higher math achievement on SATs but lower high school graduation rates (St. John, 2006). The current high school graduation requirements are presented below (Table 10.1).

Florida has raised its course requirements for high school graduation over the past 20 years. The state required three math courses but did not specify the level in 1990. By 1995, they adopted the National Council of Teachers of Math (NCTM) standards, and by 1998, they specified that students should complete at least three math courses, including Algebra I. At the time of the first edition of this book, Florida had just passed the Next Generation Sunshine State Standards, which became the foundation for the curriculum requirements today. In 2011, the state phased out the Florida Comprehensive Assessment Test (FCAT); it began the implementation of FCAT 2.0 and a series of

Table 10.1 Florida High School Graduation Requirements (Class of 2014)

Standard Diploma	Alternative Courses
English—4 credits	English—none
Math—4 credits, Inc. Algebra I & Geometry	Math—Industry certification or computer science
Social Studies—3 credits, world & US history, gov't, & economics	Social Studies—none
Science—3 credits, Biology, and 2 lab courses	Science—Industry certification or computer science
Personal Finance—½ credit (class of 2028)	Personal Financial Literacy—none
Visual and Performing Arts—1 credit	Visual and Performing Arts, Speech, Debate, CTE—1 credit
Physical Education & Health—1 credit	Physical Education & Health—1 credit

Source: Florida Department of Education (2023). Student Support Services—Graduation Requirements. Retrieved from https://www.fldoe.org/schools/k-12-public-schools/sss/graduation-requirements/

end-of-course (EOC) tests, which include Algebra I, English 10, Geometry, Biology, and Civics in 2023 (Florida Department of Education, 2024a, 2024b).

As the Minnesota case (Chapter 8) illustrates, more rigorous course requirements can increase graduation rates by expanding opportunities for groups to access formally the college preparatory curriculum. Changes from the FCAT assessment to the EOC assessments or the development of alternative course requirements to meet the state expectations may have contributed. It will be interesting to see if eliminating several EOC assessments will have any further relationship with high school graduation rates. Since Florida's eased graduation requirements, including tinkering with tests, it is impossible to untangle the impact of the two conflicting policies from the review of trends.

College Admissions

Affirmative action was a high-profile issue in Florida in the late 1990s. In 1996, the Fifth Circuit Court of Appeals ruled to strike down the use of affirmative action in the *Hopwood v. Texas* case, and the Supreme Court chose not to take the case, making it the law in Texas, Louisiana, and Mississippi (Hurtado & Worthington-Cade, 2001). In 1999, by executive order, Governor Jeb Bush banned affirmative action in Florida and instead guaranteed access to state universities to the top 20% of a high school's graduating class (Florida Department of Education, 2023b). These debates were settled in Florida 20 years before the Supreme Court decision in *Students for Fair Admission, Inc. v. University of North Carolina* (2023), which struck down the use of race-based forms of affirmative action in college admission in public colleges nationwide.

State Financing of Postsecondary Education

Public Tuition Charges

The price of higher education in Florida varies from other states. Two-year colleges are more expensive than the national average and have been for many years (Figure 10.1). In 2022, the cost of a community college was over $5,700 compared to the national average of $3,860. The higher tuition may result from the changing missions of many of the two-year colleges across the state. Florida has been at the forefront of the community college baccalaureate movement, and most of the state's 2-year colleges now offer 4-year degrees. Rationalized by speculation about the demand for 4-year degrees in the state, mission creep in community colleges has a lower cost for the students and the state than higher-cost 4-year colleges and universities. On the other hand, 4-year in-state tuition is more than $2,000 lower than the national mean, just above $8,500.

State Appropriations for Public Higher Education

Florida appears to be reinvesting in higher education by 2022, but they have not yet returned to 2000 levels (Figure 10.2). The V-shaped trend in state appropriations has been consistent nationally, and it reflects the balance wheel phenomenon that Delaney and Doyle (2007) describe when examining the role of higher education funding in state budgets. The state hit a low for appropriations per FTE in 2010, following the great recession, and it briefly fell below national averages per FTE. Florida appears to be reinvesting more aggressively than other states, but in inflation-adjusted terms, they are still behind 2000 levels by more than $900 per FTE.

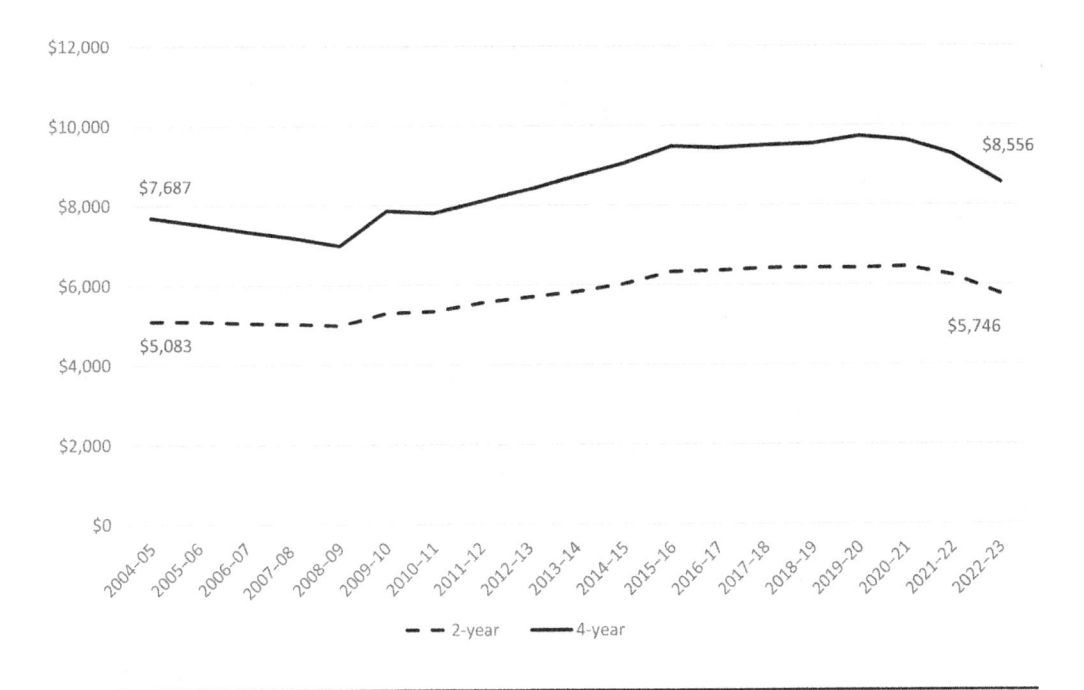

Figure 10.1 Trends in Florida Public Tuition & Fees (in 2022 Dollars)
Source: Ma & Pender (2023). Trends in College Pricing and Student Aid 2023. New York: College Board.

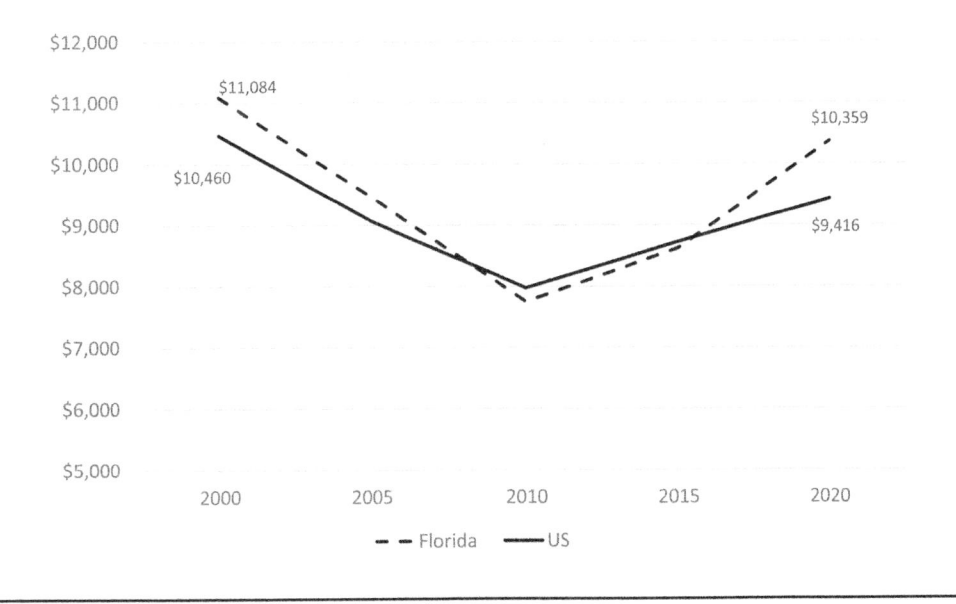

Figure 10.2 Florida State Appropriations per FTE (2020 Dollars)
Source: State Higher Education Executive Officers (SHEEO) Grapevine Annual Reports and NCES, Digest of Education Statistics (2023) Table 307.20.

Florida is experiencing a period of increasing appropriations per FTE, a decline in tuition and fees over the past two years, and an increase in spending on non-need-based aid, as we show next. These recent trends shift some of the burden of costs from students to taxpayers, a seemingly progressive state. Since Bright Futures covers tuition for some, the shift in revenue from tuition to the state partially functions as a shift in the source of state. At the very least, however, lower tuition favors low-income students who do not receive Bright Futures.

Funding for Non-Need-Based (Merit) Grants

Florida's signature financial aid program is Bright Futures, distributed based on merit rather than financial need. As such, non-need-based aid is much more important in Florida than in many other cases. Figure 10.3 shows that in 2000, Florida spent over four times as much as the national average per FTE on merit aid ($993 v. $201 per FTE). The Bright Futures funding may have hit a high-water mark in 2000 as the state investment declined steadily for the next ten years. The reasons for the rise of non-need-based aid after 2015 are not evident, especially given the decline in tuition. Florida added vocational programs to the four Bright Futures scholarships already in existence and experienced enrollment declines during that year.

Prior research found that public funding for non-need-based grants is associated with modest improvement in enrollment rates, mainly for whites (Dynarski, 2002). Over the past decade, Florida has experienced just the opposite. High school graduation rates are up, and enrollments of the proportion of 18- to 24-year-olds is declining. Non-need-based

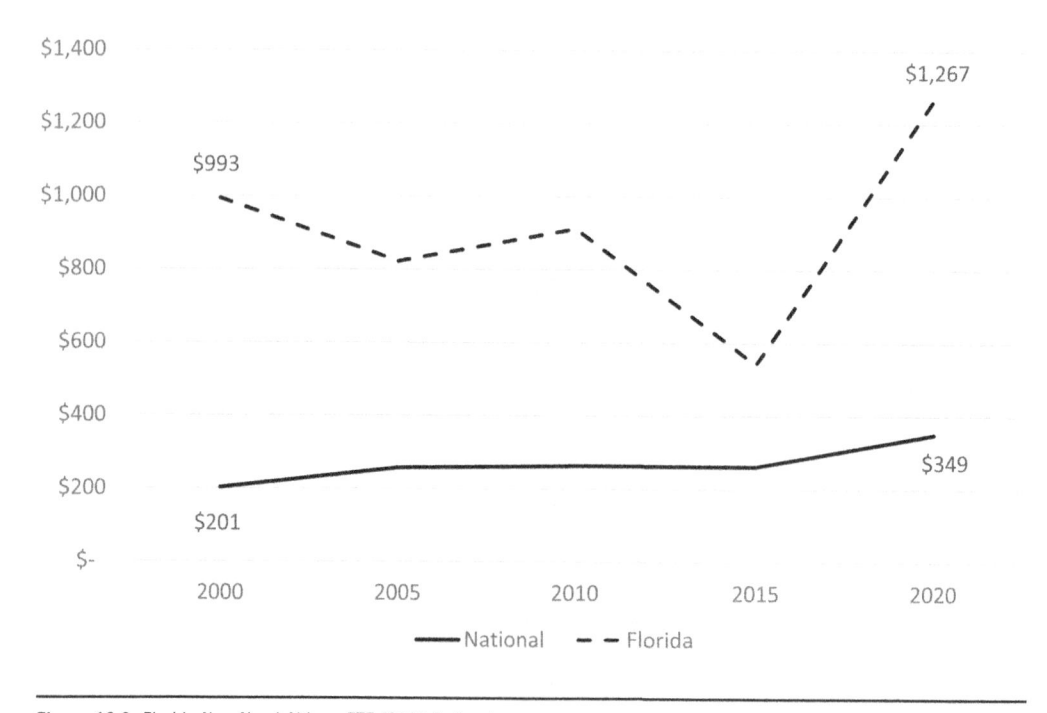

Figure 10.3 Florida Non-Need Aid per FTE (2020 Dollars)

Source: National Association of State Student Grant & Aid Programs (NASSGAP) (2023). Annual Survey Report. NCES, Digest of Education Statistics (2023) Table 307.20.

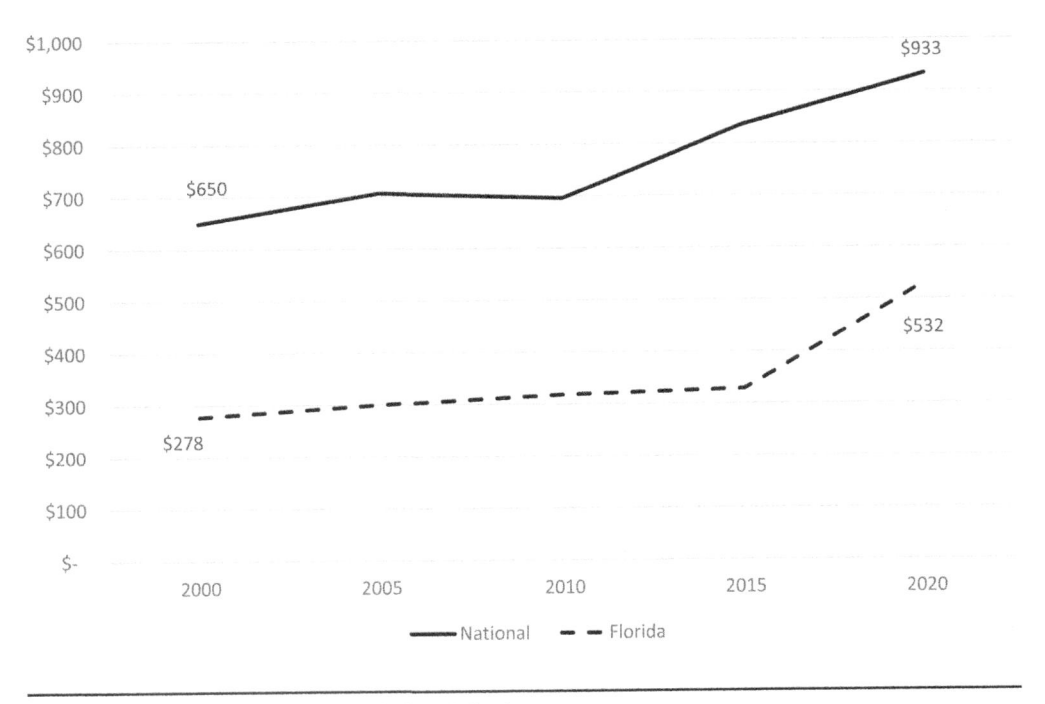

Figure 10.4 Florida Need-Based Aid per FTE (2020 Dollars)

Source: National Association of State Student Grant & Aid Programs (NASSGAP) (2023). Annual Survey Report. NCES, Digest of Education Statistics (2023) Table 307.20.

grants have increased per FTE, and tuition rates are declining, suggesting that college may be growing more accessible in Florida. Some Florida students may avoid taking more advanced courses in high school to keep their grades high enough to qualify for a Bright Futures scholarship. These scores may also reflect the growing proportion of high school students attending college who may not have done so in years past.

Need-Based Grant Aid

Need-based student financial aid is linked to improvement in college enrollment rates, especially for low-income students (Leslie & Brinkman, 1987; St. John, 2006). State funding for need-based grant aid has historically been meager in Florida; it was only $208 in 2000, compared to the national average of $477 per FTE (Figure 10.4). Florida remains committed to a merit-based financial aid system but has also experienced growth in spending per FTE on need-based aid, increasing from $208 to $377 per FTE. The state of Florida supports the Florida Student Assistance Grant (FSAG) program, which funds students with demonstrated need in eligible Florida institutions prioritized as part of Talented Twenty program.

TRENDS IN STUDENT OUTCOMES

In theory, a merit program like Bright Futures could improve preparation by incentivizing students to focus on grades during high school. In contrast, the follow-through on the state's commitment to funding could improve access to and retention in 4-year institutions. If other state funding strategies changed—for example, increasing tuition owing

232 • State Cases

to the decline in state support to colleges—they could offset the impact of the grant programs. Price increases, on the other hand, could eliminate the positive effect of grants and scholarships unless low-income students borrowed more to pay the increased costs. Building an understanding of the timing of the implementation of grants and other policies is central to untangling the ways the implementation of Bright Futures influenced student outcomes, which was our intent in the first edition when we found an impact on racial disparity. These analyses examine the ongoing pattern, informing the reader about the continuation or mitigation of systemic inequalities caused by the implementation of Bright Futures.

Trends in College Preparation

The Bright Futures program provides financial incentives for students to achieve high grades as they complete the courses required for college. Not all students have the same opportunity to prepare for postsecondary education. The development of flexible graduation options and the growth of the K-12 voucher program may also influence students' preparation for college. A review of trends does not allow distinguishing between the effects of different policy changes.

High School Graduation Rates

The Bright Futures program, implemented in 1998, could have influenced education choices, including study habits, by the time the students in the class of 2000 were sophomores (Figure 10.5). It is possible, therefore, that the program influenced their graduation rate as well. However, the trends inform readers about the effects of sustaining financial incentives for college preparation.

Florida graduation rates lagged national averages in 2000 but grew steadily over the next 20 years. In 2020, Florida's high school graduation rate was 3 percentage points

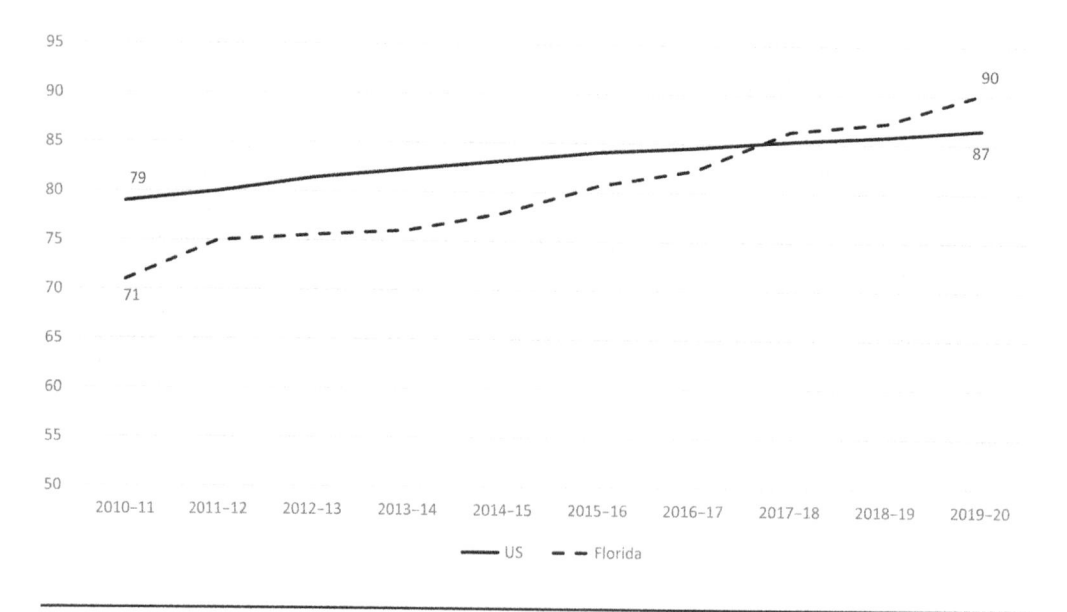

Figure 10.5 Public High School Graduation Rates in Florida, 2010–11 Through 2019–20

Source: National Center for Education Statistics (2023). Digest of Education Statistics, Table 218.46.

higher than the national average of 90%. Bright Futures, especially the implicit program of merit scholarships for high achievement, probably influenced Florida's improvement compared to national trends, but it is not the only policy variable. They do indicate a sustained positive relationship with high school graduation rates. Therefore, maintaining the merit program over time corresponded with Florida's improvement in graduate rates, which outpaced national trends.

School Voucher Program

It is also possible that the voucher program has contributed to increases in Florida's high school graduation. The Family Empowerment Scholarship is relatively new, but since 2019, when the program was announced, the number of program participants has grown from approximately 13,000 students to 136,087 in 2023–24 (Ed Choice, 2023). However, from these trends, ending in 2019–20, it is too early to know the impact of vouchers on high school graduation rates or college access. The program has grown with political support from the conservative state legislature and governor, largely because the cap on the award is set at 100% of unweighted state funding, less exceptional services education expenses, and the eligibility criteria has a generous threshold for family income (185% of poverty for priority and up to 400% for the second tier).

Test Scores

College admissions test scores play an entirely different role in Florida than in the other state cases. The Bright Futures program sets its eligibility thresholds according to high school GPA and SAT, ACT, or the Classic Learning Test (CLT) scores. The CLT tests for the classics, a strategy aligned with the MAGA theory of school curriculum. This K-12 test option aligns with "traditional" education. With the theocratic twist in course content in some Christian schools, the CLT may provide an alternative path for voucher students choosing Christian schools. However, it is not a college admissions test like the ACT or SAT.

Even in cases where colleges have elected for test-optional or removal from the admissions decision, students' eligibility for Bright Futures relies on taking at least one of these tests. Therefore, test-taking patterns did not change much during the pandemic. The number of test takers grew steadily through 2019 to 190,000, dropped modestly in 2020 and 2021 to a low of 172,000, and rebounded the following year. By 2023, the state of Florida had already exceeded its highest test-taking numbers from before the pandemic (over 205,000 test-takers).

The mean test score dropped slightly in the years after the pandemic, corresponding to an increase in test-takers—a finding we would expect. As a more significant proportion of students take the test, the growth is among those who would not have done as well, which brings the average scores down. In the final section, we will discuss the possible implications of the CLT since Florida has endorsed the new "admissions" test alternative.

Trends in College Enrollment and Diversity

A second intent of Bright Futures is to improve the retention of high-achieving Floridians in the state. Although we do not have a direct measure of this outcome, college enrollment rates and representation of racial diversity provide related indicators. College enrollment rates measure the percentage of resident students (18- to 24-years-old) who enroll in both in-state and out-of-state universities. The Bright Futures is just one policy affecting enrollment. Tuition, need-based aid, and state funding reducing college costs

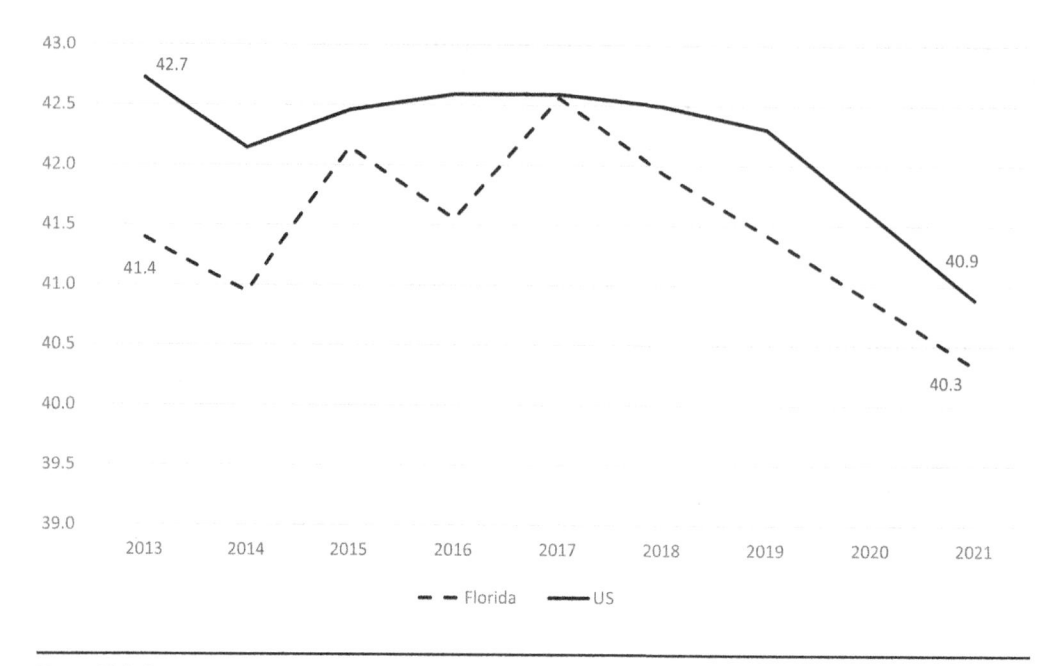

Figure 10.6 Percentage of 18- to 24-Year-Olds Enrolled in Degree-Granting Postsecondary Institutions: Florida & U.S.
Source: National Center for Education Statistics (2023). Digest of Education Statistics, Table 302.65.

have long been the primary policy variables influencing predicting enrollment rates. Bright Futures and other merit grants may influence enrollment, but the impact is usually less substantial than need-based grants (see Chapter 5).

College Enrollment Rates for College-Age Students Starting in Florida Degree-Granting Colleges

The trends reported in the first edition considered college continuation rates, a measure of whether high school graduates enrolled in the fall after graduation. We found that college enrollment rates increased faster than the national after the implementation of Bright Futures (St. John et al., 2012). The college-age population examined in Figure 10.6 includes new and continuing students in the age group, a different measure. The trends show that sustaining Bright Futures had a continued association with college participation.

These recent trends in college participation rates for Florida lagged slightly behind the national enrollment averages by about 1 percentage point between 2013 and 2021 (Figure 10.6), except for 2017, when the rates were identical. Florida has had a capacity issue across its public higher education system, which may be related to the availability of the Bright Futures program. The combination of lower average tuition at public in-state 4-year colleges and Bright Futures sustained enrollment. In addition to the monetary effect, the incentives to prepare provide a link to the college application process, something like Indiana's Twenty-first Century Scholars and Encouragement programs (Chapter 9). Regardless, the higher enrollment rate is a positive finding from the perspective of advocates for Bright Futures and low tuition.

In addition, Bright Futures may hold down tuition increases by limiting the necessity of institutional merit aid to induce and sustain enrollment for high-achieving students, many from upper-middle-income families. Given the lower tuition and the reduced need for campus-based merit scholarships, we caution readers not to conclude that sustaining

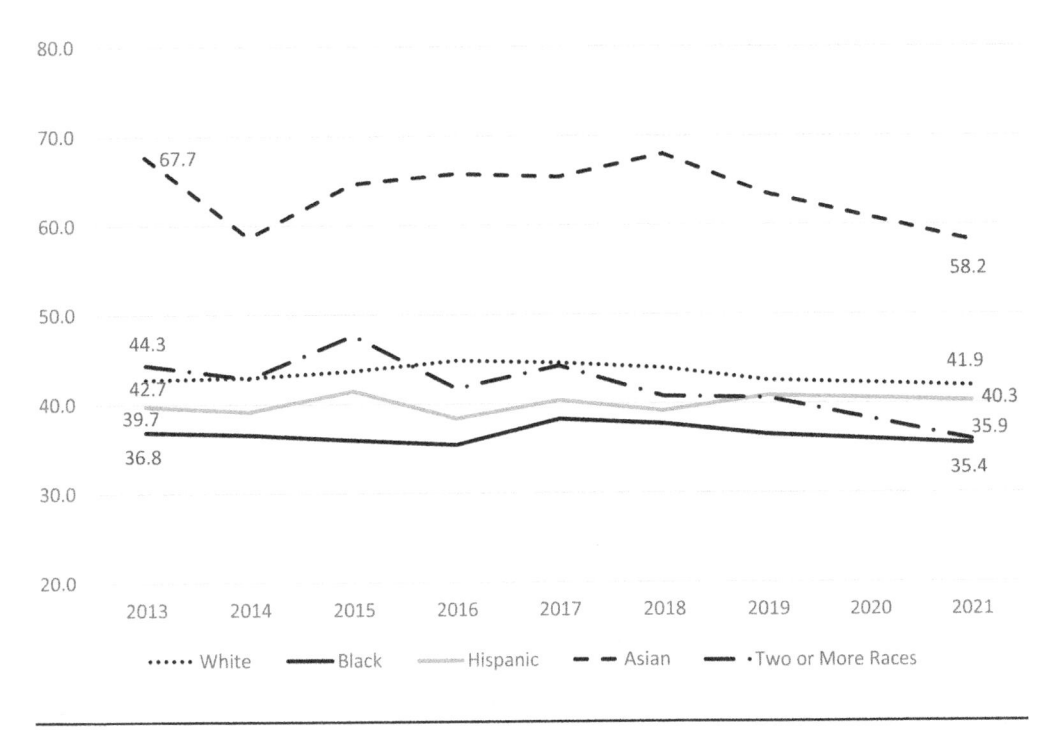

Figure 10.7 Percentage of 18- to 24-Year-Olds Enrolled in Degree-Granting Postsecondary Institutions, by Race/Ethnicity: Florida

Source: National Center for Education Statistics (2023). Digest of Education Statistics, Table 302.65.

Bright Futures caused higher in-state enrollment. However, Bright Futures appears to have direct and indirect associations with higher in-state enrollment in Florida.

Diversity in Florida Postsecondary Education

The trends in college enrollments by race and ethnicity at 4-year public colleges (Figure 10.7) show that the patterns are consistent, and the gaps remain substantial. In 2013, the gap between Asian and Native American students was nearly 35 percentage points, and that gap has narrowed by about 10 points by 2021. The gap between Black and white students continues to be approximately 10 points, with some narrowing by 2017, followed by a period of divergence through 2021. From the social justice perspective, the only positive trend is the progress Native students have made since they hit a low of 29% going to college in 2015. As a group, they increase college participation among 18- to 24-year-olds by 12 percentage points to 41%.

Proportional Representation by Race and Ethnicity

In Florida, white students are under-represented in higher education relative to their proportion of the state population, while all other groups are over-represented to some degree (Figure 10.8). It is helpful to consider an illustration to make sense of these data. In 2020, the population of Florida was 21.5 million people, and of those, 3.1 million were Black (15%). During that same year, just over 1 million students enrolled in college across the state, and 172,000 were Black (17%). As a result, Black students were over-represented in higher education, relative to their proportion of the state population, by 9 percentage points (17/15 = 1.09).

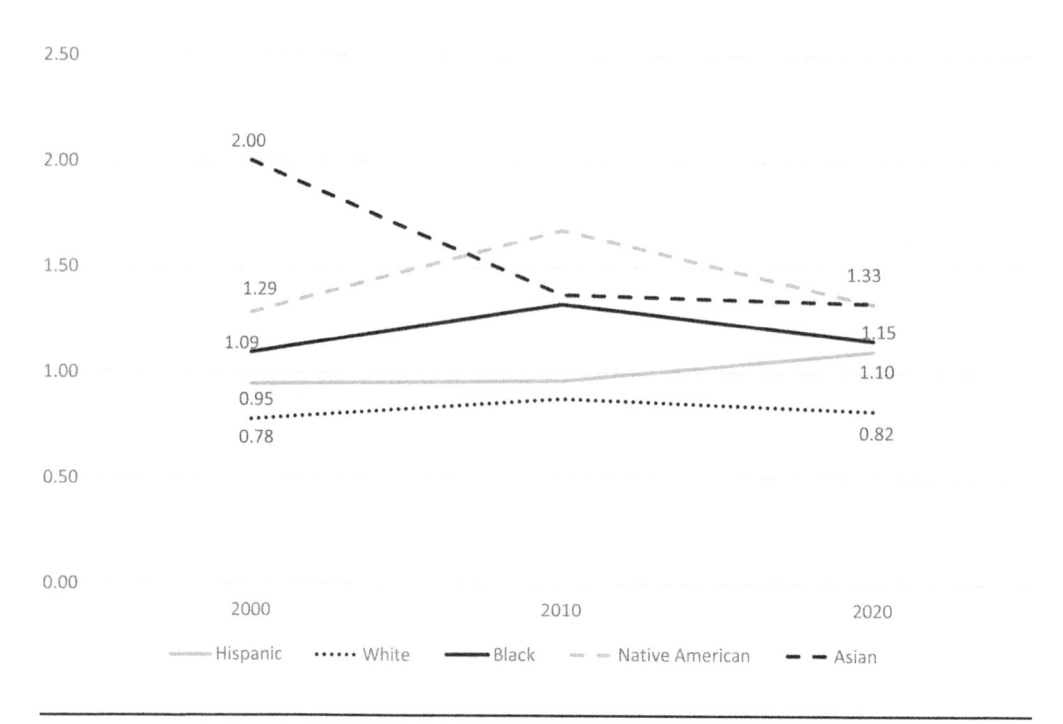

Figure 10.8 Racial/Ethnic Representation in Florida Postsecondary Education as a Proportion of the State Population
Source: National Center for Education Statistics (2023). Digest of Education Statistics, Table 306.70 & Table 266 & US Census Bureau.

The difference is likely to be found in the relative age of each population. In Florida, for example, it is expected that more older adults are white and fewer are in the 18- to 24-years-old range due to the elderly retired population. In the US, the average age of the white population is 44, compared to 35 for Black and 30 for Latinx (National Equity Atlas, 2024). Since the white population skews older, especially in Florida, even a more substantial percentage of that group going to college will still be under-represented relative to the entire white population in the state.

In addition, it is possible that white Floridians do not enroll in 2-year colleges at the same rates as non-white students. White high school graduates who are not in college may find it easier to find a job with sufficient income to support their life choices. Minoritized students often find it harder to find a good job without college, so they may have an added incentive to work instead of attending community colleges. In the final section below, we discuss this hypothesis with trends in earnings and debt. In this trend analysis (Figure 10.8), we do not have the statistical breakdowns in place of enrollment that would be necessary to explain enrollment destinations further.

Postsecondary Attainment

The National Student Clearinghouse (NSC) provides data for diverse students, tracking them from their campus of origin through transfers and stop out across six years to degree completion. It provides a measure of degree attainment related to social uplift and economic development. We examine trends for six cohorts who began their undergraduate careers in 2012–17, starting at either a public 4-year (Figure 10.9) or a private 4-year (Figure 10.10) college and finishing within six years.

From Merit Aid to MAGA Reforms • 237

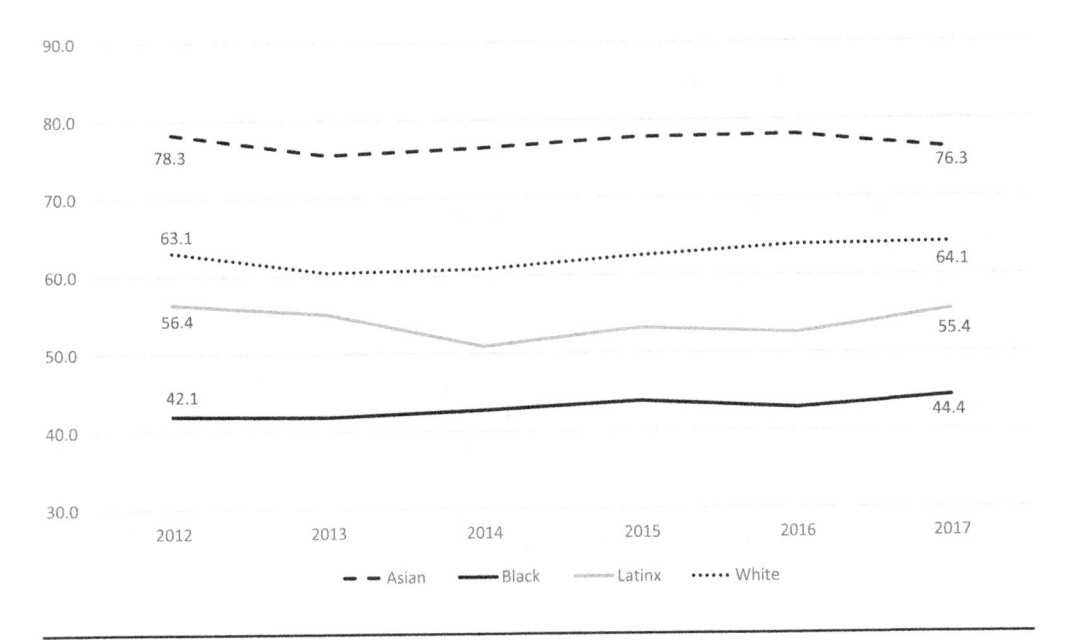

Figure 10.9 Trends in 6-Year Degree Attainment Rates for all Florida Public 4-Year Postsecondary Institutions

Source: National Student Clearinghouse Research Center (2023). Completing College: National & State Reports. Retrieved from https://nscresearchcenter.org/completing-college/

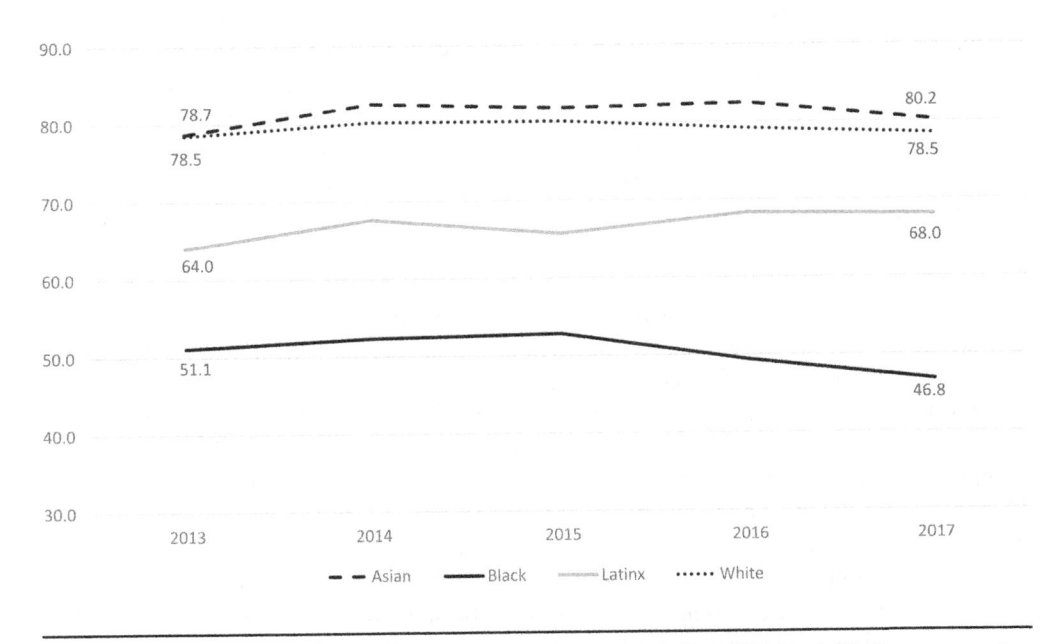

Figure 10.10 Trends in 6-Year Degree Attainment Rates for all Florida Private Nonprofit 4-Year Institutions

Source: National Student Clearinghouse Research Center (2023). Completing College: National & State Reports. Retrieved from https://nscresearchcenter.org/completing-college/

Degree Attainment for Students Starting in Public 4-Year Colleges
Completion rates by race and ethnicity demonstrate persistent inequality in Florida's public colleges and universities for the six cohorts (Figure 10.9). Nationally, the most substantial gap in degree completion rates is between Asian and Black students at about 30 percentage points, which has been consistent for a decade. The gap between white and Latinx students is about half that at 15 percentage points, and the gaps have not declined.

In Florida, the gaps have declined modestly between Asian and Black students, from 38 percentage points for the 2012 cohort to 32 percentage points for the 2017 cohort, which is still slightly larger than the national gaps. These trends illustrate the central systemic inequality associated with Bright Futures. This state program invests substantially in merit scholarships to retain high-achieving students. This design intent explicitly favors whites because it does not provide sufficient aid to mitigate loan dependence by lower-income minority students. These trends illustrate success for whites, the highest income group. The inequality in 4-year degree attainment illustrates systemic inequality, providing substantially less opportunity for degree attainment by Latinx students and, especially, Blacks. The systemic inequality and Florida student debt crisis create an economic disaster for the state (see the final section).

Degree Attainment for Students Starting in Private 4-Year Colleges
Some groups started at Florida's private colleges and universities and completed at higher rates than those who enrolled in public institutions; others did not (Figure 10.10). Many private campuses, like the University of Miami, attract students from other states and nations. White students starting in the 2012–17 cohorts at private nonprofit colleges graduated nearly 80% compared to 64% of the time at Public 4-year colleges. Similarly, the degree completion rate for Latinx students was 15 percentage points higher at the private colleges. In contrast, Asian and Black students see no appreciable difference in completion rates. The disparities in completion rates for Blacks and other groups are more substantial for students starting at private colleges. Bright Futures is not a substantially influential program concerning private college choice, so the finding has only modest implications for state policy development.

Linking Policies and Outcomes

The structure of Florida's education policies and postsecondary funding strategies was relatively stable in the early 2000s, and there were no substantial changes in educational outcomes. High school graduation and enrollment rates for 18- to 24-years-olds improved. The enrollment rates for traditional college-age Asian students were consistently higher than for other groups, without substantial disparity between whites, Hispanics, and Blacks. The academic preparation policies—the combination of requirements, encouragement services (not reviewed), and incentives provided by merit aid—appear to promote uplift. However, the racial disparities in bachelor's degree attainment were problematic. Black students were closer to the state averages in getting into college but much less likely to complete in six years at either public or private 4-year campuses.

Much like Minnesota, African Americans, the lowest income group of college students in Florida, were left behind during their college years, a problem because the state's merit aid strategy was inadequate for the highest-need students. Specifically, if graduation disparities are higher than for academic preparation, financial ability to pay is likely the problem. Students with higher unmet needs borrow more, drop out of school to work or enroll only in part-time—intermediate outcomes that undermine attainment. In Florida, the merit financial aid strategy perpetuated the state's historical pattern of racial discrimination.

THE CURRENT POLICY CONTEXT

Like many states, Florida focused on merit aid programs to create an incentive for more substantial preparation in high school and to keep top academic talent in the state through the Bright Futures scholarship program, the key higher education policy issue. In the years following the implementation of higher standards, there was a negative association with high school graduation rates (Daun-Barnett & St. John, 2012). With the extended time past the original implementation of higher standards in the 2000s, Florida continues to invest in merit aid and expand eligibility for Bright Futures. Aside from eliminating the book scholarship for FAS students, it has not significantly limited the size of the awards. Florida's high school graduation rates have increased more than the national average, and those policies have been and continue to be in effect. SAT participation and scores remained higher than the national average. However, racial disparities in attainment continued and widened, a key indicator of sustained educational inequality. The merit aid policy continued Florida's legacy of segregation and education discrimination. Below, we note the limitations of the state's strategy and the complications created by the social conservative agenda.

Limitations of Florida's Merit Strategy

Florida is among the country's most reasonably priced public postsecondary education systems, at least in terms of public, 4-year, in-state tuition. Combined with Bright Futures, the moderate costs of 4-year colleges provided incentives for enrollment and completion by middle-income and high-income students. However, the strategy is inadequate for low-income students, resulting in severe disparities in attainment for Blacks compared to whites, extending the state's history of racial inequality. There was also a substantial gap in attainment for Hispanics compared to whites and Asians. The NSC did not have sufficient data to report on Native American student attainment, adding to the unequal shadow haunting Bright Future's legacy.

The most severe problem with Florida's merit aid strategy, the racial disparities in college attainment, are best mitigated by investing in need-based student aid. Merit aid is unequal on its face, placing low-income students with substantial unmet financial need at risk of dropping out. The Florida case proves the proposition. In contrast to Florida, other cases illustrate funding of state need-based grants in apparent efforts to narrow racial and class disparities in attainment—for example, California, Minnesota, and Indiana are all reinvesting in need-based aid. While the new strategies in the other state cases will not equalize attainment, they have taken corrective steps to narrow racial disparities. Not in Florida, where the political discourse has tumbled more deeply into racially charged politics.

It is also problematic that Florida's community colleges are more expensive than many of their peers around the country. We suspect that there are higher than average costs for public 2-year colleges, at least in part because of the community college baccalaureate efforts in the state. Most Florida community colleges now offer bachelor's degrees, and many have since dropped "community" from their names. The cost of providing baccalaureate education is higher than it costs to provide a 2-year education; the result is higher-than-average community college tuition.

Complications with Conservative Shifts in Education

Florida's most significant changes align closely with the conservative priorities emerging since 2019 when the passage of the Family Empowerment Scholarship created the state's K-12 voucher program. The program began with strict income eligibility requirements and a cap on the maximum award, but both have changed dramatically in the intervening years. According to Ed Choice (2023), the Florida program is "the most expansive education savings account (ESA) program in the United States, with nearly 3 million students eligible for a flexible education, chosen by their parents." (n.p.). In only four years, participation grew to more than 136,000 students, which is still only a fraction of the eligible students, but the growth rate is dramatic. The program is increasing demand for Catholic schools, and with growing wait lists, they are expanding their enrollment capacity (Costantino & Tavel, 2024), an expansion of educational opportunities that could attract Hispanics from the public. The more considerable concern for a program like this is that it has been opened to families whose incomes are 400% of poverty, meaning that more middle-class and upper-middle-income families can take those resources away from public schools and shift their students to private education, including religious institutions.

Florida's second ultra-conservative trend is toward banning books and eliminating public support for DEI initiatives in education. The banning of books and the restrictions imposed on the teaching of Black history and LGBTQ topics in K-12 schools create hostile learning environments, placing minoritized and LGBTQ students at greater risk of harm through social discrimination. Changes in laws and regulation of content, a penchant toward textbook wars that go back in Florida history, have manifested in extreme, perhaps even savage, ways that intrude into the ability of collegiate education faculty to teach about diversity and to use pedagogical practices that focus on race and cultural strengths of racial/ethnic groups. These practices could further accelerate disparities in educational outcomes in Florida. The state has recently placed limits on individuals' ability to call for the banning of books, but it remains a politicized issue (Atterbury, 2024).

As a MAGA state, Florida has gone to war against the DEI programs and culture, a strategy shaking the foundation of postsecondary education (Associated Press, 2024). Expanding opportunities to enroll in Catholic high schools could appeal to Latinx families, possibly reinforcing the appeal of MAGA's political ideology and social agenda. The attacks on academic freedom are equally concerning in higher education. Governor DeSantis' move to replace the entire Board of Trustees at the New College in Florida—with a reputation for being a more liberal space—with a slate of conservative Board members is a signal that the conservative right does not simply want to ban DEI programs on campus or weaken the tenure process by implementing a 5-year post-tenure review process.

Finding Balance and Hope

The ultra-conservative forces in Florida are also evident in the other states' cases, but not to the extent evident in the Florida case. The conservative tensions are especially high in Indiana and North Carolina, but their histories of progressive education bring balancing forces into the policy discourse. Like Florida, North Carolina and Indiana have consistently pursued conservative social policies. The major difference in comparing these cases is that Indiana and North Carolina have progressive student aid and conservative social policies. Florida's merit, voucher, and MAGA strategies make no pretense of mixing conservative social policies with progressive education policies. The combination of K-12 and merit student aid builds on an elitist model that disadvantages poor people, Black and white. Ironically and sadly, these policies alienate poor whites, pushing them to the MAGA political extreme where policies are constructed that defy their economic and educational interests.

REFRAMING COLLEGE SUCCESS

Emphasizing merit over need as a basis for student aid redirects support from college students from high-poverty to high-achieving high school graduates, many of whom are middle-class students with collegiate opportunities even without grants. Florida's strategy advantages economically privileged families, further increasing cross-generation wealth inequality. The state's history of education discrimination preceded the Bright Futures and the MAGA anti-woke policies that are now transforming Florida's schools and colleges. To frame the challenges facing Floridians—their economic and social circumstances—we consider the lingering problem of student debt before considering the status of degrees attainment and earnings, setting the stage for questions for readers.

Florida's High Debt for College Graduates

Floridians across age groups have debt from college (Hanson, 2023). Adults over 61 still owe $7.1 billion, indicating this problem has a long history. The 25- to 34-years-old cohort owes $31.6 billion, an age group benefiting from Bright Futures, while the 35–49 group that completed college before Bright Futures owes $43.2 billion. It appears Bright Futures reduced reliance on debt for 24- to 34-years-olds who received tuition reductions or achievement. Also, if it had passed, Biden's loan forgiveness efforts would have eased the burden for some low-income earners in Florida (Bridges, 2024). The easing of debt burden benefits low-income adults with some college or college degrees, many of whom would not have benefited from Bright Futures.

Given the state's history of racially unequal schooling, an underlying problem is the debt disparities across racial groups among current students. In 2019–20, Florida A & M, 82% borrowed and had an average debt of $26,819. At Florida State, a predominantly white university across town, only 44% of students borrowed and owed an average of $21,425 (The Institute for College for College Access & Success, 2021). This difference further reveals the consequence of state financial aid policies emphasizing merit instead of financial need. While the race disparity in debt burden is national (Hanson, 2023), Florida's merit program exacerbates the inequality by denying need-based had to high-poverty students who do not have high achievement in high school, an artifact of the state's legacy of race inequality in public education in K-12.

Economic Benefits of College for Floridians

Education attainment in Florida still lags the nation, indicating that Bright Futures directed aid toward students who probably would have gone to college without the grant aid instead of uplifting new groups. Using Census data, we consider attainment and earning in Florida. Given Florida's systemic inequality, this section concludes by examining poverty rates by race, a key issue in Florida because the state's higher education finance policies accelerated wealth inequality gaps in education attainment.

242 • State Cases

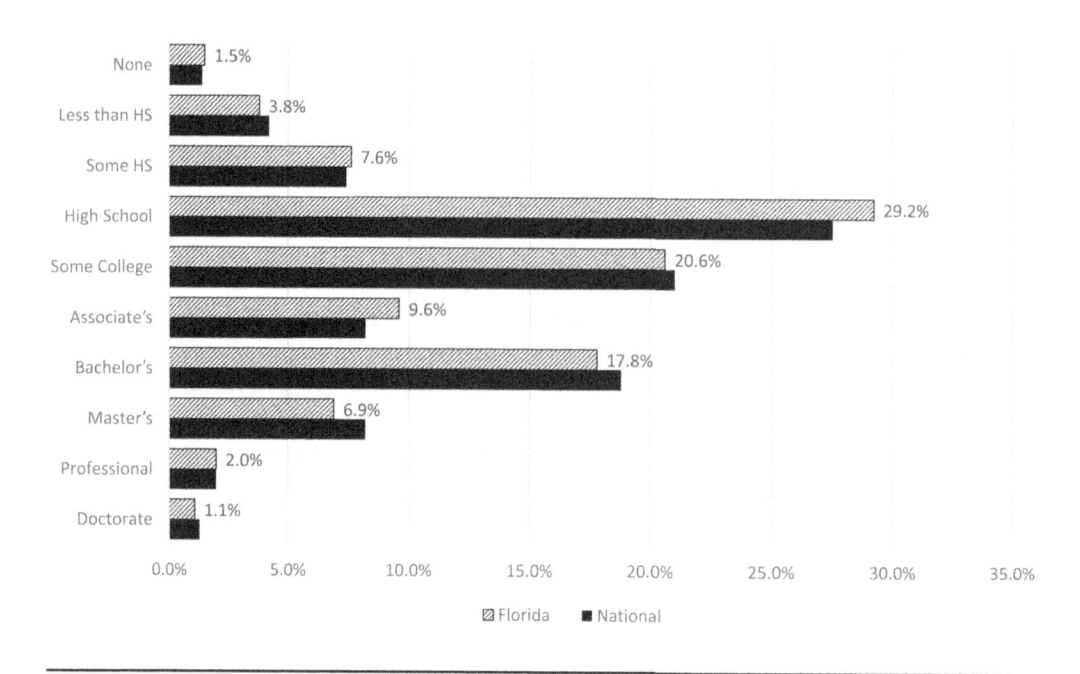

Figure 10.11 Highest Level of Educational Attainment for People 25 or Older in Florida (2020)
Source: Statistical Atlas (2023). Educational Attainment. Retrieved from https://statisticalatlas.com/United-States/Educational-Attainment

Educational Attainment Among Florida's Adult Population

According to the 2020 Census, compared to the nation, higher percentages of Floridians have high school diplomas or lower levels of education. The percentage of Floridians with associates degrees exceeds the national average (Figure 10.11). At the same time, those students who attain some college with no degree comprise a lower percentage of Floridians than the national population. The associates degree and some attainment, in combination, indicate that Florida's 2-year systems have a successful legacy in graduating students, at least compared to the nation. Whether upgrading community colleges to baccalaureate awarding campuses will change this accessibility pattern to 2-year completion is an open question.

Compared to the rest of the nation, bachelor's degree attainment remains low among the adult population in Florida. Another dilemma of merit aid may be that it eases education barriers for people who will likely move anyway after attaining their degrees. The merit subsidies eased the pressure on middle-class parents with high achieving students to pay rising tuition costs and reduced the necessity of borrowing. Given Florida's relatively high enrollment and completion rates for whites and Asians with high achievement during high school, the low percentage of 4-year degree recipients raises questions about the out-migration of educated labor, especially given earnings for the state's college-educated population.

Earnings by Education Level

In 2023, Floridians across the attainment spectrum earned less than the national average. Florida has a lower cost of living than other states used as cases. The gaps in earnings are most substantial for people who earned bachelor's or advanced degrees (Figure 10.12). Florida does not provide a nationally competitive economic environment

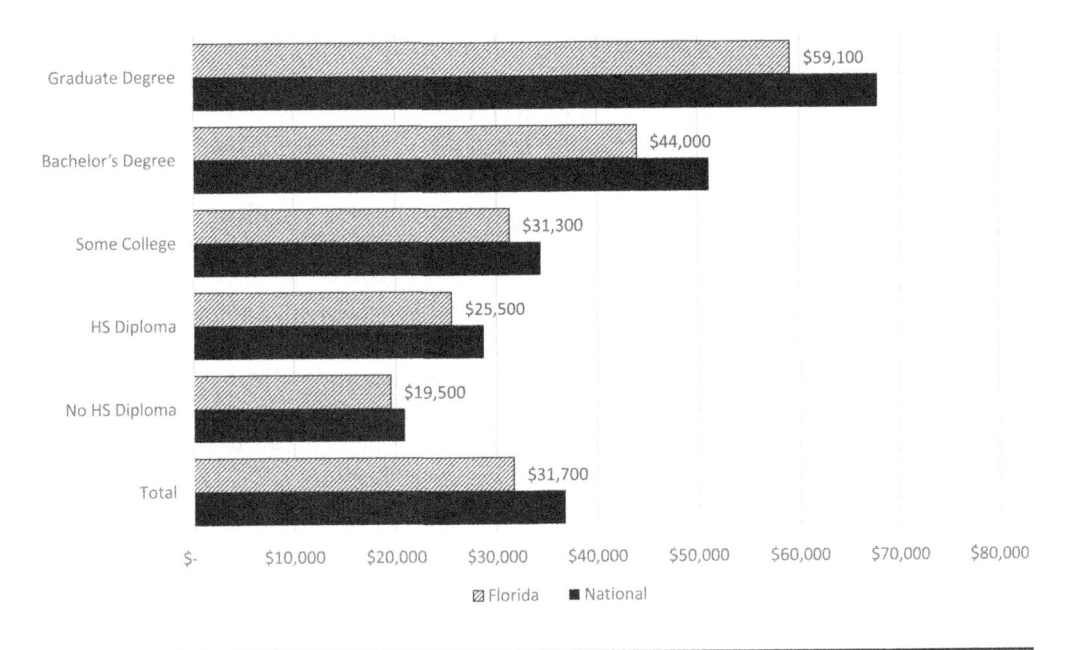

Figure 10.12 Median Annual Earnings in Florida by Level of Education (2023)

Source: Statistical Atlas (2023). Educational Attainment. Retrieved from https://statisticalatlas.com/United-States/Educational-Attainment

for degree recipients, so it is unlikely to attract working-age, college-educated migrants from out of state.

Poverty Rates by Race in Florida

With postsecondary education policies emphasizing merit aid and high prices in 2-year colleges, Florida discriminates against poor children more than other states studied. According to the 2020 Census, Florida's poverty rate was 13%, ranking 32nd among states (Center for American Progress, 2022). The poverty rate for whites was 9%. The Black poverty rate was 20%, more than double the rate of whites. The poverty rates of Hispanics (16%) and Native Americans (15%) were also substantially higher than whites. Asians had a 10% poverty rate, nearly equal to whites. Because of high tuition in community colleges and reliance on merit scholarships, Florida's postsecondary education policy discriminates against people experiencing poverty, not only denying them equal chances of college access but penalizing them because high debt is the only way most of them can pay for college. High debt upon graduation limits the net earnings of college graduates, worsening the cross-generation cycle of wealth inequality. Instead of lifting families, Florida's policies increase wealth inequality across generations.

Financial Wellbeing of Floridians

The Sunshine State offers warm weather, beaches, low costs, and high vulnerability to severe weather. It does not have the high-knowledge, high-tech economy of other large states like California, Texas, and New York. The cultural richness of Caribbean infusion into southern culture offers alternative lifestyles, including retirement communities attracting older citizens from other states. Even with the migration of the Northern snowbirds for their senior years, college degree attainment remains low among the general population, possibly because graduates find better jobs out of state. The state's education policies improved pathways to college for high achievers choosing academic and vocational options, but they do not benefit from a robust economy if they stay in the state. Educated young adults may be one of Florida's major exports.

The challenges left unaddressed are the educational pathways for students of average ability and the capacity of low-income high achievers to afford a livable lifestyle whether they receive Bright Futures awards or not. The debt burden accrued by low-income students is an outcome of policies that transfer income—through state income tax and lottery revenue—from low-income families to wealthier families who benefit from vouchers and Bright Futures. The poor whites left behind educationally are prone to buying into MAGA ideologies that support merit and voucher policies that undermine their interests and the future financial wellbeing of their children—a better blend of progressivism with the dominant commitment to conservative social values is a necessity. Backing off extremist education policies on curriculum and academic freedom is essential as well if Florida is to overcome the dramatic inequalities and divisiveness inherent in the current trajectory.

Questions

1. How does Florida's development before the Civil War compare to states in the Northwest Territory (Minnesota, Indiana, and Michigan)?
2. What difference did Florida's Spanish history and alignment with the South influence the evolution of race relations after the Civil War? How does the history of Spanish influence in Florida compare to and contrast with California?
3. How did the fear of slave rebellions before the Civil War in Florida morph across generations in education policy?
4. How do the incentives for college preparation in Florida's Bright Futures compare to incentives in Indiana's and Minnesota's approaches to college preparation?
5. How does the efficacy of Florida's approach to merit aid and schools compare to the education finance policies in California and Minnesota? How do Florida's MAGA education policies compare to and contrast with the emphasis on Christian nationalism in Indiana?

REFERENCES

Altschuler, G. C., & Wippman, D. (2023). *Florida Is Trying to Roll Back a Century of Gains for Academic Freedom.* https://www.washingtonpost.com/made-by-history/2023/02/06/academic-freedom-florida/

Associated Press (2024). *U. of Florida axes DEI office under GOP-led law aimed at ridding similar programs.* National Public Radio. Retrieved from https://www.npr.org/2024/03/04/1235725631/university-florida-cuts-dei-office.

Atterbury, A. (April 16, 2024). *DeSantis signs law limiting Florida book challenges.* Politico. Retrieved from https://www.politico.com/news/2024/04/16/desantis-book-challenge-law-00152515.

Bateman, R. B. (1990). Africans and Indians: A comparative study of the Black carib and Black seminole. *Ethnohistory*, 37(1), 1–24.

Bates, T. (1928). The legal status of the negro in Florida. *The Florida Historical Society Quarterly*, 6(3), 159–181.

Bennett, W. (1987, February 18). *Our greedy colleges.* New York Times.

Bishop, J. H. (2005). *High school exit examinations: When do learning effects generalize?* Center for Advanced Human Resource Studies. Retrieved from http://www.wiroundtable.org/Web_Site_PDFs/2010_pk12_committee/Bishop%20Paper.pdf

Black, M. W. (1964). The Battle over uniformity of textbooks in Florida, 1868–1963. *History of Education Quarterly*, 4(2), 106–118.

Borg, J. R., & Borg, M. O. (2007). The reverse robin hood effect: The distribution of net benefits from the Florida bright futures scholarship. *Florida Political Chronicle, 18.* https://stoppredatorygambling.org/wp-content/uploads/2012/12/The-Reverse-Robin-Hood-Effect-The-Distribution-of-Net-Benefits-From-the-Florida-Bright-Futures-Scholarship.pdf

Bridges, C. A. (2024). *Biden plan cancels $1.2 billion in student loans. Do Florida students qualify?* Retrieved April 20 from https://www.news-journalonline.com/story/news/state/2024/02/21/student-loan-forgiveness-biden-administration-qualify/72681677007/

Ceballos, A. (2021, April 27). Florida's top college students to lose $600 stipend for textbooks. Tampa Bay Times. https://www.tampabay.com/news/florida-politics/2021/04/26/floridas-top-college-students-to-lose-600-stipend-for-textbooks/

Census Bulletin. (1890). Population of Florida by Counties and Minor Civil Divisions. Retrieved from https://www2.census.gov/library/publications/decennial/1900/bulletins/demographic/16-population-fl.pdf

Center for American Progress. (2022). Talk Poverty - Florida. Retrieved from https://talkpoverty.org/state-year-report/florida-2020-report/index.html

Colavecchio-Van Sickler, S. (2007, February 25). Higher education for a better Florida: Too many students, too little money don't bode well for the state. St. Petersburg Times.

Costantino, L., & Tavel, J. (2024, March 31). The voucher effect? South Florida Catholic schools see more kids, even wait lists. Miami Herald. https://www.miamiherald.com/news/local/education/article286344395.html

Daun-Barnett, N., & St. John, E. P. (2012). Constrained curriculum in high schools: The changing math standards and student achievement, high school graduation and college continuation. *Education Policy Analysis Archives*, 20(5). http://epaa.asu.edu/ojs/article/view/907

Delaney, J. A., & Doyle, W. R. (2007). The role of higher education in state budgets. In K. Shaw, & D.E. Heller (Ed.), *State postsecondary education research: New methods to inform policy and practice.* Stylus.

Dodd, W. G. (1948). Early education in Tallahassee and the West Florida seminary, now Florida state university. *The Florida Historical Quarterly*, 27(1), 1–27.

Doyle, W. R. (2006). Adoption of merit-based student grant programs: An event history analysis. *Educational Evaluation and Policy Analysis*, 28(3), 259–285. https://doi.org/10.3102/01623737028003259

Doyle, W. R. (2010). Does merit aid "crowd out" need-based aid? *Research in Higher Education*, 51(5), 397–415. https://doi.org/10.3102/01623737028003259

Dynarski, S. M. (2002). The Consequences of Merit Aid. National Bureau of Economic Research *(9400).*

Dynarski, S. M. (2004). Who should we help? The negative social consequences of merit scholarships. *State Merit Scholarship Programs and Racial Inequality, Issue.*

Ed Choice. (2023). Florida: Family Empowerment Scholarships for Education Options Program. Retrieved from https://www.edchoice.org/school-choice/programs/florida-family-empowerment-scholarship-program/

Florida Department of Education. (2023a). 2021-22 Florida Statewide End-of-Course Assessments Fact Sheet. Retrieved from https://www.fldoe.org/core/fileparse.php/5663/urlt/EOCFS2022.pdf

Florida Department of Education. (2023b). Talented Twenty Program. https://www.fldoe.org/core/fileparse.php/7754/urlt/TT-PBOG.pdf

Florida Department of Education. (2023c). *High School Graduation Requirements.* https://www.fldoe.org/schools/k-12-public-schools/sss/graduation-requirements/

Florida Department of Education. (2024a). Assessments and Publications Archives: FCAT Historical. Retrieved from https://www.fldoe.org/accountability/assessments/k-12-student-assessment/archive/fcat/#:~:text=During%20the%202010%2D11%20school,last%20time%20in%20Spring%202015.

Florida Department of Education. (2024b). End-of-Course Assessments. Retrieved from https://www.fldoe.org/accountability/assessments/k-12-student-assessment/end-of-course-eoc-assessments/

Hanson, M. (2023). *Student loan debt statistics.* Education Data Initiative. Retrieved from https://educationdata.org/student-loan-debt-statistics

Harkreader, S., Hughs, J., Hicks Tozzi, M., & Vanlandingham, G. (2008). The impact of Florida's bright futures scholarship program on high school performance and college enrollment. *Journal of Student Financial Aid*, 38(1), 1.

Heller, D. E. (2002). Is merit-based student aid really trumping need-based aid? Another view. *Change, July/August*, 6–8.

Heller, D. E. (2004a). State merit scholarship programs. In E. P. St. John (Ed.), *Public policy and college access: Investigating the federal and state roles in equalizing postsecondary opportunity* (Vol. 19, pp. 29–64). AMS Press, Inc.

Heller, D. E. (2004b). State merit scholarships: An overview. In D. Heller & P. Marin (Eds.), *State merit scholarship programs and racial inequality.* The Civil Rights Project.

Heller, D. E., & Rogers, K. R. (2003). Merit Scholarships and Incentives for Academic Performance. *Annual Conference of the Association for the Study of Higher Education, Portland, OR.*

Hurtado, S., & Worthington-Cade, H. (2001). Time for retreat or renewal? Perspectives on the effects of hopwood on campus. In D. E. Heller (Ed.), *The States and public higher education policy: Affordability, access, and accountability* (p. 271). Johns Hopkins University Press.

Kleinberg, E. (September 7, 2019). What is Florida's oldest university? It depends. *The Ledger*. Retrieved from https://www.theledger.com/story/news/education/2019/09/07/what-is-floridas-oldest-university-it-depends/3470657007/.

Lapovsky, L. (April 3, 2023). Political Climate and Educational Policies May Lower Enrollment At Florida Colleges, *Forbes* https://www.forbes.com/sites/lucielapovsky/2023/04/05/political-climate-and-educational-policies-may-lower-enrollment-at-florida-colleges/?sh=48575e3242f6.

Leslie, L., & Brinkman, P. (1987). Student price response in higher education: The student demand studies. *Journal of Higher Education*, 58(2), 181–204.

Martin, S. W. (1944). The public domain in territorial Florida. *The Journal of Southern History*, 10(2), 174–187.

McGrory, K. (March 22, 2014). Feds investigate Florida's Bright Futures scholarship program. *Tampa Bay Times*. Retrieved from https://www.tampabay.com/news/education/college/feds-investigate-floridas-bright-futures-scholarship-program/2171469/

Moody, J. (2024). DEI Spending Banned, Sociology Scrapped in Florida. Inside Higher Ed. Retrieved from https://www.insidehighered.com/news/governance/trustees-regents/2024/01/18/dei-spending-banned-sociology-scrapped-florida?utm_source=Inside+%E2%80%A6

National Equity Atlas. (2024). Median age: Shared prosperity requires setting up young people of color to succeed. Retrieved from https://nationalequityatlas.org/indicators/Median_age

National Student Clearinghouse Research Center. (2023). *Completing College: A State-Level View of Student Attainment Rates*. Retrieved December 20 from https://nscresearchcenter.org/completing-college/

Newman, M. (1999). The Florida baptist convention and desegregation. *The Florida Historical Quarterly*, 78(1), 3.

News Service Florida. (2023). New report shows nearly 123,000 new students received Florida school vouchers in 2023. https://www.nbcmiami.com/news/local/new-report-shows-nearly-123000-new-students-received-florida-school-vouchers-in-2023/3112869/

Office of Student Financial Assistance. (2023). *Bright futures student handbook*. Florida Department of Education. Retrieved from https://www.floridastudentfinancialaidsg.org/PDF/BFHandbookChapter1.pdf

Olschki, L. (1941). Ponce De Leon's fountain of youth: History of a geographical myth. *Hispanic American Historical Review*, 21(3), 361–385.

Russell-Brown, K. (2024). The multitudinous racial harms caused by Florida's stop woke and anti-DEI legislation. *51 Fordham Urban Law Journal*, 785. https://papers.ssrn.com/sol3/papers.cfm?abstract_id=4573301.

Sachs, S. (Feb 28, 2023). *Florida college Enrollment won't hit pre-pandemic level in the next six years*. https://www.wfla.com/news/education/florida-college-enrollment-wont-hit-pre-pandemic-level-within-next6years/#:~:text=The%20same%20data%20showed%20the.

St. John, E. P. (2006). *Education and the public interest: School reform, public finance, and access to higher education*. Springer.

St. John, E. P., Daun-Barnett, N., & Moronski, K. (2012). *Public policy in higher education* (1st ed.). Routledge.

Sterling, R. (2023) Bright Futures Scholarships gets mini-makeover. *The FAMUAN* https://www.thefamuanonline.com/2023/09/22/bright-futures-scholarships-gets-minimakeover/#:~:text=With%20the%20signing%20and%20a,the%20passage%20of%20HB%2025.

Stranahan, H. A., & Borg, M. O. (2004). Some futures are brighter than others: The net benefits received by Florida bright futures scholarship recipients. *Public Finance Review*, 32(1), 105–126.

The Institute for College for College Access & Success. (2021). Student Debt for College Graduates in Florida. Retrieved from https://ticas.org/wp-content/uploads/2021/11/Student-Debt-for-College-Graduates-in-Florida.pdf

Tomberlin, J. A. (1974). Florida and the school segregation issue, 1954-1959: A summary. *The Journal of Negro Education*, 43(4), 457–467.

Tyack, D. B., & Lowe, R. (1986). The constitutional moment: Reconstruction and Black education in the South. *American Journal of Education*, 94(2), 236–256.

Winsboro, I. D., & Bartley, A. A. (2014). Race, education, and regionalism: The long and troubling history of school desegregation in the sunshine state. *The Florida Historical Quarterly*, 92(4), 714–745.

Woo, A., Diliberti, M. K., Lee, S., Kim, B., Lim, J. Z., & Wolfe, R. L. (2024). The Diverging State of Teaching and Learning Two Years into Classroom Limitations on Race or Gender: Findings from the 2023 American Instructional Resources Survey. https://www.rand.org/pubs/research_reports/RRA134-22.html

Zhang, L., Hu, S., & Sensenig, V. (2013). The effect of Florida's bright futures program on college enrollment and degree production: An aggregated-level analysis. *Research in Higher Education*, 54, 746–764.

11

CONSERVATIVE-PROGRESSIVE TENSIONS

*The North Carolina Case**

North Carolina has been a consistent example of progressive change in higher education compared to other *Adams* states. From the development of the Research Triangle in the 1960s through the response to federal desegregation mandates in 1978 and the state's investment in need-based student financial aid in the early twenty-first century. Although North Carolina continues a progressive education trajectory, it is also an extremely conservative state. From school privatization to gendered bathroom regulation, the Republican legislature has set conservative education agendas for Southern conservatives (Gaylord & Molony, 2016). Indeed, North Carolina has demonstrated a pattern of turning progressive agendas into education policies favoring whites and segregation, especially in K-12 education (Thompson Dorsey & Roulhac, 2019). Given its history of diversity, religion, and race inequality in public education, its effort to maintain a progressive higher education strategy is noteworthy. This case describes some of the critical developments in the North Carolina higher education system, the trends in policies and outcomes, and recent policy developments before raising questions for readers.

A HISTORY OF CONSERVATIVE-PROGRESSIVE CONFLICT

Throughout its history, North Carolina has struggled to overcome systemic inequality in the governance of the state, especially in efforts to expand educational opportunities. The North Carolina story is not merely about white supremacy resisting advocacy for equality. In the colonial and Early American periods, North Carolina governing authorities, confronted by converging and conflicting groups with oppositional goals, faced challenges not evident in New England—the region for most of the education histories. The white resistance to race equity solidified after reconstruction, shattered public K-12 education after *Brown*, and resurfaced as activists pursued equal education rights. In this troubled and strident context, North Carolina's higher education system found ways

---

* Ontario Wooden, Senior Associate Dean in the University College at North Carolina State University, provided a thoughtful review of this chapter, an appreciated collegial contribution.

DOI: 10.4324/9781032724867-13

through separate but equal, desegregation, and student support for equal opportunity during the neoliberal transition.

The Oscillating State of Unequal Opportunity

The tensions evident in North Carolina's Colonial and Early American periods provide a framework for viewing the tensions between religious conservatism and progressive education politics that have evolved in recent decades. As one of the first colonies, this state's history remains integral to the evolution of US education policy.

From Colonial Disputes to Education Diversity During Early American Period

The national themes of white male education and Christian domination were undoubtedly evident in North Carolina. The social contexts and educational aspirations were diverse and lingered in the state's discourse on education policy, differing from other states in the North and South.

North Carolina's history of diverse tensions between African, European, and Native American traditions is evident over five centuries, starting with the early seventeenth-century settlements (Fenn, 1983). The colonists initially had two different ideas about governance. In the European tradition, the Anglicans argued for alignment of church and state—the Puritan tradition in the North—but this wasn't a common purpose among the settlers: "Colonists attracted by promise of religious freedom and the agrarian dreams rebelled against these forces pushing for alignment" (Conkin, 1955, p. 1) Agrarian idealism, trading of European goods with Native Peoples (Rodning, 2010), and tensions between church and government, as an early shift toward secularism emerged. The Piedmont was fertile land where trade developed with Natives (Dobbs, 2009). There were agreements to govern fairly toward Native people, but Coastal tribes complained to the NC governor in the 1600s without resolution. The 1711–1713 War began the decline of tribes in the region (Denson, 1995). Quasi-secularization through regulation evolved as a governing mechanism for social control of the colonial rules and as a strategy for reducing conflict among settlers (Dobbs, 2009). Attracted to the new land by an Agrarian ideal of land ownership, extra-legal activities evolved, as did rebellious attitudes among settlers. "Regulators" became instrumental in enforcing the rules (Watson, 1994). The prevalence of firearms and liquor intensified disputes among Europeans and between them and Native tribes (Wetmore, 1979). In the midst of this contested diversity, "schoolhouses" developed in Eastern NC in the seventeenth century (LeMaster, 2006).

The Early American period did not bring socio-political stability, especially for the ethnically and socially diverse population. "From the colonial period through the Civil War, freed people of color in North Carolina held a sociopolitical status that firmly placed them legally above slaves and below whites" (Milteer, 2014, p. 1). The freed people were caught in a social status between whites and enslaved people without full rights before the Civil War. People of color had tensions between the rights of males and females and between servants and landowners, as did whites in North Carolina during this period. Some acquired wealth, and a few owned enslaved Africans. Encouraged by abolitionists, freed Blacks organized and advocated for formal and informal schooling in the state before the Civil War (Woodson, 1919).

Diverse educational opportunities emerged during the Early American period. Quakers and well as Anglicans formed schools, academies, and early colleges (Klain, 1925), but the Anglican seminary model dominated (Coon, 1915). The University of North

Carolina was chartered in 1785 as one of the nation's earliest public colleges (Battle, 1907). The nation's first colored normal school was open in Fayetteville, North Carolina, from 1865 until 1877 (Huddle, 1997), illustrating temporary gains in opportunities for freed Blacks during Reconstruction.

Education, Reconstruction, and White Resistance

Under federal control for a period, the Civil War became a transitional period; freed Blacks advocated for access to education. One historical account tells this story: "When Union armies arrived in Eastern North Carolina in 1862, they encountered escaped slave's eager to acquire education. Soon after the armies occupied the region, missionaries and teachers arrived seeking to educate and uplift these former slaves" (Browning, 2008, p. 1). Historical documents reveal that between 1861 and 1875, at least 1,400 teachers taught Black school children in North Carolina and that white southern and northern women teachers had different attitudes about the purposes of the schools (Brosnan, 2016).

By 1868, white males began organizing to reassert supremacy, framing their agenda as white rule (Zipf, 1999). Between 1880 and 1910, legislation promoted a white middle-class progressive and exclusionary regime (Kousser, 1980). Blacks continued to advocate as separate and unequal schools and collegiate systems developed.

Progress and Student Choice

Underfunded and racially isolated, progressive support of diverse groups languished until the *Brown* decision, as white advocacy shifted toward privatization and school choice (Thompson Dorsey & Roulhac, 2019). North Carolina pioneered legislation supporting privatization to resegregate: "With the 1954 *Brown v. Board of Education* decision opening the doors to integration, the state General Assembly passed a bill known as the Pearsall Act to provide vouchers for families to attend nonpublic schools. Since tax money would flow toward private institutions, the legislature instituted new standard, supervision, and inspection mechanisms to look after the taxpayers' investment" (Young, 2005, p. 34).

Progressive Policies in Public Higher Education

The University of North Carolina is among the nation's oldest and most esteemed public systems of higher education. It comprises 16 campuses—including the flagship research university at Chapel Hill—and an accelerated high school for gifted students. The University of North Carolina prides itself as the first public university in the nation and the only one to graduate students during the eighteenth century (University of North Carolina General Administration, 2011), which distinguishes it from the College of William and Mary in Virginia and Rutgers University in New Jersey, both of which make claims about their early founding. A 24-member board of governors elected by the general assembly oversees the multicampus institution. The board, in turn, elects a president for the institution, and a chancellor runs each of the campuses. The chancellors report to the institution's president and are responsible to an eight-member trustee board for their respective campus. The 17 campuses serve more than 221,000 students, and nearly a quarter are graduate students (North Carolina Community College System, 2010).

The UNC system has demonstrated an openness to innovation within the campuses that strengthens higher education in the state. There has been systemic support for campuses to provide national leadership. We use a couple of illustrative examples: North Carolina's historical leadership in desegregation and the development of the North Carolina Covenant at the flagship campus to improve economic and racial diversity and as a stimulus for improving student aid funding in the state.

Desegregation of the North Carolina System

UNC was one of the state systems that complied soon after the federal government guided the desegregation of public systems of higher education (Williams, 1997). Several UNC historically Black colleges and universities (HBCUs), adopting the *Adams* guidelines for systemwide desegregation and strengthening developing institutions, had been involved in the federal Title III developing institutions program since its inception. For example, North Carolina A&T University, designated as exemplary of the advanced program under Title III, was one of the first HBCUs to develop doctoral programs, including in Engineering (St. John, 1981).

The amalgamation of HBCUs into the North Carolina system helped provide a framework for developing these campuses using systemwide numbers to claim desegregation. This approach to system integration and development was a stark contrast to states like Alabama, Mississippi, and Louisiana, which maintained separate systems, resisted the *Adams* framework, and instead used the *Fordice* framework, which supported program development at HBCUs only if that new development could attract white students (St. John & Hossler, 1998).

The success of the North Carolina model rests on the full acceptance of HBCUs as partners systemwide in providing accessible college opportunities. Unfortunately and ironically, the strategy enabled the state to retain an essentially segregated system while complying with federal requirements to desegregate. Unequal funding for state HBCUs was an additional risk. Despite these limitations, North Carolina avoided the extremely conservative remedies that evolved in the midsouth, where the post-*Fordice* decisions forced HBCUs to develop programs for whites to get additional funding. This strategy failed to remedy the unequal treatment of institutions (St. John & Hossler, 1998). In contrast, becoming part of the UNC system initially uplifted the HBCUs, at one time becoming some of the best-funded HBCUs.

North Carolina's HBCUs continue to provide national leadership in advocacy for strengthening and developing these vital institutions. For example, in June 2010, North Carolina Central University hosted a national meeting on the future of HBCUs. An analysis completed for the symposium found that despite differences in preparation at the time of admission (HBCUs have primarily taken on a developmental focus), HBCUs had similar graduation rates for African Americans as the predominantly white public universities in the state (St. John, 2010), The trends in graduation rates from HBCUs illustrate a stable pattern of graduation for African Americans (45% in 2002 and 44% in 2007) at the majority at these colleges. After the symposium, NCCU issued a report, *Strengthening America's Historically Black Colleges and Universities: A Call for Action* (Nelms, 2011), calling for continued federal support for the HBCUs as a vital resource in a global period emphasizing increased achievement.

The Carolina Covenant and Commitment to Need-Based Student Aid

In 2003, the University of North Carolina at Chapel Hill implemented the *Carolina Covenant* as a comprehensive approach to improving access to and retention of underrepresented low-income students; it rapidly became a national model for ensuring student financial support. The Covenant guaranteed low-income students would receive sufficient grant aid to ensure that borrowing would not be necessary during college if they were willing to work 15 hours a week on College Work Study. At the time, the idea was that the new program would "send a message to young people harboring aspirations of attending UNC: if they worked hard in high school and gained admission, lack of money would not be an obstacle to becoming a 'Tar Heel'"(Fiske, 2010, p. 17).

Although the financial aid guarantee provided by UNC received national attention, most campuses that adapted the strategy failed to deliver the services that were part of the institutional commitment. The UNC program also developed comprehensive support services, including orientation, mentoring, academic workshops, special programming, cultural events, and other programs and services. The institutions across the country that have adopted the aid guarantee overlooked the integral role of the support services. The documented success of the program, summarized below, is attributable to the guaranteed aid and support services.

The Covenant came at a time when the test scores of admitted low-income students were rising. The percentage of low-income minority students remained constant as the number of low-income students rose, illustrating that the strategy did not increase the total number of low-income, high-achieving students of color at UNC; it improved the graduation rate of Black undergraduates over the following decade. The success of the Carolina Covenant is demonstrated by the improved economic and racial diversity on the Chapel Hill campus and, ultimately, improvement in long-term outcomes—degree completion and employment. The early analysis indicates improved retention. A comparison of fourth-year retention by the 2004 cohort (i.e., the first Covenant group) to the 2003 ("control") cohort that entered the year before the establishment of the Carolina Covenant indicated a 5 percentage point gain for the Covenant students. Additional analysis examined graduation rates, finding a substantial improvement in graduation rates for white males (33 percentage point gain from the 2004 cohort to the 2003 cohort), followed by Black males (20 percentage point gain) and Black females (12 percentage point gain); white females showed a slight drop in 4-year graduation (St. John et al., 2012). The cohort comparison indicates a reduction of the racial gap in retention and completion rates for African American and white males compared with females. The Covenant program supported equitable completions over two decades (Ort, 2023).

With research as evidence of success, the UNC system has successfully lobbied the state to increase its funding of need-based grants for students in public 4-year colleges. These gains in state funding for grants (discussed below) have reduced the costs of maintaining the commitment to meeting tuition for UNC and improved funding for students at other college campuses. It may be helpful to note that the UNC System has held tuition flat for 8 years through 24–25 AY.

Community College System

The North Carolina community college system epitomizes the state's progressive shift. The community college system was born during the tumultuous decade of the 1950s when desegregation efforts in the South were in full force and, as Wescott (2005) notes, the community colleges were never segregated, accepting both whites and students of color from the beginning. Therefore, the North Carolina Community College System (NCCCS) was emblematic of the progressive shift in the state and across much of the

South. However, recent trends in completion rates indicate race disparities are once again evident (see outcomes trends below).

The mission of NCCCS narrowly defines the role of the community college relative to other systems across the country. Although Michigan allowed community colleges to operate largely independently of the state, Florida community colleges could broadly interpret their mission, including access to baccalaureate education. In contrast, North Carolina community colleges focus on technical and vocational preparation and training. According to NCCCS (2008, p. 12),

> The major purpose of each and every institution operating under the provisions of this Chapter shall be and shall continue to be the offering of vocational and technical education and training, and of basic, high school level, academic education needed in order to profit from vocational and technical education, for students who are high school graduates or who are beyond the compulsory age limit of the public school system and who have left the public schools.

Like most community college systems, NCCCS also provides academic pathways to the 4-year degree, allowing for systemwide articulation to the UNC system and agreements with private colleges across the state. However, this is secondary to vocational and technical education.

The early establishment of the NCCCS is reminiscent of the dual public systems of Indiana and Purdue Universities in Indiana. In 1950, the North Carolina Superintendent of Public Instruction convened a statewide commission headed by Allan Hurlburt to consider the question of the establishment of postsecondary alternatives to 4-year institutions; two years later, the Hurlburt Commission issued its recommendation to create a state-funded system of community colleges (Wescott, 2005). The 1957 general assembly passed acts providing funding for a community college system intended for the arts and sciences (reminiscent of public junior colleges) and industrial education centers. These two systems mainly operated independently for the first five years of their establishment. Governor Terry Sanford convened the Commission on Education beyond High School in 1962. The Carlyle Commission (as it was known) called for consolidating these two systems under a single administrative unit in the state board of education. Once officially established, the merged system had 20 industrial centers and 6 junior colleges (North Carolina Community College System, 2008). In 1981, the Department of Community Colleges moved out of the state board of education and established itself as a separate entity; it became the North Carolina Community College System in 1999. By 2013, the system had 59 (there are currently 58 community colleges in NCCS) institutions serving more than 358,000 students (U.S. Department of Education & National Center for Education Statistics, 2013).

Fiscally Progressive and Socially Conservative

In previous editions of *Public Policy and Higher Education*, we described North Carolina as the "new progressive South." With the passage of time and the addition of a historical perspective, we understand the tensions between white conservativism and progressive ideals, which have a long history in North Carolina. It is a complex case in 2024 because, in this state, periods of education progress and regress recur. Given the ideological forces affecting education policy development, the North Carolina case now demonstrates the importance of examining trends in policy and outcomes.

The progressivism is evident in their financial support for higher education. As we explore in the next section, North Carolina continues to provide higher appropriations to higher education than most states. Its public 4-year institutions have a lower average in-state tuition rate, and its need-based aid programs are at the national average of nearly $1,000 per FTE. Few states provide this level of support to their higher education systems. What is new about the North Carolina version of progressive education policy is the persistent and growing social conservatism emblematic of current trends across the South and among conservative states in the interior portions of the US. The contemporary issues section below discusses recent developments that reflect this antagonism to socially progressive policies. Two developments that we had not yet considered—school vouchers for K-12 school students and anti-transgender legislation that was prominent in the national news, referred to as the "Bathroom Bill"—illustrate how conservative reform can reverse the trajectory of progressive reforms.

Private School Vouchers

In 2017, Betsy DeVos and the Trump administration proposed providing federal funding for school choice, including money to support school vouchers for students to attend private schools. The Trump administration reflected the groundswell of support that was bubbling up across states, including North Carolina, which had launched their "Opportunity Scholarship" program in the 2014–2015 school year. The program was designed to provide school choice to low-income families, which in 2020 was the equivalent of $65,000 annual income for a family of four. In the initial year, approximately 1,200 students received a voucher to attend a private school and by 2020, that number had grown to 12,000 (Wattach, 2020).

In October 2023, the NC legislature passed House Bill 259, which removed the income cap for families to receive the scholarship, meaning that all students K-12 will be eligible for the scholarship, regardless of their family's income (North Carolina State Education Assistance Authority, 2024). The amount of the scholarship will still be determined by family income and the amounts will range from $3,000 to $7,000 per year, per child. The legislature plans to grow the program by 2,000 students each year, through 2027 and increase appropriations from $75 million in 2020 to $145 million once the program is fully implemented. The policy change is not surprising given trends across other states, but as Wattach (2020) points out, there is very little evidence that the program has any effect, beyond giving parents choice. The legislation calls for an evaluation of the programs' outcomes, but by 2024, no independent study has been conducted and the private schools receiving vouchers are not required to collect or provide the sort of data that would allow for a rigorous evaluation. Critics point out the program discriminates against students and families based on their religious beliefs and sexual orientation and that many of the schools that receive these public subsidies teach a curriculum shaped by religious fundamentalism that rejects the science of evolution and sanitized to minimize what is taught about slavery and the African American experience in the US (Schofield, 2023). Another subset of critics argue that the program is poorly run and fiscally irresponsible. A North Carolina Justice Center report found dozens of examples where schools received more vouchers than they enrolled total students, amounting to what they estimate as more than $1.6 million in fraudulent payments to schools (Nordstrom, 2023). They also point out other circumstances when payments went to schools in years where they appeared to be closed.

The program is no longer designed to help low-income families exclusively, and it is likely to subsidize many wealthier families to pursue a private school education they were already going to utilize. And the current versions of the legislation do not include any meaningful accountability mechanisms, nor does it limit which private schools are eligible to receive the scholarships.

Trans-Gender Rights and the 2016 "Bathroom Bill"

Public opposition was fierce in 2017, when Governor Pat McRory signed House Bill 2, effectively limiting protections for LGBTQ students. The legislation was wide-reaching, but the provision that received the most visible attention in the national media was the restriction that would require transgender people to use the bathroom consistent with their biological sex at birth. The issue became a firestorm at UNC-Chapel Hill and a US District Court struck down the provision requiring the state institution to enforce that provision. The public outcry over the policy resulted in the cancellation of sporting events, the banning of national meetings to be held in the state and affected business decisions of major national and multi-national corporations (Petrow, 2016). In 2017 the law was repealed and the court challenges that followed the law's passage were settled two years later. The following year, the Republican incumbent was defeated narrowly for the governorship by the Democratic challenger.

In 2023, the state legislature passed several new bills that affect the transgender community, but the context has changed considerably, and the public resistance was not as vocal. Despite vetoes from Democratic Governor Roy Cooper, the legislature barred medical professionals from providing hormones, puberty-blocking drugs, and surgical transition procedures for anyone under the age of 18. They also prohibited instruction about gender identity and sexuality in elementary school classrooms and banned transgender girls from playing sports on girls sports teams from middle through high school (Schoenbaum & Robertson, 2023).

POLICY CHANGES

In the early 2000s, North Carolina took a different path concerning K-12 and higher education policies than most other states. It is one of the few states that has maintained a commitment to low tuition and high aid, which aligns with a progressive set of priorities. However, as discussed in the next section, North Carolina continues to pursue a socially conservative agenda. Below, we review trends in policies on academic preparation and higher education finance before reviewing related outcomes.

Policy Trends in North Carolina

Coordination of Academic Preparation and College Access

North Carolina is the archetype for the pathways approach to high school graduation requirements. Currently, the state identifies two overarching pathways for students: the Future Ready Course of Study (FRC), which is the expectation for most students, and the Occupational Course of Study (OC) for students with disabilities identified explicitly for the program (North Carolina Department of Public Instruction, 2023). The basic FRC framework requires all students to complete four years of English, three years of social studies, four math courses, and three years of science (including one physical, one biological, and one environmental science). In the past, they stipulated that students must complete Algebra I, Geometry, and Algebra II as part of their math requirement. More recently, the state shifted that level of detail by adopting a series of endorsements that students can earn.

Shifting the more specific requirements to the endorsements allows the state to provide one framework for all while differentiating pathways through the four endorsement options—Career, College, UNC, and NC Academic Scholars. All four endorsements require math through Algebra II but differ in the fourth math requirement. The key curricular differences focus on science and foreign languages. The Career and Initial College endorsements have no science or foreign language requirement, whereas the UNC and the Academic Scholars endorsements include both. The unique feature of the North Carolina policy is that they also require all students to earn "at least the benchmark reading score established by a nationally norm referenced college admissions test." They do not stipulate which test to take, and they also allow students to take it as frequently as they need to earn that minimum score. In 2010, North Carolina eliminated the high stakes, mandatory end-of-course exit exams, making those tests part of the overall grade and not a separate requirement; the addition of the reading benchmark on one of the college admissions tests re-invigorates our discussions about high-stakes testing. They do not specify the threshold for passing the reading benchmark, so it is difficult to know how demanding the expectation is for students.

The Financing of Higher Education in North Carolina

In the 2000s, North Carolina adhered to a public finance model of high public subsidies to institutions, low student tuition, and high need-based student aid, counter to the other state cases. For over two decades, the average in-state tuition and fees at 4-year public universities was approximately $2,000 below the national average. In contrast, the 2-year colleges were just the opposite and nearly $2,000 more than the national average for community colleges. The narrower gap between the cost of 2-year and 4-year institutions in NC is striking (Figure 11.1). The average price for tuition and fees, adjusting for inflation, is about $2,700, which is the difference between public 4-year and community college tuition and fee rates.

The trends in state and local higher education funding per FTE (Figure 11.2) have varied in predictable ways, with a significant decline around the Great Recession. The critical story for NC is that they continue to contribute more per FTE than most states. Between 2010 and 2020, NC appropriations per FTE rose from a low of about $12,000 to more than $13,300 in 2020 while this is indeed an increase, I would argue that appropriations are flat. The state's commitment to providing state appropriations to higher education has made it possible for NC to keep its sticker prices down, particularly at 4-year institutions. On the other hand, tuition and fees for the state's public 2-year colleges have been consistently higher in NC than the US average, which was only $3,860 in 2022 (Ma & Pender, 2023). NC prioritized 4-year affordability over 2-year college opportunities for career-minded students, the opposite of California's approach to financing access (Chapter 6).

North Carolina is unique because it shifted funds to expand need-based undergraduate aid in the 2000s (Figure 11.3). The state's growing commitment to meeting student's financial needs is a response to a growing progressive sentiment in the state. Even with its historic commitment to maintaining low tuition in the public sector, NC invested little in need aid through the 1990s. Late in the decade, the state increased its investment

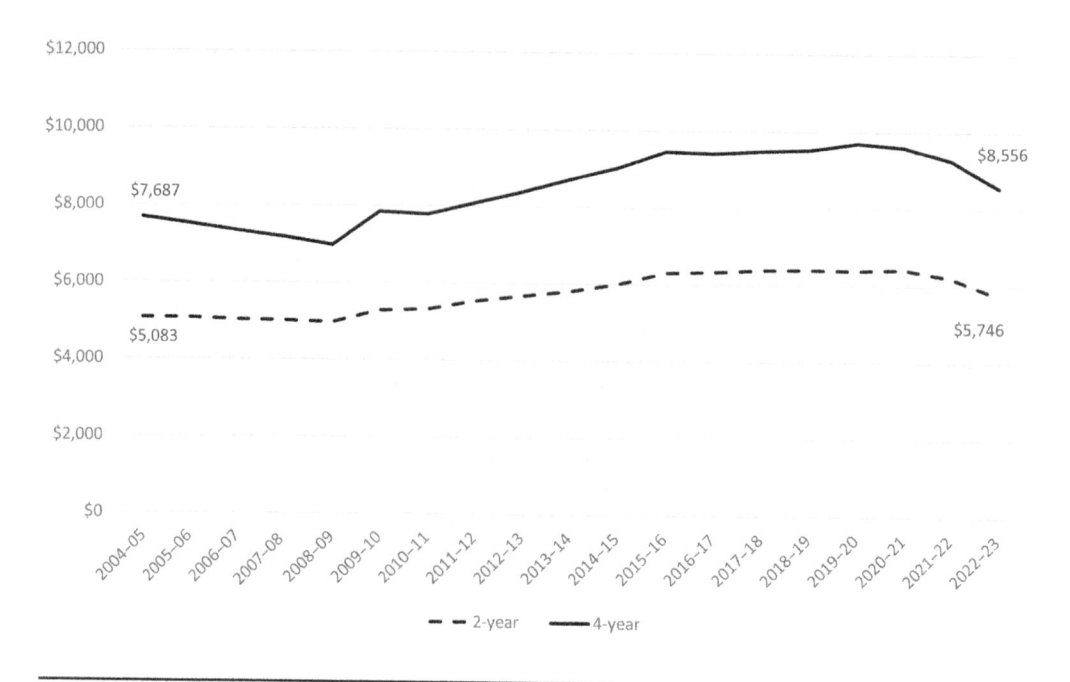

Figure 11.1 Trends in North Carolina Public Tuition & Fees (in 2022 Dollars)
Source: Ma and Pender (2023). Trends in College Pricing and Student Aid 2023. New York: College Board.

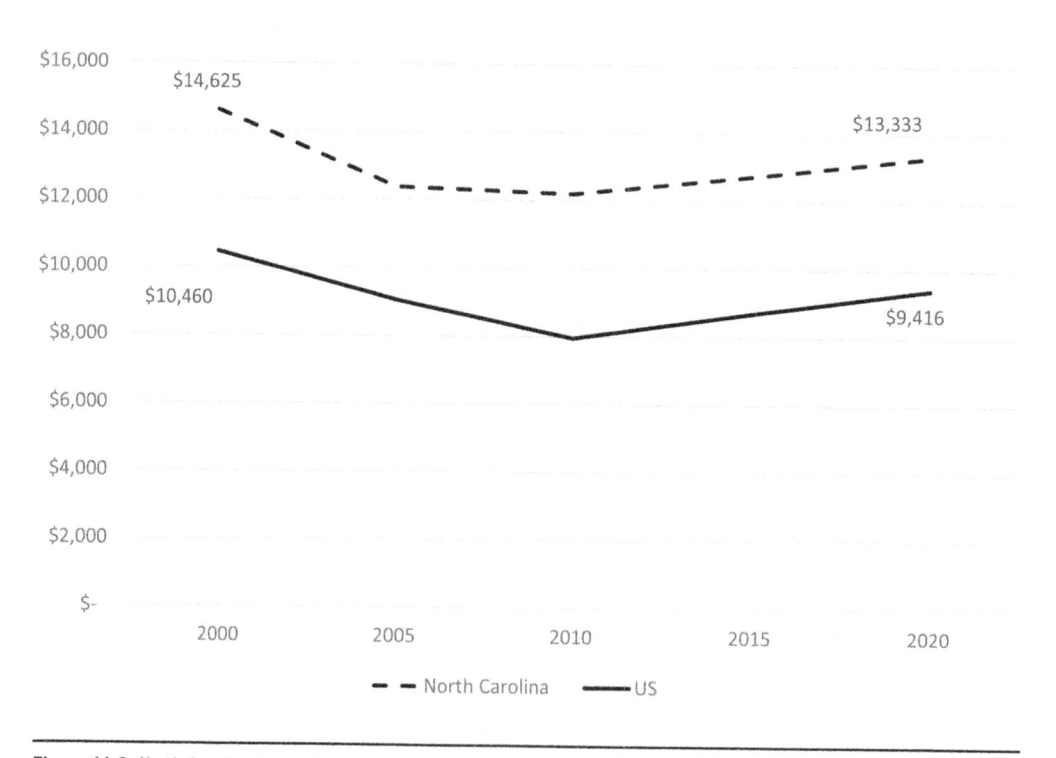

Figure 11.2 North Carolina State Appropriations per FTE (2020 Dollars)
Source: State Higher Education Executive Officers (SHEEO) Grapevine Annual Reports and NCES, Digest of Education Statistics (2023) Table 307.20.

Conservative-Progressive Tensions • 257

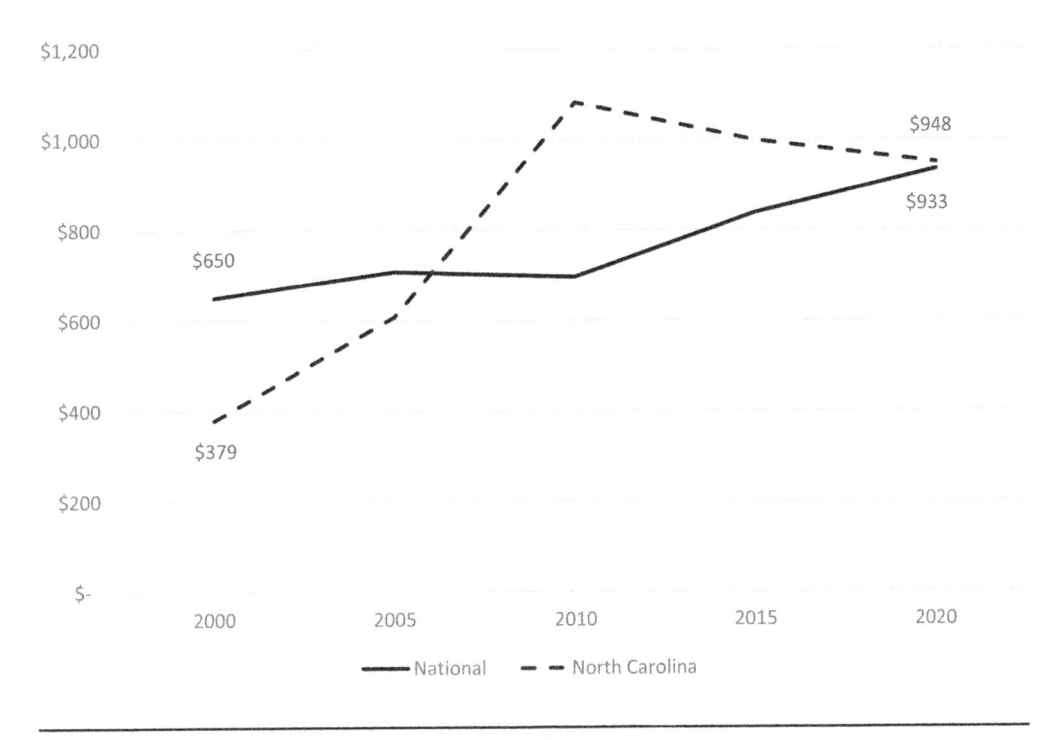

Figure 11.3 North Carolina Need-Based Aid per FTE (2020 Dollars)
Source: National Association of State Student Grant & Aid Programs (NASSGAP) (2023). Annual Survey Report. NCES, Digest of Education Statistics (2023) Table 307.20.

substantially, and by 2006, North Carolina's investment per FTE in need-based aid substantially exceeded national averages. In 2010, the state's investment per FTE in need-based aid was nearly $1,100 per year, compared to $700 per FTE nationally. In the past decade, the trends appear to be changing. By 2020, the North Carolina commitment to need-based aid dropped to $948 and the national average per FTE rose to nearly the same amount, meaning North Carolina has slowed down its investment in need-based aid while other states have increased their commitments.

North Carolina's increases in need-based aid corresponded to declines in non-need or merit aid (Figure 11.4). In 2000, before North Carolina shifted toward need-based aid, it spent more than $400 per FTE on non-need assistance, double the national average across all states. What is most interesting about these trends, taken together, is that North Carolina has reduced its investment in total aid compared to the national averages. In 2000, states spent $850 per FTE on need and non-need forms of assistance, while North Carolina spent roughly $780. In 2020, the combined investment in aid nationally was $1,280, compared to only $979 in North Carolina. Maintaining a lower cost for tuition and fees at 4-year colleges created favorable conditions for the North Carolina Scholarship—the signature program in the state. It is a last-dollar scholarship that requires the FAFSA and is capped for families below $75,000 adjusted gross income (AGI) with $7,500 or less expected family contribution (EFC). An eligible student is guaranteed at least $5,000 from the combination of Pell and the state grant program. Subtracting Pell from the maximum award and capping the combined award at $5,000 is especially problematic for high-poverty students with zero EFC.

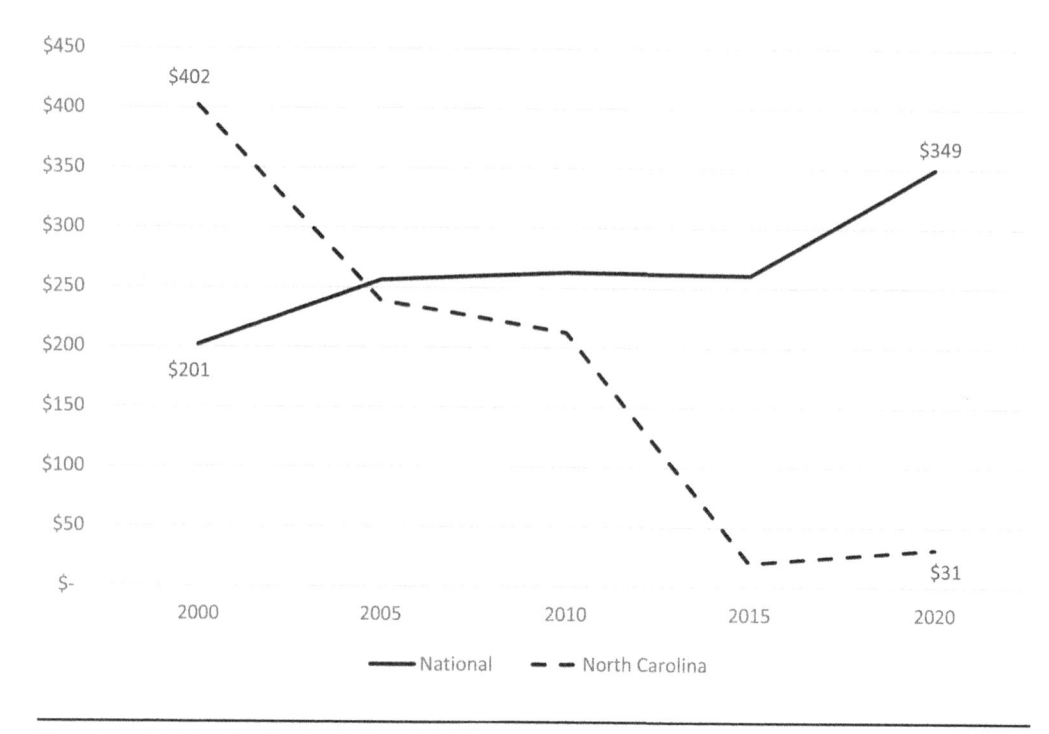

Figure 11.4 North Carolina Non-Need Aid per FTE (2020 Dollars)
Source: National Association of State Student Grant & Aid Programs (NASSGAP), 2023. Annual Survey Report.

TRENDS IN STUDENT OUTCOMES

We examine trends for outcomes related to academic preparation, access and diversity, and degree completion. We also consider how these trends compare and contrast with changes in policy and funding.

Academic Preparation

High School Graduation Rates

Trends in high school graduation rates across North Carolina over time are consistent with the trends in other states (Figure 11.5). Students in North Carolina are graduating at rates slightly above the national average in 2020. The more significant part of the story appears to be that in 2010, the state graduation rate was just below the national average at 78%, and within a few years, it surpassed the national average. This trend corresponds with changes to the high school graduation requirements, including eliminating the mandatory exit exams for graduation. The state now has multiple curricular pathways during this improvement period, so more restrictive course requirements do not explain this positive change.

SAT Scores

We previously described North Carolina as an SAT state, meaning that most college admissions test takers chose the SAT. In 2012–13, North Carolina required the ACT for all 11th-grade students in the state (My Future NC, 2020), much like Michigan had

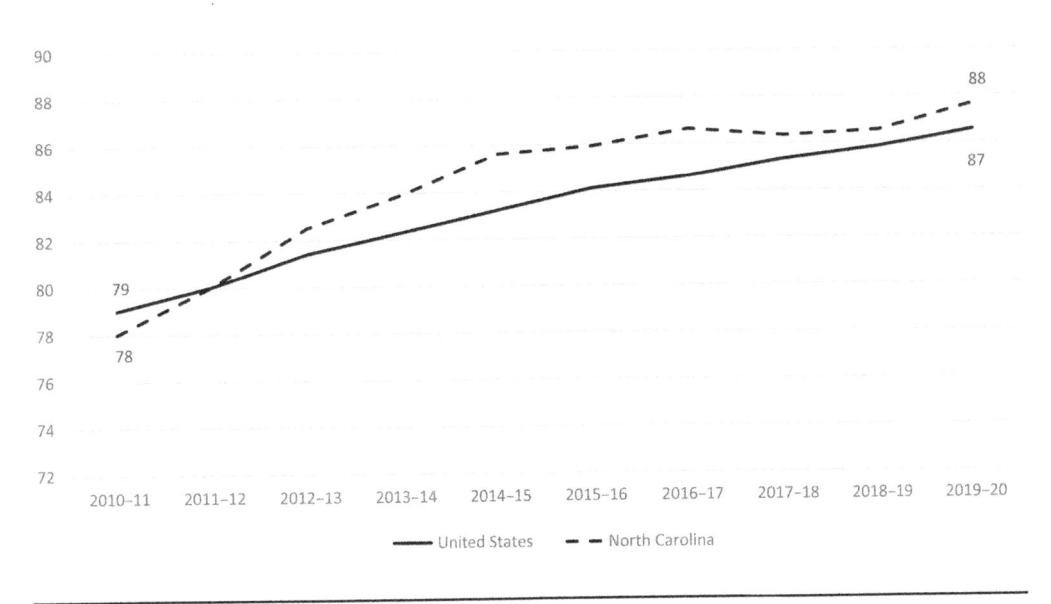

Figure 11.5 Public High School Graduation Rates in North Carolina, 2010–11 Through 2019–20
Source: National Center for Education Statistics (2023). Digest of Education Statistics, Table 218.46.

done for several years. In 2022, 88% of the state's graduates took the ACT for an average score of 18.5 composite. Despite that policy change, more than 50% of the graduating class continued to take the SAT until the pandemic and the national trend to make tests optional in college admissions. After that point, ACT taking remained high, but SAT participation rates declined by 50%.

Access and Diversity

Each year, the American Community Survey (ACS) conducted by the U.S. Census Bureau asks a representative sample of state residents about college participation for household members, providing a measure of enrollment rates and diversity among traditional college-age students. We examine trends in North Carolina compared to the nation using both indicators.

College Enrollment Rates

North Carolina consistently fell below the national average in the percentage of young adults (18–24) enrolled in college, indicating fewer traditional-college-age adults in college (Figure 11.6). In 2013, North Carolina lagged the nation by nearly 2 percentage points and experienced a considerable drop between 2015 and 2017 before recovering slightly. By 2021, the percentages in North Carolina were 40%, slightly below the national mark at 40.9%. These numbers are surprising given the relative affordability of the North Carolina 4-year system. The higher-than-average community college tuition rates may account for some of that difference. The lower costs can also be a matter of supply and demand. When demand is lower, one might expect prices to drop. Higher education prices have not always behaved this way, but we have seen evidence in the first part of the 2020s.

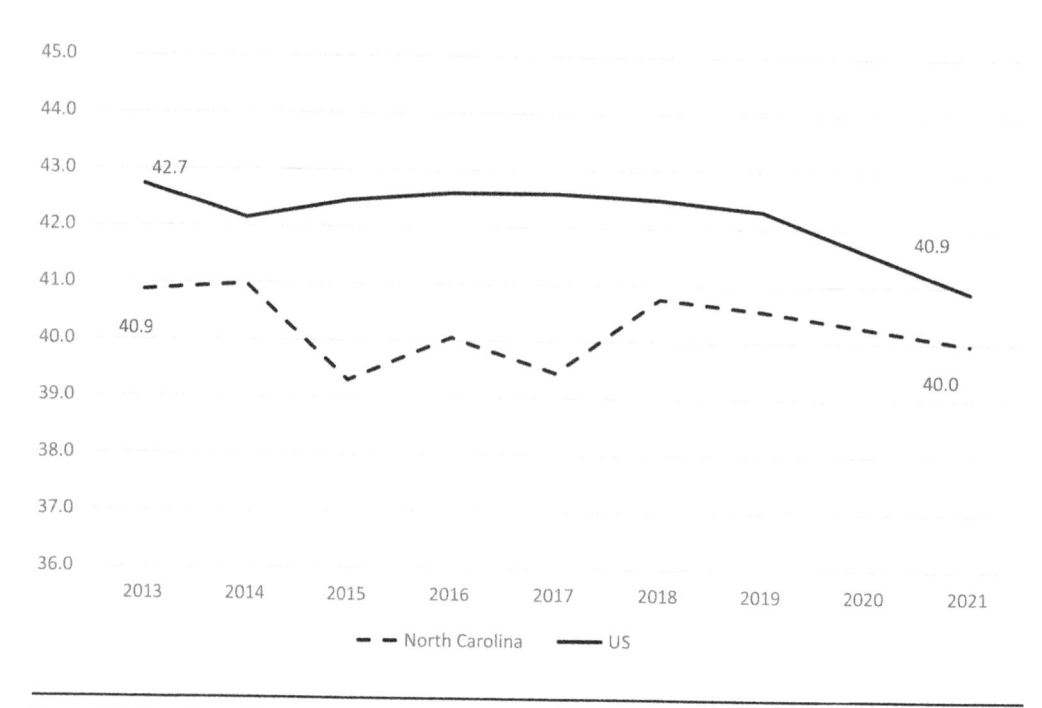

Figure 11.6 Percentage of 18- to 24-Years-Olds Enrolled in Degree-Granting Postsecondary Institutions: North Carolina & US
Source: National Center for Education Statistics (2023). Digest of Education Statistics, Table 302.65.

Diversity in Enrollment Rates

There were modest differences in college enrollments for whites, Blacks, and multi-race students of college age (Figure 11.7). Asian students attended at nearly 70% from 2013 to 2021, with a sizable gap between them and other populations of students. Asian students only account for 3% of the state population, so their participation rates moderately affect the overall trends. Over 60% of the state population identifies as white; approximately 50% of white young adults enrolled. The gaps between white and under-represented minority groups remained about 15 percentage points through 2021 despite volatility in the middle years.

We also consider whether enrollment patterns reflect the state's current population (Figure 11.8). The graph illustrates that white student enrollments began roughly proportional to their representation in the state population but declined slightly by 2020. The under-representation may be a function of an aging white population and growth in birth rates among racially minoritized groups. The denominator in this calculation is the percentage of all adults over age 18, but the younger subset of the population has fewer white students. On the other hand, Black students reflected their proportion of the population in 2000; they were over-represented in 2010 by 20 percentage points before returning to a point just slightly above their representation in the state population in 2020.

The most intriguing trend in these data is among Latinx students. College enrollments among Latinx students accounted for less than half of their proportion of the population in 2000. To put it differently, if 7% of the state population identified as Hispanic/Latinx, only 3% of students enrolled in college identified the same way. However, by 2020, they improved to 90% of their proportion in the population. An upsurge in Latinx enrollment was also evident in California (Chapter 6).

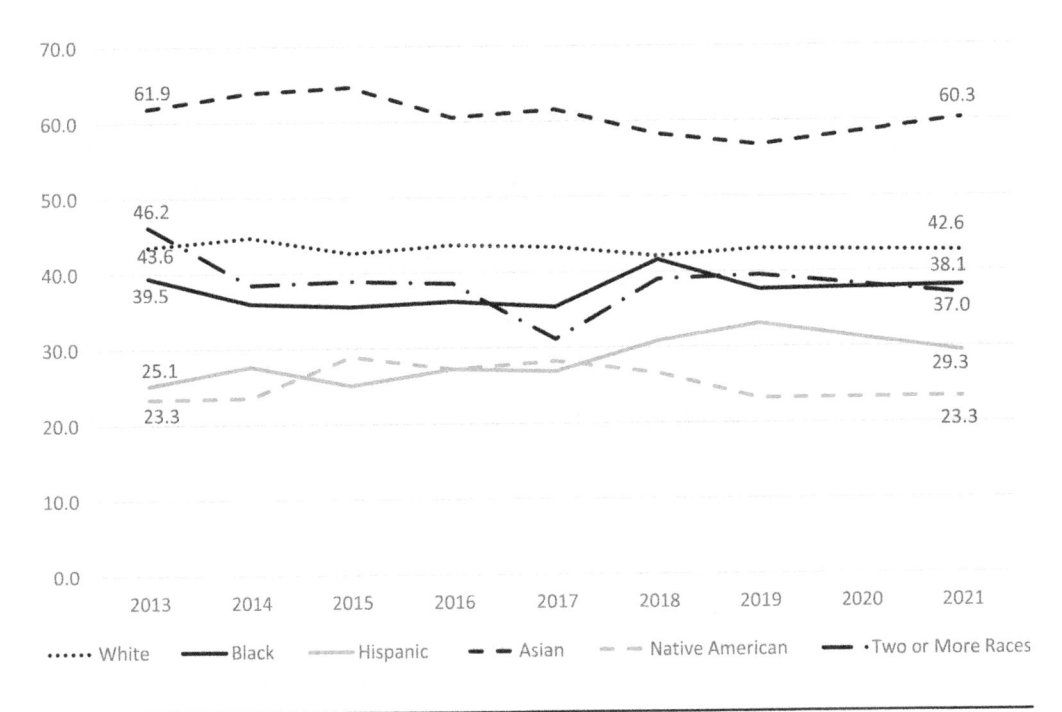

Figure 11.7 Percentage of 18- to 24-Year-Olds Enrolled in Degree-Granting Postsecondary Institutions, by Race/Ethnicity: North Carolina

Source: National Center for Education Statistics (2023). Digest of Education Statistics, Table 302.65.

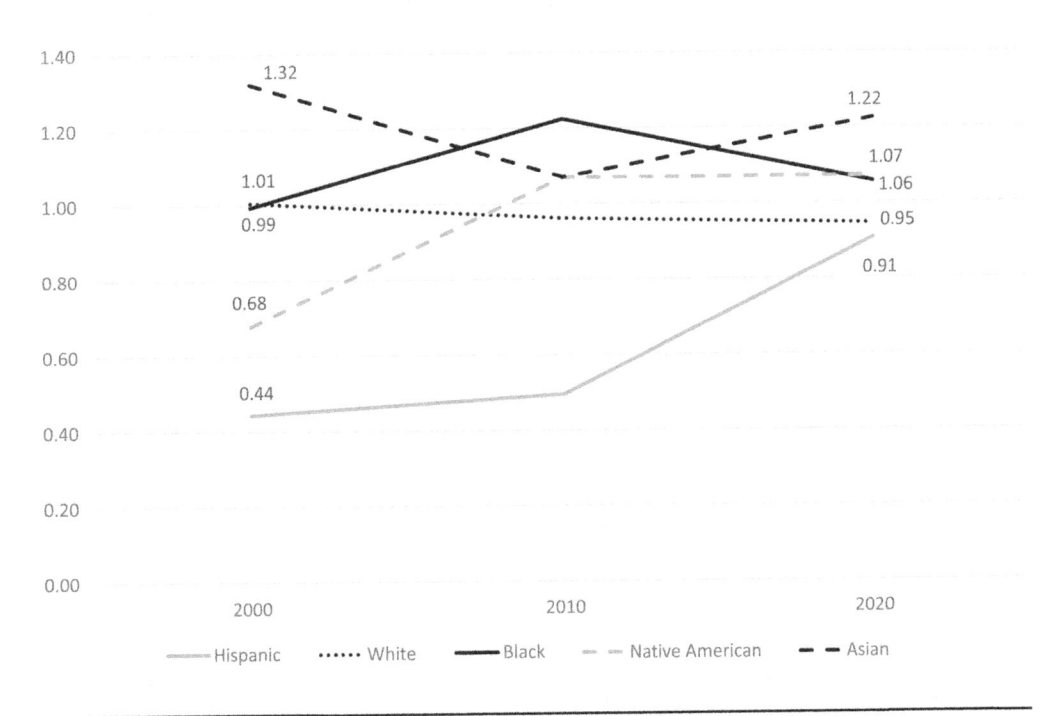

Figure 11.8 Racial/Ethnic Representation in North Carolina Postsecondary Education as a Proportion of the State Population

Source: National Center for Education Statistics (2023). Digest of Education Statistics, Table 306.70 & Table 266 & US Census Bureau.

Graduation Rates

In this section, we consider 6-year graduation rates for public 4-year, private nonprofit 4-year, and public 2-year colleges and universities. The numbers we report are based on whether students in the cohort identified graduated within six years of when they started. Figure 11.9 provides trend data for public 4-year colleges in North Carolina and the data suggest a modest narrowing of the graduation gaps by race over time. The gap between Black and white students' graduation rates for the 2012 entering cohort was 24 percentage points, with white students graduating at about 77% in six years and Black students at nearly 53%. Six years later, that gap shrunk to approximately 17 percentage points. In fact, graduation rates among Black students in North Carolina grew consistently over this time, while the results were mixed for other groups. Perhaps the more troubling trend is that while enrollments grew for Latinx students, their graduation rates declined during this period.

The most alarming trends, when considering college graduation rates by race and ethnicity, are evident in the data for private nonprofit colleges. Figure 11.10 shows that while white and Asian students fare extremely well at these institutions, Black students struggle. In fact, based on these data, Black students are more likely to graduate if they attend a 4-year public institution than an institution in the private sector, which is not true of any of the other groups. The graduation rates among Asian students are 10 percentage points higher among private colleges than public institutions. Meanwhile, white students graduate at comparable rates at both types of institutions, even if modestly higher at the private colleges, and Latinx students appear to be much more successful at private colleges with an increase in their 6-year graduation rate of 13 percentage points among the 2017 entering cohort.

Consistent with other state and national trends, community college students are less likely to earn degrees within six years (Figure 11.11). The racial gaps are slightly

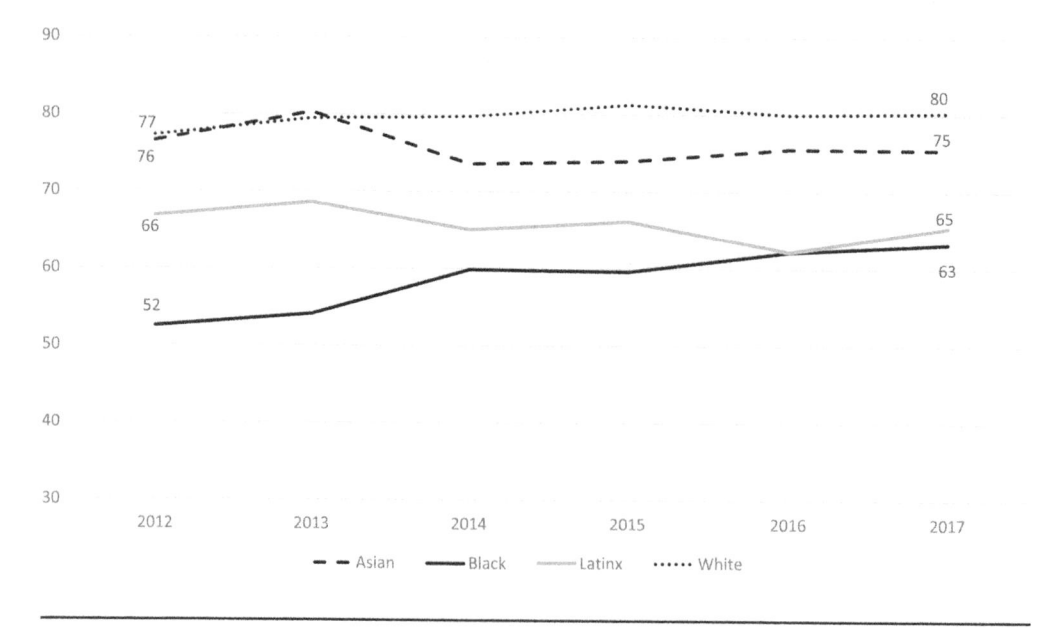

Figure 11.9 Trends in 6-Year Degree Attainment Rates for all North Carolina Public 4-Year Postsecondary Institutions

Source: National Student Clearinghouse Research Center (2023). Completing College: National & State Reports. Retrieved from https://nscresearchcenter.org/completing-college/

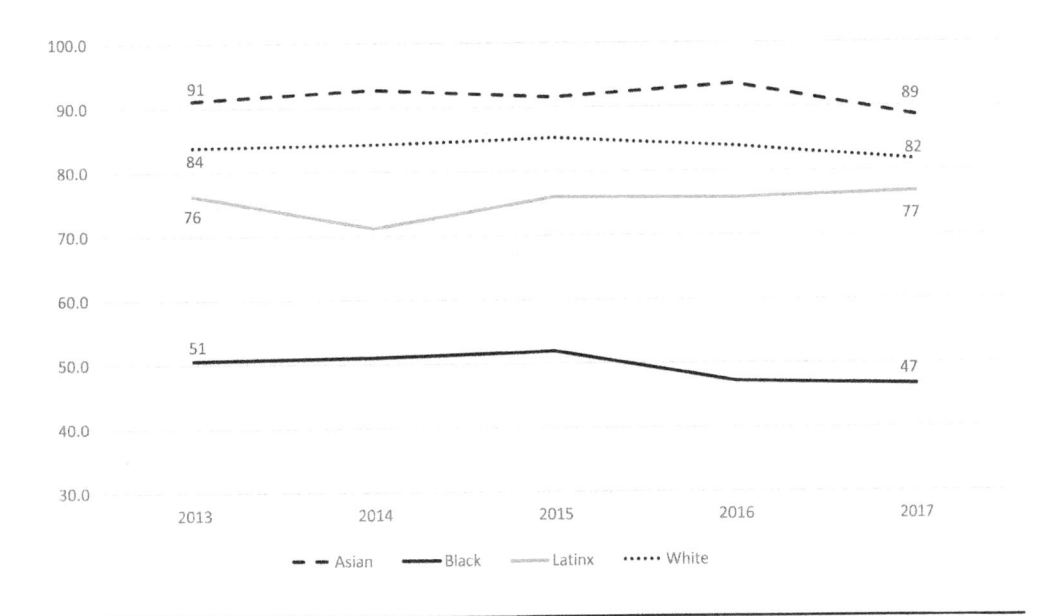

Figure 11.10 Trends in 6-Year Degree Attainment Rates for all North Carolina Private Nonprofit 4-Year Institutions
Source: National Student Clearinghouse Research Center (2023). Completing College: National & State Reports. Retrieved from https://nscresearchcenter.org/completing-college/

smaller (25 points v. 30–40 points among 4-year institutions), but all groups show degree completion rates that are nearly 30 percentage points lower than their 4-year degree completion rates. Black and white students show improvements in their graduation rates across the five cohorts, but the gap remains roughly the same at 23 percentage points.

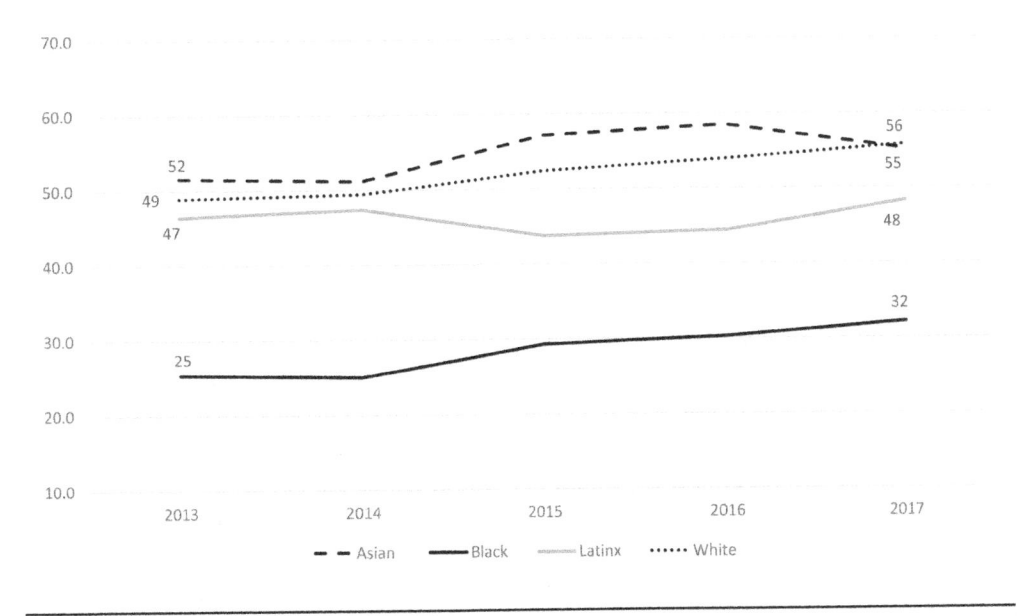

Figure 11.11 Trends in 6-Year Degree Attainment Rates for all North Carolina Public 2-Year Postsecondary Institutions
Source: National Student Clearinghouse Research Center (2023). Completing College: National & State Reports. Retrieved from https://nscresearchcenter.org/completing-college/

CONTEMPORARY ISSUES

As noted earlier, despite the fiscally progressive approach North Carolina has maintained, there is a growing social conservatism that directly impacts higher education across the state. Earlier, we discussed the private school voucher movement and the anti-transgender legislation that played out at UNC in fights over the "Bathroom Bill" (HB 2). Both issues remain on the state political agenda with the new anti-transgender legislation in the state legislature and the move to lift the caps off the state voucher program to allow virtually all students to be eligible. Below, we discuss three additional issues indicative of the state's growing social conservatism in its higher education policy—anti-DEI efforts, the erosion of tenure and academic freedom, and changing system-level governance structures that create and enforce institutional policies.

Dismantling Diversity, Equity, and Inclusion Initiatives

North Carolina's opposition to DEI initiatives has flown under the national news radar, mainly because Florida has been the lightning rod of controversy. It has also not been as explicit in its opposition to DEI initiatives, but they are moving in this direction. During the summer of 2023, the General Assembly's Joint Legislative Commission on Governmental Operations requested a comprehensive list of training programs and other expenses associated with DEI efforts on campuses, including anything that refers to "… 'diversity,' 'equity,' 'inclusion,' 'accessibility,' 'racism,' 'anti-racism,' 'anti-racist,' 'oppression,' 'internalized oppression,' 'systemic racism,' 'sexism,' 'gender,' 'LGBTQ+,' 'white supremacy,' 'unconscious bias,' 'bias,' 'microaggressions,' 'critical race theory,' 'intersectionality,' or 'social justice.'"(Public Ed Works, 2023). By the time this volume was published, the state had not yet acted on these data in the way that Florida banned funding for DEI initiatives, but it appears to be the next step in a systematic process by the state legislature.

While this inquiry occurred, the UNC System Board of Governors introduced a policy that would ban discussion of "political debates, beliefs, affiliations, ideals, or principles" in either admissions or employment (Killian, 2023). The policy will effectively eliminate the use of diversity statements in either employment or college admission. Subsequent legislation calls for viewpoint neutrality across the higher education system. SB 195 calls for the UNC system to "remain neutral, as an institution, on the political controversies of the day," and HB 607 extends the prohibition of "compelled speech" across both UNC and the community college system, meaning that officials cannot ask students and employees to declare their positions on current political or social issues (Warta & Robinson, 2023). It is not yet evident how the law will impact colleges and universities. In 2024, the Board responded by cutting diversity staff, following Florida in the assault on DEI in public universities (McClellan, 2024).

Changing Community College Governance

Under normal circumstances, policies pertaining to higher education governance would receive less attention. However, given the changes Florida has implemented, the fact that other states are beginning to consider similar policy changes concerns higher education policy leaders. During the 2023 legislative session, both HB 149 and SB 692 called for changes to community college governance in two ways. First, it would reduce the size of the state board for community colleges to 21 members and give nine appointments each to the Senate and the House and the Governor would lose appointment power. Next, they would allow the state board to continue identifying its system president, but the assembly would be asked to give final approval. Similarly, changes would be made at the local level where board of trustees of individual colleges would have 12 members, two-thirds appointed by the legislature and one-third by the local municipality. Local boards will continue to select their presidents, who will then require approval from the state board. With changes to the makeup of both the state board and the local boards, the legislature is attempting to exert maximum influence on the system's governance. The policies have not yet passed, but there is support in both chambers of the state Assembly.

Eroding Tenure and Academic Freedom

North Carolina was one of five states to entertain legislative attempts to eliminate or significantly curtail tenure and promotion. HB 715 Higher Education Modernization and Affordability Act, proposed in the spring of 2023, has provisions that would have eliminated tenure for anyone hired after July 1, 2024. Although the Bill did not make it out of committee, it reflects a growing antagonism to tenure among conservative policymakers who perceive higher education as too liberal and biased against conservative perspectives (Quinn, 2023). Tenure remains intact in North Carolina, at least for now. But battle lines are evident. When considered, in combination with the anti-DEI efforts—including anti-transgender legislation discussed earlier—and the changes to community college governance, it appears that the conservative legislature is dismantling features of the higher education system they believe are sustaining a liberal political agenda on college campuses, effectively minimizing conservative perspectives. The University of North Carolina now appears to be taking steps that will cost academic freedom in the 17 UNC campuses (McClellan, 2024).

REFRAMING COLLEGE SUCCESS

Using these traditional indicators, the status of college access and success in North Carolina remains mixed, echoing the state's contested history of race inequality. The state has maintained multiple academic pathways through high school to earn the diploma, and they appear aligned with college prep and workforce development. Their high school graduation rates continue improving, surpassing national averages. They have maintained a testing requirement, with the ACT as the benchmark for reading proficiency among high school students. At the same time, the state continues to be a model for relatively affordable public higher education, particularly among 4-year institutions. Community colleges are costlier than the average across states, but that may be related to the structure of the financial aid programs. Despite what appears to be favorable conditions for college access and success, the state trends tell a different story. Fewer young adults are choosing higher education than the national average, and the gaps in college completion across the various sectors remain stark. Assessing how these extremely conservative social policies will likely affect higher education is difficult. Indeed, North Carolina appears to be moving in a similar direction to Florida in the MAGA-DEI debate. The one crucial takeaway from the college completion data is that Black students are served better at public 4-year colleges and Latinx students are more successful at the private institutions. Below, we reconsider the success of the North Carolina system in the context of the financial wellbeing of its citizens.

Financial Wellbeing

North Carolina faces challenges similar to those in other states concerning the financial wellbeing of college graduates and departers. After examining student debt, degree attainment, and earnings, we reflect on college success in the contemporary state context.

North Carolina's Legacy of Student Debt

In North Carolina, as in most other states examined, the legacy of federal neoliberal finance policies is high cross-generation student debt. More than 60% of North Carolina private or public college graduates have student loan debt. The average student loan among borrowers is more than $25,000, according to the State Department of Justice (2024). Reporting on student debt is a critical social issue in North Carolina, as in other states.

The historical disparities in education contribute to cross-generation wealth inequality. The shift in federal policy from emphasizing need-based grants to loans for all not only reaches nearly two-thirds of students but impacts low-income students more substantially than whites, a story reaching the news: Black borrowers had the most federal student loan debt, averaging almost $53,000 per borrower in money in 2022, Hispanic borrowers averaged $26,000 in student loan debt (Murry, 2024). North Carolina's continued investment in grants did not reduce the severity of inequality in borrowing, indicating a lingering gap in the purchasing power of combined federal and state grants. HBCU graduates face exceptionally high debt, and activists are pursuing collective legal action against the state for discriminatory state finance policies (Lang, 2022; Mohammed, 2023).

Education Attainment Among Adults

Compared to national educational attainment in 2020, North Carolina has substantially higher percentages of adults with high school only or some college, modestly higher associates degree completion, and lower rates of 4-year degree attainment or higher (Figure 11.12). Four-year degree completion was higher for adult whites (37%) than Blacks (23%), Hispanics (18%), and Native Americans (13%) (NC Department of Commerce, 2023). Disparities in 4-year college attainment persist in North Carolina. In contrast, more Black adults had associate degrees (34%) than Hispanics (22%), whites (31%), and American Indians (30%). Sixty percent of Asian Americans in North Carolina have 4-year degrees, indicating they are the highest-achieving group. The race disparities in debt contrast with the attainment differences, given that Blacks have higher average debt and a lower percentage attain their 4-year degrees.

Earnings by Degree Level

Adult earnings for college degrees and less were lower in North Carolina than in the nation (Figure 11.13). Adults with bachelor's and advanced degrees had earnings' closer to the nation's average in 2023 but were still slightly lower. The differential between average earnings for high school graduates and adults with some college (associate degrees, certificates, and departers) was about $4,000 per year, a modest amount given the high debt levels for degree recipients. While we did not find data on the subject, because of the

Conservative-Progressive Tensions • 267

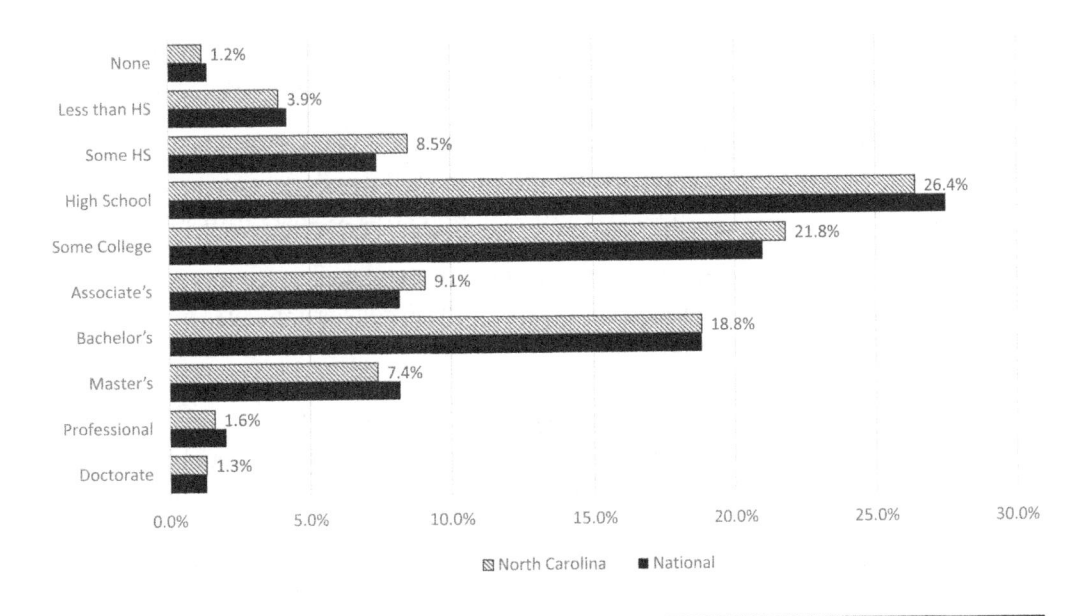

Education Level	North Carolina	National
None		1.2%
Less than HS		3.9%
Some HS	8.5%	
High School		26.4%
Some College		21.8%
Associate's	9.1%	
Bachelor's		18.8%
Master's	7.4%	
Professional	1.6%	
Doctorate	1.3%	

Figure 11.12 Highest Level of Educational Attainment for People 25 or Older in North Carolina (2020)
Source: Statistical Atlas (2023). Educational Attainment. Retrieved from https://statisticalatlas.com/United-States/Educational-Attainment

high cost of attending 2-year colleges, we suspect students who drop out have high debt, which could influence departure. College graduates had a higher differential than those with some college, about $18,000, presumably making it easier to pay off debt associated with the additional college necessary to attain the degree.

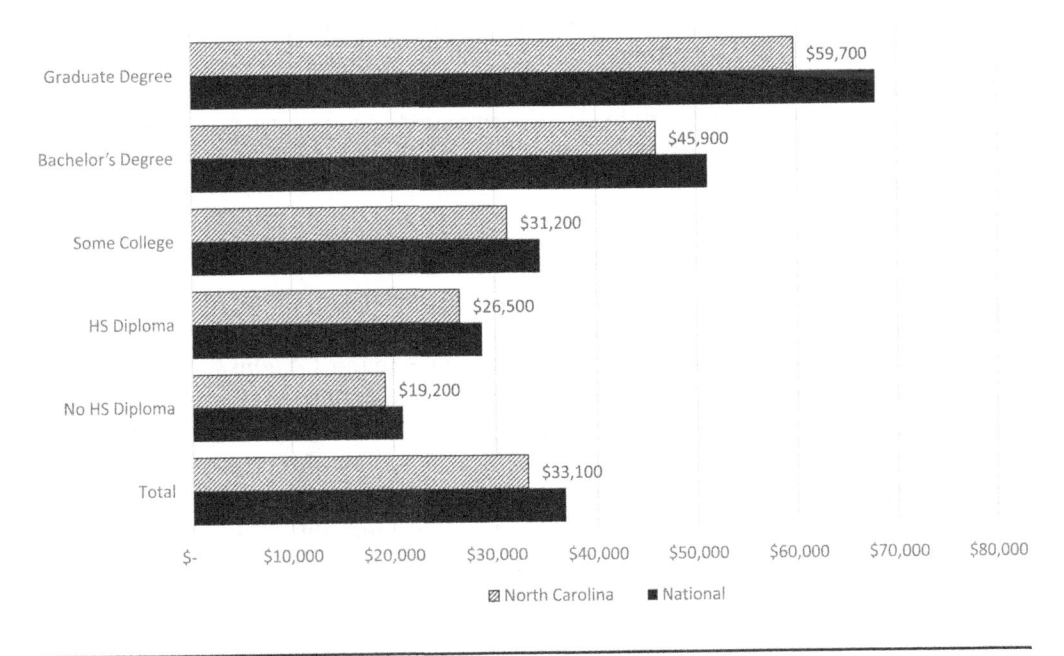

Level	North Carolina
Graduate Degree	$59,700
Bachelor's Degree	$45,900
Some College	$31,200
HS Diploma	$26,500
No HS Diploma	$19,200
Total	$33,100

Figure 11.13 Median Annual Earnings in North Carolina by Level of Education (2023)
Source: Statistical Atlas (2023). Educational Attainment. Retrieved from same issue

There are also earnings differentials for whites and Blacks in college attainment. For example, there is a long history of unequal pay for white and Black teachers in North Carolina and other southern states (Margo, 1990). The differentials in school achievement result from racial isolation, poverty, and inequality in North Carolina school funding (Sharma et al., 2014). Black teachers continue to earn less than white teachers. Most recently, North Carolina implemented a program that gives teachers with student's high achievement gains more pay (BESTNC, 2023). Careful impact monitoring is crucial, given the base disparities in teacher pay. It is difficult for college graduates with average student debt to earn a living, a tough challenge for Black college graduates in North Carolina, given the differentials in debt burden.

Debt, Attainment, Earnings, and Financial Wellbeing

The large amount of public reporting as studies of racial and pay inequality in North Carolina provide a baseline of information that activist scholars can use to support interest groups promoting race equity. The tuition levels for 2-year technical and collegiate programs are about $2,000 higher than the national average, increasing the necessity of loans in a 2-year system with high Black representation. Given the low earnings of adults with 2-year degrees, the high cost and debt, the overrepresentation of Blacks in the system, and low completion rates for Blacks, the limited financial access at 2-year colleges accelerated wealth inequality for Blacks in North Carolina.

North Carolina's history of race, education, wealth, and income inequality remains problematic. Education finance policy alone cannot fully resolve the underlying issues. Yet, the reconstruction of school finances to promote equity remains a crucial element of the necessary change process, as are continuing efforts to promote fairness in collegiate opportunities through lower-than-average costs at public 4-year colleges and encourage uplift through affordable 2-year technical and community colleges. However, the failure to ensure affordability at 2-year colleges, along with the apparent reliance on loans in this sector, places many low-income Blacks at long-term risk of poverty, including an inability to pay off loans across their work lives. The current strategy shows progress for some, causes severe economic inequality for others, and accelerates economic stratification in college destinations in the state.

Rethinking College Success

The struggles for fairness through governance reforms have a long history in North Carolina, spanning centuries. Given this history, it remains notable that higher education desegregation was achieved earlier in North Carolina than most *Adams* states by merging into one state system of colleges and universities. Higher education has, at times, been a shining light leading to fairness and uplift. Progressive initiatives in North Carolina often transform to favor whites, a plot line that repeats across decades. The state has repeatedly demonstrated an ability to adapt, expanding opportunities for underrepresented groups, at least for periods of time. At present, racial inequalities in higher education attainment, debt, and earnings for college graduates are severe issues in North Carolina. Recent changes further constrain diversity and equal opportunity to earn wages sufficient to support families. The silencing of the diversity dialogue on university campuses reinforces the systemic inequality for at least the near future.

Questions

1. How does the history of conflicts in colonial North Carolina—disputes between loyalists and agrarian idealists, between Indians and colonists, and between freed Blacks and Europeans—inform understanding of contemporary racial tensions in North Carolina? How were these tensions manifested in the development of schools and colleges?

2. How did policies evolving from white advocacy after the Civil War and after *Brown* interact with diversity in high school and college attainment? Consider how white activism after Reconstruction links to school choice funding over the decades since the Supreme Court's decision in *Brown v. Board of Education*.

3. How did changes in North Carolina education policy and finance, from Reconstruction through the Neoliberal Period, influence the progress toward diversity and swing back toward racial inequality? Consider how the state's preemptive strategy after the two *Adams* decisions prompted federal oversight of college desegregation compares to the state/s student aid programs that developed this century.

4. How have the shifts in federal education policy across periods, from the Early American period to the current Post Neoliberal period (discussed in Chapter 1), influenced the shifts in North Carolina education and finance policies across these periods?

5. What role have the Supreme Court Decisions (discussed across chapters) influenced federal policies and state strategies for improving college access, diversity, and attainment? How might the current Supreme Court's stance on affirmative action and school choice alter the context for Black activism and advocacy promoting race equity and fairness in higher education?

REFERENCES

Battle, K. P. (1907). *History of the university of North Carolina: From its beginning to the death of president swain, 1789-1868* (Vol. 1). Edwards & Broughton Printing Company. https://www.google.com/books/edition/History_of_the_University_of_North_Carol/n3l3nJjwr5EC?hl=en&gbpv=1&dq=North+Carolina+first+college+founded&pg=PA294&printsec=frontcover.

BESTNC. (2023). Teacher pay in North Carolina: A smart investment in student achievement. Business Round Table. https://www.bestnc.org/wp-content/uploads/2023/03/BEST-NC-Teacher-.

Brosnan, A. (2016). *Contested goals and competing interests: Freedpeople's education in North Carolina during the civil war and reconstruction era, 1861-1875*. Mary Immaculate College, University of Limerick.

Browning, J. (2008). "Bringing light to our land ... when she was dark as night": Northerners, freedpeople, and education during military occupation in North Carolina, 1862–1865. *American Nineteenth Century History*, 9(1), 1–17.

Conkin, P. (1955). The church establishment in North Carolina, 1765-1776. *The North Carolina Historical Review*, 32(1), 1–30.

Coon, C. L. (1915). *North Carolina Schools and academies, 1790-1840: A documentary history* (Vol. 5). Edwards & Broughton printing Company.

Denson, A. C. (1995). Diversity, religion, and the North Carolina regulators. *The North Carolina Historical Review*, 72(1), 30–53.

Dobbs, G. R. (2009). Frontier settlement development and "initial conditions": The case of the North Carolina piedmont and the Indian trading path. *Historical Geography, 37*(1), 114–137.

Fenn, E. A. (1983). *Natives & newcomers: The way we lived in North Carolina Before 1770* (Vol. 1). UNC Press Books.

Fiske, E. B. (2010). The Carolina covenant. In R. D. Kahlenberg (Ed.). *Rewarding strivers: Helping low-income students succeed in college* (pp. 17–70). The Century Foundation Press.

Gaylord, S. W., & Molony, T. J. (2016). Individual rights, federalism, and the national Battle over bathroom access. *North Carolina Law Review, 95*, 1662–1699.

Huddle, M. A. (1997). To educate a race: The making of the first state colored normal school, Fayetteville, North Carolina, 1865-1877. *The North Carolina Historical Review, 74*(2), 135–160.

Killian, J. (2023). In 2023: Conflict over politics, diversity and shifting leadership in NC higher education. States Newsroom. Retrieved from https://ncnewsline.com/2023/12/29/in-2023-conflict-over-politics-diversity-and-shifting-leadership-in-nc-higher-education/

Klain, Z. (1925). *Quaker contributions to education in North Carolina* (Vol. 31). Westbrook Publishing Company.

Kousser, J. M. (1980). Progressivism-for middle-class whites only: North Carolina Education, 1880-1910. *The Journal of Southern History, 46*(2), 169–194.

Lang, H. (2022, November 20). HBCU grads can face lifelong student debt burdens. Here's what that looks like in NC. *Charlotte Observer*.

LeMaster, M. (2006). In the" scolding houses": Indians and the law in Eastern North Carolina, 1684-1760. *The North Carolina Historical Review, 83*(2), 193–232.

Ma, J., & Pender, M. (2023). Trends in College Pricing: 2023. Trends in Higher Education Series, Issue. https://research.collegeboard.org/trends/college-pricing

Margo, R. A. (1990). Teacher salaries in black and white": Pay discrimination in the Southern classroom. In R. A. Margo (Ed.), *Race and schooling in the South, 1880-1950: An economic history* (pp. 52–67). University of Chicago Press.

McClellan, H. V. (April 18, 2024). UNC System committee votes to repeal diversity goals and jobs at 17 campuses across NC. EDNC. https://www.ednc.org/04-17-2024-unc-system-committee-votes-to-repeal-diversity-goals-and-jobs-at-17-campuses-across-nc/

Milteer, W. (2014). *The complications of liberty: Free people of color in North Carolina from the colonial period through reconstruction*. University of North Carolina. https://cdr.lib.unc.edu/concern/dissertations/zp38wd52g.

Mohammed, O. (2023, October 23). Activists Canceled Millions of Student Debt for HBCU Grads: Who Qualifies?. *Newsweek* https://www.newsweek.com/activists-cancel-student-debt-hbcu-grads-who-qualifies-1837000

Murry, K. (2024). Here's why black college graduates are more likely to have greater student loan debt. WCNC. Retrieved from https://www.wcnc.com/article/money/personal-finance/debt-disparities-racial-breakdown-student-loans-money-personal-finance/275-e35fcb62-9d32-4dd7-9b75-da6fc5958cda.

My Future NC. (2020). ACT Performance. Retrieved from https://dashboard.myfuturenc.org/college-and-career-access/act-performance/

Nelms, C. (2011). *Strengthening America's historically black colleges and universities: A call to action*. NCCU Office of the Chancellor.

Nordstrom, K. (2023). *New analysis shows many private schools in N.C. Have more vouchers than students*. North Carolina Justice Center. https://www.ncjustice.org/analysis-nc-private-school-voucher-program/

North Carolina Community College System. (2008). A Matter of Facts: The North Carolina Community College System Fact Book.

North Carolina Community College System. (2010). History of the North Carolina Community College System. Retrieved from https://www.nccommunitycolleges.edu/about-us/system-office/history/.

North Carolina Department of Public Instruction. (2023). High School Graduation Requirements. Retrieved from https://www.dpi.nc.gov/districts-schools/high-school-graduation-requirements.

North Carolina State Education Assistance Authority. (2024). The 2023 Appropriations Act Expands Eligibility for the Opportunity Scholarship Program. Retrieved from https://www.ncseaa.edu/2023/10/the-2023-appropriations-act-expands-eligibility-for-the-opportunity-scholarship-program.

Ort, S. (2023). *Structuring opportunity for low-income student access and success in co-learning in higher education: community wellbeing, engaged scholarship, and creating futures*. Routledge.

Petrow, S. (2016, August 28). Ruling against 'bathroom bill' enforcement on UNC campuses is a memo to the GOP: Tell the truth, rely on the facts. *Washington Post*. https://www.washingtonpost.com/news/arts-and-entertainment/wp/2016/08/28/ruling-against-bathroom-bill-enforcement-on-unc-campuses-is-a-memo-to-the-gop-tell-the-truth-rely-on-the-facts/.

Public Ed Works. (2023, March 23). North Carolina joins the DEI inquisition.

Quinn, R. (2023, July 21). In Statehouses, Tenure Was Bruised, but DEI Was Walloped. *Inside Higher Ed*. https://www.insidehighered.com/news/faculty-issues/diversity-equity/2023/07/21/statehouses-tenure-was-bruised-dei-was-walloped.

Rodning, C. B. (2010). European Trade goods at Cherokee settlements in southwestern North Carolina. *North Carolina Archaeology*, 59, 1–84.

Schoenbaum, H., & Robertson, G. (2023, August 18). North Carolina laws curtailing transgender rights prompt less backlash than 2016 'bathroom bill.' Associated Press. https://apnews.com/article/transgender-health-north-carolina-new-laws-b28aed0d20d363c22b1107135125c2d6.

Schofield, R. (2023, July 5, 2023). NC school vouchers: a decade of failure…and now this? NC Newsline. https://ncnewsline.com/2023/07/05/nc-school-vouchers-a-decade-of-failureand-now-this/.

Sharma, A., Joyner, A. M., & Osment, A. (2014). Adverse impact of racial isolation on student performance: A study in North Carolina. *Education Policy Analysis Archives*, 22, 14.

St. John, E. P. (1981). *Public policy and college management: Title III of the higher education act*. Praeger Press.

St. John, E. P. (2010). *Access and success: Strategies for historically black colleges and universities*. Setting an Agenda for Historically Black Colleges and Universities.

St. John, E. P., & Hossler, D. (1998). Higher education desegregation in the post-Fordice legal environment: A critical-empirical perspective. In Fossey, R. (ed.), *Readings on Equal Education, Vol. 15, Race, the Courts, and Equal Education: The Limits of the Law* (pp. 101–122). AMS Press.

St. John, E. P., Ort, S., & Williford, L. (2012). Carolina Covenant: Reducing the retention gap. In E. P. St. John (Ed.), *Expanding postsecondary opportunity for underrepresented students: Theory and practice of academic capital formation* (Vol. 26, pp. 235–254).

Thompson Dorsey, D. N., & Roulhac, G. D. (2019). From desegregation to privatization: A critical race policy analysis of school choice and educational opportunity in North Carolina. *Peabody Journal of Education*, 94(4), 420–441.

U.S. Department of Education & National Center for Education Statistics. (2013). Digest of Education Statistics, 2012 (NCES 2014-015).

University of North Carolina General Administration. (2011). The University of North Carolina: A Multicampus University. Retrieved from http://www.northcarolina.edu/

Warta, A., & Robinson, J. A. (2023). *The general Assembly's long higher-ed reach*. James G. Martin Center for Academic Renewal. Retrieved from https://www.jamesgmartin.center/2023/05/the-general-assemblys-long-higher-ed-reach/.

Watson, A. D. (1994). The origin of the regulation in North Carolina. *The Mississippi Quarterly*, 47(4), 567–598. https://www.jstor.org/stable/45237209.

Wattach, J. (2020). School Vouchers in North Carolina: 2014-2020.

Wescott, J. W. II (2005). *A vision of an open door: The establishment and expansion of the North Carolina community college system*. Dissertation, North Carolina State University.

Wetmore, R. Y. (1979). The role of the Indian in North Carolina history. *The North Carolina Historical Review*, 56(2), 162–176.

Williams, J. B. (1997). *Race discrimination in public higher education*. Praeger.

Woodson, C. G. (1919). *The education of the negro prior to 1861: A history of the education of the colored people of the United States from the beginning of slavery to the civil war*. Associated Publishers.

Young, H. (2005). North Carolina's educational wall of separation. *Freeman New Series Foundation for Economic Education*, 55(6), 34.

Zipf, K. L. (1999). "The whites shall rule the land or die": Gender, race, and class in North Carolina reconstruction politics. *The Journal of Southern History*, 65(3), 499–534.

EPILOGUE

States continue to adapt their education policies and public finance strategies to respond to the lingering remnants of flawed neoliberal education framework. When we started working on the third education of *Public Policy and Higher Education*, we naïvely assumed we could reframe our argument given the changing global context and could add some recent trends. So much has changed since 2017, when we finished the second edition. It was impossible to update; instead, we needed a new approach. We focused on education development as an ongoing challenge for states; we examined whether the K-12 improvements and higher education financial strategies ensured their residents' economic and social wellbeing. This epilogue identifies policy themes emerging globally as nations and states adapt in this challenging period:

- *Transforming Global Contexts:* The 1980s education reforms in K-12 and higher education were in a new historical period of economic globalization. The liberal theories that guided education policy in the 1960s and 1970s broke down as neo-liberal political ideologies promoted fragmented policies, and public education in most states lost the capacity to ensure the economic and social wellbeing of their residents.
- *State Politics and Education Development:* States adapted their historical education development policy frameworks to meet the challenges created by federal K-12 and higher education. With few exceptions, states approached reforms as adaptations of their inner systemic frames, but new political ideologies emerged, complicating these attempts to change systems. Tensions between MAGA and DEI overshadowed the deep, cross-generation wealth inequality that neoliberal policies had created.

TRANSFORMING GLOBAL CONTEXTS

Looking at national and state education trends, as intended and unintended outcomes of neoliberal policies on marketization and college for all, does not tell the story of transformation in K-12 and higher education since 1980. The shift to student loans to fund expanded college access was a global phenomenon, placing education reform and development for a new age into the context of international economic globalization. In the US, public college privatization introduced by the federal market strategy using loans instead of grants did not work. States innovated to correct the severe problems across their education systems. Emphasizing loans over grants spurred the privatization of higher education, a complex development not fully anticipated by advocates for this policy approach in the US and internationally.

The push for college for all was primarily an American narrative. There was evidence in some states that raising high school graduation requirements improved college access, one of the central claims of neoliberal reformers. It is apparent, however, that during the 2010s and early 2020s, improvements in high school graduation resulted from adding career and technical education (CTE) diploma options. CTE adapts and revises the older vocational and technical education (VTE) to make the college for all narrative work. Western Europe modernized VTE rather than abandoning it in favor of college for all; they led the transition to CTE, and most developing nations in Asia, the Middle East, and Africa also kept and improved dual systems, sometimes using privatized methods. The US skipped upgrading VTE as a bridge to CTE, so adjustments are slower and more costly than in the EU.

There is less comparability and commonality across states than before the radical neoliberal turn. We examine the cross-cutting theme from our national and state studies of preparation, access, and success as outcomes of systemic reforms. We identify emerging themes within post-neoliberal globalization as states adapt and evolve their K-20 systems in this evolving US context.

Adapting K-20 Systems in Post-Neoliberal Times

Federal studies used the end of the Cold War and rapid economic globalization to promote rationales for turning K-12 schools into college prep schools for all and using loans to finance higher education expansion. Eight themes emerged from the analyses of national and state policy trends.

1. ***The transition to Mass Higher Education Increased Government Spending.*** The transition to mass higher education, first in the US followed by Western Europe, was viewed as an investment for national governments. In the US before and during World War II, President Roosevelt's agenda of promoting social programs and the GI Bill were catalysts for massifying states' higher education systems. States massified state systems in the 1950s and 1960s, as federal student financial aid for low-income students began with the *National Defense Education Act of 1958*, early in the Cold War Era. President Johnson's K-12 and higher education legislation formalized and extended the federal role. The Marshall Plan brought Roosevelt's social policy framework to Europe. It provided a process that engaged Western European nations in developing social programs, K-12 education, and massifying higher education. After the Cold War, the US radically departed from the human capital investment strategy and turned its trajectory using new unfounded claims. European nations and, eventually the European Union adapted the human capital investment strategies instead of replacing them.
2. ***STEM College Prep for All.*** In the early 1980s, US federal agencies—the National Endowment for the Humanities and the US Department of Education—advocated

liberal arts as the basis for college preparation for all students. With support from the National Science Foundation, the education establishment seized the idea of college for all, abandoning the liberal arts ideal—humanities and social sciences in addition to science and technology—in favor of the Science, Technology, Engineering, and Math (STEM) version of college prep. This neoliberal tactic put off the culture wars, at least until this more recent period when social divisiveness haunts all public discourse, threatens academic freedom, and leaves higher education in chaos.

3. ***The US Failed to Reinvest in Vocational School-to-Work Education.*** The European Union (EU) focused on education exchange; workers and students could migrate within the EU, and most countries upgraded VTE to promote workforce development. The US federal government, in contrast, lodged their liberal arts college-prep ideas in the argument that the US was at risk—a reactionary claim emerging from neo-conservative advocacy of the liberal arts curricular reforms. The neoliberal educationists, economists, and industrial advocates seized on the math part of the college prep argument, arguing that students in high schools and colleges should prepare to be the designers for a global supply chain, assuming the American workforce could not compete with lower-cost workers in the other nations. The STEM for all arguments used faulty conclusions from research about math education—math is essential, but learning Algebra cannot expand college access when low-income students cannot afford to attend. It took another 30 years to rediscover that our cultural history and competitive economic forces necessitated that the nation's schools educate and empower students for working-class jobs and elite STEM professional opportunities.

4. ***US Policy Reports Conveyed Misunderstanding of this Nation's Competitive Position in the Global Economy.*** America's global economic competitors in Western Europe (i.e., the European Union) and Asia (e.g., India, China, and Southeast Asia) expanded education for the working class and the new generation of STEM professionals. The US's business, engineering, science, and computer professionals were among global leaders, but this nation had stiff competition for leadership in these fields. The overt failure to provide VTE education haunted the US, undermined the working class, and drove down wages. The combination accelerated wealth inequality even more than was evident in the EU.

5. ***In the 2010s, States Responded to the Need for More Flexible K-12 Pathways.*** After difficult times delivering STEM college prep for all, states began to promote career and technical education, allowing for college prep for technical fields at universities but not quite reinvesting modernizing vocational education in high schools and community colleges to support students who sought to move from school to work. The Obama administration eased federal standards, allowing for adaptation; Trump pushed CTE, emphasizing private delivery along with some modernization of technical education; and Biden pushed vocational education for school-to-work. Most states embraced CTE, and some reinvested in vocational programs for students seeking technical vocational preparation in high school and 2-year colleges.

6. ***Paying for Higher Education Expansion with Student Debt Created New Problems.*** The "Washington Consensus" argued that high loans and high prices were the best (i.e., lowest cost) way to expand access. This political-right narrative argued that since students benefited financially from higher education, they should pay for it—with loans in lieu of grants—as the privatized market induced innovation and

lowered prices. Latin American nations, Pacific region nations, and especially the US bought into the strategy, a libertarian free-market approach. However, the STEM ideal dominated K-12 and higher education planning in the US, where vocational pathways were dysfunctional. This strategy was a disaster in the US, as discussed across chapters. Latin American and Southeast Asian countries used different education and economic development strategies but used student loans; they also found that debt was too high for the financial wellbeing of workers who'd financed their postsecondary education with borrowed money.

7. *The US Education Strategy Accelerated Wealth Redistributed from the Poor and Middle Class to the Rising Corporate Elite.* The STEM prep for all strategy aligned with reductions in tax rates and education spending. It was a tradeoff the US education establishment made when they accepted money from NSF and the US Department of Education for STEM reforms. There were modest critiques from left-leaning educational researchers, including our prior editions of *Higher Education and Public Finance*—the counterview did little to alter the STEM strategy, nor was that the intent. Arguing for inclusive and diverse pathways does not marginalize STEM; STEM dominance marginalizes these alternative pathways. Economic globalization worked exceedingly well for some, but not the majority in industrialized nations. Northern European nations continued taxing for education, health, and social services, but the US and many others did not. Wealth redistribution became a severe problem in the US and, to a lesser extent, in Western Europe.

8. *Readjustments in Global Economic Alliances Create Opportunities to Rethink National and State Strategies for Education Development.* The economic battles between China and the US, wars in Eastern Europe and the Middle East, and the international COVID pandemic altered the global economy. Nation shutdowns slowed the global supply chain, igniting inflation; international education competition and student exchange are reshaping with changing economic alliances. This new global context complicates planning for new directions in international higher education and student exchange, and the nation's repositioning alters the contexts for states' education development. State- and campus-based planning for CTE program development should consider the broader context of economic restructuring, including the rising minimum wage in some states, competition for workers across industries, and prospects for community-based renewal. We argue that these local and state strategies must consider the social and economic wellbeing of diverse groups in their communities.

State Politics and Education Development

When framing this edition of *Public Policy and Higher Education*, we traced the history of ideologies that influenced education development, a process that informed the development of human capital theory in the 1960s, and its application in planning for higher education finance in the 1970s. Rather than contend with mainstream economic theory, Reagan's US Department of Education first turned to Milton Friedman's *Capitalism and Freedom* before slipping entirely into making flawed claims about markets in K-12 and higher education that morphed into the STEM pipeline for all. The big change ushered in by the neoliberal turn and accelerated by the MAGA ideology is that facts—the evidence-based approach advocated in the 1980s and 1990s—have given way to beliefs-driven policy. Themes emerged related to the influence of political ideologies on education development, the changes in state policy frames as K-12 systems adjusted to and accommodated ideological policy developments, and the prospects of reframing state strategies for promoting college success, given realities of college student debt as an accelerant to wealth redistribution.

Political Ideologies Reshaping Education Development

After World War II, applications of human capital theory in systems planning for education development were a guiding hand in the development and reauthorization of the *Higher Education Act*, with the pivotal versions being the original HEA and the 1972 reauthorization since they used the human capital theory and education research in the design of the federal role in 1962 and the reframing of the federal and state roles in 1972. In this new world of ideologically informed policy swirl, we were dismantling cross-cutting programmatic logic previously used for policy development (i.e., human capital coupled with systemic approaches). While the older logic was outdated, replacing it with unfounded ideological claims did not work well for the US. We started this by viewing the MAGA-DEI discourse as a debate; in the reality revealed by the cases, the conversation is being quieted, in some states at least, by radically conservative laws.

1. ***The MAGA-DEI Turmoil Undermines US Civic Leadership in Global Economic Development and Societal Uplift.*** Florida and North Carolina have adopted laws and policies silencing the diversity discourse, shutting down prospects of discussion of the underlying problems. Education curricula and policies promoting difficult dialogues have become as divisive as the idea of desegregation had been after *Brown*. In Florida, North Carolina, and Indiana, students educated in private Christian academies and schools funded by state-funded vouchers can enroll in Christian colleges and enter the workforce without experiencing racial and cultural diversity in high school or college. These patterns of educational choice undermine the diverse democracy arguments that persuaded the Supreme Court to extend affirmative action in the *Gratz* and *Grutter* decisions. The more recent conservative Court reversed course on affirmative action, reflecting the growing MAGA conservatism and its response to DEI on the left. Rather than establishing diverse pathways, the vision for an earlier generation of conservatives and liberals. Christian nationalist education finance policies undermine this priority set in the period of economic globalization. Legislation banning conversation about diversity moves the nation another step further from global leadership by example in promoting openness, fairness, and justice worldwide. The idea of a global community is deconstructing within embattled communities across this nation.

2. ***Eurocentrism Undermined the Liberalization in Education Development.*** In the 1980s, in *To Reclaim a Legacy*, William Bennett argued for restoring the humanities as foundations for the liberal arts, and in *The Closing of the American Mind*, Allan Bloom argued that the student movement stimulated gender and ethnic studies, fragmenting undergraduate liberal arts education. These ideas were not new. In reaction to student protests and higher education changes, Sidney Hook argued similarly in *Academic Freedom and Academic Anarchy* in 1970. Student advocacy for curriculum change in the 1960s and 1970s had spilled over from classrooms using humanist literature, theory, and pedagogies. Centuries earlier, the opposite argument opened the liberal arts to new theories and methods. At the time of the

American Revolution, for example, Adam Smith's *The Wealth of Nations* criticized the clerics and philosophers who defended overly narrow notions of knowledge that excluded science. Liberalizing curriculum took centuries, including student activism in the 1960s and 1970s. The irony is that these debates among old European men—from Smith to Hook, Bennett, and Bloom—have permeated academic traditions for centuries; now, states' polities are silencing the discourse in school and college classrooms. Listening to new voices and ideas has often been difficult for American white men, as demonstrated by centuries of oppression, from the Indian Wars and slavery in English colonies and American states before the Civil War to contemporary fear of immigrants in a nation with many states and communities perched on the edge of armed civil conflict.

3. *The Leap from Liberalism to Progressivism in Education Development Side Steps the MAGA-DEI Debate.* During the progressive periods at the turn of the twentieth century through the Cold War, both Republicans and Democrats promoted progressive social policies. The comparison of California's liberal-progressive building of the three collegiate systems evolved parallel with Indiana's conservative-progressive development of two university systems with 2-year campuses and, eventually, a community college system. The US is now in a period when unequal progress in education development addressing unequal opportunities across groups should alarm Republicans and Democrats—MAGA and DEI advocates alike. Whites and Blacks are being left behind economically due to college costs and the effete academic battle between STEM and liberal arts ideologues. The fact that the education system leaves so many on the outside of education for economic wellbeing should be alarming to all. Progress in education development should be prioritized over battles about course content and regulating professional practices inside colleges and universities.

4. *The STEM Education Movement and Higher Education Privatization Were Promoted by Extreme Conservatives Seeking to Reduce Their Tax Burdens.* Wealthy, conservative southern California Republican transformed the state's liberal Republican party before 1968 when Ronald Reagan was first elected Governor. After the election, the reconstituted California Republicans constrained taxes, implemented tuition in the University of California system, and Governor Reagan's appointees on the University of California Board of Regents fired Clark Kerr, the visionary behind the development of elite research universities across the US. After the 1976 election, President Jimmy Carter used efficiency arguments for legislation, creating means for restructuring the federal role in K-12 and higher education. Reagan's 1980s presidential election was a widely viewed start in neoliberalism. However, in the 1960s, the elite conservative tax-cutting faction infused their agenda into the core values of the Western Republican party and, in the 1970s, the political interests reshaped Southern Democrats' agenda, a transformation symbolized by the elections of Carter, Reagan, and subsequent presidents, at least until Obama began to make regulatory changes enabling flexibility in K-12 education. These "neoliberal" forces transformed the US liberal education strategy, moving the nation from a human capital public investment framework to the belief that unfettered markets and tax cuts would "trickle down" to benefit the middle class and lift people out of poverty, the origin narrative shaping the neoliberal turn.

5. *Alignment of Catholic and Protestant Interests Accelerated Christian Nationalist Policies on Education Development.* For far more than a century, from the 1870s

through the 2010s, the idea that religious artifacts in schools undermined communitarian learning prevailed in the mid-twentieth century in the US but not in Europe. The flight of white Christians from public schools in the South left many in the same bind as Catholics faced since the school wars of the 1880s: their beliefs led them outside of the public school system. Using social media, conservative billionaires infused their tax-cut agenda into misinformation about the social and educational aspirations of conservative Catholics and Protestants, aligning their interests with the nationalist MAGA movement. The US Supreme Court's decision in *Carson v. Makin* opened the doors wider for voucher programs for students enrolling in religious schools, and students go through them, the doors regularly used for learning, when their parents respond to vouchers. This fracture within states' polities—the divide between Christians and progressives supporting education development for this new period—can be healed through dialogue. Indiana seems the closest to discovering an alternative neutral ground of the states we studied.

6. ***Through Social Media, The Tax-Cut Ideology of Conservative Billionaires Inhibits Rebuilding a Liberal-Progressive Strategy in the US.*** It will take more funding and a willingness of billionaires to pay higher taxes, as argued by progressive Democrats, for the federal government and states more fully to address the systemic challenges of opening religious and public schools to all and financing higher education to promote fair opportunities to learn and earn a livable wage after monthly payments on student debt. In the US, conservative billionaires promoted the nationalist social agenda; they reinforced the notion that middle-class taxes are too high, which is true because the wealthy manipulated the tax system during the neoliberal turn. Like the US, European nations have clashes between the extremes of the political left and right, yet they maintain affordable pathways to universities and technical institutes. The paths forward in American states can learn from and adapt European strategies to provide affordable postsecondary academic or career opportunities within their distinctive cultures and traditions. A different approach to federal education policy could facilitate such a transition, especially if it creates discursive space for states to resolve the MAGA-DEI tensions rising from the history and evolution of states' polities.

EVOLVING STATE POLICY FRAMES

When we began working on the first edition in the 2010–2011 academic year, distinct patterns were evident in how states adapted to neoliberal federal policies. All states complied with raising standard, but there were variations in how they adapted state financing for higher education, mainly based on the history of governance and funding. As severe problems with the neoliberal consensus emerged, states adopted new strategies, altering their frameworks. These emerging themes revealed states' finance and governing tactics accelerated privatization.

1. ***The Low-Tuition and High-Grant Aid, the Core of the Old Liberal Model, Has Proven Difficult to Maintain.*** Indiana managed to sustain grant investments and keep public tuition lower than most of the nation. Yet, it had a lower-than-average enrollment rate among the traditional college-age population. After years of tax constraints, California moved to high tuition with high grants but found ways

to maintain low tuition in 2-year colleges. North Carolina's constrained tuition increases and investment in need-based grants have increased since 2005, keeping 4-year colleges more affordable than California's; however, North Carolina's 2-year colleges are not as inexpensive as in California. Florida held down tuition increases in 4-year colleges, but community colleges evolved toward the 4-year model, further complicating fairness in access.

2. ***High Tuition High Aid Has Also Been Difficult for States to Maintain.*** Higher education programs have been one of the few areas around which states have flexibility. There was a rationale for institutional building into the annual budget process when funding formulae crafted higher education budgets. Minnesota's high tuition and grant strategy required public colleges and universities to forgo direct funding, let tuition rise, and accept the idea that student grants would enable students to continue their enrollment. In Minnesota, funding for institutions declined, but funding for student grants rose to provide an even hand of support. Ensuring funding for grants and institutions proved a bit too fungible when states faced growing prison populations, expanding welfare demands, and increasing healthcare costs. Further, like California, many states weathered periods of taxpayer revolts constraining tax increases. Reductions in funding need-based grant programs accelerate cross-generation wealth disparities by delaying timely college attainment, whether tuition is high or low. With high tuition, failure to fund state grants squeezes more students out or results in higher debt, remedies that further increase wealth disparities.

3. ***High Merit Aid Reinforces Structural Inequality in Educational Attainment.*** High merit aid can improve enrollment, but the strategy is not the remedy for inequality in opportunity, according to findings established by economic research on access. Florida maintains low tuition fees and makes substantial investments in merit grants. In addition to keeping college affordable for many students, it holds some high-achieving residents in the state. However, in Florida, the MAGA ideology has become a counterforce, motivating liberal-minded young adults out of state for college. Further, enrollment declines in state universities seems related to the high net cost for most low-income students who do enroll.

4. ***Last Dollar Schemes Can Worsen Wealth Inequality Across Generations.*** Consider two hypothetical students at a college with tuition of $5,000 and a $10,000 Cost of Attendance (COA), including the expected cost of living at the college or in the community. Assume a maximum Pell is $5,000, and the state has a last-dollar promise grant of $5,000 that uses tuition as the maximum award for the last dollar award (subtracting the Pell Grant). *Student 1* has a zero expected family contribution (EFC), and *Student 2* has $5,000 EFC. In this example, *Student 1* would receive a full Pell ($5,000) and no state grant; *Student 2* would receive no Pell and a $5,000 state grant. *Student 1* would have to borrow $5,000, and *Student 2* would attend college for free if the parents paid their expected contribution. This simplified example illustrates the cross-generation wealth inequality resulting from last-dollar programs that set the combined maximum for state and federal award at tuition instead of net costs after federal grants. It leaves out self-help, work, and financial strategies that are part of campus aid packaging. Even with the complete packaging methodologies, this inequality results from state last-dollar grants with maximum award below the COA (e.g., tuition) when they subtract Pell and other grants from the maximum award. Too many last-dollar schemes are deceptive mechanisms that push

cross-generational debt onto low-income families. It is far more equitable to base these awards on financial need and avoid inequality created by these problematic subtraction methods.

5. ***The Current Structure of Federal and State Grant Programs Sentences Low-Income Families to Excessive Cross-Generation Debt.*** Starting in the 1980s, the shift from federal grants to federal loans had a high cost for middle- and low-income families because of the debt carried across lifetimes and generations. The debt burdens of middle-aged and older adults can discourage college-age students from attending college. The economic wellbeing of generations of Black families, undermined as many families have cross-generation student debt, cannot be remedied by the wages they make, even with some college or 2-year degrees. Now that Latinx Americans are enrolling at higher rates, they, too, could be headed toward cross-generation debt if their education investment doesn't result in substantially higher earnings. Let's hope it is not beyond repair. The decline in white college enrollment further indicates the severity of the financial challenge in some states. However, ill-conceived promise programs that use last-dollar grants may advantage working-class families, but they worsen the extreme wealth inequality that now haunts our nation. Applying basic math to problems of inequality, as in the simple example above, can educate policymakers and analysts caught up in the neoliberal idea of serving all through efficient mechanisms, the values that entered education policy in the late 1970s and set the stage for savagely unequal neoliberal public finance policies that rooted the trajectory stared in the 1980s.

INDEX

Note: *Italicized* page references refer to figures, **bold** references refer to tables, and page references with "n" refer to endnotes.

academic access 51, 226–228
academic communities 4, **4**, 6
academic debates 64; polarization 74
academic discourse 1–3, 6, 64
academic freedom 212, 215, 219, 221–222, 240, 244, 264–265, 274
ACT scores 81, 174, 233, 258–259, 265; in admissions at CSU 157; Black/white gap in 174; for college admission 173–174; Florida Bright Futures program 223; in Michigan 81; requirement 157
Adams v. Califano 26
Adams v. Richardson 26
Advisory Committee of Student Financial Assistance 58
African American 37, 72, 83–85, 152; and ANAR 77; in California 144; college preparatory options 75; education 84; ethos of 84; experience in US 253; graduation rates for 250; high debt burden 184; high school graduation rates for 173; in Minnesota 174, 238; research on 84–85; scholarship 85; in UC system 143
Afro-Indian 220
Allen, Walter 84
American Association of University Professors (AAUP) 212, 215
American Community Survey (ACS) 90, 259
American Dream and Promise Act of 2023 34
American (white) nationalism *see* white nationalism
American Revolution 9, 43, 112, 277
analysis/analyses: communicative 64–65; cross-state 51; data 14, 47; databases 49–50; of diffusion of merit aid programs 225; of education statistics 53; experimental 75; frameworks for reliable trend 55–62; higher education policy 48–52; history of 48–52; of longitudinal cohort 120; of national and state policy trends 273; of national trends and state cases 65; of policies 77, 79; of policy changes 42; of school reform initiatives 11; of state student records 51–52
ANAR *see A Nation At Risk* (ANAR) (National Commission on Excellence in Education, 1983)
Anderson, M. S. 167
anticommunist movement 9
anti-DREAM Act 34
antislavery movement 9
anti-transgender legislation; *see also* transgender rights
anti-woke movement 11, 63, 220–221
Archaeology of Knowledge, The (Foucault) 6
Asian students 11
attainment 120–121, 268; adult education 184–185; college 153–156, 206–209; college-degree attainment rates 177–180; degree 121, *123*, *124*, *125*, *127*, *155*, 173, 177–180, 238; and economic development 213–214; education/educational 23, 37, 46, 53, 56, 59, 62, 76, 107, 119, 185–186, 242; framework 55; outcomes 12; and persistence 120–121; postsecondary *57*, 57–58, 184, 236–238; race/ethnic gaps in 120; timeliness of 121; timely 120
Avery, C. 58

Baby Boomers 2, 5
Basic Educational Opportunity Grants (BEOG) *see* Pell Grants

282 • Index

'Bathroom Bill' (HB 2) 253, 254, 264
Bayh-Dole Act (1980) 29
Bear Flag Revolt 138, 144
Becker, Gary S. 71
Begin Again: James Baldwin's America and Its Urgent Lessons for Our Own (Glaude) 3
Bell, Daniel 7, 26
Bell, Ted 10
Bennett, W. 7–8, 10, 98, 224
Berkner, L. 54
Berkner-Chavez report 55
Bettinger, Eric 58
bias 6, 62, 117, 157; collective 11; convergence of 12; cultural 11; gender 11–12; unconscious 264
Bible 3, 118
Biden, J. 3, 33–34, 46, 82–83, 85, 186
Biden, President of the United States, et al. v. Nebraska 33
"big lie" 3
Black Caribe 220
Black Lives Matter (BLM) movement 2–3
Black Seminole 220
Black students 11, 25, 54, 85, 150, 153–155, 175–180, 184, 187, 202, 203, 206–208, 238, 260, 262
Bloom, Allan 7–9
"blue line" budget process, California 29
Brenan, M. 212
BREXIT 22
Bright Futures program 219–226; critiques and reform efforts 224–225; examine of 225–226; merit grants 223–224
British common law 23–24
British legal system 114
Brown, Pat 141
Brown v. Board of Education 8, 26, 94, 221, 249
Build Back Better agenda 33
Bush, George W. 146
Bush, GHW 55
Bush, Jeb 228

California case study 137–160; adults with bachelor's degree 144; African American 144; Asian Americans 144; "blue line" budget process 29; California Master Plan 137–138, 139–140; college admissions test scores 150–151; college attainment 153–156; college attainment rates 153–154; college participation rates 151–153; college preparation 149; college success 158–160; current issues 156–158; demographic changes 143–144; department of education 145–150; diversity 144; educational policies 145–149; education outcomes, trends in 149–156; elimination of SAT/ACT in admissions at CSU 157; expanding opportunity 142–143; financing of higher education 146–149; free community colleges 157; funding per FTE 147, *147*; higher education enrollment 151–153; high school diploma 144; high school graduation rates 149–150; high school graduation requirements 145; high school reform 145–146; high tuition/high aid model 156–157; investment 148; Latinx 144; legacy of excellence and equity 138–144; legacy of political, social, and economic change 144; Master Plan for Higher Education 45; median annual earnings in *159*; Native Americans 144; need-based aid per FTE *148*, 154–156; open-access education system 144; overview 137–138; political storms, weathering 140–141; from revolt to public systems 138–139; system-wide administrations in 45; tax revenue constraints 141–142; tuition rates 147; UC tuition stability plan 158; working class, undereducated 144
California College Promise Act 46
California College Promise Grant 157
California Community Colleges (CCC) 46, 140
California Education Code 145
California High School Exit Exam (CAHSEE) 146, 149–150, 158
California Master Plan 137–138, 139–140
California Postsecondary Education Commission (CPEC) 141, 142
California State University (CSU) 46, 145, 148, 150, 157–158
Callan, Pat 141
career and technical education (CTE) 33, 46, 47, 54, 82, 146, 150, 158, 170, 273–274
career preparation 71–78; adding financial wellbeing to 82–83; integrating math into 82
Carnegie Commission on Higher Education 50–51, 94, 140
Carnevale, Anthony 77, 95
Carroll, E. Jean 11
Carruthers, C. K. 60
Carson v. Makin Supreme Court 33, 74
Carter, Jimmy 7, 29–30, 43, 45, 49, 112, 118
Castaneda v. Regents of the University of California 142
Catholic 8, 113, 277–278; children 74; colleges and universities 10, 93, 138; high school curriculum 8; judges 74; and school choice 240; schools xiii, 73–74, 93, 215
change in policy 79–81
Chavez, L. 54
Child Tax Credit (CTC) 84
CHIPS and Science Act of 2022 33
Christian: academies 46, 221, 233, 276; -centric historical themes 11, 138, 192–193, 248, 278; colleges 115; denominations xiii; education **21**, 43, 46; nationalism 3, **4**, 10–11, 44, 46, 212, 214–215, 276; theology 10; values 197; view of science 74
civic leadership 126, 276
civics education 82
Civil Rights movement 5, 7, 8–9, 107, 117, 118
Civil War 8–9, 30, 43–44, 113–114; amputation of limbs 114; antislavery movement before 9; college for privileged 91; colleges amid social stress 114–115; legal education 114; national pension

system 93; public and private colleges in nation building before 22–24; public education before 138; public higher education after 192–193; from Spanish origins to 220–221; successful college development after 115–116; women's right to vote movement 8
closed-strategic ideologies 64
Closing of the American Mind, The (Bloom) 7
Cold War 5, 9, 10, 22–24, 26–27; education expansion during 75; expansion of public systems 94–95; investing in education development 116–118; liberal education establishment of 72
college access 20, 29, 56, 62–65, 90–108; Cold War expansion of public systems 94–95; college choice 102–106; development of competing college systems 93–94; diversity 102–106; enrollment 102–106; enrollment stratification 107–108; federal role 98; finance policies 96–102; history of US education 106–107; inequalities in 71; legislation 27; and neoliberal turn 91–96; overview 90–91; pathway of privilege 91–93; policy changes 107–108; policy indicators for **56**; post-neoliberal uncertainty 96; public and private colleges 96–98; purchasing power of Pell Grants 98–99; state and local subsidies 100; state funding for colleges and students 100–102; state need-based grants 100–102; state non-need-based grants 100–102; through privilege of ancestry 28; trends in student debt 99
college attainment 153–156, 206–209; Florida 236–239; Indiana 190, 206–209; Minnesota 176–181; North Carolina 262–264, 279
college choice xi, xiv, 60, 90, 97, 102, 104–106, 120–121, 177, 211, 221; debt and 99; private 238; process 70; theory 50–51, 70
college costs ix, 2, 7, 30, **38**, **56**, 82, 90, 97–100, 111, 120–121, 127–128, 277; California *146*, 157; Florida 225–226, *229*, 233; Indiana 191, *199*, 206; Minnesota *171*, 172, 184, 187; North Carolina *256*
college development **112**, 112–113; after Civil War 115–116; and community development 113–114; and economic development 114; and social stress 114–115
college finance 61–62
"college for all" model 29
college-founding movement 91
College Leadership for Community Renewal; Beyond Community-Based Education (Gollattscheck) 125
college participation rates 151–153
college preparation 71–78, **73**; California case study 149; and financial wellbeing 82–83; pathways for high-school graduates and dropouts 83–84; reconstructed reasoning about 82–86; reconstructing theory and practice 85–86; research on African American 84–85
college success 111–131; civic leadership 126; economic uplift 126–128; financial wellbeing 128–130; historical perspectives on 112–120; overview 111; and social stress 114–115; for students in their states 130–131; timely college completion across race/ethnicity 120–125
Collom, Gresham 165, 188n1
Columbia University 25
Commission on the Future of Higher Education 78
communicative: action 62–63; ideology 64–65; practices 64–65
communism 64; Cold War 116; Russian 118
community-based liberal ethos 115
community colleges 104–105, 126, 130, 137, 140–141, 143, 147, 149, 153; *see also* free community colleges
community development 113–114, 117, 118–119
competing college systems 93–94
competing systems 74–75
conflict/conflicting beliefs 4–9; about education 5–6; about racial and ethnic diversity 28; from Civil Rights to DEI 8–9; conflict about education 5–6; between education and contingent in polity 6; MAGA-DEI 6; policy trajectories 32; political ideologies 42–47, **43**; during progressive Cold War 45; Western Civilization 7–8
conservatism 3, 5, 9, 190, 214, 222, 248, 253, 264, 276
Cooper, Roy 254
cooperative learning 76
Coronavirus Aid, Relief, and Economic Security Act of 2020 (CARES Act) 2, 33
Cosby, Bill 11
cost of attendance (COA) 61, 96–99, 100, 184, 279
creative work 78
cultural biases 11; *see also* bias
cultural differences 30, 123
current issues: California case study 156–158; Indiana case study 210–212; Minnesota case study 181–183
curriculum: Catholic high school 8; college preparatory 53, 145, 170, 190, 228; Core 40 194–195, 198; CTE 54; diversity 73–74; evolving structure of 5; K-12 9, 11; K-20 7, 33; reform traditions 72–75; in schools and colleges **4**; student advocacy for 276; vocational 74–75

Dakota-Indian War 165
Daniels, Mitch 198–199
Dartmouth decision 19, 23–24, 38, 106, 113, 115
Daun-Barnett, N. 61
debt burden 129–130; California 158; Florida 241–244; Indiana 215; Minnesota 184–187; North Carolina 268
Deferred Action for Childhood Arrivals (DACA) 156
degree completion xi, 54, 122, 181, 251; across race/ethnic groups 121–122; as attainment process 121; data in California 156; in Florida 236–238; in Indiana 206–207; institutional vantage on 207; in Minnesota 177, 181; in North Carolina 251, 258, 263, 266; by race and ethnicity 56–57; rates 120, 121–125, 177, 206, 238, 263; for students of color 52; substantial gap in 238

Delaney, J. A. 228
Department of Education (US) 7–8, 46, 53, 63, 95, 178, 275; math standards 77–78; studies 49
DeSantis, R. 37, 219, 222, 226
desegregation **27**, 28, 46, 74, 77, 84, 276; in Florida 220–221; in North Carolina 247, 248, 250–251, 268
De-valuating of America: The Fight for the Culture of Our Children, The (Bennett) 8
DeVos, Betsy 253
Dewey, John 7, 72
Diversity, Equity, and Inclusion (DEI) xii, **xiii**, 3, **4**, 5–14, 221, 240; from Civil Rights movement to 8–9; limitation of 9; movement 1, 9; and North Carolina case study 264; practices and guidelines 12; programs 222, 240; strategies for promoting hope 9; of twenty-first century 9; v. MAGA 1, 4
Doyle, W. R. 225, 228
Doyle-Bayh Act 35
DREAM Act 34, 156, 157
Dresch, Stephen 51, 52
Du Bois, W. E. B. 115
Dumke, Glenn 137
Dynarski, Susan 57

Early America 73–74; college founding in 192; colleges 91–93, 115; education development in 113–115; faith traditions and curriculum diversity 73–74; origins 5; period 19, 83, 93, 248–249
Earned Income Tax Credit (EITC) 84
earnings by education level 127–128, 185, 242–243
East Florida Seminary 220
East India Company 23
economic development 24, 37, 114, 276; and attainment 213–214; college development interacts with **112**; and colleges 114; national 127; as outcomes of public spending on education 116
economic globalization 2, 7, **21**, 276; advocates of 107; Cold War 273; from empires to 20; and international education policy 64; university engagement in 29
economic uplift 126–128
Ed Choice 240
educational cross-generation 8
Education Amendments of 1972 90
Education and the Public Interest: School Reform, Public Finance, and Access to College (St. John) 57
Education Commission of the States 70
Education Consolidation and Improvement Act of 1981 (ECIA) 29, 77
education development: colleges development 113–115; community development 113–114; in early America 113–115; economic development 114; economic growth form investment in 117–118; investing in 116–118; social stress 114–115
education/educational attainment 23, 37, 46, 53, 56, 59, 62, 76, 107, 185–186, 190, 207, 242, 266, 279; highest level *127–128, 159, 185, 213–214, 242–243, 267*

education expansion 75
education expenditures 61
education marketplace 47
education savings account (ESA) program 240
egalitarianism 43, 44
Elementary and Secondary Education Act (ESEA) 7, 27, 29, 32, 65, 74, 76, 117, 146
encouragement 58–61
enrollment: by college type 104–106; management 36, 51, 71; rate 152; stratification 107–108; by traditional-college-age students 103
Eurocentric: beliefs 9; education 9; nationalism 8; values 8
Eurocentrism 10
evangelism **43**, 44
Every Student Succeeds Act (ESSA) of 2015 **32**, 65, 78, 80, 96
expected family contribution (EFC) 257, 279

Fair Test 182
faith traditions 73–74; *see also* Christian
fake news 3
family finances 120–121
Father Knows Best 118
federal funding 29–30, 35, 51; GEAR UP 196; Pell grant 98, 123–124; school choice 253
federal government 2, 76, 107; debt 2, 78, 278; education and social agencies in 49; education statistics 47; funding strategies 29; marketized higher education 2; partnership with state 66n3; policy frameworks 65; supported planning for state systems 26
federal legislation **24**, **27**, **28**, 28–29, 34, 36
federal need-based grants 61
federal policy/policies 22, 57–58, 146, 266; flexibility in 65; from grants promoting equity 165–166; history of higher education in 19; mechanisms 29
federal research 35, *36*
Federal Reserve Bank of Minneapolis 169, 173
federal role 98–99, 106–107
federal-state partnership 96
Fenwick, Leslie T. 85
finance policies 96–102; cost of attending public and private colleges 96–98; federal role 98–99; trends in state funding 100–102
financial access ix, 83, 173, 180, 268
financial inequality 29–34
financial wellbeing: and career preparation 82–83; college success 128–130; Florida 243–244; Minnesota 183–186; North Carolina 266–268; preparation for 70–71, **73**, 81–83
financing higher education 35, 137, 278
Florida Academic Scholarship (FAS) award 223, 224
Florida case study 219–244; Afro-Indians 220; balance and hope 240–241; Black Caribe 220; Black Seminole 220; Bright Futures grant in context 222–226; Bright Futures program 221–222; college

admissions 228; college enrollment 233–236; college preparation 232–233; college success 241–244; complications with conservative shifts in education 240; current policy context 239–241; degree attainment 238; Department of Education 222, 227–228; diversity 233–236; earnings by education level 242–243; East Florida Seminary 220; economic benefits of college for Floridians 241–243; educational attainment 242; education development 220–221; financial wellbeing 243–244; funding for non-need-based (merit) grants 230–231; high debt for college graduates 241; high school graduation rates *232*, 232–233; high school graduation requirements **227**, 227–228; limitations of Florida's merit strategy 239; linking policies and outcomes 238–239; Native Americans 220; need-based grant aid 231; overview 219–220; policy implementation 226–231; postsecondary attainment 236–238; poverty rates by race 243; proportional representation by race/ethnicity 235–236; public tuition charges 228; school voucher program 233; from Spanish origins to Civil War 220–221; state appropriations for public higher education 228–230; state financing of postsecondary education 228–231; state policy related to academic access 226–228; student outcomes 231–239; test scores 233; West Florida Seminary 220; white-Black tension 221

Florida Comprehensive Assessment Test (FCAT) 227–228

Florida Financial Aid Application (FFAA) 223

Florida Gold Seal Vocational (FSV) award 223, 224

Florida Medallion Scholars (FMS) award 223, 224

Florida State Board of Education 222

Florida Student Assistance Grant (FSAG) program 231

Fogel, Robert 44

Ford, Henry 25

Foucault, Michael 6

Fourth Great Awakening and the Future of Egalitarianism, The (Fogel) 44

Fox, W. F. 60

Franklin, Benjamin 24

Free Application for Federal Student Aid (FAFSA) 61, 98, 257

free community colleges 157; *see also* community colleges

free or reduced lunch (FRL) 211

Free Speech Movement (FSM) 7, 140

French-Indian War 116, 166

Fugitive Slave Law 115

full-time-equivalent (FTE) *147*, *148*, 149; amount of subsidy per 100; average annual state and local appropriations per *101*; average state funding per 100; average state need-based/non-need-based undergraduate grants per *101*; average undergraduate in-state tuition & fees *97*; California need-based aid per *148*; California's funding per 147; California trends in state appropriations per *147*; Florida need-based aid per *231*; Florida non-need aid per *230*; funding of need-based grants *102*; Indiana need-based aid per *201*; Indiana state appropriations per 200, *200*; Minnesota need-based aid per *172*, 181–182; Minnesota state appropriations per *171*; need-based grant awards per 102; North Carolina need-based aid per *257*; North Carolina non-need aid per *258*; North Carolina state appropriations per *256*; state grant funding per *172*

Future Ready Course of Study (FRC) 254

Gaines v. Canada 25
Gann Amendment 141
Garland, Merrick 22
Gates Millennial Scholars (GMS) 60; program 84–85
GEAR UP (Gaining Early Awareness and Readiness for Undergraduate Programs) 195, 196, 210
gender biases 11–12
GI Bill 48, 50, 71, 94, 98, 116, 139–140, 193, 273
Gillie, Scott 199
Glaude, Eddie 3
Glazer, Nathan 26
global competitiveness 20
global consensus 2, 64
globalism 20
globalization: democratic 20; economic theories of 64; higher education 19; post-neoliberal 273; US education development 31; *see also* economic globalization
Golden Age of higher education **xiii,** 26–27, **27**, 28, 43, 45, 48, 53, 85, 96, **112**, 113, 116
Gold Seal CAPE Scholars (GSC) 223
Gold Seal Vocation Scholars (GSV) 223, 224
Gollattscheck, James 125
Gorbachev, Mikhail 20
graduation rates across periods 79–81
Gross State Product (GSP) 143
guarantees of student 58–61

Habermas, J. 62
Hamas-Israeli war 46
Harvard university 11, 22, 64, 93; presidency 2; supreme court case 28, **32**, 34, 142, 145, 150, 178, 180, 194
HB 715 Higher Education Modernization and Affordability Act 265
health systems 2
Hearn, J. C. 167
HEA Title IV Programs 49
higher education 1; administrative regulation in 9; Cold War **21**; conflict about 5–6; DEI as core issues 8; enrollment 151–153; federal legislation and court decisions 24; finance 2; foreign threat to 11; global consensus 2, 64; globalization 19, **21**; global

uncertainty 22; Golden Age of 26–27, **27**; history of federal policy in 19; international alliances 20–22; marketization of 1–2, 19, 29, 31, 53; mass systems of 91; new uncertainty **21**; polycentric governance in 19; pre-WWII **21**; as professional field of study 6; and public policy 19–38; specializations in 6; state data collection 49; women in 8
Higher Education Act of 1965 (HEA) 7, 27, **27**, 34, 50, 98, 276
Higher Education General Information Survey (HEGIS) 49–50
higher education policy: analysis 48–52; conflicting beliefs 4–9; development of databases and analysis methods 49–50; evolution of 1; federal studies 49; global and national contexts for 20–31; impact of tuition and grants 50–51; institutional surveys 49; longitudinal student studies 49; state data collections 49; troubled contexts for 1, 3–12
Higher Education Relief Opportunities for Students Act of 2003 33
High School and Beyond (HSB) 51
high-school graduates and dropouts 83–84
high school graduation rates: for African American 173; California case study 149–150; Florida case study *232*, 232–233; Indiana case study *202*, 202–203; North Carolina case study 258; U.S. Public High School Graduation Rates *80*
high school graduation requirements 8, 29, 31, **56**, 60, 70–71, 273; in California **145**; in Florida 222, **227**; in Indiana **197–198**, 202, 210; in Minnesota **169**; in North Carolina 254, 258
Hispanic Serving Institutions (HSI) 50, 124
Historically Black Colleges and Universities (HBCUs) 7, 26–27, 250
Hoachlander, Gary 82
Hook, Sidney 8
Hopwood v. Texas 228
Hossler, Don 195
Houston Chronicle, The 3
Hoxby, C. 58
Hudson Bay Company 165
human capabilities theory 37, 71
Human Capital Theory (Becker) 71
Hurlburt, Allan 252

ideologies *see* political ideologies
increased reliance on loans 76–78
independent colleges 24–25
Indiana Career and Postsecondary Advancement Center (ICPAC) 195, 198–199, 203–204, 214
Indiana case study 190–216; 6-year attainment by race 207; academic preparation 202–204; academic preparation policies 197–198; ambiguous outcomes 209–210; attainment 213–214; balanced approach 194–197, 215; college attainment rates 206–209; college founding in early American period 192; college success 212–215; comprehensive approach 190–192, 201; current issues 210–212; decline in white student enrollment 206; Department of Education 190, 195, 198, 211; diversity 204–206; economic development 213–214; enrollment 204–206; funding for public colleges and universities 199–200; gains in preparation 203–204; high school graduation rates *202*, 202–203; integrative approaches to school reform 191; K-12 policy issues 191, 198; low-income students 191; overview 190; period of change 193–194; from political balance to reactionary conservatism 214–215; private nonprofit colleges and universities 208; Promise programs 191; public 2-year colleges 208–209; public and private colleges 192–193; public college tuition charges 199; public higher education, restructuring 193; public higher education after Civil War 192–193; SAT test scores 203; SB 202 Bill 212; school choice voucher program 211–212; school graduation requirements 197, **198**; state financing of higher education 198–201; state funding for need-based grants 200–201; state policy and funding 197–201; student outcomes 202–210; support services 191–192
Indiana Commission for Higher Education 45, 193–194, 197, 208, 214
Indiana Education Policy Center (IEPC) 190–191, 194–195
Indiana Project on Academic Success (IPAS) 206–207
Indiana Twenty-First Century Scholars 60
Indiana University Bloomington (IUB) 200
Inflation Reduction Act of 2022 33
Infrastructure Investment and Jobs Act of 2021 33
institutional surveys 49
instrumental ideology 63
Integrated Postsecondary Education Data Surveys (IPEDS) 49
international wars 22
Israel-Hamas War 2
Ivy League 93
Ivy Tech 45, 193–194, 208

Jackson, G. A. 51
Jefferson, Thomas 24
Jim Crow 10
John Birch Society 26
Johnson, Hiram 45
Johnstone, D. B. 182
Jones, Stan 194–195, 213

Kane, M. 54–55, 66n1, 85
Kennedy, Peggy Sue Wallace 12
Kerr, Clark 117, 137, 140–141
Khun, Thomas 6
Kirst, M. 77
Klan activism 10
knowledge economy 54

Land Grant Act 23, 74, 116, 139
Land Grant universities 5, 24–25, 75, 93, 115–116, 125, 222
LA Times 141

Latinx students 11
Leave It to Beaver 118
legacy of resisting social progress 7–8
"Lemon Test" 74
Lemon v. Kurtzman 74
liberal education establishment 1–2
liberalism 22, 25
Liberty of Conscience: In Defense of America's Tradition of Religious Equality (Nussbaum) 24, 44
Lilly Endowment 190, 191
Lincoln, Abraham 45
Lindberg, Charles 25
"line-item veto" 29
loan repayment 129, **129**
Long, B. T. 58
Long, Huey 10
longitudinal student studies 49
Loper Bright Enterprises v. Raimondo 34
low-income families 121
Lumina Foundation 215

Ma, J. 147
MAGA-DEI: battles 6, 13, 106, 221; debates 3–5, 42, 265, 276; divisiveness 10, 37, 119; tension 44, 278
majority-minority state 144
Make America Great Again (MAGA) movement 1, 3, 10–12, 37, 63, 219, 240; academic conservatism 9; American (white) nationalism 10–11; Christian nationalism 10; gender discrimination 11–12; ideology 46; quasi-inclusive nature of 11; v. DEI 1, 3–5, 6, 9, 10–12, 13, 37, 42, 44, 106, 221, 265
Mann, Horace 92
Manski, C. F. 51
Marcuse, Herbert 26
marketization: agenda 46; of higher education 19, 53; outcomes of 56
McRory, Pat 254
McVan, Madison 184
merit (and other non-need grants) 61
"Me Too" movement 11–12
Middle Income Student Assistance Act of 1978 (MISAA) 29–30, 95, 98
Miller, L. S. 50
Minding the Gap (Hoffman) 78
Minneapolis Federal Reserve Bank 181
Minnesota case study 164–187; access to higher education 174–177, 181; adult earnings by education attainment level 185–186; adult education attainment 184–185; bachelors' degree attainment rates 177–179; changes in state grant programs 182–183; changing graduation requirements 182; college debt by Minnesota graduates 184; college-degree attainment rates 177–180; college enrollment 175–177; college success 181, 183–187; current issues in 181–183; degree attainment rates by race 180; degree attainment rates by race/ethnicity 179–180; Department of Education 169–170; development of market model 164–169; diversity 174–177; evolution of strategy 168–169; financial wellbeing 183–186; funding higher education in 170–173; high school graduation 173–174; high school graduation requirements **169**; high school preparation policies 169–170; high-tuition/high-aid approach 182; high-tuition/high-grant aid market model 164, 181–182; K-16 policies, trends in 169–170; market model 166–167; North Star Promise 187; overview 164; performance funding 183; policy developments 166–167; public in-state tuition and fees 170, *171*; state financing of higher education 170–173; state funding of public higher education 170–172; state need-based grants 172–173; student academic achievement 173–174; student aid strategy 168–169; student outcomes 173–181
Minnesota Higher Education Coordinating Board (MHECB) 166–168
Minnesota Office of Higher Education (MOHE) 168, 182
Minnesota Reformer (McVan) 184
Minnesota State College and University (MNSCU) 182
minorities 11
Morrill Land Grant Act of 1862 24
Morrill Land Grant Act of 1890 220

National Association for the Advancement of Colored People (NAACP) 8, 25
National Bureau of Economic Research (NBER) 57–58
National Center for Education Statistics (NCES) 26, 49, 64, 203, 204, 207
National Center for Higher Education Management Systems (NCHEMS) 49, 51
National Center on Education Statistics (NCES) 54
National Commission on Excellence in Education 29
National Commission on the Financing of Postsecondary Education (NCFPE) 50–52, 71
National Council of Teachers of Math (NCTM) 227
National Defense Education Act 27, 75, 94, 95
National Institute of Education (NIE) 26
nationalism 20, 25; Christian 10; Eurocentric 8; nationalist groups 10–11; populist 3
nationalizing K-12 education 29
National Longitudinal Study of the High School Class of 1972 (NLS-72) 51
national pension system 93
National Student Clearinghouse (NSC) 120, 130, 180, 207, 236
A Nation At Risk (ANAR) (National Commission on Excellence in Education, 1983) 7, 29, 31, 47, 53, 76, 78
need-based scholarship 93
neoliberal consensus 32
neoliberal education establishment 7, 54, 111

neoliberal education policy ix, 63, 70, 75, 197, 207, 272
neoliberal education regime *see* neoliberal education establishment
neoliberalism xii, 20, 44, 46, 48, 277; critique of 48; ironies of 118–120; neoliberal haziness of 58; political ideologies 46; public policy x, 14, 30–31
neoliberal national policy 33, 45, 49, 106, 278
neoliberal period x, xv, 1–8, 13, 37, **43**, 53, 70–71, **73**, **112**, 146
neoliberal political theory 22
neoliberal trajectory 2, 7, 22–30, 56, 112
neoliberal transition 34, 81, 90–91, 248
neoliberal turn xi, xiii, xiv, 5, 27–30, 47, 64, 91–96, 275; consequences of 53; in education 9; nationalizing education standards 76–78
Newman, John H. 73
New York Times 3
No Child Left Behind Act of 1983 29
Noell, J. 66n1
non-need grants 100–102
North Carolina case study 247–269; academic freedom 265; academic preparation 258–259; academic preparation and college access 254–255; access 259–261; adjusted gross income (AGI) 257; attainment 268; 'Bathroom Bill' (HB 2) 254, 264; changing community college governance 264–265; college enrollment rates 259, *260*; college success 265–268; from colonial disputes to education diversity 248–249; community college system 251–252; conservative-progressive conflict 247–254; contemporary issues 264–265; debt 268; and DEI 264; Department of Public Instruction 254; desegregation of 250; diversity 259–261; early American period 248–249; earnings 268; earnings by degree level 266–268; education 249; education attainment among adults 266; eroding tenure 265; expected family contribution (EFC) 257; financial wellbeing 266–268; financing of higher education in 255–257; fiscally progressive and socially conservative 252–254; graduation rates 262–263; high school graduation rates 258; legacy of student debt 266; need-based student aid 250–251; oscillating state of unequal opportunity 248–249; overview 247; policy changes 254–257; policy trends in 254–257; private school vouchers 253–254; progress and student choice 249; progressive policies in public higher education 249–252; reconstruction 249; SAT scores 258–259; student outcomes 258–263; trans-gender rights 254; white resistance 249
North Carolina Community College System (NCCCS) 251–252
North Carolina Justice Center 253
North Star Promise 187, 188n2
Northwest Ordinance of 1787 22
Northwest Territories Act 221
Northwest Territories Ordinance 192
Nussbaum, Martha 24, 44, 71

Oakes, J. 77
Obama, Barack (Obama administration) 3–4, 9, 22, 31–34, 70, 78, 80, 95–96, 274
Occupational Course of Study (OC) 254
open-strategic ideology 63–64
"Opportunity Scholarship" program 253
Orfield, Gary 193

pathways: align with college and career 70; to high-school completion 70; for high-school graduates and dropouts 83–84; model 59, 59–60; options in 2020s 78; in policy 70; of privilege 91–93
patriotism 11
Pelavin, S. H. 54–55, 66n1, 85
Pell Grants 30, 50, 61–62, 96–99, 107, 167–168, 173, 175, 184, 196–197, 224, 257, 279; impact of 51–52, **56**, 207, 210; *see also* Basic Educational Opportunity Grants (BEOG)
Pence, Mike 211
Pender, M. 147
people of color 8, 129, 148
persistence 120–121
Plessy v. Ferguson 25, 116
policies: analysis/analyses of 77; beliefs, ideologies, and experience 13; changes 107–108; educational 145–149; finance 96–102; frames 278–280; indicators 55, **56**, 79, 225; legal history 13; linked to educational outcomes 55–57; and outcomes 14; pedagogical design 13–14; purposes 12–13; trajectories **32**; *see also* federal policy/policies; finance policies; higher education policy; public policy
policy matters 42–65; assumptions 62–65; closed-strategic ideologies 64; communicative ideology 64–65; data collection 47–55; frameworks for reliable trend analyses 55–62; framing processes 63–65; instrumental ideology 63; open exchanges about troubling, problematic issues 65; open-strategic ideology 63–64; political ideologies 42–47
policy-related variables **79**
political divisions 31–37; into academic organizations 36–37
political ideologies ix, xii, 13, 34, 42–47, **43**, 63; competing beliefs 43–44; conflict during progressive Cold War 45; conservative 214; education development 276–278; from equity to policy outcomes 52–55; MAGA 244; nationalist 25; neoliberalism 46, 272; post-neoliberal malaise 46–47; race equity to academic preparation for all 53–55; research evidence 47
political stressors 116
populist nationalism 3
postmodernism 6
post-neoliberal legislation **32**
post-neoliberal malaise 46–47
post-neoliberal period 5, 8, 46–47, 53, 71, 81, 113
post-neoliberal transition 3, 79
post-neoliberal uncertainty 96

postsecondary attainment: impact of federal and state policy on 57, 57–58
postsecondary education 70
preparation 70–86; career preparation 71–78; change in policy 79–81; college preparation 71–78, 82–86; for financial wellbeing 70–71, **73**, 81–83; graduation rates across periods 79–81; for meaningful work 72; overview 70–71; pathway options in 2020s 78; periodization of 72; for work opportunities 71
private colleges 22–24, 96–98
private school vouchers 46, 50, 74, 276; in Florida 227, 233, 244; in Indiana 197, 211; in North Carolina 249, 253
program advocacy 60–61
Project on Academic Success (PAS) 207
Promise programs 34–35, 52, 55, 58–61, 65, 96, 98, 108, 280; California 157; Indiana 191; Minnesota 182
proofiness 58, 77, 81–83
proofy *see* proofiness
public colleges 22–24, 96–98
public four-year college 105–106
public policy: corporatized neoliberalism 30–31; from empires to economic globalization 20–22; global and national contexts for 20–31; global competition 30–31; and higher education 19–38; neoliberal trajectory 22–30; and political divisions 31–37; reframing strategies in chaotic times 37–38; *see also* policies
public–private cooperation 23
Public Service Loan Forgiveness (PSLF) program 82
public systems: creation of 5; emergence of 24–25
Purdue University 45
Puritan 44, 248

Quaker 44, 192, 215, 248

racial wealth gap 129–130
Radner, R. 50
Ravitch, Diane 7
Reagan, Ronald 7, 10, 29–30, 34, 43, 45, 46, 55, 63, 112, 119, 140, 156
Reed, Suellen 194
reframing strategies in chaotic times 37–38
Regents of the University of California v. Bakke 28, 142
region-based culture 23
Reisman, David 26
religious differences 23–24
research evidence 62
research-informed planning 48
resistance in public and academic communities **4**, 6
room & board 61
Roosevelt, Franklin 25, 48, 85
Roosevelt, Teddy 45
Russia-Ukraine War 22

Sanford, Terry 252
San Jose State University 138

SAT scores 80, 203, 258–259
SAVE plan policy 83
school curricula **4**, 5
school reform initiatives 11
school tracking schemes 63
school voucher program *see* private school vouchers
Science, Technology, Engineering, and Math (STEM) 1, 7; agenda 1, 5, 46, 53–55, 70, 75, 78, 81, 83, 85, 91, 119, 126–127, 130; inspired national education standards 8; pipeline 6, 7, 46; science establishment 2
secularization of public schools 74
Seife, C. 58
Serviceman's Readjustment Act see GI Bill
Shopping Mall High School (Powell et al.) 47
social agenda 3, 240, 278
socialism 3, 25; critiques of 63
social justice 8, 9; pedagogies 9
social media 11
social stress 118; and college development 114–115; and college success 114–115; education development 114–115
social stressors 116
Spellings Commission *see* Commission on the Future of Higher Education
standardized price response coefficients (SPRCs) 51
state data collections 49
state need-based grants 61; college access 100–102; Minnesota case study 172–173; purchasing power of 102; trend analyses 100–102
state policy 57–58
state politics and education development 275–276
State Student Aid Commission of Indiana (SSACI) 195
STEM agenda 46, 70; adaptations 79–81; neoliberal support of 75; transformation of high schools 91
STEM movement 72
STEM paradigm 72
St. John, E. P. 66n1
Strengthening America's Historically Black Colleges and Universities: A Call for Action (Nelms) 250
Strengthening Career and Technical Education for the 21st Century Act of 2018 32
stressors: political 116; social 116; in uncertain times 119–120
Structure of Scientific Revolutions, The (Khun) 6
student debt 7, **28**, **32**, 33–34, 38, 82–83, 99–100, 106, **112**, 129–131, 274–278; in California 137, 160; in Florida 238, 241; in Minnesota 168, 184; in North Carolina 266–268
student funding for public colleges 61
Student Price response 50–51
Students for a Democratic Society (SDS) 7
Students for Fair Admission, Inc. v. University of North Carolina 34, 228
Students for Fair Admissions, Inc. v. Harvard College **32**, 142, 160
Students for Fair Admissions, Inc. v. President & Fellows of Harvard College 33–34

Success For All (Slavin) 76
Supplemental Educational Opportunity Grants (SEOG) 30, 66n2
Supreme Court **xiii**, 9, 19, 82; appointments 22, 74; decisions **24**, 25–26, **28**, **32**, 33–34, 142, 160, 178, 197, 228, 276, 278; judges 74
systemic inequality 26, 238, 241, 247, 268

technical high schools 31, 93
Tennessee Promise program 60, 157
theory of change 55, *59*, 81
theory of communicative action *see* communicative action
Tierney, W. G. 143
timely attainment 120
timely college completion across race/ethnicity 120–125
To Reclaim a Legacy (Bennett) 7
Toutkoushian, R. 52
transgender rights 254, 264–265
trend analyses 96; in average annual state and local appropriations *101*; in average state need-based and non-need-based grants *101*; non-need grants 100–102; in per FTE funding of need-based grants *102*; in policies linked to educational outcomes 55–57; policy reframing 55–62; research-based model of college finance 61; state and local subsidies to public colleges/universities 100; in state funding for colleges and students 100–102; state need-based grants 100–102; in student debt 99
Trent, William T. 84
Trump, Donald (Trump administration) 1–4, 10–11, 22, 31, 32–33, 35, 46, 253
tuition and fees 61, 96–97, *146*, 148–149; *see also* college costs
Twenty-First Century Scholars program 52, 58, 60, 191, 194–201, 207, 209–211, 214–215, 234

UC Tuition Stability Plan 158
Union of Soviet Socialist Republics (USSR) 20, 22
university budget 35–36
University of California (UC) 25, 28, 93, 137, 139–140, 142, 145, 158, 277
University of California, Berkeley (UCB) 25–26
University of California, Davis (UCD) 117, 137–142, 158
University of Chicago 25–26, 97
University of Michigan 8–9
University of San Francisco 138
University of Texas 143
US Capitol Building 3
U.S. Census Bureau 90
US–China conflict 22
US Constitution 19, 23, 28, 63
Usdan, M. 77
US Department of Education (USDE) 7–8, 30, 46, 49, 53–55, 80, 178, 273–275; argument for higher math standards 77–78; Office and Planning and Budget 54; Reagan's- 63, 95
U.S. Public High School Graduation Rates *80*
US Supreme Court *see* Supreme Court

Venegas, K. 143
Venezia, A. 77
Vesper, Nick 195
Vietnam War 2
vocational curriculum in high schools 74–75
vocational education 75, 82, 94
vocational and technical education (VTE) 273
vouchers *see* private school vouchers

Walker, Venessa Siddle 84
Wallace, George 10, 12
Warren, Earl 45, 141
"Washington Consensus" (Gore) 20, 33, 90, 274
Washington State achievers 60
Wattach, J. 253
wealth disparities 37, 130, 279
Weathersby, George 45, 194
Weinstein, Harvey 11
Wescott, J. W. II 251
Western Civilization 7–8, 9–11, 93
West Florida Seminary 220
White House 3
white nationalism 10–11, 12
white students 52, 54, 152–154, 175–177, 180, 184, 203, 205, 207
William, Roger 44
Wise, D. A. 51
women: in higher education 8; rights cases in the Supreme Court 9; right to vote movement 8
World Bank and the International Monetary Fund 20, 90
World War I (WWI) 48
World War II (WWII) 2, 9, 71, 116, 140, 191; American war effort in 25; civil unrest before 25–26; federal research funding during 25

Made in the USA
Middletown, DE
18 August 2025